W9-BGW-384

AMERINDIAN IMAGES AND
THE LEGACY OF COLUMBUS

SEP - 2 1994

Hispanic Issues

HISPANIC ISSUES
VOLUME 9

AMERINDIAN IMAGES AND THE LEGACY OF COLUMBUS

RENÉ JARA AND NICHOLAS SPADACCINI
◆
EDITORS

UNIVERSITY OF MINNESOTA PRESS
MINNEAPOLIS   LONDON

Copyright 1992 by the Regents of the University of Minnesota

The editors of this volume gratefully acknowledge assistance from the Program for Cultural Cooperation between Spain's Ministry of Culture and United States' Universities; the College of Liberal Arts and the Department of Spanish and Portuguese at the University of Minnesota.

All rights reserved. No part of this publication may be reproduced, stored in a retrieval system, or transmitted, in any form or by any means, electronic, mechanical, photocopying, recording, or otherwise, without the prior written permission of the publisher.

Published by the University of Minnesota Press
2037 University Avenue Southeast, Minneapolis, MN 55414
Printed in the United States of America on acid-free paper

Library of Congress Cataloging-in-Publication Data

Amerindian images and the legacy of Columbus / edited by René Jara and
    Nicholas Spadaccini.
       p. cm. — (Hispanic issues ; 9)
    Includes bibliographical references and index.
    ISBN 0-8166-2166-7 (hc). — ISBN 0-8166-2167-5 (pb)
    1. Indians—History—Sources. 2. Indians in literature.
3. Indians—Public opinion. 4. Public opinion—Europe. 5. America—
Discovery and exploration. 6. Spain—Colonies—America. I. Jara,
René, 1941– . II. Spadaccini, Nicholas. III. Series.
E58.A532 1992
970.01'5—dc20   92-22084
                                                 CIP

The University of Minnesota is an
equal-opportunity educator and employer.

Hispanic Issues

Nicholas Spadaccini
Editor in Chief

Gwendolyn Barnes-Karol   Antonio Ramos-Gascón
Jenaro Talens
General Editors

Jennifer M. Lang
Donna Buhl LeGrand
Associate Editors

Monica Allen
Assistant Editor

Advisory / Editorial Board
Rolena Adorno (Princeton University)
Rodolfo Cardona (Boston University)
Jaime Concha (University of California, San Diego)
Tom Conley (University of Minnesota)
Patrick Dust (Carleton College)
Ruth El Saffar (University of Illinois, Chicago)
Eduardo Forastieri-Braschi (Universidad de Puerto Rico, Río Piedras)
David Foster (Arizona State University)
Edward Friedman (Indiana University)
Wlad Godzich (Université de Genève)
Antonio Gómez-Moriana (Université de Montréal)
Claudio Guillén (Universidad Autónoma de Barcelona)
Hans Ulrich Gumbrecht (Stanford University)
Javier Herrero (University of Virginia)
René Jara (University of Minnesota)
Susan Kirkpatrick (University of California, San Diego)
María Eugenia Lacarra (Universidad del País Vasco/Euskal Herriko
Unibertsitatea)
Tom Lewis (University of Iowa)
Jorge Lozano (Universidad Complutense de Madrid/Fundación José
Ortega y Gasset)
Michael Nerlich (Technische Universität Berlin)
Margarita Santos Zas (Universidad de Santiago de Compostela)
Iris M. Zavala (Rijksuniversiteit Utrecht)

Contents

◆ Introduction

The Construction of a Colonial Imaginary
Columbus's Signature

René Jara and Nicholas Spadaccini

Reading Columbus

Few tales in the history of the world are more familiar than the one relating the adventures of Columbus, the fabled Admiral of the Ocean Sea who, prisoner of his dreams, sailed West in search of the fabulous riches of Cathay or Cipangu, only to trip on America, a mass of then "unknown" land that was soon to become the fourth terrestrial continent.

The Admiral's story has become a piece of art in the sense that it has acquired its own truth, a truth that in addition to being self-validating and indisputable is also ambiguous and contradictory. That he landed in Guanahani in 1492 seems of little consequence as other events of his life still demand explanation. It is widely known that Christopher Columbus won royal backing for his enterprise of the Indies, although nobody knows how. Columbus's life remains a problematic puzzle, despite the voluminous body of critical attention that it is receiving, now more than ever on the occasion of the quincentennial anniversary of the "discovery" or "encounter" between two worlds.

We know little about the man himself, and the myth of Col-

1

umbus as "hero" and miracle worker who brought progress to humankind is now being stripped of its luster. The historian John Noble Wilford has speculated recently:

> The world and America are changing... and Columbus's reputation is changing. Modern life has made disbelievers of many who once worshipped at the altar of progress. In the years after World War II, nearly all the colonies of the major empires won their independence and, like the United States in its early days, began to view world history from their own anticolonial perspective. The idol had been the measure of the worshipers, but now there were atheists all around. To them, the age of Discovery was not the bright dawning of a glorious epoch, but an invasion. Columbus became the avatar of oppression. Another Columbus for another age. (48)[1]

Of the man Columbus one might say that he opened the gates of the ocean to the flux of Christianity, which was truly a Greek present for the aboriginal peoples; that as the first overseas Spanish viceroy for the Catholic Crown he was the epitome of failure in colonial administration; that he was an explorer and discoverer without a fixed name, a certain place of birth, or even a definite tomb; that he was a skillful and lucky sailor who knew how to read the winds and find his way back; that he was also less than magnanimous, as was the case when he did not give proper credit to the lookout who had cried "¡Tierra!" and instead proceeded to reserve for himself the lifetime pension promised by the Crown to the first individual who saw land. It has also been said that Columbus was a mystic in the tradition of St. Francis of Assisi, perhaps, as we shall see later in greater detail, because during his third voyage he identified the earthly Orinoco River as one of those flowing out of the Garden of Eden and because he was eager to help finance the liberation of the Holy Sepulcher in Jerusalem (see Jane, Boorstin, Granzotto, Las Casas, Morison, Sale). Finally, he was a man who never found a place to call his own, a man who continues to be a cipher like the signature he crafted for himself, a signature whose graphemes no one has been able to decode.

The decade of the 1990s promises to be a trying one for Columbus's myth and memory, for discoverers and colonial powers.

Columbus's legacy of discovery and colonization will be the subject of scholarly and public debate and if, in the process, he should become the scapegoat, we might thank him for it. What is certain is that we cannot afford the luxury of ignoring him, precisely because exploitation and imperialism may not be ignored, for in the end the analysis of those scourges is apt to provide a clearer picture of the world we live in, even if we are still unable to decode Columbus's signature.

The world is changing and a new age seems to have dawned, when the voices of those Native Americans and African Americans who suffered the consequences of the encounter and contact between two different civilizations are clamoring to be heard. The time is ripe to remember the rape of the land that is still rampant in Brazil and the Amazons. It is time to defend the value and the right to existence of endangered cultures. It is the time to recall the bravery, the endurance, and the ingenuity needed for the constitution of an Amerindian world that was born of resistance against imperial cultural assimilation.

Five hundred years ago Columbus landed on an island that was to become a palimpsest of civilizations and geographies. It was one of the islands of the Lucayos, who were peoples from Asia. Columbus was to name that island San Salvador, acknowledging that his inscription was another trace upon that of the native topogram: Guanahani. The year 1992 marks one more centennial, half a millennium of resistivity, in which America has endeavored to demonstrate that absolute conquest is impossible and that for all of its brutality and injustice, colonization is a double-edged sword.

In its chiaroscuro, the story of Columbus seems to belong to the world of myth, to another universe, to a cosmic *tableau vivant*, in which everything is definitely different and inaccessible, because in it the issue of authenticity is suspended. It is precisely for this reason that one ought not to forget Columbus, even if one does not choose to forgive him or the historical processes that he set in motion in 1492. More often than not, myth is but the reverse of prestigious history, and the history of peoples falls into the cracks of narrativity. In the Amerindian landscape, popular narratives have coined together myth and history, and the critic is compelled to be the guest of both.

The Discourse of Exploration and Conquest

Columbus's story has come to us in the narration, the paraphrases, and the marginal annotations made to his diary by the Dominican friar Bartolomé de Las Casas and through the biographical materials written by his own son Hernando (see Fernández de Navarrete, Jane, Sale, and, in this volume, Zamora and Henige). The original diary has been lost, but we know that Las Casas worked effectively to make of the mariner the hero he needed to inspire the Christianization of the natives. John Leddy Phelan claims that Las Casas patterned his hero on the models of classical antiquity, bestowing upon him the high lineage, the intellectual gifts, and the human virtues that characterized the Roman nobility. The very origin of his first name, "he who carries Christ," not only made of Columbus a metaphor for the transfer of Christianity to the Indies, but also pointed to the lofty mission that Providence had assigned to him. In Las Casas's tale, the culmination of this assignment in the discovery of the new lands would determine Columbus's rise from obscurity to fortune and prosperity. Las Casas, however, chose to give a tragic twist to Christopher's story, thus sparing the reader the image of the misery and solitude that framed his final years in Spain. In Las Casas's narration Columbus's fall served the need of poetic and divine justice, as the viceroy's mistreatment of the Indians could only provoke divine anger and punishment. Phelan has argued:

> By casting Columbus in the mold of a classical hero, Las Casas was able to regard him as a divine instrument, and yet Las Casas was still free to criticize the discoverer for his oppression of the Indians. Las Casas, however, was moved by both the splendor of his hero's rise and the crash of his fall. For this reason Columbus was spared the vituperative treatment that Las Casas ordinarily reserved for all those who had a hand in exploiting the natives. (31)

Born in 1484, Las Casas was a contemporary of Columbus (born ca. 1451), but Las Casas's writing gives the navigator's life the aura of earlier heroic times. Jason, Hercules, Achilles, Odysseus, and Aeneas participated with the help and company of their gods in the morass of human affairs, which, willy-nilly, was an interesting aspect of godly behavior. Las Casas himself, a devoted Aristotelian and a man of law who seemed unwilling to meddle in other-worldly matters, used the rhetorical effects of the chronicle and the historiography of the period in order to detach himself from Columbus's character. The third-person narrative, the techniques of hagiography, the marginal annotations framing the text of the Admiral's diary (see Zamora in this volume), and the conscious manipulation of the historical record (see Henige in this volume) point to a fascinating phenomenon: Columbus is the double of Las Casas, inscribed by the latter in his own texts. In turn, from Las Casas's texts Columbus's own seems to have originated. It is as if Las Casas had sought to assume the guilt of the very conquest he fought to erase, while enjoying the happenstance of discovery and taking charge of the commitment to Christianization of the new peoples. For this reason the reading of Las Casas's *Historia de las Indias* locates Columbus on the other side of the chronicler's temporal horizon. The Admiral seems to be one of the last productions of a mythical universe who is forced to act on a less prestigious terrain.

Columbus continued to believe in the fantastic world of medieval bestiaries and chivalresque romances, and, as a result, he reduced their creatures to the mode of the present, to the experiences of everyday life. Las Casas's transcription of Columbus's *Diary* shows that the paths that took the Admiral to the New World were paved with the medieval imaginary. For present-day readers, to navigate through those routes is like zigzagging among imprecise boundaries between the realms of the quotidian, the marvelous, and the fantastic. One senses the entrapments of the chivalric world.

The chivalric mode, as Manuel Alvar suggests in this volume, became a blueprint for the understanding of the New World, whose reality might otherwise have been incomprehensible to the European mind. The adventures of the knight-errant served as analog to the heroic feats of the conquistadors. While the lives of Cortés, Valdivia, Montejo, and Coronado were to be transformed into literature, it also happens that literature—because of the wealth of exemplary feats represented by the genealogies of knights-errant—was translated into the grammar of American life.

Amadís de Gaula (*Amadis of Gaul*) became a sort of a symbol of the New World, and this book brought with it the imagery of the time period to which it belonged. On their journeys, the conquistadors would encounter dragons, a good number of mermaids and mermen, even a few damsels in distress. These elements of chivalric literature, more often than not, found a different meaning on this other shore of the Atlantic; for example, the unicorn, which in Europe was tied to the conventions of chivalry and courtly love, became in America a glyph of the devil (see Gisbert in this volume) and a favorite icon of satanic worship.

It may be useful to recall at this point that the overthrow of the indigenous empires of Mesoamerica and the Andes was achieved by a handful of men—less than a thousand in all—mostly drawn from the Crown of Castile (the legal owner of America) and, within it, from Andalusia and Extremadura. Most of them were young, unmarried, professional soldiers who came from the gentry class and below. But if the aristocracy did not play an important part in the Conquest (Elliott, *Imperial Spain*), the strictures of the system of entail (*mayorazgo*) in Castile did provide "a strong incentive for emigration by younger sons of aristocratic and gentry houses, who hoped to find in the New World the fortune denied them at home. *Hidalgos* in particular were well represented in the *conquista*—men such as Cortés himself, who came from noble but impoverished families, and were prepared to try their luck in an unknown world" (62; see also Elliott, *The Old World and the New*).

The predominance of these "sons of somebody" (*hidalgos*) in positions of leadership gives a characteristic shape to the enterprise of Conquest, for they had brought with them a collective memory that spanned centuries of struggle against the infidels in the wars of the Spanish Reconquest. The final bastion of Moorish resistance had surrendered in Granada in 1492, the year of Columbus's first voyage. Many Spaniards who migrated to the New World seem to have maintained great discipline under pressure.[2] After all, as career soldiers in Old Spain, they had suffered hardships and had learned to overcome them.

Their discipline was accompanied by an exuberant imagination that had been generously fed both in the actual feats of the Reconquest and in the delirious fantasies of the romances of chivalry.[3] The latter's emphasis on intrigues of love and sensuality, on the atmosphere of mystery and fantasy, on the construction of a loosely episodic plot with room for chance, spontaneity, and lightly motivated adventure, and the presence of a visible narrator who kept the reader's trust and confidentiality unshaken were sufficient reason for the popularity of the genre among the very men who decided to try their fortunes in the New World.

The advent of printing in Spain (ca. 1473) and its expansion toward the end of the fifteenth century and in the first two decades of the sixteenth century had increased the popularity of these stories and had also made possible their circulation in chapbooks or *pliegos sueltos*, which served as digests of the traditional culture of the Middle Ages and early Renaissance to various types of "readers," regardless of where they were located in the cultural and social spheres (Godzich and Spadaccini 52-54). J. H. Elliott (*Imperial Spain*) has remarked on the impact of these books on the Spanish psyche and on the importance of America as a theater where fantasies could be played out:

> *Amadis of Gaul* (1508), the most famous of them all, was known in affectionate detail by a vast body of Spaniards who, if they could not read themselves, had heard them told or read aloud. A society soaked in these works, and touchingly credulous about the veracity of their contents, naturally tended to some extent to model its view of the world and its code of behaviour on the extravagant concepts popularized by the books of chivalry. Here was an abundance of strange happenings and heroic actions. What more natural than that the mysterious world of America should provide the scene for their enactment? (63)

Columbus, Hernán Cortés, Vasco Núñez de Balboa, Diego de Almagro, Hernando de Soto, Juan Ponce de León, Bartolomé de Las Casas, Diego de Landa, Francisco Vásquez de Coronado—any of them could have been cast as the protagonist or antihero of one of these romances of chivalry. The model is clear as those romances follow the loose pattern of the quest: the character embarks on a journey in order to accomplish some goal that may involve meeting a challenge, obeying a royal command, seeking gold, finding El Dorado or the Fountain of Eternal Youth, punishing the Indians for their idolatry, or, perhaps, championing their cause against the Spaniards' abuses. On this journey he finds numerous adventures, many of them apparently unrelated to the original quest, except a posteriori, when reason imposes scrutiny, selection, and organization to illustrate a new goal and thus justify the telling.

Strategies of Domination and Resistance

If the first European contribution to America was the chivalresque program of truth, the immediate Amerindian response was the transformation of this program into the exigencies of American reality. And if the Reconquest of Spain from the Moors had given it a set of values that the conquistadors brought in earnest to the New World, it is also the case that the events of Conquest were to teach the native Amerindians strategies and techniques of both incorporation and cultural resistance, strategies that, several centuries later in the twentieth century, would still shine as powerful examples of cultural strength and vitality.[4] At the same time, one must keep in mind that the Spaniard who, for the first time, set foot in the New World was immediately transformed into a different human being, into another cultural specimen—an individual who suffered a radical change of skin. The contact with the new soil would soon plant in his mind the seeds of independence. This happened at the same time that the Spaniards were fighting and making alliances with the racial and social groups with which they would collaborate in the making of the material and cultural circumstance of the Amerindian continent. Francisco Roldán, Gonzalo Guerrero, Martín Cortés, Gonzalo Pizarro, Lope de Aguirre, Santos Atahuallpa, Antonio Pérez, Tupac Amaru II, Manuel Rodríguez, and Manuel Hidalgo are just the first in a long list of Spanish, Creole, and *mestizo* rebels and revolutionaries.

From the very beginning of the encounter the natives were confronted with the previously unknown experience of reading. That lack of European knowledge was to reinforce the native tendency toward interpretation, a characteristic that is common to oral culture. There was the strange appearance of the conquerors, some of them red-skinned, bearded, heavily clad in the midst of tropical heat and humidity, armed with movable orifices that vomited fire on the enemy, knocked down walls, demolished trees, and made stone fortresses tremble. They were strange men who were smelly and sweaty, ignorant of the delights of a frequent bath, hungry for gold and precious stones. The anonymous *Tragedia del fin de Atahuallpa* (*Tragedy of the End of Atahuallpa*) dramatizes the moment when the Inca leader is apprised by the supreme priest of the aliens' arrival:

> They wear three-pointed horns
> just like the *tarukas* [deer]
> and their hair
> is sprinkled with white flour,
> and on their mandibles they boast
> blazing red beards,
> similar to long strands of wool
> and they carry in their hands
> extraordinary iron slings
> whose occult power
> is to vomit flaming fire
> rather than launching stones.[5]

The experience of seeing those strange creatures is converted into an even more inscrutable trauma when Huascar, serving as royal emissary, must bring to his half brother Atahuallpa the written decree signed by the King of Spain granting Pizarro ownership of the conquered lands. The document is interpreted by the Inca through a code that reveals a lack of knowledge of alphabetic writing:

> Seen from this angle
> it is an anthill
> seen from this other side
> the traces they leave
> seem to me like those left by birds' feet
> in the muddy banks of the river.

Seen in this way it looks like deer upside-down
with the legs straight.
And if we simply look at it this way
it is similar to the llamas with their heads down
and with deer horns.
Who can make sense out of this![6]

The accumulation of material traces—those of the ants and the birds, the deer and the llama, even the mixture of them, such as the slow and parsimonious demeanor of the llama that is dressed up with a deer's headdress—will not be sufficient to solve the mysteries of artificial writing, the fanciful European alphabet that threatened the transmission of a culture based on tradition and orality (see Bermúdez-Gallegos, Gisbert, and Mignolo in this volume; see also Mignolo, "Literacy and Colonization").

One is thus confronted with a struggle of images. Now we know that an image of something—especially if that something is the Other—usually testifies to the failure of human mental schemata to deal with alterity as difference; it is not simply the duality of Self and Other, which is the way the Western mind operates. It seems, however, that the images forged by the Amerindian peoples in order to confront the results of the Encounter will, in the long run, ensure the permanence of their culture, for without renouncing their imaginary, they modified it in order to integrate in it the facts of Conquest and Westernization—they became their own others. Thus, to study the emergence of these images is to watch the Other rising within the Self, the Amerindian self. The Amerindians in effect have understood the Other; that is, they have stood underneath the Other in order to accept its substantial alterity and, in the process, they have realized that absolute assimilation is impossible.[7] Spain and Europe have value for what they are, for their Otherness. Yet most of the literature dealing with the Encounter has originated in the European model doing exactly the opposite: it has tried to assimilate the Other, to stand on top of it, deprive it of its exteriority, and, in the final analysis, colonize it (see Piedra, Johnson, Carey-Webb, López Maguiña, Pratt, Reis, and Arrom in this volume).

The first voyage of Columbus provides the clues to this co-nundrum. Where the Admiral was confronted with the peoples of the Caribbean, they became Arawaks when they succumbed to the Spaniards' demands. Inversely, they became Caribs when they decided to defend their way of life and their territories against the Spaniards. The labels are not ethnographic ones. Rather, they correspond to the response of the Amerindians to the invaders. Ethnography is no better than translation. The New World had to be commensurate to the Old. When something did not fit the pattern, violence ensued. Such is what happened with religion. In Middle America things were simple enough. There were visible signs of religious practices that were repulsive to Catholic Europe. Yet, despite the differences in the religious practice of the Aztecs and the Incas, Viceroy Francisco de Toledo was to impose the same solutions in the Andean region: those peoples were idolaters and could well be assimilated to other pagans. In some cases, however, definition was a bit more complex and confusing. Such was the case with the shamanistic behavior of the Tupinamba in Brazil, with their belief in spiritual beings, sorcerers, and magic. Those Indians would soon be assimilated into a demonological frame-work. Thus the problem had been solved: the Tupinamba did have a recognizable religion, they were idolaters, and their spiritual be-ings were devils. "In the process," Peter Mason has written, "the freshness of the discovery of a people without religion, without superstition and yet with some notion of a universal God grew stale in the course of its reduction to the familiar. The New World lost its novelty" (Mason 25; Jara and Spadaccini).

The projection onto Amerindian reality of the images that the Europeans had of their own Other was a favorite discursive strat-egy. Perhaps the central axis in the medieval European imaginary relative to the embodiment of its own Other is that of savagery ver-sus nobility. In the extremities of this axis one finds the figurations of the Noble Savage and the Wild (Wo)Man. Columbus, however, could perceive only mercantile advantage and profit in this Other who was not European. Accordingly, his first presupposition was the inferiority of the natives. Their beautiful nakedness unleashed in his mind a chain of figurations: technological backwardness, hence docility; absence of weapons, hence no defense; lack of religion, hence suspicion of bestiality. In the Admiral's mind, that simple signifier, nakedness, which in the mind of the native was an adequate response to Guanahani's weather, transformed the Amerindians into creatures fit for captivity and serfdom, into commodities to be used for the European's profit. Significantly, slavery would be the next signifier in Columbus's semiotic chain: he ordered the capture of several "heads" of women and children. For Columbus, Amerindians were a historical conundrum whose solution was to strip them of their humanity: they lived in an Edenic world that they did not deserve; their barbaric innocence was such that neither greed nor robbery nor the very idea of private property crossed their minds. Their generosity, gentleness, and naïveté could only be despised by the powerful man of the Old World. No matter that those Indians had lived in the area for almost 1500 years, that they possessed a rational agricultural system that fed everybody, that they lived in harmony with their ecosystem, that they had a well-organized and clean social and domestic life, and that they had developed a polity composed of villages of ten to fifteen families ruled by a *cacique* (leader) who was, in turn, counselled by an assembly of elders. Columbus could only see exchange value. His views of both humanity and nature were conditioned by greed.

As inventor of European colonialism in America, Columbus decreed the construction of the first of many fortresses in order to better subject and take advantage of the Indian labor force; he ordered that the only trade with the Indians be in gold, although none was available; and he assumed uncontested European sovereignty of the land. His editor, Las Casas, who was so keen in defending the human and property rights of the Amerindians, did not have time to claim the restitution of the Taíno territories and property. By the middle of the century all Taíno people were dead (Las Casas, Cook and Borah, Crosby). Columbus did not have time for Noble Savages. Wild Men and Women were always more convenient. The myth of the Golden Age and the concept of the Noble Savage would gain impetus in the eighteenth century, but the concept may be recognized in some of its modern manifestations in the writings of the Christian humanists of the sixteenth century. We might also add that the clearest conception of the Amerindian as Noble Savage seems to appear in the writing of Sigüenza y Góngora and in the political-religious utopia of reformist friars such as Las Casas, Motolinía, Torquemada, and Friar Jerónimo de Mendieta, who thought of the possibility that Indians could achieve terrestrial perfection if they were kept under the exclusive supervision of the friars. In effect, Mendieta and Friar Juan Focher earlier (*Itinerario del misionero en América* [1574]) pictured a theocracy run by ecclesiastical authority.

The Utopian Project of the Franciscans

The Franciscans pondered the psychological qualities that they assumed existed in the Indians: they possessed natural reason and thus were capable of receiving grace, which was the most simple denominator of humanness; they also lacked the superfluous emotions and desires that had transformed Europe into a continent of sinners. Significantly the same features that served Columbus to pile them up as merchandise—features such as poverty, humility, obedience, generosity, and meekness—were used by the Franciscans to endow them with childlike innocence. The image of the Amerindian emerging from Franciscan writings is that of a child to be reared, disciplined, and guided by proper fathers and teachers. Yet, this apparent benevolence also has its underside, for as children the Indians could not assume certain responsibilities; they were to be students and parishioners rather than instructors or priests.

On the surface the notion of Indian inferiority might appear to be placing Mendieta on a par with the most ferocious attacks on the Indians proffered by the jurist Sepúlveda in his polemics with Las Casas in the middle of the sixteenth century (see Jara and Spadaccini; Pagden, *The Fall of Natural Man;* Rabasa), but a closer analysis reveals a striking difference between their respective positions. For Sepúlveda the Indians' mental inferiority was their greatest defect; Mendieta considered their simplicity their greatest asset, one that made them ripe for rewards in the hereafter. Mendieta even contended that he could build a terrestrial paradise while the Millennium was approaching, provided that the Spanish king granted him exclusive rights to rule his Indian flock, thus isolating them from the contamination of the Spaniards. Many of the latter were, after all, of suspect religious allegiance, contaminated with non-Christian blood. The Amerindians, on the other hand, provided the Franciscans with the possibility of fashioning a return to a pristine Christianity and a pristine Church "in a place that did not allow for laziness and indigence" (Maravall, "La utopía político-religiosa" 108).

Mendieta, in effect, likens his image of terrestrial paradise to the seven cities of Antillia of the Ancients,

> which some say is enchanted and which is located not far from Madeira. In our times it has been seen from afar, but it disappears upon approaching it.... They say that on this island there are seven cities with a bishop residing in each one and an archbishop in the principal city.... It would be ... appropriate to ask of our Lord that the Indians be organized and distributed in islands like those of Antillia; for they then would live virtuously and peacefully serving God, as in a terrestrial paradise. (*Historia eclesiástica indiana* 3: 103-104)[8]

The Antillian paradise of Mendieta—a paradise ruled by bishops—makes the New World the geographical location of the millennial kingdom of the Apocalypse. Mendieta's creation seems a replica of another feat of the imagination by another *fratello*, the very Christopher Columbus. For some reason in 1496 Columbus was back in Spain dressed as a Franciscan (Granzotto, Sale). Nobody knows if the gesture was due to a sudden attack of anonymity, a penitential mood, or remorse for the misadministration of the lands he had encountered. In any case, something was forcing him to seize the moment, which was full of surprises. In 1497 John Cabot discovered New England for Henry VIII. On May 20, 1498, Vasco da Gama gave Manuel I of Portugal the Indies that Columbus had dreamed of. Columbus must have recalled then that on June 12, 1494, he had forced his men to swear that Cuba was not an island but the beginning of the Indies. Now, suddenly enlightened, the Admiral begins a third voyage, realizing that he has found an unknown continent. In the Venezuelan Peninsula of Paria he observes the mouth of the Orinoco River, which he identifies as one of the four waterways flowing from the Garden of Eden, the very place where humankind was created in the image of God. Columbus had found a new continent, and this was none other than Paradise. There he has a vision of an *orbis terrarum* shaped as a woman's breast. The Terrestrial Paradise could be found in the nipple. Columbus's paradise on earth, in the lands that he had claimed in the name of the Catholic Kings, may now be read as a compensatory fantasy, almost a subconscious mechanism for self-restitution of peace and tranquillity after turmoil and failure. Let us dwell for a moment on Columbus's image of Paradise.

For the Western world the signifier "Paradise" connotes a pre-lapsarian existence, abundant, healthy, and peaceful. These were the same notions that Columbus had fought so hard to eliminate from the human bodies and the environment of the New World. It is not surprising that very soon after his vision, Columbus instituted the *encomienda* system in Santo Domingo and that from this moment on the gentle Taínos or Arawaks became savages, wild men, and natural slaves. Paradise also signifies the absence of war, laws, rulers, greed, fortresses, hierarchies, and private property. When those things do not exist, as was the case among the Taíno people, for example, Western man had to make an effort to create them in order to accomplish man's mission on earth: to expiate the sins of the first parents as Augustine had commanded. The sense of tragedy and loss, pilgrimage and a lack of roots, which came with the idea of Paradise Lost, were necessary evils for civilization, for there was no doubt that civilization was one—it was Western—and that the Amerindians had no right to live outside the constraints of this culture. Man could not avoid the Faustian imperative of the search for knowledge, a search that had produced discovery and that was affected by both good and evil. In the meantime a fallen humanity, exclusively European, had to await the Millennium in order to recapture the Lost Paradise.

The Taínos had to be subjected to the same condemnation. It did not matter that they were a people who believed that they had surfaced from the underworld, that they did not think of condemnation and guilt, and that they were inherently healthy, happy, and self-sufficient. There was no room for exceptions. Columbus had found Paradise in the nipple of this earthly breast and would waste no time in exterminating the native Amerindians in order to accelerate the coming of the Millennium. Columbus himself would probably be the Messiah. In this manner he does it all, as the beginning and the end of time coincide in him on the land of Paradise. When Columbus wore the Franciscan habit in 1496, he did not do so out of sheer vanity. It is more likely that he had formulated his own theory squarely in the center of the Franciscan scheme of things. Such a theory is contained in his *Libro de las profecías* (*Book of Prophecies*), an unfinished booklet that consists of a number of documents collected by himself, his brother Bartolomé, his son Hernando, and Friar José Gorricio. The writings are collected from a number of classical and medieval authors—among them Seneca and Joachim of Fiore—and include some fragments of poetry and selections from the Church Fathers. The booklet also contains a puzzling introduction by the Admiral.[9] The goal of his *Libro de las profecías* is to convince the king of Spain that his adventures and his figure are of cosmic importance and that the results of his enterprise will be crowned with eternal recognition. His signature, Xpo Ferens, with a crusader's flavor, allows one to read that he is not justifying himself in front of the Spanish monarchs, but in front of all Christendom, both present and future. He affirms that he has been chosen by God as his instrument in order to bring to completion the ancient prophecies that would rescue Christianity before the Apocalypse. The latter event, according to his calculations, was only 155 years away. Xpo Ferens, the Messenger of God, would help to expand Christendom to all the heathen in the world and would provide the gold needed to finance the great crusade that would recapture the Holy Sepulcher from the infidels. The metaphysical bent of Columbus is here full blown.

In the realm of the profane, the images that one finds of Paradise in the writings of Columbus, Vespucci, and Léry, among others, show a scopophilic inclination. The naked bodies of the men and women, especially those of the women—as Michel de Certeau has indicated (246)—in being transferred into writing produce a surplus that can be defined in terms of savagery and pleasure (see also Conley in this volume). Columbus builds a mystic image of the New World as Paradise, and the resulting metaphor is that of a woman's breast where the majestic beauty of the nipple hides the pleasure of sucking the wealth of a whole world. Peter

Mason suggests that the emphasis in the visual erotic component of the perception of the New World may well be connected to a sadistic strain of the conquistadors. In sadism, he says, it is the surface, the skin, that operates as erotogenic and in it the aggressors inscribe their desire (150). Most telling, in this respect, is the rape of an Indian woman by Michele de Cuneo during the second voyage. Tired of the woman's resistance to his demands, he whipped her with a cord and proceeded to brutalize her. Inscription and penetration go hand in hand. The target of the gaze is possession rather than contemplation; even seduction is out of the question.

Columbus's first observation on October 12 relates to the nakedness of the natives. We have already commented on the political economy of this nakedness. The bodies of the people and the continent itself are eroticized, and those bodies are always female. Love and awe are the obliged responses to the Master and the Messenger of the True God. The Spaniards desire to use those bodies and to penetrate the continent. The economic motif of the search for wealth substitutes for the erotic without canceling it. The beauty of native bodies will become a source of profit derived from the slave trade.

Likewise, for Vespucci the New World is also an object for penetration and scrutiny. His gaze is that of the voyeur. He looks at women's breasts, at their genitals, at their lovemaking. He is comfortable when they remain passive, but as soon as they act as subjects they become monsters. A good example is Vespucci's account of the cruelty of the women who enlarge the penises of their partners, introducing herbs and insects, sometimes producing the need for castration of the affected individual. The Amerindian female had to continue to be lascivious, overactive, and wasteful in order to accommodate the European ideal of exploitive behavior translated as economic moderation. But there is more to this story. José Piedra, for example, argues convincingly in this volume that twentieth-century Latin Americans still maintain the stereotypes of gender and sexuality that came out of the colonial period. The impetus for native conversion was but another form of defense in order to deal with the temptation of the Other in regard to the notions of gender and sex. After all, the very concept of Western civilization might be at stake if male domination, heterosexuality, hierarchies of gender and power, and notions of property and land tenure came tumbling down. Acculturation was a European necessity against which the Amerindian world would learn to struggle.

The Wild (Wo)man's Excesses:
The Need for European Intervention

One might observe the phenomenon in Fernández de Oviedo, López de Gómara, Vespucci, and De Bry (see Conley in this volume) where a strategy of moral and physical remaking of the Amerindians is undertaken. The Amerindians were the opposite of the Europeans. Lacking body hair, the males were effeminate and, therefore, inclined to Socratic love. Excessively masculine for European tastes, the Amazon-like woman was a sexual deviation with lesbian overtones. Such images were a strong call for European intervention to redress the balance. Let us not forget that these texts are the results of political, sexual, and economic principles. They are not reflections of something external to them; the text gives reality to political, sexual, and economic practices. So if these texts are imaging or inventing America, they constitute the reality of America. The study of images is useful both as a building and as a debunking practice.

One of the favorite European constructs of the colonial period was that of the Amerindian as Savage Beast or as Wild (Wo)man.[10] According to Christian belief, those who live too close to nature become savages and acquire bestial features; they become less than human in the chain of being. In European folklore, the Wild Man was a hairy giant who lived in the woods and was armed with a club, his large genitals exposed, mute and therefore without reason, slave to natural desires and uncontrollable passions. His diet of raw vegetables and meat brought him close to bestiality, insatiability, and lack of discrimination in sexual and dietary matters. The Wild Man and the Wild Woman were the inscription of the Europeans' fear of the elements of the natural world (Sale 74+). Mountains and forests were dreadful. The wilderness was unruly, out of control, uncivilized, unpredictable, and chaotic. Opposed to the fear of the wild is the love of the tamed, that is, of domination and control of the natural world symbolized by the Renaissance garden. The roots of this attitude are biblical: Yahweh creates Man to have dominion over all animals and to replenish and subdue the Earth. A discernible image emerges, writes Sale, "of a world more mechanistic than organic, more artificial than intrinsic, more corporeal than numinous, from which intimacy, sacredness, and reverence have all but vanished" (81). In America the habitat of the Wild Man, the European Other, was precisely the home and hearth of the Taíno: they were beardless, they had a language, they cultivated their land, they loved their families, and they had a beautiful lore of legend and myth in which they showed their love for their environment. They also had a healthy diet that allowed ten of them to feel satisfied with the same amount of food a Spaniard consumed in one meal. They became savages because it was convenient for the invaders.

This is precisely the image that Columbus gives of the Caribs: they had bows and arrows and were uglier than the Taínos; their faces were painted with charcoal; they had very long hair, tied behind with parrot feathers; and they were stark naked. Vespucci's astonishment at the beauty of the Indian woman's bosom is due to the lack of flabby and hanging breasts characteristic of the European Wild Woman. Similarly, the castrating power that he attributes to the Amerindian women belongs to European witches whose magic was supposed to produce impotence in males. Columbus soon adds that the Caribs had contact with the women who lived on the island of Matinino, which sometimes he calls Matrimonio (Spanish for marriage), a place with no men and where once a year the women mated with the cannibals. The races gathered by Pliny begin to occupy the stage. In a different region Columbus heard of peoples who were born with tails. He also learned of another place populated with people who had no hair. He mentioned three ugly mermaids and a report about an island where everything was made of gold. In the absence of his regular interpreters, some Indians informed Columbus that there was another island whose inhabitants were either cyclops or dogheaded. Moreover, they were not only anthropophagi but would also castrate and drink the blood of anyone who came within their reach. In this case Columbus speculated that the report had been concocted by the natives in order to keep strangers away, and so he decided that it was preferable to believe that the island was inhabited by the subjects of the Great Khan. Pliny's races were everywhere in America, but nowhere could Columbus, Vespucci, or anyone else for that matter, see them.

Demonization is a feature that usually accompanies the image of the Wild Man and other monstrous beings (Mason, Arens). In one of his engravings, De Bry depicts a group of Tupinamba grilling on a bonfire. Although the Tupinamba used a slow burning method to cook their meals, the artifact manages to achieve a coalescence of cannibalism and infernal fire. Such is precisely the intention of Sepúlveda's *Democrates Segundo* in which, according to Pagden, the author makes "use of images of inversion, commonly reserved for witches and other deviants, and of such descriptive terms as homunculus, which suggests not only stunted growth but, since homunculi were things created by magic, also unnatural biological origins, the persistent reference to animal symbolism, monkeys, pigs and beasts in general—was intended to create an image of a half-man creature whose world was the very reverse of the 'human' world of those who by their 'magnanimity, temperance, humanity and religion' were the Indians' natural masters" (*The Fall of Natural Man* 117-118; also Todorov). During the eighteenth century the writings of Robertson, Reynal, and de Paw, among others, resuscitate these images, although the target would be broadened to include all inhabitants of the continent in the dispute of the New World (Jara, "The Inscription"; Commager and Giordanetti; Keen, *The Aztec Image*).

The central feature of the natives' inferiority—noticed by Francisco de Vitoria (see Scott, Grisel)—was their inability to discriminate, as seen in their culinary, religious, and sexual habits. Thus, in this discourse, the consumption of human flesh and of lower species of animals and plants signaled the natives' failure to distinguish between the edible and the inedible. Devil worship was also a result of the same characteristic: the Indians could not distinguish between genuine faith and a set of false beliefs crafted by satanic cunning (see Reis in this volume). Sexual deviations were explained by the generalized selection of the wrong mates indulging in bestiality, lesbianism, sodomy, incest, and other unnatural practices. The central Indian offenses—sodomy, idolatry, and cannibalism—were thus explained.

A discussion of cannibalism deserves some special attention here because one of the most recurrent rhetorical devices in European chronicles concerning Amerindian anthropophagy is removal of that practice to somewhere else or to some other time. Many alleged cases of man-eating episodes evaporated as scholars found that the practice had either vanished before their arrival or that the people questioned attributed it to their neighbors. Columbus located cannibalism in the islands of the Caribs, which, incidentally, he never visited. Vespucci's letter of 1500 also used the "neighboring" device. Anthropophagy is almost a cliché in the woodcuts and engravings representing the Amerindian peoples in the postdiscovery period. Sometimes, in ironic reversal, the man-eating neighbors happened to be Europeans, and around 1600, the Protestant De Bry used Las Casas's depiction of Spanish cruelty to make of them not only consumers of human flesh but efficient brokers for Western commercial ventures (see Conley in this volume). This is an interesting fictional twist that, in our judgment, comes to confirm the research of Arens, an anthropologist who has demonstrated convincingly that there is a striking contrast between the numerous references to anthropophagi found in various regions of the world and the failure to find a single eyewitness account of a cannibal feast or even a single description that does not rely on elements taken from classical accounts of anthropophagy. The image, however, continues to be a powerful one (see also Pagden, *The Fall of Natural Man;* Mason).

Cannibalistic feasts—as can be gathered from many of the illustrations accompanying Léry's travels through Brazil and Vespucci's voyages—are in metonymic relation with sexual disorder. Eating, drinking, and sex go together in medieval and early Renaissance mentality; all three are failures of temperance. Socratic love is a good way to end a feast of barbecued human. Léry makes a clear connection on this matter. Moreover, it is not rare to find paintings in which the joys of eating are associated with female lesbianism and masturbation. Nakedness in women— and Amerindian women are always without clothes in these portrayals—was associated with witchery and devil worship. European witches of the sixteenth and seventeenth centuries wore no clothing.

According to Michelet, the figure of the devil evolved from French folklore. By the end of the Middle Ages this character, the devil, had become an ally of the peasantry oppressed by the landlords and the Church. The most vulnerable sector of this society was composed of women who turned to the devil as the principal deity in a pantheistic cult concerned with healing and surviving. As we have suggested in relation to Columbus's image of Paradise and in connection with Western ecological theories of domination and conquest of territory, nature becomes closely associated with women: both have to be conquered, controlled, possessed, and raped—as Cuneo had done with the body of the young Indian female and as the Admiral had done with the continent and the world through his imaging of the Edenic breast. The colonies were also women who had to be conquered, penetrated by gaze, sword, pen, and penis, because their only ally and protector was none other than the crafty devil.

European witch-hunts of the sixteenth and seventeenth centuries also were to be translated to America where they became known as extirpation of idolatries. Their mechanism was to impose on a dialectical vision of the universe—such as the Andean—a Manichaean view organized by the dichotomy of good and evil. Everything that did not fit such a scheme smelled of idolatry and had to be persecuted and suppressed. Thus Polo de Ondegardo and Bernabé Cobo dedicate some of their writing to identifying witches, sorcerers, and women who had the power to kill (Silverblatt). In the case of Brazil, Léry adds that older women and witches had a special inclination for human flesh. Columbus, the friars, the conquerors, and the colonizers had not yet found their counterparts in image building. The discoverers were inventing America, and their imagination was working at full speed. As Edmundo O'Gorman has said in his now-classic book (*La invención de América*) America was invented, named, and historicized before its territory and its peoples had been encountered. It was an imagination that operated by *transpositio* rather than *translatio* of the known into the unknown, with unexpected results (see also Washburn, Hanke, Trinkaus, Greenblatt).

Columbus seems to have been looking for the kinds of signals that would confirm his expectations. Communication was simply a European monologue. This situation must have heightened the anguish of the Amerindians when confronted with the violence and communicative ineptitude of the invaders. As Mignolo shows in this volume, the alphabet was presented both as a means to improve conquest and as an instrument for colonization. The rush to impose the tyranny of the alphabet was, however, one battle that the invaders were going to lose (see León-Portilla and Gisbert in this volume). The alphabet was the first cultural weapon that the colonized learned from the colonizer. Moreover, they managed to use it early on in order to protect the secrets and "architexture" of their world. The natives used the European script to guard the secrets of their cultures and to keep the memory of their elders, but the European scientific community was unable to accumulate enough experience and firsthand observation to decode the scintillating messages in the Mayan and Aztec calendars. Did the Indians—one might ask—try to understand the secrets of European culture? The answer must be in the affirmative, with one consideration added: the natives had learned through centuries of familiarity with their environment how to cope with the strictures of material life; they had lived in agreement with their ecosystem; and they had even managed to prosper and defeat the ghost of hunger during the rule of the Inca. As we indicated earlier, something similar seems to have been achieved by the Taíno people in the pre-Columbian Antilles; and, though the situation was not as promising in the Mexica empire, the commoners there were not starving. The point is that the Amerindians did not need the Europeans. Rather, the Europeans needed them to revitalize the economy of the Old World. Once conquered by the forces of technology and disease, the Amerindians were to keep their native traditions through a thorough process of domestication of European rituals and beliefs. But in order to do so, they first had to understand them. The possibility of such an understanding was remote but they were comforted by the sense of certainty that their gods would return.

Thus while the conquered natives assimilated and appropriated the culture of the invaders within their own Amerindian worldview, the conqueror—schooled in the strictures of a one-track mind—not only considered Indian beliefs to be illegitimate but also chose to condemn them as works of the devil. The Spaniards had the sword, the pen, and the cross; they had weapons of war, the Inquisition, courts of law, and corregidors. The Indians, on the other hand, had an uncanny ingenuity to make their culture survive against all odds and regulations. The images of the peoples of Amerindia are those that allow us to define their overcoming of the trauma of contact. They are not connected only with economic and historical iron laws acting as a secular Providence; they are those representations that permit the spectator or the reader to discover the materiality of Amerindian difference permeating all structural sectors of life. In short, those images have to do with the cultural unconscious of the peoples of America.

History, Myth, and Memory

The so-called facts of conquest and colonization are of the same nature as any other facts: they are human constructions, and the reading of those constructions depends on a point of view. Thus in the same manner that nothing may be considered inherently fictional, no event can be read as absolutely real. Because "the difference between fiction and reality is not objective and does not pertain to the thing itself; it resides in us, according to whether or not we subjectively see in it a fiction. The object is never unbelievable in itself, and its distance from 'the' reality cannot shock us; for, as truths are always analogical, we do not even see it" (Veyne 21). Thus, a resistive interpretation of the "historical facts" is always possible even when least expected. Teresa Gisbert suggests that if there is a single feature of Amerindian arch-writing or primal inscription whose presence can be felt even in the absence of writing, such a feature is that of resistance, which is evident in the craftsmanship of vases and weavings, as well as in theatrical spectacles and festivals, architecture, and folklore. And although an openly rebellious attitude toward the preservation of indigenous values can be found parallel to a Herod-like disposition to accommodation and compromise, the latter—which is expressed in the language of the conqueror—does not permit the intruder to come out of the experience unscathed. In the end, an undercurrent of cultural syncretism undermines the grammar of the dominant idiom (see Gisbert and Bermúdez-Gallegos in this volume). This is, perhaps, the reason why so many first-rate critics, like those in this volume, have made colonial "writing," as conceptualized above, a centerpiece of their scholarly activities.

The chronicles, the plays, the theatrical activities, the monuments, the crafts and arts, the legends and myths transmitted by oral tradition take us from Spain to America, and from the New World to the Old and back again—from one truth and one program of truth to another. We experience them as literature, as a sort of anonymous writing whose narrator is the voice of the Amerindian peoples. One may pass from Columbus to Las Casas or from Acosta to Pané with little or no discomfort. When one encounters a new truth, the reconsideration of the old realm becomes necessary: Garcilaso and Guaman Poma shake the reader's lethargy and force a reaccommodation of the strategies of understanding. They are different points of view—often conflicting and contradictory, as we have shown in our *1492-1992: Re/Discovering Colonial Writing*—whose common target is the programming of American identity. The truths and perspectives we find in the books and artifacts that come to our attention are not the end result of natural illumination. Rather, they are born of the imagination; they belong to what may be called the Amerindian imaginary.

This Amerindian imaginary might be identified with the historical tradition only if one has in mind that this historical tradition, instead of conforming to a linear masterplot, is a weaving or an "architexture" of different cultural threads. When these threads make contact—those of the Castilian conquistador, the Seraphic friar and the down-to-earth Dominican and Jesuit, the indigenous Man-God and the shaman, the native animistic populace with its faith in the efficacy of ancient beliefs—they produce a texture that brings to light the existence of another set of images for identification. They are mixed, *mestizo* images, which imprint new wealth in shades and nuances to the Amerindian imaginary: the Creole patriot, the revolutionary native, the assimilated Indian, the poor Spaniard, and an army of social deviants such as witches and wizards, bandits and rebels, mystics and travelers.

This tradition is not only mythical (although myth plays an important part in it), and it does not only repeat what was said of gods and heroes. It is also a historical tradition, at least if, for a moment, one wishes to maintain the distinction between historical and mythical narration. The narrator or interpreter of these images and traditions does not always "speak of this superior world by putting his own words into indirect discourse" (Veyne 23) as happens with the mythographers who seem to repeat what the People, the Word, or the Muses have already told them. Myth is always a kind of information that the exegete has stumbled upon. Neither revelation nor arcane knowledge, the mythical plot is always already known, and the function of the Muse is to repeat to the poets what they already know and what is available to all interested parties. Friar Servando de Mier's quilt of Mexican history, his battle against Enlightened prejudice, his disarmingly candid apology for independence are precisely the case of a mythographer-historian in full performance (Jara). From this emerges what one could call historical mythology.

This Amerindian imaginary is also historical as it is often substantiated by the memories that contemporaries of the events have transmitted to their descendants. Here again the image of the weaving imposes itself. Who are those Amerindians who are operating as transmitters? What is their audience? Are they whites talking to Indians? Creoles to *mestizos?* Indians to whites? A white friar to a mixture of all of the above? Indians to Indians? Whites to whites? What tales are being told? Are they their own tales or do they belong to other racial or social groups? Are they ancient or contemporary narrations? These are questions one should ask in each case, but what interests us here is how the answers to these questions, however precarious, affect and provide a figuration in the form of a commentary on the Amerindian imaginary. Exclusion and inclusion, foreign and native cultural elements, play within a dialectic of imaginary identification that is not always easy to pinpoint. Some of the older preserved manifestations of Mayan culture can serve as a starting point of discussion. The quilt has to be explained and contextualized.

As is well known, the roots of Maya culture reached the Olmec period on the Gulf coastal plain some three thousand years ago. So Maya hieroglyphic writing and calendrical reckoning might have originated at that time, although inscriptions dated prior to the first century B.C.E. do not seem to exist. The Maya were conquered by the militaristic Toltecs, whose culture, according to Tedlock,

> is thought to have originated among speakers of Nahua languages. In the Mayan area, Toltec culture was notable for giving mythic prominence to the use of spear-throwers in warfare, and sacrificial prominence to the human heart. Mayan monuments and buildings no longer featured inscriptions after the end of the classic period, but scribes went right on making books for another six centuries, sometimes combining Mayan texts with Toltecan pictures. (24-27)

Thus, a common hero of Toltec, Maya, and the newer Mexica or Aztec cultures was the image of the Plumed Serpent, a cultural hero with messianic overtones.

When the Europeans arrived in Mesoamerica in the sixteenth century, hundreds of hieroglyphic books were burned by missionaries and religious fanatics. Only a few of the pre-Conquest books have survived, and they still present daunting problems in decipherment and interpretation (Clendinnen 134). So the survival of Mayan literature, culture, and thought—whose brilliance one can contemplate in the massive work of Nobel Prize–winning novelist Miguel Angel Asturias—is not dependent on the survival of its outward forms.

Rather, this survival is the result of a subtle strategy of resistance and counteracculturation. The massive old books—painted on both sides, folded like screens, made of bark, a quarter of a yard high, some five fingers broad—were a sore thumb for the friars. They had to be disguised. Inga Clendinnen writes:

> The men trained in their [the books'] elucidation were ageing, and there was little hope of their replacement, as the sons of the lords who would once have been trained in the glyphic mode had been rounded up and sequestered by the friars' schools. So that new training was turned to the service of the old ways. Men who had learned in the mission

schools how to write a European script, and had some access
to European writing materials, were brought together with
ah-kines [Maya priests, eds.], and wrote down as best they
could the words softly chanted by the interpreter-priests as
they scanned the painted pages, so translating both mode
and form to produce "books" of a new, externally European
kind. (134)

Thus, in the same manner that the ancient gods donned the garb
of Christian saints, the Roman alphabet served to mask the words
of ancient aboriginal texts.

As Walter Mignolo (in this volume and "Literacy and Colonization") reminds the reader, the sixteenth-century privileging
of writing over speech was to handicap gravely the interpreter's
performance of the Nahuatl or the Mayan text. One may consider it poetic justice that the very friars who vandalized Mayan
and Nahuatl manuscripts, tossing them into bonfires, were the
ones who worked out the adaptation of the alphabet to the
sounds of the Amerindian languages, the ones who wrote native grammars and compiled dictionaries. The purpose of the
friars' program was twofold: first, it sought the domestication of
the native idiom and the reproduction of the colonial effect by
imposing the alphabet on languages that were not of the Romance family; second, it endeavored to facilitate the writing and
dissemination of Christian prayers, catechisms, sermons, and religious instruction and propaganda in the native languages. But
the alphabet, as we indicated earlier (see also Jara and Spadaccini), was a double-edged sword, so that, as Tedlock reminds us,
"very little time passed before some of their [the friars'] native
pupils found political and religious applications for alphabetic
writings that were quite independent of those of Rome. These
independent writers have left a literary legacy that is both more
extensive than the surviving hieroglyphic corpus and more open
to understanding" (28). At least part of this problematic may be
understood through glosses of the *Popol Vuh* and the books of
Chilam Balam, both written as alphabetic substitutes for hieroglyphic books.

Writing and Performance:
Bodily Practice among the Maya

As a result of Diego de Landa's efforts to suppress idolatry, by the end of the sixteenth century most villages in the Yucatan peninsula had their sacred writings transliterated into the new form. Fourteen of these writings are known, and scholars have given them the generic title of the books of Chilam Balam. In the Mayan language "Chilam" (or "Chilan") means "spokesman" or "prophet." "Balam," meaning "jaguar," also connotes lordly guardianship, and the seer named Balam had prophesied the coming of the Spaniards. Thus the series could be named "The Books of the Spokesmen of the Jaguar Lords" (Clendinnen 134; Gallenkamp 28-29). There is a strong similarity in the record of events as narrated in all these books, revealing the presence of a deep structure, a common frame, an Ur-account that underlies the particularities of the reading of each of the Chilam Balam books. It is useful to recall that each of these texts chronicles the life of a lineage, and that the opposition and war between lineages defined the boundaries of the Mayan territories. Yet despite these conflicts, a more profound commonality structured Mayan life. Frontiers would melt away in times of famine, times in which the woods provided a hope of refuge and survival for individuals whose social life had dissolved. The collective life followed the rhythm of the seasons, the times of sowing and of harvesting. Lineages, social conflicts, wars, the affairs of men and women were subordinated to the sacred order of the universe.

The Spanish invasion brought disruption to this orderly world. The strangers and their god meant misery and destitution. But the European new order would not abrogate the rule of the legitimate Mayan lords. The books continued to be written and revised, the events continued to be recorded in order to discover their secret pattern in this untiring search for knowledge. The continuity of the lords' rule was unchallenged. There we find—writes Inga Clendinnen—"a major diagnosis: the Spaniards were identified with the Itza, those earlier, ambivalent invaders, and their destructive, fructifying presence. That creative identification rendered the flood of novel experience intelligible in familiar terms, providing a formidable shield against cognitive and emotional demoralization" (157). In time those foreigners would withdraw, or be absorbed or driven out. The lords of the peninsula would rule again.

The new and transient overlords were to be used by the Maya people. The Maya were to select from the foreigners what they could incorporate as their own. Thus, the donning of European dress and the riding of horses by the Maya nobles were unconscious strategies through which the aboriginal structures of authority and legitimacy were represented as alternatives to the Spanish system. Similarly, despite the inquisitorial eye of the friars, the Maya continued to cultivate their religious practices, which were in consonance with the pulse of nature and the gods. They inflicted and blessed themselves with physical anguish; they staged self-laceration and fasting as well as fire-walking dramas and daylong warrior dances. They viewed pain as a path to ecstasy and ingested drugs in order to explore the ways of the transcendental. They had a material, existential, and collective notion of religion quite different from the Christian postmortem salvation of the individual.

During 1562 the violence and cruelty inflicted on the Indian population by the friars under the leadership of the Franciscan Diego de Landa culminated in a wholesale destruction of the idols and in a series of confessions of ritual crucifixion and other human sacrifices concocted by Landa and spelled out to the natives with the persuasion of the instruments of torture. It seems that in that fateful year two native youths stumbled upon a cave crowded with idols and human skulls. When Diego de Landa surmised that pagan practices were continuing despite years of teaching by the Franciscans, he resorted to violence in the form of public displays of torture in order to reestablish Franciscan authority over the Indians. Clendinnen recalls this bloody episode, in the words of a Spanish eyewitness:

> When the Indians confessed to having so few idols (one, two, or three) the friars proceeded to string up many of the Indians, having tied their wrists together with cord, and thus hoisted them from the ground, telling them that they must confess all the idols they had, and where they were. The Indians continued saying they had no more...and so

the friars ordered great stones attached to their feet, and so
they were left to hang for a space, and if they still did not
admit to a greater quantity of idols they were flogged as
they hung there, and had burning wax splashed on their
bodies. (74)

It seems that 158 natives died under duress, 30 committed suicide, a great number were crippled, and some 4,500 were tortured.
No matter that physical punishment was the preserve of the secular government. Despite the illegality of the friars' actions, violence
continued for three months under the leadership of the provincial Diego de Landa, who ordered mass arrests and the savage
and indiscriminate application of torture. The culmination of the
macabre festival took place on July 12, 1562, with a great *Auto de
Fe*, which Landa managed to legitimate with the presence of the
Spanish civil authority in the person of Don Diego Quijada. The
carnival, after all, had a very clear discursive and political motif:
the elimination of all doubts regarding the Franciscans' rule in the
peninsula.

The Maya seem to have understood at this point that their cultural survival depended on a new choice. They decided that the
time of the old gods was indeed over, and that the rule of new
gods, those of Christianity, had to begin. The point of departure of
the new era is almost catachrestic in its coincidence with the death
of the Franciscan provincial and then bishop of Yucatan, Diego de
Landa, whose *Relación de las cosas de Yucatán (Yucatan, Before and After the Conquest)* is one of the few original sources from that area
that survived his Vandalic tantrum. The terse comment of William
Gates in the Introduction to his edition of *Yucatan, Before and After
the Conquest* is worth reproducing:

The position of Diego de Landa in history rests upon two of
his acts, one the writing of the book [on Yucatan], and the
other the famous *Auto de fé* of July 1562 at Maní, at which,
in addition to some 5000 "idols," he burned as he tells us
twenty-seven hieroglyphic rolls, all he could find but could
not read, as "works of the devil," designed by the evil one
to delude the Indians and to prevent them from accepting
Christianity when it should in time be brought to them.
Both acts were monumental, one to the ideas of his time,

and the other as the basis and fountain of our knowledge of a great civilization that had passed. (iii)

There is something more to bear in mind at this point. The Franciscan image of the Indians as childish in their physical and mental constitution, which we have seen in Mendieta and which Georges Baudot analyzes in this volume in reference to Motolinía, assumes perverse and hyperbolic representation in Friar Diego de Landa. During his rule as provincial, the Franciscans toughened their regulations for religious instruction as well as the coercive context in which this teaching took place. The obligatory instruction of catechism, the forced baptism for Indian leaders, the sequestering in schools of the sons of the native lords to be drilled in Christian Hispanic ways of living and in the contempt for the manners and values of their parents, were practices that were rigorously enforced. Moreover the friars showed little enthusiasm to teach Spanish to the Indians, not only—as we stated earlier in our discussion of Mendieta and Motolinía—because they thought it would open the way to corrupting influences, but also because their role as mediators between Spaniards and Indians could be challenged. For Landa and his brethren of Yucatan, the Indians were not the property of the *encomenderos;* all physical and spiritual control over the Indians belonged to the friars, and the settlers had only some limited rights to Indian labor and tribute. The Franciscan discourse in Yucatan is tinted with a vicious chiliastic strand, for the Franciscans believed that the rapid death of the Indians would be followed by the end of all things. It seems that Landa wanted to hasten this end: his temperament did not call for resignation, as was the case with Jerónimo de Mendieta at the end of his life, but one of feverish, paranoiac activism inspired by the need to secure Indian souls and bodies—for the Franciscans first and for salvation next. His millenarianism was closer to Columbus's than to Mendieta's. If one looks at this consideration, the delightful irony of Maya historiographic behavior comes to light.

The Maya decided to end the era of the old gods with the death of Landa. The ancient deities had permitted the double encounter: with Jesus Christ and with Diego de Landa, with the principle of good and with the prince of evil. They saluted Diego de Landa's death, perhaps with some rejoicing, as an anticipation of the sufferings that would envelop the Millennium according to the friars' teaching, a suffering that they, the Indians, had already been subjected to since the arrival of the European strangers:

Then, with the true God, the true Dios, came the beginning of our misery. It was the beginning of tribute, the beginning of church dues, the beginning of strife with purse-snatching, the beginning of strife with blow-guns, the beginning of strife by trampling on people, the beginning of robbery with violence, the beginning of debts enforced by false testimony, the beginning of individual strife, a beginning of vexation, a beginning of robbery with violence. This was the origin of service to the Spaniards and priests, of service to the local chiefs, of service to the teachers, of service to the public prosecutor by the boys, the youths, of the town, while the poor people were oppressed. These were the very poor people who did not depart when oppression was put upon them. . . . But it shall still come to pass that tears shall come to the eyes of our Lord God. . . . (Prophecy for *Katun 11 Ahau*)

They also decided to appropriate the Christian ideal of the Millennium. Christ would mean the end of the domination of foreigners. From then on, Jesus and the Maya lords would begin their kingdom on this earth. Christ became an Amerindian deity. What would become of the rights of the colonizers? The idea of a colonial period itself was being put in question. Just one more cycle had come to pass, as so many others in Mayan myth-history. In *The Book of Chilam Balam of Chumayel*, one can read:

Then, I tell you, justice shall descend to the end that Christianity and salvation may arise. Thus shall end the men of the Plumeria flower. Then the rulers of the towns shall be asked for their proofs and titles of ownership, if they know them. Then they shall come forth from the forests and from among the rocks and live like men; then towns shall be established again. There shall be no fox to bite them. This shall be in *Katun 9 Ahau*. Five years shall run until the end of my prophecy, and then shall come the time for the tribute to come down. Then there shall be an end to the paying for the wars which our fathers raised against the Spaniards. You shall not call the *katun* [periods of twenty Mayan years, eds.] which is to come a hostile one, when Jesus Christ, the guardian of our souls, shall come. Just as we are saved here on earth, so shall he bear our souls to his holy heaven also. You are sons of the true God. Amen.

The discursive strategies for Mayan manipulation of both the text of colonization and the Christian code may be found in the very content of the books of the Jaguar Priests of the Yucatan peninsula. Scrupulous observation and careful recording of the movements in the heavens, coupled with the conviction that all things have a pattern, allowed them to discern complex recurrences. For the Maya, knowledge was not something finite that could be grasped through the interpretation or the mere reading of a simple book where all knowledge could be found. Knowledge was arrived at through the patient recording of events in the experienced world and, at the same time, through the recording of any clues regarding the deciphering of those events. Finally, through the accumulation of empirical and interpretive data, a structural model would be discerned. History, therefore, was not just causality, rational and reasonable explanation, or linear narration. Rather, it was history-in-the-writing (Clendinnen), pure dynamics and movement, predictable but always relative in its results. The events of the Spanish Conquest integrated into the whole complex of Mayan history would acquire a different meaning and might even lose their triumphant character.

In Mayan calendrical thought, for example, each day and each larger time unit were recognized as deities whose attributes would be subtly modified through association with other deities. That structure allowed for prediction, for the recurrence of the same combination of influences could be expected to produce the same effects. In the words of Clendinnen, "history was simultaneously prophecy, prophecy becoming history again with the next swing of the cycle" (146). Yet the future could not be read by just anyone; that action involved training, and only the lords of the lineages had the skills and empowerment to do so. Moreover their power was subordinate to their responsibility for that particular segment of the human order, and that responsibility was for a designated section of time. The knowledge of the lords, however esoteric, brought with it higher social utility, and this utility was expressed not in the reading of the book, but in its performance, for the performance quality of the Mayan script remained in the European transliteration of the aboriginal glyph.

One reason for the continuation of this performative quality in Mayan writing is the simple fact that the first transcribers of the manuscripts into alphabetic writing had no rules to follow. They had to guess at spellings and separation of words and sentences, which might further explain the emendations by later copyists. The translation of the oral into writing was, at the same time, made even more difficult by the Mayan language's bent toward polysemics in both word and sentence structure and its penchant for punning, wordplay, and irony. Furthermore, the original hieroglyphs were condensed statements that depended heavily for their exposition on trained and skilled performers who could read them while "fleshing out the spare shapes with memorised formulae" (Clendinnen 136). Their initial transcription into the European alphabet was purposely aphoristic. The compact and telling expression meant that it could not simply be read off by just anyone for, in essence, it was a script to be interpreted and textualized through its performance within formal rules. These texts, therefore, remained as scripts, as skeletal structures for dramatic action that allowed for a dialogic relationship between the performer and the audience whose response could shape all aspects of the performance itself.

Within this framework the prophets came to the realization that the Spaniards were just a chapter in the saga of their social existence, that like previous invaders they would be incorporated and assimilated to an order of things that could be read in nature and in the stars. The responsibility of the lords was to precipitate the downfall of the Spanish dominion in order to accelerate the victory of Jesus Christ, the new Maya god, and the coming of the cherished Millennium. The books of Chilam Balam had announced the events that were to follow, and each reading/performance pointed unambiguously to the end of Spanish rule and to the aboriginal appropriation of selected aspects of European culture.

The *Popol Vuh* is the most prestigious Amerindian representative of this fusion and mixing of history and myth. The text was written in Quiché using Spanish script between 1554 and 1558. It chronicles the creation of humankind, the actions of the gods, the origin and history of the Maya-Quiché people, and the chronology of their kings down to 1550. The original was discovered by Francisco Ximénez, the parish priest of Chichicastenango in the highlands of Guatemala. He copied the original Quiché text, which is now lost, and proceeded to translate it into Spanish. Ximénez's work is now at the Newberry Library in Chicago.

According to the *Popol Vuh*, at the beginning the first four humans could see everything on earth to the limits of space and time. The gods decided to limit the sight of their human creation to what was obvious and nearby. But the lords of the Quiché also had an instrument that was used to overcome their nearsightedness and assess future and distant events. That instrument was a book, the *Popol Vuh*, or the "Council Book," which spoke of the "Dawn of Life." These two alternate meanings of its title make reference to the duality of writing and painting in both the Mayan and the Nahua languages. In ancient Mayan books both skills were practiced by the same artisan and had the same patron deity known as One Monkey. Dennis Tedlock has written perceptively:

> In the books made under the patronage of these twin gods there is a dialectical relationship between the writing and the pictures: the writing not only records words but sometimes has elements that picture or point to their meaning without the necessity of a detour through words. As for the pictures, they not only depict what they mean but have elements that can be read as words. When we say that Mesoamerican writing is strongly ideographic relative to our own, this observation should be balanced with the realization that Mesoamerican painting is more conceptual than our own. (30-31)

The transliteration of the ancient *Popol Vuh* into alphabetic form is more than a translation on a glyph-to-glyph basis, a translation that would have produced a text for an elite of performers and diviners. Rather, it is a reader's interpretation that brought out the world behind the pictures and the plot outlines of the original book. The *Popol Vuh* is a book of quotations, and one is constantly reminded of this iterative and contextual quality by its deictic rhetoric—"as it is said"; "here is the account"; "this is the narration"—which points to the mythic demeanor of the representation. Tedlock comments that at some point the author/translators of the book assume the role of performers, speaking directly to contemporary readers as if they were members of a live audience and complaining, as performers sometimes do, of the difficulties of their task:

> This is the beginning of the ancient word, here in this place called Quiché. Here we shall inscribe, we shall implant the Ancient Word, the potential and source for everything done in the citadel of Quiché, in the nation of Quiché people. / And here we shall take up the demonstration, revelation, and account of how things were put in shadow and brought to light by the [Gods].... They accounted for everything—and did it, too—as enlightened beings, in enlightened words. We shall write about this now amid the preaching of God, in Christendom now. We shall bring it out because there is no longer a place to see it, a Council Book / a place to see "The Light That Came from Across the Sea," / the account of "Our Place in the Shadows," a place to see "The Dawn of Life," / as it is called. There is the original book and ancient writing, but he who reads and ponders it hides his face. It takes a long performance and account to complete the emergence of all the sky-earth... as it is said, / by the [Gods]. (*Popol Vuh* 71-72)

From the vantage point of the moment in which the preaching of God and Christian pedagogy take place, the authors' project is to inscribe the Ancient Word, the Prior Word, a Language other than that of Christendom. They attempt to close the gap left by the ancient *Popol Vuh* using their visual and aural memory. This is like saying that the Book is missing, and because it is missing it is there: the transliterated *Popol Vuh* is a symbolic place in which the Other comes to rejoin the Self, in which the disconcerted Christian Self subsumes the Other that was once its true Self, the Word of the ancestors. One wonders if this was the reason why the authors decided to remain anonymous. It may very well be, because this is the Book of a collective historical identity.

The spiral movement in which the Maya are going to submerge

the Spanish domination—as they had done with the Itza invasion—appears as soon as the Book is set in motion. Everything starts with a dialogue between the gods of the Ocean and those of the Sky, in which they agree to conceive of the emergence of earth from the sea and of the growth of plants and people in its surface. Tedlock explains:

> They wish to set in motion a process they call the sowing and dawning, by which they mean several different things at once. There is the sowing of seeds in the earth whose sprouting will be their dawning, and there is the sowing of the sun, moon, and stars, whose difficult passage beneath the earth will be followed by their own dawning. Then there is the matter of human beings, whose sowing in the womb will be followed by their emergence into the light at birth, and whose sowing in the earth at death will be followed by dawning when their souls become sparks of light in the darkness. (34)

The gods fail three times in the creation of living creatures who are articulate and religious and follow the rhythms of nature as expressed in the calendar. The first beings will neither work nor talk; they can only make savage noises, and their progeny are the animals of today. In their second try the gods build a creature of mud that cannot walk, turn its head, or keep its shape; its solitude negates its capacity for reproduction, and the unfortunate being dissolves into nothing. The third time the gods seek council from an elder couple who instructs them to bring to life a creature made of wood. Such a creature, though seemingly normal, is unable to organize its actions and is often oblivious of the gods. The Hurricane god floods these new creatures, and they are attacked by monstrous animals as well as by their own domestic utensils, dogs, and turkeys, which claim vengeance for the mistreatment to which they have been subjected. Their descendants are the monkeys of today.

The fourth time the gods know of a mountain filled with both yellow and white corn that has been discovered by the animals. Xmucane, the divine midwife and adviser to the gods in their previous construction of the wooden being, grinds the corn from this mountain, and the flour mixed with water provides the substance for human flesh. The four men who are formed will become the four leaders of the Quiché lineages. Still today these men are called mother-fathers, since, according to Tedlock, "in ritual matters they serve as symbolic androgynous parents to everyone in their respective lineages" (47). This time the beings are so perfect that the creators decide to curtail their access to knowledge and, after an agreement achieved through dialogue, they limit their vision of time and space. Soon they make four wives for the men, and the peoples' lineages begin to multiply. Twelve generations come to pass until Tonatiuh, or "Sun"—as the Aztecs nicknamed Pedro de Alvarado, whose troops invaded Guatemala in 1524—arrives and the leaders of the lineage are "hanged by the Castilian people." During the next generation, when the lords adopted Spanish names, the alphabetic *Popol Vuh* was written. Tedlock's fine translation into English allows one to listen to the rhythm of Mayan speech and to the movement of its historical cycles, which show a striking symbiosis between human and vegetable life. It reaches the most complete identification of the human and the vegetable in the metaphoric series on maize, whose phases of growth are represented as following the human existential curve.

At the end of the book the place named Quiché has been renamed "Holy Cross," Santa Cruz. Tedlock comments:

> Today, even when Quiché daykeepers go to a remote mountaintop shrine, sending up great clouds of incense for multitudes of deities and ancestors, they sometimes begin and end by running through an "Our Father" and a "Hail Mary" and crossing themselves. It is as if the alien eye and ear of the conqueror were present even under conditions of solitude and required the recitation of two spells, one to ward them off for a while and the other to readmit their existence. Between these protective spells daykeepers are left to enter, in peace, a world whose obligations they know to be older than those of Christianity, obligations to the mountains and plains where they continue to live and to all those who have ever lived there before them. So it is with the authors of the *Popol Vuh* who mention Christendom on the first page, Holy Cross on the last page, and open up the whole sky-earth, vast and deep, within. (62)

History and myth confuse their marks in this book, and in many of its characters the borders between human and divinity are hard to locate with precision. By the end of part 3, the characters, who are unequivocally divine, perform rituals to worship corn and dead relatives. They are gods acting like common people. Contrariwise, when part 4 begins we meet those people who were first created by the gods, their powers of vision and understanding untouched. They are people acting like gods. Once their vision is taken away, the narrative assumes the aspect of a chronicle of lineages and generations. Many characters, however, seem to refuse their simple status as historical beings and aspire to supernatural deeds. Myth and history belong here to a single whole; there is no separation between them. In primal Amerindian thought dualities do not define themselves in a play of canceling oppositions; they complement and attract each other.[11]

Christianity, the Law, and Amerindian Life

This spiral conception of human development, which seems to have been generalized in the Amerindian world, openly conflicted with the tenets of Christianization. The friars did not stop with the rituals of incorporation and participation represented by Baptism and Communion. Indians had to confess their sins, including what they had taught their own children: respect for their god, their temples, and their priests, love and veneration of their elders and extended family, and their dedication to the community. Christianization meant new rituals and a new pantheon, an exclusive monotheistic faith, emphasis on individual commitment and salvation, and the reduction of the family to a nucleus formed by the couple and their children. Christianization represented the erosion of Amerindian social, familial, and sacred structures, the loss of Indian contact with rhythms of nature that, in a last turn of the screw, was tantamount to the breakage of the link between social persona and individual self. Ironically, the breaking up of ethnic, regional, and communal solidarity was to produce effects adverse to the efforts of Spanish colonization for it increased the importance of the Amerindian village, pueblo, or town as a sort of fallback zone of resistance to the colonial regime. The natives maintained—or created, when it was lacking—a collective identity on the basis of religious, economic, and juridical cultural habits, habits that they had been able to safeguard from the ravages of colonial deculturation.

The best instrument available to the settlers in their project of eliminating the religious and mythical bases of Amerindian cultures was the law. The Spaniards had an intense legalistic mind that, trained in the discipline of writing, had a propensity for drawing up documents as well as for preparing treatises and monumental recompilations of decrees and Crown directives (Jara and Spadaccini). The legacy of this predisposition is the careful documentation kept for the most incredible events and the abundance of chronicles, historical accounts, letters, diaries, and biographies connected to the conquest and colonization of the New World. Unfortunately the colonizers did not have the same respect for the documentation of the life and traditions of those they came to conquer. In an attitude revealing an amazing lack of confidence, they burned and destroyed monuments, works of art, scrolls, and buildings, as we have seen in the Landa episode. More often than not, the gods of an absolute Other, such as the Amerindian, made the Spaniards afraid. Legality, for the Spaniards, was the private property of civilized Europe. Procedural constraints and logical rationalizations necessary to achieve legality did not immediately apply to barbarians who, after all, had been born in the Antipodes, a place where everything worked topsy-turvy. The Amerindians had to be straightened out. But as with everything else, the law proved to be a double-edged sword, and, in fact, the birth of international law can be located in the debate provoked by the encounter between Europe and America. The founding father of international law may be said to be the Dominican friar Francisco de Vitoria, and his most successful disciple in America would be the indefatigable friar Bartolomé de Las Casas (Scott; Grisel; Pagden, *The Fall of Natural Man*, "Identity Formation in Spanish America").

Under Spanish rule the law was the institutional representation of power at the same time that it legitimized power in a juridico-discursive net of royal decrees and codes of law, defining the prerogatives of the king, the rights of the courts, the functions of the viceroys and local officials, and regulations for towns, communities, and cities. The law also circumscribed the areas of influence of the secular branch of the Church and those corresponding to the monastic orders as agreed in the statutes of royal patronage.

One can imagine how difficult it would have been for a chronicler to exit safely this discursive legal grid. With many of the chronicles of the Indies, censorship was almost instantaneous. How could the chroniclers represent a world that did not fit into the representational categories of *jus civile, jus gentium,* and natural law? How could they represent a different conception of power? Of course, they always had recourse to myth, understood as superstition or legendary tale, as we indicated earlier. And there was the repository of the European Other represented in the images of the witches, the Wild Man and the Wild Woman, and the Amazons, among others; of the European Others collected in foreign lands, either of real or imaginary geography, some of whom were already present in the books of chivalry.

Yet none of those European Others could explain, for instance, the Nahuatl conception of power and its force, which, far from being legitimized in legal books, was divinely infused into the nobles and the lords. In effect, power was a call for leadership that, emanating from Quetzalcoatl's will, legitimized the authority of the *pipiltin,* or nobleman. There was no power without a body to receive it from the deity, and the body could then exercise power as the deity itself. The power, therefore, was the lord and the noble; it was the person who exercised it. The paraphernalia were, at the same time, an integral part of that power that emerged from sacred relics, ritual words, songs, intonations, and human sacrifice itself. In human sacrifice the language of the priests, the garment of the sacrificial warrior, the expectations of the crowd, the invocations to the god, and the god incarnated in the scapegoat functioned as the very script of power. Thus, to read the signs of power was to perform them.

Once again we find here the inextricability of myth and history, the incarnation of the Man-God who, in diverse garments and disguises, came to alleviate the confusion and chaos in which the Mesoamerican peoples were immersed after the close of the classical period, around the year 1000 of the Christian era. Despite the difference in values and emphasis, these figures are Amerindian equivalents for the Christian Jesus, a Jewish rabbi who, before the destruction of the Temple by the Roman armies, gathered disciples through his teachings and was condemned as an impostor and troublemaker. Among the Mesoamericans, according to Gruzinski, "the man-god had the prerogative of communicating with the tutelary god, the calpulteotl, of striking up a dialogue that was pursued by the paths of ecstasy, of possession or hallucination: 'In him the god arises.' The pact made in the course of these dialogues was the act that formed the basis of the power: through it the protective numen, the *altepetl iyollo* (the heart of the pueblo), undertook to lend his efficacious protection to the people who revered him" (21). The man-god was the skin, or the envelope, of the deity, or its *nahualli*, i.e., its receptacle or covering. The man was possessed, transformed into the god, since he partook of the divine force; in Nahuatl language and thought the man was the god. Again we see that Christian duality is canceled out in Amerindian thought.

The man-god was also a rebel in decisive struggle against the figure of the despot, as was the case against Moctezuma in Mexico. The signs of misfortune had started in 1509. For a full decade omens and miracles terrified Tenochtitlan, the other big cities, and the countryside. Inexplicable flames consumed the temple of the god of fire; monstrous beings were brought to Moctezuma's palace only to vanish in mystery; a comet spread panic. Nezahualpilli, ruler of Texcoco and himself a man-god, predicted the ruin of the Aztec empire, and a woman resuscitated to join him in claiming the end of Moctezuma's rule. Many chroniclers, including Sahagún, Durán, and Alva Ixtlilxochitl, refer to some of these omens. Now these omens may be read in two ways: as a rhetorical strategy that assimilated the events of the Conquest into the symbolic realm in order to eliminate the unforeseen—thus explaining it as something inevitable—or as a symptom of hostility against Aztec domination (Gruzinski 27-30). As in the case of the Mayas of Yucatan, the spiral of history took another Vician turn when the Mexicans experienced the Spanish invasion of 1519. Quetzalcoatl, the very symbol of the man-god, was reincarnated in Cortés the conqueror—the warrior riding deer and armored in metal. The

Toltecs' fate would now be repeated; the destruction of the Mexica was imminent. In the following monologue or harangue the
Mexica *tlatoani,* Moctezuma, is speaking to Cortés:

> Our Lord, you are tired, but you have already arrived in
> your land, Mexico. You have come to occupy your throne
> which, for a brief time, was kept for you by your substitutes.
> I wish that one of the lord kings could see now, astonished,
> what I am witnessing. It's not that I am dreaming... for
> I have already seen you and for five or ten days I was
> anguished and my gaze fixed on the world of mystery, and
> you have come among clouds and fog. The Kings who had
> ruled your city had told us that you would come back, and
> now you have arrived, even if fatigued. Come to the land,
> rest, recover your royal mansions, freshen your body. Come
> to your land, our lords.[12]

Absolute power and a fleeting lifetime bordered by death mark
the Man-God, who seeks neither everlasting power nor hereditary
status. Shamanistic, mysterious, and mystic—like Columbus—the
Man-God becomes a sign of himself, or better, a betrayal of the sign
of himself: Christopher's cabalistic signature. Orphaned, Columbus and the Man-God do not have a history to explain their power;
or, perhaps, it would be preferable to say that their history starts
with the present, or with a twist of the present; that their history
begins with them, with Quetzalcoatl and Columbus.

There seems to be a difference between this structure and that
of patriarchal societies, however. The power of the Amerindian
hero is not tied to "the name of the father." Control, coercion, the
law, institutional violence are not guarantees of its efficacy. His
power has a maternal source, a ceremonial character underscoring identification. Coming from nobody, the Amerindian hero has
to proclaim himself; like Augusto Roa Bastos's dictated-dictator,
he has to utter the magic words: "I, the Supreme." Power is a
dramatic art, its nature is aesthetic: the hero either had to display his divinity on his own or allow others to exhibit it. Tupac
Amaru's head had to be removed from public display because in
time it could become even more beautiful. The Inca's head becomes an icon of subversion, the possible undoing of the powers
that be.

The hereafter and the idea of a supernatural being do not seem to pertain to the code of Amerindian beliefs. Incas, Mayas, Aztecs, Tupis, and Taínos lived in their present. They also dreamed of a better world, that is, they had utopias, but the construction of those utopias followed rules that were quite different from those respected in the European West, for after all they were built within a colonial context. European language and writing, the artistic and literary canon, festivals, carnivals, and other popular celebrations were used to construct an Amerindian utopia. In the Andean world in particular, it was a quest for the restoration of the ideals of a defeated and conquered society. And despite certain chiliastic aspects derived from a Judeo-Christian story based on the theme of the Millennium, in this utopia, it is the Amerindian matrix that gives the quest its social and transcendental value in a radical subversion of the ideas that had served as a platform for conquest.

For the Indians Christianity meant repression of their ideas and traditions. Syncretism, as shown by Gisbert in this volume, would pave the way for utopia. It was in the Andean provinces of the empire where Inca history, which had often been hated and rejected by the conquered peoples, was to become a clear panacea of expectations and a solid ground for consciousness-raising (Wachtel, Burga, Ossio, Flores Galindo). There secular joy, profane celebrations, comedies, and popular rituals became signifiers of protest and unqualified resentment. Similarly, the Maya lords of the major provinces used to keep troops of professional comedians who performed on public occasions for the delectation of the commoners and also to satisfy the taste for low comedies and satires among the nobility (Gallenkamp 141-142; Clendinnen 140-143). These satires often indulged in criticism of the rule of the very same lords who supported the staging and representation of these events, attesting to their sense of security and confidence in their position as well as to the stability of the social order. The Spaniards, on the other hand, thought of these representations as dangerous and deleterious for society and sought legal and illegal means—from the tribunals of the Inquisition to naked force—to suppress them.

Taki Onkoy and the Resurrection of Ancestral Identity

In the Andean area things were not very different, as can be seen through various interpretations regarding the death of Atahuallpa, an event promptly seized upon by the oral tradition. Let us recall that the Inca had been baptized by the Spaniards, who also executed him by strangulation and buried him with Christian ceremony. The Inca's death produced the expectation of his resurrection, although chronicles bear witness to the sadness of the people and say that when they could not find his corpse many of them hanged themselves (Pease, *El pensamiento mítico*).

In the meantime the Inca's nobility was divided, as Teresa Gisbert reminds us in her essay. The rebels' headquarters were in Vilcabamba, but other children of Huayna Capac had concentrated in Cuzco at the service of the Spaniards. No historian can suppress the temptation of isolating Cristóbal in this adventure. Cristóbal Paullu Inca, baptized in 1543, used the patronymic of his political leader, Cristóbal Vaca de Castro. He lived in luxury, was first a partisan of Pizarro, and then sided with Almagro, Pizarro's enemy. He also owned *encomiendas* and became a good Christian (Wachtel, Burga). To understand the problem presented by this division, one must recall that the decrease of the Indian population, as shown by Cook and Borah, had acquired alarming proportions, and that the *mestizos*—individuals of mixed European and Indian blood—had become a threat to colonial stability. According to Las Casas they were the owners of the New World. These *mestizos*, allied with the Creoles, the Indians, and the Inca leaders of Vilcabamba, started a revolutionary process during the last third of the 1560s. As a result of those activities, the Augustinians were charged with the evangelization of the Vilcabamba region, and the religious movement to extirpate idolatry gained momentum. Those activities would bring about resentment and eventual counteraction: Titu Cussi Yupanqui, the emperor, decided to keep his distance from the friars while his subjects were more decisive, originating the Taki Onkoy movement of resistance to foreign oppression. That movement was discovered in 1564 by Luis de Olivera and was repressed by Cristóbal de Albornoz between 1570 and 1572, as part of Viceroy Toledo's efforts to eliminate idolatry in the Andes (Millones; Burga; Castro-Klarén; Pease, *El dios creador andino*).

The *Relación de las fábulas y ritos de los Incas* (*Account of the Fables and Rites of the Incas* [1574]), the chronicle of the Peruvian Cristóbal de Molina, broke the news on the Taki Onkoy, a heretic ritual performed in both song and dance. The activities of the *taquiongos*, the name given to the ministers of the cult, seem to have been concentrated mainly in the region of Huamanga. The *taquiongos*, who claimed to have been chosen by the deities, could communicate with the *huacas*—a place or a sacred object, a temple containing the deity, like a lake or a mountain—and were possessed by the ethnic gods of their ancestors who could speak through them. Thus, in South America one finds again shamanistic features incorporated in privileged creatures or men-gods who availed themselves of techniques that gave them access to other worlds and allowed them to rule the elements and guard against adversity. Structured in the form of rituals, those defenses were often precipitated by the consumption of hallucinogens, and they functioned as didactic and initiatory experiences in the fashion of visions and dialogues with the deities. The *taquiongos* preached the end of the Christian world, the return of the *huacas*, and the end of all injustices. According to the ministers, the Indians had not taken good care of their ancestral gods and had forgotten their *huacas*. In order to recover the favor of their gods, the Indians had to return to the Andean values and to the idea of reciprocity. Although many of the *huacas*—gods and sacred places—had been defeated by the Christian deities, some, like Pachacamac and Titicaca, had been able to resist and had good prospects for victory (Molina, Burga). Ultimately, a return to Andean values meant that believers should abandon everything foreign, including names, foodstuffs, clothing, and other objects.

In the preaching of the *taquiongos* it was said that the Inca and the Sun—the god of the Inca state—had been defeated by the Christian God. It was now up to the *huacas*, or local deities, to expel the invaders and their god. Thus, the main tenets of the movement revolved around the restoration of a collective conscience that focused on the imminent destruction of the world of the Indian, on Spanish exploitation and abuses, and on the resurrection of the

Andean order, centralized in the image of the Inca as an organizing principle. It must be emphasized, however, that the Taki Onkoy was not a movement of Inca restoration. The religion preached by the *taquiongos* was that of the ethnic groups who preceded the Inca. Their nobility would also be championed later on by Guaman Poma. Unlike Guaman Poma, however, the *taquiongos* never would have rejected the divinities of their ancestry, and never would have accepted Christians—good or bad—as Guaman, the Yarovilca prince, does.

The central motif of the Taki Onkoy was the Indian perception of a *pachacuti*, of human existence in an upside-down world produced by the trauma of a conquest that had displaced the Inca gods who now seemed to be erased from memory. The narrative singing of the past—the *taki*—is entranced by the scourge of epidemics and anguish. The Taki Onkoy was a dance of desperation and hope; it was the Andean exorcism of foreign evil. It was a ritual of singing and dancing preceded by sexual abstinence and fasting. Often the paroxysm of dance and words ended in the final exhaustion of death. The Taki Onkoy was the Andean bet for resurrection, for renewed health and well-being. The rejection both of Spanish colonization and the Inca regime meant the return to an ancestral identity. But the locus of this turn was not meant as a *tabula rasa*. Rather, it was thought of as a second chance, as signaled by the patronymics of the prophet and his comrades in the leadership of the movement. Thus, Juan Chocne, named after John the Baptist, and his two companions, Mary and Mary Magdalene, recall the Christian sacrifice; they signify a symbolic structure whose function is the reinstitution of the sacrifice and the resurrection of the body. Juan would baptize the Andean peoples a second time. Thus, after the defeat of the Christian God, the individual body—which had become a tabernacle for the *huacas*—was the sole guarantor of identity. The figure of Christ had thus become assimilated into Amerindian mental structures, as can also be seen in the case of the Maya in Yucatan.

The *taquiongos* proceeded to open the gates of repression in the Andean psyche. The body exploded in communal dance. An animistic principle seemed to orient the Andean reading of social and material phenomena. The body became a gigantic repertoire of symbols projected into the material world. Like infants, the Andean beings confused their boundaries with those of the earth and the universe.

The Spanish presence meant a brutal immersion of the Andean being into the mirror stage. The presence and the violence of the foreigners revealed to the Indians their own alterity and their difference regarding the universe they inhabited, their *Pachamama* (Mother Earth). Those strangers who had come to usurp their land had turned them into subjects of a different law: the law of a different father, far from Viracocha and the Sun. The isomorphic relation of the Amerindian with the landscape was broken by the European presence and the ensuing masquerade of war, exploitation, epidemics, famine, and death. The Taki Onkoy was the revenge of the Andean soul, a soul that sought to reconnect with communal values in order to rescue the traces of the Andean self. Once the Christian victory over the Inca was erased from memory, the new sacred pantheon would be that of the *huacas*, i.e., the ancient communal and regional gods.

The crumbling of Inca resistance against the Spaniards at Vilcabamba had been brought about by a number of factors, including epidemics, internal dissension, and sheer exhaustion. The new emperor, Tupac Amaru, was captured by the troops of Viceroy Toledo on June 27, 1572, and he was beheaded in September of the same year. It seems that prior to his execution, Tupac Amaru had embraced Christianity. But even if this were true, the event has lost its relevance, for what matters is the Indian reaction of pain and sadness, in addition to the possibility of his resurrection as the final restitution of Andean order. The emperor's body was buried in an unknown place, and his head was exhibited on the extremity of a lance to serve as a lesson to the populace. Yet, the lesson must have missed its mark for, according to a popular legend, the head began a day-to-day process of miraculous embellishment instead of experiencing decay. It is also said that the Spanish viceroy, alarmed at that development, ordered the head to be buried. The myth of the *Inkarri*, one of the most powerful images of Andean utopia, might well have its origin in the death of Tupac Amaru, which, it might be said, began to fuse significantly with the death of Atahuallpa.

Not all mythical images operate as symptoms of hope for reintegration of the Amerindians into their world. Some seem to play havoc with their history. Such was the case with the initial encounters. The European ships, coming from the East or the West, were thought to bring back the gods, Quetzalcoatl or Viracocha, to the land they had abandoned with the promise to return. It is well known that this myth has been used to explain the facility of the Spanish Conquest. But there is something else to consider: in the Amerindian world actual history becomes mythic event, and that in the final turn the gods end up deciding the fate of human beings. Wachtel, Todorov, and Burga, among others, have frequently reminded readers of this conundrum. There is always a divinity, multifaceted and metamorphic, that in popular thought can explain both victory and defeat. Such a divinity is the lord who knows, the one who is able to conceptualize and actualize a liberating project; he is the lord of order, the cultural hero; he is the Inca, the organizing principle of parthenogenetic birth.

According to legend, once upon a time, this Viracocha vanished. The myth belongs to the tradition of *Huarochiri*, which might have been parallel to the events of conquest (Taylor). The god had disappeared before the Spaniards could reach the Andes. Manuel Burga comments:

> Viracocha, father of the regional huacas, the most ancient, tied to atmospheric phenomena, this time—contrariwise to the path traveled in the course of his civilizing work— marches toward the orient, toward Lake Titicaca, from which he had originally emanated. The march toward the orient, in a direction counter to that of the Sun, is a march of punishment; it is the march followed by Tuguapaca, as he headed toward death, to the bosom of the earth. (122+)

Las Casas, Guaman Poma, and the Idea of Restitution

The colonial situation created a need to explain the defeat of the Inca through the representation of the disappearance of the foremost Andean gods. One explanation contemplated the idea of the return of Viracocha (Burga 122-136, 148+). Burga goes on to explain that the Viracocha myth is closely linked to the death of

Huayna Capac, the last legitimate Inca, as a result of a European epidemic (Crosby), in 1524, before the Spaniards' arrival to the area; thus, the Conquest occurred in a situation of religious abandonment experienced before the arrival of the Spaniards. In the meantime, the image of restitution founded in Las Casas's writings became a powerful Indian motor for the natives' cause. During the second half of the seventeenth century a combination of bad consciousness, guilt, and a sense of opportunity prompted a number of *encomenderos* to remember their Indians in their wills and even to return to the affected some of the wealth that the *encomenderos* had accumulated. With publication of his *Brevísima relación* (1552), which coincided with the New Laws, Las Casas struck a blow to the colonizers' conscience. Now, a pardon for past sins and the promise of eternal life were no longer easy to obtain as it became easier to recognize exploitation and abuse.

Perhaps the best champion of the restitution image was Guaman Poma, whose birth may be dated in 1534 or 1535, and whose observations encompass a time frame approximately from 1560 to 1620. In a fictitious dialogue between Guaman's persona and a Spaniard, the central motif of his *Primer nueva corónica y buen gobierno* is spelled out: to inform the king of the situation in the Peruvian Indies. His royal ancestry and the collaboration between his relatives and the conquistadors authorize him to claim restitution for lost privileges. His chronicle differs from the classic version in that the classic historian would directly translate or transpose oral information into the written text without interpretation (Adorno, *Guaman Poma*).

Guaman Poma's discourse seeks to document the evil, corruption, and vicious behavior that had come to plague the Indies. These evils were brought by the Spaniards, who were helped by a false and bastardized Inca nobility, since an authentic nobleman could not be an enemy of his own people. The overall image of the colony is that of *pachacuti*, a world upside-down, in which all Indians, including commoners, sought to act as Europeans (Adorno, *Cronista y príncipe*).

The disorder and confusion introduced by the Conquest were aggravated by the process of miscegenation and by the increased number of *mestizos*, many of whom were born as a result of the violence and rape perpetrated by the conquistadors upon Indian women. Hence racial segregation was deemed necessary for the recuperation of the Andean order. It was thought that whites, people of mixed blood, mulattoes, and blacks should live in the cities, and Indians should inhabit the countryside. Any contact among different racial groups was dangerous and to be avoided. Bad Christians were considered to be the very source of evil and disorder. The proposal here was to restore the traditional order that had been broken by Conquest. Ironically, on the matter of the separation of Indians from non-Indians this proposal even shares certain characteristics of the utopian program of the Franciscans in New Spain (see our earlier discussion on Mendieta).

Following Las Casas, Guaman Poma also argues that, since the natives had accepted Spanish rule peacefully, there was no war of conquest and thus the system of awards represented by the *encomienda* did not apply to the Andes (see Adorno in this volume). On this matter Guaman Poma assumes the point of view of the nobility that had collaborated with the Europeans in the defeat of the Inca administration. This nobility was more ancient than the Inca and had originated in a mythical Golden Age when everybody could eat, drink, sing, and dance in moderation, an epoch that did not experience epidemics, starvation, drought, or famine. This period—which had lasted 2,100 years and was known as Auca Pacha Runa—was marked by an Edenic tranquillity, by the founding of important political institutions, by the establishment of noble lineages such as that of Guaman Poma de Ayala, and by a respect for the principles of Christianity, which were thought to have been preached by a disciple of Christ in the early times of Christendom. It was a time of only one deity, Pachacamac, the creator and maker of everything. Even idolatry was unknown then, having first been brought to the people by Mama Huaco, the mother and wife of the Inca Manco Capac. Those ancient lineages had been conquered first by the Inca and then by the Spaniards, who had brought the Christian faith to the Andean people.

For Guaman Poma, the present *pachacuti* stemmed from the rule imposed upon the Peruvian people by Spaniards who were bad Christians. From them the Indians had learned all vices. For Guaman Poma the ideal society was modeled on Christian principles. It is also clear that he did not totally reject Inca organization; he admired the order that ruled every detail of Andean life, including the rituals, the wise codes of justice, and the calendrical rigor. The Incas, after all, were a segment of the Andean world, and the Spaniards, on the other hand, were foreigners. Because the latter were not Indians he claimed that they did not have rights to property over Indian lands and that to appropriate what did not belong to them was un-Christian. Good government, for Guaman Poma, could be achieved only if power was restored to the legitimate nobility whose lineages had originated during the Auca Runa period. In order to bring this about, "All type of bastardy had to be eliminated: false indigenous nobles, such as plebeian Spaniards or *mestizos* who wished to act as nobles. [Moreover one had to] forbid the Indians from living in the cities and [had to] prevent the Spaniards who were *mestizos*, mulattoes, and black from living in the rural areas" (Burga 269; our translation). Guaman displayed a strong political sense as he accepted the legitimacy of the Spanish king's rule over his colonies while placing directly under him the Inca king, a position that he proposed for his own son. The strategy was clever as it undermined the Conquest without questioning directly the authority of the king or the explicit ideological support on which the Conquest rested: the conversion of the native populations to the teachings of Christ. Guaman Poma's rejection of the un-Christian behavior of the Spaniards, his idealization of Andean past history, the pride in Indian identity, and the proposal for a restitution of the lost Andean order form the contours of one of the most coherent and powerful images of the Amerindian world.

As we indicated earlier, there are some points of convergence and, we might now add, many more differences between Guaman's utopia and that envisioned by the Franciscans. Mendieta, for example, thought that the Mexican natives were better off as Aztecs than as Spaniards and that they should be treated as Mexican Christians rather than as Spanish Christians. In this the Franciscan friar coincided with the Peruvian native, but the coincidence was only a surface one. Guaman's objective was very material: if we are all Christians, he argued, we are all equal, meaning that abuses of native populations by intruders may no longer take place. Hispanization, for him, was an impossibility because the Indians have an authentic view of the world that they will not abandon. One can, however, be a good Andean and a good Christian provided that rights to property of the peoples and rulers of other areas of the world within their own territories are respected. Mendieta's thinking differed from Guaman's in that for him Hispanization and Christianization were mutually exclusive, for, in practice, Hispanization would not only destroy Christianity among the Indians but would transform them into replicas of European Christians, far from the pristine Christianity that they had envisioned. The idea, then, was to keep the native Amerindians separate and pure, away from European contamination, under the theocratic domain of the friars (Phelan 89; Maravall, "La utopía político-religiosa" 86-87, 109).

Garcilaso and the *Mestizo* Utopia

In his mythical reconstruction of the Inca empire, Garcilaso de la Vega, the Inca, shapes in his discourse what Manuel Burga calls the second Andean utopia. According to Garcilaso, prior to Inca rule, the Andean peoples lived in the midst of barbarism. The previous lineages claimed by Guaman Poma were nonexistent or despicable. Cuzco would be the Rome of the New World. The Incas had not only introduced the great gods and agriculture, but they had also established lasting social and political institutions. The expansion of the Inca empire was effected through persuasion rather than by force. The Inca system of beliefs had advanced many of the Christian ideals. The Inca, for Garcilaso, was a loving and generous patriarch acting on principles of reciprocity, with a moral sense of justice and an imperative of equality for all. The ingenuity of the Incan irrigation system permitted an equal distribution of water for agriculture, and the same criterion of distributive justice was observed in a labor code that contemplated commonality of work. All individuals enjoyed enough land, and the relevant system of taxation was just. Alcoholic beverages were forbidden.

In Garcilaso's writings, little mention is made of the previous empires of Huari, Tiahuanaco, and Chimu, from which the Incas appropriated a number of political and socioeconomic techniques. Similarly, there is no mention that the imperial spread of the Quechua language meant the suppression of many other idioms, and the cruelty of the *mitimaes* system is left without analysis. The *mitimaes* were loyal colonists from older provinces of the empire called to replace departing dissident populations in the newly conquered provinces. The reader is never told that the splendid irrigation system, which formed the economic basis of the empire, was already in place when the Incas took over or that the practice of communal work was a distinct characteristic of the *ayllu*, and not an Inca invention.

The *ayllu* was a kinship group whose members claimed the same ancestors and married within the group. Each *ayllu* owned certain lands, which were assigned in lots to heads of families who could pass the land to their descendants but could not sell or dispose of it otherwise. A village community consisted of several *ayllu*, and villagers practiced mutual aid in agricultural tasks, in building houses, and in private and public projects. Before the Inca conquest the *ayllus* were ruled by the *curacas*, who were hereditary leaders assisted by a council of elders, with a superior *curaca* ruling over the whole state. This is precisely the system that Guaman Poma wished to have reinstated. The Inca rulers took over this communal principle and used it to exact unpaid forced labor; they also debilitated the kinship organization by the use of *mitimaes*. A certain amount of land was taken from the villages and vested in the Inca state and the state Church. The villagers, in addition to tilling their own land, were required to labor on those of the Inca and the Church. Keen and Wasserman explain the principle of reciprocity mentioned above:

The relations between the Inca and the peasantry were based on the principle of reciprocity, expressed in an elaborate system of gifts and countergifts. The peasantry cultivated the lands of the Inca, worked up his wool and cotton into cloth, and performed various other kinds of labor for him. The Inca, the divine, universal lord, in turn permitted them to cultivate their communal lands, and in time of shortages released to the villages the surplus grain in his storehouses. Since the imperial gifts were the products of the peasants' own labor, this "reciprocity" amounted to intensive exploitation of the commoners by the Inca rulers and nobility. We must not underestimate, however, the hold of this ideology, buttressed by a religious world view that regarded the Inca as responsible for defending the order and the very existence of the universe, on the Inca peasant mentality. (35)

This is a different shade of light to be sure from the one discovered by Garcilaso. And this is precisely the crux of the matter. Garcilaso does not attempt to tell the truth about the Incas. He is telling the Inca truth, and that truth or program of truth is that of myth. In the narration of this story the Inca rulers are idealized beings and the Spanish officers are demonized. Such is precisely the case with his portrayal of Viceroy Toledo. At the beginning of the seventeenth century, the gaze is turned over the past both to evade the sadness of current reality and to create imaginary alternatives to the colonial system. Garcilaso's truth—like any other truth—is the child of his imagination. The myth that he creates with the collaboration of others is as authentic as its debunking. Paul Veyne has written:

> The authenticity of our beliefs is not measured according to the truth of their object.... it is we who fabricate our truths, and it is not "reality" that makes us believe. For "reality" is the child of the constitutive imagination of our tribe. If it were otherwise, the quasi-totality of universal culture would be inexplicable—mythologies, doctrines, pharmacopoeias, false and spurious sciences. (113)

The Peruvian *mestizo* Gómez Suárez de Figueroa was born in the imperial city of Cuzco in 1539. He was the son of a Spanish captain, who fought with the conquistador Francisco Pizarro, and an Inca princess. In 1560, at age twenty-one, he left the New World for Spain, where he lived until his death in 1616. We might also recall here that toward the end of 1563, some three years after his arrival on the Iberian peninsula, the young Gómez Suárez changed his name to Gómez Suárez de la Vega and, soon thereafter, to Garcilaso de la Vega.[13] One might say that Garcilaso's experiences in Spain in the course of half a century, together with those of his formative years among the Incas in Peru, were to inform his writing and mark his truth and that, perhaps, nowhere is this mixed legacy more crucially felt than in his *Comentarios reales* (*Royal Commentaries of the Incas and General History of Peru* [1: 1608; 2: 1616]), a writing that sets out to contest the official Spanish interpretations of the Conquest, especially as they pertained to the character and values of the Incas. A *mestizo* writer who identified with many facets of his Inca roots, Garcilaso countered a type of European discourse that had tended to reduce indigenous cultures to an undifferentiated, non-Christian, and barbaric identity. Such a discourse, he intimated, was ultimately irresponsible as it represented native Amerindians untruthfully.

Let us recall here that truthfulness as a "program of truth" was an essential concern of humanist thinking about literature, a thinking that had strongly rejected on moral grounds those popular stories about the marvelous adventures of knights-errant and the love trials of aristocratic shepherds and shepherdesses, escapist tales that were characterized by a lack of social engagement and responsibility. For Garcilaso, the humanist writer of the *Comentarios reales*, if the truth was part of a process of cognition that could be arrived at best through an interpreter's intimate dialogue with original sources (Inca culture in his case), then its transmission and propagation depended upon the interpreter's ability to persuade the implied receiver of his commentaries and glosses. Thus, in an account published in two parts at the twilight of his life, he interpreted for a Spanish reading public the history and civilization of the Incas, doing so within a general history of Peru. His ostensible aim was to recover the original text (Inca culture) through written sources and oral traditions, and, by means of that recuperation, move the reader to question the assumptions underlying various European representations of that particular native American reality. Garcilaso's interpretation of that reality also assumed a redefinition of the function of the chronicler or historian, whose role was no longer limited to describing past events but became one of representing them for a purpose: to persuade the reader that Amerindians were not a passive, monolithic, and invisible mass and that within the heterogeneous human landscape of the New World one could find worthwhile—and even sophisticated—models of social organization and political thinking. For Garcilaso, then, the Incas had a history and a human face, and it is to this issue that this straddler of two worlds spoke most eloquently. We might also add that Guaman Poma would take this eloquence one step further as he argued for the separation and autonomy of the Andean world.

In assessing Garcilaso's writing one must keep in mind that for him, as for most Renaissance humanists, history was a branch of rhetoric (Zamora 6) and that historical truth was conceivable only within a specific linguistic context. In the *Comentarios reales* that program of truth was constructed through the interpretation of a speaker (Zamora 44) who was cognizant that its full execution relied ultimately upon the competence and persuasion of the reader. This strategy is already evident in the "Proem" to his *Comentarios reales*, where Garcilaso sets the stage for an intertextual and interdiscursive reading of the cultural and political history of the Incas. He proposes to do so through commentaries, glosses, and interpretations of the Spanish chronicles of the Conquest, which, ostensibly, were written by people who were not totally familiar with the original text or native sources: Quechua and its intimate modes of expression.

Careful not to ruffle feathers, Garcilaso goes out of his way to credit the very chroniclers from whom he ultimately seeks to wrest authority. Thus, while claiming that his own *Comentarios* gains authority from their accounts, he manages to inscribe their narratives within his own story, all the while effecting a mediation upon their message(s) and setting in motion a deauthorizing process. In the "Proem" to the reader, Garcilaso states:

> In the course of my history I shall affirm its truthfulness and shall set down no important circumstances without quoting the authority of Spanish historians who may have touched upon it in part or as a whole. For my purpose is not to gainsay them, but to furnish a commentary and gloss, and to interpret many Indians expressions which they, as strangers to that tongue, have rendered inappropriately. (*Royal Commentaries* 4)

Garcilaso's counternarrative, then, focuses on the question of authority and, in so doing, manages to problematize the concept of Western truth and its literary representation (Zamora 39+; Frankl).

From a historiography based on the authority of an "I" witness—in which the narrating "I" is the literary representation of the I, and eye, that has seen or experienced the events that are recounted—Garcilaso invests that "I" with the depth, understanding, and convictions of a *mestizo* who, having suckled those insights in the motherly milk of Inca culture, is now committed to transforming the European discourse on Amerindian reality. Thus, Garcilaso's greatest claim of authenticity for his narrative is an intimate understanding of Inca history, customs, and traditions that he now seeks to interpret for the Spanish and European reader, i.e., the discriminating reader whom he has learned to imagine from the time of his arrival in Spain in 1560 to the moment of writing and eventual publication of his *Comentarios* in the early part of the seventeenth century. This was a remarkable period in Spanish history and culture, a time marked by the continued illusion of grandeur and by the reality of despair, a time that was imprinted on the Spanish psyche through two emblems: Spain's victory at Lepanto against the Turks (1571) and the demise of its Invincible Armada when Philip II sought to invade England (1588). Ironically, Garcilaso's Spain was already an empire in decline, one whose subjects would soon be characterized as "the Indians of Europe" ("los indios de Europa").

What is often forgotten in many of the studies on Garcilaso is that he was also a contemporary of Cervantes, Lope de Vega, Góngora, Quevedo, Mateo Alemán, and other major Spanish writers who lived through a period of intense political and social ferment. The pages of this dignified, learned former soldier (for a time he fought the rebellion of the *moriscos* at Alpujarras) betray none of the pettiness that characterized some of the writings of his contemporaries. In many ways he seems closest to Cervantes, who also wrote against the grain at a time when literature and other cultural artifacts were being generated for "mass" consumption to reinforce the endangered values of the monarcho-seigniorial segments of Spanish society (Maravall, *Culture of the Baroque*).

In the midst of the crisis of baroque Spain this Peruvian *mestizo* played out his own crisis of identity through writings that he himself characterized as contestatory. His *Comentarios reales*, whose second part is entitled *Historia general del Perú*, have the ostensible aim of rescuing indigenous history from the distortions perpetrated upon it by the "modern histories of the new empire" (*Royal Commentaries* 187). Those histories are many and they include Francisco López de Gómara's account as well as other more or less "benevolent" ones (those of Cieza de León, José de Acosta, Agustín de Zárate, and Blas Valera, among others). Thus, at a time when official culture sought to exclude from its realm all traces of transgression, when continued persecution of religious minorities—let us recall that the *moriscos* were finally expelled from Spain between 1609 and 1614—and the cancer called purity of blood (*limpieza de sangre*) continued to infect the Spanish social body, Garcilaso wrote for a largely Spanish and European public for the purpose of rectifying the stilted images of the Incas that had been forged and perpetuated by "modern histories of the new Empire." Those official accounts, however well intended, had managed to distort the history of a people whose Golden Age had spanned several centuries prior to the conquest and colonization effected by Christian Spain, which had coupled its insatiable appetite for precious metals with an ideology of the spirit that conspired to demonize, suppress, and eventually appropriate the body and the material landscape of the native Amerindian.

As we hinted earlier, against those official histories, Garcilaso's *Comentarios* focus on the longevity of the Inca empire, on the Incas' social organization, and on the moral traits and political acumen of their leaders, before the civil strife between the forces of Huascar and his half brother, Atahuallpa, helped precipitate the defeat of the Incas at the hands of Pizarro and his band at Cajamarca on November 16, 1532. Yet, Garcilaso's tempered interpretation of the events leading to Atahuallpa's fall at Cajamarca not only fails to assume the combative, accusatory stance of the indefatigable Las Casas, who half a century earlier (*Brevísima relación de la destrucción de las Indias*, 1552) had cited an eyewitness, a Franciscan friar named Marcos de Niza, to attest to the cruelty and treachery of the Spaniards. It also advances a theory that could be persuasive to Europeans accustomed to political dramas connected to laws of inheritance and succession: that the fall of the Inca empire may have been fatally set into motion by Huayna Capac when he chose to disregard the established law of succession among the Incas and proceeded to split the kingdom between the legitimate heir,

Huascar, and the illegitimate son, Atahuallpa, whom he rewarded with the kingdom of Quito (*Comentarios reales* 396). The *Comentarios* endow the demise of the Inca empire with a tragic dimension, as Garcilaso makes clear that Huayna Capac's political judgment had been impaired by passion: his blind love for Atahuallpa had opened a fissure in the political fabric, a fissure that was to doom the empire and burden its subjects with tragic consequences. The *Comentarios* thus provide a political interpretation of the dissolution of the Inca empire, a dissolution attributed less to the valor of the Spaniards than to the internal division and civil wars among the Incas.

Although Garcilaso's narration of those events seeks to present a balanced approach, which many critics have attributed to his neo-Platonism (Durand), it is clear that the demise of the Incas is placed squarely on the shoulders of Huayna Capac and his illegitimate son, Atahuallpa, who is portrayed less as a tragic figure—as many other representations would have it (see also Conley and Gisbert in this volume)—than as a cruel tyrant who shattered the peaceful and utopian world built by the first Inca, Manco Capac, and his descendants (see Book 1, chap. 21: "The Inca's teachings to his vassals" [*Royal Commentaries* 53-55]).

It is interesting to note the manner in which Atahuallpa's cruelty is highlighted for Spanish and European readers as the author compares his bloodthirsty and mean-spirited inclinations to those of the Ottomans—the hated infidels who had long been part of the consciousness of the Spanish populace—through a variety of experiences:

> Suffice it to mention the evil custom of the Ottoman house, by which the successor to the empire buries all his brothers with his father for his own security. But the cruelty of Atahuallpa was greater than that of the Ottomans and he was even more avid for the blood of his own family. Not sated with that of two hundred of his brothers, the children of the great Huaina Capac, he went on to drink that of his nephews, uncles, and other kinsmen up to and beyond the fourth degree, so that no member of the royal blood, legitimate or bastard, escaped. He had them all killed in different ways. Some were beheaded; some hanged; some

were thrown into rivers and lakes, with great stones about
their necks, so that they were unable to swim and drowned;
others were flung from high crags and precipices. (*Royal
Commentaries* 616)[14]

Garcilaso's image of Atahuallpa as a bloodthirsty and power-
hungry leader even more wretched and evil than the Turks is in
sharp contrast to his general portrayal of the Incas as just and magnanimous, even with their enemies. Garcilaso's strategy is clear: if
the Inca empire had collapsed after several hundred years of existence, that collapse could be attributed, to some extent, to the
disharmony and disarray that had come to shatter its political and
social organization. And if the Spaniards had prevailed so swiftly
over the Inca empire, it was not because the conquistadors were
morally superior to their enemies. This message can be gathered
in the *Historia general del Perú*, which is dedicated to "the Indians,
mestizos and creoles of the kingdoms and provinces of the great
and very rich Empire of Peru."[15] In that text Garcilaso makes clear
that the Spaniards were less than noble souls when it came to the
important matter of Christianizing the native populations, prefer-
ring to engage in power struggles among themselves rather than
facilitating the spread of the gospel:

The devil sought to prevent the conversion of those Indians
with all his might; and although he was not successful in
preventing it altogether, at the very least he prevented it for
many years. All of these wars were exercised by the devil
in succession, for twenty-five years. For these reasons the
gospel was not preached as it would have been, for the
faithful could not teach the faith, due to the disorder they
experienced every day, nor could the infidels receive it.[16]

Although the devil is said to conspire against the conversion of the
gentiles by sowing discord among the conquistadors, what is at
stake here is a questioning of the ideological underpinnings of the
conquest and colonization of the New World (the conversion of native populations to the teachings of Christ). These underpinnings
are stripped of their certitude as they are subject to the power
struggles that take place from below, among the conquistadors, far
from Old Spain and its centers of power. The conquistadors are

moved by personal greed and, in the process, display none of the vision of the successful commonwealth of the Incas practiced before the tragic dismemberment of their empire. The reader cannot help but be captivated by a rhetorical tour de force, a powerful defense of the Inca world by a *mestizo* intellectual who writes against those official writings that, however well intentioned, because of their superficial contact with the original sources of Inca culture and civilization tended to shape what in Garcilaso's mind was a less than truthful account of the Incas. In the final analysis, Garcilaso seems to say that a more complete and truthful representation of the Amerindian past can be shaped by those who are closest to their sources, namely, Indians, *mestizos*, and creoles (*Comentarios reales* 6). They are the ones who can provide a fuller and more balanced account of their own past; they can capture the essence of those lands and peoples better than their Spanish counterparts. In this sense Garcilaso identifies with the Inca side of his mixed heritage. The entire account (*relación entera*) that he seeks to provide for European readers is also a voyage toward his own self-discovery; it is an attempt to find a sense of the whole and completeness through his writing; it is, ultimately, a way of getting at historical knowledge and at the creative forms of writing (Pupo-Walker 86). The idea of a "complete account" is connected to the notion of discovery and to a writer's need to explain in order to persuade. There are countless examples that come to mind, especially within the framework of autobiographical writing. One need only think of *Lazarillo de Tormes* (1554) or, in recent times, the *Autobiography of Malcolm X* (1965) to see how the notion of completeness is connected to the idea of truth, power, and control:

> Though there have been learned Spaniards who have written accounts of the states of the New World, such as those of Mexico and Peru and the other kingdoms of the heathens, they have not described these realms so fully as they might have done. (*Royal Commentaries* 4)[17]

Writing, as we have argued in our earlier study in this same series (Jara and Spadaccini) and as we have pointed out in the course of this introduction, is indeed a double-edged sword. In the works of Garcilaso, it is used by the *mestizo* writer to contest the values of the "victors," to vindicate the pre-Columbian world of the Incas, to question the construction of certain official truths about the Conquest, and to rediscover his own Inca roots. His is an attempt to contextualize for the European reader—and for the reader called Garcilaso de la Vega, Inca—the world of some of his Amerindian ancestors. Thus, claiming to be better and more clearly informed than the Spanish chroniclers about the Incas' history, culture, and traditions, he strives to provide the most complete account possible ("la relación entera que de ellos se pudiera dar," 4), thus allowing the reader to enter into a worldview that, however remote from that of Counter-Reformation Catholic Spain, nevertheless possesses certain characteristics consonant with contemporary theories of knowledge.

Let us recall here that Garcilaso emphasizes the importance of experience and materiality in the mentality of the native Amerindians and that his *Comentarios* are full of references to this effect. His observations on this issue may be summed up in a statement made in Book 2, chap. 21, which deals with the sciences learned by the Incas. What they learn, says Garcilaso, "is more by way of experience (schooled by necessity), than by their natural philosophy, for they speculated little about that which they did not touch with their own hands."[18] In the following chapter, discussing how the Incas came to venerate the sun above all other stars, he says that "their imagination did not go beyond what they saw, materially, with their own eyes."[19] Finally, in commenting about the Incas' lack of knowledge of theology, the queen of the sciences, he argues that they knew even less of what they knew of natural philosophy and medicine, "because they did not find a way of grasping and understanding invisible things: the entire theology of the Incas was enclosed in the name Pachacamac."[20]

Ironically, when Garcilaso wrote, the Aristotelian and Ptolemaic conception of the universe was in crisis. The old god as the creator and immovable driving force of the universe was being challenged by the Copernican theories that would soon have wide philosophical ramifications. On February 17, 1600, Giordano Bruno was burned at the stake in Rome and in the year of Garcilaso's death the Inquisition was to ask Galileo to recant his defense of the Copernican theories. Bruno had held that just as the earth was not the center of the universe, so it was that man was dissolved in the vicissitude of nature, so that every birth is death and every past is present. In this scheme, God "becomes the soul of the world, all reversed and diffused in things, to become nature."[21] Similarly, Tommaso Campanella, whose portrayal of an ideal commonwealth in *The City of the Sun* anticipated the New Atlantis of Francis Bacon, considered sensory experience as the central basis of knowledge. In *The Defense of Galileo*, composed in a Neapolitan dungeon in 1616, Campanella affirmed that, following Copernicus, "Galileo discovered new planets and new systems, and unknown changes in heaven. How ignorant and senseless they are, who consider satisfactory the theories of the heavens set forth by Aristotle" (McColley 23). For Campanella, only the senses and experience could begin to explain the mysteries of nature and only by reading the great book of nature could one arrive at truth. Says Campanella: "I learn more from the anatomy of an ant or from a blade of grass... than from all the books written since the beginning of time" (qtd. in Procacci; our translation).[22] Clearly,

> the heliocentric universe conceived by Copernicus was indeed a radical departure from orthodox cosmology. By exchanging the places of the earth and sun, Copernicus brought earth and hell within it into the pure heavens. By making the earth one of the planets he prepared the way for the corollary that the planets are earths. His belief that sun and heaven are immobile, and that all planets move in orbital revolution around the Sun, dispensed with much of the celestial machinery so beloved by the poet, theologian and astronomer of the sixteenth century. (McColley xv)

It is interesting to note that *mestizo* and Indian writers such as Garcilaso, Guaman Poma, and Alva, among others, seemed to realize that the encounter between the European and the Amerindian worlds had shattered the order of representation. Thus, the Western program of scientific and ideological truth could not continue working—neither in the New World nor in the Old. The distance produced by miscegenation allowed these writers to separate themselves from this order of things and permitted them to establish an ironic and often subversive difference between Amerindia and Europe. This is, perhaps, the best contribution of the *mestizo* in the political cleavage that occurred as America moved toward independence.

Garcilaso's truth, like Guaman Poma's, is tied to the Lascasian idea of restitution, although, as opposed to Guaman, he believed that the Incas were the legitimate lords of Peru. The program of truth emerging from the *Comentarios reales* was a powerful one that was to have repercussions for the Amerindians. There is also external evidence for this assertion. In October 1781, after the execution of the second Tupac Amaru, a decree was issued to collect all available copies of the second edition of the book, dated 1723. It seems that Garcilaso's myth had acquired a dangerous truth; it had become a weapon in the minds of the Andean nobilities. On the basis of Garcilaso's book the Incas reinscribed themselves in the Andean popular imaginary as an ordered, fair, and equalizing lineage of rulers. The Inca, as a principle of order, with no temporal consideration in mind, would subsume Guaman's regional *curacas* and Garcilaso's Cuzcan dynasty. To return to the time of the Inca was to reconquer order. As the Millennium approached, a reversion of the current order was to take place. The Andean peoples were to recover the *Hanan*, the high position they lost with the European conquest. In the new order the Indians would make whites work. The underlying, subterranean order would emerge as Inkarri.

Elsewhere we have dealt with the contrasting representation of Spaniards and Indians in the epic discourse of Ercilla and Oña (Jara, *El revés;* Jara and Spadaccini). Here we shall focus on how aspects of popular theater in seventeenth-century Peru—such as the anonymous *Usca Páucar, El hijo pródigo (The Prodigal Son)*, attributed to El Lunarejo, the pen name of the baroque poet and scholar Juan de Espinoza Medrano, and *El pobre más rico (The Richest Poor Man)*, attributed to Gabriel Centeno de Osma—incarnate a different facet of Amerindian reality. The Indian image presented here is that of an impoverished nobility in perpetual pilgrimage, one that, mired in multiple sins, is finally pardoned through the intervention of the Virgin Mary. In this popular representation one finds an impoverished Indian prince who undertakes a pilgrimage in search of fortune and, in despair, makes a contract with the devil, who promises him wealth in exchange for his soul. In a typical happy ending the youth repents, goes back to the Christian faith, and is saved by the redeeming action of Mary. This image of the pilgrimage is similar to the one found in Sigüenza y Góngora (Jara, "The Inscription"; Jara and Spadaccini). As we will be able to appreciate at the end of this essay, these popular representations are an important cog in the machinery of the Spanish American baroque.

Amerindian Baroque

From the seventeenth century on an intense duality begins to appear in the Amerindian cultural landscape. As Burga has explained, acculturation becomes a need and, as such, it has to be present on the surface of any image. One has to be Christian and look like one, belong to the Western world and show it. But the Amerindian figures of identification do not leave; they remain there in an unruly unconscious that is always threatening to erode the lustrous organization of the symbolic. Collaboration, the Herod-like attitude recognized by Gisbert (see her essay in this volume), was part of the political demeanor of the Amerindian nobilities. The Indian aristocracies among the Maya, as we have noted, and also among the Aztecs and the Incas, very soon assimilated the life-style of the conquerors: they took to horseriding, they donned Western dress and weapons, they spoke Spanish, and they assumed the Spanish diet. But, as we have observed in our analysis of Sor Juana Inés de la Cruz's sacramental play *El divino Narciso*, beneath a Western language laden with Counter-Reformation overtones, there remains a mythology as well as strong attitudes connected to the materiality of the Mexican view of the world (Jara and Spadaccini). In the same manner the invisible rules of the Andean cosmovision are latent and powerful in Guaman Poma's drawings, as Rolena Adorno has demonstrated in this volume.

Festivals, rituals, and other manifestations of popular culture are also rich in this duality, as Teresa Gisbert shows in her essay. Garcilaso describes the celebration of the feast of Corpus Christi in the city of Cuzco in 1555. It seems that at that time, lords, servants, and *curacas* continued to participate in the festival. The Indian nobility paraded in front of the Spaniards, continuing a tradition common during the times of the Inca; they represented their *pacarinas*, or places of origin, and exhibited their totems to recall the mythical roots of their lineage. The Incas paraded at the end of the procession, with their clothing diminished. Theirs was an exhibition of the poverty that they deserved for having lost the empire. To this insult was added the presence of a team of Spanish collaborators, aggressive and donning symbols of the European victory. If for the conquerors the festival was an opportunity to celebrate the Christian god, the Indian nobles took the occasion to celebrate and recall their own deities, the same deities who, in Garcilaso's thought, had abandoned the Incas, thus precipitating the events of the Conquest.

As opposed to Garcilaso's representation, which focuses on cultural coexistence, conviviality, and mutual respect, Guaman Poma's *Primer nueva corónica* echoes the Spanish intolerance embodied in Philip II's decree of August 16, 1570, which sought to prevent the native populations of America from coming in contact with heretics or individuals of doubtful orthodoxy. That same decree ordered the extirpation of all heresies and false doctrines that could have found their way into the Indies (Konetzke 260).[23]

Guaman Poma was a racial separatist who believed that the integration and salvation of the Indian world lay in Christianity. He believed, as we mentioned earlier, that if everyone was Christian then all people would be equal. For this reason, in describing the festival of Corpus Christi, he argued that Indians ought to eradicate idolatries, promote the Catholic faith, be good Christians, and dress like Spaniards. Unlike Garcilaso, whose writings champion cultural coexistence and thus move in consonance with pre-Tridentine thinking, Guaman Poma felt at ease in the closed atmosphere of the Counter-Reformation. He felt that since coexistence was no longer possible, the natives should dance like Spaniards and celebrate the Christian God. Burga believes that in Guaman Poma's drawings, such as the one representing the sons of the *curaca* dancing in Spanish costumes, one is faced with rituals in a state of transition. Burga explains:

> They were ancient, Andean dances accompanied by
> traditional music, but using Spanish disguises, thus
> insinuating the fundamental choreographic structure—
> Indians dressed as Spaniards—which would soon develop

the ancient Andean rituals. What one searches for, in a period of intolerance and repression of the indigenous, is to discover rituals in order to celebrate the Christian gods. (379; our translation)

As with the case of the Maya of Yucatan, Guaman relied on the conjunction of the tradition of the Andean ancestors and the Christian God, placing Europe in the Amerindian outline of the world (see Adorno in this volume).

Teresa Gisbert, using a number of popular artistic manifestations, makes a strong case for the resistance of native Amerindians against the European attempt to erase native cultures. She observes that even in those cases in which a rebellious attitude favoring the preservation of indigenous values is absent and in which the mood is one of accommodation expressed in the language of the conqueror, it is clear that the European does not come out of the experience unscathed. It is precisely the language of the conqueror that is undermined and utilized for the expression of an undercurrent of the native worldview. The repression undertaken by Viceroy Toledo in Peru was to trigger an Amerindian reaction through the organization of masquerades by the Andean populations in the style of the urban festivals celebrated in the main cities of the viceroyalty.[24]

The urban festival, whose theme could be religious or profane, always included a masquerade. One of the most famous was the one recalled by Arzáns in his *Historia de la Villa Imperial de Potosí*. Arzáns describes the festival to celebrate Corpus Christi, the Immaculate Conception, and the Apostle James as patron of the imperial city. It was a procession headed by fifteen Indian squadrons. Then came some two hundred members of the nobility representing the Inca court. After them the Inca kings paraded in couples. They were followed by Indian dancers representing the diverse Indian nations. The Spanish section followed with Santiago, the Holy Virgin, and a number of religious communities. The Spanish authorities closed the procession. The festival lasted fifteen days. During that time, eight comedies were presented, four of them dealing with native topics, for example, the origin of the Indian kings, the victories and successes of Huayna Capac, and the ruin of the Inca empire, which included the unjust imprisonment of Atahuallpa and his death in Cajamarca. Arzáns, a historian, dated the festival in 1555, which was impossible since there was full-fledged armed resistance in Vilcabamba at that time. Moreover, it seems that Atahuallpa was despised and mocked, and the fall of the empire was considered to be a liberation for most Andean peoples. Garcilaso described the celebration in Cuzco and did not mention the one in Potosí. Arzáns was to attribute his information to a fictional witness, a sort of Borgian character. Burga thinks that the representation is modeled on the parade of the native counterpart of the viceroys. Such parades were customary by the end of the seventeenth century. Through Garcilaso, the Incas had reentered the soul of the populace, even if his negative portrayal of Atahuallpa was not to take hold. Arzáns's strategy of fusing Atahuallpa's disgraceful strangulation with Tupac Amaru's actual beheading under Viceroy Toledo's order was true to popular wisdom and mythical imagination.

García Pabón (in this volume) argues that Arzáns fills the gaps of history, creates fictional narrators, and eliminates some historical threads in order to construct his own Creole story. Thus, the mountain of Potosí is a symbol of colonial encounters and disencounters. The mountaintop is the Virgin's head, and its sides and lap are her dress and skirt. Under the appearance of the Christian myth the fluidity of liquid metaphors and a semiosis of mirroring and doubling project the presence of monstrous and sensuous forms in open contrast with the homogeneity and singularity of European and Christian history. Instead of being rejected, the acts of sinning and the devil himself inhabit the interior of the Virgin-Mountain's body, whose opening is guarded by el Tío (the Uncle), a phallic deity who gives structure to Andean life and work.

The Myth of Inkarri

The myth of Inkarri is a good example of the resilience of Andean cultural memory and mythologizing. The Conquest had decapitated the Inca; thus the Inca had been separated from his body. The period of disorder, confusion, and darkness unleashed by the defeat ends only when the body and the head of the Inca meet again.

Only then will the Andean peoples recuperate their own history. One variant of the myth tells us that the Inca was decapitated by the Spaniards after his death by strangulation. The head was taken to Cuzco to be buried. While it lies underground the head grows, and the body begins a process of rebirth and re-creation of itself. When the Inca is totally reconstituted he will come to the surface. At such time the Spaniards will be expelled, and the empire will be reestablished. One must recall at this juncture that the return to order is not an analogue of a return to the past. In every society, but especially in oral cultures, the past is not separate from the present; moreover, the past is remodeled in the present (Heller). In Amerindian mythical history, time is represented as a series of cycles, each ending in some sort of cataclysmic catastrophe; therefore, according to this program of truth, to think in terms of a return to the previous cycle is out of the question.

The myth of the Inkarri must have been reinforced in its messianic content by the revolt of Tupac Amaru II in 1780. Tupac Amaru became the embodiment of his followers' hopes. The leader, José Gabriel Condorcanqui Noguera, was a direct descendant of the Inca executed in Vilcabamba. What matters here is not the lineage but the symbolic importance of the Quechua word *amaru*. While *túpac* means "the real thing" and has the connotation of eminence, *amaru* means "ophid," "serpent," an animal that in the Andean world is connected to the subterranean. This characteristic is assumed by the Inca in the colonial context. It is interesting to note, as Flores Galindo has done, that another of the leaders of the 1780s revolt took the name of Tupac Catari, Catari being the Aymara counterpart of Amaru, serpent. The Amaru is also identified with a subterranean deity that, emerging from lagoons in the shape of a wild bull, is a sign of floods and other natural catastrophes. The phallic importance of the character cannot escape the post-Freudian reader.

Tupac Amaru's uprising was directed against the colonial powers and the peninsular aristocracy. He attempted to expel the Spaniards from the territories of the Tahuantinsuyo; he tried to reinstitute Inca rule, as called for by Garcilaso, and sought to promote substantial changes in the political organization. Among the proposed changes were the elimination of the *corregidores*, the abolition of the *mita*, the appointment of Indian governors for the provinces, and the abolition of the *alcabala* and other taxes. On the surface the Andean leader proclaimed his loyalty to the Spanish king and to the Church while, at the same time, he styled himself Inca-King of Peru. The leadership of the movement was undertaken by the *curacas* and the Inca nobility. Distrustful of the Spaniards whom he wanted expelled from his lands, he was conscious of the need of Creole support as a condition for victory. Condorcanqui's protonationalism implied the formation of a body politic integrated by Creoles, Indians, *mestizos*, and blacks. Only the *chapetones*, who were the peninsular Spaniards, would be excluded.

The events of the uprising, however, were determined by the preferences and objectives of Indian-peasant demands. The collective memory of the group was fixed on the return of the Tahuantinsuyo. This was a society that, as it was crystallized in the learned imagination of the *mestizo* Garcilaso de la Vega, was unassailed by merchants, colonial authorities, great landholders, and mineowners. The populace wanted an egalitarian and homogeneous society integrated by Andean peasants. The ancient nobility of the *curacas* and the Inca lineages were both accepted as ground on which to cultivate, on the one hand, the ideas of Guaman and the Taki Onkoy and, on the other, those of Garcilaso, those inferred from representations of the death of Atahuallpa and the narratives of the myths of Inkarri.

The violence of this uprising was produced, at least in part, by an inversion of the discourse of Conquest. It was an effect of the appropriation by the Indians of the discourse of the Inquisition at its worst. The Spaniards deserved torture and death because they did not practice what they preached. They were hypocritical and heretics and thus they could not be good Christians; they appeared to be the embodiments of the devil and the Antichrist, and, as such, they had to be ritually exterminated once and for all so they could not produce further damage.

At this point the leader's motivation clashed with that of the Indians and peasants, his most dedicated followers. A simple break with the colonial system, free trade, and modernization were not enough. The Indian imaginary needed a *pachacuti*, a forceful reversal of the world, which Tupac Amaru, because of his acculturation, could not lead. Neither could Tupac Catari, his Aymara brother in arms, who was duly executed after being betrayed by one of his friends. Catari was the war name of an Aymara Indian, Julián Apaza, who was bold enough to proclaim himself viceroy of the lands to be called Bolivia. He was backed by an army of some 40,000 Indians, which gave brave and effective battle to the troops of the viceroy. This illiterate Indian, ignorant of Spanish, had indeed turned the world upside-down. After his defeat his wife, Bartolina Sisa, and his sister Gregoria were brutally stoned and mocked in the public plaza. After both women were hanged in the gallows, their heads and hands were paraded through the towns of the region on orders of the viceroy.

Tupac Amaru was also betrayed by one of his men, Chief Pumacahua, who had Inca ancestors. Once he was defeated on the battlefield, the general visitor José de Areche ordered Tupac Amaru hauled to the scaffold and had his tongue cut out by the executioner. Tied to four horses by hands and feet, he was quartered. His head was sent to the town of Tinta, the place in which the Indian leader had the *corregidor* Antonio de Arriaga put to death at the beginning of the uprising. Each of his limbs was sent to a different location in the region. Eight other individuals were executed in the macabre celebration; among them were Tupac Amaru's wife, Micaela, and one of his sons, whose torture he was forced to watch. The event was not a rapid one. It took place between 10 A.M. and 5 P.M. on May 18, 1781.

The barbarity of this execution, surpassing those of Atahuallpa and Tupac Amaru I in Vilcabamba, can be explained only by the masses' response to Condorcanqui's call. They thought he could be king. Tupac Amaru's execution by the Spaniards, the quartering of his body, was both a symbol of the colonial fragmentation of Indian nationhood and a proof of its imminence. Tupac Amaru's war, however, did not end with him. It was continued by Diego Cristóbal, who decided to sign a truce with the colonial authorities in exchange for a general amnesty for his Indian warriors. Soon after he also hung in the gallows, his flesh torn to pieces next to the torn body of his mother. The sentence read that it was not fitting for the king or the state that any relative of Tupac Amaru should remain, considering the enthusiasm his name had aroused among the natives.

In Galeano's rendition the sentence against Tupac Amaru reads as follows:

> Indians are forbidden to wear the dress of the gentry, and especially of the nobility, which serves only to remind them of what the ancient Incas wore, bringing back memories that merely cause them to feel more and more hatred for the ruling nation; apart from looking ridiculous and hardly in keeping with the purity of our religion, since it features in various places the sun which was their first deity; this order extends to all provinces of this Southern America, totally abolishing such clothing... and at the same time all paintings or portraits of the Incas.... And to the end that these Indians should rid themselves of the hatred they have conceived against Spaniards, that they should dress in clothing prescribed by law, and that they should adopt our Spanish customs and speak the Castilian language, schools shall be more vigorously encouraged than heretofore, with the most stern and just punishment for those who do not use them, after a due period of time for their enlightenment. (159)

The Inca was not dead, despite his condemnation to a kingdom of shadows—to the subterranean world of the serpent and the wild bull—since the murder of Atahuallpa at the hands of Pizarro in 1533, despite the fact that his death had been ritually confirmed, or denied, by that of the last Inca of Vilcabamba, and further reiterated by the martyrdom of the second Tupac Amaru in 1781.

The myth of "the School," registered by Alejandro Ortiz Rescaniere and told to him by a Quechua elder, goes as follows. The God Father made everything on earth using the body of the Pachamama, Mother Earth. Peru came to be identified with Lima, which is Pachamama's mouth. Lima became the language of Peru, that language being Spanish, a foreign language that, in time, seems to have displaced the native ones. It happens that the Creator, while wandering around the world, had two children, Inca and Jesus Christ. Very soon Inca became a cultural hero: he taught the people to speak and introduced them to agriculture, inaugurating a period of abundance and happiness. He built Cuzco and grew fond of Pachamama until he married her and procreated two sons. Unlike Inca, Jesus was an envious character and decided to take revenge on his brother's fortune for having procreated two children. Ironically, Jesus is an image of the Antichrist, which is tantamount to saying Anti-Inca, an evil hero. Jesus' markers are darkness and writing—night, moon, puma, traces on a sheet of paper—while those of the Inca are identified with light and clarity. Jesus defeated the Inca and decapitated Pachamama, Mother Earth, establishing a link between Atahuallpa, the Amarus, and the Inca.

A third character now enters the scene. He is a sort of evil wizard who had been forced to live in hiding while the beneficent powers of the Inca and Pachamama ruled the world. His home is "La Escuela" (The School), where he preaches to the children of the Inca that there is no difference between the Andean and Creole cultures, that the Inca had made friends with Jesus, and that both the Inca and Pachamama are alive. He invites the Inca's children there in order to indoctrinate and devour them, after convincing the two boys that the scriptures—his scriptures—will confirm his words. The boys escape.

The end of the story, as recorded by Ortiz Rescaniere, deserves transcription:

> Since the Inka's children escaped it has been ordered
> that all children must go to school, but it happens that all
> children, such as the Inka sons, do not like school, and
> they manage to escape. Nobody knows the whereabouts
> of the Inka's children, but it is said that when the elder is
> already grown up he will come back to the lands of Peru.
> His return will coincide with the Day of Judgment, although
> it is uncertain he will come back. Children, the people say,
> are looking for him, and they might be able to find him.
> As to his whereabouts, he could be in Lima—which is the
> mouth of Peru [Rima=*hablar*, to speak], the capital city
> founded by Pizarro, the conqueror—or in Cuzco, which is
> the heart of the land, the omphalos of Tahuantinsuyo. If
> we are unable to find him, the story ends, the elder boy of
> the Inka could starve as his father did. Will he? ("El mito";
> our translation)

Writing as a producer of fear and ideological manipulation, as a weapon of the conquistador to erode the values of the vanquished through the educational institution, establishes the structural matrix of this story, which shows a surprising continuity with the mythology surrounding Cajamarca and the deaths of both Atahuallpa and Tupac Amaru II.[25]

The theme of writing as a sign of Spanish superiority goes hand in hand with the motives of misunderstanding and the lack of cultural communication. It is enough to recall here the scene in the *Tragedia del fin de Atahuallpa* (*Tragedy of the End of Atahuallpa*) when the Inca, intrigued by the message sent by Almagro on something similar to a husk of corn, puts the message close to his ear but is unable to understand anything. This episode is a reiteration of the interview between Pizarro and Atahuallpa at Cajamarca when Valverde hands the Bible to the Inca, who examines the mysterious object, opens it, listens to it, and, infuriated at his own inability to understand, throws the book to the ground, unleashing the Spaniards' rage and the ensuing massacre.

The stories we have reviewed here have as a common denominator the Amerindian notion of Conquest as an inversion of the world order, a *pachacuti*. The Inca has transferred his kingdom to the darkness of the underground, to the realm of the wild bull and the serpent. The identification of the Inca with Amaru predicates the new existential condition of the Andean beings representing both dereliction and faith in a forthcoming revival of the Andean order.

The Creole Utopia: Independence

Very early indeed the Spaniards built the scaffoldings for their own utopia. But if the Andean utopia still has to approach its Millennium and the pious Earthly Paradise of the Franciscans was doomed to failure by circumventing the interests of the Crown, the Creole fantasy came to realization in the first quarter of the nineteenth century, during the years of emancipation. This fantasy had a long elaboration. The death of the Amerindian emperors, both in Mexico and in the Andes, had left those regions without kings, and the Spanish emperor was too far removed to have any real effect. Meanwhile, the *encomenderos* aspired to become an autonomous military nobility. This desire was the background for the frequent battles between the conquistadors and the metropolitan administrators.

Perhaps the epitome of these desires and battles might be represented by the deeds and image of the infamous Lope de Aguirre (1518-1561), who arrived in Peru belatedly in 1544. Aguirre took part in the Spanish suppression of Indian rebellions and in the wars that broke out between the partisans of Almagro and Pizarro. In 1560 he joined an expedition led by the explorer Pedro de Ursúa to find El Dorado, which was thought to be located at the headwaters of the Amazon River in Western Brazil. An uprising was headed by Aguirre, and Ursúa, the leader, was murdered. Soon after Aguirre killed Fernando de Guzmán, who had succeeded Ursúa in the leadership of the expedition. Aguirre not only had those who opposed his plans summarily executed but also killed his own beloved daughter so she would not become the mistress of anybody in the crew. Finally, after raiding successfully a number of towns in Venezuela, he was caught and executed by the Spaniards. The most important document we have inherited from Lope de Aguirre is a letter to King Philip II, in which he proclaims himself traitor in an open challenge to the monarch. The rage of the conquistador is raw:

> Listen, listen, Spanish king, stop being cruel and ungrateful
> to your vassals, because with your father and you
> comfortably back in Spain away from all worries, your
> vassals have given you at the cost of their blood and treasure
> all the many lands and dominions that you have in these
> parts, and listen, king and sir, you can't call yourself a
> just king and take any part of these lands for which you
> ventured nothing without first rewarding those who toiled
> and sweated.... Alas, what a terrible pity that the imperial
> Caesar your father should have conquered proud Germany
> with the forces of Spain, spending so much money brought
> from these Indies discovered by us, that our old age and
> exhaustion doesn't pain you enough for you to relieve our
> hunger even for a day! (Galeano 136)

Hypnotic violence, cruelty, and irrationality came to define Lope de Aguirre in the chronicles of his adventures, as Beatriz Pastor has clearly noted. He was the very image of the Antichrist, a man with no king and no rules. There is a different story to be pulled from the records of his trial, which reveals the picture of a charismatic man who was popular among the Spaniards and *mestizos* who surrounded him (Pastor 88+). His rebellion was produced by the decline of heroic values. Aguirre wanted to return to the ideals of the Reconquest (Pastor 92-93). He was indeed a baroque soul caught in despair and solitude, foreshadowing Sigüenza and Sor Juana. They all had a fate of change and doubt; they shared the impossibility of a perfect present. In a sense, they embodied the baroque soul, which would forge a Creole identity and provide a profile for Hispanic American literature.

Let us recall that the life of the conquistadors was directed by archaic ideals. Lope de Aguirre is not an isolated case. Hernán Cortés, just a bit more modern than Columbus, was a feudal vassal of the Spanish monarch and an instrument of a providential undertaking. Anthony Pagden has written that "the whole history of the conquest of Mexico was conceived as a *translatio imperii* from the old world to the new. It was the secular equivalent of the Franciscans' dream of a new apostolic Church, to replace and surpass in piety that which had been lost to Luther" ("Identity Formation" 52). The society of the conquistadors' dream, the one they came to found, in which their ambitions would be fulfilled, was a mirror image of that they left in Castile or Extremadura. Medieval contractual practice, as it is evident in the letters of Cortés, regulated the relations between these men and the Crown. The *encomienda*, a grant of Indians and land made to an individual conquistador for a lifetime, was the reward for his military service. But, as Pagden observes,

> like the Cid in the land of the Moors, the conquistadors considered themselves to be the founders of a new kingdom that would be a fief of the Spanish Crown but in all important respects a self-governing polity. Those who, on their arrival in America, had masses said for the soul of the Cid were stating quite clearly that in this land, among the heathen God had given them to conquer, they were to be

their own masters. Like the Cid they had endured a long
and dangerous journey to a land inhabited by alien and
hostile peoples; and although, unlike the Cid, they had gone
of their own free will, it was not difficult later for them to
see themselves in the role of "good" vassals ill-treated by a
misguided lord. ("Identity Formation" 53)

There was something wrong in the Crown's decision, and the
encomendero was ready to fight in order to redress it. For the soldier of conquest only the conversion of his grant, or *encomienda*,
into a perpetual institution would benefit his family and descendants and provide the conditions of noble status to which he had
aspired when he sailed for America. To a large extent this attitude
would define the demeanor of the elites of the nations that became
independent in the first quarter of the nineteenth century.

Triggered by rumors that the Crown intended to eliminate
the *encomienda* system, a conspiracy arose in Mexico in 1565 to
bring about emancipation from Castile. One night two members
of the conquistador elite, the brothers Alonso and Gil González de
Avila, dressed as Mexican lords, marched in procession through
the streets of Mexico City escorted by a group of servants who were
masked and garbed as Indian warriors. They marched toward the
mansion of Martín Cortés, the second Marqués del Valle. They carried a crown, which Cortés received in all solemnity before with-
drawing. The event, conceived as a prologue for an uprising that
never took place, is faithful to the image that the children of the
conquistadors sought to create for themselves. Oblivious of their
obligations to the Crown, they wanted independence, ground-
ing their claim in the elder Cortés's account that Moctezuma had
granted him the Mexica empire to dispose of it as he saw fit. One
must recall that the donation was received in the name of the
Emperor Charles V, who, in the conqueror's mind, had adhered
to medieval contractual law. The tensions between the conquistadors' sons and the Spanish Crown were to heighten when Philip II
attempted to suppress the *encomienda*. The conquistadors' sons felt
betrayed; they felt that the blood and anguish spilled in the battles
for conquest of the territory had bound them to the land. They
were the lords of the land, and no memory of a previous contract
with Spain or Castile should remain. This behavior shows some

similarities with that of the Aztecs when they established their empire (León-Portilla).

One has to keep in mind that during these times the nobility was the objective of life and that a society of merchants and miners could not be a substitute for a landed aristocracy. For the Creoles the seventeenth century was a world upside-down, a *pachacuti* as dramatic as that of Guaman Poma de Ayala. But it was a *pachacuti* of a very different sign. The *gachupines*, the Spaniards coming to America for profit in lowly trades, did not even share a stake in the land. The self-image of the Creole was that of a nobility of service that was developed into citizenry at the beginning of the eighteenth century. It is at that point that the Creoles began to appeal to a genealogy based upon a history of service to the land rather than to one of conquest, bloodshed, and extermination. The Bourbon attempt to restrict important offices to peninsular Spaniards was perceived as a direct challenge from the Crown. With that challenge it became clearer that a genealogy different from Europe's was needed, and very often the answers to their predicaments were to be found in the ancient past of the Inca and the Mexica. The military imaginary of the Creole was to find its traces in an Amerindian heroic past.

Creole Consciousness: Mythologizing the Amerindian Past

A difference must be established here regarding the utilization of Amerindian nobility in the Andean region and that in the Mexican plateau. Andean mythologizing was an activity championed by the *mestizo* and the Indian sectors of the population that searched its past to find the traces of a utopian future. The Indians were far more numerous and more densely concentrated in the Andes than in the Mexican lands, and in the Andes revolts and uprisings were regular events. Thus, the Peruvian Creoles had reasons to be apprehensive about awakening old loyalties and ambitions among the Indians. The Tupac Amaru uprising was a lesson that the Peruvian elites learned well. In Mexico, on the other hand, the native Amerindians had been crushed early on by European epidemics and conquest, so uprisings were few and sparse. The Mexican Creoles, therefore, could safely reflect upon the glories of the Mexica and Toltec past.

This mythologizing is rooted in the image of the Amerindian as Noble Savage. For Cortés the Mexica were a warrior race of great sophistication. The technical achievements of the Inca and the Mexica, their wealth and bravery, gave more splendor to the victory and future glory of both Cortés and Pizarro. In the beginning phase of the Conquest and colonization, marriages between Spanish men and women belonging to the Indian nobility were seen as a sign of social advance for some of the more plebeian members of the Spanish armies. By the end of the sixteenth century, however, this image had all but vanished because the Spaniards were not fond of associating with the next echelons of Amerindian nobility, that is, with the *caciques* and *curacas* who had become little more than tribute collectors for the *encomenderos*. Nonetheless, this image was revived by the Amerindian elites during the eighteenth century, in order to vitalize the emerging idea of American nationhood. Anthony Pagden has written, "The criollos wished to assume a direct link through kin with an ancient Indian past that would provide them with an independent historical identity; at the same time they needed to avoid, in a society so obsessed with racial purity, any suggestion that this association might have contaminated their blood" ("Identity Formation" 68). Thus, a line was being drawn between living Indians and the ancient Amerindian nobility.

One must recall that, since the sixteenth century, these Creoles were living in a multiracial society (López García 91). The introduction of large numbers of blacks resulted in a variety of racial mixtures, which were to invite the taxonomic inclinations of the eighteenth century. These mixtures were classified as castes (Zavala, Morner) forming a pyramid in which the Indian occupied the lowest position. Thus interbreeding with Indians, however noble, would become very unattractive. The Americans "were to have a culture that was Mexican or Peruvian, Spanish in customs and rooted in an understanding of a mythical Indian past. But it was to be white, *español*, by blood" (Pagden, "Identity Formation" 70). The *mestizos* were not to be foreign. In Mexico the counterparts of Garcilaso de la Vega, the Inca, were Diego Muñoz Camargo, tied to the house of Tlaxcala, and Fernando de Alva Ixtlilxochitl of Texcocan lineage. The Conquest represented for them a joint venture in which the Indian played a major role. Since they were convinced that the actions of their ancestors had made the Conquest possible, they demanded that the historical role of the Amerindian be taken into account in the formation of a *mestizo* society in which Spanish laws and Indian customs, Christian and native religious practices, would mix harmonically. Creole nationalism was to take good advantage of these developments.

The idea of a Creole nationalism based on the prestige of ancient Amerindians was fully developed by the Mexican savant Carlos de Sigüenza y Góngora (Jara and Spadaccini). In our previous volume we saw how in his *Theatro de virtudes políticas* Sigüenza substituted Mexican models for Greco-Roman ones, although the values they represented continued to be Western. Significantly, Sigüenza's text manages to link effectively the Old World and the New, picking up on the attempt of his contemporaries to account for the origin of the Indians. They had to prove that the Indians were true sons of Eve and Adam. Sigüenza made an elaborate interpretation of the name Neptune, the ocean deity, which was instrumental in establishing the connection between the Mexica, the ancient Greeks, and the sons of Noah. "Neptune" was a corruption of the historic "Nephthuym," the son of Misraim and grandson of Shem, one of Noah's children. At the same time this Neptune was the historical leader whose return the Indians were waiting for under the guise of the Plumed Serpent, or Quetzalcoatl. Later, Servando de Mier concluded that Quetzalcoatl was none other than St. Thomas, who had come to preach the gospel to the Indians during the first century of the Christian era, thus eroding all legitimacy for the presence of the Spaniards in America (Jara).

At the same time, in his narrative Sigüenza uses the myth that Moctezuma had donated his empire to Cortés in the belief that he was Quetzalcoatl. Now if Neptune and Quetzalcoatl were the same individual, the Spaniards by virtue of the donation became the heirs of Nephthuym. Thus, on the one hand, the Indians' lineage was as old as those of the Greeks and the Hebrews, and they could be considered, like everyone else, as the prestigious and proper children of Adam and Eve. On the other hand, the Spanish conquerors were the natural rulers of the newly found kingdom. The Spaniards had become Creoles; they were different and, because of their difference, they had a claim to the land. The logic is nearly impeccable. The Creole descendants of the conquistadors, their blood enriched with the plasma of the Amerindian past, were thus the natural rulers of the soil that their parents and grandparents had come to conquer. Here Sigüenza joins the earlier and frustrated effort of the second Marqués del Valle.

The Dispute of the New World

It is here where the creativity of the peninsular Spaniard came to play a role in the pantheon of the Amerindian imaginary that we are trying to describe. Similarities were found between the behavior of Indians discovered by the likes of Sepúlveda and that of the Creoles. Cornelius de Pauw and William Robertson, following Buffon and Reynal, among others, viciously reinscribed in their writings the environmental theory sponsored by Sahagún, who had noted that, because of the climate of the land, the Spaniards born in the New World were Spaniards in appearance only but not in disposition. Through this very audacious principle, the moral and social instability of the Creoles and the weaknesses of the Indians were explained.

At this point in our narrative we reencounter the Plinian mythology found in the writings of the American forefathers: Columbus, Vespucci, Léry, and Anghiera. The American continents were primitive and degenerate; they were lands where men had less strength and courage than the Europeans. The Amerindian men supposedly did not have as much hair as the Europeans, and they were not even very good at loving their women. The great Reynal wrote that Amerindian males often had milk in their breasts and that, as a result of mothering their children, they were unable to procreate. This was for him a reasonable explanation of America's decline in human population. Thus, the discovery of America had been a mistake. Besides, America had infected Europe with venereal disease. The sexual metaphor will never fade. The price of conquest had been shame, death, misery, and slavery (Commager and Giordanetti).

In Sigüenza's narrative the living Indian is a ghost, just a mne-monic trace to work against. But in Francisco Xavier Clavijero's eighteenth-century writings there is an edge favoring the natural constituency of the Creole and the clear defense of an Amerindian being who could be Indian, *mestizo*, or Creole. His *Storia antica del Messico* (*Ancient History of Mexico*) is geared to show that the Indi-ans were every bit as gifted as any white. Exploitation, disdain, and enslavement under the guise of legality had produced the miser-able condition of alcoholism, mistrust of whites, and criminality. The living Indians had been wronged by the Conquest. They had been forced to forget the high culture and civility of their ances-tors. There is a Lascasian tone to Clavijero's argument. He still condemned the Mexica religion as an aggregate of superstitious practices, but he was quick to establish the superiority of Aztec pa-ganism over that of the European world. For him the Mexica gods were more virtuous than those of the Greeks and Romans. And al-though he did not defend human sacrifice, he asked the reader to recall that it was also practiced among the Greeks, the Carthagini-ans, and the Scythians. To de Pauw's charge that Mexican writing was limited to a crude representation of objects, he countered with proof that this writing was hieroglyphic and that the char-acters were arbitrary and conventional. He also argued that if the Mexicans lacked words for the categories of matter, substance, and accident, so did Cicero when he endeavored to translate for-eign ideas—in his case Greek. As a truly enlightened individual, Clavijero argued that conditions of inferiority and degradation of the living Indians were easily treated with good education. If the image of the Indians was disastrous, something could be done to educate them, for the problem was one of ignorance rather than stupidity and that ignorance had been cultivated through brutality and despoliation.

Let us pause for a moment to explain Clavijero's image of the Amerindians, starting with his Jesuit background. We must recall that the Society of Jesus was expelled by royal decree from Amer-ica in 1767. Since their arrival in America, the Jesuits had been an ally of the Creole cause, and because of their prowess in academic institutions they became the instructors of the colonial elites. In regard to the Indians, in a bold foreshadowing of modernity, the

Jesuits believed in the technical and scientific development of the economic system of the Amerindians. They did not think in terms of charity toward, or protection of, the natives but of their ability for production. The Jesuits are identified with the mission, which was one of the three institutions designed to help imperial expansion and defense on the northern frontier (Gibson). The other two were the garrison and the civil settlement. The missions were supposed to gather native converts into communities that would train them to practice various crafts, to till the land, to herd cattle, and to take care of themselves until they were fully Christianized. The *presidio*, or garrison, would serve as military protection for the missions, and the civil settlement would attract Spaniards into the area.

The Jesuit establishments in Paraguay are the most notable example of their success. Discipline, honesty, and organization turned the missions into a highly profitable undertaking. To protect the Indians against the Portuguese slave raiders known as *bandeirantes*, the Jesuits created a native army that sometimes fought successfully against Portuguese greed (Johnson in this volume, Caraman, Rubert de Ventós). The Jesuits promoted an image of the Indians that was close to reality and that was sensitive to social and political abuses committed against them. In Brazil they insisted on Indian segregation from the harmful influence of the whites. They were echoing the protest of Guaman Poma de Ayala in the Andean mountains and prairies. The Jesuits, however, were the champions of assimilation; with them sacrifice became sacrament, and fertility rites were changed into processions, masquerades, and religious plays. One of the tools of assimilation used by the Jesuits was the theater, as Garcilaso reminds us in his *Comentarios reales* (95-97) when he refers to the participation of Indian children in the religious plays staged by the order in the cities of Cuzco and Potosí.

Every gesture of the Indian was to be contained in the universalizing worldview of these Christian missionaries. The sheer size of the new continent needed to be contained. The men who confronted this problem had to render to subjectivity: there was no objective measurement for this kind of reality. Often reason became a handicap. The American experience, in the eyes of the

European man, could only be considered as baroque. Closure, solitude, and the inability to rationalize what was happening under
their own eyes invited men to develop their conscience in darkness and thus to act with irrational gestures. Lope de Aguirre and
Martín Cortés, rationally although unconsciously, knew what they
were doing. They left us images rather than books, a very human
text of the period. Theirs is the praxis of the baroque. Lope de
Aguirre lived out his disillusionment in the midst of a landscape
of plenitude that reduced him to insufficiency, solitude, and madness. His letter to the king of Spain is testimony to his errant life
and to the fact that his dream had become a nightmare. One has
to entrap the baroque gesture: America is in it. America was the
opposite of anything that the European Renaissance meant. After
the encounter with America, the world was an image, a baroque
image, a conjunction of worlds, a universe.

People like Garcilaso, the Inca, Guaman Poma de Ayala, Carlos
de Sigüenza y Góngora, Arzáns de Orsúa y Vela, and Sor Juana
Inés de la Cruz are self-enclosed beings made of solitude. In a
sense, they had to be like that, for who can confront Latin America
with the burden of solitude and misunderstanding inherited from
Columbus's signature? Their relationships with other human beings are just a tactic, not a need. They are pilgrims in the world.
Their search is directed either by utopia or nostalgia. Their present
is always imperfect, made of change and doubt. The subject is always alien, exiled, as Sor Juana, that extraordinary woman in a
world of men (see Feder in this volume), testifies in her life and
work.

America perceives itself as a heterogeneous locus. Lacking a
visible center, works like those of Guaman, Arzáns, and Sor Juana
define themselves in pilgrimage and transience, in instability and
perpetual movement, with no precise here and there. From 1492
America was a *mundus alterius*, another world, in which linearity
was absent. In any case the goal was not the destination but traveling itself, a displacement born of the dislocation of similitude in
the primary scene of the encounter.

From then on, representation did not mean an accord between
the word and the world. The search for identity in America does
not seem to have an end; the search itself is the end and the goal.

Anguish for an identity will become a perennial fellow-traveler of the individual searcher. Mexicanhood, Peruvianhood, Chileanhood remain the ghosts that, from the beginning of the sixteenth century on, Latin Americans were to capture.

As Djelal Kadir has explained, topographics, which expresses the need to make discourse of a place, is the one instrument that defines America. For America is not an entity of the world, but a fiction of a world created by its men and women. America is a discursive entity: it is what has been said about America and what its men and women have told us and the world about it. America becomes such when language discovers its autonomy, when it discovers its ability to serve itself as a system. Sor Juana and Arzáns exemplify the praxis of minds in search of truth, debating with uncertainty, far from truth but searching for it with anxiety. Errors and lies will always be present on the horizon. Columbus, Garcilaso, Guaman Poma sometimes assumed the belief in an absolute knowledge, but they knew that this knowledge was always already out of reach. Two fictions, one of prophecy and the other of memory, utopia and nostalgia for a Golden Age, have been the alternatives. Both have one key feature. That feature is resistance, which, like Columbus's signature, will not reveal its secrets.

America has been the fruit of Columbus's error. But this error produced a history, and that history could only be grounded in the fictions that gave it credibility. Latin American history is nothing more than fiction. Politically correct people will ask us how one can forget and, apparently, justify events such as the genocide of the Caribbean Indians and the injustice of wars triggered in order to establish, or to reestablish, the victory of capitalist greed. We are not forgetting injustices, for, after all, fiction is the image through which empirical events are articulated, an image that helps to integrate the history that has engendered those events. Through fiction, injustices and inequalities acquire a living and bothersome presence.

The novelty of America is not only the result of Columbus's errors. It is above all the result of a need to articulate a narrative for a continent that had a different history: a history that was narrated in the *Popol Vuh*, in the books of Chilam Balam, in the words of the informants of Sahagún and Durán, in the anonymous authors of the myths of Inkarri and the legend of the School, in Sor Juana's dream and Arzáns's fictional narrators. This history has not rejected myth and has moved in a dialectic of search, error, and accommodation, far from linearity and totalization. The New World could only be new(s) because it was already old. The signature of the Admiral of the Ocean Sea—almost a cabalistic cipher—as much as the final destination of his body, still traveling in the minds of novelists, scholars, and filmmakers, is a glyph for America, at least the America that lies south of the Rio Grande.

Notes

1. See also Wilson.

2. One example of this behavior was the conquest of the Yucatan peninsula, one of the most arduous episodes in the war of Spanish expansion. Referring to the final stages of Montejo's campaign against the Mayan natives, Inga Clendinnen writes: "The last stages of the conquest were fought by seasoned [Spanish] men, who learnt to move almost instinctively into the tight formation fighting which had made the steadiness of Spanish swordsmen and pikemen a legend in Europe. Awareness of the military value of every Spanish life, intensified by the deeper loyalty to one's own kind in a world both alien and hostile, meant that no man in jeopardy would be abandoned if his comrades could prevent it. In warfare at least, Spanish lives were neither lightly wasted nor easily yielded. Above all, while the Indians were fighting on their home ground, with all that implies of inhibition, vulnerability, and anxiety for the morrow, the Spaniards could move through the land with no scruple as to destructiveness and the human cost of their actions: those considerations could wait on victory" (33).

3. The concept of chivalry, which finds its clearer definition during the twelfth and the thirteenth centuries, was strengthened by the Crusades, which led to the foundations of the earliest orders of chivalry, the Hospitallers and the Templars, both originally devoted to the service of the pilgrims to the Holy Land. Antiquity—ancient Rome and Greece, Thebes, Troy—Charlemagne, William of Orange, and King Arthur were among the favorite topics of the medieval romances of chivalry.

4. It is a vitality that often stems from their recuperation and interpretation of the colonial motives. Such happens in the works of the Argentinians Juan José Saer and Abel Posse, the Chileans Gabriela Mistral and Pablo Neruda, the Colombian Gabriel García Márquez, the Cuban Alejo Carpentier, the Guatemalan Miguel Angel Asturias, the Mexicans Carlos Fuentes and Octavio Paz, the Paraguayan Augusto Roa Bastos, among others.

5. "llevan tres cuernos puntiagudos / igual que las tarukas / y tienen los cabellos / con blanca harina polvoreados / y en las mandíbulas ostentan / barbas del todo rojas; semejantes a largas vedijas de lana / y llevan en las manos / hondas de hierro extraordinarias / cuyo poder oculto / en vez de lanzar piedras / vomita

fuego llameante" (Lara 34). All translations into English are our own except where otherwise indicated.

6. "Vista de este costado / es un hervidero de hormigas / la miro de este otro costado / se me antojan las huellas que dejan / las patas de los pájaros / en las lodosas orillas del río. / Vista así se parece a las tarukas puestas con la cabeza abajo / y las patas arriba. / Y si solo así la miramos / es semejante a llamas cabizbajas / y cuernos de taruka. / ¡Quien comprender esto pudiera!" (Lara 35).

7. For the European view of assimilation see Elliott, *The Old World and the New*.

8. One must recall at this point the feverish search for those cities throughout the mainland of North America by the fellow Franciscan Marcos de Niza in 1536 and the Coronado expedition, which, sponsored by Viceroy Mendoza, allowed the exploration of a large part of the Southwest of the United States (Bandelier, Phelan, Winship).

9. The first edition was published by Cesare de Lollis in 1892. An excellent *en face* edition is now available: *The* Libro de las profecías *of Christopher Columbus*, translation and commentary by Delno C. West and August Kling.

10. For an interesting survey of the chronicle's creation of the pre-Columbian mind see the catalog of quotations reproduced in Guerra. For the image of the Wild Man see also Dudley and Novak.

11. "If we had an English word that fully expressed the Mayan sense of narrative time," Dennis Tedlock has written, "it would have to embrace the duality of the divine and the human. . . . In fact we already have a word that comes close to doing the job: mythhistory, taken into English from Greek by way of Latin. For the ancient Greeks, who set about driving a wedge between the divine and the human, this term became a negative one, designating narratives that should have been properly historical but contained mythic impurities. For Mayans, the presence of a divine dimension in narratives of human affairs is not an imperfection but a necessity, and it is balanced by a necessary human dimension in narratives of divine affairs. At one end of the *Popol Vuh* the gods are preoccupied with the difficult task of making humans, and at the other humans are preoccupied with the equally difficult task of finding the traces of divine movements in their own deeds." This is not a contrast between Amerindian cyclical time and European linear time, for "Mayans are always alert to the reassertion of the patterns of the past in present events, but do not expect the past to repeat itself exactly." Unique events are allowed but they always carry "echoes of the past." "The effect of these events . . . is cumulative, and it is a specifically human capacity to take each of them into account separately while at the same time recognizing that they double back on one another" (64).

12. "Señor nuestro: te has fatigado, te has dado cansancio: ya a la tierra tú has llegado. Has arribado a tu ciudad: México. Allí has venido a sentarte en tu solio, en tu trono. Oh, por tiempo breve te lo reservaron, te lo conservaron, los que ya se fueron, tus sustitutos. Los señores reyes, Itcoatzin, Motecuhzomatzin el Viejo, Axayácacn Tízcoc, Ahuítzotl. Oh, que breve tiempo tan sólo guardaron para ti, dominaron la ciudad de México. Bajo su espalda, bajo su abrigo estaba metido el pueblo bajo. ¿Han de ver ellos y sabrán acaso de los que dejaron de sus pósteros? ¡Ojalá uno de ellos estuviera viendo, viera con asombro lo que yo ahora veo venir en mí! Lo que yo veo ahora: Yo el residuo, el superviviente de nuestros señores. No, no

es que yo sueño, no me levanto del sueño adormilado: no lo veo en sueños, no estoy soñando.... ¡Es que ya te he visto, es que ya he puesto mis ojos en tu rostro!... Ha cinco, ha diez días yo estaba angustiado: tenía fija la mirada en la Región del Misterio. Y tú has venido entre nubes, entre nieblas. Como que esto era lo que nos iban dejando dicho los reyes, los que rigieron, los que gobernaron tus ciudades: Que habrías de instalarte en tu asiento, en tu sitial, que habrías de venir acá.... Pues ahora, se ha realizado: Ya tu llegaste, con gran fatiga, con afán viniste. Llega a la tierra: ven y descansa; toma posesión de tus casas reales; da refrigerio a tu cuerpo. ¡Llegad a vuestra casa, señores nuestros!" (775).

13. For a biography of Garcilaso, see Varner.

14. "Mayor y más sedienta de su propia sangre que la de los otomanos fue la crueldad de Atahuallpa que, no hartándose con la de doscientos hermanos suyos, hijos del gran Huaina Capac, pasó adelante a beber la de sus sobrinos, tíos y parientes, dentro y fuera del cuarto grado, que, como fuese de la sangre real, no escapó ninguno, legítimo ni bastardo. Todos los mandó matar con diversas muertes: a unos degollaron; a otros ahorcaron; a otros echaron en ríos y lagos, con grandes pesas al cuello, porque se ahogasen sin que el nadar les valiese; otros fueron despeñados de altos riscos y peñascos" (430).

15. "a los indios, mestizos y criollos de los reinos y provincias del grande y riquísimo imperio del Perú" (9).

16. "Mas el Demonio... procuraba... con todas sus fuerças y mañas, estorvar la conversión de aquellos indios; y aunque no pudo estorvarla del todo, a lo menos la estorvó muchos años... Todas estas guerras exercitó el Demonio sucessivamente, por espacio de veinte y cinco años... Por estos impedimentos no se predicó el Evangelio, como se predicara si no las hubiera, que ni los fieles podían enseñar la fe, por los alborotos que cada día tenían, ni los infieles recebirla" (*Historia general del Perú* 1: 124-125).

17. "Aunque ha habido españoles curiosos que han escrito las repúblicas del Nuevo Mundo, como la de México y la del Perú y las de otros reinos de aquella gentilidad, no ha sido con la relación entera que de ellos se pudiera dar" ("Prohemio al Lector" 4).

18. "más por experiencia (enseñados de su necesidad), que no por su filosofía natural, porque fueron poco especulativos de lo que no tocaban con las manos" (82).

19. "no pasaron con la imaginación más adelante de lo que veían materialmente con los ojos" (84-85).

20. "porque no supieron levantar el entendimiento a cosas invisibles; toda la teología de los Incas se encerró en el nombre Pachacámac" (89).

21. Procacci 221-222. Bruno indeed had a cosmic vision that foreshadows Spinoza. On the latter, see Negri.

22. "Io imparo piu dalla anatomia di una formica o d'un'erba... che non da tutti i libri che sono scritti dal principio dei secoli."

23. The tribunals of the Inquisition, however effective Landa's repression of Indian idolatry might have been, did not have competence over the native Amerindians, and the first of them was instituted only in 1571, nine years after the Franciscan's great *auto de fe*.

24. For a description of masquerades in ancient Mexico see Leonard.

25. For other Andean myths related to these topics, see Ortiz Rescaniere, *De Adaneva a Inkarri* and *Huarochiri: 400 años después;* also Pease (*El dios creador andino* and *El pensamiento mítico*) and Ossio.

Works Cited

Adorno, Rolena. *Cronista y príncipe: La obra de don Felipe Guamán Poma de Ayala.* Lima: Fondo Editorial de la Pontificia Universidad Católica del Perú, 1989.

————. *Guaman Poma: Writing and Resistance in Colonial Peru.* Austin: Univ. of Texas Press, 1986.

Aguirre, Lope de. "Letter to King Philip II." Galeano 136.

Arens, W. *The Man-Eating Myth: Anthropology & Anthropophagy.* New York: Oxford Univ. Press, 1979.

Bandelier, Adolf F. *The Golden Man (El Dorado).* New York: Appleton and Company, 1893.

The Book of Chilam Balam of Chumayel. Ed. Ralph Roys. 2nd ed. Norman: Univ. of Oklahoma Press, 1967.

Boorstin, Daniel J. *The Discoverers.* New York: Vintage Books, 1985.

Borah, Woodrow, and S. F. Cook. *The Aboriginal Population of Central Mexico on the Eve of the Spanish Conquest.* Berkeley: Univ. of California Press, 1963.

Burga, Manuel. *Nacimiento de una utopía: Muerte y resurrección de los Incas.* Lima: Instituto de Apoyo Agrario, 1988.

Canny, Nicholas, and Anthony Pagden, eds. *Colonial Identity in the Atlantic World, 1500-1800.* Princeton, N.J.: Princeton Univ. Press, 1987.

Caraman, Philip. *The Lost Paradise: The Jesuit Republic in South America.* New York: Dorset Press, 1975.

Castro-Klarén, Sara. "Discurso y transformación de los dioses en los Andes: Del Taki Onqoy a 'Rasuñiti.'" Millones. 407-423.

Chiappelli, Fredi, ed. *First Images of America: The Impact of the New World on the Old.* 2 vols. Berkeley: Univ. of California Press, 1976.

Clavijero, Francisco Xavier. *Storia antica del Messico.* Cesena: G. Biasini, 1780-1781. Spanish trans. *Historia antigua de México.* Mexico City: Porrúa, 1945.

Clendinnen, Inga. *Ambivalent Conquests: Maya and Spaniard in Yucatan, 1517-1570.* New York: Cambridge Univ. Press, 1987.

Columbus, Christopher. *The Libro de las profecías of Christopher Columbus.* Trans. and commentary by Delno C. West and August Kling. Gainesville: Univ. of Florida Press, 1991.

Commager, Henry Steele, and Elmo Giordanetti. *Was America a Mistake? An Eighteenth-Century Controversy.* Columbia: Univ. of South Carolina Press, 1967.

Cook, S. F., and Woodrow Borah. *Essays in Population History: Mexico and the Caribbean.* 3 vols. Berkeley: Univ. of California Press, 1971-1979.

Crosby, Alfred W. *The Columbian Exchange: Biological and Cultural Consequences of 1492.* Westport, Conn.: Greenwood Press, 1972.

De Certeau, Michel. *The Writing of History.* Trans. Tom Conley. New York: Columbia Univ. Press, 1988.

Dudley, Edward, and Maximilian E. Novak, eds. *The Wild Man Within: An Image in Western Thought from the Renaissance to Romanticism.* Pittsburgh: Univ. of Pittsburgh Press, 1972.

Durán, Diego. *Historia de las Indias de Nueva España e islas de la tierra firme.* 2 vols. Mexico City: Porrúa, 1967.

Durand, José. *El Inca Garcilaso clásico de América.* Mexico City: Secretaría de Educación Pública, 1976.

Elliott, J. H. *Imperial Spain, 1469-1716.* New York: St. Martin's Press, 1963.

———. *The Old World and the New, 1492-1650.* Cambridge: Cambridge Univ. Press, 1970.

Etienne, Mona, and Eleonor Leacock. *Women and Colonization: Anthropological Perspectives.* New York: Praeger Publishers, 1980.

Fernández de Navarrete, Martín. *Viajes de Colón.* Mexico City: Porrúa, 1986.

Fernández de Oviedo, Gonzalo. *Historia general y natural de las Indias, islas y tierra firme del mar océano.* 5 vols. Madrid: Biblioteca de Autores Españoles, 1959.

Flores Galindo, Alberto. *Buscando un Inca.* Lima: Editorial Orizonte, 1988.

Focher, Juan. *Itinerario del misionero en América,* 1574.

Frankl, Victor. *Antijovio de Gonzalo Jiménez de Quesada y las concepciones de realidad y verdad en la época de la contrarreforma y del manierismo.* Madrid: Ediciones de Cultura Hispánica, 1963.

Galeano, Eduardo. *Memory of Fire I: Faces and Masks.* Trans. Cedric Belfrage. New York: Pantheon Books, 1987.

Gallenkamp, Charles. *Maya: The Riddle and Rediscovery of a Lost Civilization.* 2nd ed. New York: Penguin Books, 1981.

Garcilaso de la Vega, El Inca. *Comentarios reales.* Ed. José de la Riva Agüero. Mexico City: Editorial Porrúa, 1984.

———. *Historio general del Perú.* 3 vols. Ed. Angel Rosenblatt. Buenos Aires: Emecé, 1944.

———. *Royal Commentaries of the Incas and General History of Peru.* Trans. with an introduction by Harold V. Livermore. Foreword by Arnold J. Toynbee. Austin: Univ. of Texas Press, 1987.

Gates, William. Introduction. *Yucatan, Before and After the Conquest.* By Diego de Landa. New York: Dover Publications, 1978. iii-xvi.

Gibson, Charles. *Spain in America.* New York: Harper and Row, 1966.

Godzich, Wlad, and Nicholas Spadaccini. "Popular Culture and Spanish Literary History." *Literature among Discourses: The Spanish Golden Age.* Minneapolis: Univ. of Minnesota Press, 1986. 41-61.

Granzotto, Gianni. *Christopher Columbus.* Norman: Univ. of Oklahoma Press, 1987.

Greenblatt, Stephen. "Learning to Curse: Aspects of Linguistic Colonialism in the Sixteenth Century." Chiappelli 2: 561-580.

Grisel, Etienne. "The Beginnings of International Law and General Public Law Doctrine: Francisco de Vitoria's 'De Indiis Prior.'" Chiappelli 2: 305-325.

Gruzinski, Serge. *Man-Gods in the Mexican Highlands: Indian Power and Colonial Society, 1520-1800.* Trans. Eileen Corrigan. Stanford: Stanford Univ. Press, 1989.

Guaman Poma de Ayala, Felipe. *Primer nueva corónica y buen gobierno.* Segunda edición crítica de John V. Murra, Rolena Adorno, and Jorge L. Urioste. 3 vols. Madrid: Historia 16, 1987.

Guerra, Francisco. *The Pre-Columbian Mind: A Study into the Aberrant Nature of Sexual Drives, Drugs Affecting Behaviour and the Attitude towards Life and Death, with a Survey of Psychotherapy, in Pre-Columbian America.* London: Seminar Press, 1971.

Hanke, Lewis. "The Theological Significance of the Discovery of America." Chiappelli 2: 363-389.

Heller, Agnes. *Teoría de la historia.* 2nd ed. Barcelona: Editorial Fontamara, 1985.

Ixtlilxochitl, Fernando de Alva. *Obras históricas publicadas y anotadas por Alfredo Chavero.* Mexico City: Oficina Tip. de la Secretaría de Fomento, 1891-1892.

Jane, Cecil. *The Four Voyages of Columbus.* 2 vols. New York: Dover Publications, 1988.

Jara, René. "The Inscription of Creole Consciousness: Fray Servando de Mier." Jara and Spadaccini 349-379.

———. *El revés de la arpillera.* Madrid: Hiperión, 1988.

Jara, René, and Nicholas Spadaccini, eds. *1492-1992: Re/Discovering Colonial Writing.* Hispanic Issues 4. Minneapolis: Prisma Institute, 1989.

Kadir, Djelal. *Questing Fictions: Latin America's Family Romance.* Minneapolis: Univ. of Minnesota Press, 1986.

Keen, Benjamin. *The Aztec Image in Western Thought.* New Brunswick, N.J.: Rutgers Univ. Press, 1971.

———, and Mark Wasserman. *A History of Latin America.* 3rd ed. Boston: Houghton Mifflin Company, 1988.

Konetzke, Richard. *América latina: La época colonial.* 16th ed. Mexico City: Siglo XXI, 1984.

Landa, Diego de. *Yucatan, Before and After the Conquest.* Trans. William Gates. New York: Dover Publications, 1978.

Lara, Jesús. *Tragedia del fin de Atahuallpa.* Cochabamba, 1957; rpt. Cochabamba: Amigos del Libro, 1989; Buenos Aires: Ediciones del Sol, 1989.

Las Casas, Bartolomé de. *Brevísima relación de la destruición de las Indias.* Ed. André Saint-Lu. 2nd ed. Madrid: Cátedra, 1984.

———. *Historia de las Indias.* Ed. Agustín Millares Carlo y estudio preliminar de Lewis Hanke. 2nd ed. 3 vols. Mexico City: Fondo de Cultura Económica, 1965.

Leonard, Irving A. *Baroque Times in Old Mexico.* Ann Arbor: Univ. of Michigan Press, 1959.

León-Portilla, Miguel. *Aztec Thought and Culture.* Trans. J. E. Davis. Norman: Univ. of Oklahoma Press, 1963.

Léry, Jean de. *Histoire d'un voyage faict en la terre du Brésil.* Paris: Plasma, 1980.

López de Gómara, Francisco. *Historia de la conquista de México.* Mexico City: P. Robredo, 1943. English trans. *Cortes: The Life of the Conqueror by his Secretary.* Trans. and ed. Leslie Bird Simpson. Berkeley: Univ. of California Press, 1964.

López García, Angel. *El sueño hispano ante la encrucijada del racismo contemporáneo.* Mérida: Editora regional de Extremadura, 1991.

McColley, Grant. Introduction. *The Defense of Galileo of Thomas Campanella.* Smith College Studies in History 22.3-4 (April-July 1937): v-xliii.

Maravall, José Antonio. *Culture of the Baroque.* Minneapolis: Univ. of Minnesota Press, 1986.

———. "La utopía político-religiosa de los franciscanos." *Utopía y reformismo en la España de los Austrias.* Madrid: Siglo XXI, 1982. 79-110.

Mason, Peter. *Deconstructing America: Representations of the Other*. New York: Rutledge, 1990.

Mendieta, Jerónimo de. *Historia eclesiástica indiana*. 4 vols. Mexico City: Salvador Chávez, 1945.

Michelet, Jules. *Satanism and Witchcraft: A Study in Medieval Superstition*. Trans. A. R. Allison. New York: Citadel Press, 1973.

Mignolo, Walter. "Literacy and Colonization: The New World Experience." Jara and Spadaccini 51-96.

Millones, Luis, ed. *El retorno de las huacas: Estudios y documentos sobre el Taki Onqoy, siglo XVI*. Lima: Instituto de Estudios Peruanos, 1990.

Molina, Cristóbal de. *Relación de las fábulas y ritos de los Incas*. C. de Molina and C. de Albornoz. *Fábulas y mitos de los Incas*. Ed. Henrique Urbano y Pierre Duviols. Madrid: Historia 16, 1988.

Morison, Samuel Eliot. *The Great Explorers: The European Discovery of America*. New York: Oxford Univ. Press, 1978.

Morner, Magnus. *Race Mixture in the History of Latin America*. Boston: Little Brown, 1967.

Motolinía (Fray Toribio de Benavente). *Historia de los indios de la Nueva España*. Ed. Georges Baudot. Madrid: Castalia, 1985.

Negri, Antonio.*The Savage Anomaly: The Power of Spinoza's Metaphysics and Politics*. Minneapolis: Univ. of Minnesota Press, 1991.

O'Gorman, Edmundo. *La invención de América*. Mexico City: Fondo de Cultura Económica, 1958.

Ortiz Rescaniere, Alejandro. *De Adaneva a Inkarri. Una visión indígena del Perú*. Lima: INIDE, 1973.

———. "El mito de la escuela." *Ideología mesiánica del mundo andino*. Ed. Juan Ossio. Lima: Colección Biblioteca de Antropología, 1973. 237-250.

———. *Huarochiri: 400 años después*. Lima: Pontificia Universidad Católica del Perú, 1980.

Ossio, Juan. Introducción. *Ideología mesiánica del mundo andino*. Lima: Colección Biblioteca de Antropología, 1973. xi-xlv.

Pagden, Anthony. *The Fall of Natural Man*. New York: Cambridge Univ. Press, 1982.

———. "Identity Formation in Spanish America." Canny and Pagden 51-93.

Pastor, Beatriz. "Lope de Aguirre the Wanderer: Knowledge and Madness." *Dispositio* 11.28-29 (1986): 85-98.

Pease, Franklin. *El dios creador andino*. Lima: Mosca Azul Editores, 1973.

———, ed. *El pensamiento mítico*. Lima: Mosca Azul Editores, 1982.

Phelan, John Leddy. *The Millennial Kingdom of the Franciscans in the New World*. 2nd ed. Berkeley: Univ. of California Press, 1970.

Popol Vuh: The Mayan Book of the Dawn of Life. Preface and trans. Dennis Tedlock. New York: Simon and Schuster, 1985.

Procacci, Giuliano. *Storia degli Italiani*. Bari: Laterza, 1987.

Pupo-Walker, Enrique. *Historia, creación y profecía en los textos del Inca Garcilaso de la Vega*. Madrid: José Porrúa Turanzas, 1982.

Rabasa, José. "Utopian Ethnology in Las Casas's 'Apologética.'" Jara and Spadaccini 263-289.

Rubert de Ventós, Javier. *El laberinto de la hispanidad*. Barcelona: Planeta, 1987.

Sahagún, Bernardino de. *Historia general de las cosas de Nueva España*. Ed. Angel María Garibay. Mexico City: Porrúa, 1989.

Sale, Kirkpatrick. *The Conquest of Paradise: Christopher Columbus and the Columbian Legacy*. New York: Alfred A. Knopf, 1990.

Scott, James Brown. *The Spanish Origin of International Law: Francisco de Vitoria and His Law of Nations*. Oxford: Clarendon Press, 1934.

Sepúlveda, Ginés de. *Democrates Segundo*. Ed. Angel Losada. Madrid: Consejo Superior de Investigaciones Científicas, 1984.

Silverblatt, Irene. "Andean Women under Spanish Rule." Etienne and Leacock 149-184.

Taylor, Gerald. *Ritos y tradiciones de Huarochiri del siglo XVII: Estudio biográfico sobre Francisco de Avila de Antonio Acosta*. Lima: Instituto de Estudios Peruanos, 1987.

Tedlock, Dennis. Preface. *Popol Vuh* 13-65.

Todorov, Tzvetan. *The Conquest of America: The Question of the Other*. Trans. Richard Howard. New York: Harper and Row, 1985.

Torquemada, Juan de. *Monarquía indiana*. Introduction by Miguel León-Portilla. 6th ed. 3 vols. Mexico City: Porrúa, 1986.

Trinkaus, Charles. "Renaissance and Discovery." Chiappelli 2: 3-9.

Varner, John Grier. *El Inca: The Life and Times of Garcilaso de la Vega*. Austin: Univ. of Texas Press, 1968.

Vespucci, Amerigo. *El nuevo mundo: Cartas relativas a sus viajes y descubrimientos*. Introduction by Roberto Levillier. Buenos Aires: Editorial Nova, 1951.

Veyne, Paul. *Did the Greeks Believe in Their Myth? An Essay on the Constitutive Imagination*. Trans. Paula Wissing. Chicago: Univ. of Chicago Press, 1988.

Vitoria, Francisco de. "The First 'Relectio' on the Indians Lately Discovered." Trans. John Pawley Bate. Appendix A to Scott i-xlvi.

———. "The Second 'Relectio' on the Indians, or On the Law of War Made by the Spaniards on the Barbarians." Trans. John Pawley Bate. Appendix B to Scott xlvi-lxx.

Wachtel, Nathan. "La visión de los vencidos: La conquista española en el folklore indígena." *Ideología mesiánica del mundo andino*. Ed. Juan Ossio. Lima: Colección Biblioteca de Antropología, 1973. 35-81.

Washburn, Wilcomb E. "The Meaning of Discovery in the Fifteenth and Sixteenth Centuries." *American Historical Review* 68.1 (Oct. 1962): 1-21.

Wilford, John Noble. "Discovering Columbus." *New York Times Magazine* (Aug. 11, 1991): 25+.

Wilson, Samuel M. "Columbus My Enemy: A Caribbean Chief Resists the First Spanish Invaders." *Natural History* (Dec. 1990): 45-49.

Winship, George Parker. *The Journey of Coronado, 1540-1542*. Golden, Colo.: Fulcrum Publishing, 1990.

Zamora, Margarita. *Language, Authority, and Indigenous History in the Comentarios Reales de los Incas*. Cambridge: Cambridge Univ. Press, 1988.

Zavala, Iris M. "Representing the Colonial Subject." Jara and Spadaccini 23-48.

◆ Chapter 1
Word and Mirror
Presages of the Encounter

Miguel León-Portilla

(translated by Jennifer M. Lang)

The announcer of the portent was born in Córdoba many centuries ago. The testimonies of the fulfiller of the presage are still found today in Seville, beside the Giralda. And upon the realization of the portent, from the coasts of Andalucia, facing the Atlantic, the ocean ceased being an encircling barrier to become a path of encounters.

There are crystal balls and mirrors in which one sees what is about to happen. There are also prophetic words pronounced by soothsayers and, at times, even by circumspect men renowned as philosophers. Such words and mirrors are magic bearers of presages; they are early images of portents.

◆

Moctezuma, the Aztec sovereign, contemplated in a mirror a portent never seen before. The fishermen of the lakes on which his metropolis stood had found that mirror on the head of a rare, ash-colored bird that looked like a crane. In the mirror, with the bird's head opened, and in daylight, the fishermen had seen reflected the stars that they called *Mamalhuaztli,* "sticks which are rubbed together to light the fire," for as such they shone in the sky.

Moctezuma was in *Tlilancalco,* his house of darkness, a place of retreat and meditation. To that refuge they brought him the

rare, ashen bird that looked like a crane, on whose head the mirror rested. With reverence and trepidation, the fishermen placed
the bird and mirror in the hands of the great lord's servants, who
brought it to him, interrupting his meditation.

He gazed at the mirror found on the bird's head. Like the fishermen before him, he saw how there shone in it the stars they
called *Mamalhuaztli*. Moctezuma and the others knew that when
those stars reached their zenith, every fifty-two years, the New
Fire was to be lit at the summit of a mountain. That ceremony
took place amid cries and sacrifices. For if the Fire was not lit, the
shadows would rule the world forever.

For an instant, Moctezuma put aside the head of the strange
bird. Then he looked again. The stars of *Mamalhuaztli* could no
longer be seen in it. Instead there were reflected in it, as if in the
distance, people who hurried forth, arrogant men who advanced
by pushing and shoving. They were people of war, and they rode
what looked like large deer.

Moctezuma contemplated the stars of *Mamalhuaztli* and the
men riding those strange animals, in a year designated by his
calendar as 12-House, as recorded in books of painting and hieroglyphic signs. That year corresponds to 1507 according to the
Christian calendar. Moctezuma did not know that fifteen years had
passed since the ocean—the *téoatl*, "divine waters"—had stopped
being a barrier to become a path of encounters.

◆

We are once again in Andalucia. The one who had conquered the
ocean barriers was now moving on from Granada and Seville to
Sanlúcar to undertake his fourth voyage. He was leaving behind
a book in which he had copied many texts of the Bible and of
the Holy Fathers. The book also reproduced some of his letters,
accounts of eclipses, words about Ophir, Tharsis, and Jerusalem.
That strange volume is entitled the *Libro de las profecías* (*Book of
Prophecies*).

The Admiral of the Ocean Sea was to add other paragraphs to
his *Book of Prophecies* upon returning from his fourth trip. Was it in
1504 or 1505? In fact, he recorded an eclipse that he had witnessed
in Jamaica on February 29, 1504. Such additions in his book ante-
ceded by only two or three years the moment in which Moctezuma

gazed at the mirror on the head of the strange, ash-colored bird that looked like a crane.

Of interest here is an addition to the *Libro de las profecías* in which, only a couple of years before his death, Admiral Christopher Columbus was to quote the one born in Córdoba many centuries earlier who had foreseen the portent. But the Admiral's quote in his *Libro de las profecías* goes beyond a mere literal transcription.

Lucius Annaeus Seneca, the master who was born in Córdoba more than a thousand years earlier, was to have the chorus of his tragedy *Medea* utter the following words at the end of the second act:

> Times will come with the passage of time
> in which the ocean will loosen the barriers of the world
> and the earth will open itself in all of its extension
> and Tethys will discover new worlds for us and
> Thule will no longer be the farthest part of the earth.

With the passage of time, the prophetic word of the chorus, and of Seneca, was to impress more than a few distinguished people. The last Thule, the Iceland colonized by the Danes, would no longer be the edge of the earth, which was to see its vast horizons open as the ocean loosened the frontiers of the world.

◆

It is important to clarify here that in some of the ancient manuscripts, in which the text of Seneca's *Medea* is conserved, it is said that Tethys would discover new worlds. Tethys was a goddess, the wife of Father Okeanos. Now there are variants in other ancient transcriptions. Instead of the name of the goddess Tethys, there appears that of Typhis. In Greek mythology the latter was a famous mariner who knew of winds and stars, who served at the same time as guide to Jason, of the Golden Fleece. In the text handled by the Admiral of the Ocean Sea, most likely a printed text, one could read the variant that adjudicated to the mariner Typhis the task of opening the earth in all of its extension and of discovering new worlds. Christopher Columbus was to copy

Seneca's words in his *Libro de las profecías*. It is important to point out, however, that in doing so he was going beyond a literal transcription.

The original *Libro de las profecías* is in the Columbian Library in Seville, which was founded by Columbus's son, Hernando. On the reverse side of page 59, the Admiral wrote in his own handwriting:

In the latter years of the world certain times will come,

in which the ocean sea will loosen the bonds of things

and a great land will open up,

and a new mariner, like the one who served as Jason's guide,

by the name of Typhis,

will discover a new world

and then the isle of Thule will no longer be

the end of the earth.

Vernán a los tardos años del mundo ciertos tiempos,

en los cuales el mar océano afloxerá los atamentos de las cosas

y se abrirá una grande tierra,

y un nuevo marinero, como aquel que fue guía de Jasón,

que obe nombre Tiphi,

descobrirá nuevo mundo

y entonces non será la isla Tille

la postrera de las tierras.

Like Jason's guide Typhis, the Admiral was the new mariner. And like Typhis, as he explicitly proclaims in his transcription, *he will discover a new world*.

Another book from the Columbian Library is of interest here. It is also an edition of Seneca's tragedies, printed in Venice in 1510. Hernando Columbus, son of the Admiral, was also unable to resist the idea of including a gloss or notation in the margins, next to the text in which it is said that times will come in which the earth will open itself up in all its extension and Typhis will discover new worlds. Don Hernando's annotation, in Latin, reads as follows:

Haec prophetia impleta est per patrem meum,
Christophorum Colom, admiraltem, in anno 1492.

This prophecy was realized by my father, Christopher
Columbus, the Admiral, in the year 1492.

Among other distinguished persons who were profoundly impressed by Seneca's presage stands out Father Bartolomé de Las
Casas, the first to preserve in detail the account of Columbus's
enterprise in his *Historia de las Indias*. After explaining there that
the isle of Thule "is in the ocean near Norway, between the North
and the West" ("está en el océano desa parte de Noruega, entre el
Septentrión y el Poniente"), he says:

Could anything clearer have been said by Seneca about
the discovery of these Indies? And by saying "Typhis ["the
first to set sail," clarifies Fray Bartolomé] will discover new
worlds, he gives to understand *automatice* or *par excellence*,
specialty, knowledge, and grace, which God was to instill in
Christopher Columbus for that task; as if he were saying:
no one but the excellent and distinguished mariner—like
Typhis, inventor of notable and admirable novelty in matters
pertaining to navigation—will discover new worlds....

¿Qué más claro pudo decir Séneca del descubrimiento
destas Indias? Y diciendo "Tiphis ["el primero que hizo
navío," aclara fray Bartolomé] descubrirá nuevos mundos,
da a entender *automatice*, or por excelencia, la dignidad y
especialidad y sabiduría y gracia que Dios había de infundir
para ello en Cristóbal Colón, como si dijera, el excelente
y señalado marinero y no otro tal, como el inventor de
señalada y admirable novedad en cosas pertenecientes
al navegar como lo fue aquel Tiphis, descubrirá nuevos
mundos....

The list of prominent people impressed by Seneca's presage
is a long one. I shall at least recall the name of Francisco López
de Gómara who, in his *Historia general de las Indias*, published
in 1552, adduced, once again, the words of Seneca in his commentary. Those words were "like a saying about the New World
which seems to be a prophecy" ("como un dicho acerca del Nuevo
Mundo que parece adivinanza").

The ocean's boundaries loosened and the ocean became a path

of encounters. It is true that the Admiral expressed many times the idea of having reached the frontiers of Asia. Yet, in his *Libro de las profecías*, he wrote in his own hand that in those last years of the world, when "a great land will open up, a new mariner, like the one who had been Jason's guide ... will discover a new world ... " ("se abrirá una grande tierra, un nuevo marinero, como aquél que fue guía de Jasón ... descobrirá nuevo mundo ... "). What was the Admiral thinking when he thus altered what Seneca had expressed in his tragedy *Medea?* Let the erudites and the recalcitrant polemists rack their foggy brains. It is best to seek awareness of the fact that, beyond the ancient barriers of the world according to Ptolemy's maps, there existed many diverse peoples, some with great cities, temples, and palaces, such as the Mayas, Aztecs, and the Quechuas of Peru.

◆

A chain of encounters occurred from the moment the new mariner, like the one who served as Jason's guide, "discovered a new world" ("descobrió nuevo mundo"). Columbus discovered the Taínos of the islands and the fear-inspiring Caribs from whom he derived, rightfully or not, the sad name of cannibals. The Admiral also touched the shores of *terra firme.* Others followed him and the chain of encounters ensued, with ever greater frequency.

Moctezuma contemplated the presage in his mirror. And much earlier, as recalled by the hermit Ramón Pané, the first chronicler of the New World, and by Cacibaquel, the Taíno lord of Hispaniola, Moctezuma claimed to have been told by his god Yucahuamá "that a clothed people would come to the land, and would dominate and kill them ... " ("que llegaría al país una gente vestida, que los dominaría y mataría ... " [48]). At the same time the Mayan priests of the Yucatan and Guatemala foretold their arrival, interpreting the sequence from their calendars. And it is said that, in the south, the Inca Huayna Capac learned of a portent and ill omen that would soon be connected with the arrival of a vessel carrying bearded white men.

The barriers of the world forever broken, the earth opened in all its extension, peoples of different worlds came to meet. The encounter produced stupor, followed by conflict, struggle, deaths, and cultural ruin. The encounter also brought with it exchanges, and a fusion of peoples and ways of life. New peoples began to exist who looked and felt like *mestizos*.

To explain the unforeseen is always a human urge. In order to make sense of the previously unknown, one must appeal to what belongs and corresponds to the ancestral vision of the world. Beliefs, ancient tales, and prophecies are elements found in any vision of the world. The unusual becomes comprehensible only when placed in the context of what is known to have occurred or what might occur. To witness the unknown other at times implies foretelling its appearance, even if, paradoxically, after the encounter.

◆

Were the words and visions of the Taínos, Mayas, and Quechuas prophetic? Did Moctezuma really contemplate that mirror and in it the stars and the men threatening war "riding on deer-like beasts"? What is clear is that, if one places those "men of Castile" ("los hombres de Castilla"), who came from beyond the great waters, in the context of the ancient indigenous conceptions of the world, those who were radically strange ceased to be so.

The Admiral also found in his reading of Seneca's *Medea* a principle of understanding of which speaks his *Libro de las profecías*, the half-forgotten testimony preserved to this day in Seville, next to the Giralda. The portent indeed came true. No longer confining, the ocean became a path of encounters. After thousands of years of separation, humankind started to become one; it was already the *Encounter of Two Worlds*. That encounter made possible the existence of only one world.

Works Cited

Columbus, Christopher. *The* Libro de las profecías *of Christopher Columbus*. Trans. and commentary by Delno C. West and August Kling. Gainesville: Univ. of Florida Press, 1991.

Las Casas, Bartolomé de. *Historia de las Indias*, Ed. Agustín Millares Carlo. Intro. Lewis Hanke. Mexico City: Fondo de Cultura Económica, 1951.

López de Gómara, Francisco. *Historia general de las Indias y vida de Hernán Cortés*. Intro. Jorge Gurria Lacroix. 2 vols. Caracas: Biblioteca Ayacucho, 1979.

Pané, Ramón. *Relación acerca de las antigüedades de los indios*. Ed. José Juan Arrom. Mexico City: Siglo XXI, 1974.

Seneca, Lucius Annaeus. *Medea*. Ed. C. D. N. Costa. Oxford: Clarendon Press, 1980.

Chapter 2

De Bry's Las Casas

Tom Conley

Many of the images we know of the European encounter with the New World come to us through Théodore De Bry and his two sons. Currently adorning posters and brochures announcing conferences celebrating the Columbian Quincentennial, they offer an allure of "authenticity" of first-hand contact of new and old cultures. Their engravings are sharp and clear, and their figures of Europeans and Indians accompany folio texts with innovatively drawn maps.[1] One of the smaller illustrated volumes is a Latin edition of Bartolomé de Las Casas's *Brevísima relación*, issued by Théodore De Bry in Frankfurt in 1598. In the paragraphs that follow I would like to investigate how and why a Protestant artist takes up a Catholic work written almost fifty years before. For what ostensive purposes were the engravings made? In view of our own investments in the Quincentennial, with what implications? What, we can ask, are the perspectives that De Bry's Las Casas opens about the Conquest, and how are we conditioned to receive them? The questions can be broached through first-hand contact with the images themselves.

Théodore De Bry was the first in a family of engravers who undertook publication of the series of "Great" and "Lesser" *Voy-*

ages that run from 1590 to 1634. The first volumes, entitled the *Grands voyages*, contain accounts and illustrations of European travel to the West Indies, while the *Petits voyages* retrace colonial expansion to the East, or "Oriental," Indies. The collection was begun when Théodore De Bry (b. Liège, 1528, and d. Frankfurt, 1598) saw Thomas Hariot's account of Raleigh's expedition to Virginia (1590). De Bry printed multilingual editions with illustrations copied from the artist John Wright, who accompanied Raleigh and made sketches of the New World colony for the sake of documentation and promotion of the venture. The success of De Bry's enterprise led his sons, Jean-Théodore and Jean-Israël, to develop and complete the collection over the next forty-four years. As Bernadette Bucher has noted, the work "involves a large communication network" running from the publication to his sources of information and to the places from which the work was distributed.[2] De Bry exploited new copper-plate engraving in order to launch a quasi-synoptic treatment of Europe's initial contact with the Americas.

Dissemination of illustrated accounts of the Conquest came late. The first English publication of Columbus's voyages came more than fifteen years after the fact. While travelogues did increase over the years, their audience was so limited that most of Europe had little inkling of the existence of lands to the West. De Bry's copper drawings supplanted woodcuts of fanciful flora and fauna that mark Mandeville's travels, the *Nuremburg Chronicle,* and marginalia in early editions of Ptolemy's *Geographia.* Some detail is no doubt informed by illustrated editions of Oviedo's reports. Two definite origins of De Bry's inspiration are found in the woodcuts, drawn in the Fontainebleau style (long attributed to Jean Cousin) that come with André Thevet's *Singularitez de la France antarctique* (1557). Later, and in less elaborate depiction, the illustrations accompanying Jean de Léry's *Histoire d'un voyage faict en la terre du Brésil* (1578) are used as a point of departure.[3]

We should recall that, as a Protestant who moved from war-torn Belgium in 1570 to Huguenot strongholds in northeastern France and western Germany, De Bry did not handle his material neutrally. He sought previously published works that he could translate and then illustrate in the service of a Protestant vision. He went to London in 1586 to draw illustrations of Sydney's funeral, and there he met Richard Hakluyt, who was obtaining texts and documents of the New World for the purpose of selling the idea of colonization to the English public. By the time of De Bry's death in 1598 the foundation of a project was complete: he and his sons would select and interpret materials in handsome accounts of the colonial venture. They were to gather any available sources and interpret them according to their view of religious history. The father gathered his materials primarily from England and France, while the two children drew on reports filed in the archives of the Dutch East India Company.[4]

A significant background to Théodore De Bry's acquaintance with Las Casas is found in the Spanish materials that inform his illustrations, in part 2 of the *Grands voyages*, taken from René de Laudonnière's relation of the French Protestant attempt to colonize Florida in the 1560s. A Spanish fleet massacred the French expedition, but one survivor, the artist Jacques Le Moyne de Morgues, fled to England with illustrations that De Bry was able to copy.[5] Girolamo Benzoni published an *Istoria del nuovo mondo* in mid-century, which Urbain Chauveton, a Huguenot theologian from Geneva, translated into French in 1579 as the *Histoire nouvelle du Nouveau monde*. His version interprets the Catholic original for the ends of the Reformation, especially to indict the Spanish for their treatment of the Indians. By way of Chauveton, Benzoni's history takes up Las Casas's descriptions that mark the first manifestations of the "Black Legend." Later, the seventh part of the *Grands voyages* (1599) depicts Spaniards engaged in anthropophagia before De Bry's 1619 edition of Vespucci's travels show the conquistadors seducing native women who offer them gifts.

Théodore De Bry's edition of Las Casas's *Brevísima relación* falls in the midst of the *Grands voyages* and thus appears to represent an ancillary labor that endorses the vision of the overall project. Its circumstances do, however, separate it from the *Grands* and *Petits voyages*. Las Casas published his account of Iberian cruelty in the vernacular and in the context of the debate held at Valladolid with Sepúlveda on the humanity of the Indians. Apparently the early editions never reached De Bry. In 1579 Jacques de Miggrode published a French translation, in Antwerp, with the intention of spurring anti-Catholic sentiment in Belgium and the low countries. It was entitled *Tyrannies et cruautez des Espagnols, perpetuees es Indes occidentales, qu'on dit nouveau monde: Briefvement descrite en Espagnol, par Dom Frere Barthelemy de Las Casas ou Casaus, Espagnol, de l'ordre de S. Dominique, & Evesque de la ville Royalle de Chiappa, fidellement traduictes par Iaques de Miggrode pour servir d'exemple & advertissement aux XVII provinces du pais bas* (A Anvers: chez François de Ravelenghien joignant le portail septentrional de l'Eglise Nostre Dame. M. D. LXXIX) (*Spanish Tyrannies and Cruelties, perpetrated in the West Indies that are called the New World: Briefly Described in Spanish by the Dominican Brother Bartholomew de Las Casas, or Casaus, a Spaniard, and Bishop of the Royal city of Chiappa, faithfully translated by Jacques de Miggrode to serve as an example and warning to the 17 Provinces of the low countries*). A Parisian edition soon followed (G. Julian, 1582) to serve the Huguenots in the French civil wars, and in 1630 Jacques Caillové published another edition of the same French text.[6] The first two French editions bear the same couplet on the title page:

> Happy are they who become wise
> By seeing in others their demise.[7]

Apparently De Bry obtained the Antwerp edition of 1578 and had the text translated into Latin and accompanied with his copper engravings, performing what the translator proposes in rhyme.[8] The Latin text follows that of Miggrode and is carefully edited to be circulated on a fairly extensive scale. Numbers are placed in a corner of each of the copper plates to match the page on which they appear. An elaborate title page tells a tale, in clockwise sequence, of the meeting and eventual torture of the natives, around the cartouche containing the title translating the French original thus: *Narratio Regionum Indicarum per Hispanos Quosdam devastatarum verissima: priùs quidem Episcopum Bartholemæm Casaum, natione Hispanum Hispanicè conscripta, & anno 1551. Hispali, Hispanicè, Anno verò 1598. Latinè excusa, Francoforti, Sumptibus Theodori De Bry, & Ioannis Saurii typis. Anno M.D. XCVIII.* By contrast, the 1664 edition (Heidelberg) shows that De Bry's scheme has eroded: the plates as numbered in 1598 do not exactly correspond to the new pagination, and are renumbered on the upper left or right corner. the same illustrations make their way into *Le miroir de la cruelle, & horrible Tyrannie espagnole perpetuee au Pays bas, par le Tyran Duc de Albe, & Aultres Commandeurs par le Roy Philippe le deuxiesme. On a adjoint la deuxieme partie commise aux Indes occidentales par les Espagnols. Nouvellement exorné avec taille douce en cuyvre* (*The Mirror of the Cruel and Horrible Spanish Tyranny Inflicted on the Low Countries by the Tyrant Duke of Alba, and Other Commanders by King Philip the Second. Adjoined is the Second Part Given Over to the Western Indies by the Spanish. Newly Illustrated with Copper Plate Drawings.*)(Newberry Library copy, Amsterdam, 1620, but first edition dating to 1604). Paginal indications are effaced, the first sequence is changed, and the stamp loses much of its definition. Suscriptive quatrains in French alexandrins are fashioned to make emblems that "fix" the image in the mind of the reading spectator.

The edition of Frankfurt in 1598 appears to serve as paradigm for everything that follows. Its material is rigorously set in place but is general enough to be adapted for different contexts. The illustrations betray an ideological mobility insofar as they can at once represent the *Brevísima relación*, be used to "imprint" the image of horror perpetrated by whomever the editor wishes to mark in adjacent writing, and, as we shall see, have a covert relation with other genres, especially accounts of martyrdom that pass as prototypical manuals of torture and insurrection.

De Bry's illustrations appear to use the stylistic innovations that come synchronously with the *Grands voyages*. Ten of the seventeen (the title page not included) are chosen here for study of the emblematic process that the relation of text and image strives to develop. The images, to repeat, avail themselves for both specific and general use. They work in tandem with the Latin translation of Las Casas's Spanish by "fixing" or eternizing expressions that might otherwise not be deemed historical. Las Casas's vernacular, a language of transition between immortal writing and speech or one social class and another, is implied not to be appropriate for the heroic representation of infamy. At the same time, the *gap* between the immediate and graphic horror of the pictures and the Latin text underscores a difference between what is taken to be seen and what must be imprinted as immutable history: those who are not versed in Latin have access to the contents by way of the image, a stratagem that in turn entices the reader to learn Scripture at the same time he or she is taught to hate Spanish Catholics. Even if, for De Bry's most pragmatic ends, the French translation serves as the "original" for the new edition, an agency of subjectivity is set in the gap between the visual discourse and the Latin. The Latin lends a greater aura of "truth" to the document by the presence of its iconic authority. The same authority wills to lend an effect of veracity to the visual propaganda.[9]

The seventeen images display no single choice of theme except, perhaps, for De Bry's penchant for telling a coded pictorial narrative through the figures of Moctezuma, seen on the frontispiece and, later, in the Mexican sequence of the account.[10] Otherwise, violence seems to be depicted to give a documentary air to Las Casas's discourse, and to essay superimpositions of spatial planes of diegetic materials (to code descriptions in tabular fashion) for sake of compression and efficacity. On a broader scale the engravings appear to be asking if violence, like death itself, can be grasped through visible representation. A serial review of selected figures will allow us to wonder if De Bry was indeed posing this question. What follows is a comparison of the images with the French that De Bry ostensibly had translated into Latin.

Figure 1 conflates two descriptions taken from Las Casas's account of Hispaniola. The background is general (no pertinent feature in the text being illustrated). In the foreground to the left, a baroque image is made of "They took the little creatures by their feet, ripping them from the breasts of their mothers and smashing their heads against rocks."[11] To the right, the portrayal of a mass execution depicts the following: "They made certain gallows long and low, such that the feet almost touched the ground, each one for thirteen people, in honor and reverence of our Redeemer, and of His twelve apostles, as they used to say; and putting fire to it they thus burned alive those who were attached. They commonly killed lords and nobles in this way."[12]

De Bry represents the gibbet in detail and places it in a diagonal, receding view that heightens the illusion of spatial depth. The Spanish are huge in proportion to the victims, who are small. So baroque are the effects that the torturer's immense left hand

Figure 1. Las Casas 1598, page 10. All reproductions are derived from the Latin edition of Bartolomé de las Casas, Brevísima relación de la destrucción de las Indias: Narratio Regionum indicarum per Hispanos Quosdam devastatarum verissima. *Frankfurt, 1598 (with 17 engravings by Théodore De Bry). Courtesy of the James Ford Bell Library, University of Minnesota.*

touches the minuscule left foot of the native being tortured. An Indian woman—not specified as a mother of one of the babies crushed—is presented almost attractively, if not pornographically (a svelte body and pudenda in view as she looks down, not to encounter the viewer's gaze). The fifth victim from the right is depicted with an open mouth, as if miming the shrieks described in the text. Two narrative elements are set adjacent to each other and play on the tension of two sides and two areas of depth.

The image in Figure 2 picks up the description in the sentence following the last description: "They made certain grills with sticks erected on forks, and made little fires beneath so that, little by lit-

Figure 2. Las Casas 1598, page 12.

tle, in crying and despairing in these torments, they would render their soul."[13]

Here a method of torture renders depth and illusion that complement the first image. De Bry adds salient detail, in the bellows one Spaniard aims at the fire along with the sight of a Spaniard putting wood into the blaze (hardly the "petit feu" as described above). As usual, the Spaniards are clothed while the natives are nude. The effect underscores the relation of power held between the colonizer and the natives, but it also engages prurience in the viewer's relation to the scene. Despite the indictment of the Spanish Catholics, the natives are in fact coded to be below the dignity of the Europeans. The scene of amputation in the background generalizes the torture; no contextual element from Las Casas is being illustrated. The scene in the foreground resembles a Christian martyrdom at the same time an element of sadism is introduced: a stake enters the victim's rectum.[14]

In Figure 3 the first of two adjacent engravings tells of two mo-

Figure 3. Las Casas 1598, page 38.

ments of the story of Moctezuma in the chapter on New Spain. The first image is directly opposite the description on the following page.

From Cholula the Spaniards went toward Mexico. King Moctezuma sent before them a thousand presents, lords and people moving along the road in festivity and play. And at the road's entry to the city of Mexico, which is of two leagues' length, he also sent them his own brother accompanied by many great lords bearing great gifts of gold, of silver, and clothing; and at the entry to the city, the king in person with his entire court went to receive them, carried on a golden litter, and accompanied them as far as the palace that he had prepared for them.[15]

The engraving offers a grand perspective of the Mexican plains, but in fact underscores the moment of meeting and of gift-giving

Figure 4. Las Casas 1598, page 40.

that precedes its inversion. The illustration narrates, as it were, the first moment of a "total social fact" that involves the initial contact with the Indian Other and the phatic gestures that precede exchange: meeting, offering of signs, and gifts that mediate the affrontment of two cultures. One group belongs to the space by virtue of following the sinuous road from the walled city to the Spaniards. The latter are few but loom large where the others are small and of great number. The illustration offers a view of one of the first signs of difference, the "litter," which demarcates the Americas as a culture that does not know the wheel. The Spaniards offer a lance where the natives, in festive mood, offer the gifts that Las Casas reports in the text. The picture appears to work a part of a diptych with what follows on page 40.

Figure 4 offers a view of the inside of the city with the background—just seen on pages 38-39—visible beyond the frame of the windows. The picture displays Moctezuma as captive (to the left) and underscores the Spaniards' deceit. Where social practices and archaic versus modern exchange had been taken up in the preceding illustration, now the engraver shows how the indigenous space is entered and violated. The theme binding the two illustrations appears to be that of the dancing Indians. Whereas they announced the coming of the exchange just before, now they are surprised at the inversion of fortune. De Bry appears to apprehend the irony of the text and use it to develop a picture-narrative that plays on the difference of outdoor as opposed to intimate space, and multitudes versus a limited number of individuals. These scenes reproduce the recent history of the Wars of Religion in Europe, perhaps St. Bartholomew's massacre of 1572, in which similar twists of destiny took place: an outer peace was betrayed by French Catholics' invasion into the private space of Huguenot dwellings. A *theatrical* decor (on which all torture depends) is put forward.

The text reads thus:

> And the most noble lords and princes of royal blood all, according to their degree held balls and festivals nearest the house where their lord was held prisoner. Right next to the said place were more than two thousand young men, children of the lords who were the flower of the nobility of Moctezuma's aura. The captain of the Spanish went against them with a number of soldiers, and sent the others to all corners of the city where festivals and dances were being held, and all of them feigned going only to watch them. The captain had commanded that at a certain hour they would ambush these dances, and throwing themselves into them, the Indians, fearing nothing and merely taking pleasure in their festivities, he ordered, "Saint Iago, jump in, and on them!" And thus they began to open these delicate and nude bodies with the tips of their swords, and to spread this generous and noble blood.[16]

The chapters on the province of Guatemala rank among the bloodiest of Las Casas's descriptions. In Figure 5 De Bry uses a "rotative" display of torture in a circle that turns inside of a theatrical

Figure 5. Las Casas 1598, page 47.

arrangement of thatched huts. Most representations of the New
World portrayed Indians' domiciles as long huts; here they are set
in the dramatic space of a half-decagon that backgrounds a theater
of blood. The text notes that the Spanish

> took account of how to make certain ditches in the middle
> of the roads in which horses would fall, and piercing their
> bellies inside with sharpened and burnt stakes, and placing
> above clumps of earth so adroitly that nothing seemed
> amiss. Horses fell in once or twice: for the Spaniards know
> how to watch out for them. And to take vengeance, they
> passed a law that as many Indians that could be taken alive
> of whatever age or sex would be thrown into these same
> ditches. They also threw in as many pregnant women,
> women with infants, and old people as they could find until
> they were filled.[17]

Once again, a native practice or stratagem is turned against itself in order to propagate its opposite. A theater of cruelty results,
with emphasis on erotic penetration mixed with bodily violence:
spikes run through a woman's breast and a pregnant belly. The
murder describes a circle around the pit and includes five scenes
[clockwise: (1) a women is pushed out of her hut with a baby in
her arms; (2) a woman is pierced by a lance as she holds a child;
(3) three men are flogged and one is pierced by a sword; (4) men
are felled by lances; (5) a woman is pushed into the pit]. The concentric disposition of the scene reproduces a common narrative
and dramatic pattern in De Bry's emblematic practice in the *Grands
voyages*.

A signature might indeed be present in the lower right corner.
At the threshold of her hut, a woman with pendant breasts lurks
in shadow. According to Bucher, the same figure marks the entry
of the devil or the sign of the pregiven maculation of the world
that confirms the Protestant vision of history. It could be that the
engraver has thus interpreted the collection of images according to
the allegorical schemes that structure the greater sum of his work.

Figure 6, also from the Guatemala sequence, arranges Las
Casas's text according to another circular disposition at the same
time it redoes former depictions of anthropophagia in Thevet's
Singularités de la France antarctique. An infant is roasted on the
boucan, or grill, the familiar apparatus that organizes ritual space
through cannibalism. The natives' practice is seen under the eyes
of the Spaniards, while at the center of the picture a butcher's
stand puts human flesh on display for sale to the natives. A woman
exchanges a necklace for the meat of her own people. The Indians
swap their valuables in order to gain access to the former rituals
they had used to define their identity. A collective activity of an
archaic society is now put forth as a model for capital investment
in the third world: one needs only turn indigenous practices into
commodities sold back to the natives for gain in the first world.
An allegory indicts the Spanish at the same time it puts forward
a model for development of third-world nations. In addition, the
copper-plate technique offers detail that is part of an erotic agenda
that complements the economic paradigm. The point of the anchor
that the Indian bears in the foreground covers his pubis: a "penal"

Figure 6. Las Casas 1598, page 50.

region happens to be aligned with the very art of engraving, as if the artist were confusing a narrative means of covering the genitals with the stylus that is both a part of his metier and a figure of what subjugates the natives. Most of the figures in the image are doubled, so as to offer in both foreground and background two perspectives of the same practice. The rotative model does, however, carry Las Casas's depiction in and through the depth of the pictorial field, and in detail. The Spanish had the custom,

> when they warred in the cities or provinces, to bring along as many captured Indians as they could in order to have them fight against the others: and as they never fed the ten or twenty thousand men they brought, they allowed them to eat the seventeen or twenty thousand Indians they took. Thus in the camp there was an ordinary stockyard with human flesh; in the Spaniards' presence children were killed and roasted. They killed men only to take the hands and feet that they held to be the best pieces.... They

brought an infinite number of Indians to their demise in
shipbuilding, whom they delivered to the North and South
Seas, that are one hundred and thirty leagues away, having
them bear anchors weighing hundreds of pounds. Thus
they transported a great deal of artillery that they placed
on the shoulders of these poor naked men, of whom I have
seen many fall by the wayside, because of the great and
heavy loads. They broke up their families, tearing men
from their women and children, whom they gave to help
sailors and soldiers: who led them in their armies. They
filled all their ships with Indians, in which they died of
thirst and hunger.[18]

In the chapter on New Spain, Miggrode's translation runs thus:

The king and lord of the country, accompanied by an infinite
number of followers rendering a thousand services and
courtesies, going to receive him, because it was known that
he was rich with gold and silver: and so that they would
give him great treasures, he began administering torture.
And putting his feet in irons, his body stretched out, and
his hands bound to a stake, he placed a fire by his feet, and
a boy with a sprinkler with his hand daubed with oil with
which he basted him little by little in order to roast his skin.
Next to him was a cruel man armed with a taut crossbow
aimed right at his heart: on the other side was another who
held a dog and who feigned having it jump on the victim
and that, in a flash, would have torn him to pieces. Thus
they tortured him to get word of the treasures they wanted,
until a Franciscan cleric removed him. Nonetheless he soon
died of the same tortures.[19]

De Bry's image in Figure 7 uses the stake to provide a center
around which the depiction can turn (an earlier state of the drawing evident in the stake first angled along the lines of the chain that
the torturer holds to the left of the victim). Details of the mode
of torture are adumbrated: the boy's apparatus to one side, the
feet being burned, the irons and pillory, and the crossbow. Once
again the background provides the curtains of a theatrical decor
that stages the scene. A technical description of efficient torture is
included.

It appears that the engraver favors a circular disposition of nar-

Figure 7. Las Casas 1598, page 53.

ration, as on pages 47, 50, and 53. The circle of torments is slanted into the field of illusion to articulate the common space and time of the account. In Figure 8 the most complete expression of the same form is accomplished, in fact so well that the association of the circle with time and money saved—part of the ethic being advanced in the margins of the narrative—becomes evident. Miggrode's origin offers a volley of facts that the image turns into a closed form: The Spanish conqueror

> burned cities, took the Chiefs as prisoners, and tortured them: they enslaved everyone whom they captured, and they led thousands bound to chains. Women with infants went laden with the evil Christians' baggage, and unable to carry their little children because of the labor and hunger, they threw them by the roadside where infinite numbers of them died.[20]

Figure 8. Las Casas 1598, page 55.

Once again the theatrical space is defined by the circle that narrates the scene, from the burning city in the background to the woman bearing her burden with her child in the foreground, at the bottom of which lies an infant between her legs. The naked Indians carry the clothing of the conquerors. At the axis of the picture is a scene of motherly love—a woman embracing her child—in a visual rhetoric that counterpoints the surrounding torture. Three natives in the foreground decline in progression (in a montage resembling Bosch's painting of the blind leading the blind). Ambivalence is thus evinced in the depiction of the natives. They are heroic but nonetheless own a lower social rank than that of the implied viewer.

As for the Yucatan peninsula, Las Casas reports,

No one can believe or express the particular cases of cruelties that were committed. I shall tell of only two or three that come to mind right now. The evil Spaniards went with their

Figure 9. Las Casas 1598, page 59.

enraged dogs seeking their way along which the Indian men
and women were coming: a sick Indian woman, seeing that
she could neither flee nor evade the dogs that would tear
her to pieces as they did the others, took a cord and hanged
herself from a beam, attaching her one-year-old child to
her feet; and she would have done no less, except when
the dogs came to devour the boy, a monk just happened to
baptize him before he died.[21]

De Bry changes the narrative slightly in Figure 9. The woman
hangs from the molding of a building that allows the figure to be
framed—or visually sanctified—in a tabernacle of darkness. The
nudity and nubile body eroticize the description. The child hangs
such that the bandoleer covers the woman's sex. In a tradition of
simultaneous representation of two elements in sequence, the dog
attacks the boy as he is being baptized. A virtual rebus is offered
in the dog, tugging the right foot as the monk lets three drops of
water fall from his hand, that is identified as a *Spaniel*, a canine fig-

ure of the Spanish torturers. The scene is complicated by a split perspective in which one half of the child's body, in a serial representation of the scene simultaneous to the event on the left, is seen in profile hanging from a Spaniard's right hand, while the identical other half of the body is suspended from his left. Torture and the mode of representation appear to be identical. A dog behind the Spaniard eats the head on the left while another, to the left and front, nibbles at the head and right forearm. Movement in the background generalizes the descriptions of dogs chasing the Indians.

The chapter on Peru takes up the story of Emperor Atahuallpa (Attabalipa). The engraver returns to the rhetoric that was used in the depiction of Moctezuma. A long depiction in Las Casas's account is summarized. In Figure 10 a tapestry-like representation of the first sequence in the narrative is found on the wall (when the king is thrown from his litter), while his strangulation takes place in the foreground. The picture economizes the description through appeal to simultaneous actions seen at different depths in the image. The Latin text immediately below the image keys the relation of the king's name to the narrative ("Paulò post Rex, & supremus Imperator omnium horum Regnorum, Ataliba nomie..." [A few days later arrived the universal king and emperor of these kingdoms, who was named Ataliba...]). In contrast to Las Casas and Miggrode, the picture shows that the murder is accomplished by what appear to be professional hangmen, *verdugos*, in heroic guise. A strangling machine is shown. A bar and rope are placed on the neck, a mechanism not mentioned in the text. Spectators are added to complete the theater of torture. In the middle ground is Atahuallpa, captured, giving gifts as mentioned in the text. Yet the scene of battle and butchery that lead to his capture are depicted in a picture in the scene. The Spaniards beat the Peruvians to the left and knock the king off his litter to the right. The picture is "read" in a semi-circular movement that runs clockwise, from back to front, registering three stages of Atahuallpa's demise. Implied is that a representation of a mode of torture is coextensive with the story of Atahuallpa.

A similar rhetoric informs the depiction of torture in Granada. De Bry translates the following:

Figure 10. Las Casas 1598, page 86.

Another time, because the Indians did not give him a golden casket that the cruel Captain wished, he ordered men to make war, where they killed an infinite number of people. And they cut off the noses of an inestimable number of women and men. They threw others before packs of enraged dogs that tore them to pieces and devoured them.[22]

Figure 11. Las Casas 1598, page 95.

Again the composition offers two different events simultaneously. Figure 11 is a circular depiction of the "theater" of torture prevails in a landscape that calls attention to the New World through the straw huts in the background (whereas in the text they are burned to the ground). The engraver can register bodily mutilation and scattering in detail: ten arms are seen without their hands. A woman is depicted having her nose amputated, but the scene suggests that enucleation is taking place. The object of fear, the Spaniard wielding a sword, figures at the axis of the composition.

The last engraving, Figure 12, accompanies Las Casas's remedies that supplement the text, in the eleventh reason adducing the truth in the report about the horrors of Spanish torture that are written into the system of the *encomienda*. The scene is taken from the mines at Lares, where the colonists impress the natives to dig for the gold the Iberians will circulate in Europe. The back-

Figure 12. Las Casas 1598, page 123.

ground displays men and women enslaved: they till fields, work in the mines, and draw water from the wells. As in the depiction of anthropophagia, their natural modes of life are seen subjected to commercial exploitation. The natives now are enslaved or salaried to do what they practiced in traditional labors that defined the community. In the foreground, instruments of torture are shown adjacent to a general—undifferentiated—violence in which the Spaniards beat the women tilling the soil. Natives are also forced to break their land with pickaxes. An allegory of (Catholic) violence exercised on nature is articulated. The text reads,

> The visitor heedlessly bound them to a stake; and himself
> with his own hands, taking a weighted rope, that in
> the galleys is called a cat-o-nine-tails, that resembles an
> iron whip, administered so many blows and beat them
> with such cruelty that blood flowed from them in many
> places.[23]

The description in the text allows the engraver to adumbrate the means and methods of torture. Here the viewer senses that Las Casas's indictment is turned, as in the treatment of Atahuallpa, into a practical manual that depicts apparatus that can be used to subjugate others.

So ends the series of illustrations. The style resembles the pictures of larger dimension in the *Grands voyages*, but the effects appear more focussed and local. De Bry's design that tells of the Fall and of Protestant destiny does not emerge from the scenes of torture. De Bry recounts images efficiently, according to an emblematic tradition that distinguishes narrative from images that obey laws of spatial logic. Recessional and circular designs prevail, and often simultaneous depictions of events in different time and space are found in single images. The engraver and typographer select or summarize descriptions that are immediately adjacent to each copper plate. A double symbolical efficacity is obtained insofar as each image can both distill a pertinent unit of description in the surrounding text and provide a lesson for deciphering of the Latin. In the latter way the scenes of torture serve in the role of propedeutic devices that "teach" lessons to students by offering images that can be seen through the foreign text. But the content is multiple: it is ideologically charged and tilts in favor of eliciting violence through images of violence. In this way a teaching "aid" of audio-visual character imprints figures of horror in detail that woodcuts had been technically unable to represent; it provides a Berlitz-like immersion to Latin; it inculcates a Protestant ideology at a time of war with Spanish Catholicism in Northern Europe. On a broader level, the engravings institute division or "subjectivity" among readers and spectators by means of the multiple differences that the discrete relations of text, image, and idiom are inaugurating.

The pictures are not exactly what they purport to be. They come to us not as false or veracious images of the Conquest, but as elements of a more persistent and subterranean genre that runs from hagiography and martyrology[24] to CIA manuals of torture: the pictures tell us to strengthen our souls at the sight of excess, but only in such a way that we are also being told that we have to see it in order to know it. Prurient enticement, in which the viewer is asked to behold the invisibility of the violence or read of its ineffable nature (as in Las Casas's apostrophes that utter how he cannot describe what he saw), is used to mask and to circulate religious propaganda.

A mimetic dialectic common to Catholic practices is now mobilized for Protestant ends, but over the passage of four centuries we see that little has changed from De Bry to Goya or to Francis Bacon. Torture begets a sense of violence that the images cannot assuage. We realize that their excess can be channelled for ideological purposes, as here, or it can be used pragmatically, as it is in what American expeditionary forces have used nowadays in Guatemala, El Salvador, and other nations, in manuals that tell their users how to foment strife and to strike fear into indigenous masses. The artist's image of the Conquest tells us what the economy of the copper-plate engravings had been in the years following the Columbian discoveries. De Bry seems to be accomplishing in 1598 what we have seen more recently in the practices that North American ideologues have brought to the same countries that Las Casas reviewed in the *Brevísima relación*.[25] The figures represent what appears to be the sum of the image-makers' investment in the New World, in short, a massive production of debris.

Notes

1. A symposium on European encounters held by the Center for Early Modern History at the University of Minnesota (October 4-7, 1990) superimposed its title over maps taken from De Bry's *Voyages*. In 1988-1990, the Hermon Dunlap Smith Center for the History of Cartography advertised its "Transatlantic Encounters" seminars at the Newberry Library with drawings taken from the same work. Michel de Certeau uses an engraving from the tenth volume of the same work as a frontispiece to *L'écriture de l'histoire*. Other manifestations abound.

2. Jacques-Charles Brunet's bibliography in the *Manuel du libraire* 1 (Paris: Dorbon-Aîné, n.d.), 1310-1363, still commands authority, as do his pages on the translations of the *Brevissima relacion de la destruycion de las Indias occidentales* (Seville, 1552), 1611-1612. The most accessible history in English of the fortunes of publication and single study of the *Greater Voyages* is that of Bernadette Bucher. She provides a background (5-42) that informs and recoups many of the hypotheses advanced above.

3. See, for example, Michèle Duchet's study of De Bry's elaboration of a complex representation of an Indian dance from a detail in Léry.

4. Biographical materials on De Bry are available in Eisenstein, Evans, Moran, Retamar, and Yates. The ideology of the image is taken up in Alexander, Bataillon and Saint-Lu, Chiappelli, and Conley.

5. Only one watercolor remains and is now located in the New York Public Library.

6. The 1630 edition in the Newberry Library of Chicago begins the text with a historiated initial *T* shown over the body of a decapitated women. It does not include other images of cruelty. Brunet reports that the 1579 edition is the same as the Paris 1582 reprint as well as another edition (*Histoire admirable des horribles insolences, cruautez, et tyrannies exercees par les Espagnols*), also 1582, and another of Lyon (1594). In the seventeenth century, editions appeared in Lyon (1642) and Amsterdam (1692). The work appears to gain a "Northern" tradition that begins with Miggrode's French translation.

7. "Heureux celuy qui devient sage
   En voyant d'autruy le dommage."
(This and other translations from the French are mine.)

8. The intentions are spelled out twice in the 1578 edition. A prefatory sonnet (fol. 7 v°) confirms again the message of the couplet:

> Happy he who wisely will behold
>
> The ills of others by prudence matured,
>
> To use as a mirror and example
>
> In hope he won't be disillusioned.

> Heureux celuy qui sagement contemple
>
> Les maux d'autruy par prudence murie
>
> Pour s'en servir de miroir, & d'exemple,
>
> Qu'il ne se laisse à la fin decevoir.

The ideology is redundantly clear. The Newberry Library catalogue entry notes that the Latin editions "appear to be based on the French edition, Antwerp, 1578, which appeared with the title, *Tyrannies et cruautez des Espagnols....*"

9. In his essays on "truth" in painting, Jacques Derrida shows how Kant attempts to stabilize the terms of his mobile concepts by putting their key components in Latin. A similar desire to elevate an image into a permanent form is apparent here. In "Montaigne and the Indies," I have argued that "truth" is made manifest in the media where images are used to confirm what is stated in a text (and vice-versa). One is used to be the authenticating agent of the other (239).

10. By 1598 the king had become a stereotype in literature of the Conquest. See, for example, appropriate images in Parent and Marchard, or the description at the end of Montaigne's "Des coches" (*Essais*, III, vi).

11. "Ils prennoyent les petites creatures par les pieds, les arrachans des mammelles de leurs meres, & leur froissoyent la teste contre les rochers" (14).

12. "Ils faisoyent certains gibets longs et bas, de maniere que les piedz touchoyent quasi à la terre, chacun pour treize, à l'honneur & reverence de nostre Redempteur, & de ses douze apostres, comme ils disoyent; & y mettant le feu bru-

loyent ainsi tout vifs ceux qui y estoyent attachez. Ils tuoyent communement les seigneuers & nobles de ceste façon" (14).

13. "Ilz faisoyent certaines grilles de perches dressees sus des fourchettes, & faisoyent petit feu dessoubs, à fin que peu à peu, en donnans des cris, & desesperans en ces tormens, ilz rendissent l'esprit" (14-15).

14. De Bry uses this detail to depict the practices of the Florida Indians in the *Grands voyages* (*Brevis narratio ... secunda pars americae* [Frankfort, 1592], chap. 9, 179); he notes (by way of Le Moyne's legend) that he does not know why Indians penetrate the dead enemy as they do, and that they never do so without escorts nearby to assure that the enemy will not catch them in the act. In the context of Las Casas, De Bry seems to be turning a social activity—a delimitation of space—that the natives practice into a form of prurient torture among Spanish Catholics.

15. "De Cholula [the Spaniards] allerent vers Mexico. Le Roy Motençuma leur envoya au devant un milier de presens & des Seigneurs & des gens menans festes & esbatemens par le chemin. Et à l'entrée de la chaussée de Mexico, qui dura deux lieuës, il leur envoya aussi son propre frere accompagné de beaucoup de grans seigneurs portans de grans presens d'or, d'argent & de vestemens; & à l'entrée de la ville, le roy en personne avec toute sa grande cour, les alla recevoir, estant portée en une litiere d'or; & les accompaigna iusques au palais qu'il leur avoit faict apprester" (46).

16. "Aussi les plus nobles & les princes de sang royal tous selon leur degré faisoyent leurs bals & festes plus proches à la maison où estoit tenu prisonnier leur Seigneur. Tout au plus pres dudit palais estoyent plus de deux mille jeunes gens, enfans des Seigneurs qui estoyent la fleur de la noblesse de tout l'esbat de Motençuma. Contre ceux-cy alla le capitaine des Espagnolz avec un nombre de soldats, & envoya les autres en tous les endroits de la ville où se faisoyent les festes & danses, & tous faisoyent semblant de les aller seulement voir. Le capitaine avoit commandé, que à certaine heure ils se jettassent sus ces danses, & luy se jettant dedans, les Indiens ne se doubtans de rien, & seulement s'amassans à leurs danses, il dict, Sant Tiago, donnons dedans & sus eux. Et ainsi commençerent les espees au point à ouvrir ces corps nuds & delicats, & à espandre ce sang genereux & noble" (47-48).

17. "s'adviserent de faire certaines fosses au milieu des chemins ausquelles tombassent les chevaux, & se perçassent le ventre dedans des pieux aigus & brulez, y mis tout à propos & couvers si bien de glazons qu'il sembloit n'y avoit rien. Il y tomba des chevaux dedans une fois ou deux: car les Espagnols s'en sceurent après donner de garde. Et pour se venger, ils firent une loy, qu'autant d'Indiens qu'on pourroit prendre vifs de quelque aage ou sexe qu'ils fussent, ils seroyent jettez dedens ces mesmes fosses. Ils y jetterent aussi des femmes enceintes & accouchees d'enfant et vieilles gens autant qu'ils en purent prendre, jusques à ce qu'elles furent remplies" (56).

18. "avoit pour coustume quand il alloit faire guerre à quelque ville ou province, d'y mener des Indiens des-jà subjuguez, autant qu'il pourrait, pour faire guerre aux autres: & comme il ne donnoit point à manger à dix ou vint mille hommes qu'il menoit, il leur permit de manger à dix-sept ou vint mille hommes qu'ils prenoyent. Et par ainsi il avoyt en son camp une boucherie ordinaire de chair humaine; où en sa présence on tuoit ou rostissoit des enfans. Il tuoyent les hommes seulement

pour en avoir les mains & les pieds, lesquelles parties ils tenoyent pour les meilleurs morceaux. . . . Il faisoit mourir de travail une infinité d'Indiens à faire des navires, lesquelles il menoit de la mer de Nort, à celle de Midi, qui sont cent & trente lieuës, la chargeant d'ancres pesantes trois ou quatre quintaulx. Il transportoit en ceste maniere beaucoup d'artillerie qui se chargeoit sur les espaules de ces povres gens nuds, dont j'en ay veu beaucoup defaillir par le chemins, à cause des grands & pesans fardeaux. Il desfaisoit les familles ostant aux hommes leurs femmes et filles, lesquelles il donnoit aux mariniers & soldats, pour les contenter: qui les menoyent en leurs armées. Il emplissoit tous les navires d'Indiens, où ils moururent de soif & de faim" (59-60).

19. "Le Roy & Seigneur du païs l'allant recevoir, avec une compagnie d'une infinité de gens qui leur faisoyent mille services & courtoisies, il le print incontinent, par ce qu'il avoit le bruict d'estre fort riche d'or et d'argent: & à fin qu'il luy donnast de grans tresors, il commença à luy donner les tormens. Et le mettant en un cep par les pieds, le corps estendu, & les mains liées à un pal, il luy mit une brasière contre les pieds, & un garçon avec un arrousoir en main mouillé dedans l'huile qui arrousoit peu à peu, à fin de rostir la peu. Il y avoit à costé un homme cruel, lequel avec une arcbalestre bandée visoit droict au coeur: de l'autre costé il y avoit un autre qui tenoit un chien, faisant mine de la faire courrir sus, qui en moins d'un Credo l'eust peu deschirer: et ainsi le tormenterent il à fin qu'il descouvrit des tresors qu'il desiroit; jusques à ce que un religieux de Saint François l'osta: toutesfois il mourut en fin de ces tormens" (62).

20. "brusloit les villes, il prenoit les Caciques prisonniers, & les donnoit des torments: il faisoit esclaves tous ceux qu'il prenoit, dont il en menoit une infinité attachez des chaines. Les femmes accouchées allans chargées de bagages des mauvais Chrétiens, & ne pouvans porter leurs petis enfans à cause du travail & de la faim, elles les jetterent par le chemin, dont il mourut une infinité" (64).

21. "Il n'ya homme qui peust croire ne dire les cas particuliers des cruautés qui se sont commises. J'en racompteray seulement deux, ou trois, dont il me souvient à cest'heure. Comme les malheureux Espagnols alloyent avec leurs chiens furieux cerchans au trac, & venans les Indiens femmes et hommes: une Indienne malade voyant qu'elle ne pouvoit fuir ne eschapper des chiens qu'ils ne la deschirassent, comme il faisoyt les autres, elle print une corde, & s'en pendit à une poutre, ayant attaché à son pied un enfant de l'age d'un an qu'elle avoit; & ne l'eust point si tost fait, voicy les chiens venir despescher l'enfant, combien que devant qu'il mourut, un frere religieux le baptisa" (68).

22. "Une autre fois par ce que les Indiens ne luy donnoyent point un coffre d'or, que ce cruel Capitaine leur demandoit, il envoya des gens pour leur faire la guerre, où ils tuerent une infinité de personnes; & ils coupperent le nez à tant de femmes et hommes, que l'on n'en sçauroit dire le nombre. Ils en jetterent d'autres devant des chiens acharnez, qui les despeschoyent & mangeoyent. . . . Le Capitaine commanda, qu'ils tuassent & jettassent de la montaigne, laquelle estoit fort haute, tous ceux qui estoyent demeurez en vie: et il fut faict ainsi" (119).

23. "Le visitateur les lioit incontinent à un pal; & luy mesme avec ses propres mains prenant une corde poissée, laquelle on appelle sus les galeres Anguille, qui est comme un verge de fer, leur donnoit tant de coups, & tant cruelement les battoit, que le sang descouloit d'eux en beaucoup d'endroits" (162).

24. See, for example, Gallonio.

25. A case in point: in a publication similar to De Bry's Las Casas, Verstegen 66-67, a man is portrayed tied to a table, his torso bared, and an inverted copper pot placed on his belly. A fire is shown placed on top, while the text reports that a rat is enclosed beneath. Alarmed at the heat, the rat burrows into a slit the Spaniards (seen in Verstegen as Protestants) have cut on the victim's skin. It frantically digs downward and escapes through the man's innards. The same torture can be found in the 1980 film (shown on most American PBS television stations) recounting the life and career of the notorious Frank Terpil, a gunrunner that the CIA hired to foment unrest in third-world countries. After firing him, the agency scapegoated Terpil by accusing him of doing what it had advised him to do. In the story, Terpil recalls how, in Uganda, Idi Amin used the same "copper pot" torture to strike fear in the heart of his enemies.

Works Cited

Primary Materials

Bry, Théodore de. *Americae Tertia Pars*. . . . Frankfurt, 1592.

———. *Brevis narratio eorum quæin Florida*. . . . Frankfurt, 1591.

Las Casas, Bartolomé de. *Narratio Regionum Indicarum per Hispanos quosdam devastatarum verissima*. Frankfurt, 1598; with 17 engravings by Théodore De Bry.

———. *Tyrannies et cruautez des Espagnols perpetrees es Indes occidentales, qu'on dit Nouveau monde. Brievement descrites en Espagnol par Don Frere Bartelemy de la Casas ou Casaus, Espagnol, de l'ordre de S. Dominique . . . fidelement traduictes par Iaques de Miggrode: pour servir d'exemple & advertissement aux XVII Provinces du Païs bas*. A Anvers, chez François de Ravelenghien ioignant le portail Septentrional de l'Eglise Nostre Dame. M. C. LXXIX. (1579)

———. *Tyrannies et cruautez des Espagnols, perpetrees es Indes occidentales, qu'on dit le Nouveau monde*. . . . Paris: Par Guillaume Iulien, à l'enseigne de l'Amitié, près le collège de Cambray. M. D. LXXXII. (1582)

Léry, Jean de. *Histoire d'un voyage fait en la terre du Brésil*. 1578. Ed. Sophie Delpech. Paris: Plasma, 1980.

Gallonio, Antonio. *Trattato degli istrumenti di martirio*. Rome, 1591; with engravings by Antonio Tempesta.

Thevet, André. *Les singularités de la France antarctique*. Ed. Frank Lestringant. Paris: La Découverte/Maspéro, 1983.

———. *Les singularitez de la France antarctique, autrement nommée Amerique: et de plusieurs terres & isles descouvertes en notre temps*. Paris: Maurice de la Porte, 1557.

Verstegen, Richard. *Theatre des cruautez des Hereticques de nostre temps*. Antwerp: Adrien Hubert, 1588.

Secondary Materials

Alexander, Michael, ed. *Discovering the New World: Based on the Works of Theodore De Bry*. New York: Harper and Row, 1976.

Bataillon, Marcel, and André Saint-Lu. *Las Casas et la défense des Indiens*. Paris: Julliard, 1971.

Bucher, Bernadette. *Image and Conquest: A Structural Analysis of De Bry's "Grands voyages."* Chicago: Univ. of Chicago Press, 1981.

Certeau, Michel de. *L'écriture de l'histoire*. Paris: Gallimard, 1982.

Chiappelli, Fredi, ed. *The First Images of America: The Impact of the New World on the Old*. Berkeley: Univ. of California Press, 1976.

Conley, Tom. "Montaigne and the Indies: Cartographies of the New World." *1492-1992: Re/Discovering Colonial Writing*. Ed. René Jara and Nicholas Spadaccini. Hispanic Issues 4. Minneapolis: Prisma Institute, 1989. 225-262.

———. *Theatres of Cruelty: Wars of Religion, Violence and the New World*. Slide Set 14. Chicago: Newberry Library, 1990.

Derrida, Jacques. *La vérité en peinture*. Paris: Aubier-Flammarion, 1978.

Duchet, Michèle, ed. *L'Amérique de Théodore de Bry*. Paris: Centre national de la recherche scientifique, 1987.

Eisenstein, Elisabeth. *The Printing Press as an Agent of Change*. 2 vols. Cambridge: Cambridge Univ. Press, 1979.

Evans, R. J. W. "The Wechel Presses: Humanism and Calvinism in Central Europe 1572-1627." *Past and Present*, Sup. 2 (Oxford, 1975).

Moran, Michael G. *Renaissance Surveying Techniques and the Mapping of Raleigh's Virginia*. Slide Set 19. Chicago: Newberry Library, 1990.

Parent, Alain, and André Marchard, eds. *La Renaissance et le nouveau monde*. Québec: Bibliothèque Nationale, 1984.

Retamar, Roberto Fernández. Introduction to Bartolomé de Las Casas, *Très brève relation de la destruction des Indes*. 1552. Trans. Fanchita González Bataille. Paris: La Découverte/Maspéro, 1987.

Yates, Frances. *The Rosicrucian Enlightenment*. London: Routledge and Kegan Paul, 1972.

◆ Chapter 3
(Re)discovering Aztec Images

Eloise Quiñones Keber

Encountering the Aztecs

> Gazing on such wonderful sights, we did not know what to
> say, or whether what appeared before us was real, for on one
> side, on the land, there were great cities, and in the lake ever
> so many more, and the lake itself was crowded with canoes,
> and in the Causeway were many bridges at intervals, and
> in front of us stood the great city of Mexico.... (Díaz del
> Castillo 192)

With these awe-struck words the Spanish conquistador Bernal
Díaz, writing decades later in distant Guatemala, vividly recalled
his first glimpse of the Aztec capital of Mexico Tenochtitlan, which
in 1519 he was among the first Europeans to see (Fig. 1).[1] He marveled at the sumptuous attire of the city's ruler, Moctezuma II, and
the noble entourage that had come to greet Hernán Cortés and his
retinue after they had crossed the broad southern causeway leading into the island city. And once inside he was impressed by the
spacious oratories, halls, and chambers of the palace complex that
had once belonged to Moctezuma's father and predecessor Axayacatl, where they were housed (192-196). Eyewitness narratives
like those of Díaz and Cortés (1986) are invaluable records of contact and conquest.[2] These and a wealth of other sixteenth-century
ethnohistorical sources written by Spanish, Indian, and *mestizo*
authors have made the Aztecs the best documented indigenous
people of the New World.[3]

But valuable as they are, the biases, agendas, and limitations
of these ethnohistorical materials must be considered. The abbreviated, pictographic writing of the Aztecs was essentially an
esoteric system, intended to be supplemented, even during the
pre-Hispanic period, by oral tradition and explicated by priestly

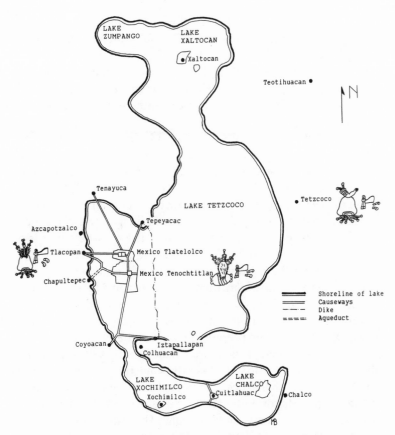

Figure 1. Map of the Basin of Mexico in 1519. Courtesy of Michel Besson.

interpreters. Yet the guardians of these traditions, the educated nobility and the priesthood, had been decimated by the Conquest
as well as the traumas of a tumultuous post-Conquest period.
When Spanish missionary writers or bureaucrats sought information about native culture, those most informed about it may
have been unavailable or unwilling to divulge their knowledge to
those whom they regarded as its destroyers. One does not have
to venture far in reading these ethnographic works to learn that
information is partial, confusing, sometimes contradictory, and often undifferentiated as to the place or ethnic group from whom it

derived. It was, moreover, filtered through a European consciousness, and expressed in outside intellectual categories and modes
of communication. Even the Indian and *mestizo* writers were educated in missionary schools and writing in a colonial setting, often
in a foreign language. These documents must be seen as products of their time, representative of sixteenth-century attitudes and
understandings.

Nevertheless, in contrast to other Mesoamerican groups for
whom we lack comparable sources, the colonial texts have greatly
enhanced our understanding of Aztec culture in general and of
those particular visual manifestations of it that we call "art."[4] Because of them, for example, we know the names of Aztec deities;
we can recognize their painted or carved images and place them
in ritual contexts. We can even interpret the esoteric symbols of
complex monuments in light of their data.

Issues regarding colonial writing have been dealt with elsewhere.[5] For the art historian, there is another consideration: ethnographic texts represent but one source of information about Aztec
culture. Objects (art/artifact) are a discourse in themselves, as is
archaeology, where the present encounters the past. Yet although
art, archaeology, and texts are our major sources of information
about Aztec art, they do not all say the same thing. As Esther Pasztory points out in her article "Texts, Archaeology, Art, and History
in the Templo Mayor: Reflections," there are no exact correlations
among them and many contradictions. There are things they tell
us, things they do not tell us, and things they tell us differently.

The fortuitous existence of these ethnohistorical materials for
Aztec studies, even if problematic, is balanced by other losses.
Chief among these were those indigenous oral traditions that were
never transcribed into a written (alphabetic) form and the pre-
Hispanic pictorial manuscripts in which the Aztecs recorded their
traditions figurally and pictographically.[6] Many stone monuments
and objects made of fragile or perishable materials such as wood,
feathers, and paper were also destroyed in the fierce fighting that
accompanied the crushing Aztec defeat of 1521 at the hands of
Cortés and his combined force of Spanish soldiers and Indian
allies. Items made of gold were a predictable early casualty, for
most were melted down and converted to bullion, some even be-

fore they left Mexico. Equally devastating, what was left of the imposing architecture once admired by Díaz was dismantled to provide materials for colonial buildings or buried under the viceregal capital of Mexico City, which arose over the ravaged Aztec capital.

In New Spain after the Conquest Aztec images continued to be demolished in the name of conversion.[7] What we would call "religious" images, that is, deity figures or images that encode myths, ritual practices, cosmic-calendric beliefs, or worldview, constitute much of Aztec art. These were particularly suspect since the Spanish missionaries regarded them as diabolical relics, visible reminders of the idolatry, superstition, and bloody sacrifices that they associated with indigenous religious concepts and practices.[8] Surprisingly, some monuments escaped for a time. Writing in the 1570s, the Dominican missionary Diego Durán unhappily reported seeing carved pre-Hispanic stones still conspicuously visible in Mexico's Zócalo, or main plaza, and at the cathedral (*Historia* 2: 180-181). And it was not until the mid-eighteenth century that Aztec ruler images carved on rocky outcrops in Chapultepec were finally destroyed.[9]

Even in Europe few people who saw the first treasures shipped by Cortés to the emperor Charles V recognized them as having any value other than that of exotic curiosities. Among the exceptions was the German artist Albrecht Dürer, whose attitude combined interest and admiration. When he saw the materials on display in 1520 at the Hôtel de Ville in Brussels, he marveled not only at their "strangeness" and value but at their beauty and inventiveness. Some Aztec items that found their way to Europe during the following centuries were also prized for their exotic appeal and incorporated into royal collections or placed in the cabinets of curiosities assembled by wealthy collectors.[10] Over the years, however, many fragile objects deteriorated, and others were forgotten, lost, or misidentified as interest in pre-Hispanic Mexico waned.

The nineteenth century marked a turning point in the rediscovery of Aztec art, as well as the art of other Mesoamerican cultures. In Mexico the quest for Mexican identity, spurred by independence from Spain in 1821, stimulated a search for its pre-Hispanic roots. A national museum formally established in 1825 included a collection of ancient Mexican monuments (Bernal 134-137).[11] The opening of Mexico to foreign visitors after independence also encouraged the arrival of European and North American diplomats, merchants, and travelers, who often published accounts of their journeys, sometimes accompanied by illustrations.[12] Some of them developed a keen interest in Mexico's pre-Hispanic past and returned home with collections of antiquities. In many cases these objects, along with those that had arrived earlier, came to rest in newly established public museums of ethnography or natural history that sought to preserve the exotic relics of preliterate and preindustrial cultures. Objects produced by the Aztecs and other pre-Columbian groups were initially of greatest interest to the developing discipline of anthropology, which viewed them primarily as ethnographic specimens shedding light on these little-known peoples. Exploration of Mesoamerican sites, which had begun in the eighteenth century and became increasingly ambitious in the nineteenth, began to unearth not only artifacts but whole sites and cultures that over time had been forgotten or "lost."

In the late nineteenth and early twentieth centuries, when some early modern European artists and art critics started to notice the exotic or "primitive" items exhibited in museums and galleries and at international expositions, they began to see them in a different light. Although viewed most often from a purely formal perspective, apart from the cultural contexts that clarified their meaning and use, they were recognized as having some esthetic merit. The shift from artifact to art had begun.[13] With the increasing receptivity in the second half of the twentieth century to artistic traditions outside the Western canon, greater attention has been directed to cultures such as those of pre-Hispanic Mexico, including Aztec.[14] About this time too art history departments started expanding their course offerings beyond the standard Western art sequence, and art historians began studying Aztec and other pre-Columbian objects as "works of art."[15]

In recent years Aztec images have gained familiarity as parts of permanent museum collections of pre-Columbian art, often donated by private collectors, that are now increasingly housed in "fine arts" museums as well as in earlier types of repositories. Aztec art has been included in temporary exhibitions offering broad surveys of Pre-Columbian or Mexican art that have been held in the United States since the 1930s, but it has been the focus of special exhibitions to a far lesser extent.[16] Through accompanying exhibition catalogues and other publications, knowledge of Aztec art has begun to grow, along with a fuller understanding of the historical, socio-political, and cultural forces that produced it, and that it in turn reflected and reinforced.[17]

While available ethnohistorical texts have enabled us to decipher much of the iconography of Aztec art, they by no means answer all our questions about it.[18] We are unable to date many pieces that have been found outside of the archaeological contexts that might have provided chronological clues. Since we lack the names of artists or patrons, we do not know who made the pieces, who commissioned them, or why they were made. In most instances we do not know how objects were displayed or may have functioned. While many figural works can be categorized according to the type of deity or personage they may represent, nonfigural works are less easily classified. Monumental works, in particular, exist as singular examples, and in many cases we are unsure about their relationship to other works or to their society.

That is why the archaeological excavation of the main temple (Templo Mayor) of the Aztecs in downtown Mexico City, in the area adjoining the present-day cathedral and Zócalo, or central plaza, has been such a landmark event.[19] It was carried out under the direction of Eduardo Matos Moctezuma and the Instituto Nacional de Antropología e Historia (INAH) intensively between 1978 and 1982, with minor probes continuing since then. Earlier chance discoveries as well as finds encountered during lesser excavations or when digging for building foundations, the city's subway system, and installation of public utilities had given some indication of the riches buried beneath Mexico City's concrete and asphalt surfaces. But this marked the first intensive archaeological project carried out in the ruins of ancient Mexico Tenochtitlan, and it involved the most important structure in the ritual heart of the empire.

Most directly, the Templo Mayor project has revealed the architectural history of the building, enabling archaeologists to reconstruct its sequential building stages, chronology, and significance.

It has also provided dates and information for other structures un-covered in the ceremonial precinct, as well as for architecturally related sculptures and other objects found in situ.[20] Additionally, thousands of artifacts were unearthed at various levels where they had been deposited in offertory caches during successive renovations of the Templo Mayor, a practice barely mentioned in the written sources. The products of both past and contem-poraneous cultures, they had been obtained through trade and tribute exacted from subject peoples. Particularly numerous were materials from the present-day state of Guerrero, the probable result of extensive military campaigns begun by the ruler Itz-coatl and continued by his successors. Results thus far have given us greater understanding not only about objects and buildings but about the relationship between Aztec art, empire, and ide-ology. The differences and inconsistences exposed between the written and archaeological records has been another unintended but important outcome.

The Aztecs

Who were the Aztecs, who have continued to surprise observers from the time of the conquistadors to the present day? In Nahuatl, the language they spoke, the word "Aztec" (*azteca*) means person of Aztlan, the legendary homeland of several different groups who migrated into the Basin of Mexico during the thirteenth century. Although widely used today, the name "Aztec" was popularized only in the nineteenth century. Alexander von Humboldt adopted it in his writings as a generic term for the ancient Nahuatl-speaking peoples of Central Mexico.[21] In his best-selling history of the Con-quest of Mexico first published in 1843, William Prescott further disseminated its use. Bernal Díaz and other early writers referred to them as "Mexicanos" (Mexicans) and to their city as México (place of the Mexica), both derived from the name that they called themselves, "Mexica." Cortés variously refers to them as Mexicans, those of Temistitan (Tenochtitlan), or those of Culhua (Culhuans). The latter name derives from Colhuacan, a city in the southern basin with ancient Toltec connections from which the Mexica also claimed to descend, at least politically and dynastically. Some historians also use the name "Tenochca" to refer specifically to the people of Mexico Tenochtitlan to distinguish them from other Mexica like the Tlatelolca, who inhabited the neighboring community of Tlatelolco.[22] The name "Mexica" is preferred in Mexico although "Aztec" has continued to be used in the United States.

According to tradition, after wandering without a permanent home for many years after departing Aztlan in the twelfth century, in 1325 the Aztec migrants claimed as their new homeland a small island near the western edge of Lake Tetzcoco. They chose the site under the guidance of their patron god Huitzilopochtli, who had instructed them to select the place where they sighted an eagle perched upon a nopal cactus. This gave them the second part of the name for their city, Tenochtitlan (next to the place of the nopal cactus). This founding myth simplifies a complicated and less romanticized historical situation, for other texts reveal that during their early years in the Basin of Mexico the Aztec newcomers, rough and unruly, remained subservient to other more established and powerful peoples. For many years after the founding of their city, they continued to serve as mercenaries for the militarily aggressive Tepanec city of Azcapotzalco, located on the northwestern mainland of Lake Tetzcoco. Rebelling against the Tepanecs only in the late 1420s, the Aztecs became partners in a triple alliance that included the Tepanec city of Tlacopan and the Acolhuaque city of Tetzcoco. A series of vigorous Aztec leaders beginning with Itzcoatl (1428-1440) then proceeded to make Mexico Tenochtitlan the hub of a political and commercial empire that stretched from the Pacific Ocean to the Gulf of Mexico and extended even beyond the Isthmus of Tehuantepec to the border of present-day Guatemala (Fig. 2). Lasting less than two hundred years, and fully independent for less than a hundred, Mexico Tenochtitlan was destroyed at its height by the Spanish Conquest.

Aztec Art and Artists

Although colonial texts do not provide the name of a single Aztec artist during the pre-Hispanic period, some pictorial and written documents give us some general information about the role of the Aztec artist. The third, ethnographic section of the *Codex Mendoza*,

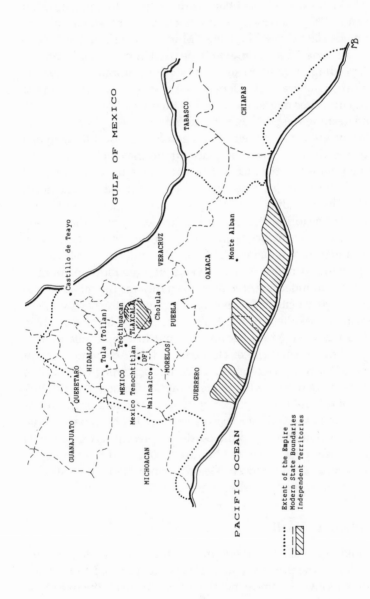

Figure 2. Map of the Empire of the Triple Alliance in 1519. Courtesy of Michel Besson.

a sixteenth-century pictorial Aztec manuscript, illustrates certain types of artisans, including a master feather worker, carpenter, stone worker, painter, and silversmith. Women are also shown spinning and weaving in a domestic setting. The *Florentine Codex*, compiled in Mexico by the sixteenth-century Franciscan missionary writer Fray Bernardino de Sahagún, provides more details about certain pre-Hispanic crafts than any other single source.[23] Descriptions of three major elite arts of feather work, gold work, and lapidary work identify the patron deities of the groups and provide details about the techniques used to fashion their wares (Figs. 3, 4, 5). The *Matrícula de Tributos*, a pictorial Aztec tribute list, and the second section of the *Codex Mendoza* that was copied from it (or a common source) picture the tribute the Aztecs received from various regions of the empire. They show both raw materials (e.g., wood, cotton, gold, turquoise, feathers, dyes) and finished articles (e.g., clothing, warrior outfits, shields, ceramics, bead necklaces, bracelets, lip ornaments, various jade and gold jewels, copper bells). These pages provide valuable information on the materials that were most valued and requisitioned by the Aztecs.

From these sources as well as actual examples, we know that Aztec artists worked with an assortment of materials, using a variety of techniques to produce forms characterized by fine workmanship. Presumably the most accomplished artists worked with precious materials that required mastery of complex processes. The *Florentine Codex* makes a distinction between feather workers who created for the ruler and those who produced works for the marketplace, and other artisans may have been similarly ordered. Public monuments were also produced by the most competent artists and undoubtedly represented the prevailing standards and collective values of Aztec society. Personal expression was not a primary motivation for creating works although a certain degree of individuality may be apparent in the differing ways that the standard themes and forms supplied by the culture were handled. Although there was no concept of "art for art's sake" among the Aztecs, an artist's skill and the quality of finished works were highly esteemed.[24] Master craftsmen could be lavishly compensated. According to the late sixteenth-century Indian chronicler

*Figure 3. Feather worker with feather items
(drawing from* Florentine Codex, *Book 9).
Courtesy of Michel Besson.*

Figure 4. Gold workers (drawing from Florentine Codex, Book 9).
Courtesy of Michel Besson.

Tezozomoc (409), as a reward for carving his relief image in Chapultepec, where he was depicted wearing the costume of the fertility and war god Xipe Totec, Moctezuma II presented the sculptors
with the rich tribute collected from the province of Cuetlaxtlan in
the present-day state of Veracruz.

Despite the widespread destruction of much Aztec art, an astonishing number of major sculptural works have survived. Judging from them, the main subjects of Aztec monuments were cult
images of the gods and pieces that depicted sacred or mythological
subject matter. Although historical and overtly political images are
few, a number of the "religious" works clearly had "political" implications.[25] Aztec images did not depict the natural world of human
activities. They depicted a world of belief, expressing ideas about
the cosmos, its perceived structure, and one's place in it. The relationship of human beings to the gods was critical. Blood sacrifice
was a commonly represented theme because it was thought that

Figure 5. Lapidary worker (drawing from Florentine Codex, *Book 9).*
Courtesy of Michel Besson.

through this ritual offering one honored the gods and sustained
the world order.

Because of the esoteric symbolism that was often included,
it seems most likely that the planning of major monuments and
their religious or political agendas were worked out in conjunction with the rulers or administrators who commissioned them,
as well as with priests and scribes who were most familiar with
the pictorial manuscripts that preserved the written lore of the
community. In their related histories Durán (*Historia* 245-246 and
Tezozomoc 170-171) explicitly describe, and Durán also illustrates,
how the Chapultepec image commissioned by Moctezuma I was
carried out by a team of artists. From this we can assume that
monumental public images were made by cooperative groups
of artists, possibly under the direction of a master artist in es-

tablished workshops, working within a hierarchically controlled system that specified the nature of the images to be produced. Master craftsmen were probably also patronized by nobles and aristocrats who had large household establishments. Priests, especially those dedicated to a particular deity, may have had a direct hand in specifying the kinds of images to be placed in the temples and shrines in their care. Aside from elite commissions such as these, the general population might have fashioned their own kinds of images for household shrines and ritual occasions or purchased them in the market place.

Aztec style primarily refers to the artistic forms and conventions that are characteristic of works produced in Mexico Tenochtitlan. From surviving sculpture deriving from different regions of the empire, it is evident that this style was shared by the other major polities of the Basin of Mexico and beyond. For example, a huge disk with a relief image of a sun deity, carved in a style indistinguishable from that of Mexico Tenochtitlan, originated in the allied city of Tetzcoco near the lake's eastern shore. Outside the basin the style appears to have extended west into the Toluca Basin, which had been colonized under the rulers Axayacatl and Ahuitzotl. Dynastic connections also provided an opportunity for influence at Malinalco, even further southwest, where a temple dedicated to the elite eagle and jaguar warriors as well as associated sculpture were cut into the living rock. Sculpture close to the metropolitan style of the capital has also been found in the present-day states of Guerrero to the southwest, Puebla to the southeast, and Veracruz on the east coast, especially at the site of Castillo de Teayo. From this distribution it appears that the style of the capital rapidly spread throughout the empire, although it should also be recognized that it shared in a common Mesoamerican cultural inheritance and borrowed from its predecessors and neighbors when formulating its own style. Also, works in some areas displayed provincial or strongly regional manifestations. For example, little monumental sculpture has been found to the far southeast in Oaxaca, where relief sculpture and works in other media retained a distinctive local style into the late pre-Hispanic period.

Architecture

When the Spaniards first saw the twin cities of Mexico Tenochtitlan and Tlatelolco, they beheld a bustling metropolis of about
a quarter of a million inhabitants. Divided into quarters and organized along a grid plan, the capital was crisscrossed by canals
and streets, which led the Spanish soldiers to compare it to the
island city of Venice. It was connected to the mainland by four
main causeways, which extended outward from the main ceremonial center toward the west, north, and south. With his ever
watchful eye Cortés (85-86) noted the causeways, bridges, towers,
walls, fortifications, gates, temples, and dwellings that marked the
southern part of the city where he first entered. The main marketplace, which astonished Cortés and Díaz by its size, crowds,
and quantity of merchandise, was located in nearby Tlatelolco.[26]
Descriptions of ritual activity in Book 2 (The Ceremonies) of the
Florentine Codex indicate that in addition to the Templo Mayor numerous other temples and shrines dedicated to other deities were
scattered throughout the city.

According to Sahagún's enumeration (2: 179-193), the central Templo Mayor precinct consisted of a walled compound
enclosing seventy-eight structures. In addition to temples and
shrines dedicated to the major gods of the populous Aztec
pantheon, other structures included ballcourts, skullracks, and
residences for priests. Dominating the sacred complex at the
eastern end was the main temple, or Templo Mayor proper,
which was topped by two shrines, one dedicated to the ancient
god of rain, Tlaloc, and the other to the Aztec solar patron of
war, Huitzilopochtli. Together they expressed the two forces that
sustained the Aztec world. Tlaloc's beneficence produced the life-
giving water that assured physical existence; the martial activities
promulgated by Huitzilopochtli sustained the cosmic order by
furnishing the precious liquid, blood, believed to strengthen the
sun in its daily battle with nocturnal forces. The astronomical
orientation of the Templo Mayor also reveals the cosmic symbolism the Aztecs devised to express their relationship to the
gods and the universe. The structure was positioned with regard to the rising of the sun. For part of the year it rose above

the Tlaloc shrine and for another part above the Huitzilopochtli shrine.

Sculpture

As heirs to a Mesoamerican cultural tradition stretching back over two millennia, much Aztec art had its historical roots in the art types and forms of earlier cultures.[27] From the Toltecs, who had ruled Tollan (Tula) centuries earlier, sculptors adopted upright, rigid warrior statues holding weapons at their sides, extended low relief panels featuring processions of warriors, and the reclining but alert figure called a Chacmool. A Chacmool painted in still vivid colors, found at the entrance of what Matos Moctezuma has designated Stage 2 of the Templo Mayor and datable to about 1400, is one of the earliest Aztec sculptures yet found. These Toltec adaptations reveal a strong historical consciousness on the part of the Aztecs. They were no doubt intended to forge an artistic continuity between them and the revered Toltecs, whom they regarded as their political and cultural predecessors in Central Mexico. Artists also imitated the even earlier, large-scale ceramic sculptures that are best known from sites in what is today Veracruz. The most impressive examples of this type are the spectacular pair of life-size warrior figures dressed in eagle costumes, which were found flanking a doorway in a structure called the Platform of the Eagles in what corresponds to Stage 5 of the Templo Mayor. The Aztecs also imitated forms typical of Teotihuacan. One colonial text reveals that Moctezuma made pilgrimages to the great ruined city of Teotihuacan, which had flourished several centuries earlier to the northeast, and the *Florentine Codex* relates how the Aztecs set the mythical creation of the fifth sun at this impressive site, which they called "the place of the gods" (Sahagún 3: 4-8). Thus Teotihuacan imitations also communicated their reverence for this once mighty civilization and their desire to establish visible signs of their participation in the great cultural traditions of the past.

The sequence of sculpture discovered in the Templo Mayor dramatically illustrates the rapid progress of the Aztecs in forging their own distinctive artistic identity and cohesive iconographic program. Sculptures found in the earliest Stages 1 through 3 (ap-

Figure 6. Drawing of the Coyolxauhqui Stone. Courtesy of Michel Besson.

proximately 1390 to 1440) are rough, derivative, and schematic. By Stage 4b (about 1470), however, the massive serpent heads found at the bases of Templo Mayor balustrades and especially the circular relief with the splendidly carved dismembered image of the goddess Coyolxauhqui already exhibit the mastery of formal and iconographic features that we associate with the best of Aztec sculpture. This immense disk illustrates a central myth that became a powerful instrument of Aztec political ideology (Fig. 6). As told by Sahagún (3: 1-5), the myth relates the story of Coatlicue's miraculous conception of Huitzilopochtli, and the plot of his sister Coyolxauhqui and his numerous brothers to kill their mother because of this unseemly incident. Even as they attacked

Coatlicue, Huitzilopochtli was born, grown and fully armed, and vanquished his treacherous siblings, decapitating and dismembering Coyolxauhqui. In one of the most successful correlations of text and image, the German Mesoamericanist Eduard Seler first identified a colossal stone head as an image of the decapitated Coyolxauhqui and interpreted the myth as the battle waged by the sun (Huitzilopochtli) to overcome the nocturnal forces of the moon (Coyolxauhqui) and stars (his brothers) (Seler 2: 327-328; 4: 157-167). Even more, Huitzilopochtli's conquest presaged the political and military destiny of the Aztecs. Placed as it was at the base of the stairway leading up to the Huitzilopochtli shrine, this uncompromising monument proclaimed for all to see the prevailing power of Huitzilopochtli and the Aztecs over their enemies. The Coyolxauhqui sculptures are consummate examples of how through their art the Aztecs strove to make visible the structures and beliefs that validated their rule and gave direction to their society.

Why did Aztec art develop so rapidly and in the way that it did? Its artistic development clearly parallels the military expansion and political consolidation of the empire. Stage 4a can be associated with the reign of the great Moctezuma I (1440-1469), under whom the Aztecs began their ambitious program of conquest. Contact with other areas gave them access to new materials and techniques and exposed them to a range of art forms produced by various groups, some of them more culturally advanced than they were. Certainly the "foreign" materials buried in the Templo Mayor attest to their increasing authority to command vast quantities of objects from all corners of the empire. As their power grew, the need also arose to create the public architecture, monuments, and goods commensurate with an imperial center and expressive of imperial aims. Art provided the great organizing symbols of the society. Sculpture, especially, was a theophanic window through which the Aztecs glimpsed the powers under which they led their lives, that is to say, it not only represented these powers but participated in their sacred character.

Stone sculpture is the most abundant and impressive of all Aztec art forms, although Sahagún and other authors say relatively little about it.[28] These works are generally skillfully carved

Figure 7. "Calendar Stone." Photo by Eloise Quiñones Keber.

and finished, a remarkable achievement given the stone tools that were the chief instruments used by the Aztec sculptor. Although the overall shapes of three-dimensional objects are usually simple, incised details often convey complex religious and political ideologies through the use of a coherent and intricate symbolic system. Nowhere is the Aztec ability to express abstract concepts in a compelling visual mode more evident than in the famous relief carving known as the Sun Stone or "Calendar Stone" (Fig. 7). In fact, its rediscovery in the main plaza in 1790 along with the massive and terrifying figure of the earth goddess Coatlicue launched the period of the material rediscovery of the Aztec past. A colossal circular disk, it is called the Sun Stone because of the concentric rings and triangular rays that overall form a schematic representation of this celestial body. It is also named the "Calendar Stone" because it expresses some basic cosmic-calendric concepts known from the ethnohistorical texts. The face of the sun god Tonatiuh, the center of the stone as it was the pivot of the Aztec universe, lies at the intersection of an X-shaped Ollin symbol signifying movement or earthquake.[29] The Aztecs believed that on a future 4 Ollin day the era of the fifth sun in which they were living would terminate in catastrophic earthquakes. It was only the sacrifice of human blood that kept the sun in its orbit and their universe in existence. Within the arms of the Ollin sign are symbols of the four previous suns, or cosmic eras, that had been terminated by similar cataclysms caused by winds, jaguars, a rain of fire, and floods. Symbols of the twenty day signs, which together with the numbers one to thirteen formed the repeating 260 days of their ritual-divinatory cycle, fill one concentric ring. Other symbols include the date 13 Acatl (Reed), the date of the creation of the fifth sun, and the possible name sign of the ruler Moctezuma II, in whose reign and by whose mandate the monument was carved.

Many figural stone sculptures also survive. In the rare depictions of ordinary human figures emphasis was on a collective Aztec type. The few ruler representations that exist in relief carvings also show the same generalized, expressionless features; they are not portraits in our sense. Those gods represented anthropomorphically were conceived in the same manner. Individualization in all cases was achieved by the depiction of characteristic attire and insignia. For example, the bells (*coyolli*) carved on the cheeks of the goddess Coyolxauhqui identify her as the goddess "painted with bells." For deity images the limiting of the marks of individuality to details external to the physical form, like apparel and ornamentation, may point to their identities as concrete representatives of more abstract forces. Since rulers were often represented in the costumes of gods, the lack of individualized features for their images may have been intended to communicate the role of rulers as mediators between supernatural and natural powers.

It is interesting that while deity images are described (and denounced) in the colonial sources, whole categories of objects are not mentioned, much less explained. Among these are deftly carved animals like serpents, jaguars, eagles, monkeys, canines, grasshoppers, and even insects. Aztec sculptors were excellent observers of flora and fauna, and many of these were produced with a remarkable if streamlined realism. Some animals were alter egos of certain gods and thus bore deity insignia or other symbols.

While the actual function of these pieces is not known with certainty, they and sculptures of other natural forms, like shells and squashes, may have been placed in appropriate sacred structures as offerings. Numerous stone carvings of ritual items, recognizable from their depictions in pictorial ritual manuscripts, include containers for offerings, braziers, and masks of human or deity faces, many of them carved with sacred symbols.

Pieces with overt "historical" connotations form a small but important group of sculptures. Among the most significant is the Stone of Tizoc, a huge cylindrical monument with relief carvings that depicts the ruler Tizoc (1481-1486) in the guise of the Aztec patron god Huitzilopochtli. With his short and undistinguished reign, this monument confers a celebrity on him that the historical sources do not support. Appearing fifteen times around the surface of the stone, the patron deity is shown conquering the patron deities of communities that can be identified by their distinctive place signs.[30] The schematic sun disk at the top of the monument recalls both the sanction and the cosmic context for such conquests. Another significant historical example is the Dedication Stone, a greenstone slab with relief carvings, which probably commemorates the last major renovation of the Templo Mayor in 1487 (Fig. 8), an event notorious in historical sources for the great number of people sacrificed. This year date (8 Acatl or Reed) appears prominently on the stone, along with the images of two successive rulers, Tizoc and his brother Ahuitzotl, garbed as priests, under whom the renovations were carried out. They are shown drawing blood offerings from their ears, an act that they probably performed in conjunction with the temple dedication. Another monument that may also be a dedicatory stone, the enormous rectangular slab with relief carvings commonly called the Acuecuexatl Stone, also shows the ruler Ahuitzotl attired as a priest and performing the same sacrificial act on both sides. These monuments demonstrate how visual images served to connect the ruling dynasty with the service of the gods, giving further cohesion to the different levels of Aztec society.

Because it is such a perishable material, not much wood sculpture has survived. One of the few extant examples, whose superb carving gives some idea of this mostly destroyed category of ob-

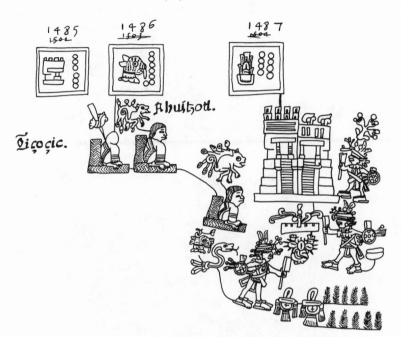

Figure 8. Drawing of a detail of Codex Telleriano-Remensis, *fol. 39r: Dedication of the Templo Mayor in 1487. Courtesy of Michel Besson.*

jects, is an intricately carved, cylindrical, upright drum found in Malinalco (Fig. 9). Expertly carved relief images of eagles and jaguars, symbols of Aztec warriors, parade around its circumference. Bearing sacrificial paper banners, they emit war cries of *atl tlachinolli* ("water-fire"), the symbol of sacred warfare that is expressed by the intertwined water and fire streams. The central emblem of the drum is the large 4 Ollin (Movement) symbol of the fifth sun, in whose honor the Aztecs waged warfare and performed sacrificial rites. These images suggest that the drum may have been used in ritual activities related to the solar cult, possibly in the mountain shrine at Malinalco dedicated to eagle and jaguar warriors. Although using different components, this ceremonial object vividly expresses the same connection seen in monoliths between warfare, sacrifice, imperial power, and the cosmic order.

Figure 9. Roll-out drawing of the Malinalco Drum. Courtesy of Michel Besson.

Other Arts

Beyond their concern with grand cosmological ideas, the Aztecs also produced luxury items of a more personal nature, items whose precious materials and expert workmanship are described by numerous chroniclers. Elegant apparel and accessories were produced by skilled masters of the craft of feather working, which involved the meticulous combining of the colorful feathers of exotic birds. The most spectacular example is a large headdress made of brilliant green quetzal feathers, with supplementary designs worked in gold. First thought to have been a cape because of its large size, it may have been one of the many feather items presented by Moctezuma to Cortés and forwarded to Charles V. The *Florentine Codex* tells how the feather workers of the palace, who worked exclusively for the ruler, made adornments for him, items for his treasury store house, and gifts for rulers of other cities. Private feather workers made and sold such specialized luxury items as shields, back standards, banners, shirts, bracelets, arm bands, and fans (Sahagún 9: 69-97). Another mosaic craft, utilizing precious materials like turquoise, shell, coral, jadeite, and mother-of-pearl usually mounted on a wooden base, produced luxury items like masks, shields, ornaments, and handles for ceremonial flint knives.

To judge from the listing of gifts presented to Cortés (39-46) and shipped to Charles V, Aztec artists produced a variety of exquisitely worked jewels in gold, silver, and precious stones. Of the few metal pieces that have survived are several gold labrets (lip ornaments) worn as status items by warriors and Aztec aristocracy, deity and animal figures, pendants, and bells. Lapidaries used such prized stones as rock crystal, amethyst, jade, and turquoise to make necklaces, bracelets, lip pendants, ear ornaments, and other desirable items.

Another major area of artistic endeavor among the Aztecs was manuscript painting, which represents both an art work in itself and a source of information about religious, ritual, calendric, genealogical, economic, and historical matters. Despite the fact that apparently no Aztec manuscript has survived from the pre-Conquest period, some idea of their quality may be gleaned from copies of Aztec originals made by indigenous artists in post-Conquest Mexico under both Spanish and Indian sponsorship. Ironically, even as colonial authors sought to preserve Aztec cultural traditions in alphabetic form, authentic pictorial versions of them were being deliberately destroyed or altered during copying. Despite their artistic and historical value, ancient Mexican manuscripts are little known to the public since they are rarely displayed because of their fragility.

The *Codex Borbonicus,* which was probably painted on native paper soon after the Conquest, is one of the earliest post-Conquest manuscripts known, and its high quality makes it a touchstone by which to gauge the features of pre-Hispanic Aztec manuscript painting (Fig. 10). Its brilliantly painted images convey visual information about the deities in different ritual contexts. One section portrays the deities who were invoked during divinatory activities, and another depicts the ceremonies that marked the eighteen feasts of the annual ritual cycle, where celebrants dressed in the costumes of various deities who were being honored. Several lengthy texts, including those of Sahagún (Book 2) and Durán describe these events. Another outstanding example is the *Codex Telleriano-Remensis,* which was painted on European paper by Indian artists in the mid-sixteenth century. In addition to the two sections represented in the *Codex Borbonicus,* it also contains an extensive pictorial chronicle that begins with the legendary migration period, continues with dynastic events in the Basin of Mexico under the nine pre-Hispanic rulers of Mexico Tenochtitlan, and concludes with a selection of events occurring during the first decades of colonial rule. One of its most famous images shows the ruler Ahuitzotl presiding over dedication of the newly renovated Templo Mayor in 1487 (Fig. 8).

(Re)discovering Aztec art, and the Aztecs themselves, is an ongoing enterprise, a continuing discourse, in many ways dependent on but not limited by the ethnohistorical or archaeological materials that exist. Learning how to read and use the colonial texts is a challenge. An equal challenge is learning how to read the works of art in themselves: how to understand the kinds of information art objects can give us; how to make sense out of similarities *and* differences, presences *and* absences, continuities *and* changes; how

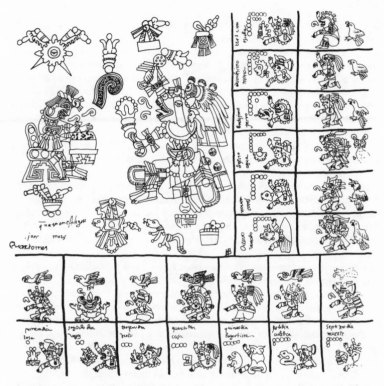

Figure 10. Drawing of Codex Borbonicus 4. Courtesy of Michel Besson.

to read forms as well as meaning, styles as well as symbols; how to relate these considerations to ethnography and archaeology; how to assess all our sources, recognizing their values and limitations and dealing with their contradictions. We must be aware that Aztec images were tied to a worldview that encompassed religious beliefs, political ideologies, and moral ideas. Because our own attitudes toward art derive from different values, when we look at those objects that we call Aztec art today we must recall that to the Aztecs these were not merely art objects but reminders of the deep structures of the world and the powers that animated it.

Notes

1. All maps and drawings are the work of Michel Besson. The photograph of the Calendar Stone is by the author.

2. The incentive for writing, as well as the attitudes expressed toward the conquered and their culture, must of course be kept in mind. Cortés was a keen observer but eager to justify his unauthorized actions and to secure both recognition and tangible rewards for what he had accomplished. Díaz the foot soldier, ostensibly writing in reaction to his commander's version of events, produced a highly readable and dramatic account of the Conquest but one that contains a number of exaggerations and inaccuracies. His account must be read critically.

3. For a comprehensive survey of the major Central Mexican ethnohistorical sources, see the four volumes of the *Guide to Ethnohistorical Sources* (Cline).

4. A comment typical of our ironic age must be made here. The discourse of contemporary interpreters makes use of terms and categories equally foreign to Aztec culture as those whose distortions they intend to redress. Without this foreign discourse the Aztecs seem incapable of speaking for themselves in a way comprehensible to the late twentieth century. We might ask ourselves if knowledge of "the other" must always be mediated by a foreign discourse ever unsure of its distorting effects.

5. See, for example, the various essays in Jara and Spadaccini that explore different aspects of this problem (*Re/Discovering Colonial Writing*).

6. Although several Aztec pictorial manuscripts exist, some of them drawn by Indian artists on native paper in screenfold form, these are regarded by most scholars as post-Conquest copies of indigenous books. Most exhibit some degree of European influence. For information on existing pictorial manuscripts, see my article, "Central Mexican Pictorial Manuscripts: An Introduction," and Glass and Glass and Robertson in vol. 14 of the *Guide to Ethnohistorical Sources* (Cline).

7. As Octavio Paz (1990) reminds us, insofar as their attitudes toward the Aztec image of the goddess Coatlicue are concerned, the Spanish friar comes closer to the Aztec priest than does the modern secular scholar. For both the friar and the priest the image represented a supernatural reality: to the Aztecs it was a goddess, to the priest a demon.

8. David Carrasco's book *Religions of Mesoamerica* includes an overview of the various Mesoamerican religious traditions, including that of the Aztecs. A chapter on the Aztecs specifically discusses their sacred myths, religious symbolism, and worldview. H. B. Nicholson's 1971 synthesis, "Religion in Pre-Hispanic Central Mexico," remains a reliable introduction to the religious ideology of this area. Broader considerations of Aztec ideology can be found in López Austin's insightful *The Human Body and Ideology: Concepts of the Ancient Nahuas* and León-Portilla's classic *Aztec Thought and Culture*.

9. See Nicholson ("The Chapultepec Cliff Sculpture") for a comprehensive discussion of these Aztec ruler images. Fortunately, despite efforts to obliterate them, remnants of the carvings can still be seen in Chapultepec Park in Mexico City.

10. Several works explore the early history of Mexican items in European *kunstkammern*, among them Heikamp and Nowotny.

11. After years of tentative starts the Museo Nacional Mexicano was installed in

rooms set aside at the National University. It was the precursor of the current Museo Nacional de Antropología e Historia in Mexico City, where the largest collection of Aztec (and other pre-Columbian) art can be found today.

12. An interest in Mexico had already been prepared by earlier visitors, especially the gifted naturalist Alexander von Humboldt, who traveled extensively in Latin America from 1799 to 1804. A curious and alert observer, his writings included illustrations of pre-Hispanic archaeological sites, manuscripts, and sculpture.

13. George Kubler's recent work on the aesthetic recognition of ancient American art provides the first major consideration of the ways Pre-Columbian objects have been evaluated over time.

14. It should be noted that interest in Aztec art initially lagged behind that in other groups, such as the Maya or Olmec. There were no picturesque Aztec sites to visit and few archaeological discoveries to capture interest and headlines. Perhaps more important, Aztec art was often regarded as crude, overpowering, and excessively preoccupied with death and sacrifice. Benjamin Keen's *The Aztec Image in Western Thought* offers an enlightening historical overview of shifting Western attitudes toward the Aztecs.

15. Because of the historical development of the field of pre-Columbian art, art historians working in this area have continued to depend on the fields of anthropology and archaeology for much of their data and to interact with other area specialists whatever their academic disciplines. As a result, they have tended to favor a broad, contextual approach to the study of objects traditionally classified in the Western tradition as "works of art."

16. Mexico Tenochtitlan was one of the eight archaeological sites selected for the pre-Columbian section of the mega-exhibition "Mexico: Splendors of Thirty Centuries," shown in 1990-91 at the Metropolitan Museum of Art in New York City, with additional venues in San Antonio and Los Angeles. The exhibition "Art of Aztec Mexico: Treasures of Tenochtitlan," held at the National Gallery of Art in 1983 under the curatorship of Elizabeth H. Boone and H. B. Nicholson, marked the first comprehensive international exhibition of Aztec art ever held in the United States (see Nicholson with Quiñones Keber).

17. As Esther Pasztory points out in her preface, although numerous books on pre-Columbian art exist, her 1983 publication was the first comprehensive book to be published on Aztec art.

18. As with many other areas of non-Western art for which written records are limited, the field of pre-Columbian art for the most part lacks the types of historical, civic, commercial, ecclesiastical, biographical data, etc. that are often available to scholars of Western art.

19. A body of specialized and popular literature on the Templo Mayor has already accumulated and continues to grow, particularly in Mexico. Among the most useful and easily available sources in English are *The Great Temple of the Aztecs* and the lavishly illustrated *Treasures of the Great Temple* by Matos Moctezuma, the project director, as well as the 1983 symposium volume, *The Aztec Templo Mayor*, edited by Elizabeth H. Boone.

20. Another significant resource for study of the excavated materials is the museum of the Templo Mayor adjoining the archaeological site, where an attempt

has been made to display the objects with respect to the archaeological contexts in which they were found.

21. The word "Nahua" is also used as an encompassing term for the Nahuatl speakers of Central Mexico, of which the Mexica were a group.

22. Founded on a nearby island to the north of Mexico Tenochtitlan, Tlatelolco was a competing community until it lost its independence after being conquered by the ruler Axayacatl in 1473.

23. The most comprehensive ethnohistorical source of information on Aztec culture at about the time of the Conquest is the encyclopedic manuscript called the *Florentine Codex* (*Historia general de las cosas de Nueva España*), with information collected and written from about 1547 to 1580. The project was undertaken by Sahagún in collaboration with a team of indigenous assistants, artists, and scribes. See Klor de Alva, et al. for a recent series of articles on ideological, historical, artistic, and linguistic aspects of this indispensable source on Aztec Mexico.

24. In Book 10 of the *Florentine Codex* (Sahagún 10: 25-28), the good craftsman is not only praised for his abilities but for his moral character; conversely, the bad craftsman is condemned not only for his shoddy workmanship but for his personal failings.

25. See note 4.

26. In Tlatelolco Díaz (217-219) was also impressed by a great courtyard that he estimated was larger than the plaza at Salamanca. Although disdainful of the "cursed idols" in the shrine at the top of Tlatelolco's great temple, he admired the spectacular view of the city and the lakeside setting afforded from this vantage point.

27. In her article "The Return of Mexica Art to Its Toltec Past," Beatriz de la Fuente discusses this phenomenon, which she sees as part of a larger cultural-artistic situation involving all Mesoamerican civilizations as well as a universal tendency of the present to establish contact with the past.

28. For the most comprehensive overviews of Aztec sculpture, see Nicholson with Quiñones Keber, and Pasztory.

29. The identification of the central figure as the sun god is the traditional (and embattled) one. Other scholars have suggested that this figure may represent the night sun or the monster-like conceptualization of the earth called Tlaltecuhtli.

30. A close relative of this piece was recently found in the courtyard of the former archbishop's residence, located today just inside what was formerly the southern boundary of the Templo Mayor precinct.

Works Cited

Bernal, Ignacio. *A History of Mexican Archaeology*. New York: Thames and Hudson, 1980.

Boone, Elizabeth Hill, ed. *The Aztec Templo Mayor*. Washington, D.C.: Dumbarton Oaks, 1987.

Carrasco, David. *Religions of Mesoamerica*. San Francisco: Harper & Row, 1990.

Cline, Howard, et al., eds. *Guide to Ethnohistorical Sources*. Handbook of Middle American Indians 12-15. Austin: Univ. of Texas Press, 1972-1975.

Codex Borbonicus. Ms.Y 120. Bibliothèque de l'Assemblée Nationale, Paris. Commentaries by Karl Anton Nowotny and Jacqueline de Durand-Forest. Graz, Austria: Akademische Druck- und Verlagsanstalt, 1974.

Codex Mendoza. Ed. James Cooper Clark. London: Waterloo & Sons, 1938.

Codex Telleriano-Remensis. Manuscrit mexicain du cabinet de Charles-Maurice le Tellier, Archêveque de Reims. Ms. Mexicain 385. Bibliothèque Nationale, Paris. Commentary by E. T. Hamy. Paris: Bibliothèque Nationale, 1899.

Cortés, Hernán. *Letters from Mexico.* Ed. and trans. Anthony Pagden. New Haven: Yale Univ. Press, 1986.

Díaz del Castillo, Bernal. *The Discovery and Conquest of Mexico.* Trans. and ed. A. P. Maudslay. New York: Farrar, Straus and Cudahy, 1956.

Durán, Fray Diego. *Book of the Gods and Rites and The Ancient Calendar.* Ed. and trans. Fernando Horcasitas and Doris Heyden. Norman: Univ. of Oklahoma Press, 1971.

———. *Historia de las Indias de Nueva España e Islas de la Tierra Firme.* Ed. Angel Ma. Garibay K. 2 vols. Mexico City: Editorial Porrúa, 1967.

Fuente, Beatriz de la. "The Return of Mexica Art to Its Toltec Past." *Artes de México* 7 (1990): 71-77.

Heikamp, Detlef. *Mexico and the Medici.* Florence: Editrice Edam, 1972.

Humboldt, Alexander von. *Vues des cordillères et monumens des peuples indigènes de l'Amèrique.* Paris: F. Schoell, 1810.

Jara, René, and Nicholas Spadaccini, eds. *1492-1992: Re/Discovering Colonial Writing.* Hispanic Issues 4. Minneapolis: Prisma Institute, 1989.

Keen, Benjamin. *The Aztec Image in Western Thought.* New Brunswick, N.J.: Rutgers Univ. Press, 1971.

Klor de Alva, Jorge, H. B. Nicholson, and Eloise Quiñones Keber, eds. *The Work of Bernardino de Sahagún: Pioneer Ethnographer of Sixteenth-Century Aztec Mexico.* Austin and Albany: Univ. of Texas Press and the Institute for Mesoamerican Studies, SUNY, 1988.

Kubler, George. *Esthetic Recognition of Ancient Amerindian Art.* New Haven: Yale Univ. Press, 1991.

León-Portilla, Miguel. *Aztec Thought and Culture.* Trans. Jack Emory Davis. Norman: Univ. of Oklahoma Press, 1963.

López Austin, Alfredo. *The Human Body and Ideology.* Trans. Thelma Ortiz de Montellano and Bernard Ortiz de Montellano. 2 vols. Salt Lake City: Univ. of Utah Press, 1988.

Matos Moctezuma, Eduardo. *The Great Temple of the Aztecs.* Trans. Doris Heyden. New York: Thames and Hudson, 1988.

———. *Treasures of the Great Temple.* Trans. Richard Lindley. La Jolla: Alti Publishing, 1990.

Metropolitan Museum of Art. *Mexico: Splendors of Thirty Centuries.* Boston: Little, Brown and Company, 1990.

Nicholson, H. B. "The Chapultepec Cliff Sculpture of Moctezuma Xocoyotzin." *El México Antiguo* 9 (1959): 379-443.

———. "Major Sculpture in Pre-Hispanic Central Mexico." *Archaeology of Northern Mesoamerica.* Ed. Gordon F. Ekholm and Ignacio Bernal. Handbook of Middle American Indians 10. Austin: Univ. of Texas Press, 1971. 92-134.

———. "Religion in Pre-Hispanic Central Mexico." *Archaeology of Northern Meso-america*. Ed. Gordon F. Ekholm and Ignacio Bernal. Handbook of Middle American Indians 10. Austin: Univ. of Texas Press, 1971. 395-446

———, with Eloise Quiñones Keber. *Art of Aztec Mexico: Treasures of Tenochtitlan*. Washington, D.C.: National Gallery of Art, 1983.

Nowotny, Karl A. *Mexikanische Kostbarkeiten aus Kunstkammern der Renaissance*. Vienna: Museum für Völkerkunde, 1960.

Pasztory, Esther. *Aztec Art*. New York: Harry N. Abrams, 1983.

———. "Texts, Archaeology, Art, and History in the Templo Mayor: Reflections." Boone 451-462.

Paz, Octavio. "The Power of Ancient Mexican Art." *New York Review of Books* 38 (Dec. 6, 1990): 18-22.

Quiñones Keber, Eloise. "Central Mexican Pictorial Manuscripts: An Introduction." *Latin American Indian Literatures Journal* 2 (1986): 162-171.

Sahagún, Fray Bernardino de. *Florentine Codex: General History of the Things of New Spain*. Trans. Arthur J. O. Anderson and Charles E. Dibble. 13 vols. Santa Fe, N.M.: School of American Research/Salt Lake City: Univ. of Utah, 1950-1982.

Seler, Eduard. *Gesammelte Abhandlungen zur Amerikanischen Sprach-u. Altertum-skunde*. 1902-1923. 5 vols. Graz: Akademische Druck-u. Verlagsanstalt, 1960-1961.

Tezozomoc, Hernando Alvarado. *Crónica Mexicana*. Ed. Manuel Orozco y Berra. Mexico City: Editorial Leyenda, 1944.

◆ Chapter 4

Fantastic Tales and Chronicles of the Indies

Manuel Alvar

(translated by Jennifer M. Lang)

This is not the first time that, in one way or another, the manner in which chivalric literature formed part of the nascent New World has been addressed. It is customary, however, to speculate with relative success based on very little information. I do not intend to enter into questions of either the personal or the collective psychology of the conquistador. Rather, I propose to examine the code of chivalry as a principle that makes possible the transmission and understanding of the New World for the West. It is also the case, though not for the first time, that either life was transformed into literature or literature brought to life through exemplary attitudes.

Thus, it turns out that fantastic tales are just as true as classical stories and the knowledge brought forth by the old naturalists. Thus, an interesting paradox arises: those who move about in a world of prodigies see reality only insofar as it justifies the learning of what is already known. There exists a medieval attraction that leads people to fuse (and confuse) what has been studied, and yet remains uncertain, with what is certain in that it belongs to human experience. Hence, for these individuals there are no frontiers between fantasy and reality. This task of differentiating between them is reserved to Renaissance thinkers who moved within a renewed intellectual world (see Cioranescu as well as Cioranescu's observations on Columbus in "Prólogo," *Diario* 55). The chivalric literature of all nations shows this differentiation, one which comes to full fruition in the figure of Charles V, who embodies the plenitude of the Renaissance. While one cannot ignore Garcilaso's verses, Valdés's dialogues, or Titian's paintings as clear symbols of the times, it was Charles V who signified the permanence of medieval chivalry—as witnessed, for example, in his efforts to save a Christendom that was breaking apart; in his notion of individual valor in his defiance of Francis I on that famous Monday before Easter in 1536 (Alonso 112-119); and, especially, in some of his readings.

The emperor always favored Olivier de la Marche's *Le chevalier délibéré* (*The Knight Delivered*), a work which he translated into Spanish and carried with him to Yuste. His preference is not surprising, for it is a typical poem of Burgundian literature that exalts the dukes of Burgundy. Its interest lies not so much in symbolism or the moral, but in the manner of resolving the knight's final struggle against sickness and death. Carlos Clavería has described it as "the sensation of a marvelous adventure lived by the author in a dream world from which he comes back to reality with a wealth of experiences used to instruct his readers" ("sensación de aventura fantástica vivida por el autor en un mundo irreal de ensueño desde el que vuelve a la realidad con un caudal de experiencias con que aleccionar a sus lectores" [16]). De la Marche's rhetoric is replete with devices that manage to transform the fantastic into a palpable presence. The struggle against Athropos and his followers is deeply connected to chivalric life. One must also bear in mind that the union of the Hapsburgs and the Spanish kings (which Erasmus foresaw and praised) created a cult of mystic chivalry that was said to have culminated in the creation of the Order of the Golden Fleece. It was in Flanders that the spirit of Burgundy survived, that an attempt was made to relive the marvelous Middle Ages where Charles the Fearless, the emperor's grandfather, lived his own book of chivalry. In America we will find again that fantastic world, one in which were interwoven, as if (re)gaining new life, Jason's voyage, the impossible Colchis, the Argonauts, the capture of the Golden Fleece, and Gideon's biblical stories. It should not surprise us, then, that in a world more fantastic than Flanders, more real than the nonexistent Colchis, less cultured and sophisticated than that of the Burgundian court, there again should arise heroes, places, and marvelous treasures that had never before existed, yet could be touched, seen, and possessed in a new reality.

The transformation of the legend began before the three caravels unfolded their sails, for it was already in the mind of a visionary known to us as Christopher Columbus. One need only to read the *Diario* (*Diary*) of the discovery. The path that takes him to the New World is paved with fantasy. His obsession was "to go to terra firme and to the city of Quisay and present Your Highnesses' letters to the Great Khan and return with his answer" ("ir a la tierra firme y a la ciudad de Quisay, y dar las cartas de Vuestras Altezas al Gran Can y pedir respuesta y venir con ella") (Columbus 2: 79 [October 21, 1492]). These simple lines become the goblin that produces his nightmares. His imagination forges new and fantastic adventures of Marco Polo, and he dreams of battles on land or in the islands against the Great Khan. The kingdoms that he encounters are inhabited by cyclops and cynocephali (see Columbus, "Prólogo," *Diario* 54-55; Cioranescu; Alegría). These ghosts fled upon his awakening. Yet it is clear that if fantasy had been able to transform itself into tangible reality, then contact with material life would have been of little use. And it is also clear that Columbus had a very keen sense of observation, even if the reality represented by him is valid only to a certain point. For if the catalyst that had set it in motion was the blind belief of a visionary, he was soon forced to harness those very visions when ordinary experience was not deemed to be sufficient. Thus, his images were of "one-eyed men and other dog-faced ones who ate people" ("los hombres de un ojo y otros con hocicos de perros que comían los hombres" [2: 96]) or of Amazons, or of the fantastic Isle of San Borondón. Let us refer to Columbus's chronology. The problems begin on August 6, when the *Pinta*'s helm breaks apart (something that happens again the next day). Columbus leaves the caravel on the Grand Canary Island and goes on to Gomera. On August 9 he begins an account that relates fewer problems:

The Admiral says that many honorable Spaniards swore to have been with Doña Inés Peraza on Gomera... that they were neighbors of the Isla del Hierro, that each year they saw land to the west of the Canaries, which, in turn, lies west; and others of Gomera also swore this to be true. The Admiral says here that he remembers how, while in Portugal in 1484, a man came from the island of Madeira to ask the king for a caravel to go to that land that he saw, which he claimed to see every year and always in the same manner. He also says that he recalls that the same thing was said in the Azores—always as a route, as a sign, as something of grandeur. (1: 68-69)[1]

An old myth has reached Columbus—the story of St. Brendan of Conflert (480-576), an Irish monk who discovered a paradise on a moving island, which turned out to be a whale (see Benito Ruano, Vigneras, and Cabrera Perera). The story is connected to the classical myth of the Hesperides, the Celtic legends of Mag Mell, the land of eternity, and the Arabian fable of Sinbad the Sailor; the story, reelaborated in numerous ways, was that of the very mystery of the unknown. The folkloric versions of this tale became the stuff of science, and beginning in the second half of the fifteenth century, the Esquivas Islands appeared in navigational charts. It is not surprising, then, that the King of Portugal (1483) should grant to the Flemish Fernando van Olm and the German Martin Behaim the Grand Island of the Seven Cities. Later, this island would become the fantastic Cíbola, which Fray Marcos de Niza believed to have discovered in 1539 (Benito Ruano 24).[2] The seven enchanted cities escaped discovery, as did the island where poor mortals sought the immortality denied them.

It is true that Columbus was unable to separate reality from fantasy and that soon after the discovery many people thought so. Nevertheless, in 1721 an expedition was organized to discover the mysterious island. The commander-in-chief of the Canaries gathered the wisest and most responsible people of his jurisdiction. They discussed their plans in the city of La Laguna and, finally, the ship *Nuestra Señora de Regla* set sail. The vessel was commanded by Captain Juan Fernando Franco de Medina, who waited anxiously on the Isla del Hierro and spent a month searching for the remains of the sought-after land (Benito Ruano 36). Once again the search turned out to be futile. San Borondón (St. Brendan) was but a mirage, even though his profile was still being traced in the eighteenth century.[3]

> Facing Gomera
> in all of its resplendence,
> the skipper told
> things which he invented.
> Since he never
> found that island,
> he neither saw it
> nor drew near it in his life.
> the enchanted one
> that disappeared
> was the island called
> San Borondón.[4]

The Admiral and many of his contemporaries carried with them a world constructed with more than rational knowledge. Merlin and Amadís were more real to them than the material landscape that they contemplated. Thus, they felt a desperate need to test their imagination, one formed by fables and books of chivalry. Such is the case when Columbus encounters the people of Caniba, who "are nothing but the people of the Great Khan, who must reside nearby, and surely have ships and will come to capture them. And, since they do not return, they believe that they have been devoured" ("no es otra cosa sino la gente del Gran Can, que debe ser aquí muy vecino, y tendrá navíos y vendrán a cautivarlos, y, como no vuelven, creen que se los han comido" [2: 143]). The popular etymology is thus on its way: the peoples of the Great Khan consume their captives (hence the association between the emperor, *Can*, and dogs as well as the connection Bishop Alessandro Geraldini made between the *Caribs* or *cannibals* and the Latin *can*).

This is not a unique case, for the ancient myth of the Amazons reappears on the Island of Matininó. Thus, on Wednesday,

January 9, Columbus recalls how he circled Monte Christi on Hispaniola, and relates the following:

> The other day, when the Admiral was heading toward the River of Gold, he said that he had seen three sirens who arose from the sea, but they were not as beautiful as they are usually depicted in paintings, that in some way they possessed the face of a man. He said that he had seen them on other occasions in Guinea, on the coast of the Manegueta. (2: 196-197)[5]

There is no need for greater clarification. The inventory of fables and legends continues to operate on the narrator's consciousness, even though upon writing to the treasurer Rafael Sánchez he is forced to admit: "I never saw such monsters" ("Itaque monstra aliqua non vidi" [Cioranescu 62]). While reality struggles against fantasy, it is difficult to renounce dreams. Unheard-of beings such as cyclops, cynocephali, and Amazons came to inhabit, as in tapestries or in romances of chivalry, the bestiaries that were to lend prestige to the New World. Yet, this imagery did not always enrich the imagination. The Spaniards saw iguanas in the voyage of discovery (Columbus 2: 68, 76; see Castellanos and Alvar, *Juan de Castellanos*). Columbus called them serpents (*sierpes*) and directed us toward the books of chivalry. For a serpent (*sierpe*) was for Covarrubias "a type of snake we imagine as having wings and large claws on its feet" ("un género de culebra que fingimos tener alas y grandes uñas en los pies" [935a]). Fernández de Oviedo defined the modest iguana in these terms: "It is a *serpent* or *dragon* ... it is ugly and frightful to the eye ... in the middle of its spine there rises a crested backbone, like a saw or thorn, and it seems very fierce in itself. It has sharp teeth and a tongue that is both long and wide and extends from its chin to its chest, just like that of the ox" (chap. 7).[6] But the iguana is imagined as taking pleasure in its ugliness; of the dragon it retained only its appearance and nothing else. No longer enchanted, the Spaniards began to see in the American iguana the symbol of the enemy—the devil—but were not able to act as paladins in order to free the guarded damsels or creatures in distress. The chivalric tales were reduced to a few descriptive lines (see Nieremberg 271-272).

If the bestiary of the Indies seems to dry up, it is because the books of chivalry and chivalry itself also fade away. Let us consider an example. The medieval unicorn is a symbol of power (represented by its horn), grandeur, and purity. The interpretations begin to emerge: the lone horn symbolizes the spiritual era, God's sword, the penetration of the Divinity in human creation (*la criatura*), that is, the impregnation of the Virgin by the Holy Spirit or the symbol of the incarnation of the Divine Word in Mary's womb (see Gheerbrant). This prestige leads to the concept of courtly love, where the fascination with purity is felt even in the most corrupt of hearts. Here we are faced with a motif that extends from the medieval bestiaries[7] to the chronicles of the Indies through a complex interpretation of this world of fantasy. Let us recall, for example, the oldest known bestiary, that of Philip of Thaun, which already in the twelfth century tried to moralize with its ingenuous verses. It is clear that the description that it gives of the unicorn is not a model of beauty: "The unicorn is a beast / it has a horn upon its head" ("Monosceros es beste / un cor at en la teste"),[8] but it is valuable in that it suggests a type of literature that in the thirteenth century would become the *Bestiario moralizzato* (*Moralized Bestiary*), a mixture of didactic-moral poetry, fable, and treatise of natural history.[9] Let us recall the painting of Schongauer in Colmar. The Virgin Child strokes and pacifies a unicorn that, according to Honorius of Autun, is a difficult animal to capture and can only be controlled by a maiden. Psychoanalysis will provide other interpretations.

This type of fable and natural history will comprise many episodes of the chronicles of the Indies—as if the mythology represented in the French and Flemish tapestries lived on or as if the chivalric fictions of fantastic animals were the stuff of nature. In other words, the chronicles reenact the feats of knights defeating dragons or monsters. Moreover, the manatees are transformed into sirens,[10] iguanas into serpents, and—why not?—the purity of the unicorn is debased by descriptions unworthy of its legendary beauty. Similarly, referring to the unicorn, Fernández de Oviedo brings up the testimony of Rodrigo de Albornoz, a bookkeeper in New Spain, who saw in the lands of Cíbola "animals that have only one horn, which reaches its feet, for which reason he says that it eats on its side" ("animales que tienen un cuerno solamente, que le

allega hasta los pies, a cuya causa dice que come echado de lado"
[11: 1]). Indeed, in the tapestries of Cluny this poor beast has a
horn whose size confers on it a grieving presence. We do not learn
much more from the *Comentarios* (*Commentaries*) of Alvar Núñez
Cabeza de Vaca, who, as he was being taken down the Paraná
River by his captors, relied on a piece of unicorn for his welfare.
We are told that he "caught realgar three times, and to remedy this
he brought with him an oil jug and a piece of unicorn and whenever he felt something he took advantage of these remedies night
and day with great difficulty" ("le dieron tres veces rejalgar, y para
remedio de esto traía consigo una botija de aceite y un pedazo de
unicornio, y cuando sentía algo se aprovechaba de estos remedios
de día y de noche con muy gran trabajo" [549-599]).[11] It seems that
the piece of unicorn [horn] carried by the intrepid traveler was acquired in the Indies. To have brought it from Spain would have
entailed a great deal of planning and foresight, even if in many
latitudes there prospered the belief in its antipoisonous nature, as
noted by Gougaud, who would have its prodigious horn guarded
in the cathedrals.

But while the fantastic history of the American unicorn leaves
us with an image as poor as that displayed in the descriptions of
Amazons and of mermaids, there is a beautiful passage by Fray
Pedro de Aguado in which the story of a fantastic animal is interwoven with a romantic one (one that would have moved the
Bécquer of *La corza blanca* [*The White Doe*]). The end of the narrative, however, leaves the mystery of the story up in the air and
does not bring us a dangerously wounded damsel when the shots
of the lover have revealed the mystery of the deceitful appearance.
But let us read Fray Pedro de Aguado in his *Historia de Santa Marta*
(*History of Saint Martha*):

> In the wilderness of this valley of Santo Domingo, a most
> remarkable thing happened, and because it seemed such to
> me I wanted to write it here. Two soldiers, honest men, of
> faith and trust, called Juan del Rincón and Juan de Maya,
> climbed to the top of the moor [*páramo*] to hunt or kill deer
> with harquebuses, where, after becoming somewhat tired
> from their travels, there appeared before them a doe, a
> harquebus and even a crossbow's shot away, and so near

was she that they clearly saw the shots reaching it; and although they directed against it many harquebus shots, not only did they not kill it, but they did not even seem to have wounded it. Rather, it continually became visible and invisible to them, so that the soldiers came to surmise that it was not a doe but some evil spirit that had placed itself before them transformed into the figure of that animal; and while in this state of confusion and wonder, they heard great shouts from atop a nearby hill, which, in the Spanish or Castilian language, called these two soldiers by their names. Twice-over terrified of hearing voices from a place to which Spaniards could not have climbed, they left hunting aside and, scared and astounded by what they had seen and heard, they went back to where their captain was billeted and managed to inquire and ascertain if that day a Spaniard had gone to the place where they had heard voices; but they found no trace of this, which had utterly convinced them to believe that some evil spirit was roaming those wildernesses and deserts. (2: 253-254)[12]

The story has a surprising and uneasy romantic air. There is no need to add embellishments, but only to clarify meanings. Let us recall that *páramo* is a Ligur-Illyrian word, but what proves most remarkable is its appearance on a Leonese votive altar, in the days of Hadrian: Tulio, the lucky hunter, offers Diana the horns of the deer that he had hunted in *parami aequore*, that is, in the plains of the wilderness (Menéndez Pidal 17). And centuries later, Antonio de Alcedo in his *Vocabulario de las voces provinciales de América* (*Vocabulary of Provincial Words of America*) was to describe *páramo* as "a very high place in the mountain range, always covered with snow, where it is extremely cold" ("paraje muy alto de la cordillera, cubierto siempre de nieve, donde hace un frío intensísimo"). If we adduce real data, the plot thickens: a sixteenth-century Augustinian monk has transcribed a brief story that both reminds us of tales recalling the beliefs of peoples who existed almost two thousand years ago and brings to mind Bécquer's fantastic creation. I am thinking, for example, of that white doe that, in the poem *Guigemar*, speaks of cursing the evil hunter (qtd. in Faral 361); I am also thinking of the *Lai* of Marie de France, as told in *Éric et Énide*, by Chrétien de Troyes:

On Easter Sunday in Spring, King Arthur had gathered his
court in Cardigan, his castle; there had never been such
a rich court, for there were many and good noblemen—
fearless, brave and fierce—and ladies and damsels as well,
daughters of kings—beautiful and genteel; before the court
dispersed, the King told his knights that he wanted to hunt
the White Deer in order to reestablish the custom. (47-48)[13]

To assume that legends repeat themselves would be to deny a
principle that the chroniclers of the Indies continually respected:
the truthfulness of their accounts. Fray Pedro takes what he relates to be true, and those two honest men of faith and trust
called Juan del Rincón and Juan de Maya are absolved after
an investigation. If this is true, it is no less true that the event
matches conventions of an old literary tradition: the tales of deer
that speak or are able to bring about misfortune; the rituals of
the hunt; or, many centuries later, the mystery of the metamor-
phoses. Or, one might ask, is there no hidden symbolism in Pero
Meogo's love poems, in which the gallant is a hunter and the
deer appears "overloaded with such a variety of meanings" (Asensio 50-53)?

There is no doubt that in the Renaissance these anecdotes
reveal the fascinating power of classical antiquity and that the
chroniclers used this mythical tradition in order to tell the truth.
Nevertheless, one must keep in mind that this fantastic truth was
necessitated by the exigencies of reception at that time. Thus, dragons, sirens, and centaurs were there for a reason and became a
part of the representation of the New World. Classical knowledge
was transliterated into a new reality. The Middle Ages were to in-
terpose their adaptive, exemplary capacity in the representations
of the unknown, especially for those people living in Renaissance
times who did not have access to classical knowledge. The world
of Antiquity was kept alive through its adaptation to new realities. Hence, we have the dragon described in the *Roman de Thèbes*
(Faral 360), the sirens of Benoît de Sainte-Maure (Faral 360), or
the centaur that is transformed into an archer in Leomarte's *Las
sumas de historia troyana* (*Compendium of Trojan History*) (194-199).
And it is that medieval interpretation which carries over to fantastic literature and, from it, to the chroniclers who wanted only

to tell the truth, even though the truth unwittingly became filled with a fantastic world in which they did not want to believe, but to which they were forced to turn in order to tell their own truths. These individuals carried a culture that was, at the same time, learned and popular. The former characteristic they had drawn from authorities such as Aristotle or Pliny or from cosmographers, while the latter they derived from books of chivalry, collections of ballads (*romanceros*) and the traditional collections of lyrics (*cancioneros*). Everything had a purpose. The names that I put forth earlier need not be considered as definite or necessary links, but are testimony of a continuity that one day would be established in the New World. That day could be any day in 1521.

The testimony recounted by a prodigious writer who was called an "uneducated idiot" ("idiota sin letras") leads us to the second part of this essay. The exemplary text written by Bernal Díaz del Castillo, *Historia verdadera de la Conquista de la Nueva España* (*True History of the Conquest of New Spain*), is quite valuable in discovering the unheard-of astonishment felt by the conquistadors as they moved through a land that could only be circumscribed by the fantastic creation of incredible narratives. Indeed, no book of chivalry equalled its greatness. In a fabulous land, peoples of a different complexion and with little clothing, cut a path for the gods: "We could not walk and the very leaders told their vassals to make room and to behold that we were gods" ("No podíamos andar y los mismos caciques decían a sus vasallos que hiciesen lugar, e que mirasen que éramos teules" [Díaz del Castillo 171]).[14]

Neither Esplandián, nor Florisel, nor Tirante had ever dreamed so much. Nor was such a triumph ever painted in even the most daring gallery. But this was the least of it, for later on, the backdrop is removed. It is no longer possible to praise the gods. Bernal Díaz del Castillo, a poor soldier from Medina del Campo, conscious of his descriptive limitations, is drawn to the rhetoric of the romances of chivalry in order to represent the heretofore unseen. In so doing, he manages to write an important page in the history of humankind. The quote that follows illustrates his need to represent the New World following conventions drawn from the books of chivalry:

And another day in the morning we arrived at the road
that we took to Estapalapa. And from that road we saw
so many populated cities and villages on water, and other
great towns on land. And that road, which lead us straight
to Mexico, astonished us, and we said that it was like the
enchanted things found in the book of Amadís... and some
of our soldiers wondered if they were not seeing things
while half-asleep. And it is not surprising that I should write
of it in this manner, for in it there is so much to praise that
I do not know how to tell it; I see things which have never
been heard, seen, or even dreamed before. (171)[15]

The conquistador was to convert into life the fiction of chivalry
at the same time that his life would become a literary paradigm.
One must not forget that from the *Sergas de Esplandián* was taken
the name of California—a certain island "very close to terrestrial
paradise" ("muy próxima al paraíso terrestre") where there were
vast quantities of gold and precious stones (Leonard 47-48; Rosenblat 26-27). One must also bear in mind that the *Sergas* are merely
the continuation of Book 5 of *Amadís* and that Feliciano de Silva
wrote *Amadís de Grecia*, a book that is purged from Don Quijote's library. It is also interesting to note that Feliciano de Silva's son, Don
Diego, might have traveled to the New World in order to live out
the story written by the father. In the same vein, a man as serious
as Agustín de Zárate, a chronicler of the conquest of Peru, makes
a reference to the life of "Diego de Silva, son of Feliciano de Silva,
a native of Ciudad Rodrigo" ("Diego de Silva, hijo de Feliciano de
Silva, natural de Ciudad Rodrigo" [Alvar, *España y America*, Note
1, 98]).

The matter of life imitating fiction is also raised in Juan de
Castellano's *Elegías de varones ilustres de Indias* (*Elegies to Illustrious
Men of the Indies*), in which one of the most celebrated and mur-
derous characters of the conquest is a dog called Amadís, to which
the poet devotes stanza after stanza, sparing us none of the savage and gory details, however concealed they may have been in
the memory of Gonzalo Fernández de Oviedo (323-329).

Indeed, Amadís is present at every crossroad, and Bernal Díaz
del Castillo becomes a transformed image of Pedro Ircio (Martínez
Ruiz and Bataillon). The latter was a presumptuous soldier who

spoke only about his life while serving in the house of the Count of Ureña and proved to be more of a hindrance than a source of help. When the soldier portrays him, he gives one of his unforgettable descriptions:

> Captain Pedro de Ircio was of medium height, lame (*paticorto*), and had a cheerful face. And he talked excessively, which thus brought about his constant tales of Don Pedro Girón and the Count of Ureña. And he was a schemer, and for this reason we called him "Agrajes sin obras," and without doing things worthy of being told, he died in Mexico. (353)[16]

Agrajes was the cousin of Amadís, the son of the King of Scotland and the Lady of the Guirnalda. His presence in the knight's four books and in the *Sergas de Esplandián* is justified by his resolute courage and the spirit of his heart. His importance in the story is highlighted in chapter 16 of the book that is dedicated wholly to him and recounts his encounter with princess Olinda, who was rescued from a storm, and his struggle with the nephew of the dwarf. Thus, while Agrajes represented the prototype of the chivalric hero, Pedro Ircio was its antithesis. He who lacks valor but possesses an abundance of words may be called "Agrajes sin obras" ("a deedless Agrajes").

We have already mentioned the presence of Amadís in the work of Bernal Díaz del Castillo, who arrived in the Indies in 1514 at age twenty-two, carrying with him a considerable cultural baggage—including the *romancero*, the *cancionero*, and a copy of *Amadís*. Between 1504, when Cortés journeyed to Hispaniola, and 1514, which marks Bernal Díaz's arrival, Jorge Coci Alemán's presses had printed the *Amadís* of Zaragoza, a beautiful book of which only one copy remains (Menéndez y Pelayo 1: 315).[17] The 1508 edition is the one that the conquistadors were to read and take to the Indies. The books of chivalry were very popular and widely published—so much so that at the beginning of his *Historia general de las Indias* (*General History of the Indias* [1535]), Gonzalo Fernández de Oviedo excuses himself for not dealing with extravagant accounts such as the ones found in *Amadís*:

> Moreover wise and natural men will heed this lesson, with greed and desire only to know and hear the works of nature.

And thus with less concern for understanding they will have to listen to me for their own good (since I do not relate the nonsense of either the lying books of Amadís or of those which depend on them). (1: 431)[18]

Fernández de Oviedo was either an exceptional or somewhat oblivious witness, for in 1519 he had written precisely one of those "preposterous and lying" books, which he entitled *Libro del muy esforzado e invencible caballero de la Fortuna propiamente llamado don Claribalte* (*Book of the Wilful and Invincible Knight of Fortune Properly Named Claribalte* [Menéndez y Pelayo 1: 432]).

Amadís, however, was not just a reference, nor the power of abstraction, nor the mockery of a brazen individual. It was one of the best-known books, and it came to adapt the art of narrating in writers such as Bernal Díaz del Castillo, whose erudition consisted of a few books of a very popular nature. Thus it has been possible to compare the portrayals of their heroes with those of *Amadís* (Gilman) or with those found in the ballads (*romances*) of Calaínos and Roland (Alvar, *El mundo americano* 4, note 2). A whole world of chivalry was replanted and from it sprang forth a way of life and a way of writing. Rosenblat, in his edition of *Amadís*, and Gilman have pointed out those key traits of the books of chivalry that were to go on to frame the details and descriptions of the New World (Gilman 108-109). Not even Cortés was free from this influence as he makes us think of himself as a loyal soldier.

I will now close with a remarkable quote from Bernal Díaz del Castillo that tells of a city upon the water, with a wide road—a city of people who, astonished, cleared the way for the Spaniards. This was Mexico's miracle in the eyes of a soldier from Medina del Campo. Cortés, in the presence of similar vistas, wrote:

The city is so grand and worthy of such admiration that, although I have said much of what could be said of it, I believe that what little I will say is almost unbelievable, for it is much grander than Granada. (336)[19]

Cortés, the former student from Salamanca, confronts the ineffable while Bernal Díaz, the uneducated soldier, draws back the curtain and speaks to us of the enchantments that appear in the books of chivalry. The key to those representations may be in chapter 11 of *Amadís:*

> and on the third day...they left that place and took to the road, and on the fifth day they found themselves near a very secure castle that stood upon sea water and the castle was called Bradoid, and it was the most beautiful castle of that land...and from one part there ran that water and in the other there was a great marsh, and the only way to enter the part that contained the water was by boat, and running across the marsh there was a path so wide that two wagons could travel upon it, one going and one coming, and at the entrance of the marsh there was a narrow bridge...and at the opening of the bridge there were two tall elm trees and the giant and Galaor saw two damsels and a nobleman beneath them. (qtd. in Gilman 111)[20]

The chronicles of the Indies have a dazzling and brilliant face. The Cuban poet José María Heredia (1842-1905) said in a renowned sonnet that to follow the footsteps of the conquistadors is to gallop while stirring up a north wind of dust. This is one side of it; the other is the world of fantasy, for only in this manner could the new reality be understood.

We have been talking about fantastic tales of ancient authors, about the fabulous medieval bestiary, and of unheard-of beings who dwell in the margins of maps and navigational charts. These are the paths which lead to the books of chivalry. In turn, these preposterous and lying works were to give meaning to the unexpected prodigy of a new life. And in the madness of those deluded men lie the belief that literature was life and that everyday actions could be transformed into a most fantastic chivalric tale.

Notes

1. "Dize el Almirante que juraban muchos hombres honrados españoles que en la Gomera estaban con doña Inés Peraza...que eran vecinos de la isla del Hierro, que cada año veían tierra al oeste de las Canarias, que es al poniente; y otros de la Gomera afirmaban otro tanto con juramento. Dice aquí el Almirante que se acuerda que estando en Portugal el año de 1484 vino uno de la isla de la Madera al rey a le pedir una carabela para ir a esta tierra que vía, el cual juraba que cada año la vía y siempre de una manera. Y también dice que se acuerda que lo mismo dezían en

las islas de los Açores y todos estos en una derrota, y en una manera de señal, y en una grandeza."

2. See also the valuable observations of Angel Rosenblat, 32-37. Here one would need to refer to the story of *El Dorado*, another chapter in which unbound imagination, greed, and the meaning of fantasy are interwoven (see Chapman). In addition, the natives of both the Canaries and America created their own fantasies, such as the story of the priest Guañañeme or the return of Quetzalcoatl, which I have dealt with, along with others, in "Canarias en el camino de las Indias" (see *España y América*).

3. See Benito Ruano for numerous illustrations and photographs.

4. This dirge appears transcribed by Bonnet in "La Isla de San Borondón."

> Frente a la Gomera
> con todo claror,
> el patrón contaba
> cosas que inventó.
>
> Porque aquella isla
> jamás la encontró,
> ni viola en su vida,
> ni a ella arribó.
>
> Era la encantada
> que desapareció
> la isla llamada
> de San Borondón.

5. "El día passado, cuando el Almirante iba al río del Oro, dixo que vido tres serenas que salieron bien alto de la mar, pero no eran tan hermosas como las pintan, que en alguna manera tenían forma de hombre en la cara. Dixo que otras veces vido algunas en Guinea, en la costa de la Manegueta." (See also 1: 19 and Rosenblat 15-38.)

6. "es una *serpiente o dragón* ... es fea de espantosa vista ... tienen por medio del espinazo levantado un cerro encrestado a manera de sierra or espinas, e paresce en sí sola muy fiera. Tiene agudos dientes e un papo luengo e ancho que le va e cuelga desde la barba al pecho, como al buey."

7. Bestiaries come from the Greek *Physiologist* (second century), a description of forty-eight animals, plants, and rocks (see Bompiani). On the medieval bestiaries see Jauss; *El Fisiólogo; Bestiaris; Bestiario medieval;* and Sebastián.

8. His *Bestiaire* dates before 1135 and the unicorn is found among the thirty-four animals that he includes in *Fisiólogo*. This text was begun with verses of six syllables and was completed in octosyllabic verses.

9. This comes from a fourteenth-century manuscript, published by G. Mazzatini in 1889 (probably written by an Umbrian author in the thirteenth century). It contains sixty-four sonnets, each devoted to an animal (Bompiani, vol. 2, s.v.). The "debased" (*envilecidas*) descriptions of the text would find themselves within what Buffon considered the inferiority of the animal species of America (see Gerbi). Regarding these texts I must point out that the *Libro della natura degli animali* is

found in two editions: the Venetian, edited by Goldstanlo and R. Wendriner (*Ein tosco-venezianischer Bestiarius*, 1892) and the Tuscan, edited by M. S. Garver and K. McKenzie.

10. This is already present in the *Diario del Descubrimiento*. One should consult, however, José Durand's thought-provoking book, *Ocaso de sirenas, esplendor de manatíes*, which, unfortunately does not take into account Nieremberg's book. In Nieremberg's work, the manatee is found (along with its corresponding illustration), and its description (247-249), taken from Oviedo, is enriched with numerous observations. See my *Juan de Castellanos* for an examination of the word (250-252) and reproductions of illustrations of manatees by Gilii (plate 12) and Rochefort (plate 14).

11. In the sixteenth century, Ambrosio Par, a surgeon with a critical spirit, wrote: "everything which is said of unicorns is something [which is] invented for the pleasure of painters and historians" ("tout ce que l'on dit des licornes est chose inventée à plaisir par les peintres et les historiographes" [Gougand, 43, 55]). In this book may be found curious and abundant documentation on the virtues of the unicorn.

12. "En el páramo de este valle de Santo Domingo, sucedió una cosa muy de notar, y por parecerme tal, la quise escribir aquí. Dos soldados, hombres de bien, y de fe y crédito, llamados Juan del Rincón y Juan de Maya, subieron a lo alto del páramo a cazar o matar venados con los arcabuces, donde, después de algo cansados del camino que habían llevado, se les puso delante una cierva a tiro de arcabuz y aun a tiro de ballesta, y tan cerca que claramente vían dar las balas en ella; y aunque le dieron muchos arcabuzazos, no sólo no la mataron, pero ni aun parecía haberle herido, antes por momentos se les hacía invisible y visible, donde los soldados vinieron a conjeturar no ser aquélla cierva, sino algún maligno espíritu que, transformado en la figura de aquel animal, se les había puesto delante; y estando ellos en esta confusión y consideración, oyeron dar grandes voces desde lo alto de un cerro que cerca de sí tenían, que en lengua española o castellana llamaban a estos dos soldados por sus nombres, y cobrando doblado espanto de oir las voces desde un lugar que era imposible haber subido españoles a él, dejaron la caza y, espantados y admirados de lo que habían visto y oído, se volvieron a donde su capitán estaba alojado, y procuraron inquerir y saber si aquel día había algún español andado de aquella parte donde habían oído las voces; pero ningún rastro dello hallaron, lo que de todo punto les hizo creer andar algún espíritu maligno por aquellos páramos y desiertos."

13. "El día de Pascua, en Primavera, el rey Artús había reunido la corte en Caradigán, su castillo; nunca se vio tan rica corte, pues tenía muchos y buenos caballeros, atrevidos, valerosos y fieros, y también ricas damas y doncellas, hijas de reyes, hermosas y gentiles; antes que la corte se separara, el rey dijo a sus caballeros que quería cazar el Ciervo Blanco a fin de restablecer la costumbre."

14. On *teul*, 'god,' see Alvar, *El mundo americano*, 97-98.

15. "Y otro día por la mañana llegamos a la calzada ancha y vamos camino de Estapalapa. Y desque vimos tantas ciudades y villas pobladas en el agua, y en tierra firme otras grandes poblaciones, y aquella calzada, tan derecha y por nivel cómo iba a Méjico, nos quedamos admirados, y decíamos que parecía a las cosas de encantamiento que cuentan en el libro de Amadís . . . y algunos de nuestros soldados decían que si aquello que veían, si era entre sueños, y no es de maravillar que yo lo

escriba así desta manera, porque hay mucho que ponderar en ello que no sé cómo lo cuente: veo cosas nunca oídas, vistas, ni aun soñadas, como víamos" (171).

16. "El capitán Pedro de Ircio era de mediana estatura y paticorto, y tenía el rostro alegre, y muy plático en demasía, que así acontecería que siempre contaba cuentos de don Pedro Girón y del conde de Ureña, y era ardid, y a esta causa le llamábamos Agrajes sin obras, y sin hacer cosas que contar sea, murió en México."

17. Alejandro Cioranescu in *Estudios* places some importance on *Amadís* and the conquest, but follows Leonard's line of thought (39-41). The burning of Cortés's vessels as a chivalric episode that comes from *Palmerín de Inglaterra* is recorded in the same work (44).

18. "Mas los hombres sabios y naturales atenderán a esta lección, no con otra mayor codicia y deseo que por saber y oir las obras de natura; y así con más despreocupación del entendimiento habrán por bien de oirme (pues no cuento los disparates de los libros mentirosos de Amadís ni los que de ellos dependen)." See also the *Quincuagenas*, which Menéndez y Pelayo cites in *Orígenes de la novela*, 431, Note 2.

19. "La cual ciudad es tan grande y de tanta admiración que aunque mucho de lo que de ella podría decir dije, lo poco que diré creo que es casi increíble, porque es muy mayor que Granada."

20. "y al tercer día...partieron de allí y fueron su camino y al quinto día halláronse cerca de un castillo muy fuerte que estaba sobre un agua salada y el castillo había nombre Bradoid, y era el más hermoso que había en toda aquella tierra...y de la una parte corría aquel agua y de la otra había un gran tremedal, y de la parte del agua no se podía entrar sino por barca y de contra el tremedal había una calzada tan ancha que podía ir una carreta y otra venir, mas a la entrada del tremedal había una puente estrecha...y a la entrada de la puente estaban dos olmos altos y el gigante y Galaor vieron debajo de ellos dos doncellas y un escudero." (See also Cortés 406 and 41a-b.)

Works Cited

Aguado, Fray Pedro de. *Historia de Santa Marta*. Ed. Jerónimo Bécker. Madrid: J. Rates, 1961.

Alegría, Ricardo. *Las primeras representaciones gráficas del indio americano 1493-1523*. San Juan: Instituto de Cultura Puertorriqueña, 1978.

Alonso, Amado. *Castellano, español, idioma nacional*. 2nd ed. Buenos Aires: Losada, 1943.

Alvar, Manuel. *España y América cara a cara*. Valencia: Bello, 1975.

———. *Juan de Castellanos, tradición española y realidad americana*. Bogotá: Instituto Caro y Cuervo, 1972.

———. *El mundo americano de Bernal Díaz del Castillo*. Santander: Bedia, 1968.

Amadís de Gaula. Ed. Angel Rosenblat. Madrid: Castalia, 1987.

Asensio, Eugenio. *Poética y realidad en el cancionero peninsular de la Edad Media*. 2nd ed. Madrid: Gredos, 1970.

Bataillon, Marcel. "Agrajes sin obras." *Studi Ispanici* (1962): 29-35.

Bécquer, Gustavo Adolfo. "La corza blanca." *Selección de Leyendas*. Montevideo: C. García, 1938.

Benito Ruano, Eloy. *La leyenda de San Borondón, octava isla canaria*. Valladolid: Casa-Museo de Colón, Seminario de Historia de América de la Universidad de Valladolid, 1978.

Bestiario medieval. Ed. I. Malaxeverría. 3rd ed. Madrid: Siruela, 1963.

Bestiaris. Ed. Saverio Panunzio. 2 vols. Barcelona: Barcino, 1963-1964.

Bompiani, Valentino Silvio. *Diccionario literario de obras y personajes de todos los tiempos y de todos los países*. Barcelona: Hora, 1988

Bonnet, B. "La isla de San Borondón." *Revista de Historia de la Laguna* 4-7 (1927-1929).

Cabrera Perera, Antonio. *Las islas Canarias en el mundo clásico*. Canary Islands: Vice Consejería de Cultura y Deportes, Gobierno de Canarias, 1988.

Castellanos, Juan de. *Elegías de varones ilustres de Indias*. 1589. Biblioteca de Autores Españoles. Madrid: M. Rivadeneyra, 1874.

Chapman, Walker. *The Golden Dream*. Indianapolis: Bobbs-Merrill, 1967.

Chrétien de Troyes. *Erec y Enid*. Trans. Carlos Alvar. Madrid: Editora Nacional, 1982.

Cioranescu, Alejandro. *Colón humanista*. Madrid: Editorial Prensa Española, 1967.

————. *Estudios de literatura española y comparada*. La Laguna de Tenerife: Univ. de la Laguna, 1954.

Clavería, Carlos. Le chevalier délibéré *de Olivier de la Marche y sus versiones españolas del siglo XVI*. Zaragoza: Institución "Fernando el Católico," 1950.

Columbus, Christopher. *Diario del descubrimiento*. Ed. Manuel Alvar. 2 vols. Las Palmas de Gran Canaria, 1976.

Cortés, Hernán. *Segunda carta de relación*. Ed. Manuel Alcalá. Mexico City: Porrúa, 1963.

Covarrubias Horozco, Sebastián. *Tesoro de la lengua Castellana o española*. 1611. Ed. Martín de Riquer. Barcelona: S.A. Horta, 1943.

Díaz del Castillo, Bernal. *Historia verdadera de la conquista de la Nueva España*. Biblioteca de Autores Españoles. Madrid: Espasa-Calpe, 1933.

Durand, José. *Ocaso de sirenas, esplendor de manatíes*. 2nd ed. Mexico City: Fondo de Cultura Económica, 1983.

Faral, Edmond. *Recherches sur les sources latines des contes et romans courtois du Moyen Age*. Paris: H. Champion, 1967.

Fernández de Oviedo, Gonzalo. *Historia general y natural de las Indias, Islas y Tierra Firme del Mar Océano*. 1535. Biblioteca de Autores Españoles. Madrid: Atlas 1959.

The Fifth Book of the Most Pleasant and Delectable History of Amadis de Gaule, Containing the First Part of the . . . Acts of Esplandian. London, printed by T. J. for A. Kembe and C. Tyus, 1664.

El Fisiólogo: Bestiario medieval. Ed. N. Guglielmi. Buenos Aires: Editorial Universitaria de Buenos Aires, 1971.

Gerbi, Antonello. *La disputa del Nuevo Mundo*. Trans. A. Alatorre. Mexico City: Fondo de Cultura Económica, 1963.

Gheerbrant, Alain Jean Chevalier. *Dictionnaire des symboles*. Paris: Seghers, 1974.

Gilman, Stephen. "Bernal Díaz del Castillo and Amadís de Gaula." *Studia Philologica*. Madrid: Gredos, 1961. 2: 99-114.

Gougand, Henri. *Les animaux magiques de notre univers*. Paris: Solar, 1973.

Heredia, José María de. "The Conquerors of Gold." *The Trophies with Other Sonnets.* Trans. John Myers O'Hara and John Hervey. New York: John Day, 1929. 207-241.

Jauss, Hans Robert. "Entstehung und Strukturwandel der allegorischen Dichtung." *Grundriss der romanischen Literaturen des Mittelalters.* Vol. 6.1. Heidelberg: C. Winter Universitätsverlag, 1968. 146-244.

Jérez, Francisco de, Pedro de Cieza de León, and Agustín de Zárate. *Crónicas de la Conquista del Perú.* Mexico City: Editorial Nueva España, 195-?.

Leonard, Irving A. *Los libros del conquistador.* Trans. Mario Monteforte Toledo. Mexico City: Fondo de Cultura Económica, 1953.

Leomarte. *Las sumas de historia troyana.* Ed. Agapito Rey. Madrid: S. Aguirre, 1932.

Libro della natura degli animali. Ed. M. Goldstanlo and R. Wendriner. Halle: S. Niemayer, 1982.

⸻. Ed. M. S. Garver and K. McKenzie and C. Segre. *Studi Romanzi* 8 (1912). Rome: Società filologica romana, 1912.

Martínez Ruiz, Juan. "Agrajes sin obras." *Ibérida* 2 (1959): 103-130.

Menéndez y Pelayo, Marcelino. *Orígenes de la novela.* 4 vols. Madrid: Bailly-Baillere e hijos, 1905-1915.

Menéndez Pidal, Ramón. *Manual de gramática histórica.* 6th ed. Madrid: Espasa-Calpe, 1941.

Nieremberg, P. Juan Eusebio. *Historia Naturae.* Antwerp, 1635.

Núñez Cabeza de Vaca, Alvar. *Comentarios.* 1555. Biblioteca de Autores Españoles 22. Madrid: Rivadeneyra, 1852.

Rosenblat, Angel. *La primera visión de América y otros estudios.* 2nd ed. Caracas: Ministerio de Educación, Dirección Técnica, Departamento de Publicaciones, 1969.

Sebastián, Santiago. *El fisiólogo, atribuido a S. Epifanio, seguido de El Bestiario Toscano.* Madrid: Ediciones Tuero, 1986.

Thaun, Philippe de. *Bestiaire.* Ed. E. Walterg. Lund-Paris, 1900.

Vigneras, Louis André. *La búsqueda del Paraíso y las legendarias islas del Atlántico.* Valladolid: Casa-Museo de Colón, Seminario de Historia de América de la Universidad de Valladolid, 1976.

◆ Chapter 5

Reading in the Margins of Columbus

Margarita Zamora

In a recent study on the colonization of Peru, Steve J. Stern traced the political and economic processes that transformed various and distinct Andean groups into a homogeneous, subordinate, and marginalized caste of "Indians." Stern's analysis reminds us that whether we use the colonial term "Indian," or the more geographically precise "Amerindian," or even the more politically correct "Native American," we are in each case speaking of a European construction that arose in the concrete historical circumstances of the conquest of America. The pre-Columbian world knew no such category of humankind. Columbus introduced the term "Indian" to refer to the indigenous peoples of the Caribbean in order to designate a political entity that would complement his geographic conception of the Asiatic nature of the lands he discovered. His testimony suggests that for him "Indians" were simply those who inhabited the territory he called "las Indias Occidentales," the Western Indies, a rather imprecise geographical entity comprised of over 700 islands and a mainland situated somewhere beyond the "India of the Ganges." He apparently believed most of its inhabitants were subjects of the Great Khan, or at least economically and militarily subordinate to him.

183

Columbus's testimony suggests that in his view Indians differed from Europeans in various ways, all of which facilitated
their exploitation by the Spanish. His testimony on the peoples
of the Caribbean often reads like a military scouting report.[1] In
fact, to scout or reconnoiter for the purpose of gaining an advantage were important connotations of discovery in the fifteenth
and sixteenth centuries. To Columbus the inhabitants of the territory he surveyed seemed a clean slate. They had no religion, or at
least none worthy of the name.[2] They also lacked a government,
a true language, real weapons, courage, and so on. Columbus's
Indians seem to be defined precisely by what they lack, in a sort
of what's-missing-in-this-picture strategy of representation. Such
observations are not to be understood literally, of course; they are
value judgments whose strength lies not in their empirical accuracy, but in their resonance with the ideological expectations of
the interpretive community from which they arise and to which
they are addressed. Columbus's image of the naked Indian—"All
of them go around as naked as their mothers bore them" ("ellos andan todos desnudos como su madre los parió"[3] [64-65])—responds
to the desire to discover a vulnerable and pliable other as counterpart of the European in the enterprise of political, economic, and
cultural expansion initiated by Spain in 1492. The effectiveness
of Columbus's representation of Amerindian reality is confirmed
by the elevation from image to icon of the naked Indian in the
woodcuts illustrating the various editions of the Columbian letter announcing the Discovery. The natives of the Indies, as they
appear in these illustrations, reproduce the main features of the
Columbian verbal image, strikingly contrasted to Europe's conceptualization of its own plenitude, as if to underscore the significance of Indian lacking through the juxtaposition. On one side
of the picture King Ferdinand (no Isabella in sight) is seated on
his throne, bearded, fully clothed, scepter raised commandingly
in hand. An ocean separates him from the Indian shores where a
group of naked adolescent-like Indians cower at the sight of the
approaching caravels.[4] What is missing in the Indians is constituted by association with the figure of Ferdinand—virility, civility,
and authority—the fundamental attributes of human plenitude
according to both classical and Judeo-Christian conceptions.

Yet one searches in vain in Columbian writing for a theory of "Indianness," akin to those available for Jews, Moslems, or heathens in the European thought of his time and for the Indians themselves in the second half of the sixteenth century. The observation is, of course, not intended to chastise Columbus for some intellectual shortcoming, but to point out that his testimony is not concerned with articulating a theory on the nature of the Amerindians (a theological or ethnological question), but with defining their political and military status with respect to the Spanish. His descriptions of the natives usually go only as far as is necessary to define the types of political, economic, and military relations the Spanish would be able to establish with them in a manner consistent, ideologically and pragmatically, with the terms and stated goals of the enterprise of discovery set forth in the "Capitulations of Santa Fe."[5] Addressing Ferdinand and Isabella in the "Diario" Columbus testifies:

> this island and all the others are as much yours as Castile, for nothing is lacking except settlement and ordering the Indians to do whatever Your Highnesses may wish. . . . they do not have arms and they are all naked, and of no skill in arms, and so very cowardly that a thousand would not stand against three. And so they are fit to be ordered and made to work and plant and to everything else that may be needed. (235-237)

And yet a very different image of the Indian attaches itself stubbornly to Columbus:

> And the natives very willingly showed my people where the water was, and they themselves brought the filled barrels to the boat and delighted in pleasing us. (87)

> They are the best and most gentle people in the world. (231)

> Such good-hearted people, so open in giving and so fearful that all of them outdo themselves in order to give the Christians all that they have, and when the Christians arrive they run to bring everything. (257)[6]

These passages are representative of what I would like to call the image of the beatified Indian as a sort of Christian *avant la lettre*, existing in a spiritual Golden Age where all that is missing to attain salvation is the news of Christ. It is this image that came to be identified with Columbus's original testimony on the Discovery. Moreover, it has become the West's culturally sanctioned image of the Indian informing, in varying degrees, the romantic "noble savage," the multiple permutations of the "indigenista" movement in Latin America throughout the twentieth century, and the revaluation of Native American cultures currently underway in the United States.

Assumptions about the special authority and privilege of this "founding image" explain its cultural resilience and longevity, assumptions that ultimately depend on the affirmation of Columbus's authorship. But can the beatification of the Indians be attributed to Columbus and maintained on his authority? I believe not. This position is not in and of itself original. Recent criticism has pointed out the duplicity of Columbian testimony on the Indians. But it seems to have overlooked the paradox implicit in maintaining the testimonial authority of Columbus to support not only different but even contradictory interpretations of Columbian writing.[7] What has been put into question is either the acuity of Columbus's readers or Columbus's moral fiber, not the textual fabric from which the image is cut. It is a fact, however, that the Columbian texts have suffered various alterations throughout the history of their transmission to present-day readers. I will be focusing on two of those alterations in this essay: the addition of marginal annotations to Columbus's testimony on the Discovery and the subsequent suppression of that marginal writing. Each of these interventions was posterior to Columbus's, yet they constitute decisive mediations in the formation of the image of the Indians associated with the Discovery.

In the remainder of this essay I will argue that the source of this image is found, not in Columbus's testimony but in the margins of Columbus. That is, it is the product of a particular reading of the Columbian text. I will be using the notion of marginality both literally—to refer to a concrete physical aspect of the "Diario" as we have it and its suppression throughout the editing history of the text—and metaphorically, as a theoretical orientation for a discussion of the consequences of reading Columbus in and from the margins of the "Diario."

The first European image of the Indian appears in the so-called "Diario" of the first voyage, the only surviving version of the journal presumably kept by Columbus and later extracted, corrected, and annotated by Bartolomé de Las Casas. In the Las Casas manuscript the "Diario" is presented with the "Relación del tercer viaje" on seventy-six continuously numbered folios. The main text attributed to Columbus, the marginal comments, and the numerous revisions are all in Las Casas's hand. The manuscript is striking in that the margins are very generous, in contrast to Las Casas's other holographs, where each page is typically filled to the maximum with text, notes, and corrections.[8] Las Casas's marginal commentary assumes three distinct forms: there is a sketch of a quill pen in the left margin opposite the entry for October 11, where the narrative of the Discovery begins, the abbreviation "n—" (for "Note") appears frequently throughout the text, as does a more elaborate commentary that ranges from a single word to several phrases. Sometimes the main text is scored with a line in the left margin or by underlining. Also in contrast to his practice elsewhere, as Varela points out, Las Casas is careful to distinguish the commentary from the corrections by consistently placing it in the left margin, while the revisions are typically placed on the right-hand side. The commentary usually appears boxed-off from the main text, further accentuating its presence and autonomy. The entire text is written with a careful hand, in a clear and legible script.

Las Casas's edition of the "Diario" (he called it the "libro de su primera navegación y descubrimiento d'estas Indias" ["Book of His First Navigation and Discovery of These Indies"]) was published for the first time in 1825 by Martín Fernández de Navarrete as part of a multivolume collection of writings dealing with Spanish exploration. The Navarrete edition appeared without most of the marginal notes by Las Casas, however, nor was any mention made of the more than one thousand revisions to the primary text also contained in the margins and between the lines of the manuscript, thereby effectively erasing Las Casas's pen from the text and leaving the impression that the "Diario" was a simple and straightforward transcription of Columbus's "journal." All subsequent editions and translations between 1825 and 1892 were based on Navarrete and thus also suppressed the marginal text.

It was not until the edition known as the *Raccolta* appeared in 1892 that the presence of Las Casas in the Columbian text was acknowledged, though only partially. Cesare de Lollis returned to the original manuscript and included most, but not all, of the marginal commentary, without any explanation of the criteria employed in his selection.[9] Since then most of the Spanish editions of the "Diario" and all of the English translations I am aware of suppress the presence of Las Casas's pen in the text.[10] This despite the fact that as of 1962 a facsimile of much of the manuscript has been available in Carlos Sanz's facsimile edition. Ironically, Sanz himself silently omitted many of the marginalia in his transcription. Even the latest diplomatic edition and English translation, done by Oliver Dunn and James E. Kelley in a bilingual format, omits the marginalia, also without explanation, from the English half of the book. Recent editions and translations, beginning with Manuel Alvar's transcription in 1976, include most of Las Casas's commentary. But it is usually relegated to the notes, which, at the very least, implies a statement on its inferior status with respect to the main text. Such a subordination of the marginalia graphically renders the commentary an isolated and disjointed writing rather than the integral component of the "Diario" Las Casas conceived it to be.[11] The physical integrity of Las Casas's text is respected only in Consuelo Varela's 1989 edition. Varela appears to hedge her bet in the introduction, however, when she anticipates the surprise that the inclusion of the "Diario" and the "Relación" in an edition of the collected works of Las Casas is likely to cause. Rather than affirm the decisive mediation that their inclusion in the Las Casas collection suggests, she gingerly sidesteps its boldest implication—that Las Casas's pen and not Columbus's defines these texts—merely pointing out the importance and value of the marginal annotations themselves.[12]

In outlining the editing history of the Las Casas manuscript my purpose is not to criticize editorial practices, but to call attention to an integral part of the text as we have it—the marginalia—and to point out what to my mind has become an institutionalized editorial fiction—creating the illusion of the pristineness and absolute authority of Columbus's voice in the "Diario" through the wholesale suppression or selective manipulation of the marginal commentary.[13] In fact, the marginalia play a fundamental role in the text that has come down to us. For this reason, I will consider some of the consequences of reading without the marginalia and examine what happens to the image of the Indian when one reads it from the margins of Columbus.[14]

The positivist notion that the past is readily accessible through the study of documentary and physical evidence has undoubtedly contributed in no small way to the persistent editorial resistance to the fact that the only source we possess on the Discovery is not a fair copy of a primary source, or even a copy of a copy, but a highly manipulated version of a copy of whatever Columbus may have written.[15] Even those who acknowledge Las Casas's intervention in the text typically feel obliged either to shield Columbus's integrity from the onus of the Lascasian violation by accusing Las Casas of wholesale fabrication of the text or, conversely, to insist on his absolute fidelity to the Admiral's *ipsissima verba* in the transcription of the first-person passages and to the substance, tone, and tenor of the original in the paraphrases that constitute some 80 percent of the text as we have it.[16] Although these two positions appear to represent opposite views with respect to Las Casas's handling of the primary text, they share nevertheless a fundamental belief in the need to maintain the integrity and authority of the Columbian word. In suggesting that Las Casas was a ventriloquist speaking through a Columbus-dummy or, conversely, a faithful and passive conduit for Columbus's voice, what is ultimately affirmed is the privilege of the Admiral's testimony and the fiction that it is available to us in a fundamentally pristine text. Yet in the final analysis neither those who vituperate Las Casas nor those who hold him up as a model of editorial fidelity can ignore the presence of another's pen in the Columbian "Diario."

The unique physical appearance of the Las Casas manuscript, with its ample margins and highlighted commentary, suggests that it not only served the likely purposes of *aide-memoire* and citation source for Las Casas's treatises and histories, but also that it may have been destined for publication or, at the very least, for circulation among other readers. One thing is clear, Las Casas assigns an exceedingly prominent role to the margins of this work. But the very nature of the commentary itself is perhaps the strongest evidence that he was not writing for himself alone. While many of the annotations simply call attention to material contained in a particular portion of the main text, others correct Columbian errors (usually of a geographic or linguistic nature), or interpret passages of the main text based on Las Casas's personal experience in the Indies. For example, a linguistic note on the Arawak word *bohío,* which Columbus confused for the name of an island, reads as follows: "The Indians of those islands called houses *bohío* and for this reason I believe that the Admiral did not understand correctly; he must have been referring to the island of Hispaniola, which they called Haiti."[17] It seems unlikely that this type of simple linguistic explanation, of which there are many in the text, would have been intended for Las Casas himself. But there are other dimensions to these annotations that bear noting. In the editor's corrective stance with respect to Columbus's linguistic incompetence there is an ostentation of the commentator's superior familiarity with the subject matter and a questioning of the Admiral's perceptions and judgments, which ultimately result in the adoption of a critical reading posture with respect to the primary text.

Perhaps the most significant aspect of the marginal commentary is the degree of control it exercises over the primary text. The "Diario" is commonly described as a summary of Columbus's journal. Yet in the absence of the original there is no way to tell if Las Casas's paraphrase is reductive or expansive. Moreover, a close analysis of the main text shows that not all the commentary resides in the margins. Some obviously explanatory and anachronistic observations are interpolated in various places, sometimes in parentheses or, more disturbingly for those concerned with the integrity of the Columbian word, embedded almost seamlessly in the paraphrase. Let us recall the reservation expressed in the entry for October 30 about the accuracy of the copy with which Las Casas was working, or the anachronistic intrusion of the Arawak name of the island of Guanahani (Columbus's San Salvador) before the first contact with the natives from whom Columbus would have learned it, or speaking of Florida many years before it was discovered, or the comical exclamations of incredulity regarding the ephemeral islands Columbus was seeking in the vicinity of what later was to be known as the Floridean peninsula. How many more are there that cannot be detected? Clearly the primary text has been violated, not only by the relatively benign operation of paraphrasing, but by the physical invasion of the marginal discourse into the presumably unadulterated Columbian narrative.[18] In instances like these, and others less readily detectable, the editorial voice is affecting to speak through Columbus. The distinction between the author's enunciation and the editor's has been effectively blurred.

So far we have seen that the physical disposition of the text in Las Casas's manuscript underscores the margins. The main text takes shape inside and in relation to them. It is in fact impossible to read Columbus without also reading the Las Casas marginalia unless one physically manipulates the page to block out the commentary. The eye continually skips from the body text to the border and back. From Las Casas's explanations, additions, corrections, and signals we learn to depend on the marginal writing to understand the primary text. And before long we sense that the text is simply not complete without it. Its very existence speaks of the necessity of the supplement, of the insufficiency of the main text.

And what exactly do we read in the margins of Columbus? What insufficiency does it address? What can the marginal reading yield? First and perhaps most importantly, it situates us in a critical stance with respect to the primary text. To the extent that it puts in question Columbus's judgments, interpretations, representations, actions, and so forth it renders his authority a relative value. Moreover, in questioning the accuracy of the source Las Casas himself was working with, it calls attention to the fact that even the text's integrity is relative. The commentary leads one to the conclusion that the primary text is neither an infallible nor even a stable and complete entity. Ultimately, it argues for the need to question, criticize, and revise Columbus.

The marginal text draws the reader's attention to those portions of the primary text where Columbus's testimony speaks of Arawak generosity, intelligence, diligence, and the Arawaks' peaceable and welcoming reception of the Christians. More importantly, the marginal reading renders these passages ironic, since such encomiastic observations by Columbus are frequently joined to an affirmation of the ease with which Spanish domination and exploitation could be established and maintained. The editorial voice's critical appraisal of the patently un-Christian intentions expressed by Columbus is explicit, and often even bitingly sarcastic or openly denunciatory. On November 12, for example, Columbus testifies that the previous day six young men in a canoe came alongside the ship, and when five of the six boarded he ordered them to be detained. Later he sent some of his crew ashore to take female captives so that the Indian men "would behave better in Spain, having women from their country, than without them" ("porque mejor se comporten los hombres en España aviendo mugeres de su tierra que sin ellas" [146]). Las Casas quips sarcastically in the margin, "this was not the best thing in the world" ("no fue lo mejor del mundo esto" [146]). A few lines later Columbus relates that a single man in a canoe had approached the ship later that evening and asked to be taken with the others. Apparently he was the husband of one of the captives and father of her three children who were also being held on board. The marginal annotation demands, "Why didn't you give him back his children?" ("porque no le distes sus hijos" [148]). On December 25 one of Columbus's ships runs aground on a reef and must be abandoned. The Admiral describes at some length the invaluable help he and his crew received from the local Indian *cacique:*

> when he learned of it [the disabled ship], they said that he cried and sent all his people from the town with many large canoes to unload everything from the ship. And thus it was done and in a very brief time everything from the decks was unloaded, so great was the care and diligence that that king exercised. And he himself and his brothers and relatives were as diligent [unloading] the ship as in guarding what was taken to land in order that everything would be well cared for. From time to time he sent one of his relatives to the Admiral, weeping, to console him, saying that he should not be sorrowful or annoyed because he would give him all that he had. (Dunn and Kelley 281)[19]

The image of the good Indian is the product of Las Casas's pen, not Columbus's. But it is not merely a pretty picture, product of some bucolic nostalgia for a lost Golden Age. The marginal reading

yields the corrosive, subversive intentionality of Las Casas's idealization. The image of the Indian that arises from the margins of
Columbus is contrastive, oppositional, polemical, and ultimately
condemnatory. Las Casas turns Columbus's own words against
him; his testimony becomes a witness against itself. Even when
the marginal note is not explicit, its function only to call attention
to particular passages, it is frequently an accusatory finger pointed
at the main text. The annotation to the passage cited above reads,
"Note here the humanity of the Indians in contrast to the tyrants
who have extirpated them" ("nótese aquí la humanidad de los yndios contra los tyranos que los an estirpado" [280]). Such comments
are reminiscent of the tone and tenor of the denunciatory *Brevísima
relación de la destrucción de las Indias*, in which Las Casas painstak-
ingly documents, place by place, the genocide perpetrated by the
Spanish. It is in the context of Lascasian discourse against the conquest that the image of the beatified Indian must be situated. Read
from the margins of Columbus, it is a disturbing, haunting image
not just, or even primarily, of the Indian but of European injustice.
The marginal writing inscribes the reproach into the image, which
finally comes to embody the condemnation.

The strategy is no doubt self-serving, since Las Casas's editorial
prerogative is the direct beneficiary of the undermining of Columbus's authority. But it is more than that. It is consistent with the
position he championed in all his written work and political practice: the negotiation for the Indians of a definitive and unassailable
place at the center of the human community.[20] The ideological de-
marginalization Las Casas advocated for the Indian is mirrored in
the interpretive strategy he applied to the Columbian text through
a commentary that invades and finally transforms the primary
text. For Las Casas writing in the margins of Columbus was a
choice with profound ideological consequences. The marginal text
is, in fact, Las Casas's reading of Columbus, an interpretation that
becomes a creative act, fundamentally altering whatever text may
have existed before him.

The marginal text does not coerce us to accept the image of the
Indian it promotes; it does, however, make it impossible for us to
read Columbus unquestioningly. To read in the margins of Columbus requires only that we assume a critical posture. In choosing

to suppress the marginalia we do not eradicate Las Casas's pen from the text, but merely fail to recognize the critical nature of the mediation. In so doing, we lose sight of the fact that the image of the Indian that has endured in our culture is not the product of an original, authoritative, definitive word but of a critical reading, a supplemental writing that questions, corrects, protests, and condemns.

Notes

1. I would like to thank the Institute for Research in the Humanities of the University of Wisconsin for its support of research contributing to this essay. I have discussed this aspect of the Columbian Discovery in "Abreast of Columbus: Gender and Discovery."

2. "I believe that they would become Christians very easily, for it seemed to me that they had no religion" ("y creo que ligeramente se harían cristianos que me pareçió que ninguna secta tenían" [68]); see "Diario," Sat., October 13; Dunn and Kelley 69. Statements to this effect appear repeatedly throughout the "Diario."

3. All English translations are from Dunn and Kelley's diplomatic transcription of Las Casas's manuscript. I have converted all Spanish abbreviations in order to facilitate reading.

4. See Alegría, especially figures 1, 3, and 5.

5. This is the contractual agreement between the Crown and Columbus signed on April 17, 1492. An English translation of this document can be found in Gómez Moriana and Mantini 383-385.

6. "esta Isla y todas las otras son así suyas como Castilla: que aquí no falta salvo assiento y mandarles hazer lo que quisieren.... ellos no tienen armas y son todos desnudos y de ningún ingenio en las armas y muy cobardes que mill no aguardarían tres. Y así son buenos p[ar]a les mandar y les hazer trabajar y sembrar y todo lo otro que fuere menester" (234-236).

"y ellos de muy buena gana le enseñavan a mi gente adonde estava el agua y ellos mesmos trayan los barriles llenos al batel y se folgavan mucho de nos hazer plazer" (86).

"son la mejor gente del mundo y mansa" (230).

"gente de tan buenos coraçones y francos p[ar]a dar y tan temerosos que ellos de deshazían todos por dar a los cristianos quanto tenían" (256).

7. The works of Carpentier, Hulme, Pastor, Sale, and Todorov are the most recent representatives of this reading tradition.

8. I am relying to a great extent on Varela's description of the manuscripts in Fray Bartolomé de Las Casas, *Obras Completas* 14: 12, since I have been able to consult only Sanz's photocopy.

9. The abbreviation "ño" was acknowledged by de Lollis only the first four times it appeared.

10. Most of the major translations into other European languages follow this

same pattern. On the editing history of the "Diario" see Morison, Fuson, and Henige.

11. Of the most recent and important translations Cioranescu's French version presents a limited selection of Las Casas's commentary in the notes. The prevailing criterion of selection here appears to be geographical. Ferro's Italian translation similarly omits some commentary, at times justifying it with pronouncements on its irrelevance. See, for example, note 1, "Due irrelevanti postille del Las Casas richiamano qui l'attenzione date delle partenze da Granada e da Palos" (20). The question such a pronouncement immediately raises is, of course, to whom is it irrelevant? Certainly not to Las Casas, who penned the comments.

12. "At first glance the inclusion of the "Diario" and the "Relación" in the *Colección* may seem surprising, an inclusion that nevertheless is its own justification. Las Casas was not only a faithful copyist of the Columbian works, as will be seen ahead, but also an annotator of the text in whose margins he left many very valuable postilles" ("A primera vista puede que sorprenda la inclusión [del Diario y la Carta] en la *Colección*, inclusión que se justifica por sí misma: Las Casas no fue sólo un copista fiel de la obra colombina, como se verá más adelante, sino también un anotador del texto en cuyos márgenes dejó muchas apostillas valiosísimas" [11, my translation]). Varela may feel some personal awkwardness here since in her *Cristóbal Colón: Textos y documentos completos* she includes both the "Diario" and the "Letter of the Third Voyage" and characterizes Las Casas's role as that of a faithful copyist: "Las Casas was a faithful copyist, even when he did not understand the passage" ("Las Casas era un copista fiel, incluso cuando no acertaba a dar con el sentido del pasaje" [xxiii]). I consider the significance of the "Diario"/"Relación" relationship in Las Casas's text in *Reading Columbus*, forthcoming.

13. For a critique of modern editing practices with respect to the "Diario" see Morison, Fuson, and Henige.

14. Vázquez has done a valuable preliminary study of the nature and content of the commentary itself. Note that what I am proposing here is significantly different—that the annotations and the main text be read organically. This, of course, requires that the text be published integrally, as it appears in Las Casas's manuscript.

15. Rumeu de Armas has argued that Las Casas was working with an already-summarized version of the Columbian text, to which he then added his own commentary and corrections. This, of course, would make the Las Casas text at least twice removed from the original.

16. The original has been lost, and the Las Casas version is the only one we have with the exception of a few quotations, apparently derived from a copy of the Columbian text different from the one used by Las Casas, which appear in Ferdinand Columbus's biography of his father. Ferdinand's *Historie* survived only in an Italian translation; the Spanish original is lost.

17. "bohío llamavan los indios de aquellas islas a las casas y por eso creo que no entendía bien el almirante, ante devía de dezir por la isla española que llamavan haití." The marginalia have not been translated into English, therefore I have provided my own translations of the commentary.

18. I discuss the nature, extent, and consequences of Las Casas's manipulation

of the primary text in "Todas son palabras formales del Almirante: Las Casas y el Diario de Colón."

19. "como lo supo dize que lloró y enbió toda su gente de la villa con canoas muy grandes y muchas a descargar todo lo de la nao. Y así se hizo y se descargó todo lo de las cubiertas en muy breve espacio: tanto fue el grande aviamiento y diligencia que aquel rey dió y el con su p[er]sona con hermanos y parientes estavan poniendo diligençia asi en la nao como en la guarda de lo que se sacava a tierra p[ar]a que todo estuviese a muy buen recaudo. De quando en quando enbiava uno de sus parientes al almirante llorando a lo consolar dizendo que no rescibiese pena ni enojo que él daría quanto tuviese."

20. I am paraphrasing Anthony Pagden's lucid assessment of Las Casas's contributions to the debate on the nature of the Indians in *The Fall of Natural Man*, 119.

Works Cited

Alegría, Ricardo E. *Las primeras representaciones gráficas del indio americano, 1493-1523.* Barcelona: Instituto de Cultura Puertorriqueña, 1978.

Carpentier, Alejo. *El arpa y la sombra.* Mexico City: Siglo XXI, 1979.

Columbus, Christopher. "Diario." *Colección de los viages y descubrimientos que hicieron por mar los españoles.* Ed. Martín Fernández de Navarrete. 5 vols. Madrid: Imprenta Real, 1825.

————. *Diario del Descubrimiento.* Ed. Manuel Alvar. 2 vols. Grand Canary Island: Cabildo Insular de Gran Canaria, 1976.

————. *Diario di bordo: Libro della prima navigazione e scoperta delle Indie.* Ed. and trans. Gaetano Ferro. Milan: Mursia, 1985.

————. *The Diario of Christopher Columbus' First Voyage to America.* Ed. and trans. Oliver Dunn and James E. Kelley, Jr. Norman: Univ. of Oklahoma Press, 1989.

————. *Oeuvres de Christophe Colomb.* Ed. and trans. Alexandre Cioranescu. Paris: Gallimard, 1961.

————. *Scritti de Cristoforo Colombo.* Ed. Cesare de Lollis. Vol. 1, pt. 1: *Raccolta di documenti e studi pubblicati dalle Commissione Colombiana.* Rome: Ministerio della Pubblica Istruzione, 1892.

————. *Cristóbal Colón. Textos y documentos completos. Relaciones de viajes, cartas y memoriales.* Ed. Consuelo Varela. Madrid: Alianza, 1984.

Fuson, Robert H. "The *Diario de Colón*: A Legacy of Poor Transcription, Translation, and Interpretation." *In the Wake of Columbus: Islands and Controversy.* Ed. Louis de Vorsey, Jr., and John Parker. Detroit: Wayne State Univ. Press, 1985. 51-75.

Gómez Moriana, Mario, ed., and Lawrence Mantini, trans. "The Charter of the Admiral Columbus (17 April 1492)." *1492-1992: Re/discovering Colonial Writing.* Ed. René Jara and Nicholas Spadaccini. Hispanic Issues 4. Minneapolis: Prisma Institute, 1989. 383-385.

Henige, David. *In Search of Columbus.* Tucson: Univ. of Arizona Press, 1991.

Hulme, Peter. *Colonial Encounters: Europe and the Native Caribbean, 1492-1797.* London: Methuen, 1986.

Las Casas, Bartolomé de. *Brevísima relación de la destrucción de las Indias*. Ed. André Saint-Lu. Madrid: Cátedra, 1987.

———. "Diario del primer y tercer viaje de Cristóbal Colón." *Colección de Obras Completas de Fray Bartolomé de Las Casas* 14. Ed. Consuelo Varela. Madrid: Alianza, 1989.

Morison, Samuel Eliot. "Texts and Translations of the Journal of Columbus' First Voyage." *Hispanic American Historical Review* 19.3 (August 1939): 235-261.

Pagden, Anthony. *The Fall of Natural Man*. Cambridge: Cambridge Univ. Press, 1982.

Pastor, Beatriz. *Discurso narrativo de la conquista de América*. Havana: Casa de las Américas, 1983.

Rumeu de Armas, Antonio. "El *Diario de a bordo* de Cristóbal Colón: el problema de la paternidad del extracto." *Revista de Indias* 36 (1976): 7-17.

Sale, Kirkpatrick. *The Conquest of Paradise*. New York: Alfred A. Knopf, 1990.

Sanz, Carlos. *Diario de Colón*. Madrid: Bibliotheca Americana Vetustissima, 1962.

Stern, Steve J. *Peru's Indian Peoples and the Challenge of Spanish Conquest: Huamanga to 1640*. Madison: Univ. of Wisconsin Press, 1982.

Todorov, Tzvetan. *La conquête de l'Amérique: la question de l'autre*. Paris: Seuil, 1982.

Vázquez, J. A. "Las Casas' Opinions in Columbus' Diary." *Topic* 21 (Spring 1971): 45-56.

Zamora, Margarita. "Abreast of Columbus: Gender and Discovery." *Cultural Critique* 17 (Winter 1990-91): 127-49.

———. *Reading Columbus*. Berkeley: Univ. of California Press, 1993.

———. "Todas son palabras formales del Almirante: Las Casas y el Diario de Colón." *Hispanic Review* 57 (1989): 25-41.

◆　Chapter 6

To Read Is to Misread,
To Write Is to Miswrite
Las Casas as Transcriber

David Henige

I

I have ventured to inquire, but without presuming to decide.[1]

Since they first appeared, the works of Bartolomé de Las Casas have been both the object of encomium and the target of obloquy. In particular his *Brevísima relación de la destrucción de las Indias* aroused passions on its publication in 1552 and has managed to excite controversy ever since.[2] Even his most fervent admirers have found it difficult to accept the surfeit of almost comically implausible scenarios and numbers he used to document his account of Spanish atrocities toward the Indians.[3] Recently there has been a move afoot to vindicate Las Casas in this respect, particularly by those intent on postulating huge populations in the New World at contact, but these efforts lack all credibility.[4]

But Las Casas never intended the *Brevísima relación* to be more than a tract for its times, a polemic prepared and published as a corollary to his other work, particularly his monumental *Historia de las Indias,* on which he busied himself intermittently for more than thirty years. The *Historia* is undoubtedly the work by which Las Casas would have posterity judge him, but whether as a historian or as a defender of the Indians *par excellence* is less clear. At any rate, since its belated publication in 1875, the *Historia* has on the whole excited less debate than some of Las Casas's other work. In fact, the consensus of recent scholarship would probably be similar to the view taken by Morison that, despite its ponderous, repetitive, and frequently polemical style, the *Historia de las Indias* is "the one book on the discovery of America that I should wish to preserve if all others were destroyed" (*Admiral of the Ocean Sea* 1: 70).[5]

In no small measure this sense of surpassing value derives from the fact that in the *Historia* Las Casas collocated and quoted from many sources no longer extant, rendering his work a primary source as well as a secondary one. Among the most precious of these is the account of Columbus's first voyage, which occupies chapters 35 to 75 of Book 1 of the *Historia*.[6] Although the original log is not known to have survived, Las Casas transcribed a copy of it and then transplanted this almost bodily into the *Historia*. Needless to say, since its discovery some two hundred years ago the *diario* has been regarded as a capital source by historians eager to understand in detail the circumstances of the first (or rather the last) discovery of the New World.

The fact that what has survived is not the original document but a copy that is about four-fifths admitted paraphrase has seldom deterred historians from using the *diario* repeatedly and intensively, and not a little boldly. Only Henry Vignaud at the turn of the century and Rómulo D. Carbia in the 1930s sought to impugn the integrity of Las Casas to the extent that it encompassed the basic authenticity of the *diario* as well. Carbia claimed that the transcription was a deliberate—if wildly overwrought—*ex post facto* forgery by Las Casas, designed to put the lie to Oviedo's recently published work. Such wholesale condemnation lacked both evidential support and the requisite cooperation from Las Casas, and has generally been ignored, if not entirely refuted.[7]

In contrast, criticism of Las Casas has of late been held tightly in check; the fashionable view of the *diario* has been that Las Casas transcribed it faithfully and with scrupulous accuracy. There are, to be sure, numerous small, if obvious, errors, but once these are divined and "corrected," this orthodoxy goes, historians will be in possession of a full and accurate rendition of Columbus's words, sufficient to develop detailed hypotheses about every important aspect of the first voyage, all thanks to the industry of Las Casas. In fact, most accept that for one-fifth of the *diario* we are privy to Columbus's *ipsissima verba*. To no one's surprise, this portion consists almost without exception of Columbus's observations on the Indians; Las Casas would have had it no other way.[8]

Despite this prevalent view, the confidence expressed in Las Casas the transcriber, however reiterated, can ultimately only be faith, since there is no original with which to test it.[9] Scholarly opinion perforce falls back on veneration rather than analysis: Las Casas was (take your pick) too saintly, too concerned with the well-being of the Indians, too near the modern view in this matter not to be a trustworthy guide. To disbelieve his capacity in this regard would be tantamount to rejecting his interpretation of early Spanish treatment of the Indians. In a real sense his texts have come to engross quasi-scriptural status because they say what those who accept them most want to hear.[10]

While there is necessarily a role for predispositions in assessing the value of any source, it is possible to proceed at least a bit beyond them in this case and to make a more considered judgment of Las Casas's proficiency as transcriber *cum* paraphrast by comparing relevant portions of the *diario* with corresponding passages in the *Historia*. This procedure offers the opportunity to bring direct textual analysis to bear on faith.

The passages I have in mind are those in the *Historia* in which Las Casas claims to be quoting Columbus, via the *diario*, verbatim.[11] The number and nature of the passages falling into this category is to some extent the function of modern editorial practice and its means of denoting such text, the quotation mark (a matter that is further explored below).

To indicate quoted text, Las Casas, quite in tune with his times, typically reverted to the first person or showed Columbus as apostrophizing Ferdinand and Isabella. He also frequently noted that a particular passage was in "the very words" of Columbus, but since he often used the outward forms of indirect discourse (third person verbs in the past tense) in the *Historia* while retaining virtually intact the text of the *diario*, the issue is anything but clearcut. Here, if only for expedience and convenience, I confine discussion to some twenty passages in the *Historia* that meet one or more of these criteria *and* for which modern editions employ quotation marks.[12]

Here I can look at only a few such passages. The selection is hardly random—for instance I immediately eliminated six very short passages from consideration. For the rest I have chosen to illustrate the variety of issues rather than their ubiquity. In any case the selection process is mildly complicated by the fact that there are two surviving manuscripts of the complete *Historia*.[13] One, the so-called original, is entirely in Las Casas's hand. The other is a fair copy that Las Casas partly annotated. Taking a unitary stand, scholars have adopted the argument that the former *in toto* is to be preferred to the latter *in toto*, but most textual critics would look at the matter differently. For them the "authoritative" text would be a composite text as well: Books 1 and 2 of the fair copy as annotated by Las Casas, and Book 3 of the holograph text. This might seem unduly eclectic to some, but textual critics would point out that this combination best and most explicitly reflects Las Casas's last expressed authorial intentions. He accepted Books 1 and 2 of the fair copy as authoritative both by annotating them in certain places and by refraining from doing so in others.[14]

But there are special circumstances with verbatim material that subvert the usual doctrine of authorial intent in this instance. It would probably be unreasonable to expect that in his correcting Las Casas would have taken pains to ensure the *exact* verbal integrity of the quoted passages in the fair copy. On these grounds I use the text of the holograph copy of the *Historia* in all comparisons here.[15]

But therein lies another, if derivative, problem. The two recent editions embodying this text, one published in Mexico City in 1951, the other in Madrid six years later, do not always agree with each other, partly through different interpretations of the handwriting, partly through differences in editorial mechanics, and partly no doubt through printing variations.[16] Forced to choose between them, I have preferred to use the Madrid edition as my text of comparison since it is marginally closer to its exemplar, the *diario*, than the Mexico City edition, at least for the texts considered here.[17] I must point out, though, that the arguments that follow would not have varied markedly had I chosen otherwise. A point to remember is that when Las Casas incorporated most of the text of the *diario* into the *Historia,* he was transcribing, not Columbus or another scribe, but himself. In judging Las Casas as a transcriber in these circumstances then, we are affording him every possible advantage.

II

> ...*quotation is good only when the writer whom I follow goes my way, and, being better mounted than I, gives me a cast, as we say.* (Emerson 549)

The first passage discussed here is also the first in which Las Casas quoted Columbus in the *Historia.*[18] Symptomatically, it refers to Columbus's first impressions of the Indians of Guanahani, as recorded in the *diario* under the date of October 11 (*sic* for October 12).[19]

HISTORIA[20]

Yo, porque nos tuviesen mucha amistad, porque cognoscí que era gente que mejor se libraría y convertiría a nuestra santa fe con amor que por fuerza, les di a algunos dellos unos bonetes colorados y unas cuentas de vidro, que se ponian al pescuezo, y otras cosas muchas de poco valor con que hobieron mucho placer, y quedaron tanto nuestros, que era maravilla; los cuales después venían a las barcas de los navíos, adonde nos estábamos, nadando, y nos traían papagayos y hilo de algodón en ovillos y azagayas y otras cosas muchas, y nos las trocaban por otras cosas que nos les dábamos, como cuentecillas de vidro y cascabeles. En fin, todo tomaban y daban de aquello que tenían, de buena voluntad; mas me pareció que era gente muy pobre de todo; ellos andan todos desnudos como su madre los parió, y también las mujeres, aunque no vide más de una, farto moza, y todos los que

DIARIO[21]

Yo [dize él] porque nos tuviesen mucha amistad, porque cognoscí que era gente que mejor se libraría y convertería a Nuestra Sancta Fe con amor que *no* por fuerça, les di a algunos d'ellos unos bonetes colorados y unas cuentas de vidro que se ponían al pescueço, y otras cosas muchas de poco valor, con que ovieron mucho plazer y quedaron tanto nuestros que era maravilla. Los cuales después venían a las barcas de los navíos a donde nos estábamos, nadando. Y los traían papagayos y hilo de algodón en ovillos y azagayas y otras cosas muchas, y nos las trocaban por otras cosas que nos les dábamos, como cuentezillas de vidro y cascabeles. En fin, todo tomaban y daban de aquello que tenían de buena voluntad. Mas me pareció que era gente muy pobre de todo. Ellos andan todos desnudos como su madre los parió, y también las mujeres, aunque no vide mas de una yo vide eran mancebos, que ninguno vide *que pasase* de edad de más de TREINTA años, muy bien hechos, de muy fermosos *y lindos* cuerpos y muy buenas caras, los cabellos gruesos cuasi como sedas de cola de caballos y cortos; los cabellos traen por encima de las cejas, salvo unos pocos detrás, que traen largos, que jamás cortan. Dellos se pintan de prieto, y ellos son de la color de los canarios, ni negros ni blancos, y dellos se pintan de blanco, y dellos de colorado, y dellos de lo que hallan; dellos se pintan las caras, y dellos los cuerpos, y dellos solo los ojos, y dellos SOLA LA nariz. Ellos no traen armas, ni las cognoscen, porque les amostré espadas y las tomaban por el filo y se cortaban con ignorancia. No tienen algún fierro; sus azagayas son unas varas sin hierro, y algunas dellas tienen al cabo un diente de pece, y otras de otras cosas. Ellos todos a una mano son de buena estatura de grandeza, y buenos gestos, bien hechos. Ellos deben ser buenos servidores y de buen ingenio, que veo que muy presto dicen todo lo que les decía, y creo que ligeramente se harían cristianos, que pareció que ninguna secta tenian, etc." Todas éstas son palabras del Almirante.

harto moça. Y todos los que yo vi eran *todos* mancebos, que ninguno vide de edad de más de XXX años. Muy bien hechos, de muy fermosos cuerpos y muy buenas caras. Los cabellos gruessos cuasi como sedas de cola de caballo, y cortos. Los cabellos traen por encima de las cejas, salvo unos pocos detrás que traen largos, que jamás cortan. D'ellos se pintan de prieto, *y* ellos son de la color de los canarios, *y* ni negros ni blancos, y d'ellos se pintan de blanco, y d'ellos de colorado, y d'ellos de lo que fallan. Y d'ellos se pintan las caras, y d'ellos *todo* el cuerpo, y d'ellos solos los ojos, y d'ellos SOLO EL nariz. Ellos no traen armas ni las cognoscen, porque les amostré espadas y las tomaban por el filo, y se cortaban con ignorancia. No tienen algún fierro. Sus azagayas son unas varas sin fierro, y algunas d'ellas tienen al cabo un diente de pece, y otras de otras cosas. Ellos todos a una mano son de buena estatura de grandeza y buenos gestos, y bien hechos. *Yo vide algunos que tenían señales de feridas en sus cuerpos, y les hize señas qué era aquello, y ellos me amostraron cómo allí venían gente de otras islas que estaban acerca y los querían tomar y se defendían. Y yo creí, y creo, que aquí vienen de tierra firme a tomarlos por captivos.* Ellos deben ser buenos servidores y de buen ingenio, que veo que muy presto dizen todo lo que les dezía. Y creo que ligeramente se harían cristianos, que *me* pareció que ninguna secta tenían. *Yo, plaziendo a Nuestro Señor, levaré de aquí al tiempo de mi partida seis a Vuestras Altezas para que deprendan fablar. Ninguna bestia de ninguna manera vide, salvo papagayos en esta Isla.* Todas son palabras del Almirante.

In this passage (which happens to be one of the longest of the direct quotations in the *Historia*) Las Casas omitted words, added words, changed the form of words, added phrases, changed singulars to plurals as well as the converse, and changed a masculine form to a feminine.[22] Some of these changes (e.g., omitting the "no" and making "nariz" feminine) corrected apparent errors of Columbus.[23] Others were mistakes by Las Casas, while yet others constituted discretionary—and pointless—editorial tampering. Yet in a sense none of this is really the point. By claiming to be *quoting* Columbus, Las Casas automatically undertook the obligation to do just that rather than silently to emend that which he found wanting.[24]

As it happens, in this case these changes, as numerous as they are, pale in comparison to Las Casas's adroit expunging of no fewer than fifty-four words from the midst of the "quoted" passage. Ellipses as an editorial device were unknown to Las Casas, but of course there were other ways of signalling omissions, such as the "etc" Las Casas employed just a few lines further along. Could this omission have been accidental, an unlucky case of haplography? Or was it more artful? Regrettably, it can hardly be counted ungenerous to suppose that it was deliberate. After all, the passage expressed Columbus's impression, based on physical evidence, that the inhabitants of Guanahani were subject to raids from nearby islanders (or mainlanders, as Columbus believed).

The notion of Indians' enslaving other Indians was of course anathema to Las Casas, who was prepared to countenance only the thought that slave raiding in the Caribbean was an innovation of the Spanish. He may well have thought that he had no choice but to allow the passage to disappear from its new context. Perhaps he even convinced himself that Columbus had been in error, despite his unwonted reiteration ("creí y creo").[25]

To reinforce this conjecture we note that Las Casas's "etc" at the end of this passage of the *Historia* appears to be further editorial legerdemain on his part. Why use "etc" instead of quoting the few remaining words in this already long passage? Could it have been because these words described Columbus's intention (duly carried out) of kidnapping several Indians to be returned to Spain? Las Casas certainly did not take every opportunity to sanitize either Columbus's thoughts or his deeds—far from it—but here he seems to have grasped the need and the chance to do so. Throughout these chapters of the *Historia*, in fact, Las Casas employed the handy "etc" to mask unwelcome text, and this forces us to wonder in turn just how Las Casas put the term to use in the *diario*. Unfortunately, of course, we can hardly do much more than wonder.[26]

The unavoidable impediments to perfect transcription reveal themselves as well in the two modern editions of the *Historia*. In this passage, for example, there are five differences between the two. The Mexico City edition uses "vidrio" twice whereas the Madrid edition uses "vidro" in each case, as did Las Casas in his transcription of the *diario*.[27] In turn the Mexico City edition uses "andaban" in place of "andan" in the Madrid edition (and in the *diario*). The Madrid edition inserts an extra "de más," in effect fusing the discrepant transcription of Las Casas in the *Historia* to his phrasing in the *diario*. Thus, combined, it is indeed "de más"! Finally, the Mexico City edition transcribes "cerdas" whereas the Madrid edition (and the *diario*) both show "cedas."[28]

Shortly after this long quoted passage Las Casas quoted another and much shorter one, adding somewhat incongruously (and incorrectly) that he had taken it from "another chapter" of the *diario*.

HISTORIA[29]

Todos de buena estatura, gente muy hermosa, los cabellos no crespos, salvo CORRENTIOS y gruesos, y todos de la frente y cabeza muy ancha, y los ojos muy hermosos y no pequeños, y ninguno NEGRO, salvo de la color de los canarios, ni se debe esperar otra cosa, pues están Leste Güeste con la isla del Hierro, en Canaria, so una línea; las piernas muy derechas, todos a una mano, y no barriga, salvo muy bien hecha, etc." Estas son sus palabras.

DIARIO[30]

Y todos de buena estatura, gente muy fermosa. Los cabellos no crespos, salvo CORREDIOS y gruesos, *como sedas de caballo.* Y todos de la frente y cabeça muy ancha, *más que otra generación que fasta aquí haya visto.* Y los ojos muy fermosos y no pequeños. Y *ellos* ninguno PRIETO, salvo de la color de los canarios. Ni se debe esperar otra cosa, pues está lestegüeste con la isla del Fierro, en Canaria, so una línea. Las piernas muy derechas, todos a una mano, y no barriga, salvo muy bien hecha...

We see here again the unindicated omission of a fair proportion of a text—a practice that in fact does not occur so much in the other passages in the *Historia* purporting to quote Columbus. Las Casas's reasoning is not so obvious here but there is room for some suggestions. In one of the omitted phrases Columbus had compared the Indians' hair to that of horses, and Las Casas might well have found the analogy invidious.[31] More intriguing is Las Casas's substitution of "negro" for "prieto." It is almost as if he were intent on making it unambiguously clear that the Caribs were racially distinct from African blacks, by then (in the 1550s?) a differentiated socioeconomic category in the Spanish New World, rather than simply reiterating Columbus's observation that they were only slightly darkish in complexion.

On a noncontextual level "negro" and "prieto" are interchangeable terms, but here of course context is all. And in Las Casas's hands it is no longer the context of the Discovery but of the introduction and triumph of African slavery. Las Casas's apparently thesaurial change matters then, not least in its supererogation, inasmuch as Columbus had already taken pains in his text to distinguish the appearance of the Indians from that of Africans he had met.

While describing Columbus's first contacts with the *cacique* Guacanagarí, Las Casas entered the following statement in the *Historia* against the date of December 30, 1492:

> Vuestras Altezas hobieran mucho placer de ver la manera dellos. De creer es que el rey Guacanagarí los debía mandar venir para mostrar mejor su grandeza.[32]

Unfortunately it is not possible to pair this passage with a counterpart in the *diario;* there is no corresponding passage in the *diario.*

Columbus, via Las Casas, referred several times to Guacanagarí by name, but never quite in the terms alleged here by Las Casas. In effect this passage is a pastiche—not even a paraphrase really—that Las Casas turned into the appearance of a direct quote by adding the apostrophic "Vuestras Altezas." Modern editions have concurred in the illusion by providing quotation marks.

One can raise questions as to why Las Casas took this particular liberty—it seems utterly inconsequential—but to do so seems futile. No less idle would be speculation regarding the provenance of the "quotation" as it appears in the *Historia.*

Finally we reach the last instance in the *Historia de las Indias* in which Las Casas purported to quote directly from the *diario*. Oddly, in this one case it is not Columbus that he quotes, but João da Castanheira, commandant of the island of Santa Maria in the Azores, which Columbus visited briefly on his way home. Here is Las Casas's version as offered in the *Historia*, carefully couched in the first person:

> No cognoscemos acá al rey e reina de Castilla ni sus cartas, ni le habían miedo, antes les darían a entender qué cosa era Portogal.[33]

Compare this with the text of the *diario:*

> Entonces respondió el capitán y los demás no cognoscer acá Rey y Reyna de Castilla, ni sus cartas, ni le habían miedo; antes les darían a saber qué era Portugal. . . .[34]

In sum the correspondence between the two passages is tolerably close—at least meaning is not affected. But then there is the not so minor detail that in the *diario* Las Casas used indirect speech, as Columbus himself must have, whereas in the *Historia* he claims to be quoting Castanheira verbatim. Las Casas's gratuitous—in fact bizarre—claim that he was directly quoting is at least mildly disquieting, particularly when considered in conjunction with the previous passage cited. It is especially perplexing since the occasion was a minor one and the comment of Castanheira, whatever it might have been, was contextually and historically trivial. Regardless of Las Casas's reasons (and I have none to suggest), the example can only reinforce the doubts of those inclined to wonder about the reputation of Las Casas as meticulous copyist.

III

But I am afraid lest some graver errors escape our notice. For I always find more when I examine the work closely.[35]

Las Casas vs. Columbus

Besides instances of expunging or changing quoted materials, Las Casas indulged in the cardinal sin of any editor/transcriber; he introduced materials that to all appearances were not an integral part of the original.[36] While not a case of direct quotation, this seems a matter worth investigating since it directly reflects on Las Casas's propensities as a transcriber.

The most mortal of these sins was certainly the grandiloquent speech that Las Casas attributed to Columbus in the *Historia*. The occasion was his departure from Navidad, leaving behind a complement of men to build a fort, explore for gold, and generally provide a base to which Columbus could return. To judge from Las Casas's rendition of this speech, though, Columbus's principal concern was that the Spanish treat the Indians just as Las Casas himself would have. We find Columbus piously exhorting his men in a manner that reads as though this was a polished text, one carefully crafted point leading inexorably and logically to the next until no fewer than eight precepts had been carefully laid out.

When we turn to the *diario* we search in vain for this edifying homily, or even a passing mention of it. Nor do its sentiments come remotely close to matching Columbus's actions toward the Indians—earlier, then, or later. It appears then that Morison drew the only possible conclusion when he concluded that this microtext was "an invention of Las Casas" (*Admiral of the Ocean Sea* 1: 401-402).[37] Most others, though, have managed to overlook the textual and transmissional incongruities and have followed Las Casas in treating this speech as a historical event.[38]

The most recent and most unequivocal statement of this view is that of Fuson, who resolutely ignores all the perplexities and actually includes the speech as *part* of his conception of Columbus's original log. With enviable certitude Fuson assures readers that it "was certainly a part of the original log," even while conceding that "it does not, however, appear in the abstracted log [the *diario*]" (162-163). Fuson fails to suggest why Las Casas would have omitted this congenial tidbit from his transcription of the log, as well as how he was then able to coax the extensive text (some 700 words long) back into existence in time to use it in the *Historia*.[39] Certainly he was not able to borrow it from Ferdinand's *Historie*, which is as innocent of mentioning it as is the *diario*.

A lesser, but still intriguing, example of Las Casas's apparent urge to improvise is his description of a belt sent to Columbus by

Guacanagarí. The incident is briefly mentioned in the *diario*, but the following is all—and only—Las Casas:

> Este cinto era de pedrería muy menuda, como aljófar, hecha de huesos de pescado, blanca y entrepuestas algunas coloradas, a manera de labores, tan cosidas en hilo de algodón y por tan lindo artifício, que por la parte del hilo y revés del cinto parecián muy lindas labores, aunque todas blancas, que era placer verlas, como si se hobiera tejido en un bastidor y por el modo que labran las cenefas de las casullas en Castilla los brosladores. Y era tan duro y tan fuerte, que sin duda creo que no le pudiera pasar, o con dificultad, un arcabuz. Tenia cuatro dedos en ancho, de la manera que se solían usar en Castilla por los reyes y grandes señores los cintos labrados en bastidor o tejidos de oro, e yo alcancé a ver alguno dellos.[40]

Las Casas ended his description by noting that he had seen "some of [the belts]" himself, and the visual detail of his account suggests either an eyewitness account or a fabrication. Morison thought that Las Casas was actually "quoting from the original journal" here, whatever that means (Columbus, *Journals and Other Documents* 132 n. 2). Las Casas's use of the first person "creo" is slightly ambiguous and could conceivably refer to Columbus, although probably it does not. But if it was Columbus speaking through Las Casas, we can only ask—again—how the latter was able to omit the passage from the *diario*, yet retrieve it for later use. The verbal hints—particularly the use of "yo" at the end—suggest that this passage is a gloss, but it is insinuated into the context of the *diario* quite smoothly. Again there is no help to be found from Ferdinand, who failed to mention the occasion at all in his much condensed version of things (*Histoire* 198-200).[41]

It is no exaggeration to characterize these interpolations (and interpolations they must be despite some modern reluctance on this point) as ominous. In their frequency they do no less than suggest that Las Casas felt no inhibitions about adding to the text of the *Historia* whatever he thought ought to be there, just as he showed no compunction in subtracting things he thought ought *not* to be there.[42]

IV

It seemed to many that there was an error in the last word. For they thought that futuram *should be written instead of* futurum, *and they were sure that the book ought to be corrected.... But an expert, on examining the book, declared that there was no mistake in writing or grammar in that word, but that Cicero had written correctly and in accordance with early usage.* (Aulus Gellius 1: 37 [Bk. 1, vii, 3-6)

Modern Editors vs. Las Casas

As we have had occasion to mention, some of the difficulties Las Casas had with his own text have been compounded by practices of modern editorship of the *Historia*. Like his contemporaries Las Casas was guided in the ways in which he indicated direct quotation by a tradition much different from our own. When he was writing, direct discourse was distinguished (if at all) from indirect discourse verbally rather than visually.[43] Although italics were sometimes used in printed texts, the quotation mark as we know it had not yet made its appearance beyond a limited area.[44] Las Casas necessarily resorted to the then usual verbal indicators to signal quoted material.

While the advent of the quotation mark as a standard typographical sign was a distinct benefit to authors and readers alike (but especially a belated courtesy to those quoted), applying it anachronistically to early texts carries with it certain risks, as the following examples from the *Historia* indicate.

HISTORIA[45]

...Esto dice el que lo hizo porque mejor se comportan los hombres en España habiendo mujeres de su tierra que sin ellas; porque ya otras VECES MUCHAS se acaeció traer hombres de Guinea en Portogal, y después que volvían y pensaban de se aprovechar dellos en su tierra, por la buena compañía que les habían hecho, y dádivas que se les habían dado, en llegando en tierra jamás parecían. Así que teniendo sus mujeres, ternán gana de negociar lo que se les

DIARIO[46]

...Esto hize porque mejor se comportan los hombres en España habiendo mujeres de su tierra que sin ellas, porque ya otras MUCHAS VECES se acaeció traer hombres de Guinea *para que deprediesen la lengua* en Portugal, y después que volvían y pensaban de se aprovechar d'ellos en su tierra por la buena compañía que le habían hecho y dádivas que se les habían dado, en llegando en tierra jamás parecía. *Otros no lo* encargare, y también estas mujeres mucho enseñarán a LAS NUESTRAS su lengua, la cual es toda una en todas estas islas de Indias y todos se entienden, y todas las andan con sus almadías, lo que no hacen en Guinea, adonde es mil maneras de lenguas, que la una no entiende *a* la otra." Todas estas son palabras formales del Almirante.

hazían así. Así que, teniendo sus mujeres ternán gana de negociar lo que se les encargare, y también estas mujeres mucho enseñarán a LOS NUESTROS su lengua, la cual es toda una en todas estas islas de India,[47] y todos se entienden y todas las andan con sus almadías, lo que no han en Guinea, adonde es mil maneras de lenguas que la una no entiende la otra.

What are we to make of this farrago? In the *diario* this passage is in the first person, but Las Casas converted this into indirect discourse in the *Historia* with the unusual (for him) phrase: "esto dice el que lo hizo," while yet asserting in conclusion that the words were the very words of Columbus. In itself his practice of "third-person quoting" is common enough in the *Historia*, and editors have customarily avoided introducing quotation marks into these hybrid citations. In this case though they have not and, as if in collusion, the editors of both the Mexico City and the Madrid editions have inserted closing quotation marks but omitted opening ones, leaving readers in perplexity.[48]

If Las Casas really intended to quote "the very words" of Columbus here, he was unusually inept. He included two phrases not in the *diario* while omitting two that were, including one whose absence in the *Historia* renders a passage meaningless. In one of his omissions, once again apparently purposeful, Las Casas consigned to oblivion Columbus's criticism of the lack of gratitude he felt that certain Lusitanized Africans had exhibited on returning home.[49] Perhaps the passage merely reminded Las Casas of his own part in introducing African slavery into the New World.

All in all this passage is tribute neither to Las Casas's transcribing standards nor to modern editorial practice, but we cannot tell in what proportions the blame is to be distributed. At the same time it is a striking example of the depth of Las Casas's feelings about Spanish treatment of the Indians as well as of the textual aftereffects of this.

That the problem may in some degree be endemic in modern editions is suggested by a second example:

HISTORIA[50]
"vinieron tantos, que parecía cobrir
la tierra, dando mil gracias, hombres
y mujeres y niños. Los unos corrían
de acá, los otros de acullá, a LES
traer pan de ajes muy blanco y bueno,
y agua, y cuanto tenían y vían que lós
CRISTIANOS querían, y todo con un
corazón tan largo y tan contento que
era maravilla; y no se diga que
porque lo que daban valía poco, por
eso lo daban liberalmente, porque lo
mismo hacían, y tan liberalmente,
los que daban pedazos de oro, como
los [que]daban la calabaza de agua;
y fácil cosa es de congnoscer cuando
se da una cosa con muy deseoso corazón de dar." Todas estas son
palabras del Almirante. Dice más:
"Esta gente no tiene varas ni azagayas, ni otras ningunas armas, ni
los otros de toda esta isla, y tengo
que es grandísima."

DIARIO[51]
... venían tantos que cobrían
la tierra, dando mil gracias,
así hombres como mujeres y
niños; los unos corrían de acá y
los otros de allá a NOS traer pan
que hazen de niames, a que ellos
llaman ajes, que es muy blanco y
bueno, y nos traían agua en cala-
baças y en cántaros de barro de
la hechura de los de Castilla, y
nos traían cuento en el mundo
tenían y sabían que EL ALMIRANTE
quería, y todo con un coraçón
tan largo y tan contento que era
maravilla; "y no se diga que
porque lo que daban valía poco por
eso lo daban liberalmente (dize
el Almirante), porque lo mismo
hazían y tan liberalmente los que
daban pedaços de oro como los que
daban la calabaça de agua; y fácil
cosa es de cognocer (dize el
Almirante) cuándo se da una cosa
con muy deseoso coraçon de dar."
Estas son sus palabras. "Esta
gente no tiene varas ni azagayas
ni otras ningunas armas, ni los
otros de toda esta isla, y tengo
que es grandíssima...;

Here again the apparently gratuitous placement of quotation
marks—and again in both modern editions alike—conspires to indict Las Casas as a very lax transcriber indeed. But in fact there are
not the slightest grounds for introducing any quotation marks before the phrase "y no se diga...." From this point until the word
"grandísima" Las Casas set a very high standard of transcription.[52]

Still, it hardly seems entirely fair to accuse modern editors of
outright sabotage when they face a text in which Las Casas alter-
nated frequently between clearly quoting Columbus, possibly (or
even apparently) quoting him, and merely citing and paraphrasing him. From all appearances Las Casas used phrases like "the
Admiral says" indiscriminately, sometimes following it with text
in the first person, sometimes not. To complicate matters, in purely
descriptive passages, which predominate in the text, there is sometimes no opportunity to indicate the person in which the text is

written. In these cases there is no knowing whether Las Casas intended to quote these passages or simply to cite them in language close to, but not identical with, the *diario*.[53]

The matter of quotation marks (and of "etcs") might well seem trifling, even pettifogging, but looking at it closely helps to appreciate the hazards implicit in applying modern editorial and typographical standards to a text that was created in an intellectual and discursive ambiance far different from ours.[54] Even so, for a modern edition to provide only partial sets of quotation marks (which come only in full sets . . .) without explanation is to betray a fundamental confusion of purpose.

V

I do not recognize my own books. . . . Things are left out, things are transposed, things are falsified, things are not corrected. (Luther 17/2: 3)[55]

Most of the instances in which the text of the *Historia* differs from its presumed exemplar while claiming to be quoting directly stem from sheer carelessness, the corrosive effects of ennui on transcribing accurately. Such slips of the pen accompany any effort to replicate that lacks the vigilance to ensure that the effort is successful. The additional leavening of prepositions and conjunctions, but more obviously the omission of these, points out that transcription can be as much a betrayal of a text as translation.

The other principal occasion of discrepancy has a less creditable stimulus—Las Casas's application of that particular species of editorial impertinence called silent emendation. Above all an editor speaks, not for the author, but for the text. Whenever editors (and transcribers are low-grade editors) emend a text, they take it upon themselves to decide what an author "really" meant to say and then boldly says it for the author, thereby becoming, if only in a minor way, co-authors. In the passages surveyed here Las Casas reveals himself as a fairly diligent emendator—and always silently, even stealthily. Perhaps he was merely displaying the typical humanist's overriding concern with style and expression; we know that he was occasionally critical of Columbus's style.

The extent and insidious effects of silent emendation, without doubt a mischievous defacer of texts, has largely been addressed by literary critics, who have found in their work that the practice is more widespread because the variants of a single literary text are usually more numerous than for the typical historical document. Nonetheless, it behooves historians to listen more carefully to the disquieting testimony of the literary critics who, to their chagrin, are constantly unearthing the practice, which is clearly universal in the legitimate sense of that word.

At the same time historians must develop a different strategy in dealing with errors and discrepancies detected in a text. Their goal must be first to discover the authoritative text and then to base historical conclusions both on its testimony and on the changes that have occurred in it. The study of history is the study of change, and this premise applies as much to texts as to events and processes.

Given this argument, and given the circumstances of the case at hand, the question naturally arises: whom was Las Casas emending in the *Historia*. Assuming (as we must) that he transcribed this part of the text of the *Historia* directly from the *diario* (that his, his earlier transcription of earlier transcriptions of the original log), we can wonder whether, in some cases, Las Casas was convinced that an "error" was his own and not Columbus's. It is of course not at all clear how he would have been able to be quite so discriminating at this later stage, unless one transcription followed the other very quickly, which seems not likely.[56] Nor can it be ruled out of hand that somehow Las Casas was bypassing his own transcription and was using the original log, but this is even less likely and can only be regarded as an exceedingly desperate *deus ex machina*.

If the charge of silent emendation is to be leveled at Las Casas, it must be leveled at modern editors of the *diario* as well, forbidding us to be very censorious of Las Casas's aptitude in this respect. In fact modern editors have shown a marked propensity for changing the text of the *diario* without feeling a need to let their readers in on the secret. Until 1984 only two of the numberless editions of the *diario* attempted to present the text as Las Casas left it to us.[57] All others to one degree or another—sometimes to a very great degree—are replete with unannounced changes. Worse yet, some editors have not even taken the trouble to indicate beforehand, even generally, their manner of proceeding.

VI

... y es cosa maravillosa cómo lo que el hombre mucho desea y asienta una vez con firmeza en su imaginación, todo lo que oye y ve, ser en su favor a cada paso se le antoja.[58]

The sample I have used here is a very small one, even in the context of the *Historia de las Indias*, let alone the vast corpus of Las Casas's writings, but it does serve to suggest that casually regarding Las Casas as a transcriber *ne plus ultra* is no more than a prospect devoutly to be wished. Of the problems discussed here, by far the most serious is the way in which Las Casas censored his private text of the *diario* in the version that he expected would be its public *alter ego*. Las Casas regarded the *Historia* as his case to posterity that the course of Spanish conquest and settlement fully justified his condemnation of their treatment of the Indians. To the extent that the *diario* contributed to this larger purpose, he made heavy and fairly careful use of it. But, alas, Columbus testified that he believed—and offered evidence for his belief—that the Indians of Guanahani were subject to raids from neighboring Indians. For Las Casas this notion was unthinkable and the passage disappeared entirely from this section of the *Historia* (though we must be grateful that Las Casas did not, on this occasion at least, exercise this judgment when transcribing the *diario*).

If Las Casas had a secular hero, it would have been Columbus, whom he regarded as the hand of providence made manifest. Yet he must also have realized that, as *homo oeconomicus*, Columbus seemed less divinely inspired. At any rate Las Casas saw fit to expunge from the *Historia* an apparently innocuous statement of Columbus's views on African "ingratitude." Inconsequential it was, perhaps, but no less deliberate and no less suggestive of the light in which Las Casas viewed the *diario*.

Ineluctably this brings us to the question of fairness. Should we reproach Las Casas simply because he failed to subscribe to

the standards that, we fancy, are the norms of the present? Not
unless we are able to show that he was markedly less careful
than his contemporaries, a task I doubt is possible, for by the
standards of his time Las Casas measured well.[59] But it seems
that many modern scholars believe that Las Casas both sub-
scribed to *modern* transcriptional standards and then met them
triumphantly, a view that resonates throughout the literature on
the matter.

For Morison, Las Casas's transcription of the *diario* was "well
and honestly made" ("Texts and Translations" 239). Leonard
Olschki, by no means an uncritical observer, believed that Las
Casas omitted "nothing essential" from his transcription (650).[60]
J. H. Parry was confident that the *diario* "represents, as clearly as
a summary by another hand could do, Columbus's own experiences and thoughts" (231). Galmés in his turn is certain that Las
Casas "wrote simply in defense of the pure truth [*sic*] and without
concessions" (233). The most recent assessment of Las Casas in this
regard is among the most laudatory and unequivocal. For Fuson
Las Casas was no less than "a slave to exactness" (*Log* 6). And the
examples of heroic praise, sometimes savoring of piety, could well
be multiplied (*Admiral of the Ocean Sea* 1: 20n).[61] Clearly though, if
Las Casas was a slave to anything, it was as much to his deeply
held convictions about the nature of the Indian as to the need to
preserve the integrity of his texts.

Such endorsements, which are seldom based on anything as
concrete as comparing Las Casas with himself, beg a more important question: to what extent should modern scholarship demand,
or even expect, the kind of textual fidelity that these apologetic
outbursts presuppose? To apply exacting standards to a text written over a long period of years and finished in old age over four
hundred years ago and with partisan ends in mind is, as Morison
put it in quite another context, "captiousness" ("Texts and Translations" 239).[62] Yet modern historians, and none more prominently
than Morison himself, have proceeded to treat Las Casas's transcription of the *diario* in the *Historia* as if it were the *diario* itself,
and the *diario* as if it were the original log.

VII

No one ever checks anybody else's collations (or his own for that matter) without finding mistakes in them. (West 63)

I have tried to test this point of view by comparing Las Casas as transcriber of the *diario* with Las Casas as transcriber of the log, and it seems to me that this comparison raises doubts as to the soundness of following Las Casas's transcription of the latter blindly—or even with one eye wide open. The difficulties arise from the natural slippage that the tedium of any transcribing exercise involves, from Las Casas's desire to "improve" on Columbus's expression, and from his more deliberate excisions and additions. The sample is the largest available, but necessarily small, and might well tempt the critic to recall Morison's criticisms of Vignaud and Carbia: "neither author makes a thorough analysis...but picks out isolated phrases and words to sustain his thesis" ("Texts and Translations" 239). Be that as it may—or rather as it must—to argue that Las Casas was uncommonly careful and remorselessly objective is, as Samuel Johnson observed on another matter, the unwarranted triumph of hope over experience.

The perspective I have adopted here derives in no small part from my understanding of the results of textual criticism, specifically as it relates to transcription, whether by hand or by printing. Recourse to this literature is ordained by both ordinary scholarly rigor and by the fact that the absence of Columbus's log has encouraged historians to wax sanguine without fear of contradiction about Las Casas's rare (and it would have been exceedingly rare) knack for faultless transcribing.[63]

Besides being untestable, these arguments suffer from their own brand of isolation, in this case from the overwhelming experience of scholarship in fields where the transmission and transformation of texts have long been a center of interest. There the ambiguous and unsatisfying role of transcribers have bedeviled study from the very beginning and, if anything, the problems continue to snowball as more and more texts are subjected to scrutiny.[64] Study after study has shown that the term "perfect transcription" is both an oxymoron and a null category—is in fact a concept that needs to be banished from Columbian studies in favor of a more rigorous and skeptical posture toward the sources, whether major or minor.[65]

Notes

1. See Robertson 9: 48-49, on the first peopling of the New World.

2. The best bibliography of Las Casas is that by Pérez Fernández.

3. For one who did find it possible see Martínez, "Valor histórico" and "Notas críticas."

4. Las Casas's estimates of population and mortality are actually held to be too low by Cook and Borah 1: 376-410. For a comment on this point of view see Henige, "On the Contact Population of Hispaniola" 222-225.

5. Even Menéndez Pidal, whose *El Padre Las Casas: su doble personalidad* is the most vitriolic attack on Las Casas ever published, found the *Historia de las Indias* fairly innocuous; see 293-296.

6. A word on nomenclature is in order at this point. Throughout the paper I use "log" to refer to whatever document Columbus turned in on his return, which has been lost. We can only assume that it closely resembled the transcription Las Casas made from a copy of it. In turn I refer to this transcription as the *"diario,"* a term that has achieved a certain modern vogue, though it was never used by Las Casas, who called it the "Libro de la primera navegación." For my purposes the two texts are regarded as alike, but also as different enough that it is necessary to distinguish between them at all times. I would go so far as to suggest that Las Casas, and not Columbus, should be regarded as the 'author' of the *diario,* but that is another matter. Perhaps it is worth mentioning in this regard that Rumeu de Armas has argued that Las Casas transcribed literally a text that had *already* been abridged, on the grounds that Las Casas's "habitual inclination" was to preserve the writings of Columbus "in all their integrity" (see 10, 14n).

7. This argument of Carbia is measurably weakened by the fact that Las Casas took so long to complete the *Historia,* took no apparent steps to abridge it in any way thereby completing it sooner, and then enjoined a forty-year delay in its publication. See, among others, Marcus 612-613.

8. On this disproportion see Olschki 639-641.

9. There exists, however, a tiny fragment of what appears to be the log of the first voyage, some fifty words that do not appear in the *diario,* and which may of course represent another kind of text. For this fragment see Columbus, *Textos y documentos completos* 138, where it is described as a "fragmento de un escrito en el *Cuaderno* de a Bordo," thus describing its actual format rather than its possible content.

10. For interesting observations on our sometimes dangerously anachronistic preconceptions and on the reliability and authority we ascribe to texts see Orgel.

11. In his edition of the *diario* for the 1892 festivities, Cesare de Lollis noted differences between the *diario* and the *Historia,* basing himself on the fair copy manuscript, the only one then known. Although he did not draw out the implications of these differences, his attempt still represents the only serious effort to

view the two texts in close juxtaposition. The comparisons I have made here may not always agree with de Lollis's, though I have noticed no differences.

12. The following are the passages in question, including citations to the edition of Bartolomé de las Casas, *Historia de las Indias*, by Pérez de Tudela Bueso and López Oto as well as the book and chapter number to facilitate consultation in other editions:

1: 143-44 (1/40)	1: 159 (1/45)	1: 169 (1/47)
1: 144 (1/40)	1: 163 (1/46)	1: 171-72 (1/48)
1: 149 (1/42)	1: 164 (1/46)	1: 184 (1/54)
1: 151 (1/42)	1: 165 (1/46)	1: 186 (1/55) 1: 188-89 (1/56) 1: 198 (1/60)
1: 192 (1/58)	1: 201 (1/62)	
1: 193 (1/58)	1: 219 (1/69)	
1: 197-98 (1/60)	1: 222 (1/71)	

13. See Hanke, *Las Casas, Historian* 32-34; Pérez Fernández 210-218; Wagner and Parish 290-292; Hanke, "The *Historia de las Indias*" 143-144.

14. For a brief conspectus of the matter of authorial intent see Henige, "In Quest" and the sources cited there. Despite its intrinsic historical interest, once again it has been the literary critics who have monopolized this field.

15. But I do have occasion to note the fair copy text edition, which is Bartolomé de las Casas, *Historia de las Indias*, edited by Marqués de la Fuensanta del Valle and José Sancho Rayón.

16. Las Casas, *Historia*/Madrid (Madrid: Rivadeneira, 1975); Las Casas, *Historia de las Indias*, ed. Agustín Millares Carlo, 3 vols. (Mexico City: Fondo de Cultura Económica, 1951), henceforth *Historia*/Mexico. Several reprints of the latter have appeared in various guises during the 1980s, occasionally with a new introduction but with untouched texts.

17. For some examples of these discrepancies see below.

18. In all juxtapositions the text of the *Historia* appears first, followed by that of the *diario*. Many modern(ized) editions of the *diario* exist, some better than others. Here I use the modernized edition of Manuel Alvar, which appears in tandem with a quasi-diplomatic edition, and which I have found to be the most thorough and dependable.

19. In the parallel passages, wording *not* in one text is indicated by italics in the other while substitution of one term or phrase for another is shown by capital letters. Differences in spelling, punctuation, capitalization, and other "accidentals" do not seem important here and are ignored, although these have been known to assume critical significance in many textual studies.

20. Las Casas, *Historia*/Madrid 1: 143-144. English trans. in Appendix, no. 1.

21. Colón/Alvar, *Diario* 2: 49-53. English trans. in Appendix, no. 2

22. "Transcriptional" errors as distinct from "substantive" errors; that is, these are "wrong" only in the sense that they do not replicate their originals while professing to do so.

23. Unless of course Las Casas's transcription of the log (or earlier transcriptions of it) were in error. Much of the tidying-up changes could be attributed to Las Casas correcting himself, or at least thinking that he was doing so, but any such arguments can only be formal and unprovable.

24. Other examples of silent emendation, inflicted by and on Las Casas, are discussed at various points below.

25. Incidentally, Columbus's belief on this matter also appears in the text of the *Historie* attributed to his son Ferdinand, a source that many believe was the inspiration for much of Las Casas's text. See Ferdinand Columbus 1: 169.

26. As noted below, the modern view is to regard any omissions in the *diario* as of exceedingly minor consequence, referring to such matters as weather conditions, minor changes of course, and the like. The evidence for this view is nonexistent and the peculiar absence of virtually all references to, e.g., mutinous behavior is suspect.

27. For "vidro"/"vidrio" see Colón/Alvar, *Diario* 2: 49n.

28. Las Casas, *Historia*/Mexico 1: 204. These two words have virtually identical meanings so that differences in transcriptions could have occurred with particular ease.

29. Las Casas, *Historia*/Madrid 1: 144. English trans. in Appendix, no. 3.

30. Colón/Alvar, *Diario* 2: 53-54. English trans. in Appendix, no. 4.

31. On the other hand he included much the same comparison in the first passage quoted.

32. Las Casas, *Historia*/Madrid 1: 201. English trans. in Appendix, no. 5.

33. Las Casas, *Historia*/Madrid 1: 222. English trans. in Appendix, no. 6.

34. Colón/Alvar, *Diario* 2: 230. English trans. in Appendix, no. 7.

35. Samuel Collins, *Increpatio Andreae Eudaemono Iohannis* (Cambridge, 1612), as quoted in Binns 17.

36. As distinct from much other matter that Las Casas added to the account of Columbus's first voyage in the *Historia*, but in clearly interpolative terms—any editor's prerogative if carefully exercised.

37. Morison, *Admiral* 1: 401-402. De Lollis, *Raccolta* I/1, 87n was more cautious than Morison intimated, thinking it not impossible that Las Casas had "amplified" some less ambitious address of Columbus. There seems, however, to be no need whatever for such caution.

38. For example, see Thacher 1: 632; Columbus, *Journal of Christopher Columbus* 146nl. Emiliano Jos believed the speech "in character" for Columbus and concluded that "any words added by Las Casas are innocuous, and more grammatical than anything"[!] (359n).

39. All that proponents of the historicity of this speech can do is to attribute its survival to "the truly elephantine memory" with which Hanke credits Las Casas. See Hanke, *Las Casas, Historian* 81.

40. Las Casas, *Historia*/Madrid 1: 190-191; see also Colón/Alvar, *Diario* 2: 166. English trans. in Appendix, no. 8.

41. Ferdinand Columbus, *Historie*, 198-200. Typically, de Lollis, *Raccolta* I/1: 74n., declined to pass judgment either way, but Cioranescu saw the passage as "in the guise of elucidation," as did Alvar: *Oeuvres* 411 n.298; Colón/Alvar, *Diario* 2: 166.

42. But probably not merely for picturesque effect, since the description (and the belt itself?) was of a nature as to highlight the artisanal skills of the Taínos, whether or not at the price of textual integrity.

43. Some recent studies of the signs and aspects of indirect/direct discourse are Thomson, Banfield, Richman, Chickering, and Gerardi.

44. It seems that the quotation mark first appeared in printed texts in Strasbourg early in the sixteenth century, but it was slow to establish itself as *the* sign to indicate direct discourse unambiguously. For its early development see Compagnon 246-263 and McMurtrie 133-134. For its fitful and variegated progress to the end of the eighteenth century see Mitchell 259-284. Although the quotation mark *per se* originated as a printer's mark, the need for it arose in part as a reaction to the unrestrained, unabashed, and unacknowledged borrowing in literary works from predecessors, usually the Bible and classical authors in high esteem. Some of the philosophy of quoting and of its symbol, the quotation mark, is discussed in Compagnon 48-93+.

45. Las Casas, *Historia*/Madrid 1: 163-164. English trans. in Appendix, no. 9.

46. Colón/Alvar, *Diario* 2: 106. Las Casas added about 300 words at this point in his rendition of the *diario's* account, but they are clearly enough his. English trans. in Appendix, no. 10.

47. This is one of the many instances where Las Casas corrected Columbus's naturally hazy geographical impressions of the New World, which he had barely encountered. Merely by adding an "s" to "India" Las Casas transformed completely Columbus's lifelong certainty that he had reached the Far East.

48. Truer to its text, the 1875 edition of the *Historia*, the first to be published and based on the fair copy manuscript, used no quotation marks at all in this instance: Las Casas, *Historia* 1: 335-36. De Lollis, *Raccolta* I/1: 40n., considered, probably correctly, that the "verbatim" passage began with "esto hize."

49. Although he would not have been directly involved, Columbus must have had in mind here such cases as that of Bemoy, a mediatizing Wolof ruler who was taken to Portugal in the late 1480s and who, on returning home, broke with the Portuguese and was killed by them. On this episode see Teixeira da Mota. More generally see Hair.

50. Las Casas, *Historia*/Madrid 1: 188-189; Las Casas, *Historia*/Mexico 1: 269. English trans. in Appendix, no. 11.

51. Colón/Alvar, *Diario* 2: 162. English trans. in Appendix, no. 12.

52. In the introduction to his edition of the *diario* Alvar points out that he and Carlos Sanz, who produced another edition of the *diario*, occasionally disagree as to the matter to be treated as direct quotation. Colón/Alvar, *Diario* 2: 10n. However, this is not such a case.

53. By extension this ambiguity applies to any interpretation of Las Casas's transcription of the log, a matter I hope to deal with elsewhere.

54. For attitudes to quotes in the Renaissance see Reynolds and Wilson 148-150.

55. For the circumstances see Newman.

56. The most widely advocated date for Las Casas's transcription of the *diario* is 1552, and in the following seven years or so Las Casas is thought to have refurbished an inchoate draft of the *Historia* into the text as we now have it.

57. I refer to those of de Lollis and Alvar, of which the latter is much more successful. I deal with the remaining editions in *In Search of Columbus*.

58. Las Casas, *Historia*/Madrid 1: 156. English trans. in Appendix, no. 13.

59. Although no doubt without realizing it, Las Casas had no less an example in this attitude than the apostle Paul; see Stanley; Koch, esp. chapter 3.

60. Even Marcelino Menéndez y Pelayo, no partisan of Columbus, regarded

that part of the *Historia* that covered Columbus's activities as "meriting much more credit" than the remainder of the work because of the superior qualities of the sources (249).

61. For example see Saint-Lu; Gandía 37-38.

62. Morison was criticizing Carbia here and went on to add that it was ludicrous to "demand of fifteenth-century documents a scrupulous exactitude as if they were pleadings in modern civil suits." Unless they happened to support his own version of Columbus's activities, one presumes.

63. And then to assume that the log *in absentia* faithfully reproduced a reality even beyond Columbus's perceptions. I have in mind principally the innumerable proponents of one landfall or another, since each argument depends on accepting in the most minute detail (with an occasional twist to suit) the testimony of the *diario*. For another facet of the *Historia* see Benítez-Rojo.

64. In order to make my case more explicit let me cite a few general studies as well as some particular studies of very recent vintage, with a design to suggest on how broad a front the problem is being investigated: Reynolds and Wilson 137-162; West 49-59; Willis 47-102; Castellani 167-172; Timpanaro; Mattina; Kaiser; McBain; Easson; Brodsky; Holmes; Fahy; Hay; Burkhardt; Neumann; Emerton; Elias; Dawson.

65. The fact that the first full diplomatic edition of the text of the *diario* appeared only in 1989 (Columbus, *The Diario of Christopher Columbus's First Voyage*), some 175 years after the first published edition—a long overdue step that is bound to raise far more questions than it answers—speaks eloquently of the cavalier attitude for the underlying texts in Columbian studies. For another text with a similarly checkered textual history see Mantello.

Works Cited

Aulus Gellius. *The Attic Nights*. Ed. and trans. E. Capp, T. E. Page, and W. H. D. Rouse. 3 vols. Cambridge: Harvard Univ. Press, 1927-1928.

Banfield, Ann. "Narrative Style and the Grammar of Direct and Indirect Speech." *Foundations of Language* 10 (1973): 1-39.

Benítez-Rojo, Antonio. "Bartolomé de las Casas entre infierno y la ficción." *MLN* 103 (1988): 259-288.

Binns, James. "STC Latin Books for Printing-House Practice." *The Library* 5/32 (1977): 1-27.

Brodsky, Louis D. "William Faulkner's 1962 Gold Medal Speech." *Studies in Bibliography* 41 (1988): 315-322.

Burkhardt, Frederick. "Editing the Correspondence of Charles Darwin." *Studies in Bibliography* 41 (1988): 149-159.

Castellani, Arrigo. "Transcription Errors." *Medieval Manuscripts and Textual Criticism*. Ed. Christopher Kleinheinz. Chapel Hill: Univ. of North Carolina Press, 1976.

Chickering, Howell. "Unpunctuating Chaucer." *Chaucer Review* 25 (1990): 96-109.

Columbus, Christopher. *Diario del Descubrimiento*. Ed. Manuel Alvar. 2 vols. Gran Canaria: Ediciones del Cabildo Insular, 1976.

————. *The Diario of Christopher Columbus's First Voyage to America. 1492-1493.* Ed. and trans. Oliver Dunn and James E. Kelley, Jr. Norman: Univ. of Oklahoma Press, 1989.

————. *Journal and Other Documents on the Life and Voyages of Christopher Columbus.* Ed. Samuel Eliot Morison. New York: Heritage Press, 1963.

————. *The Journal of Christopher Columbus.* Ed. Clements R. Markham. London: Hakluyt Society, 1893.

————. *The Log of Christopher Columbus.* Ed. and trans. Robert H. Fuson. Camden, Maine: International Marine Publishing Co., 1987.

————. *Oeuvres de Christophe Colomb.* Ed. and trans. Alexandre Cioranescu. Paris: Gallimard, 1961.

————. *Scritti di Cristoforo Colombo.* Ed. Cesare de Lollis. Vol. 1, pt. 1: *Raccolta de documenti e studi pubblicati dalle Commissione Colombiana.* Rome: Ministerio della Pubblica Istruzione, 1892.

————. *Textos y documentos completos. Relaciones de viajes, cartas y memoriales.* Ed. Consuelo Varela. Madrid: Alianza Editorial, 1982.

Columbus, Ferdinand. *Le Historie della vita e dei fatti di Cristoforo Colombo.* Ed. Rinaldo Caddeo. 2 vols. Milan: Edizioni Alpes, 1930.

Compagnon, Antoine. *Le séconde main, ou le travail de la citation.* Paris: Editions du Seuil, 1979.

Cook, Sherburne F., and Woodrow W. Borah. *Essays in Population History I.* Berkeley: Univ. of California Press, 1974.

Dawson, Marc H. "The Many Minds of Sir Halford J. Mackinder: Dilemmas of Historical Editing." *History in Africa* 14 (1987): 27-42.

Easson, Angus. "Reviewing Editions: Letters, Journals, Diaries." *Literary Reviewing.* Ed. James O. Hoge. Charlottesville: Univ. of Virginia Press, 1987. 56-69.

Elias, Robert H. "Eighteenth-Century Thorns, Twentieth-Century Secretaries, and Other Prickly Matters." *Text* 3 (1987): 347-353.

Emerson, Ralph Waldo. "Quotation and Originality." *North American Review* 106 (April 1868): 543-557.

Emerton, J. A. "An Examination of Some Attempts to Defend the Unity of the Flood Narrative in Genesis." *Vetus Testamentum* 37 (1987): 401-419.

Fahy, Conor. "More on the 1532 Edition of Ludovico Ariosto's Orlando Furioso." *Studies in Bibliography* 41 (1988): 225-233.

Galmés, Lorenzo. "Cristóbal Colón y el descubrimiento de América a la luz de P. Las Casas." *Escritos del Vedat* 16 (1986): 225-251.

Gandía, Enrique de. *Historia de Cristóbal Colón.* Buenos Aires: Editorial Claridad, 1942.

Gerardi, Pamela. "Thus, He Spoke: Direct Speech in Esarhaddon's Royal Inscriptions." *Zeitschrift für Assyrologie* 79 (1989): 245-260.

Hair, P. E. H. "The Use of African Languages in Afro-European Contacts in Guinea, 1440-1560." *Sierra Leone Language Review* 5 (1966): 5-26.

Hanke, Lewis. "The *Historia de las Indias* of Bartolomé de las Casas." *Essays Honoring Lawrence C. Wroth.* Portland, Me., 1951.

————. *Las Casas, Historian.* Gainesville: Univ. of Florida Press, 1952.

Hay, Louis. "Does Text Exist?" *Studies in Bibliography* 41 (1988): 64-76.

Henige, David. "In Quest of Error's Sly Imprimatur: The Concept of 'Authorial Intent' in Modern Textual Criticism." *History in Africa* 14 (1987): 87-112.

———. *In Search of Columbus: The Sources of the First Voyage*. Tucson: Univ. of Arizona Press, 1991.

———. "On the Contact Population of Hispaniola: History as Higher Mathematics." *Hispanic American Historical Review* 58 (1978): 217-237.

Heers, Jacques. *Christophe Colomb*. Paris: Hachette, 1981.

Holmes, Frederic L. "Scientific Writing and Scientific Discovery." *Isis* 78 (1987): 220-235.

Jos, Emiliano. "Las Casas, Historian of Christopher Columbs." *The Americas* 12 (1955/56): 355-362.

Kaiser, Rudolf. "Chief Seattle's Speech(es)." Swann and Krupat 97-536

Koch, Dietrich-Alex. *Die Schrift als Zeuge des Evangeliums: Untersuchungen zur Verwendung und zum Verständnis der Schrift bei Paulus*. Tübingen: J. C. B. Mohr, 1986.

Las Casas, Bartolomé de. *Brevísima relación de la destrucción de las Indias*. Ed. André Saint-Lu. Madrid: Cátedra, 1987.

———. *Historia de las Indias*. Ed. Marqués de la Fuensanta del Valle and José Sancho Rayón. 5 vols. Madrid: Imprenta de Miguel Ginesta, 1875-76.

———. *Historia de las Indias*. Ed. Agustín Millares Carlo. 3 vols. Mexico City: Fondo de Cultura Económica, 1951.

———. *Historia de las Indias*. Ed Juan Pérez de Tudela Bueso and Emilio López Oto. 2 vols. Madrid: Rivadeneira, 1957.

Luther, Martin. *Fastenpostille*. Vol. 17, part 2 of *Martin Luthers Werke*. Ed. Paul Petsch. 62 vols. Weimar: Hermann Böhlaus, 1883-1985.

McBain, William. "Remembrance of Things Still to Come: Scribal Memory and Manuscript Tradition." *Manuscripta* 31 (1987): 77-88.

McMurtrie, Douglas C. "The Origin and Development of the Marks of Quotations." *The Library* 4/2 (1921/22): 133-136.

Mantello, F. A. C. "The Editions of Nicholas Trevet's *Annales sex regum Angliae.*" *Revue d'histoire des textes* 10 (1980): 257-275.

Marcus, Raymond. "Las Casas: a Selective Bibliography." *Bartolomé de las Casas in History*. Ed. Juan Friede and Benjamin Keen. De Kalb: Northern Illinois Univ. Press 1971, 603-616.

Martínez, Manuel M. "Notas críticas: réplica a la conferencia de don Ramón Menéndez Pidal sobre el P. Las Casas." *Ciencia Tomista* 286 (1963): 236-318.

———. "Valor histórico de la 'Destrucción de las Indias.' " *Ciencia Tomista* 244 (1952): 441-468.

Mattina, Anthony. "Native American Mythography: Editing Texts for the Printed Page." Swann and Krupat 129-148.

Menéndez Pidal, Ramón. *El Padre Las Casas: su doble personalidad*. Madrid: Espasa-Calpe, 1962.

Menéndez y Pelayo, Marcelino. *Estudios de Crítica Literaria*. 2d ser. Madrid: Estudio tipográfico de Rivadeneira, 1893-1900.

Mitchell, C. J. "Quotation Marks, National Compositorial Habits and False Imprints." *The Library* 6/5 (1985): 259-284.

Morison, Samuel Eliot. *Admiral of the Ocean Sea: A Life of Christopher Columbus*. 2 vols. Boston: Little, Brown, and Co., 1942.

————. "Texts and Translations of the Journal of Columbus's First Voyage." *Hispanic American Historical Review* 19 (1939): 239-265.

Neumann, Gerhard. "Script, Work, and Published Form: Franz Kafka's Incomplete Text." *Studies in Bibliography* 41 (1988): 77-99.

Newman, Jane O. "The Word Made Print: Luther's 1522 New Testament in an Age of Mechanical Reproduction." *Representations* 11 (Summer 1985): 95-133.

Olschki, Leonard. "What Columbus Saw on Landing in the West Indies." *Proceedings of the American Philosophical Society* 84 (1941): 633-659.

Orgel, Stephen. "The Authentic Shakespeare." *Representations* 21 (Winter 1988): 1-25.

Parry, J. H. *The Discovery of the Sea*. London: Weidenfeld and Nicolson, 1975.

Pérez Fernández, Isacio. *Inventario documentado de los escritos de Fray Bartolomé de las Casas*. Bayamón: Centro de Estudios de los Dominicos del Caribe, 1981.

Reynolds, L. D., and N. G. Wilson. *Scribes and Scholars*. Oxford: Oxford Univ. Press, 1968.

Richman, Gerald. "Artful Slipping in Old English." *Neophilologus* 70 (1986): 279-291.

Robertson, William. *The History of America*. Vol. 9 of *The Works of William Robertson, D. D.* 12 vols. Edinburgh: Peter Hill, 1818.

Rumeu de Armas, Antonio. "El 'diario de a bordo': el problema de la paternidad del extracto." *Revista de Indias* 36 (1976): 7-17.

Saint-Lu, André. "La marque de Las Casas dans le 'Journal de las Découverte' de Christophe Colomb." *Langues Néo-Latines* 239 (1981): 123-134.

Savran, George W. *Telling and Retelling: Quotation in Biblical Narrative*. Bloomington: Indiana Univ. Press, 1988.

Stanley, Christopher D. "Paul and Homer: Greco-Roman Citation Practice in the First Century CE," *Novum Testamentum* 32 (1990): 48-78.

Swann, Brian R., and Arnold Krupat. *Recovering the Word: Essays on Native American Literature*. Berkeley: Univ. of California Press, 1987. 129-148.

Teixeira da Mota, Avelino. "D. João Bemoim e a expedição portuguesa ao Senegal em 1489." *Boetim Cultural de Guiné Portuguesa* 26 (1971): 63-111.

Thacher, John Boyd. *Christopher Columbus: His Life, His Work, His Remains*. 3 vols. New York: G. P. Putnam's and Sons, 1903-1904.

Thomson, Robert W. "Vardan's Historical Compilation and Its Sources." *Le Muséon* 100 (1987): 343-352.

Timpanaro, Sebastiano. *The Freudian Slip: Psychoanalysis and Textual Criticism*. London: NLB, 1976.

Wagner, Henry R., and Helen Rand Parish. *The Life and Writings of Bartolomé de las Casas*. Albuquerque: Univ. of New Mexico Press, 1967.

West, Martin L. *Textual Criticism and Editorial Technique*. Stuttgart: B. G. Teubner, 1973.

Willis, James A. *Latin Textual Criticism*. Urbana: Univ. of Illinois Press, 1972.

Appendix

1. Same as 2, with italicized portions omitted.

2. I (he says), in order that they would show us goodwill, because I realized that they were people who could more easily be freed and converted to Our Holy Faith by love rather than *not* [sic] by force, gave to some of them red hats and some glass beads which they put around their necks, and many other things of little value, with which they took great pleasure and were so pleased that it was marvelous. Later they came to the ships' boats, where we were, swimming. They brought us parrots and balls of cotton thread and spears and many other things, and they traded with us for other things which we gave them, like small glass beads and bells. In short, they took everything and gave of whatever they had with goodwill. But it appeared to me that they were a people poor in everything. They go about as completely naked as their mothers bore them, even the women, although we did not see more than one young girl. All of them that I saw were *all* young men, none of them I saw was more than thirty years old. They are very well made, with very handsome bodies and very nice features; their hair is coarse like the tail of a horse, and short. They wear their hair almost over their eyebrows, except for a little in the back that they wear long and never cut. Some of them paint themselves black, and they are of the color of the Canarians, neither black nor white. And some of them paint themselves with white and some of them with red and some of them with whatever they find. And some of them paint their faces and some of them their *whole* body and some of them only the eyes and some of them only the nose. They do not carry arms nor are acquainted with them because I showed them swords and they grasped them by the edge and cut themselves through ignorance. They have no iron; their spears are rods without iron and some of them have at the end a fish tooth and others have other things. All of them are of good stature and well made. *I saw some who had signs of wounds on their bodies and I made signs as to what they were, and they showed me how people from other nearby islands came there and wanted to seize them and they defended themselves. And I believed and believe that they came here from the mainland to take them* *captive*. They should be good servants and [are] of good ability; I see that they very quickly repeat everything that is said to them. And I believe that they would all readily become Christians, for it appears to me that they have no religion. *Our Lord being pleased, I will bring from here when I leave six [of them] to Your Highnesses in order that they might learn to speak. I saw no animal of any kind on this island except parrots. All these are the words of the Admiral.*

3. Same as 4, with italicized portions omitted.

4. And all of them are of good stature, very handsome people. Their hair is not curly but sleek [?] and coarse like *horsehair*. And all are very broad in the forehead, *more than any other that I have yet seen*. And their eyes [are] very beautiful and not small. And none of them is black but rather the color of the Canarians. Nor should anything else be expected since this [island] is east-west with the island of Hierro in the Canaries on a line. Their legs are very straight, all alike and no belly, but are very well made.

5. Your Highnesses would be much pleased to see their demeanor. I believe that the king Guacanagarí must have commanded them to come in order better to show his grandeur.

6. We do not recognize here the king and queen of Castile, nor their letters-patent, nor had they [*sic*] fear of them, but would have them understand what thing was Portugal.

7. Then the capitão-mor replied that he and the others did not recognize the King and Queen of Castile, nor their letters-patent, nor did they have fear of them, but would have them know what Portugal was.

8. This belt was made of very small stones, like dewdrops, made of fish bones, white with some colored ones interspersed. [It was] sewn with cotton thread. The workmanship was so beautiful that the obverse was as beautiful as the front, although all white. It was as if it had been done on an embroidery frame, as the embroiderer of Castile makes the borders on chasubles. It was a pleasure to see it. And it was so hard and strong that I believe, without a

doubt, that a shot from a harquebus could not have penetrated it—or could have done so with difficulty. It was four fingers wide, so that belts embroidered on a frame or woven with gold were worn by the king and grandees of Castile, and I managed to see one of them.

9. Same as 10, with italicized portions omitted.

10. This I did in order that the men would behave themselves better in Spain, having women from their land, than without them, because many other times it happened that bringing men from Guinea, *in order to learn the language* in Portugal, and when they returned and [the Portuguese] sought to profit from them in their own country for the good treatment they had had and the gifts that had been given them, but on arriving on shore they never [re]appeared. *Others did not do this.* Thus having their women they would be willing to carry out the business with which they have been charged, and also these women will teach our men their language, which is the same in all these islands of India, and all understand it and all go about in their canoes, which is not the case in Guinea, where there are a thousand kinds of languages, which are mutually unintelligible.

11. Same as 12, with italicized portions omitted.

12. There came so many of them that they covered the land, men as well as women and children, giving a thousand thanks. Some ran here and others there, bringing us bread, *which they make from niames, which they call* ajes, and which is very white and good, and they *brought* us water in *calabashes and in clay pots of the style of those of Castile,* and they brought us all they had in the world and they knew that the Admiral wanted, and all with a heart so large and so content that it was marvelous. "And do not say that because what they gave had little value and so they gave truly (*says the Admiral*) because those who gave pieces of gold did the same and as freely as those who gave calabashes of water. And it is an easy thing to recognize (*the Admiral says*) when a thing is given with a heart very desirous of giving." These are his words: "These people do not have sticks or spears or any other weapons, nor do the others of this whole island, and I hold that it is very large...."

13. ... and it is a marvelous thing how when a man greatly desires something and has it firmly in his imagination, everything he hears and sees he fancies to be in his favor every step of the way.

◆ **Chapter 7**

Loving Columbus

José Piedra

Indians discovered Columbus[1]
—bumpersticker

... They also likely made love to him. The original saying appeared on a bumpersticker that was produced to exploit the "celebration" of the 500th anniversary of the "discovery" of America. It is still glued, half-torn by an anonymous hand, to the glass panel of my office door and was the gift of a Caribbean student who was taking my course "Native Revenge." I take this bumpersticker to be an icon of the paradoxes that arise from Caribbean peoples placing too little or too much love in Columbus's coming. For the purposes of this essay I will consider myself in the heritage of the Caribbean natives.

I

He [Columbus] says that at that hour he believes that more than a thousand persons had come to the ship, and that all brought some of the things they possessed, and that, before they had come within half a crossbow shot of the ship, they stood up in their canoes, and took what they brought in their hand, crying, "Take! Take!" (Journal, *Dec. 23, 117*)[2]

Sugar, tobacco, coffee, chocolate, rum, gender, and sex are not what I would consider healthy representatives of a people. Yet Caribbean production is often equated with these products, and consequently the lives and even the cultures of the people are forever coined through the ensuing "unhealthy" values. I, for one, remember from my Cuban childhood the bother of riding an outdated English-built train through sugar cane plantations, while my father smoked a cigar and my mother opened up a thermos of coffee, which an unknown hand had laced with a shot of rum. All of these actions happened over and over again on our family outing from a town called Matanzas (Massacres) to one called Hershey (as in the brand of chocolate). For me, a small-town boy, the only redeeming value of the trip was catching a glimpse of some animal exhibiting its genitals or having sex, and maybe the fake embarrassment on the faces of the adults.

We, as inhabitants of the Caribbean, have become known as users and producers of rhetorical and mercantile, as well as psychological, physical, and finally, libidinal dependencies. Alongside the rest, gender and sex would seem safer products with which to associate, with certain precautions, and yet both of these libidinally ruled notions join the rest of the Caribbean products in becoming suspiciously short-term stimulants and long-term depressants, even for insiders. The moment that gender and sex become a line of commodified identity, their users' and producers' own engenderment and sexualization, as well as those of their chosen partners, become dependent on the whims of supply and demand—no less than sugar, tobacco, coffee, chocolate, and rum. And yet we need them all in the Caribbean in order to survive. In the end, although we might consider one or all of these lifelines of commodified identity as mere accidents of nature or of nurture, they are destined to become lifelong, habit-forming pursuits for conspicuous consumers, sincere detractors, and well-meaning apologists alike.

Imagine, for example, the likely nightmare of a Christopher Columbus extending to the world the naked and wild Caribbean natives as Spanish products. Imagine, too, a Fidel Castro marketing worldwide a handful of "boyish" cigars and "girlish" lineups of Tropicana chorus members, all in a meta-Freudian and pro-

Cuban line of duty. Although Columbus allegedly never touched a native and Castro is rumored to have given up smoking and eliminated prostitution in his native country, Columbus, Castro, and I still have to deal with other equally (ob)noxious, hyper-engendered, and oversexed Caribbean images for sale. No matter how much the justification for Caribbean production radiates from a desperate need to survive by marketing people and products on alien grounds, the ongoing side effects of the exchange are bound to erode Caribbean integrity. But what if we consider hyperengenderment and oversexualization as part of *our* post-colonial identity? Could gender and sex become revealing and rebelling pillars of our identity? What if we accept these alien or alienating "traits" as postcolonial sources for a critical strategy to overcome our colonial beginnings?

The very issue of postcolonialism assumes a review and/or rejection of colonialism. This leaves the reviewer with a sense of a virtual continuum from colonialism to postcolonialism, which in the case of the Caribbean might be quite closer to the truth than we care to admit. If one is to extricate from such a setting the question of Caribbean gender and sex, the search for a libidinal aspect of the colonial–postcolonial continuum would be at best a most frustrating one, at worst a moot point. Judging by the bareness of the field, Caribbean critics as well as critics of the Caribbean seem to have convinced themselves that there could not be a troubling sense of "postcoloniality" in matters of gender and sex in which there is virtually no record, or at least no reliable record, of colonial antecedents. I suspect that those who would be willing to deal at all with the colonial search for the history of the Caribbean libido would be compelled to declare that the early chroniclers preferred not to think of themselves as having gender or sex worth debating, much less debatable gender and sex. The likely exception would have been made by the chroniclers in order to praise themselves for having the right gender and sex or to chastise others for having the wrong gender qualities and too much of the wrong kind of sex. Even such a reticence has important repercussions in our present-day libidinous clichés. The colonial precedent also aids in understanding the avoidance of open discussion about the Caribbean libido in literary circles. The

possibility of defining some libidinally informed literary continuum would arguably allow critics to face up to their dependency
on a colonial past and postcolonial present based on stereotypical
notions of engenderment and sexuality.

Christopher Columbus, the earliest chronicler of the New
World, can hardly be trusted as a fair-minded witness of gender
and sex. Even if we could trust or read through his colonial agenda,
we would have to contend with his publishing politics and the editorial policies of others. At the very least Columbus had to please
censors; at the very most his writings have survived the meddling
pens of people such as Bartolomé de Las Casas. The well-known
"editor" of the *Journal of the First Voyage*, arguably the defender
of natives' "purity" of soul and readiness for conversion, would
likely have put a damper on any mention of gender markers and
sexual activity.[3] After all, these would constitute impure obstacles
to the expected conversion. Meanwhile, Columbus, as defender of
natives' "impurity" of body and readiness for work, would likely
have found solace in the company of the peoples of the Caribbean.
I can only guess that Columbus's lost "manuscript" of the *Journal*
might have contained a great deal more wonder about gender and
sexual "difference" on this rather goldless and goalless stopover on
the interminable trip to India. At least subliminally Spaniards make
do with (West) Indians when (East) India seems to have eluded
them.

Indeed I have found enough libidinal markers and activities
in the *Journal*, even through Las Casas's publishing feat, to create a basis from which to imagine the rest. I have also compared
the "anthropoetical"[4] perception of certain islands in this joint
text with equivalent episodes in the works of ensuing chroniclers,
chiefly Fray Ramón Pané, Amerigo Vespucci, and Hernán Pérez
de Oliva. The rather more libidinally explicit comments of these
three writers on Caribbean natives have helped me understand
Columbus's/Las Casas's repression and/or self-censorship, as well
as their rare bursts of libidinal expression. In the end, I have been
pleasantly surprised about how much this odd couple of conquering men leave in their texts about their appreciation of the gender
typification and sexual practices of the men and women they discovered. Suffice it to say for the time being that they needed these

bodies and souls to feed the empire—and probably their egos. I propose to search for clues of Columbus's/Las Casas's libidinal cache, as well as to draw conclusions about the dormant infancy and latent maturity of Spanish Caribbean gender and sex studies.

At first glance, texts by Columbus and Co. provide a most surprising, preposterous, and telling rendering of the Spanish dawn of Caribbean codes and roles: that Amerindians had virtually no responsible or acceptable gender and sexual definition prior to being "discovered." Right after the "discovery," any discussion of the meeting and mating between the Spanish Self and the Caribbean Other was indeed very closely monitored. The Spanish refused to grant validity to the native hold on gender and sex or to reveal the libidinal exchange between colonizer and colonized. The very theme of gender and sex might bring about the Self's admitting being tempted by the Other. In order to combat these fears the colonizers upheld the notion of conversion by virtue of arrival. Conversion was a form of inoculation against contagion, particularly against desires not ruled by the Self.[5] Conversion was established not only in terms of the language of the Spanish empire and of the Catholic God, but also in terms of the sacred and profane language of gender and sex.

Across the board, the earliest Spanish settlers repressed and expressed Caribbean values to suit their expectations. Columbus himself died claiming to have arrived in India, having found gold, a place for God, and a large cache of naked natives ready to serve him, the Crown, and the Cross.[6] Like all of us, he expressed what was convenient to him and repressed the rest. It matters little to literary critics if in Columbus's writing the balance between repression and expression was willful and controlled or not. What is important is that largely the exceptions from official expectations were, implicitly or explicitly, rejected by the chroniclers as irresponsible acts. In turn these acts were attributed to the irresponsibility of the natives. But as we already know, those attributions were closely monitored; few dared to let loose on paper what they had lost and lusted after in life. Male chauvinism, heterosexism, and religious bigotry took care of the monitoring. Eventually, the master code and the sacred and secular legal systems censored any deviations left unchecked. However, at all sorts of levels—

ethical, aesthetic, political, and libidinal—the normative invasion was, so to speak, in the cards, and chroniclers became susceptible to the charms of the Caribbean. A steady stream of beautiful bodies and good souls paraded in naive nakedness before the incredulous eyes of the first Spanish visitors. The witnessing pen of the chroniclers discreetly followed these wonders into the Bush and onto the Book. Moreover, while playing their cards right, the newcomers also undoubtedly shuffled a full deck of gender and sexual differences in the strip-poker game of transatlantic libido.

The result is at best paradoxical, at worst playful. With a critical stretch of the imagination the long-term outcome is even helpful. On the one hand, we have the repression of gender and sex of the Other for the sake of the imperialist projection of the Self. On the other hand, the repression was far from foolproof and, to my mind, the failures remain arguably willful. After all, the chroniclers themselves were held accountable by the proper authorities for failing the norms; they were themselves prisoners of such norms. Consequently, as a measure of freedom, they could have pretended that they did not know that they were failing, even when in reality they might have welcomed or fostered such failings. This is particularly important in matters of gender and sex, toward which many chroniclers have traditionally pretended to be naive. Willful or not, libidinal naiveté is shared by colonizer and colonized, whereas libidinal intentionality is exerted by the colonizer over the colonized. Nontraditional instances of gender typification and of sexual practice became the exception to the rule. In those instances the colonized had a monopoly on the blame.

The nontraditional had to be accounted for, and it was largely cast in the role of the fantastic. Manly dragons and macho heroes, damsels in distress and powerful witches begin to foot the bill left unpaid and unsaid by forbidden gender attitudes and sexual experiences. No wonder a whole series of sexy books encoded in fantasy, ranging from romances of chivalry to *Don Quijote*, became best-sellers in the New World (Leonard 106, 270). They were eventually banned, alongside the official chronicles of the New World, because they were considered to be a pernicious influence on the transatlantic citizenry.[7] Thus the very fanciful and the very "real" were considered damaging by the powers that be—this is still so in many parts of the world if we consider "pornography" and "codified" government information as comparable extremes of fictional and factual sources of knowledge. And yet, classical and Renaissance chronicles of voyages other than those of the New World, which stand as encoded in fantasy as romances of chivalry and the *Don Quijote*, were upheld by the voyagers and their commanding authorities as vital sources of information. The fantastic divinities and monsters, as well as the tidbits of concrete information contained in such books, readily availed the chroniclers with characters to cast their libidinal lines—and hooks.

Whatever was missing in the travelers' vocabulary and view of reality, or deemed unacceptable by the pertinent authorities, was readily found abroad, wrapped in the sort of fiction that its contemporaries dreamed of turning into fact. The Other was embellished and/or doomed to play untraditional parts, to play out figments of the Self's imagination. In either case, such a Self would not have to assume much responsibility over the projections. Authorship, including that of the most fictitious books and imaginative passages, was attributed by the Self, often in the third person, to his faithful rendering of what the author witnessed. The excuse: the unknown world made me do it. Columbus, Las Casas, Vespucci, Pané, and Pérez de Oliva allude, for instance, to traditional limitations that they had to violate in order to do their job as witnesses. Pané is particularly graphic when he claims to have written in a certain way because he had only bits and pieces of paper while in the field: "Since I wrote hastily and did not have sufficient paper, I could not put in their proper place the things I had misplaced; but in spite of all of this, I have not erred, for they believe it all just as I have written it" (28).[8] He thus implicitly blamed his inexperience in dealing with unknown objects and untraditional subjects on a mechanical problem: his improvised writing on bits and pieces of paper gave witness to the experience of the New World according to an improvised order that is odd but befitting. Such an order tacitly and conspiratorially violated the rhetorical and ethical, not to mention libidinal, European standards of the time. In conclusion, the job of these witnesses was to take everything down, and likely everyone, too. In order to do so they felt justified to violate, mostly quietly, a long list of rules, ranging from the mechanics of reporting to the mechanics of meeting and mating. Whatever the Selves could not justify they blamed on something or somebody else.

Voraciousness and rejection are two of the most constant drives projected by the Spanish Selves onto Caribbean Others. The two drives go hand in hand: voraciousness—that is, take, take, take down and make yours—and rejection—take, take, take off and avoid the blame. Whatever cannot be taken down is blamed away; these are the rules of colonial assimilation.[9] And the Spaniards' affect toward voraciousness and rejection of the Caribbean natives is balanced with fear of these natives. That is, the very Americans whom the Spaniards wanted to assimilate, in writing and every other way, had to be kept at a distance, rejected to the margins, a controllable fiction of the Self's imagination. In turn, the Other could counterattack the Self's voraciousness and rejection, by eating and killing them—perhaps proof that the imaginative creations of the empire can strike back.

Many chroniclers of the Caribbean represent with cannibals and Amazons human exchanges based on voraciousness, assimilation, and swallowing, as well as distancing, rejection, and killing revenge. Dominant selves attempt to rhetorically trap and domesticate these otherwise indomitable bestial Others by "isolating" them, that is, placing them on libidinally created islands. In the interim, the pages on these islands also seem to be able to rhetorically entrap the readers who for centuries have either discriminatingly avoided on paper or indiscriminately embraced in life the gender and sexual charge of these unique Caribbean limbos, paradises, and/or human zoos.

Spanish chroniclers such as Columbus/Las Casas placed libidinally dangerous natives on islands that are definitely not in the mainstream, and thus those who are destined to share the islands with them can justify their ensuing behavior, including repressed or expressed lack, excess, or irregularities of gender encoding and sexual activity. This behavior presumably did not occur beyond the specially gender-marked and sexually coded enclaves. The allocated space provided pockets of permissiveness in the Caribbean archipelago where their "discoverers" could let their imagination loose, and possibly act out what they would consider lewd behavior back home or elsewhere. Ideally these islands would provide libidinal stages for freak shows geared toward a writing/reading/ paying Spanish public who would not necessarily mix with the actors and actresses. But what a set-up for temptation and contagion! The very isolation of such libidinally odd islanders, qualities, quantities, and mores might make them attractive and worth the side trip. Furthermore, let us also remember that the odd islanders in question aggressively traveled through the archipelago—a fact of which such chroniclers as Columbus/Las Casas constantly remind us.

If a Caribbean theater of gender and sex freaks became an escape valve for the lives of these Spanish impresarios, such a show must have spilled into the mainstream, even onto the mainland. At least the tendency is still threatening today. Among the most recent and most exploitative of Caribbean visitors there is an expectation for life in the archipelago to be a theater of obnoxious, hypergendered, and oversexed behavior, available to the paying passer-by. Customers might justify their behavior as yielding to the needs of the native performers under controlled circumstances.

I interpret cannibals and Amazons to be as repressively pregnant of the Caribbean theatrics projected onto natives by alien "discoverers" as later stereotypes are flagrantly expressive of the same. The search for colonial traces of a Caribbean libidinous past and of postcolonial libidinal liberation is enhanced by the secret love life of cannibals and Amazons. These exceptional islanders traded bites and strikes, love and war in an outrageously permissive manner that tests the limits of what to the traditional Self was the nontempting and noncontaminating manner of the untraditional Other.

Admittedly, I am building my critical strategy on a hope for libidinal liberation that has already proved costly and creates new ambivalent expectations. Reviewing a past of colonial devastation I find images of the Caribbean providing smokescreens for imperial notions of gender and sex, whorehouse islands for the Western world, and textual orgies for an increasing number of international customers. Cannibals and Amazons complete and complicate the picture. Old and new clichés have been ostensibly digested by all of the affected as a form of advertisement that subliminally presents us to the world as human bait in five hundred years of brochures for Caribbean cruising. The prospects for native revenge are ominous indeed.

For the time being you must take my word for it: a great deal of the hyperengendered and oversexed texts that derive from such a doomsday setting reserve a few trap doors for their patronizing and denigrating clients. My leader in this is Columbus, not Columbus the "discoverer" of Others but rather Columbus the "discoverer" of Self, and of himself as a compromise agent of Self and Other. I am referring to the Columbus that I have called elsewhere a mid-Atlantic colonial and the first proto-creole citizen of the New World (Piedra, "The Game" 39-50). Think of him as a recent immigrant to Spain and at best an improvised Christian, some say a convert. He becomes for me a scion of self-consciously critical writing, not of Hispanic culture as a whole, but of the Caribbean. I suspect that he was not just a target of compromised nativization or critical creolization, but also an early target of native libidinal conquest, perhaps revenge. Even his paternalism toward natives can be forgiven if we, the step- or natural children of the colonizers and the colonized, learn how to balance his love and hate toward us and ours toward him.

For Columbus the Caribbean was neither a smokescreen nor a whorehouse, nor a bargain basement of texts on sale, nor an archipelago of cannibals and Amazons. Columbus was too prudish, too prudent, and too pushy to doom us completely. He would rather have endorsed the idea that these islands I call ours provided an enormous range of possibilities for the newcomers. Indeed the notion is close to that of a "free zone" to project his dreams, and those of the Crown and Cross, through the bodies of the natives. So, at a certain level, he lives out his dreams and those of his superior commanders by way of the Caribbean natives. Shortly after Spaniards first set foot in this world, and the lack of expected values threatened Columbus's New World dreams, Caribbean natives were destined to become the consolation prize. Ostensibly this strategy saved Columbus's face by dooming our skin; but arguably we also got under his.

The Caribbean "free zone" that I envision in Columbus's consolation plans does not function as an open avenue of the libido. Far from it; that would not have been in keeping with the Columbian persona, or the imperial and religious enterprises. Instead, in matters of the libido, the Caribbean began to operate as a "gray zone" for human exchanges. As such, it provided loopholes for the untraditional. Armed with such a realization, my project entails "anthropoetically" decoding notions of gender typification and sexual practices that have been preserved, arguably for the benefit of both the native and the foreigner, under the layers of our colonizers' rhetorical debris. My target text is the communal effort by Christopher Columbus and his editor/publisher Fray Bartolomé de Las Casas, the so-called *Journal of the First Voyage*, which chronicles the outset of what was to become the European's New World.

A word of warning in the guise of self-centered apology: if, ultimately, the Spanish Caribbean heritage is the result of a multisided meeting and mating game, such a game must have been far more dangerous to play in real life than on the colonial field of the day or the postcolonial critical field of today. Furthermore, if the situation remains precarious for the colonizers' engaging in traditionally licit and namable gender and sex, it is much more so for the colonized engaging in de facto illicit and presumably unnameable gender and sex. What if the gray zone of gender and sex becomes a homoerotic or proto-gay zone?

Some of the traditional dangers of living at the edge of gender and sex still exist in the Caribbean, alongside new ones. A decade ago while in the Dominican Republic I interviewed a few European customers of a sex hotel who had been lured there by a get-to-know-the-Caribbean tour. The lodging was also advertised by the local English-language paper as a family establishment with four-poster beds. As implicit in the name of the Hotel Colón and in the advertised offerings in the Dominican paper, any paying customer could replay to the hilt the act of discovery, including unsuspected native pleasures, while moored in four-poster master beds.

Early one evening I sat on a bar stool among these intrepid travelers in the hastily spruced-up lobby of a dilapidated Victorian-style building located in the downtown area of the capital. The room was "naively" muraled to look like a postcard view of a night in the tropics. The alien customers were getting ready to mingle with the natives, who stood guard, soldier-erect, on the shores of a painterly sea framed by palms and a full moon among lazy coconuts and garlands of Christmas lights out of season. Were they ready to serve or to be served?

"Why are you here?" I finally engaged some European customers in a language improvised from international hustling English. "Because this is a people-to-people exchange." "If we weren't here someone else would be." "These people do this business on the side." "They practice their life, their love, and their art with us." "They have nothing to lose and much to gain; so do we." The answers from so many of them were not merely cynical rationalizations. Indeed they sounded unusually sophisticated and sophistic in the sweet-and-sour echo chamber of this gay bordello. From the mouths of the johns emerged a mixture of love and hate of Other and of Self, of humanitarianism and cynicism, of tourism and fatalism. I went on cruising the Caribbean, but the image remained with me.

While taking refuge from the heat in an air-conditioned Kentucky Fried Chicken franchise in the next cruise stop on the Haitian side of the same Dominican island, I told my traveling companion about the experience. "How about the natives?" he asked. "They were not available for comment." So I said.

II

New World Libido

I have found many earlier references to the secret libidinal availability of Caribbean natives who are otherwise unavailable for input. This situation is already suggested by the 1493 papal bull *Inter Caetera* (literally, "Among Other Things," or "By the Way"), by which the Pope appropriated the announcement and claimed for himself a slice of Christopher Columbus's success (Sanz López 31-32). The Spaniards, who proceeded to call this announcement "Bula de Concesión," or "Concession Bull," obviously attempted to emphasize the Vatican's sacred bond of concession to them rather than their costly indebtedness to papal bonding. To no avail. As we well know, Spain's imperial sword and word had to share the New World with the Cross. Many a document attests to such a sharing, ranging from the worldwide advertisement campaign conducted by Columbus himself, with the help of his Italian and Vatican friends, to Father Las Casas's editing of Columbus's journal of discovery. The Vatican claimed that Christopher Columbus:

> With the help of Divine Aid, navigating through the Western regions of the Ocean Sea toward the Indians SO IT IS SAID, have discovered [*invenerunt*, "came upon"] certain extremely remote islands and land mass, never before found by anyone... in which there are inhabitants who live in peace and that, SO IT IS ASCERTAINED, walk around indecently [*indecentes*] naked.[10]

The insistence of this document on phrases such as SO IT IS SAID and SO IT IS ASCERTAINED, which are capitalized in the original, might be a ready-made cliché of Vatican rhetoric, but at any rate, it sets the tone of this advertisement for Caribbean cruising as an invitation for non-Spanish travel. The same can be said about the opening phrase "With the help of Divine Aid" ("Quid tandem divino auxilio") appended to the secular aid of the Spaniards in the "discovery." While the papacy conditionally concedes to the Spaniards the success of the mission of discovery, it reserves for itself the right of witnessing and the need for corroboration, indeed religious recovery. Furthermore, the Spanish mission coopted by the Pope announces the encounters with the Indians, rather than with India, thus bypassing the problem of the original goal and thus the guidelines for the ownership of India laid out in the Crown's *Capitulations* (*Capitulaciones*). The Royal contract, which is understandably both flexible and precise in its terms—flexible for what was to be found; precise for what it expected to get—only implicitly alludes to the native "bodies" among "other Things and Merchandise of whatever kind, name, or description, which may be bought, bartered, found, acquired, or obtained within the limits of the said Admiralty" (Morison 28).

After the New World and/or Indies became a fact, the papacy actually claimed for itself Indians unspecified in the *Capitulations*.

They offered valuable souls fit to be saved that accompanied bodies fit to work and to save the face of conquerors expecting other
lands, other people, and other types of merchandise—or at least
more and better of each of the above categories. To this effect,
the 1493 bull and subsequent papal communications stressed the
newness of territory "invented" [*invenerunt*] by the Spaniards, by
"chancing upon it" or "reinventing" it in terms of the Church. After all, the word "invention," suggesting both a work of chance
and a work of genius, becomes a commonplace form of expressing the "discovery," "uncovering," and/or "recovery" of the New
World without assuming the paradoxes of all of the other words.[11]
And although the territory had "never before [been] found by anyone," this very document puts in doubt the validity of the find by
attributing it to hearsay. Such a doubt weakens the Spanish "pre-
claims" over the territory found, but does not discourage its further
exploitation, particularly of the native "souls," ostensibly under
proper Vatican supervision.

In the *Capitulations* and later on in the papal bull, Indians are
offered as a consolation prize for the possibility of missing the
route to India. To this effect, the natives' nakedness becomes an
"indecent" incentive to exploration and correction rather than an
obstacle to their validation. Their nakedness can be taken as a symbolic offering of themselves, all the more correctable because it is so
naively and openly indecent. These early Americans were ready to
receive not just the Cross and the Sword, but also the written word
and the uncharted desire, presumably monitored by the Holy See.
The subliminal message of this passage of the bull could be: "Don't
take the Spaniards' word for it. Visit the naked wonders of the
Caribbean."

An important confirmation of the secular and religious "invention" of the New World was the Spanish plan to translate into
"reality" and into "cash" classical and Renaissance projections and
fantasies of the existence of a world beyond the known, not to
mention a Third Sex or Gender able to fulfill the full range of
the Self's libidinal expectations.[12] Subliminally, all terms of this
agenda put the Other in charge of completing, or fulfilling, the
incompleteness and longing of the Self. The Others shoulder the
responsibility but not the empowering mechanics of fulfillment.

By the time he arrives in the New World, Columbus has everything to gain by pairing the authority of the Pope against that of the
Spanish Crown. There are sufficient indications to suggest that this
was part of Columbus's strategy of survival. He cannot be easily
dispossessed or disposed of by either authority, vying for a piece of
the American pie. Beyond survival, his bargaining ability would be
improved by serving as mediator not just between the Old and the
New World, but also between the Seat of the Cross and that of the
Sword. Christopher Columbus, the itinerant Other who bargained
for himself a Spanish appointment, thus becomes a Self-appointed
colonial envoy of Christ (as his first name indicates: *Christo ferens*,
"Christ's bearer"). He also subliminally appoints himself "inventor" of the American libido. Let me give you a taste of Columbus's
strategy as (re)produced by Las Casas:

> "I," he [Columbus] says, "in order that they [the natives]
> might feel great amity towards us, because I knew that they
> were a people to be delivered and converted to our holy
> faith rather by love than by force, gave to some among
> them some red caps and some glass beads, which they hung
> round their necks, and many other things of little value. At
> this they were greatly pleased and became so entirely our
> friends [quedaron tanto nuestros] that it was a wonder to
> see. Afterwards they came swimming to the ships' boats,
> where we were, and brought us parrots and cotton thread in
> balls, and spears and many other things, and we exchanged
> for them other things, such as small glass beads and hawks'
> bells, which we gave to them. In fact, they took all and gave
> all, such as they had, with good will, but it seemed to me
> that they were a people very deficient in everything. They
> all go quite naked as their mothers bore them; and also the
> women, although I didn't see more than one really young
> girl. And all those whom I did see were youths, so that I did
> not see one who was over thirty years of age; they were very
> well built, with very handsome bodies and very good faces.
> (*Journal*, Oct. 11 [an entry that includes Oct. 12, to which I
> am actually referring], 23-24)[13]

The ratio here is one female virgin to many "very well-built"
males, under thirty years of age, "of very handsome bodies and
very good faces." Their bodies and faces seem to be very much

part of an exchange that includes trinkets and "other [unnamed] things" to be "delivered" and "converted" [wrapped and ready to go Spanish and Christian] through love rather than force. At least one of the two categories, the virgin or the hunks, who become objectified and merchandised physiques in a native market "deficient in everything" else, compares favorably to the warring mature males and their gullible and easy-to-buy housemates as a potentially unreachable object of desire.

The choice of whom Columbus praised and set aside is of paramount importance to my investigation. I hope that it reveals something about Columbus's well-hidden libido. But since the issue of homoeroticism and homosexuality can hardly be taken lightly when dealing with the alleged Father of the Caribbean, let us first further set the ground for the discoverer's gray zone as a potential gay zone. What sets up the Caribbean situation as different from that of the rest of the New World? Is it simply the fact that, being the first area of the Americas to be experienced and recorded, it caught the Spaniards by surprise?

For the incoming Spaniards the Caribbean lacked the "textual" challenges that were present, for instance, in the mightier writing peoples of Mesoamerica and the equally feisty, accounting peoples of Andean America. Such perceived relative poverty in Caribbean cultural and military power, civilization, and will may have predestined my culture to be billed from the start as a parade of natives whose nakedness of body and soul was predisposed to provide libidinally charged values at the beck and call of our suitors' tradition and trampling. At any rate, textual data and common sense, including the virtual annihilation of Caribbean natives, indicate to me that we have been more effective in making love than in making war, even though the available texts make it difficult to differentiate between love and war.

As we already know, cannibals and Amazons illustrate the difficulty of differentiating the notions of love and war in the New World—in other words, the love and war between Self and Other. The Self established toward both of these exceptional variants of Otherness what in psychological terms is known as a "hostile dependency." Cannibals and Amazons are needed by the Spanish Self to complete as well as to compete with them. Beside the convergence of loving and warring, other fine lines practically vanish, such as those between witnessing and becoming, needing and being, assimilating and eating, meeting and mating, hunting and fucking, creating and procreating. The fear of undifferentiation would be a panicky state of affairs for most. It becomes a crucial issue of survival for the colonized, who are subjected to the colonizer's panic. I would argue that upon identifying the Self's panic about such a confusing state of affairs critics would uncover signs that there was some liminal consciousness of hostile dependency. Let us review the cannibalistic and Amazonic patterns of gender typification and sexual practices to attempt to uncover such signs of consciousness.

Cannibals eat mostly other males for the sake of love of the ancestors and/or for the sake of hate of the neighbor.[14] These natives presumably practiced transubstantiation of the worthy ancestor and/or of the worthy enemy, perhaps even of their unsuspecting friend—even munching away pieces from their live prey.[15] Consequently they symbolically and factually recreate procreation—passing on digestively rather than genetically precious knowledge chiefly from male to male. Presumably this practice frees them from regular procreation, something they do only in order to keep alive a critical mass of cannibals. Their mating habits can hardly be called traditional—as exemplified by the myth-weaving Pané (26-27), who mentions cannibals' trapping with their own rough bodies androgynous creatures whom they pierce at the level of the groin and transform into women.[16]

In turn, Amazons fight for the sake of love of their own kind, and when they mate with men they do it for the exclusive purpose of giving birth to females, while the male offspring are disposed of, sometimes eaten (Pérez de Oliva 50-54). Cannibals and Amazons mostly live among members of their own gender, and their sexual practices and warring activities are primarily directed toward preserving their own kind. Their existence is a veritable potpourri of homoeroticism and heteroeroticism, homosexism and heterosexism, not to mention the mixing and matching of other relative matters—above all, love and war, eating and assimilating, hunting and fucking, creating and procreating.

To me, the compounding of these factors alone allows my

zeroing in on the most extreme traditional deviations from the Self-appointed libidinal norm. However, ultimately, the issue is not so much whether particularly threatening human activities fuse with less threatening ones in the colonial mind, but why this is important as a cover-up for nontraditional forms of gender and sex that merit uncovering. Moreover, once again, the question is not so much whether or not homoeroticism and homosexism fuse with heteroeroticism and heterosexism for the sake of a rhetorical safe heaven, or that homosexuality as a singular issue is verifiable in the earliest chronicles (as I think it is), but to what degree the colonial management of each of these libidinal classifications offers a paradigm of Otherness with which we could all identify.

I assume that a likely reason for the banishment of cannibals and Amazons from our libidinal clichés would be not only their exceptionally ambivalent combination of divine and monstrous features, but also their largely implicit homoeroticism (mostly among cannibals) and rather explicit bouts of homosexuality (mostly among Amazons). And perhaps the reluctance of critics to deal with cannibalistic and Amazonic images and practices should also be linked to their special status in representing native-born aggression against the Spaniards. Cannibals and Amazons provide one of the few instances recognized by chroniclers of the natives taking them for targets of bellicose attacks and, if I am correct, also targets of libidinal threat. Leafing through early chronicles of the Caribbean one becomes aware that Spaniards are indeed eaten by cannibals and hunted down by Amazons. Mind you they also sporadically become cannibals and Amazons themselves—as illustrated by Cabeza de Vaca in Florida (*Relación de los naufragios y comentarios; Adventures* 60), in terms of a desperate measure of survival among shipwrecked sailors and as demonstrated by the life of the Monja Alférez (Erauso, *Historia de la monja alférez; The Nun Ensign*), the warring nun who lived for a long time as a man.[17]

Beyond the prospects of homoeroticism and homosexuality offered by cannibals and Amazons, we have to establish that the most obvious model for beauty and goodness for Columbus and Las Casas was male and young. Las Casas's choice of young males was a perfect one. The so-called Father of the Indians would target young males as converts, for they were most likely to be malleable to the ways of the Cross and thus to the practice of sacred love. These young males remain faithful to the image of male supremacy cherished by the Catholic Church. Columbus had a similar target group in mind. He also wanted young males to be saved but for ostensibly different reasons than those of Las Casas. Columbus's natives became human pelts or pets who were the most malleable, as slaves and citizens, to the ways of the sword and to the practices of profane love. They also proved rather faithful to the image of male supremacy cherished by the empire. Neither Columbus nor Las Casas could be readily accused of pederasty; if indeed they were guilty, they covered their tracks well.

One might also endorse the premise that Caribbean "natives" were promoted as "braves" to fulfill the Spanish urge for untamed and worthy enemies. What kind of winner would confess that the victory was a giveaway? By the same token the enemies would become tamable friends, after tasting the power of the invaders. Such are the bravado tactics of war and perhaps of feisty lovemaking between opponent factions. In both instances Renaissance tradition dictates for the chosen mates to be aggressive young males ready to capitulate to the power of a bigger male. In fact Columbus, Pané, and, above all, Vespucci and Pérez de Oliva are very worried about the presence of tall men, much more of tall women, among the natives.[18]

As soul mates, body-conscious buddies, or dream mates, the Others are forced to climb the difficult ladder of parallel Selfhood. The struggling steps to parallelism refer us to New World images of the search for the Fountain of Youth and further back to Old World images of Narcissus searching for the Fountain of Self.[19] Whereas Narcissus falls for his own image in a pool of water in the midst of the wild, the Spaniards fall for a younger and wilder image of themselves in a transatlantic whirlpool of desire. In principle, the chroniclers limited themselves to drawing a human link between themselves and the Caribbean natives who would reassuringly duplicate their maleness.

Once more, let us try to put aside the prospects of male-centered homoeroticism, this time in order to tackle the symbolic place of non-Amazonic womanhood in the earlier chronicles of the New World. The common remark—above all in Columbus's work—that postadolescent women were hiding from the new-comers might be conditionally associated with these Amerindians' reluctance to be subjected to the Spanish libido.[20] On the one hand, the women in question—or the Self-conscious Spanish chroniclers who recorded their presence on paper—might have found female beauty too risky an object to subject to the peril of male sexual con-quest. On the other hand, one could also argue that native women hid from openness in the text because, in the first place, they were not sought out by the Spaniards. Columbus gives an example that suggests the coincidence of both reasons. In this instance women other than Amazons show themselves and show off their power. In the end they objectify the Spaniards:

> Afterwards the men went out and the women entered, and sat in the same way round them [the Spaniards], kissing their hands and feet, fondling them, trying to find if they were of flesh and bone like themselves; they asked them to stay there with them for at least five days. (*Journal*, Nov. 6, 54)[21]

Some women seem to think the Spaniards to be "unreal" ob-jects of their desire, and therefore they show themselves basically uninterested in them as individuals. That is a possible reason why they shy away from the "conquerors," and why they, in turn, presume to avoid them.

Given these two possible obstacles impeding the meeting of the male colonizers and the female colonized, I have to prelimi-narily conclude that in texts written by men of the period, women might very well remain secondary targets or variants of a model of beauty and individuality that in Spanish eyes remains tradi-tionally male or traditionally *for* and/or *against* the male. In the balance, the women's ceremonious fondling and equally rituali-tic inquisitiveness have to be interpreted as a threatening act to the male conqueror—at least to the puritanical censoring practices that went with such texts.

III

*I saw some who bore marks of wounds on their bodies, and I made
signs to them to ask them how this came about, and they indicated to
me that people came from other islands, which are near, and wished
to capture them, and they defended themselves. And I believed and
still believe that they come here from the mainland to take them for
slaves. (Journal, Oct. 11 [12], 26)[22]*

*Two men showed them [the Spaniards] that some bits of flesh were
missing from their bodies and gave them to understand that the
Cannibals had bitten mouthfuls from them. The admiral did not
believe this. (Journal, Dec. 17, 102)[23]*

Name in the Hole: The Rules

Admittedly oversimplified, during the Renaissance love between
two men would be both more justifiable and more problematic
than love between two women. To illustrate the point, men were
ostensibly in charge of the politics of naming, and therefore they
could at will name or hide the name that established the de facto
and de juro distinction between Platonic love and Socratic love—
or better said, "Socratic sex," tantamount to sodomy (Dell'Orto
33-65). Thus, during the time of the Renaissance (and possibly at
any other time), men attempted to justify their right to do as they
pleased, even taking power over another man in practically any
way. Thus the full range of love and sex between men, including
the fine line between Platonic love and Socratic sex, is blurred and
the situation condensed to the question of sodomy. By virtue of
his respective positioning in the mechanics of sodomy, the naming
and fucking male could ostensibly distinguish who was gaining
and losing power.

Women were kept out of the picture, since presumably they
could neither have "meaningful" Platonic love nor "real" Socratic
sex nor could they, for that matter, presumably gain or have men
gain anything from them in the act of sodomy. I suspect that men
of that time were unwilling to talk about the possibility of a female being either the sodomizer or the sodomized. But willingness
to talk or not does not detract from the main issue: traditional
men's obsession with the hole-filling activity (or hole-making ca-

pacity) of the penis being solely responsible for settling the score of who had been empowered over whom through the mating act—particularly in a nonprocreational mating act such as sodomy.[24] The colonializing Spanish complicated matters considerably. They mixed and matched these prejudices to create their own intricate hierarchies—to a certain degree still extant today. In order to do so, they also added cannibals and Amazons as essentially Spanish exceptions to the libidinal tradition that they upheld; they offered them an opportunity to experience deviation in the libidinal plot of their voyage. Cannibalistic and Amazonic exceptions prove that release was from the self-imposed rules concerning transatlantic gender and sex.

In the texts of the transatlantic Spanish-speaking Renaissance, sodomy becomes the behind-the-scenes link between man-to-man love and man-to-man war. And as we shall see, this linkage was also projected onto woman-to-woman love and woman-to-man war. The men and women involved are ostensibly not the Self, his wife, and the Other, but the Others among themselves. However, even though to this day one's relative position toward hole-filling/hole-making is "orally" accepted as a "de facto" form of power, written discourse largely avoids the "de juro" inscription of such empowering definitions.

First of all, there is the distinction in Spanish between *bugarrón* and *maricón*, loosely translatable in English as "buggerer" and "buggered." Second, the *bugarrón* and the *maricón* are not distinctively distinguished by name in the chronicles of the New World, and to my knowledge only sporadically in the New World documents of the Inquisition. Records of inquisitorial trials embrace male homoeroticism and homosexuality under the umbrella of *pecado nefando*, the "nefarious sin" that ostensibly unites two men against God. In turn lesbians rarely appear in the texts of either the chronicles or the Inquisition. My random perusals of the documents of the Mexican Inquisition indicate that the lesbian affectional preference would be presumably neutralized under the all-encompassing, provocative heading of *pecados contra-natura*, or "sins against nature." This is a curious choice of words, because *amor contra-natura* is a euphemism for sodomy, otherwise known during the Renaissance as *amor socraticus*, "Socratic love." On this note, let me return to male-centered forms of empowerment.

According to the Spanish tradition to date, the sodomizing *bugarrón*, "buggerer" or, etymologically, "hole maker," is not a homosexual at all.[25] He is indeed empowered, even masculinized, by the act of sodomy at the expense of the *maricón*, which in Spanish does not literally translate to "buggered," or "holed man," but rather a womanized man, a "Mary Ann."[26] Thus, conveniently, the Spanish readily masculinize the sodomizer and not just emasculate but feminize the man in order I presume to complete the process of rationalization by way of which it is justifiable to make love to anyone, as a token of war—as long as the token is a woman or womanlike. Homosexual women—sinning, if not necessarily loving, "against nature" (*contra-natura*)—are also placed at the fringes of such a consideration. They take up archery in order to symbolically become a man by piercing the body and/or the heart of the males. Thus women too get to make holes and justify their lovemaking as a manly act of empowerment. The politics of naming are so strong and well digested by the system that even though colonial literature attempts to suppress direct evidence of such politics, the effects are there—particularly in the form of cannibals and Amazons.

IV

They [the all-female inhabitants of Matrimonio] do not shoot them [bows and arrows] as in other parts, but in a peculiar manner so that they cannot do much harm. (Journal, Jan. 15, 151)[27]

Name in the Hole: The Exceptions

The rule of thumb that characterizes cannibals and Amazons as exceptional natives endowed with special qualities of gender and of sex is fraught with homoerotic and homosexual potential. These aggressive males seem to have chosen, perhaps by a godly punishment, to live among themselves. At least so claims Pané, who had settled amid cannibal-fearing natives after arriving with Columbus on one of his trips to the island of La Hispaniola. The idea was in

the air and the experience certainly available, if not in his chosen
land at least close by, when Columbus implied and others testified
that cannibals were condemned by their God to live on men-only
islands.[28] Pané, for instance, takes a dramatic reinterpretation of
Christian reasoning, which would have homosexuals repent from
their sinning after the fall from Paradise; Pané, instead, has men
and women "sinning," becoming homosexuals, after being thrown
from a Paradise-like island onto others, from which they have to
reinvent their respective genders and "marital," or at least procre-
ative, relationship.[29] If the sexual activities of these cannibals can
only be deduced, their gender typification is far more obvious. Columbus and others describe these men "with very long hair, like
women wear their hair in Castile," a healthy shade of color, good
skin, and other features showing that they subject themselves to
pain for the sake of what they take to be beauty.[30] Traits such as
these remain to this day symptoms of feminine leanings and, in
a male, traditional stigmas of gay behavior. At the time, the confusion could have been the product of the utopian search for a
Third Sex or Third Gender, which I have suggested to be a revived classical theory that Renaissance explorers attempted to live
in practice.

Even when I assume homoeroticism and homosexuality
among cannibals, it is with the caveat that cannibalistic behavior is certainly a distorted picture of gay sexual practices or of the
search and experience of the Third Sex. Both pictures correspond
to Spanish images of incompleteness to be fulfilled in the New
World. Therefore, the homoerotic and homosexual images that en-
sue are imbued not just with heteroerotic imagination but also
with a heterosexual model. As I have already discussed, the idea
of cannibalistic transubstantiation complements these men's lack
of pleasure in procreation; and the idea of these men's androgyny
or hermaphroditism justifies and enhances the bodily possession
of the Other as an avenue for the colonizers' Self-empowerment.
I remind you that such a distortion is not necessarily wicked; it
might be in place merely as a condition for such libidinal material
to be discussed at all. To counter the idea of Spanish ill will toward
cannibals, let us point out that: (1) the land of the cannibals is offered by chroniclers to their readers as a dangerous lure lurking in

the Caribbean and other similarly wild enclaves; (2) cannibalistic love of Other was accepted by the Spaniards as a form of ritual warring.[31] And finally, as a state-of-the-art corollary I would argue that the global accusation of promiscuity raised against gays and the eating metaphor with which oral sex has been associated relate to the feats of voraciousness and fits of cannibalism that colonial Selves attribute to colonized Others, but presumably were enjoyed by both.

Meanwhile, lesbians, who in the nonliterary world of the Spanish Renaissance are pointedly empowered as *marimachos* ("Macho, or Butch, Maries"), travel to the New World as man-hol(d)ing Amazons ca. 1492.[32] They are portrayed as lovely images of aggressive womanhood. This is a male fantasy that backfires: they not only reject men, except as entrapped baby-makers, but be they "butch" or "fem" they also remain perfectly acceptable females in their own right—or at least on their own island. Amazons cannot be understood exclusively from the viewpoint of male-centeredness, especially from the perspective of male fantasies about lesbian "foreplay" or "coitus" interrupted by them. Amazons defy these set-ups. Arguably they surge above their comparative models, from Diana the huntress to Cupid, from the Harpies and the Furies to the Muses, from the Sirens to the Mermaids, all of which are mediators, entrappers, and doomers, love goddesses and/or androgynous warriors for love, toward which males develop hostile dependencies. In conclusion, Amazons translated themselves from objects to subjects of hostile dependency. No longer are they the target of male hostility and dependency; on the contrary, males are their targets. They interrupt their own ongoing hostility in order to engage in a mechanistic coitus that guarantees the (re)production of baby Amazons.

Beyond the mechanics of representing untraditional fact and fiction, Amazons provided Columbus and Co. with a perfect excuse for the absence of women from their lives. Maybe Columbus has become disillusioned with a series of feminized figments of the male imagination who never materialize as available women—for instance, the Sirens, whom he tentatively connects to the sighting of beautiful lower mammals in the Atlantic and ugly-looking manatees in Caribbean waters.[33] Decidedly, Columbus fails (with) heterosexual native women; arguably homosexual Amazons only fare marginally better in the Admiral's New World veiled scheme of gender and sexuality.

In the text Las Casas shared with Columbus, the Amazons essentially appear as mirages or a teasing bait. Later texts, beginning with Pané's, bill the Amazons as disappointed or betrayed females, who turn to each other for solace and to defend themselves from the disappointing or betraying males.[34] Ultimately the Amazons' veiled lovemaking among themselves, like the male bonding of the cannibals, was arguably accepted as part of their ritual warring. The islands of both are conveniently paired in the texts of Columbus, Las Casas, Vespucci, Pané, and Pérez de Oliva.[35]

But cannibals and Amazons are not only libidinally rich paradigms of Otherness. The very idea of a cultural image of the Caribbean basin is symbolically tied to cannibals and Amazons by way of Columbus. On the one hand, Columbus fantasized about fighting the troops of the Grand Khan—whose name, by corruption with the word "Carib" and identification with the alleged anthropophagy of this group, yields the words "cannibal" and "Caribbean."[36] On the other hand, Columbus's thirsty imagination rose to the need to prove that he had arrived on *tierra firme*, literally the "firm land" of continental America, by reporting on his feeling of arrival euphoria in what I would consider Amazonic terms.[37] The well-known episode of the *Account of the Third Voyage* places Columbus facing the delta of the Orinoco, about to land, or to trip, on this river that belongs to the large fluvial system of the later-to-be-named Amazonia.[38] The mouth of the river appears to his spirited male's cupidity and godfearing but fertile imagination as many things at once. Is it a pear? Is it a vagina? Is it the entrance to paradise? No, it is a super-breast, he decides—a breast cut off from America, the feisty warrior who would not give herself to him. As the euphoria subsides, Columbus's proto-scientific sense transforms the conical perspective he encounters from a river whose banks seem to come together as convergent lines on the horizon into a lesson in the nearly spherical nature of the earth. In spite of this Amazon-made hole in his imagination, the future of America is tied to the image of an Amazonic breast that stands as a synec-doche for the whole world that his erotic imagination has already conquered.

V

I saw no beast of any kind in this island, except parrots. (Columbus, Journal Oct. 11 [12], 24)[39]

Columbus's Second Coming

For the sake of enticement, Columbus includes in his account of the New World a seemingly dispassionate record of what at that time must have been considered a few divine monstrosities of the gender and sexual kind. The extraordinary human varieties thus paraded are all cagily assigned by our discoverer to specific islands for us to discover. For instance, when Columbus publishes in 1493 his letter to Luis de Santangel summing up the first voyage, he claims that among:

> these people good looks are esteemed.... Thus I have neither found monsters nor had report of any, except in an island which is the second at the entrance to the Indies, which is inhabited by a people who are regarded in all the islands as very ferocious and who eat human flesh; they have many canoes with which they range all the islands of India and pillage and take as much as they can; they are no more malformed than the others, except that they have the custom of wearing their hair long like women.... These [men] are those who have intercourse with the women of Matrimonio, which is the first island met on the way from Spain to the Indies, in which there is not one man. These women use no feminine exercises, but bows and arrows of cane ... and they cover themselves with plates of copper of which they have plenty. (qtd. in Sanz López 503)

For Columbus even the exception confirms the rule in matters of "human monstrosities," "gender ambivalence," and "sexual dif-ference." The exceptions are evident and ultimately should speak to our libidinal interests as critics and noncritics. The result, to my taste, is deliciously confusing. These divine monsters of sexuality might be men but they look and possibly behave like women who are likely to fall prey to the incoming Spaniards, while the women on the neighboring island act like fiercely voracious men who might be an enticing challenge for the Spaniards to meet, mate, and render meek. However, poetic justice is rendered in this Columbian fantasy as these natives find their perfect match. Either way, this fantasy match presumably leaves Columbus and his men safe from temptation and contagion. All of this, to my amusement, occurs around the island of Matrimonio—also spelled Mateunín in the Latin edition, Matinino, Matininno, or Martinino in other texts.[40] Experts rather link this Matrimonio, a less-than-veiled allusion to an island which in European ears would have been placed somewhere between "Child of Morning," "Marriage," and "Martyrdom," with present-day Martinique. Indeed, Columbus prefaces his description of the exceptional island of marriage with a kind of disclaimer, potentially spilling the erotic charge of this free libidinal territory onto other islands:

> In all these islands, I saw no great diversity in the appearance of the people or in their manners and language, but [furthermore?] they all understand one another, which is a very singular thing, and which I hope that will persuade Your Highnesses to convert them into our holy faith, towards which they are much inclined. (Sanz López 501)

There is indeed, in Columbus's textual and sexual perspective, an attempt to include all of us Americans within reach of the erotics of conquest, whether we place ourselves on Matrimonio, hail from Martinique, or neither.

Notes

1. I read preliminary drafts of this essay at the Cornell University 1990 Renaissance Colloquium directed by Marilyn Migiel and at the Duke University 1991 Gender Series directed by Eve Kosofsky Sedgwick and Michael Moon. I am indebted to Kate Bloodgood for her editorial comments.

2. "Dice que aquella hora cree haber venido a la nao más de mil personas, y que todas traían algo de lo que poseen; y antes que lleguen a la nao, con medio tiro de ballesta, se levantan en sus canoas en pie y toman en las manos lo que traen, dicciendo: 'Tomad, tomad.' "

3. Las Casas occasionally chastises Columbus in his marginal notes.

4. I adopt the term "anthropoetical" in the sense of a "cultural studies" approach to literature that includes the community that is represented or left on the margins of the representation, e.g. in the case of colonial chronicles, the colonized as willfully or unwillfully represented by the colonizer. For further explanation see my "The Game of Critical Arrival," 63-85. Also see Pané, Vespucci, and Pérez de Oliva.

5. Let us keep in mind that for the New World voyagers the worst "ailments" were dangerously related to the libido. They included syphilis and sodomy, incest and fraternal cannibalism. Quick conversion to Christianity and to the other ways of the Spanish would presumably prevent the above-mentioned ailments from reaching epidemic proportions. Whether as equals or as uneven partners, Spaniards must have approached proximity and intimacy with fear if not with contempt. The same could also be true of the natives, whose libidinal imprint, including curiosity and reticence, shows through Spanish inscriptions.

6. His last will testifies to this, although I wonder how much of this statement was a strategy to save for him and his progeny a measure of what had been promised to him in the *Capitulations* in terms of India—or rather "the islands and mainland of the Indies discovered and to be discovered" ("las islas e tierra firme de las Indias descubiertas e por descubrir"). That is, he had been given territory in, or on the way to, India(s), not in a New World, which so far led to "nowhere" known. His words, particularly the pluralization of India, cover all the bases. See his "Testamento y Codicilio" 359, and compare this strategic "pluralization" to the Crown's *Capitulations* (*Capitulaciones*) to Columbus—available in English in "The Capitulations of 17 and 30 April 1492," 26-31. Refer also to the text of the papal bull, which chooses to refer to the Indians rather than India (or Indies); the passage is quoted later in text.

7. On the war against reading "light literature," that is, "romances of chivalry," see Leonard's chapters "The Conquerors and the Moralists," 65-74, and "Light Literature and the Law," 75-90. For the ban on reading the *Quijote*, see 79. In reference to the chronicles themselves, although we have information only about a later ban, the fact that so many originals of these early documents have been lost, reedited, or published in truncated or adulterated forms might be sufficient proof of their danger for the powers that be. The works to be considered here—Columbus's, Pané's, and Vespucci's—all fall into this category. For information on the later ban see Cortés 1: viii.

8. "Puesto que escribí de prisa, y no tenía papel bastante, no pude poner en su lugar lo que por error trasladé a otro, pero con todo y eso, no he errado, porque ellos lo creen todo como lo he escrito." Refer also to my discussion of this subject in "The Value of Paper" 85-104, esp. 85-94. Practically all other Old World chroniclers mention some shortcoming of the actual material and/or rhetorical framework within which they inscribe the New World.

9. I deal with the colonial policy in terms of race in "Literary Whiteness and the Afro-Hispanic Difference," 303-332, also in a revised version in Dominick La Capra, *The Bounds of Race*.

10. "Quid tandem divino auxilio facta extrema diligentia per partes occidentales, UT DICITUR versus Indos in mari Oceano navigantes certas insulas remotis-

simas et etiam terras firmas, que por alios hactenus reperte non fuerant, *invenerunt*, in quibus quan plurime gentes pacifice viventes et UT ASSERITUR nudi *indecentes*" (Sanz López 31-32; translation mine).

11. My interpretation of the word "inventor" as it appears in the 1493 bull takes into consideration the problematic history of the Spanish arrival from their viewpoint as well as the natives'. The usage extends to many documents of the time and about that time—ranging from Hernán Pérez de Oliva's sixteenth-century work *Historia de la inuención de las Yndias* to Edmundo O'Gorman's twentieth-century work *La invención de América*. In fact the word "invention" attempts to overcome problems implicit in other words used to signal the meeting of the colonizers and the colonized. The term "discovery" would imply that Christ and Crown had once owned the New World or at least known about it and, consequently, the authorities would have to prove it, and "conquest" would imply justification for the use of force. Although undoubtedly all of these terms were shuffled and rationalized, particularly when it came time to "get to know" and "get to own" the Americans intimately, *invention* to this date seems much more suitable as a term particularly because its Latin etymology (the verb *invenire* simply implies "to come upon") would indicate a sense of wonder upon a chance wandering into a new continent, while the word's Romance usage favors the notion of a creative endeavor. In short, Divine Aid is followed by a lot of work—as the 1493 bull indicates. For the etymological implications of *invenire* see Pérez de Oliva, *Historia de la inuención de las Yndias*, 39. See also O'Gorman.

12. The Western notion of a Third Sex (Gender) has deep roots in the Judeo-Christian tradition—for instance, "in the writings of the Midrashim, Jehovah is both male and female; before the Fall, Adam and Eve were a single being." See van Stynwoort Logan, introduction, esp. 12. As a background to the religious tradition, let it suffice to connect the notion of a third libidinal category with the classical notion of androgyne/hermaphrodite, as suggested by Aristophanes's speech in Plato's *Symposium*, since in all likelihood before Plato—for instance in Herodotus's *Histories* 4. 67—the notion of androgyny was connected to "effeminacy." Note also that although Aristophanes is actually telling a myth of archaic unity, he also reflects on the actual condition of humanity—see for instance *Symposium*, 191d.33: "Each of us thus is a part of a man, because he has been cut like a flatfish; two were made out of one: each portion is always looking for his other half." Incidentally, the act of division of humanity into man, woman, and the androgynous, which is performed by Apollo in Plato's account, finds an echo in Pané's telling of the Arawak myth to be discussed later in this text. In this myth, sexual communication presumably leads to linguistic communication, as man creates woman from an "animalistically" self-contented being with whom he can now have "intercourse" at all levels. The notion of Arawak Otherness is thus born as a gender-, sex-, and speech-giving or subliminal voicing of womanhood through the libidinal and procreational consequences of engenderment. See Pané, 26-27.

13. "Yo (dice él), porque nos tuviesen mucha amistad, porque conocí que era gente que mejor se libraría y convertiría a Nuestra Santa Fe con Amor que no por fuerza, les di a algunos de ellos unos bonetes colorados y unas cuentas de vidrio que se ponían al pescuezo, y otras cosas muchas de poco valor, con que tuvieron mucho placer y quedaron tanto muestros que era maravilla. Los cuales después venían a

las barcas de los navíos a donde nos estábamos, nadando. Y nos traían papagayos y hilo de algodón en ovillos y azagayas y otras cosas muchas, y nos las trocaban por otras cosas que nos les dábamos, como cuenticillas de vidrio y cascabeles. En fin, todo tomaban y daban de aquello que tenían de buena voluntad. Mas me pareció que era gente muy pobre de todo. Ellos andan todos desnudos como su madre los parió, y también las mujeres, aunque no vide más de una harto moza. Y todos los que yo vi eran todos mancebos, que ninguno vide de edad de más de 30 años. Muy bien hechos, de muy hermosos cuerpos y muy buenas caras."

A similar passage occurs in Pérez de Oliva, who, after blaming the (male?) natives' fear of the Spaniards on their being taken for cannibals, deals thus with a token woman: "They were only able to hold onto one woman, whom they dressed according to our ways, and dealt with her humanly, and sent her back to her people, so that they would fill with the hope of good treatment" [the original says "conversation"—in the archaic sense of "treatment"?] ("Sola na muger alcançaron, la cual según nuestro vso vistieron, y trataron según pudieron más vmanamente, y embiáronla a los suyos, que les lleuase esperanza de buena conversación"; Pérez de Oliva 46). See also the editor's explanation of the word "conversation," 44-45.

14. Pérez de Oliva is particularly explicit in this regard: "Estos nombrauan caribes, que aunque eran codiciosos de la carne vmana, no comían las mugeres," 50, also 54, 59. For a review of the notion of symbolic versus gluttonous cannibalism see Geertz 102-28.

15. Columbus in his very first description of natives goes so far as to leave in doubt whether there are natives walking around with missing pieces of flesh because they defended themselves against the attack of cannibals or because the cannibals were able to bite off pieces of live flesh. See *Journal*, Oct. 11 [12], 24. He later confirms the possibility, *Journal*, Dec. 17, 102—quotations are given as epigraphs in part 4.

16. Refer to note 12 for a comparison with Plato's myth of gender origin. Also compare the version given by Pérez de Oliva 121-26. Note that the surprise of the Spaniards toward cannibalism underscores the apparent gluttony toward human flesh rather than the fact that it happened—presumably allowing the possibility of "symbolic" cannibalism. Furthermore, a range of chroniclers beginning with Columbus alludes to the cannibals' castration of their victims in order to fatten them up and thus improve the quality of the meat—there is also the distinct possibility of the "feminization" of the edible morsel. See *Journal*, Nov. 4, 52.

17. Columbus himself suggests that cannibals are going to imagine that when their friends did not come back from their visit to the Spaniards they would have been eaten (*Journal*, Nov. 23, 69) and, later on, through his *Letters* and other chronicles (chiefly Bernal Díaz del Castillo's), Cortés indicates that Moctezuma and other Mesoamerican natives called him "Malinche," confusing or at least fusing his persona with that of his translator/mistress.

18. It is Vespucci who is most concerned about size and strength, not just of bodies but also of male genitalia and women's superiority over men. See, for instance, the comparison between men and women in the first voyage, esp. 6-7 and the episode on the Island of Giants, esp. 27. On the issue of the male Other as genitally well endowed, consult Perry 67-89, esp. 81.

19. I am specifically referring to the accounts of the Spanish search for the

"Fountain of Youth," probably learned by chroniclers from the "romances of chivalry," whose actual search centered in Florida, and to Ovid's version of the Narcissus myth, which arguably led to the lingering medieval and Renaissance notion of writing books that acted as "mirrors of [an individual or a people's] knowledge," which constituted widespread reading among the earliest settlers to the New World. Leonard gives numerous examples of both myths read by the New World "braves."

20. It is so much the rule that women hide from Columbus—since the first encounter (*Journal*, Oct. 11 [12], 23-24, discussed in text)—that Columbus shows his surprise when women do show up alongside men, for instance, 28. Not so in Vespucci's *Letters*, where in the first encounter men and women either run away or show up together regardless of gender, for instance, 5-6. I have noticed a relationship between libidinal directness and the appearance of women in the text; that is, the more explicit the writer is about gender qualities and sexual activity, the more obvious women become in their texts. Vespucci excels in this matter; for him most native women are libidinous and desirous, for instance, *Letters* 46-47. Pané even tops Vespucci; his women are created by desperate men from androgynous beings.

21. "Después saliéronse los hombres, y entraron las mujeres y sentáronse de la misma manera en derredor de ellos, besándoles las manos y los pies, tentándoles si eran de carne y de hueso como ellos. Rogábanles que se estuviesen allí con ellos al menos por cinco días."

22. "Yo vi algunos que tenían señales de heridas en sus cuerpos, y les hize señas que era aquello, y ellos me mostraron como allí venían gente de otras islas que estaban cerca y los querían tomar y se defendían. Y yo creí y creo que aquí vienen de tierra firme a tomarlos por cautivos."

23. "Mostráronles dos hombres que les faltaban algunos pedazos de carne de su cuerpo y hiciéronles entender que los caníbales los habían comido a bocados; el Almirante no lo creyó."

24. I suspect that gestation has been traditionally seen by some males as a hole-filling compensatory activity in women, arguably even more dramatic than the tongue-piercing activities of anyone who is not a card-carrying macho.

25. I find the connection to Bulgaria, by way of a Bulgarian heresy of the Middle Ages, too fanciful, particularly in light of the fact that the well-regarded seventeenth-century dictionary *Tesoro de la Lengua Castellana o Española* by Sebastián de Covarrubias clearly identifies "buxarrón" as "horadado" ("pierced"), which was later given the opposite connotation, of "pierce." Other Romance languages have similar words, at least in the early developments of these languages. I have consulted the Barcelona edition of 1987, 244.

26. I wonder whether the word "maricón" is connected to the biblical "Malakoi," implying those who committed "delicta contra pudiciatam." See von Rosen 185.

27. "y no tiran como en otras partes, salvo por una cierta manera que no pueden mucho ofender."

28. Women cannibals do exist—mostly accompanying men—and sometimes women are victims of cannibals, but these are exceptions to the rule. Once again Vespucci provides the largest and most significant exceptions, particularly in his

description of a scene of women cannibals operating on their own and of a man devouring his wife and children; see *Letters* 38 and 47. In fact, we might think of the first instance as a case of impromptu revenge—to show women's power—and the second instance as a case of cannibalistic incest. In a sense both exceptional instances corroborate the rule that cannibalism is a form of erotic (if not always homoerotic) empowerment.

29. I am referring to Pané's telling of the myth of men and women abandoning the paradisiacal safe haven of a cave on the island of La Hispaniola, out of curiosity—i.e., the independent pursuit of knowledge, which the Judeo-Christian tradition, and Pané's version of Arawak mythology, associate with sexuality. See Pané, 22-32.

30. "When the boat reached the shore, there were behind the trees quite fifty-five men, naked, with very long hair, as women wear their hair in Castile. . . . All this the admiral says, and that he wished to take some of them. He says that they made many smoke signals, as they were accustomed to do in that island of Española [La Hispaniola]" (see *Journal*, Jan. 13, 148-49). The notion of sacrifice for the sake of beauty is related to the cranial deformation practiced by Caribs, which Columbus suggests when he says that they were dog-faced, as well as to their less dramatic cosmetic habits—consult, for instance, *Journal*, Nov. 4, Nov. 26, and Jan. 13 (52, 74, 146, and 148). Columbus also mentions that "since they were armed, they must be an intelligent people, and he believed that they may have captured some men and that, because they did not return to their own land, they may say that they were eaten" (*Journal*, Nov. 23, 69).

31. Columbus mentions a rich land of fearful people and explicitly connects cannibals and Amazons to the possession of gold and the use of arms throughout the *Journal;* the suspicion in the case of cannibals begins as early as Oct. 13, 26, where it is connected "linguistically" to the lands of the Grand Khan, Nov. 26, 74, and is finally seemingly verified on Dec. 17, 102, although other natives seem to have substantial gold objects—for instance, a mask—by Dec. 27, 125. Later, Amazons enter the picture as living on and owning islands that are rich in gold, Jan. 13, 146-47.

32. "Marimacho" already appears as a term in Covarrubias, and not surprisingly, as a derivative of "Maricón," its male equivalent; see 790. "Amazon" is also an entry in Covarrubias, its etymology debated as those who cut off one breast in order to make better use of the bow and arrow, or those who do not eat bread (but only meat instead); see "Amazona," 110. I cannot help noticing that the word also suggests "Love Zone" in Spanish.

33. What Columbus saw in the ocean were possibly sea cows or seals, but there are more interesting aspects of this issue. "The day before, he [Columbus] said that he saw three sirens, who rose very high from the sea, but they were not as beautiful as they are depicted, for somehow their faces had the appearance of a man." Las Casas cuts down on Columbus's fantasy, and yet he does not edit out (or perhaps adds himself), the manlike character of these women, as if this were enough of a libidinal detriment for the man aboard the caravels (*Journal*, Jan. 9, 143). For an excellent review of Columbus's and other chroniclers' sources, see Leonard's chapter "Amazons, Books and Conquerors, Mexico," 36-53.

34. Pané writes that women separated themselves from men because the lat-

ter had violated a taboo, which the text suggests was related to sexual curiosity/ timing/hygiene. Guahayona, a raging, godlike individual, asks them to leave their husbands, taking them to Matinino (Matrimonio in Columbus's *Letter*), while he goes to Guanín. In the rest of Pané's account, males attempt to retrieve women— from baby boys, who only want women for their teats, to adult males, who want women only for the most violent and perfunctory of intercourse, creating a new kind of woman by simply perforating androgynous creatures at the level of the groin (see Pané 22-28). The notion of Amazonhood as a form of retaliation by distraught women against taboo-breaking men moves on from the realm of the mythological to that of the concrete social reaction in the South American accounts (see Leonard 54-64).

35. Columbus is most insistent on this pairing; see for instance *Journal*, Jan. 14 and 15, 149-51.

36. The chroniclers themselves give their linguistic approximations of the word "cannibal" as connected etymologically with "caribs" and homonymally with "Grand Khan." At times the chroniclers themselves ascertain that the "cannibal" is not linguistically connected with anthropophagy, but rather to "daringness"; Columbus himself suggests this—see *Journal*, Oct. 30, Nov. 26, and Jan. 13 (49, 74, and 147). See "Caribe" in Henríquez Ureña 95-102 and Taylor 156-57. Furthermore, the commonplace attribution, most evident in Columbus, to these men of a doglike semblance is also connected to the etymology of the word—from *cane*. One should also relate the erotic quality of the cannibals' "daring" to another etymological connection—from canicular days, in which the influence of the constellation of Canis overexcites people, animals, plants, waters, even stones, in untraditional ways. The star Sirion (Siren?) is connected to this constellation. See "Caniculares" in Covarrubias y Orozco 287. Finally, this crossreferencing might explain Columbus's obsession with the extraordinary dogs that he claims to have found everywhere in the Caribbean; in fact he follows a similar earlier attitude of Europeans toward the Canary Islands—their name also related to the dogs found there.

37. After discussing the "latest" ideas about the shape of the earth: "...I am compelled, therefore, to come to this view of the world: I have found that it does not have the kind of sphericity described by the authorities, but that it has the shape of a pear, which is all very round, except at the stem, which is rather prominent, or that it is as if one had a very round ball, on one part of which something like a woman's teat were placed, this part with the stem being the uppermost and nearest to the sky, lying below that equinoctial line in this ocean sea, at the end of the East." The episode insists several times on the connection between the floating breast and Terrestrial Paradise (in "The Third Voyage of Discovery," Morison 285-287). At the end, in a section not included in the Morison translation, the breast becomes a rough hill, impossible to climb or "to mount" unless God is willing (see *Cristóbal Colón* 216).

38. This whole episode, taken from the manuscript of Columbus's letter to the Catholic monarchs copied/edited by Las Casas appears somewhat artificially inserted toward the end of a fairly routine description of the entire third voyage as if, about to return to Spain, Columbus/Las Casas were reminded of the religious/scientific reason for this voyage and had decided to recount it in large

brushstrokes from the very beginning until the end. For editorial information about this letter, see *Cristóbal Colón* 202; Morison 284.

39. "Ninguna bestia de ninguna manera vi, salvo papagayos en esta Isla."

40. See Sanz López 503 and the transcription of other versions of the letter to Santangel reproduced by Sanz López.

Works Cited

Bourne, Edward Gaylor. *Columbus, Pané and the Beginnings of American Anthropology.* Proceedings of the American Antiquarian Society Series 18. Worcester, Mass., 1906. 310-389.

Cabeza de Vaca, Alvar Núñez. *Adventures in the Unknown Interior of America.* Trans. Cyclone Covey. Albuquerque: Univ. of New Mexico Press, 1983.

———. *Relación de los naufragios y comentarios.* Madrid: V. Suárez, 1906.

Columbus, Christopher. "The Capitulations of 17 and 30 April 1492." *Journals and Other Documents of the Life and Voyages of Christopher Columbus.* Trans. and ed. Samuel Eliot Morison. New York: Heritage Press, 1963. 26-31.

———. *Diario de Colón.* 2 vols. Madrid: N.p., 1962.

———. *The Journal.* Trans. Cecil Jane. New York: Clarkson N. Potter, 1960.

———. "Testamento y Codicilio." *Cristóbal Colón. Textos y documentos completos. Relaciones de viajes, cartas y memoriales.* Ed. Consuelo Varela. Madrid: Alianza, 1984.

Cortés, Hernán. *Letters from Mexico.* Trans. and ed. Anthony Pagden. New Haven: Yale Univ. Press, 1986.

Covarrubias y Orozco, Sebastián de. *Tesoro de Lengua Castellana o Española.* Madrid, 1611.

Dell'Orto, Giovanni. " 'Socratic Love' as a Disguise for Same-Sex Love in the Italian Renaissance." *The Pursuit of Sodomy.* Ed. Kent Gerard and Gert Hekma. New York: Harrington Park, 1989. 33-65.

Erauso, Catalina de. *Historia de la Monja Alférez, escrita por ella misma.* Madrid: Tip. Renovación, 1919.

———. *The Nun Ensign.* Trans. James Fitzmaurice-Kelly. London: T. Fisher Unwin, 1908.

Geertz, Clifford. "Us/Not Us: Benedict's Travels." *Works and Lives: The Anthropologist as Author.* Stanford: Stanford Univ. Press, 1988. 102-128.

Henríquez Ureña, Pedro. *Para la historia de los indigenismos.* Buenos Aires: Imprenta de la Universidad de Buenos Aires, 1938.

Herodotus. *The Histories of Herodotus.* Trans. George Rawlinson. Ed. E. H. Blakeney. London: Dent, 1964.

Leonard, Irving. *Books of the Brave, Being an Account of Books and of Men in the Spanish Conquest and Settlement of the Sixteenth-Century New World.* New York: Gordian, 1964.

O'Gorman, Edmundo. *The Invention of America.* Westport, Conn.: Greenwood, 1961.

Pané, Fray Ramón. *Relación acerca de las antigüedades de los indios.* Ed. José J. Arrom. Mexico City: Siglo XXI, 1978.

Perry, Mary Elizabeth. "The 'Nefarious Sin' in Early Modern Seville." *The Pursuit of Sodomy*. Ed. Kent Gerard and Gert Hekma. New York: Harrington Park, 1989. 67-89.

Pérez de Oliva, Hernán. *Historia de la inuención de las Yndias*. Ed. José J. Arrom. Bogota: Instituto Caro y Cuervo, 1965.

Piedra, José. "The Game of Critical Arrival." *Diacritics* 19.1 (Spring 1989): 63-85.

———. "Literary Whiteness and the Afro-Hispanic Difference." *New Literary History* 18 (1986-87): 303-332; revised in *The Bounds of Race*. Ed. Dominick La Capra. Ithaca, N.Y.: Cornell Univ. Press, 1991.

———. "The Value of Paper." *Res* 16 (Autumn 1988): 85-104.

Plato. *The Symposium of Plato*. Ed. John A. Brentlinger. Trans. Suzy Q. Groden. Amherst: Univ. of Massachusetts Press, 1979.

Sanz López, Carlos. *El gran secreto de la carta de Colón*. Madrid: Bibliotheca Americana Vetustissima, 1959.

Taylor, Douglas. "Carib, Caliban, Cannibal." *International Journal of American Linguistics* 24 (1958): 156-57.

Van Stynwoort Logan, Marie-Rose. "Androgyne, Hermaphrodite: Interpretive Illusion and Delusion: Essays in the Rhetoric of Love." Diss. Yale Univ., 1974.

Vespucci, Amerigo. *The Letters and Other Documents Illustrative of His Career*. Trans. and ed. Clements R. Markham. London: Hakluyt Society, 1894.

von Rosen, Wilhelm. "Sodomy in Early Modern Denmark: A Crime without Victims." *The Pursuit of Sodomy*. Ed. Kent Gerard and Gert Hekma. New York: Harrington Park, 1989. 177-204.

♦ Chapter 8

Fray Ramón Pané,
Discoverer of the Taíno People

José Juan Arrom

(translated by Andrés F. Moreno and
Gwendolyn Barnes-Karol)

Columbus, seeking a shorter route to the East Indies, accidentally
found some islands not charted on European maps. During his
trip, he described the landscape of those islands and placed in
that landscape some exotic beings whom he called Indians. On his
next trip, he brought along a Hieronymite friar, whom he commissioned to investigate the "beliefs and idolatries" of those strange
beings. The friar, following these orders, went to live among the
Indians, learned their language, listened to their songs and their
tales, and wrote down what he could of their astonishing tales.
As part of this process of inquiry, he discovered the nature of
the American people and rescued for posterity the fascinating
mythical world of the ancient residents of the Antilles.

The importance of the extraordinary feat of the friar went almost unnoticed until some twenty years ago. It was known that he
had given Columbus some notes, known by the title *Relación acerca
de las antigüedades de los indios* (*Historical Account of the Antiquities of
the Indians*). But in looking for the original text, researchers found
only a defective translation into Italian, inserted into a book whose
very authenticity was doubtful. Moreover, the *real* name of the friar
was not known; was it Roman, Romano, Román, or Ramón? Pan,

Pane, or Pané? So little attention was paid to the ravaged document that in 1970 Ernesto Tabío, a competent Cuban anthropologist, summarized the state of the question in these words:

> The collector of the greatest part of those myths was a Catalonian member of a religious order who accompanied Columbus during his second voyage. Las Casas ... pointed out that he had very little culture and ... in addition, he had scant knowledge of the language of the aboriginal people. It must be very difficult for a rationalist man of science to accept this information, which from the start, has been corrupted by many difficulties. (47)[1]

Tabío was right in that the problems posed by the text were neither few nor easy to solve. However, instead of discarding the text as a result of these problems, what was urgently needed was a way to take advantage of the information that it contained. To do this, it became necessary to start from the beginning.

Initially, Fray Ramón Pané—for this was his name—landed on the island of Hispaniola in January of 1494. At first, he went to live in the province of Macorís, which was inhabited by a group of Indians who did not speak the standard language. After a few months, he realized that he had to carry out his inquiry among those who spoke the predominant language of the island: the Taíno people. Thus, in the spring of 1495, he moved to the area under the control of the Indian chieftain Guarionex. He lived with Guarionex and his subjects for about four years, sufficient time for Pané to learn enough of the language of his informants to carry out the task that had been given to him. Around 1498, he gave the Admiral the notebook in which he had been translating into Spanish the essence of the mythical tales that he had heard in the aboriginal language. The Admiral, or his emissary, took it to Seville. It was there that Pedro Mártir de Anglería read it and, inspired by the novelty of the news, hurriedly relayed the information that most interested him to Cardinal Ludovico of Aragon, in a letter in Latin. This letter was published in the first of Anglería's *De Orbe Novo Decades* (27–87). The manuscript was also seen in Seville by Fray Bartolomé de Las Casas. In his zeal to gather any information that might be helpful in defending Indian dignity, Las Casas summarized what he found most useful. These notes, along with some commentaries of his own, became part of three chapters of his *Apologética historia de las Indias* (*Apologetic History of the Indies*). Finally, Columbus's second son included the entire *Relación* in his *Vida del Almirante Cristóbal Colón por su hijo Fernando* (*Life of Admiral Christopher Columbus by his Son Fernando*). This work was unpublished when Fernando died and remained unpublished, for in those years it was extremely difficult in Spain to print a work that was essentially a plea in defense of his father's rights. For at that time, there was a campaign of defamation against the Admiral in full swing, with the evident purpose of denying him the privileges granted by the Crown in the "Charter of Admiral Columbus" ("Capitulaciones de Santa Fe," April 17, 1492). As a result of such an adverse political climate, the manuscript was taken to Italy (probably by Luis Colón, the Admiral's grandson) and translated into Italian by Alfonso de Ulloa. Nothing more has been heard about the manuscript of Fernando's *Vida* or Pané's original *Relación* since the publication of this translation in Venice in 1571 (see Pané, "Estudio preliminar" and notes).

Had Ulloa's translation been a faithful and careful rendering of the original, many of the problems posed by the work would have been avoided. But this was not the case. The inaccuracies, incongruencies, and mistakes that appear in the translation of Fernando's work are so frequent, that for many years it was thought that it might have been a fraudulent work by Las Casas or by Hernán Pérez de Oliva, a writer who was a contemporary of Fernando, whose work, *Historia de la inuención de las Yndias* (*History of the Invention of the Indies*) was also lost. Since both hypotheses have been invalidated by the discovery and publication of Pérez de Oliva's *History*, all further references will pertain to Pané's *Relación*.

Let us start by pointing out a bit of information that was not known until very recently: Ulloa translated the text while in a Venetian jail, where he died from malignant fevers in 1570. Instead of leaving a finished translation, he left a rough draft, which he was unable to revise due to his premature death. The unfinished manuscript was taken into friendly hands and was sent to press, in its current state, in 1571. It is precisely this ravaged version that became the point of departure for numerous editions and translations prepared later, in which the many initial flaws of the text were repeated and augmented.

These are some of the reasons why one can find lacunae in the text of the *Relación,* which perhaps were to be filled by the author in the final version of the work. It also explains the hasty readings that yielded missing letters in some of the Taíno words, the confusion of some letters for others, or changes in their order. To all this can be added the fact that Ulloa proceeded to Italianize, at times in a violent fashion, terms that were not always made to correspond to their original forms when the text was translated into Spanish or other languages.

Let us look at some examples. Ulloa wrote *giutola* in a context in which it is obvious that the original would be *yuca;* he wrote down *conichi* as the plural of *conuco; iobi* are *jobos; guanini e cibe* are of course, *guanines* and *cibas; cazzabi* is *cazabe;* the variants *cimini* and *cimiche* correspond to *cemíes.* In other cases the Italianizations are less transparent. He recorded that the spirit of the dead came out at night to eat a fruit, whose name is given as *guabazza.* Bachiller y Morales thought that this fruit was the custard apple (*guanábana*). But Anglería explains it as "a fruit unknown to us similar to quince" ("fructu nobis incognito cotono simili"), and the fruit that is similar to quince in form, flavor, and texture is not the *guanábana* but the guava (*guayaba*). Similarly, he called the spirit of the indigenous people, while alive, *goeiz,* a term from which he omitted the final *-a.* If complete, it would yield *goeiza,* or as Las Casas writes, *guaíza,* which is the Hispanization of *wa-* (our) and *ísiba* (countenance); that is, that which characterizes and distinguishes living people. One example of toponyms in which some letters were misread is the word *Maroris,* which should have been *Macorís.* We shall also consider three more examples of incorrectly transcribed proper names: *Caouabo* becomes *Caonabó* after the accent is placed correctly and the confusion between the *u* and the *n* is cleared up; the friar's first name is usually written as *Roman* and on one occasion *Romano;* and finally, the warden of the fortress at Concepción is called Giovanni di Agiada, a name that I have seen translated as Juan de Aguado, when his real name was Juan de Ayala.[2]

If this happened with terms whose inaccuracy could have been rectified by a careful reading of the text, one can only imagine what happened to the polysyllabic names of mythological beings mentioned in the book, which must have been totally foreign to printers and translators. It is enough to mention that one of them, *Basamanaco* or *Bayamanaco*, appears written in four different ways, and that the names of the Supreme Being and those of the Mother of God, their importance in the Taíno pantheon notwithstanding, have suffered so many alterations that it is extremely difficult to match up the transliterations left of them by Ulloa, Anglería, and Las Casas. Those names contain, nonetheless, the nature, functions, and attributes that the indigenous people assigned to their gods. It is, therefore, of paramount importance to reconstruct the original graphemes to the greatest extent possible, because only then can we proceed to the structural analysis that will reveal to us their most hidden and hermetic meanings.

As an example, let us try to analyze the various meanings attributed to the Supreme Being and the Mother of God. After Pané declares his objective in the title and the brief paragraph that acts as an exordium to his treatise, he gets to the heart of the matter immediately in the second paragraph. This paragraph, restored and translated, reads as follows:

> Every person, when adoring the idols they have at home, which they call *cemíes*, observes a particular manner and superstition. They believe that he is in heaven and is immortal, and that nobody can see him, and that he has a mother, but no beginning, and they call him Yúcahu Bagua Maórocoti, and her mother by five names, Atabey, Yermao, Guacar, Apito and Zuimaco. (Pané 3)[3]

The extreme conciseness of this note forced Las Casas to paraphrase it in the following manner:

> The people of the island of Hispaniola had a certain faith and knowledge of a single and true God, who was immortal and invisible so that nobody could see Him, who had no beginning, whose abode and dwelling place is heaven, to whom they gave the name of Yócahu Vagua Maórocon; I do not know what they meant by this name, because when I could have found out, I did not take notice. (Las Casas 71)[4]

Without pausing to consider the problem of the numerous variants of these names, the three names of the Supreme Being can be analyzed this way: *Yuccah-hu* is equivalent to "Spirit-of-the-Cassava;" *Bagua* is "sea"; and *Ma-óroco-ti* can be translated literally by "Without-Predecessor-Male." Further along in his text, Las Casas mentions again the Supreme Being, which then he calls *Yúcahu-guamá*, that is, "Lord-of-the-Cassava." In summary, the Supreme Being is "Provider of the Cassava" and "Lord of the Sea."

The names of the Mother of God differ so greatly in the translations of Ulloa and Anglería's letter that it is absolutely impossible to make the two lists coincide. Las Casas does not shed any light on this matter either, for he records only the following: "God had a mother, whose name was *Atabex*, and a brother, *Guaca*, and others in this fashion."[5]

It would be risky to comment on totally uncertain names. Consequently, I will limit my inquiry to *Atabex* and *Guacar*, which do appear in the three lists, and to the name *Mamano*, which can be found only in Anglería's list. *Atabex*, *Atabey*, or *Attabeira* seem to correspond to the vocative *Atté*, used by young people to respectfully address elderly women, which is roughly equivalent to *señora* ("Lady") or *doña* ("Madame"). The attached suffix, *-beira*, seems to be equivalent to "water"; thus, the name's meaning would seem to be "Lady or Mother of the Waters." *Guacar* could have been *Wa-katti* or *Wa-kairi*, from *wa-* which is "our" and *Katti* or *Kairi*, corresponding to "Moon," "Tide," or "Menstrual Cycle." *Mamano*, the term obtained when the misprints are corrected by transposing the vowels in the last two syllables, can be analyzed as *mama*, a root-word whose variants appear in numerous languages with the same meaning, and the suffix *-no*, a marker of the feminine plural. This yields "Mother-s" or perhaps "Universal Mother." A free translation of the preceding epithets, paying more attention to their sacred than to their literal meanings, would be "Our Lady of the Waters, of the Moon, of the Tides, and of the Menstrual Cycle, Mother Universal" (Pané 4, note 5). Such appellatives really constitute a chant in praise of the Mother of God, a prayer to the compassionate helper of pregnant women and pious protector of women giving birth.

The tone of oral poetry that can be perceived in these linguistic explorations has taken me to investigate other literary aspects of the *Relación*. With this in mind, let us go back to the title and initial paragraph of the text. Restored and newly translated, they read as follows: *Relación de Fray Ramón acerca de las antigüedades de los indios, las cuales, con diligencia, como hombre que sabe la lengua de ellos, las ha recogido por mandado del Almirante (Historical Account by Fray Ramón about the Antiquities of the Indians, Which, with Diligence, as a Man who Knows Their Language, Have Been Gathered by the Order of the Admiral)*.

> I, Fray Ramón, a poor hermit, of the Order of St. Jerome, by the mandate of the illustrious Admiral and viceroy and governor of the Islands and Mainland of the Indies, have written what I have been able to learn and understand about the beliefs and idolatry of the Indians, and how they revere their gods. This is the matter with which I shall deal in this historical account. (3)[6]

Perhaps it was pure coincidence that historical account (*relación*) is the last and first word of this passage. Yet, both the repetition and the privileged place it enjoys at the beginning and the end of the quoted text allow a glimpse into the future of our literature. It is worthwhile to remember that Columbus chose the diary and the letter as the rhetorical models through which to communicate his unusual feats in the Indies. Pané chose, perhaps innocently, the *relación* as his model to report his adventures among the Indians. The term *relación* has, among other meanings, that of "the act and effect of relating" and of a "report that an ancillary official makes of the substance of a trial or any repercussion that it might have before a tribunal or a judge" (*Diccionario de la Real Academia Española de la Lengua*, s.v.). Without resorting to more precise definitions, let this word highlight the fact that Pané relates the results of his inquiry and delivers it to the Admiral as a subordinate. This legalistic formula allows him the use of the narrative first person that will reappear in *Lazarillo de Tormes* and its considerable picaresque progeny. Pané starts: "I, fray Ramón, a poor hermit of the Order of St. Jerome, by the mandate of the illustrious Admiral and viceroy and governor of the Islands . . . have written what I have been able to learn and understand about the beliefs and idolatry of the Indians..." (21).[7] Lázaro starts his narrative in this way: "Your Excellency, then, should know first of all that I am called Lázaro de Tormes, son of Thomé González and Antoña Pérez, natives of the Salamancan village of Tejares" (*The Life of Lazarillo de Tormes*, 1).[8] It is worth noting that the same rhetorical model was used on this side of the Atlantic in some of the most prominent works of the colonial period. As examples, consider the *Cartas de Relación* sent to the emperor by Cortés and the festive observations titled *El lazarillo de ciegos caminantes... por Calixto Bustamante Carlos Inca, alias Concolorcorvo*, written by Alonso Carrió de la Vandera.

It might be worthwhile bringing to mind a work closer to us. I refer to the *Infortunios de Alonso Ramírez*, published in 1690 by Carlos de Sigüenza y Góngora. Strictly adhering to the same formula, in a paragraph that serves as an exordium, the work continues: "My name is Alonso Ramírez and my homeland the city of San Juan of Puerto Rico... My father was named Lucas de Villanueva ... and he was Andalusian, and I know very well that my mother was born in the same city of Puerto Rico, and her name is Ana Ramírez" (74).[9] But after this initial similarity, the author resorts to another rhetorical model that has older roots in Hispanic narrative: the *pereginatio vitae*. It is worth noting that this model had been used in America much earlier in the *Peregrinación de Bartolomé Lorenzo*, written in Lima in 1586 by José Acosta, a work that had mistakenly been taken as the simple biography of an obscure character of colonial times, when instead, it is a short novel of travel and adventure (see Acosta; Arrom, "Carlos de Sigüenza").

While I have taken some time to comment on the rhetorical model of the *Relación*, it is more important to emphasize the importance of its content. Pané's text goes beyond the limited objectives of a report submitted to a superior to become the first investigation of an Indian cosmogony, totally different from the European worldview. With it, he sets a precedent. This is why his inquiry is something more than rhetorical form; it is a firm root. In this sense, it is worth pointing out that the fascinating investigations of Bernardino of Sahagún and of chroniclers such as Durán, Cieza of León, Acosta, Murúa, and the Inca Garcilaso followed the route opened by Pané. These works constitute inexhaustible lodes of narrative, poetry, theater, and even the political and religious thought of vast regions of our hemisphere.

To illustrate some of the above assertions, let us look at one of the tales told by the friar, the one in which he tells us how the sea was made and narrates the arcane adventures of the four brothers that took part in its creation. This tale formulates the myth of the origin of the smiling and hospitable people that preceded us to these islands and also gives meaning to several pieces of pottery, representative of the exquisite craft of the Taínos. Pané tells it in these words:

Chapter IX

How they say that the sea was made

There was a man named Yaya, whose name no one understands; and his son was named Yayael, which means son of Yaya. This Yayael, wishing to kill his father, was banished by him, and he was thus banished for four months; and after that, his father killed him and put his bones in a gourd, which he hung from the roof of his house, where it hung for some time. It happened that one day, wishing to see his son, Yaya told his wife: "I want to see our son Yayael." And she was glad, and taking the gourd down, she spilled out its contents to see the bones of her son. And many fish, large and small, came out. Therefore, seeing that those bones had turned into fish, they decided to eat them.

They say that one day, Yaya having gone to his *conucos*, which means property that was part of his inheritance, there emerged, all from the same womb, four identical sons from a woman named Itiba Cahubaba; after dying of childbirth, this woman was opened up, and the four identical sons were delivered, and the first one they took out was *caracaracol*, which means mangy, and this *caracaracol* was named [Deminan]; the others had no name. (28-29)[10]

Chapter X

How the four identical sons of Itiba Cahubaba, who died giving birth, went together to take the gourd of Yaya, which contained his son Yayael (who had been transformed into fish), and none dared to take it, except for Deminan Caracaracol, who took it down and they all had their fill of fish.

And while they were eating, they heard Yaya returning from his estate, and wishing in their haste to hang the gourd up, they did not hang it well, so that it fell to the ground and it broke. They say that so much water came out of that gourd, that it filled the entire land, and with it, came out many fish; and this they say is the origin of the sea. They left from there, and they found a man, named Conel, who was mute. (29-30)[11]

Chapter XI

Concerning the adventure of the four brothers when they were fleeing from Yaya

As soon as they reached Bayamanaco's door, and noticing that he had cassava [*cazabe*], they said: "Ahiacabo guárocoel," which means; "Let us get to know this our grandfather." In the same manner, Deminan Caracaracol, seeing his brothers before him, went in to see if he could get some *cazabe*, this *cazabe* being the bread that is eaten in this country. Caracaracol, having entered into Bayamanaco's house, asked him for *cazabe*, which is the aforesaid bread. And Bayamanaco put his hand on his nose and spit *guanguayo* onto Caracaracol's back; that *guanguayo* was full of *cohoba*, that he had had made that day; that *cohoba* is a kind of dust, which they sometimes take to purge themselves and for other effects which will be told later. This they take with a cane half a man's arm long, and they put one end on the nose and the other on the dust; in this way they inhale it through the nose and this makes them purge themselves greatly. And it was thus that he gave them for bread that *guanguayo*, instead of the bread that he made; and he left indignant because they asked him for it.... Caracaracol, after this, went back to his brothers and told them what had taken place with Bayamanacoel and of the blow to the back that he had given him with the *guanguayo* and that it hurt him greatly. Then his brothers looked at his back and saw that it was very swollen; and the swelling grew so big that he was near death. Then they tried to excise it, but they could not; and taking a stone axe, they opened it, and a living female turtle came out; and in this way they made their house and raised the turtle. (30-31)[12]

In light of the arguments presented above, now we know that Yaya is equivalent to "Supreme Being" or "Supreme Spirit." The insurgency of his son Yayael is the oft-repeated rebellion, frequent in other mythologies, of the young prince against the older king. The cosmic *conucos* are the wide-open expanses of the universe during the first days of creation. Those who were born of the torn womb of Itiba Cahubaba, the Mother Earth, are the four gods who will later be the ones who create and civilize humankind. Deminan did not want just *cazabe* from the elder god; what this Antillean Prometheus really steals from his choleric grandfather is fire, the primordial element for the development of human society. It is the generous gift of fire that Deminan gave to the Taíno people that made them capable of cutting down and burning the forest for their *conucos,* and to be able to cook the ground *yuca* flour, from which they made their daily bread, their daily *cazabe*. The "living female turtle," prodigiously conceived without male intervention, is the mother of humankind, the Antillean Eve, the progenitor of the Taíno people. Finally, when the four brothers conclude their adventures and they "make their house," what they really do is to cross over from the risky, wandering life-style of hunters and gatherers to the higher and more developed stage of a sedentary, agricultural, and ceramic-producing society, with its permanent buildings and a safer and more organized life-style.

This unraveling of the meaning of these myths reveals that they are fictionalized narrations that take place in a totally imaginary time and space. Like all mythical tales, they have an ulterior purpose. In this case, it is the imaginative rescue of ancient historical events, lost in the penumbra of times remote: migrations, the founding of settlements, the domestication of useful plants, the discovery of processes for the manufacture and conservation of foodstuffs. If we were to take the time to transcribe and decipher other fragments from the *Relación*, we would establish how they used these and other myths to make sacred the apparition of humankind in these islands, to resolve the opposition between man and woman, to reiterate the ties of human beings to the flora and fauna in their ecological interdependence, and to transmit their most deeply held beliefs about life and death. Moreover, we would learn how they took advantage of the episodes spun around the abduction of the first Taíno women for the purpose of codifying their rules of hygiene, their social norms, and their ethical principles of conduct.

These and other myths transmitted orally since time immemorial have reached us as a compendium, written originally in Spanish, of what the Catalonian hermit had heard in the Taíno language. In the process we have undoubtedly lost much of the essence and pristine beauty of the aboriginal epic. For instance, the conventions of its metaphorical system, or the structure, inflections, and rhythm of a language totally different from ours, a tongue that Columbus had described as "the sweetest tongue in the world" ("habla la más dulce del mundo" [*Diario*, Dec. 25]). What we have left are the verbal remnants of songs, hymns, and epic legends: in other words part of the lyrics of their most solemn *areítos*. In spite of these irretrievable losses, we are still able to recognize that they are fascinating fictions in which the apparent contradictions between logical and magical thought, communicative and expressive language, imagined and seen reality have been resolved. If we would take the liberty of splitting up the sentences of each paragraph, arranging them as if they were Bible verses, their sacred character and the epic contour of their narrative form would shine through the opacity of the translation.

I will not continue my examination of other equally meaningful tales nor will I continue expounding on the literary merits of the *Relación*, since I must now deal with what is perhaps the most important value of Pané's report, that is, the correct interpretation and thus the full enjoyment of the Taíno plastic arts. In the Antilles, the predominant tendency is still to judge these creations by the standards applied to European arts, standards unsuited to authentically American art. Thus, I would like to draw attention to certain concepts formulated by the forefather of modern anthropology in Latin America, the Mexican Manuel Gamio. Applying his postulates to one of the most celebrated creations of Aztec sculpture, Gamio comments:

In order to have the Eagle Warrior arouse in us that deep, legitimate, unique aesthetic emotion that the contemplation of art makes us feel, it is necessary, indispensable, that a harmony be found in the integration of the beauty of the material form and the understanding of the idea that it expresses. The term "Eagle Warrior" is undetermined and unexpressive. We must know where and when he lived as well as the how and why of his life. The Eagle Warrior is neither a discobolus nor a Roman gladiator. He represents the hieratic attitude, the fierceness, the serenity of the Aztec warrior of the noble class. The sculptor who made it lived at the time of his flowering, was a spectator of his battles, of his defeats and triumphs, and it took form in his mind out of all these epic visions, embellished and palpitating.... Only in this manner, knowing its antecedents, can we feel pre-Hispanic art. (45-46)[13]

Let us see what happens when anthropologists and art critics ignore the criteria formulated by Gamio. Let us use as our first example the numerous artifacts known as three-pointed stones (*piedras de tres puntas*), more pompously called trigonolyths, tricorned or triphasic *cemíes*, or tricuspid icons. The ingenious invention of names did not solve anything. The three-pointed stones kept on guarding the secret of their meaning: the religious beliefs they represent, the impressive variety of their designs and dimensions, the obvious realism that some of their details reveal, the imaginative magic stored in others. With a commendable desire to try to put some order into that apparent chaos, Jesse W. Fewkes proposed a topological classification of the stones in 1907 (1-220). His good intentions were of little use in this case. A simple ordering based on their external features without decodifying their symbolic language reveals nothing about the nature and functions of the beings that they represent, nor does it help increase the appreciation of the art of the Taíno stone carvers.

On the other hand, if we resort to the reports made by the Catalonian hermit in Chapter XIX of his *Relación*, he points out that "stone *cemíes* have different purposes. There are some that are said ... to be the best for making pregnant women give birth.... others have three points and it is believed that they are helpful in making cassava grow" (42).[14] Later on in Chapter XXVI Pané mentions how the latter used to be buried in the fields and how they sprinkled them with a liquid as these words were pronounced: "Now your fruits will be good and large" ("Ahora serán grandes y buenos tus frutos" [53]). All of this is confirmed by Anglería. Calling the *yuca* from which the *cazabe* is made by the erroneous name of *ajes*, he writes: "At the roots of the *ajes* is referred to what is found among the *ajes*, that is, the kind of foodstuff of which we spoke above. They say that these *cemíes* are used to form that bread" (98).[15] It is clear that we are dealing with agricultural rites of a propitiatory nature, in which the magical presence of the *cemí* fertilized the land and multiplied the yield of crops. It has already been pointed out that the Supreme God, Provider of the Cassava and Lord of the Sea was named Yúcahu Bagua Maórocoti. Having decodified his names and functions, I only wish to add that this kind numen of three names, represented by the three-pointed stones, in itself summarizes the three primordial elements that live harmoniously in the happy islands of the Taínos: land, sea, and humankind.

Because of the numerous and well-known examples of trigono-lyths that have been preserved I will allude only briefly to the nature and functions they attributed to Yucahuguamá. Notable among them are fish, birds, turtles, manatees, and other manifestations of marine fauna; frogs that announce the rain needed for the sowed fields; reptiles that controlled harmful pests; the use of the extremities for underground locomotion; and the impressive faces highlighted in many of the most detailed and sculpted pieces (see Arrom, *Mitología y artes*).

More recently, on the cover of a 1987 issue of the *Boletín: Museo del Hombre Dominicano*, appears a *cemí* described in the following terms by the editor of the issue:

[This] amulet of white stone from the island of Santo Domingo . . . represents two human figures united. Researchers have classified it in several ways as a twin idol, twin idols, or as a Siamese amulet. Amulets similar to these have been found in the region of Chalchaqui, Argentina. Ambrosetti called them "amulets for love." Other authors consider them to be the representation of the Inca god Huacanqui Carumi. (n.p.)[16]

Amulets for love and a representation of Huacanqui Carumi: these postulates serve to highlight the imagination of the Argentinian scholar and the erudition of the Dominican editor. I believe, however that, it would have been easier and more fruitful for the editor to have started with Pané. In the *Relación*, he would have read:

> And they also say that ... in that cave there were two *cemíes*, made of stone, small, of the size of half a man's arm, with their hands tied, and it seemed that they were sweating. These *cemíes* were held in high regard; and when it was not raining, it is said that the people went there to visit them, and immediately it would rain. And of these *cemíes*, one was called *Boinayel* and the other *Márohu*. (31)[17]

And if the Dominican editor had stopped to read the notes to the text, he would have found out that *Boinayel* means "Son of Boina," the dark Snake, which is by a process of metaphorization "Son of the Gray Clouds, Loaded with Rain," and that *Márohu* means "Without-Clouds," that is, "Clear Weather." All of this is confirmed by Las Casas: "What this friar Ramón was able to gather was that they had some idols or statues.... These they believed gave them water, and wind, and sun, whenever the need arose for it."[18]

Now, regarding those "similar amulets" found in the region of Chalchaqui, I must point out that they have also been found in the Antilles. Furthermore, there are two series of amulets: one, with idols that are joined as described above, and another series, just as numerous, of the most important of the two, the rain-giver (see Arrom, *Mitología y artes*, chap. 4).

Finally, let us return to the feats of the four sons of Itiba Cahubaba. After having presented them as a narrative discourse of considerable literary merit, I would like to examine them as ethnographic sources indispensable for the interpretation of two masterpieces of Indo-Antillean ceramics. The first one of these pieces is an effigy-vessel at the Museum of the American Indian in New York. The director of the museum, Frederick J. Dockstader, was with me the day that I first saw it. When I suggested that the vessel represented Deminan Caracaracol, the cultural hero that had given fire and cazabe to the Taíno people, he gave a slight smile

Figure 1. Deminan Caracaracol. Santo Domingo. Courtesy of the Museum of the American Indian. Heye Foundation, New York.

of incredulity, which dissuaded me from providing additional information. Not surprisingly, a short time later, he produced the vessel in his book *Indian Art in Middle America.* He describes it as a "Humpbacked Clay Idol" and tells us that "the brooding cast to the countenance of this crouching figure gives it an atmosphere only augmented by the powerful modeling. It is one of the finest clay objects known from the West Indies.... The extremely thin walls make this an amazing *tour de force* in ceramic art. It was set up on an altar in a cave where it was found by Theodoor de Booy in 1916" (plate 193).

The information regarding the circumstances of its discovery confirm the religious function of the effigy. But Deminan does not have a humpback; it is a turtle, the turtle that in Pané's tale

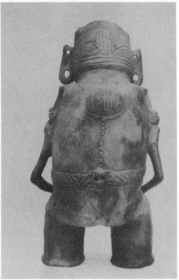

*Figure 2. Lateral and dorsal view of Deminan Caracaracol. Courtesy of the
Museum of the American Indian. Heye Foundation, New York.*

was formed by the spittle that his irate grandfather fired toward
Deminan's back and from which the Taíno nation was engendered.

The identification of Deminan's image allows us to move on
to the fragment of a vessel housed in the Musée de l'Homme in
Paris. The fragment represents a head that might be that of Itiba
Cahubaba, the fertile Mother Earth, with grooves that allowed her
to bear her quadrupled fruit. The eyes, shaped like slightly angled
coffee beans, point to the relationship between the images of the
Mother and the most intrepid of her sons, a form not found in
any other effigy of mythical beings. Signs of her representation as
the Great Birth-Giver that dies during the birth of the quadruplets,
are the bulging forehead and face and the swollen lips, unmistakable indications of a process of decomposition that has already
begun.

By opening up the scope of this inquiry it has been possible
to prove that this fragment was part of a vessel that is related to
the large and voluminous female bottles whose heads form spouts

*Figure 3. Female face in fragment of vessel effigy, terra cotta. Santo Domingo.
Courtesy of the Collection Musée de l'Homme, Paris.*

Figure 4. Dorsal view of female face in Figure 3.
Courtesy of the Collection Musée de l'Homme, Paris.

(see Arrom, *Mitología y artes*, Illustrations 52-53). We are not dealing with an isolated artifact, but rather with an impressive specimen from a series of effigies that represent the same numen. All these strange vessels have a helmet or turban on the figure's head. The prominent place that the head covering occupies, its size in relation to the face, and the extreme attention to detail lead us to believe that it was not an ordinary adornment, but an essential element in the codification of the symbolic message that the potter wanted to transmit.

In the fragment in question, the object on the top of the figure has grooves that form trapezoidals on both the front and dorsal panels. Continuing our process of decodification, it is appropriate to infer that the message corresponds to the cosmic nature of Itiba Cahubaba. With this premise in mind, let us assume that the top side represents the trajectory of the sun during the winter solstice (December 22, the shortest day of the year in the northern hemisphere); similarly, the bottom side would correspond to the summer solstice (June 21, the longest day). In this way, the sun carves the borders of the cosmos as it rises and sets daily, as perceived by observers on their islands. Therefore, what Itiba holds on her head—like Atlas on his shoulders in Greek mythology—is the world. Similarly, the imaginative design of lines and points would constitute an abbreviated chart of the universe.

The brief notes left by Pané and the scattered artifacts that serve as witnesses to their veracity might provide scant evidence for the investigation of esoteric ideas such as the concept of space in the thought of this long-gone culture. Notwithstanding, let us proceed to draw two diagonal lines starting from the corners of the drawing and crossing in the center. The drawing is thus divided into four parts, corresponding to the four points of the compass. These sectors or regions follow the model for the ordering of cosmic space used by the Aztecs, Mayas, and Incas.[19]

Following this parallel, let us remember that in Aztec mythology, the Primordial Mother also had four sons: the black Tezcatlipoca, or simply Tezcatlipoca; the blue Huitzitopochtli; the red one, named Xipe and Camaxtle; and the white one, Quetzalcoatl. They are, of course, the Lords of the Four Directions. One of them, Quetzalcoatl, was the civilizer of humankind and the one who stole maize from the gods in order to give it to the first Mexicans (Caso 19+). It would not be too daring to assume that in the Amerindian mythical context, the four quadruplets had analogous functions and that each one of them presided over one of the four segments of cosmic space.

This four-part division also serves to corroborate another of the tales rescued by Pané, the story of the original Taíno women who were abducted by the chieftain Guahayona and abandoned on the island of Matininó, so that "in this way, all the men were left without women" ("de esta manera quedaron todos los hombres sin mujeres" [24]). In order to remedy this grievous situation, the men went to bathe and "on that day, while washing themselves, they say that they saw "a particular type of people that were neither men nor women, nor did they have male or female sex. There were four sexless forms, which were captured by four men. With their arms and legs bound, the four men brought a woodpecker to them. And [the bird], believing they were logs, started doing its accustomed work, pecking and boring holes in the place where the female sex is ordinarily located. And in this way, say the Indians, they obtained women" (28).[20] Those four women, one for each region of the Antillean geography, were the ones who later populated the islands.[21]

In summary, I believe that what I have presented in these pages is sufficient to suggest that Pané's "little book"—as it was thus described by Anglería—is no longer the forgotten testimony of a humble Hieronymite friar, but the first written ethnographic investigation of the New World. Through the recovery of the mythical tales of a pre-Hispanic people, Pané revealed the roots of a native oral tradition, and by transcribing those ancient tales, he preserved elements that place him in a preeminent position among the founders of Hispanic American narrative. At the same time, his work is an indispensable source for deciphering the arcane artistic creations of the peoples that first inhabited these islands. Pané, like the Admiral for whom he wrote, was a great discoverer.

Notes

1. "El colector de la mayor parte de esos mitos fue un religioso catalán que vino con Colón en su segundo viaje. Y Las Casas... señalaba que tenía muy poca cultura y... además conocía poco la lengua de los aborígenes. Para un hombre de ciencia racionalista le tiene que ser muy difícil aceptar esta información que, de inicio, está viciada por muchas dificultades."

2. All such corrections have been clearly documented in the notes to Pané.

3. "Cada uno, al adorar los ídolos que tienen en casa, llamados por ellos cemíes, observa un particular modo y superstición. Creen que está en el cielo y es inmortal, y que nadie puede verlo, y que tiene madre, mas no tiene principio, y a éste llaman Yúcahu Bagua Maórocoti, y a su madre llaman Atabey, Yermao, Guacar, Apito y Zuimaco, que son cinco nombres."

4. "La gente de esta isla Española tenían cierta fe y conocimiento de un verdadero y solo Dios, el cual era inmortal e invisible que ninguno lo puede ver, el cual no tuvo principio, cuya morada y habitación es el cielo, y nombráronlo Yócahu Vagua Maórocon; no sé lo que por este nombre quisieron significar, porque cuando lo pudiera bien saber, no lo advertí."

5. "Dios tenía madre, cuyo nombre era *Atabex*, y un hermano suyo *Guaca*, y otros de esta manera."

6. "Yo, fray Ramón, pobre ermitaño de la Orden de San Jerónimo, por mandado del ilustre señor Almirante y virrey y gobernador de las Islas y de la Tierra Firme de las Indias, escribo lo que he podido saber y entender de las creencias e idolatrías de las indios, y de cómo veneran a sus dioses. De lo cual ahora trataré en la presente relación."

7. "Yo, fray Ramón, pobre ermitaño de la Orden de San Jerónimo, por mandado del ilustre señor Almirante y virrey y gobernador de las islas... escribo lo que he podido saber y entender de las creencias e idolatrías de los indios."

8. "Pues sepa Vuestra Merced, ante todas cosas, que a mí llaman Lázaro de Tormes, hijo de Tomé González y de Antoña Pérez, naturales de Tejares, aldea de Salamanca" (*Lazarillo de Tormes* 99-100).

9. "Es mi nombre Alonso Ramírez y mi patria la ciudad de San Juan de Puerto Rico... Llamose mi padre Lucas de Villanueva... que era andaluz, y sé muy bien haber nacido mi madre in la misma ciudad de Puerto Rico, y es su nombre Ana Ramírez."

10. Capítulo IX. *Cómo dicen que fue hecho el mar.* "Hubo un hombre llamado Yaya, del que no saben el nombre; y su hijo se llamaba Yayael, que quiere decir hijo de Yaya. El cual Yayael, queriendo matar a su padre, éste lo desterró, y así estuvo desterrado cuatro meses; y después su padre lo mató, y puso los huesos en una calabaza, y la colgó del techo de su casa, donde estuvo colgada algún tiempo. Sucedió que un día, con deseo de ver a su hijo, Yaya dijo a su mujer: 'Quiero ver a nuestro hijo Yayael.' Y ella se alegró y bajando la calabaza, la volcó para ver los huesos de su hijo. De la cual salieron muchos peces grandes y chicos. De donde, viendo que aquellos huesos se habían transformado en peces, resolvieron comerlos.

"Dicen, pues, que un día, habiendo ido Yaya a sus conucos, que quiere decir posesiones, que eran de su herencia, llegaron cuatro hijos de una mujer, que se llamaba Itiba Cahubaba, todos de un vientre y gemelos; la cual mujer, habiendo muerto de parto, la abrieron y sacaron fuera los cuatro dichos hijos, y el primero que sacaron era caracaracol, que quiere decir sarnoso, el cual caracaracol tuvo por nombre [Deminan]; los otros no tenían nombre."

11. Capítulo X. *Cómo los cuatro hijos gemelos de Itiba Cahubaba, que murió de parto, fueron juntos a coger la calabaza de Yaya, donde estaba su hijo Yayael, que se había transformado en peces y ninguno se atrevió a cogerla, excepto Deminan Caracaracol, que la descolgó, y todos se hartaron de peces.*

"Y mientras comían, sintieron que venía Yaya de sus posesiones, y queriendo en aquel apuro colgar la calabaza, no la colgaron bien, de modo que cayó en tierra y se rompió. Dicen que fue tanta el agua que salió de aquella calabaza, que llenó toda la tierra, y con ella salieron muchos peces; y de aquí dicen que haya tenido origen el mar. Partieron después éstos de allí, y encontraron un hombre, llamado Conel, el cual era mudo."

12. *De las cosas que pasaron los cuatro hermanos cuando iban huyendo de Yaya.*

"Estos, tan pronto como llegaron a la puerta de Bayamanaco, y notaron que llevaba cazabe, dijeron: 'Ahiacabo guárocoel,' que quiere decir: 'Conozcamos a este nuestro abuelo.' Del mismo modo Deminan Caracaracol, viendo delante de sí a sus hermanos, entró para ver si podía conseguir algún cazabe, el cual cazabe es el pan que se come en el país. Caracaracol, entrado en casa de Bayamanaco, le pidió cazabe, que es el pan susodicho. Y éste se puso la mano en la nariz, y le tiró un guanguayo a la espalda; el cual guanguayo estaba lleno de cohoba, que había hecho hacer aquel día; la cual cohoba es un cierto polvo, que ellos toman a veces para purgarse y para otros efectos que después se dirán. Esta la toman con una caña de medio brazo de largo, y ponen un extremo en la nariz y el otro en el polvo; así lo aspiran por la náriz y esto les hace purgar grandemente. Y así les dio por pan aquel guanguayo, en vez del pan que hacía; y se fue muy indignado porque se lo pedían... Caracaracol, después de esto, volvió junto a sus hermanos, y les contó lo que le había sucedido con Bayamanacoel, y del golpe que le había dado con el guanguayo en la espalda, y que le dolía fuertemente. Entonces sus hermanos le miraron la espalda, y vieron que la tenía muy hinchada; y creció tanto aquella hinchazón, que estuvo a punto de morir. Entonces procuraron cortarla, y no pudieron; y tomando un hacha de piedra se la abrieron, y salió una tortuga viva, hembra; y así se fabricaron su casa y criaron la tortuga."

13. "Para que el Caballero Aguila despierte en nosotros la honda, la legítima, la única emoción estética que la contemplación del arte hace sentir, es necesario, indispensable, que armonicen, que se integren, la belleza de la forma material y la comprensión de la idea que ésta expresa. El término "Caballero Aguila" es indeterminado e inexpresivo. Debemos saber dónde y cuándo vivió y el cómo y por qué de su vida. El Caballero Aguila no es un discóbolo ni un gladiador romano. Representa el hieratismo, la fiereza, la serenidad del guerrero azteca de las clases nobles. El escultor que lo hizo estaba connaturalizado con la época de su florecimiento, fue espectador de sus combates, de sus derrotas y de sus triunfos, y de todas esas visiones épicas surgió en su mente, embellecido y palpitante... Sólo así, conociendo sus antecedentes, podemos sentir el arte prehispánico."

14. "Los cemíes de piedra son de diversas hechuras. Hay algunos que dicen... son los mejores para hacer parir a las mujeres preñadas.... otros tienen tres puntas y creen que hacen nacer la yuca."

15. "En las raíces de los ajes se veneran los que son hallados entre los ajes, es decir, la clase de alimento de que arriba hablamos. Dicen que estos cemíes se ocupan de que se forme aquel pan."

16. "Amuleto en piedra blanca de la isla de Santo Domingo.... Representa dos figuras humanas unidas. Los investigadores lo han designado con varios nombres tales como: ídolo mellizo, ídolos gemelos, amuleto siamés. Amuletos similares a éstos han sido localizados en la región de Chalchaqui, Argentina y Ambrosetti los denominó como 'amuletos para amor.' Otros autores los consideran como la representación del dios inca Huacanqui Carumi."

17. "Y también dicen que... en dicha cueva había dos cemíes, hechos de piedra, pequeños, del tamaño de medio brazo, con las manos atadas, y parecía que sudaban. Los cuales cemíes estimaban mucho; y cuando no llovía, dicen que entraban allí a visitarlos y en seguida llovía. Y de dichos cemíes, al uno llamaban *Boinayel* y al otro *Márohu*."

18. "lo que pudo este fray Ramón colegir fue que tenían algunos ídolos o estatuas de las dichas.... Estas creían que les daban el agua, y el viento, y el sol, cuando lo habían menester."

19. There is abundant bibliography on this topic, and I will cite only three references. For information on the Mexican cultures see López-Baralt. In dealing with the Inca world, Sherbondy analyzes the socioeconomic consequences of the model. Finally, see Wilbert for a treatment of the barely explored ideological world of the Amerindian peoples of the vast Amazon basin and the islands of the Caribbean.

20. "Y éste, creyendo que eran maderos, comenzó la obra que acostumbra, picando y agujereando en el lugar donde ordinariamente suele estar el sexo de las mujeres. Y de ese modo dicen los indios que tuvieron mujeres."

21. The use of this model for the organization of space does not stop here. When founding their villages or *yucayeques,* the Taíno people would lay out two main streets that met in the central square, next to which they would build the *caney* of the *cacique* or chieftain. I shall provide more information in a forthcoming publication, tentatively titled "Viviendas y poblados de los primitivos habitantes de las Antillas" regarding this distribution of space, as documented by Las Casas, and the manner in which they built and conceptualized different types of living quarters that constituted what could be called the urban space.

Works Cited

Acosta, José de. *Peregrinación de Bartolomé Lorenzo.* 1586. Ed. José Juan Arrom. Lima: Petro Perú, 1982.

Anglería, Pedro Mártir de. *De orbe novo decades.* Spanish trans. *Décadas del Nuevo Mundo.* Madrid: San Francisco de Sales, 1892.

Arrom, José Juan. "Carlos de Sigüenza y Góngora: Relectura Criolla de los *Infortunios de Alonso Ramírez.*" *Tesaurus Boletín del Instituto Caro y Cuervo* 42 (1987): 23-46.

———. *Mitología y artes prehispánicas de las Antillas.* Mexico City: Siglo XXI, 1989.

———. "Viviendas y poblados de los primitivos habitantes de las Antillas." Forthcoming.

Boletín: Museo del Hombre Dominicano. 14.20 (1987): Cover and introductory pages.

Caso, Alfonso. *El pueblo del Sol.* Mexico City: Fondo de Cultura Económica, 1953.

"Charter of Admiral Columbus. Capitulaciones de Santa Fe." Trans. Lawrence Mantini and Luis A. Ramos-García. *1492-1992: Re/Discovering Colonial Writing.* Ed. René Jara and Nicholas Spadaccini. Hispanic Issues 4. Minneapolis: Prisma Institute, 1989. 423-425 (Sp.); 383-385 (Eng.).

Carrió de la Vandera, Alonso. *El lazarillo de ciegos caminantes . . . por Calixto Bustamante Carlos Inca, alias Concolorcorvo.* Forthcoming.

Colón, Fernando. *The Life of the Admiral Columbus by his Son Ferdinand.* New Brunswick, N.J.: Rutgers Univ. Press, 1959.

————. *Vida del almirante don Cristóbal Colón.* Mexico City: Fondo de Cultura Económica, 1947.

Columbus, Christopher. *The Diario of Christopher Columbus's First Voyage to America, 1492-1493.* Trans. and ed. Oliver Dunn and James E. Kelley, Jr. Norman: Univ. of Oklahoma Press, 1989.

Cortés, Hernán. *Cartas de relación.* 6th ed. Mexico City: Porrúa, 1971.

Dockstader, Frederick J. *Indian Art in Middle America.* Greenwich, Conn.: New York Graphic Society, 1964.

Fewkes, Jesse W. "The Aborigines of Puerto Rico and Neighboring Islands." *Bureau of American Ethnology, Annual Report for 1903-04,* no. 25. Washington, D.C.: 1907. 1-220.

Gamio, Manuel. *Forjando patria.* 2nd ed. Mexico City: Porrúa, 1960.

Las Casas, Bartolomé de. *Apologética historia de las Indias.* Madrid: Bailly, Baillière e Hijos, 1909.

Lazarillo de Tormes. Ed. Joseph V. Ricapito. Madrid: Cátedra, 1981.

The Life of Lazarillo de Tormes. Trans. and ed. Harriet de Onís. Woodbury, N.Y.: Barron's, 1959.

López-Baralt, Mercedes. "Tiempo y espacio en Mesoamérica." *Cuadernos Hispanoamericanos* 397 (1983): 5-43.

Pané, Fray Ramón. *Relación acerca de las antigüedades de los indios.* Nueva versión con estudio preliminar, notas y apéndices por José Juan Arrom. 8th ed. Mexico City: Siglo XXI, 1988.

Pérez de Oliva, Hernán. *Historia de la inuención de las Yndias.* José Juan Arrom. Bogotá: Instituto Caro y Cuervo, 1965. [an updated second edition is forthcoming from Siglo XXI, Mexico City]

Sherbondy, Jeanette E. "Organización hidráulica y poder social en el Cuzco de los Incas." *Revista Española de Antropología Americana* 17 (1987): 117-153.

Sigüenza y Góngora, Carlos de. *Infortunios de Alonso Ramírez.* 1690. Ed. Lucrecio Pérez Blanco. Madrid: Historia 16, 1988.

Tabío Palma, Ernesto. "El aborigen cubano: nueva versión de un mundo viejo." *Cuba Internacional* (April 1970): 47.

Wilbert, Johannes. "Warao Cosmology and Yekuana Roundhouse Symbolism." *Journal of Latin American Lore* 7.1 (1981): 37-72.

Chapter 9

Colonial Writing and Indigenous Discourse in Ramón Pané's *Relación acerca de las antigüedades de los indios*

Santiago López Maguiña

The *Relación*, written by the Hieronymite friar Ramón Pané around 1498, is the first Spanish text written with the intention of providing information about "the beliefs and idolatries" ("las creencias e idolatrías") of the Indians who lived on the island of Hispaniola—the name with which Christopher Columbus rechristened Haiti—"and how they venerate their gods" ("y como veneran a sus dioses"). It has been said (Anderson Imbert 22) that Pané initiated ethnography on this continent and that, in all probability, he was the first European to speak an Amerindian language. Pané is said to have participated in the *idiotus* tradition, in contrast to the great chronicler Gonzalo Fernández de Oviedo, who also wrote about Hispaniola, and was distinguished as a savant (Merrim 184). An *idiotus*, according to De Certeau (74), "is the illiterate who lends his word the support of what his body has experienced, and adds no 'interpretations.'" Pané's *Relación* thus allows the reader to approach the signifying universe of the Spanish conquistadors and provides concrete examples of what Lévi-Strauss has called "savage thought." At the same time, Pané's text presents the point of view of the Spanish State whose support made possible the enterprise of colonization. In focussing on the *Relación*, this essay seeks to approach from a semiotic and anthropological perspective one of the first manifestations of colonial writing produced in the New World.

The *Relación* is composed of three narrative developments: the first dealing with the Christianization and colonization of Macoris, a province on the island of Hispaniola; a second dealing with the observation and compilation of the antiquities of the Indians; and a third dealing with writing itself. The first two belong to the instance of the utterance or to that of the narrative itself, while the last is located in the discursive instance of the enunciation.

Christianization and the Colonization

Pané's participation in the evangelizing efforts in the province of Macoris was not voluntary. He supposedly did it on order of the "viceroy and governor of the island of the 'Tierra Firme' of the Indies, Christopher Columbus," who, in turn, was carrying out the orders of King Ferdinand and Queen Isabella, who were fulfilling the wishes of God. Thus, his performance is seen as the result of a chain of instructions that originated in the Supreme Being.

A similar mode of instruction gives meaning to the narration of the so-called discovery and colonization of the New World. The will of God rules the trajectory and dynamics of human history, while individual salvation depends upon the knowledge and acceptance of Christian faith. The acceptance or rejection of that knowledge is the result of a test to which subjects, both individual and collective, are submitted; it is a test in which the subjects must confront the deceptive performance of the devil, who has a powerful capacity to deceive them and lead them to sin. The subjects are thus seen in the midst of a conflict in which they are obliged to choose between Christ and the devil.

Not all are equally prepared for the test. There are those who have little or no resistance to the manipulations of the devil. Such is the case of the ignorant, the illiterate, and the simple-minded like the natives of Hispaniola who need to be brought into the faith of Christ. Pané does not seek to indoctrinate or educate the Indians. Rather, he sustains that their only alternative is to obey and accept

Christ. For this reason he does not react when a converted chieftain ("cacique") decides to return to his old beliefs:

> (Guarionex) Due to the fact that he strayed from the right path, we, seeing that he forsook and abandoned what we had taught him, decided to leave and go where we might obtain better results, teaching the Indians and indoctrinating them in matters of the holy faith. And so we went to another eminent chieftain, who demonstrated good will, saying that he wanted to be a Christian. (Pané 51)[1]

For Pané, the teaching of religion is not understood as a transmission of knowledge. Rather, it is viewed as instruction in ritual practices and gestures:

> Therefore, we were with chief Guarionex almost two years, continually teaching him our holy faith and Christian customs. At first he showed good will and gave hope of doing whatever we sought, and of wanting to be a Christian, telling us to teach him the Our Father, the Hail Mary and the Apostle's Creed, and many from his household learned the same; and he said his prayers every morning and made the members of his household say them twice daily. (Pané 50-51)[2]

Those who accept the instruction are left alone, while the natives who refuse the true religion may be subjected to the use of force and punishment:

> With others force and ingenuity are needed, because we are not all of the same nature. Just as they had a good beginning and a better end, there will be others who will begin well and laugh later at what has been taught to them; force and punishment is needed to deal with them. (Pané 55)[3]

Any unwillingness to know the true faith of Christ gives way to transgressions. Such is the case with polygamy. It is said that the cacique Mahubiatíbire "continues in his right choice, saying that he wants to be Christian, and does not want to have more than one wife." On the other hand, those who reject the Christian faith "tend to have two or three, and the leaders have up to ten, fifteen and twenty" (Pané 56).[4]

Pané maintains that the Christianization of the indigenous

population is quite easy, arguing that those people have a good disposition toward the teachings of Christ. Nevertheless, he recalls how four brothers adopted the Christian faith and how one of them, Juan Mateo, became his collaborator and was later subjected to martyrdom. Significantly, Juan Mateo's death is connected to the Indians' rejection of the foreign religion and to the expropriation of their land by the conquerors:

> Since the Christians [in the judgment of Indian leaders who advise others, according to Pané] were villainous and had taken possession of their lands by force ... they advised [their people] that they no longer concern themselves with Christian matters, but that they conspire and plot to kill them, and they had resolved not to follow their customs in any way. (Pané 51)[5]

In the *Relación*, native resistance displays a barbaric quality that is manifested in the destruction of the images of the hermitage:

> They hurled the images to the ground and covered them with earth and later they urinated on them, saying: 'Now your fruits will be good and great.' And this because they buried them in farmland, saying that the fruit which had been planted there would be good; and all this in reproach. (Pané 53)[6]

This act was followed by official repression, which Pané explains in these terms: "Bartolomé Columbus, who had been delegated to run the government by the admiral, his brother..., as deputy of the viceroy and governor of the islands ...decreed that they be burned in public" (Pané 53-54).[7] That public spectacle, which was meant both to intimidate the Indians and to mark the signs of the accusation on the bodies of the condemned, was not enough to extinguish the rebellion:

> Guarionex and his vassals did not abandon their evil plan of killing the Christians on a day designated for paying them a tribute of gold. But their conspiracy was discovered.... In spite of all this, they persevered in their perverse intention, and putting it into effect, killed four men, among them Juan Mateo, an important Christian, and his brother Antón, who had received the holy baptism. And they ran to where they

had hidden the images and shattered them into pieces. (Pané 54)[8]

The death of Juan Mateo has the characteristics of a sacrifice and evokes the story of the first Christians who suffered persecution, punishment, and death because of their devotion to the faith of Christ. This association is reinforced by the use of the lexeme "catechumen" ("catecúmenos") to designate the believers. The death of the first Christian is described in the following segment:

Juan. This was the first Christian who suffered a cruel death, and I know for certain that his was the death of a martyr. Because I have known of some who were present at his death who said: "Dios naboría daca, Dios naboría daca," which means "I am a slave to God." And his brother Antón died in the same way, saying the same thing. (Pané 49)[9]

The martyrdom and sacrifice of Juan Mateo closes the sequence of the Christianization and inaugurates another. The first stage of the sequence can be represented as a series of tests and trials that culminates in the glorification of Juan:

God, in all His goodness, gave me for company the best of the Indians, and the most versed in the holy Catholic faith; and then he took him away from me. Truly I had him as my dear son and brother; it was Guatícabanu, who was later a Christian and called himself Juan. (Pané 50)[10]

Juan's death signifies both a reaffirmation of his faith and a willingness to die for God. His words: "I am a servant of God" (soy siervo de Dios") imply a renunciation of temporal life in favor of eternal salvation. Life in God entails a renunciation of oneself in order to achieve the final goal of Christian faith: eternal salvation.

What Pané assumes in the religious sphere, he assumes in the political and socioeconomic spheres as well. Colonization, like Christianization, is an act of law; the occupation of indigenous territories implies taking possession of what belongs to one, rather than appropriating what belongs to another. The speaker does not recognize ownership for indigenous people because they lack the written documents that authorize it. Alphabetic writing is the only instrument that authorizes possession: it gives symbolic and cogni-

tive support; it registers and brings into existence what is supposed
to be real; and, it has the power to distinguish and to differentiate.
But writing is not the only instrument that guarantees property; it
often necessitates the power of arms, which belongs to the realm
of pragmatic communication and, as such, imposes knowledge on
the other. The very possession of arms allows for the possibility
of appropriating the object of desire. Thus, a writing of war is
developed.

Observation and Compilation of the "Antiquities of the Indians"

As a participant in the evangelization of the Island of Hispaniola,
Pané collected the "antiquities of the Indians" ("antigüedades de
los indios" [21]), which, as he says in the *Relación*, he did with diligence, "like a man who knows their language" ("como hombre
que sabe la lengua de ellos") and "by the order of the Admiral"
("por mandato del Almirante"). Columbus's request of Pané seems
to have originated in the need to prove the presence of the devil
among the Indians in order to justify their eventual punishment.
Let us recall that Pané writes during the early period of Spanish
colonization, at a time when the identity of the place of their arrival was unknown. Consequently, no one had yet questioned the
Indians' humanity. It is evident that for Pané they possessed a soul;
that is why he is preoccupied with pointing out that many of them
were ready to accept the tenets of Christianity. The Indians were
infidels or gentiles who could be Christianized either peacefully
or by force if needed. Since Pané saw Christianization as a necessity, he needed to prove that the indigenous people who he was to
evangelize had been deceived and controlled by the devil. Thus,
Pané's attention to the antiquities of native culture was prompted
less by an interest to understand it than by an attempt to prove
evil influences. According to the prevailing Christian ideology at
the end of the fifteenth century, there was only one true religion,
while all others were the inventions of Satan.

The "antiquities" of the Indians are also designated with the
lexemes "beliefs" ("creencias"), "idolatries" ("idolatrías"), and "fables" ("fábulas"). The word "antiquities" refers to the beliefs of the

"gentiles." The latter is a biblical term used to designate either those people and populations that were not Christianized, or those who were influenced by diabolical and pagan beliefs.The word "beliefs," in turn, stands in opposition to the lexical coinage inscribed as "knowledge of our Holy Faith" ("conocimiento de nuestra Santa Fe"): "Those things which the simple ignorant believe their idols to make, or speaking more precisely, those demons, without knowledge of our Holy Faith" (35).[11] While "beliefs" are related to simplicity, ignorance, idolatry, and the demoniacal, "knowledge" is connected to complexity, wisdom, and the divine.

On the other hand, beliefs, superstitions and fables are discursive products of deceit; they are lies transmitted to the Indians by their ancestors and the devil: "Their ancestors have made them believe all this because they do not know how to read nor how to count to ten" (22).[12] The lack of writing contributes to the maintenance of those beliefs. Pané likens the stories of the Indians to those told by the Moors: "like the Moors, they have their laws collected in old songs by which they rule" (34).[13] Loyal to a medieval conception of knowledge, Pané does not attempt to learn something new from his informants. Rather, he is interested in confirming what he already knows from the books that he is familiar with.

The learning of the "antiquities," nevertheless, tries to be exact and true. The fables and beliefs of the Indians are lies, but their cognitive acquisition should be reliable and precise: "Everything I write is as they narrate it, just the way I write it; and so I put it as I understood it from the people of the country" (26).[14] For that reason Pané was expected to know the language of the Indians.

But the value of fidelity to sources had a difficult opponent: the informants, the Indians, who lacked a writing system. The word, the oral discourse through which they transmitted their "beliefs," could not give complete, ordered, and coherent information: "And given that they do not have letters or writings, they cannot give a good account of how they have heard this from their ancestors, and for that reason there is no agreement in what they say, nor can they even write in an orderly way what they refer to" (24). "Because the Indians do not have letters or writings, they do not know how to tell fables well, nor can what they say be written with certitude" (26).[15]

Writing is an object of power and knowledge[16] that allows for the organization and coherence of the tales narrated by the informants; it controls the types of digressions common in oral discourse. In Pané's narration, orality is seen as subverting the organized knowledge produced by writing. For this reason he says, "I think that I have put first what should be last and last what should be first" (26).[17]

The compilation of indigenous beliefs is an activity of transcription (Zamora 37-38). This activity is clearly mentioned in the text: "Given that I wrote quickly and did not have enough paper, I could not put in its proper place what I transposed by mistake in a different place" (28).[18] One can assume that here Pané follows the model used by scribes in copying manuscripts in the Middle Ages, when specialized monks spent their time copying principally the Holy Scriptures, which were invested with the values of unity, order, coherence, and truth. It can be said, then, that writing is not a mere sign or instrument of knowledge, but that it is also an instrument of power that makes knowledge possible. The Taíno Indians were deprived of writing, and their knowledge was identified with beliefs that—from the Christian point of view—meant dispersion, chaos, incoherence, and falsity.

Writing

The *Relación* distinguishes the instance of the written from the act of writing. On one hand, the writer makes a direct reference to the enunciation that he actualizes: "I write" ("escribo" [21]) and "now I will concentrate on the present *relación*" ("ahora trataré en la presente relación" [21]). He refers the act of his written production—which is no more than a simulacrum since the enunciation itself cannot be represented (Blanco 269-331)—to the present moment of enunciation. At the same time, Pané assumes the role of a witness who has participated in the events that have transpired in the recent past. He writes about what he has "been able to learn and know of the beliefs and idolatries of the Indians and of how they venerate their gods" (21).[19] He recounts what he has heard, saying, "all that I write is what they narrate" ("todo lo que escribo así lo narran ellos" [48]) and about what he has "seen and experienced" ("visto y pasado"). The verbs that allude to the act of the enunciation are recorded in the present indicative, while those that refer to the narrated events are in the past perfect, a verb tense that indicates events of recent occurrence and that implies that similar actions persist.

At the level of the utterance Fray Ramón Pané occupies the position of the subject of a search that attempts to confirm a knowledge by questioning, listening, seeing, and transcribing. At the level of the enunciation, Pané is also a transcriber. In this case, however, he transcribes what has already been transcribed: "all that I write and how I write it is as they narrate it, and so I put it on paper the way I have understood it from the people" (26).[20] Pané implicitly defines his transcription as faithful and true. The friar's utterance corresponds to the events in which he has intervened as witness and participant, at the same time that it assumes the faith of Christ as an undeniable truth. Against this truth, which hinges on experience and faith, are the "beliefs"—those written transcriptions of an oral, and thus unreliable, discourse. Moreover, Pané's transcription does not attempt to reproduce the vernacular discourse, but to translate it.

The indigenous oral discourse in Pané's *Relación* is a construction produced within written discourse; it is organized according to its rules and conventions, and its values are assigned to it by the speaker. But it is important to point out that a comparison of the narrations collected by Pané with those from other native peoples of America may produce new constellations of meaning. Moreover, conjectures can be made about the semiotic roots of their signification, as Claude Lévi-Strauss has done with the mythologies of North and South America, and as was shown earlier by Montaigne (Conley 225-262).

Indigenous Utterances: "Beliefs"

The first eleven chapters of the *Relación* present the recording of a series of cosmogonic and etiological stories that narrate the origin of the native world and its culture. Within the first and ninth chapters the narration of the beginnings of culture is developed, while the last three narrate the story of the origin of the ocean, a very important factor in the native life. According to legend, the native populations of the Island of Hispaniola came from a cave called Cacibajagua (Pané 22). This sequence is composed of two temporal episodes, one comprising the time prior to the departure; the other dealing with the time of departure. The former is related to the underground and to darkness, while the latter is connected to clarity and light. The future is associated with complete luminosity.

Humankind emerges from the interior of two caves that are situated beneath a mountain that occupies a prominent position in contrast to the plains. Thus, the narration of origins presents features that could be outlined in binary terms: *past time:* underground: darkness: prominence; *present time:* surface: luminosity: flatness. This scheme may be applied to the mythology of many aboriginal populations in America.

During the time of subterranean life, the "people" (la "gente") wanted to venture out to the surface, but could not do so for fear of being captured by the sun and being turned into stones, trees, or birds. Thus, the people charged one of their own to guard the caves and to select the best places to populate. The guard carried out his task well, but one day made a mistake: "he was late in returning to the door" ("tardó en volver a la puerta"). It is inferred that he was far from the caves because he was captured and taken away by the sun. The community condemned his lack of diligence, shut the door that marked the entrance to his dwelling, and thus expelled him. Furthermore, the sun transformed him into stone. A similar transformation occurred with some men who were taken prisoner by the sun as they were fishing. The latter were turned into trees. Thus, as a consequence of a transgression of the established order, their material condition was also transformed as they were turned into entities of nature. For similar reasons of transgression a man in another story was transformed into a bird when he ventured out from his dwelling "before sunrise." In still another version of the *Relación* (ed. Alberto Wildner-Fox) a man called Yadruvava became a bird because he had moved ahead of his companions. Here the transgression is related to the cohesion and security of the group. This last conversion precipitated the emergence of human beings on the terrestrial surface.

Yadruvava had been commissioned by the leader Guahayona to gather an herb called *digo*. When Yadruvava did not come back, Guahayona punished all men for disobeying a collective rule that required having the plant available for the community. At the same time he ordered the women to abandon the caves and leave their husbands and children. Their departure was unexpected and precipitous since the dwellers of the cave had not made a rational decision to leave.

The actions that define the origins of the people of Hispaniola stem from prohibition and passion. Moreover, we are presented with an anomalous event in the sense that the women rather than the men are the ones to come out of the caves, despite the fact that the final decision regarding their exit from the underside of the mountain is made by the male leader Guahayona. The women's exit from the cave presented hardships for their children who depended on their mothers' bodies for nourishment. Their discomfort was expressed through a transformation: the children became frogs:

> Guahayona left with all the women and went in search of other countries, and arrived at Matinino, where he immediately left the women, and went to another region called Guanin . . . and so all of the men were left without women . . . . They had left the little children by the brook. Then, when hunger pains took hold of them, they say that they cried for their absent mothers; and the fathers could not remedy their children's cries of hunger, calling "mama" to speak, but, in reality, to ask for their mother's breast. And crying in that fashion and asking for their mothers' breast by crying "toa toa" like someone asking for something deliberately and with great desire, they were transformed into small animals, like frogs, called "tona" because they were asking to be breast-fed. (Pané 23-24)[21]

A psychoanalytic explanation might be that upon abandoning their children, the mothers not only leave them without protection or nourishment, but also take away the parental image of the male. Upon losing their women, men lose the Other, i.e., what gives them identity as owners of the law that makes the symbolic order possible, a law that allows them to compete, name, sanction, and prohibit. In this situation the children cannot become subjects. Their metamorphosis into animals is a logical outcome of their abandonment.

According to the *taína* narrative collected by Pané, the population of Hispaniola originates in transgression and painful rupture; in a lack of compliance by the men and through a vindictive and punitive act by the women. These founding actions are marked by misunderstanding, by the separation of men and women, and by the abandonment of the children. These actions make human reproduction and multiplication impossible. The displacement of the women and the metamorphosis of the children occurs in relation to the community of men, which, unlike the community of women and children, represents what is permanent and continuous in human society.

A significant development in the cosmogonic myth takes place in a story that recalls the recuperation of women by men:

How there came to be women again on said island of Haiti, now called Hispaniola

They say that one day the men went to bathe themselves, and while they were in the water, it rained a lot, and that they were very eager to have women; and that quite often when it rained they had gone to look for the tracks of their women, but could not find any fresh ones. But that day, while bathing themselves, they say that they saw fall from some trees, lowering themselves among the branches, certain person-like forms that were neither men nor women, nor did they have male or female sex. But as the men went to catch them they escaped as though they were eels. Since they could not catch them, they called two or three men by mandate of their chief, so that they might see how many there were, and might seek for each one of them a man who would be *caracaracol*, because these beings had rough hands, and that in this way the men might exercise strict control over them. They told the chief that there were four; and so the four men carried off those who were *caracaracoles*. The *caracaracol* is a sickness like scabies which makes the body very rough. After they had caught them, they held counsel about how they could turn these, who had neither male nor female sex, into women. (Pané 26-28)

How they discovered a remedy in order to turn them into women

They looked for a bird named *inriri*, long ago called *inriri cahubabayael*, and in our language called woodpecker, a bird who bores holes into trees, and they also took those women with neither male nor female sex, and bound their hands and feet, and brought the above-mentioned bird, and tied it to their bodies. And these birds, believing the beings to be logs, began the work they were accustomed to, pecking and perforating in the place where the sex of the woman is ordinarily found. And in this way, as recounted by their elders, the Indians say that they had women. (Pané 26-28)[22]

This sequence may be defined as the attainment of a desire on the part of men to once again have women. The recovery of women is realized as a discovery when asexual beings are captured and shaped into women through the intervention of a woodpecker who carves the female genitalia. Thus it could be said that women are a product of a transformation of natural beings into human subjects.

The story of the recovery of the women closes the narrative cycle dealing with the origins of the people of Hispaniola. Then a second cycle opens dealing with the establishment of a family order, which begins with the story of the origin of fish:

There was a man named Yaya, whose name no one understands; and his son was named Yayael, which means son of Yaya. This Yayael, wishing to kill his father, was banished by him, and he was thus banished for four months; and after that, his father killed him and put his bones in a gourd, which he hung from the roof of his house, where it hung for some time. It happened that one day, wishing to see his son, Yaya told his wife: "I want to see our son Yayael." And she was glad, and taking the gourd down, she spilled out its contents to see the bones of her son. And many fish, large and small, came out. Therefore, seeing that those bones had turned into fish, they decided to eat them. (Pané 28-29)[23]

Once again the story presents a metamorphosis: the conversion of a human subject into nature as the result of an excess and, perhaps, a transgression that may be seen in the patricidal wishes of the son. Following the model of analysis of the Oedipus myth by Freud, we can detect here a struggle for the position of power occupied by the father in relation to the mother. The Freudian tale reads as follows: the son wants the place of the father for himself and for that reason he attempts to eliminate the father. When the recognition of the father prevails, entrance in the symbolic order of society is possible; when the opposite occurs, the subject succumbs to a madness or mania that drives him to impose his own order.

In the struggle produced in Pané's story, the son disregards the authority of the father and wishes to eliminate him. But it is the father who expels the son and then kills him. Nevertheless, the conflict is not solved by that action. Both parents miss their son and desire to see him again. This desire remains unfulfilled because the mother, excessively anxious to recover her son, produces the accident that transforms her son's bones into fish.

The hypothesis of the son's disregard for the father can be confirmed if this story is connected to the one dealing with the departure of the women from the cave. Both stories emphasize the relationship and link between the mother and child while the father is disregarded. In the story of the women who surfaced from the cave, it is the children who need their mothers for nourishment and, unable to receive it, are transformed into natural entities (frogs); in the other story, the son's bones are transformed into fish by the precipitous act of the mother. At the end, the mother eats the fish, thus reintegrating the son to her body.

The story of the origin of fish is connected to the story regarding the origin of the sea:

They say that one day, Yaya having gone to his *conucos*, which means property that was part of his inheritance, there emerged, all from the same womb, four identical sons from a woman named Itiba Cahubaba; after dying of childbirth, this woman was opened up, and the four identical sons were delivered, and the first one they took out was *caracaracol*, which means mangy, and this *caracaracol* was named [Deminan]; the others had no name.

... *the four identical sons of Itiba Cahubaba, who died giving birth, went together to take the gourd of Yaya, which contained his son*

Yayael (who had been transformed into fish), and none dared to take it, except for Deminan Caracaracol, who took it down and they all had their fill of fish.

And while they were eating, they heard Yaya returning from his estate, and wishing in their haste to hang the gourd up, they did not hang it well, so that it fell to the ground and it broke. They say that so much water came out of that gourd, that it filled the entire land, and with it, came out many fish; and this they say is the origin of the sea. They left from there, and they found a man, named Conel, who was mute. (Pané 29-30)[24]

The sea originates as the effect of a series of ruptures in the cultural order: There is an attempt at parricide, there is an infanticide and the exaggerated love of the mother, all of which make possible Yayael's transformation into fish. The immediate cause of the metamorphosis is a transgression as well. It is what compels Deminan Caracaracol to lower the pumpkin, a kind of urn, which commands respect and veneration. Yet, the brothers commit a grave act of transgression, violating a commandment that obliges respect for the dead. At the same time, they also commit the crime of cannibalism: when they eat the fish that are kept in the pumpkin, they are eating the relics of Yayael.

The brothers whose transgression produces the sea had lost their mother at birth: they were born orphans. This explains their desperate search for nourishment and for a place to live. They go from house to house in search of home-cooked food. The following story expresses the brothers' desire for shelter and parental recognition:

These [the brothers], as soon as they arrived at the door of Bayamanaco and noticed that he produced cassava, they said: "Ahiacabo guárocoel," which means: "Let us meet our grandfather." In this same way Deminan Caracaracol, seeing his brothers before him, went in to see if he could obtain some cassava, which is the bread that is eaten in this region. Entering the house of Bayamanaco, Caracaracol asked him for cassava, the above-mentioned bread. And Bayamanaco put his hand into his nose and hurled a *guanguayo* at Deminan's back; this *guanguayo* was full of cohoba which he had made earlier that day; this *cohoba* is a certain powder which they take at times to purge themselves... And so he gave them that guanguayo instead of the bread which he made; and he went away, very indignant because they asked him for it.... Caracaracol, after all this, rejoined his brothers and told them what had happened with Bayamanacoel, about the blow to the back he had received with the *guanguayo*, and that it hurt intensely. Then his brothers looked at his back and saw that it was very swollen; and that swelling grew so much that he was on the verge of dying. Then they tried to excise it, but were unable to do so; and taking a stone hatchet they opened it up and a live female tortoise emerged; and so they built a house for themselves and raised the tortoise. (Pané 30-31)[25]

Although it is difficult to establish the meaning of all of the elements of this story, it is clear that the narrative tells of the search for food and parental recognition, desires that are not met. Instead, Deminan Caracaracol meets with a strong rejection which results in the deformation of his body.

The last part of the story deals with a strange metamorphosis at the end of which the brothers obtain a home and a lineage. The blow that the grandfather gave Caracaracol with the *guanguayo* caused an enormous and hard lump to grow on his back. Finally, after a number of fruitless attempts to excise it, his brothers succeeded in opening it and went on to find a live female turtle. We might ask at this point what relationship exists between the *guanguayo*, the laxative *cohoba*, the turtle, and the dwelling. The laxative allows for a cleansing of the body through the expulsion of excrement; the turtle may be interpreted as a metamorphosis of the feces within Caracaracol's body. The feces and the turtle are associated with the earth; the former has the ability to fertilize the land, while the latter is associated with nourishment and self-sufficiency as it carries its own shell or shelter.

The stories collected by Pané form two narrative sequences dealing with the social or communal origins of the inhabitants of Hispaniola (present-day Haiti). The subject of the first series is mainly the origin of the island's population, while the second deals with the establishment of a familiar order. Both the first and second sequences are composed of a series of transgressions, ruptures, separations, and effronteries, which end with the implantation of a familiar or communal order. In the final section of the first sequence the order that is established corresponds to the reconstitution of a previously broken organization: the sexual order of human life formed by men and women, not in a balanced and harmonic way, but under the authority of masculine law.

We may recall that the women who were recreated by men through the agency of the woodpecker are evidently perceived as subordinate actors in human society, and they serve as a contrast to the women who left the caves and who could be said to have committed a rebellious act, which significantly concludes with their definitive establishment on an island where there are no men. The feminine rebellion could therefore be interpreted as an act that leads to separation and exclusion. The second sequence ends with the construction of housing that, on the one hand, represents the final objective of stability and security that the four brothers are seeking. Both sequences seem to allude to the beginnings of a cultural order, which is the result of the transformation of a previous natural order. Moreover, both allude in some way to the transformation of a savage order into a cultivated order, and therefore the establishment of the law.

Three structural levels are recorded in the discursive organization of the *Relación:* the order of written enunciation; the enunciative order corresponding to Pané's compilation and actions within native society; and finally, the order of native oral discourse that is dealt with in this essay. Traditional oral narratives cannot be separated from the written discourse through which they are enunciated. It is not possible to distinguish an oral component within a written discourse since the oral, once transcribed, consists of a written discourse. Said in another way, as soon as the enunciation of native discourse is mediated by Pané's written enunciation, it is no longer native; it is a discursive construction that forms part of Pané's discourse. What is transcribed by Pané is the result of a selective operation. At the beginning of the *Relación* Pané writes that he will let people know what he has been able to learn about the beliefs and superstitions of the Indians, intimating that he has been incapable of ascertaining it in its entirety because the natives lack writing. Yet it is clear that Pané not only writes about what he has been able to collect and record, but also about what he has been interested in seeing and hearing, in accordance with his own perceptual categories.

Notes

1. [Guarionex] "Debido a que se apartó de su buen propósito, nosotros, viendo que se apartaba y dejaba lo que le habíamos enseñado, resolvimos marcharnos e ir donde mejor fruto pudiéramos obtener, enseñando a los indios y adoctrinándolos en las cosas de la santa fe. Y así nos fuimos a otro cacique principal, que nos mostraba buena voluntad diciendo que quería ser cristiano."

2. "Nosotros estuvimos por consiguiente con aquel cacique Guarionex casi dos años, enseñándole siempre nuestra santa fe y las costumbres de los cristianos. Al principio mostró buena voluntad y dio esperanzas de hacer cuanto nosotros quisiésemos y de querer ser cristiano, diciendo que le enseñásemos el Padre Nuestro, el Ave María y el Credo, y lo mismo aprendieron muchos de su casa; y todas las mañanas decía sus oraciones y hacía que las dijesen dos veces al día los de su casa."

3. "con los otros se necesita de fuerza y de ingenio, porque no todos somos de una misma naturaleza. Como aquéllos tuvieron buen principio y mejor fin, habrá otros que comenzarán bien y se reirán después de lo que se les ha enseñado; con los cuales hay necesidad de fuerza y castigo."

4. "continúa en la buena voluntad, diciendo que quiere ser cristiano, y no quiere tener más que una mujer"/"suelen tener dos o tres, y los principales hasta diez, quince y veinte."

5. "siendo así que los cristianos [para los indios principales, según Pané, que aconsejan a otro] eran malvados y se habían apoderado de sus tierras por la fuerza ... aconsejaban que no se ocupara más en las cosas de los cristianos, sino de concertarse y conjurarse para matarlos, y habían resuelto no seguir en modo alguno sus costumbres."

6. "tiraron las imágenes al suelo y las cubrieron de tierra y después orinaron encima, diciendo: 'Ahora serán buenos y grandes tus frutos.' Y esto porque las enterraron en un campo de labranza, diciendo que sería bueno el fruto que allí se había plantado; y todo esto por vituperio."

7. "don Bartolomé Colón, que tenía aquel gobierno por el almirante su hermano ... ,como lugarteniente del virrey y gobernador de las islas ... los hizo quemar públicamente."

8. "Guarionex y sus vasallos no se apartaron del mal propósito que tenían de matar a los cristianos en el día designado para llevarles el tributo de oro que pagaban. Pero su conjuración fue descubierta ... Y no obstante todo esto, perseveraron en su perverso propósito, y poniéndolo por obra mataron a cuatro hombres, y a Juan Mateo, principal cristiano, y a su hermano Antón, que había recibido el santo bautizo. Y corrieron a donde habían escondido las imágenes y las hicieron pedazos."

9. "Juan. Este fue el primer cristiano que padeció muerte cruel, y tengo cierto que tuvo muerte de mártir. Porque he sabido de algunos que estuvieron presente a su muerte que decía: 'Dios naboría daca, Dios naboría daca,' que quiere decir 'soy siervo de Dios.' Y así murió su hermano Antón, y con él otro, diciendo lo mismo que él."

10. "Dios por su bondad me dio por compañía al mejor de los indios, y el más entendido en la santa fe católica; y después me lo quitó. Verdaderamente yo lo tenía por buen hijo y hermano; era Guatícabanu, que después fue cristiano y se llamó Juan."

11. "Las cuales cosas creen aquellos simples ignorantes que hacen aquellos ídolos, o por hablar más propiamente, aquellos demonios, no teniendo conocimiento de nuestra Santa Fe."

12. "Todo esto les han hecho creer sus antepasados; porque no saben leer ni contar hasta diez."

13. "lo mismo que los moros, tienen su ley compendiada en canciones antiguas, por las que se rigen."

14. "Pero todo lo que escribo así lo narran ellos, como lo escribo, y así lo pongo como lo he entendido de los del país."

15. "Y puesto que no tienen letras ni escrituras, no pueden dar buena cuenta de cómo han oído esto de sus antepasados, y por eso no concuerdan en lo que dicen, ni aun se puede escribir ordenadamente lo que refieren."/"Como los indios no tienen letras ni escrituras no saben contar bien estas fábulas, ni yo puedo escribirlas con exactitud."

16. Roger Dragonetti points out that in the Middle Ages "les clercs détenaient en leur pouvoir le stylet de l'escriture. Semblable au geste créateur, l'escriture était capable d'en simuler la puissance. Son emprise fondamentale sur la communauté ne tenait pas seulement au fait que'écrire c'était faire acte d'autorité, mais qu'il était surtout destiné à symboliser, dans tous les secteurs du savoir, le désir de vérité par une stratégie génératrice d'exemplarité, capable de produire l'authenticité désirée."

17. "creo que pongo primero lo que debiera ser último y lo último primero."

18. "Puesto que escribí de prisa, y no tenía papel bastante, no pude poner en su lugar lo que por error trasladé a otro."

19. "podido aprender y saber de las creencias e idolatrías de los indios, y de cómo veneran a sus dioses, de lo que le han contado."

20. "todo lo que escribo así lo narran ellos, como lo escribo, y así lo pongo como lo he entendido de los del país."

21. "Guahayona partió con todas las mujeres, y se fue en busca de otros países, y llegó a Matinino, donde en seguida dejó a las mujeres, y se fue a otra región llamada Guanín . . . y de esa manera quedaron todos los hombres sin mujeres . . . habían dejado a los niños pequeños junto al arroyo. Después cuando el hambre comenzó a molestarles, dicen que lloraban y llamaban a sus madres que se habían ido; y los padres no podían dar remedio a los hijos, que llamaban con hambre a las madres, diciendo 'mama' para hablar, pero verdaderamente para pedir teta. Y llorando así, y pidiendo teta, diciendo 'toa, toa' como quien pide una cosa con gran deseo y despacio, fueron transformados en pequeños animales, a manera de ranas, que se llaman 'tona,' por la petición que hacían de la teta."

22. *Como hubo de nuevo mujeres en la dicha isla de Haití, que ahora se llama la Española*

"Dicen que un día fueron a lavarse los hombres, y estando en el agua, llovía mucho, y que estaban muy deseosos de tener mujeres; y que muchas veces, cuando llovía, habían ido a buscar las huellas de sus mujeres, mas no pudieron encontrar alguna nueva de ellas. Pero aquel día, lavándose, dicen que vieron caer de algunos árboles, bajándose por entre las ramas, una cierta forma de personas, que no eran hombres ni mujeres, ni tenían sexo de varón ni de hembra, las cuales fueron a cogerlas; pero huyeron como si fuesen anguilas. Por lo cual llamaron a dos o tres hombres por mandato de su cacique, puesto que ellos no podían cogerlas, para que viesen cuántas eran, y buscasen para cada una un hombre que fuese caracaracol, porque tenían las manos asperas, y que así estrechamente las sujetasen. Dijeron al cacique que eran cuatro; y así llevaron cuatro hombres, que eran caracaracoles. El cual caracaracol es una enfermedad como sarna, que hace el cuerpo muy áspero. Después que las hubieron cogido, tuvieron consejo sobre cómo podían hacer que fuesen mujeres, puesto que no tenían sexo de varón ni de hembra."

Cómo hallaron remedio para que fuesen mujeres

"Buscaron un pájaro que se llama inriri, antiguamente llamado inriri cahubabayael, el cual agujerea los árboles, y en nuestra lengua llámase pico e igualmente tomaron a aquellas mujeres sin sexo de varón ni de hembra, y les ataron los pies y las manos, y trajeron el pájaro mencionado, y se lo ataron al cuerpo. Y éste, creyendo que eran maderos, comenzó la obra que acostumbra, picando y agujereando en el lugar donde ordinariamente suele estar el sexo de las mujeres. Y de este modo dicen los indios que tuvieron mujeres, según cuentan los muy viejos."

23. "Hubo un hombre llamado Yaya, del que no saben su nombre; y su hijo se llamaba Yayael, que quiere decir hijo de Yaya. El cual Yayael, queriendo matar a su padre, éste lo desterró, y así estuvo desterrado cuatro meses; y después su padre lo mató, y puso los huesos en una calabaza, y la colgó del techo de su casa, donde estuvo colgada algún tiempo. Sucedió que un día, con deseo de ver a su hijo, Yaya dijo a su mujer: 'Quiero ver a nuestro hijo Yayael.' Y ella se alegró, y bajando la calabaza, la volcó para ver los huesos de su hijo. De la cual salieron muchos peces grandes y chicos. De donde viendo que aquellos huesos se habían transformado en peces, resolvieron comerlos."

24. "Dicen, pues, que un día, habiendo ido Yaya a sus conucos, que quiere decir posesiones, que eran de su herencia, llegaron cuatro hijos de una mujer, que se llamaba Itiba Cahubaba, todos de un vientre y gemelos; la cual mujer, habiendo muerto de parto, la abrieron y sacaron fuera los cuatro hijos, y el primero que sacaron eran caracaracol, que quiere decir sarnoso, el cual caracaracol tuvo por nombre [Deminan]; los otros no tenían nombre.

... los cuatro hijos gemelos de Itiba Cahubaba, que murió de parto, fueron a coger la calabaza de Yaya, donde estaba su hijo Yayael, que se había transformado en peces, y ninguno se atrevió a cogerla, excepto Deminan Caracaracol, que la descolgó y todos se hartaron de peces.

Y mientras comían, sintieron que venía Yaya de sus posesiones, y queriendo en aquel apuro colgar la calabaza, no la colgaron bien, de modo que cayó en tierra y se rompió. Dicen que fue tanta el agua que salió de esa calabaza, que llenó toda la tierra, y con ella salieron muchos peces; y de allí dicen que haya tenido origen el mar. Partieron después estos de allí, y encontraron un hombre, llamado Conel, el cual era mudo."

25. "Estos [los hermanos], tan pronto como llegaron a la puerta de Baya-manaco, y notaron que llevaba cazabe, dijeron: 'Ahiacabo guárocoel,' que quiere decir: 'Conozcamos a este nuestro abuelo.' Del mismo modo Deminan Caracara-col, viendo delante de sí a sus hermanos, entró para ver si podía conseguir algún cazabe, el cual cazabe es el pan que se come en el país. Caracaracol, entrando en casa de Bayamanaco, le pidió cazabe que es el pan susodicho. Y este se puso la mano en la nariz, y le tiró un guanguayo a la espalda; el cual guanguayo estaba lleno de cohoba, que había hecho hace aquel día; la cual polvo, que ellos toman a veces para purgarse . . . Y así les dio por pan aquel guanguayo, en vez del pan que hacía; y se fue muy indignado porque se lo pedían. . . . Caracaracol, después de esto, volvió junto a sus hermanos, y les contó lo que había sucedido con Bayamanacoel, y del golpe que le había dado con el guanguayo en la espalda, y que le dolía fuerte-mente. Entonces sus hermanos le miraron la espalda, y vieron que la tenía muy hinchada; y creció tanto aquella hinchazón, que estuvo a punto de morir. Entonces procuraron cortarla, y no pudieron; y tomando un hacha de piedra se la abrieron, y salió una tortuga viva, hembra; y así se fabricaron su casa y criaron la tortuga."

Works Cited

Anderson Imbert, Enrique. *Historia de la literatura hispanoamericana*. 6th ed. Vol. 1. Mexico City: Fondo de Cultura Económica, 1967.

Blanco, Desiderio. "Figuras discursivas de la enunciación cinematográfica." *Lienzo* (Universidad de Lima) 8 (April 1988): 239-331.

Certeau, Michel de. *Heterologies*. Minneapolis: Univ. of Minnesota Press, 1985.

Conley, Tom. "Montaigne and the Indies: Cartographies of the New World." *1492-1992: Re/Discovering Colonial Writing*. Ed. René Jara and Nicholas Spadaccini. Hispanic Issues 4. Minneapolis: Prisma Institute, 1989. 225-262.

Dragonetti, Roger. *Le mirage des sources: L'art du faux dans le roman médieval*. Paris: Editions du Seuil, 1987.

Lévi-Strauss, Claude. *Structural Anthropology*. New York: Basics Book, 1963.

Merrim, Stephanie. "The Apprehension of the New in Nature and Culture: Fernán-dez de Oviedo's *Sumario*." *1492-1992: Re/Discovering Colonial Writing*. Ed. René Jara and Nicholas Spadaccini. Hispanic Issues 4. Minneapolis: Prisma Institute, 1989. 165-199.

Pané, Ramón. *Relación acerca de las antigüedades de los indios; el primer tratado escrito en América*. Nueva versión, con notas, mapa y apéndices por José Juan Arrom. 4th ed. Mexico City: Siglo XXI, 1980.

———. *Relación de Indias*. 1496. Ed. Alberto Wildner-Fox. Buenos Aires: n.p., [1954].

Zamora, Margarita. *Language, Authority and Indigenous History in the* Comentarios reales de los incas. Cambridge: Cambridge Univ. Press, 1988.

◆   Chapter 10

When Speaking Was Not Good Enough
Illiterates, Barbarians, Savages, and Cannibals[1]

Walter D. Mignolo

Introduction: Noticing The Lack of Letters

The lack of alphabetic writing was one of the most significant trademarks, next to lack of clothing and the eating of human flesh, in the construction of the image of the Amerindians during the sixteenth and early seventeenth centuries. Not having it yet or having it in excess were two cognitive moves used by Europeans in constructing the identity of the self-same by constructing, at the same time, the image of the other. My main goal in this essay is to examine how some Spaniards represented Amerindian verbal expression in light of a Renaissance philosophy of writing. At the same time, I shall touch upon recent anthropological research in the field of ethnography of speaking in order to gain some insight into the perception of people without alphabetic writing in the sixteenth century and to see how those perceptions have remained until this day.

In a previous essay I commented on an observation made by Pedro de Gante, one of the first Franciscans to arrive in Mexico with the mission of Christianizing the natives (Mignolo, "Literacy and Colonization"). He underscored the friars' difficulties in learning native languages because they were "people without writing, without letters, without written characters and without any kind of enlightenment" (Icazbalceta; Mignolo, "Literacy and Coloniza-tion" 66). Later on, Las Casas would close his lengthy discussion in defense of the Indians' rationality by defining four classes of barbarians. The second class includes those

> ... who lack a form of literal expression which is to their language as Latin is to ours and, finally, they do not practice or study letters, and these people are known as barbarians *secundum quid*, namely, because they lack a certain talent or quality and it is this lack which makes them barbarous, for in every other respect they may be considered wise and refined, and they are neither ferocious, odd or rough and because the English did not practice or study letters, the Venerable Bede, an Englishman, translated the liberal arts into English so that the English would not be considered barbarians, he tells us in his history, and St. Thomas also tells of this incident in the first book of the Politics, lesson one. (Las Casas 2: 638)[2]

A similar argument was construed, some forty years after the Dominican Las Casas, whose experience had been mainly with the Caribbean and Middle American Indians, by the Jesuit José de Acosta, who had been mainly in Peru and Mexico (1590). Acosta re-futed those who denied rationality to the Amerindians. However, he ranked the Aztecs third in the chain of writing, after alphabetic writing systems such as Hebrew, Greek, and Latin (which came first) and the Chinese ideographic writing system (which came second) (see Book 6). Speech was not good enough to consider the Amerindians at the same level as the Spanish and the Greco-Roman tradition, which was being actively constructed during the Renaissance.[3] Nevertheless, in one of the questions he addressed to Tovar, Acosta asked specifically how the Mexicans were able to pronounce such beautiful discourses, as Tovar informed him they did, if they did not have letters "for without letters it does not seem possible to preserve long and, in their genre, elegant speeches" ("pues sin letras no parece posible conservar oraciones largas, y en su género elegantes") and how they could have history if they did not have writing (qtd. in Sandoval 80). Acosta could not have been aware of the fact that his questions, which he cast in universal terms, presupposed a regional and culturally relative concept of rhetoric, oratory, writing, and history. Let us examine Tovar's response to Acosta:

> But it must be pointed out that although they had sundry figures and characters with which they put things in writing, their writing was not as adequate as our own, which, given the same words, would lead each person to state what was written without any disagreement. They could only agree in concepts: but in order to memorize precise words and copy speeches made by orators—as well as the many poems which they had, which they all knew word for word, all of which the orators composed—even though they represented the speeches and poems with their characters, in order to preserve them in the exact same words used by the orators and poets they had daily exercises in the schools of the principal men who were to be the successors of the orators, and by dint of constant repetition they committed the material to memory, so that there were no inconsistencies, taking the most famous speeches which had been made at any given time as the method by which they would accustom the men who were to be rhetoricians. In this way many speeches were preserved, word for word, from generation to generation, *until the arrival of the Spaniards who wrote down in our letters many speeches and poems which I witnessed, and in this way they have been preserved.* Thus the previous question has been answered as to "how it was possible to retain words by memory." (qtd. in Sandoval 81-82; emphasis added)[4]

Sahagún's Perception of Aztec Verbal Behavior

The Franciscan Bernardino de Sahagún paid more attention to the Mexicans' speech than to their writing. Sahagún (whose final copy of the *Florentine Codex* was completed toward 1578), during the same years that Acosta was writing his *Historia*, did not comment on Mexican manners and uses of writing. An entire book (Book 6 of the *Florentine Codex*) was devoted, instead, to "Rhetoric and Moral Philosophy." In it, Sahagún compiled those discourses in which the elders organized and transmitted their wisdom to future generations and which, also, were examples of well constructed and sophisticated speeches. Sahagún was aware of their cultural relevance, which he made explicit in the very first paragraph of the prologue to Book 6:

> All nations, however *savage and decadent*[5] they have been, have set their eyes on the wise and strong in persuading, on men prominent for moral virtues, and on the skilled and the brave in warlike exercises, and more on those of their own generation than on those of others. There are so many examples of this among the Greeks, the Latin, the Spaniards, the French, and the Italians that books are full of this subject.
>
> The same was practiced in this Indian nation, and especially among the Mexicans, among whom the wise, superior, and effective rhetoricians were held in high regard. And they elected these to be high priests, lords, leaders, and captains, no matter how humble their estate. These ruled the states, led the armies, and presided in the temples... *I think that by means of these virtues they achieved dominion, although it lasted little time and now they have lost all, as one will clearly see who will compare that contained in this Book with the life they now lead. This being very clear, I do not tell the reason for it.* (qtd. in Dibble and Anderson 1: 65; emphasis added)[6]

It was not enough for Sahagún to compare the Mexicans with the Greeks, Italians, and Spaniards and to contrast their past glories with their present decay. He also found it necessary to defend the credibility of the speeches he was reporting to those who had viewed the Indians as barbarians because of their illiteracy; and it was also necessary to make clear that the content of Book 6 was not invented, that "all the informed Indians will assert that this language is characteristic of their ancestors and the works they produced" ("y todos los indios entendidos, si fueran preguntados, afirmarían que este lenguaje es propio de sus antepasados, y obras que ellos hacían" [Dibble and Anderson 1: 66]). If Sahagún put so much emphasis on the Aztecs' formal speeches, it was to counter the image of the barbarian, savage, and illiterate Indians that had been constructed during the process of conquest and colonization. The idea was that while oratory was a well-known kind of oral speech that had been codified since Aristotle's *Rhetoric* and, later on, by the great Roman rhetoricians (Cicero, Quintilian), the codification (rhetoric) of oral speech (oratory) was after all a written artifact.

Some thirty years later another Franciscan, Juan de Torquemada, devoted several chapters of his *Monarquía indiana* (*Indian Monarchy*, Book 13) to the discourses ("pláticas") used by parents to educate their children. He provided two examples: a speech in which a mother addresses her daughter and another by a peasant to his married son. Torquemada could not hide his admiration for the eloquence of such discourses and emphasizes the difficulties that he, Andrés Olmos, and Bartolomé de Las Casas had in translating them into Castilian:

> We have not been able to translate them into Spanish with the gentleness and mildness which these people used in their own language, and we have dwelt more on translating the meaning of the doctrine plainly and clearly than the eloquence of the language they used themselves; for I confess that when these people express themselves, be it either to tell of their good or their bad fortune, they are outstanding rhetoricians, not because they have heard the rhetorical precepts of the type taught by Quintilian or Cicero in his divisions, but rather because they have a natural capacity, and they are so eloquent that they can talk about anything they desire with great ease. *Any high-minded person who would wish to do so would conclude, given the said conversations and notices, that these poor wretches, and native Indians of Mexico, Tetzcuco, Tlaxcalla, and its environs, were able to understand and sense things by dint of natural reason, some more so than others, as with any culture, for not all of them possess the same skill and wisdom.* (Book 13, xxxvi; emphasis added)[7]

The recognition of high forms of speech was not enough to honor them as equals. They had no knowledge of God (an observation with which Torquemada ends this chapter), nor of writing (an observation with which Torquemada opened his *Monarquía indiana*):

> One of the things which causes the most confusion in a republic and which greatly perplexes those who wish to discuss its causes is the lack of precision with which they consider their history; for if history is an account of events which are true and actually happened and those

who witnessed them and learned about them neglected to preserve the memory of them, it will require an effort to write them down after they have happened, and he who wishes to do so will grope in the dark when he tries, for he may spend his life collating the version which he is told only to find that at the end of it he still has not unravelled the truth. This (or something like this) is what happens in this history of New Spain, *for just as the ancient inhabitants did not have letters, or were even familiar with them, so they neither left records of their history.* (Book J, xi; emphasis added)[8]

Not every aspect of the Amerindian cultures attracted Spanish men of letters with the same intensity. They devoted, for instance, much more time to reconstructing Amerindian genealogy, religion, and customs than to exploring Amerindian conceptualizations of their discursive practices and means of recording the past. The authority of alphabetic writing and its "natural" links with history and rhetoric furnished sufficient proofs for the Amerindians' inferiority because alphabetic writing was tied up within an evolutionary and linear model in which Western culture was the last stage of an ascending development of human cultures. The model did not allow for alternative histories; endocentric constructions of the present taken as synonyms of the last stage of an evolutionary civilizing process were aptly characterized by Fabian as the "denial of coevalness." The "denial of coevalness" hypothesis, applicable to the colonizers' description of colonized cultures, is of course apt also for the description of a particular aspect of this process that can be called "the colonization of languages" (Mignolo, "Renaissance Theory").

Formal Discourses without Writing

Sahagún's transcription of oral Mexican discourses and the subsequent compilation by Juan Bautista (1600) under the title of *huehuetlatolli* (a Nahuatl expression meaning "ancient word" or "discourse of the elders") are paradigmatic examples of the authority of the elders in a society in which oral transmission is more important than written communication, and wisdom is deposited in the living body rather than in the book. The Franciscans (Olmos,

Sahagún, Juan Bautista)[9] documented native discursive practices but not the way they categorized and evaluated verbal behavior. I am not implying that they should have, since I am well aware that this possibility was not on their horizon of knowledge and expectations. It was a natural assumption of a man of letters in the sixteenth century to consider the Greco-Roman legacy in matters of grammar and rhetoric as the true categorization and evaluation of speech, and not to worry about what the Amerindians might have thought about their own speaking and writing activities. The missionaries collected and transcribed what had been said, but did not collect Amerindian conceptualizations, nor did they describe in (ethnographic) detail various acts of saying. The classical legacy in the field of rhetoric had stressed the description of acts of saying not necessarily for purposes of understanding them, but rather to teach and encourage good discursive performances. Missionaries had, therefore, some standards for recognizing and evaluating a good speech as a good performance, but did not have the tools to undertake a description of acts of saying, taking into account communicative situations, social roles, sex, and gender in semiotic and verbal interactions. Speech and oral discursive genres were valued, but were not considered equal to written genres.

Let us take a closer look at the discourses collected by Sahagún as examples of Aztec rhetoric and moral philosophy. And let us examine critically the image of the Amerindian left by the Spanish missionaries and men of letters who judged and depicted them in relation to their lack of letters. A preliminary organization of the speeches compiled by Sahagún according to their content may be seen as follows (see also Garibay 1):

1. The first eight chapters are devoted to the monologues addressed to the gods by high religious and political officers in which the gods are asked for help to solve the problems afflicting society;

2. Chapters 9 to 16 are illustrations of human communicative situations related to public affairs and civil government. Although there are also in this group speeches by the newly appointed leader directed to the gods, they adopt the tone of thanking the gods for his new social status. What charac-

terizes this group of speeches is their function in the political administration of the society. Thus, there are speeches that the leader addresses to the nobility or to the people as well as speeches that the nobility address to the people in support of the newly appointed leader. Those who were in charge of pronouncing this kind of address were characterized as "skillful in speaking";

3. The third group comprises the leaders' addresses to their sons in order to train them in the administration of public affairs and as future leaders of their people; and the addresses to their daughters for the purpose of training and teaching them their proper role in society and in the preservation of the unblemished image of their lineage. It is also in this category that the mothers' addresses to their sons and daughters could be included, making the distinction between parental relations and social roles. This group seems to represent the discourse pronounced by social leaders and members of the nobility;

4. The fourth group embodies those speeches pronounced by the people for the education of their children. Most of them are oriented toward procreation and education of the young and are addressed by both the mother and the father. (see Figs. 1, 1a, 1b)

One of the questions that immediately comes to mind is related to the formal character of these speeches, that is, their transmission and their pronunciation in different situations by members of different generations. The question arises whether these are examples of one specific situation or models of discourses pronounced and repeated in an indefinite number of similar situations. The amount of available *huehuetlatolli* as well as the lack of information about the social condition of their production and reception does not allow for an empirical description of the role this discursive genre played in Aztec society. However, a general description could be undertaken based on both the contribution of specialists in Nahuatl culture who have studied the *huehuetlatolli* (Garibay; García Quintana; Sullivan; Abbot) and on contemporary studies

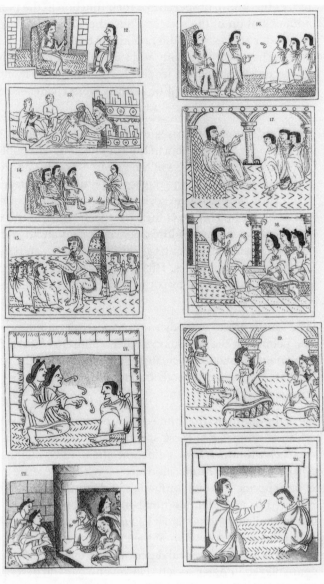

Figure 1. Graphic representations of discursive situations described in
Groups 2 to 4. Figure 1a. Redrawing and rearrangement of the drawing
in the Florentine Codex (Dibble and Anderson). Courtesy of the School
of American Research and the University of Utah. Illustrations by
Francisco del Paso y Troncoso.

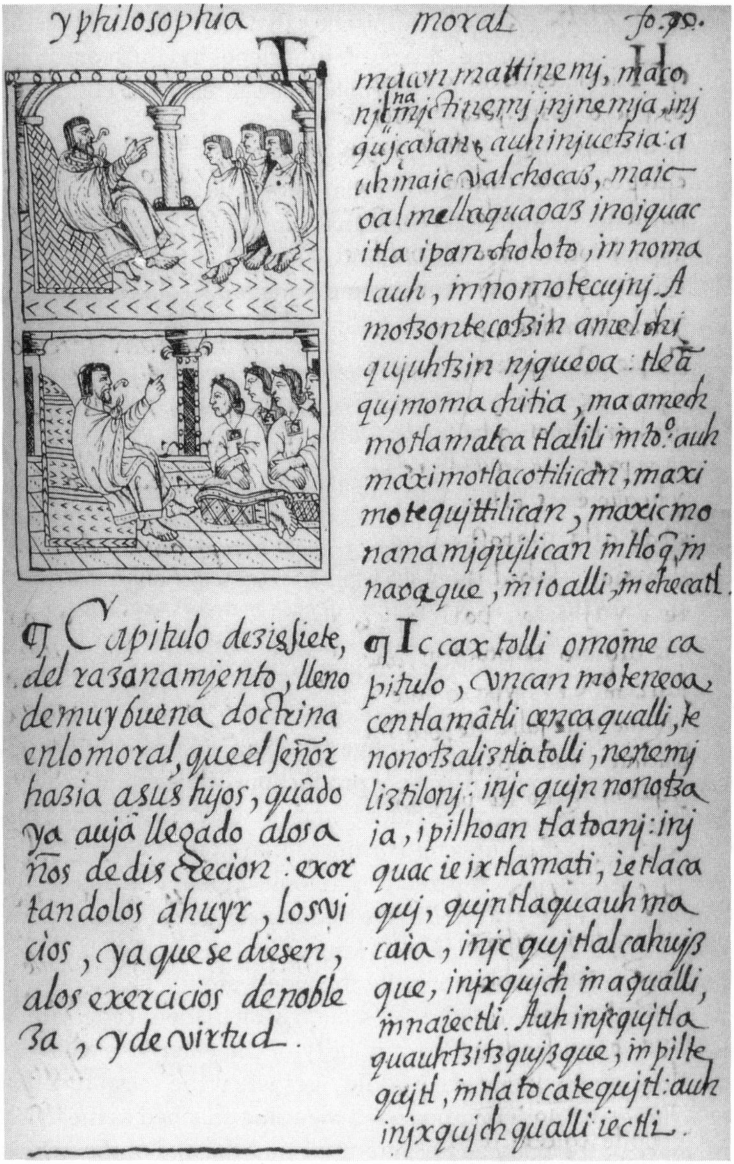

y philosophia moral fo. 78.

maçon mattinemj, maço njtlnajcetinemj injnemja, inj qujcaiati, auh injuetzia: auh maic valchocas, maic oalmellaquaoas inoiquac itla ipan chololo, in nomalauh, innomotecujnj. A motzontecotzin anoel chiquiuhtzin njqueoa: tlea qujmomachitia, ma amech motlamatca tlalili in tto: auh maximotlacotilican, maximotequjttilican, maxicmonanamjqujlican in tloq, in naoaque, in ioalli, in ehecatl.

Capitulo desisiete, del razonamiento, lleno de muy buena doctrina en lo moral, que el señor hazia a sus hijos, quãdo ya aujã llegado a los años de discrecion: exortandolos a huyr, los vicios, y a que se diesen, a los exercicios de nobleza, y de virtud.

Ic caxtolli omome capitulo, vncan motenehoa centlamantli cenca qualli, tenonotzaliztlatolli, nenemjliztiloni: injc qujnnonotzaia, ipilhoan tlatoanj: injquac ie ixtlamati, ie tlacaquj, qujntlaquauhmacaia, injc qujtlalcahujzque, injxqujch in aqualli, innaiectli. Auh injc qujtlaquauhtzitzqujzque, in pillequjtl, in tlatocatequjtl: auh injxqujch qualli iectli.

Figure 1b. One page of the original Florentine Codex *(Sahagún). Courtesy of Archivo General de la Nación, Mexico City.*

on the ethnography of communication that have shed light on the structure and function of discourse in societies in which oral communication is fundamental in politics, social relations, education, religion, etc. (Bloch).

The *huehuetlatolli* were transcribed in alphabetic writing by the Franciscan friars from 1546 (date that Andrés de Olmos might have collected them) until 1600 (date that Juan Bautista published his own collection). Angel María Garibay has asked what the relation between Olmos, Juan Bautista, and Sahagún's collections might have been. His answer is the following:

> Having examined the problem at length, I can find no other answer than the existence of two documentary resources, both of them originating in Olmos. *The first was probably elements gathered from the people, that is, from the common folk,* and Olmos himself in his *Grammar* as well as Juan Bautista in his edition must have availed themselves of this resource. *The second source probably came straight from the mouths of the principal people, the nobility and the clergy, the only ones who would be able to inform them of such matters.* And this collection is the one which Sahagún had and used for his work, which he incorporated into Book 6. (Garibay 1: 426; emphasis added)[10]

Garibay's comments underline the relationships between social stratification and discursive production. The generic name of *huehuetlatolli* ("words of the elder," "ancient word") identifying discursive genres that cut across distinct social strata accentuates the age of the person authorized to pronounce them ("words or discourse of the elder") as well as the traditional value of the discourse itself ("ancient word"). It is well known that in societies in which knowledge is transmitted orally the elders are the storehouse of wisdom (Maravall, "La idea del saber"; Mottahedeh; Pedersen). It is also well known that the authority of the elder was still relevant during the European Middle Ages when the social function of writing had not yet superseded the value attached to the living memory of the body as treasure trove and the age of the person as deposit and authority of wisdom (Maravall, "La idea del saber" 227-231, 239-250). Thus, while a society that practices writing and attributes to it a higher value over oral practices, also uses books for the organization and transmission of knowledge (García Pelayo; Chartier 45-86; Gumbrecht; Mignolo, "Signs and Their Transmission"), a society in which oral transmission is fundamental uses the elders, instead of the book, as organizers of knowledge and sign-bearers.

Although it would be difficult to make generalizations about the cultural function of speech and its relevance in social life among the Aztecs (or Mexica, as they called themselves) based on the corpus collected by Sahagún, it is nonetheless interesting to look at two aspects related to the social function of speech that emerge from this collection. The first is the uses of speech to train speaking behavior. Thus, whether it is the mother addressing her daughter or the father addressing his son, or vice versa, speech behavior appears to be very important in the social formation of the adolescent. What follows are recommendations given by the mother to her adolescent daughter, following the father's recommendations toward her general behavior in life:

> And thy speech is not to come forth hurriedly. As thou
> art to speak, thou art not to be brutish, not to rush, not to
> disquiet. Thy speech is to come forth in tranquillity and with
> gentleness. Thou art not to lift up nor to lower much "thy
> voice." As thou art to speak, as thou art to address one, as
> thou art to greet one, thou art not to squeak. Thou art not
> to murmur. Straight forward is thy speech to come forth;
> in medium voice is it to come forth; nor art thou to make it
> fanciful. (Sahagún 1578, Book VI, xix)[11]

It is interesting to observe that the mother's recommendations on verbal behavior are given in the context of other bodily related behavior. Sahagún introduced the sequence of discourse in chapter 19, from which the previous quotation is taken, recommending first "to place well within her the words of her father" (which Sahagún transcribed in chapter 18). Then the mother "told her how to live well, how to present herself, how to speak, how to look at one, how to walk, and how not to interfere in another's life and how not to abuse another." Insofar as speech, contrary to writing, presupposes the presence of the body in the very act of speaking, it is not surprising that the counseling about speech is made in the context of body-related behavior: how to walk well, how to present oneself, how to look at another. The father's advice to his son is also given in a context of body-related behavior, although the kind of acts that are mentioned mark the distinction between the social roles of male and female. Public rather than domestic life comes across in the father's advice to his son. Prudence in public, continence in eating and drinking, moderation in sleeping are some of the recommended behaviors next to speech:

> ... thou art to speak very slowly, very deliberately; thou
> art not to speak hurriedly, not to pant, nor to squeak,
> lest it be said of thee that thou art a groaner, a growler, a
> squeaker. Also thou art not to cry out, lest thou be known
> as an imbecile, a shameless one, a rustic, very much a rustic.
> Moderately, middlingly art thou to carry, to emit thy spirit,
> thy words. And thou art to improve, to soften thy words,
> the voice. (Sahagún, *Florentine Codex;* Book 6, xxii)[12]

This example illustrates that the lack of letters or of a writing system that allows for the transcription of speech does not make one a barbarian; illiterate people can have very sophisticated manners and be highly concerned with education and social behavior. While in the realm of technology there are a number of things that cannot be done without writing, in the sphere of human culture and behavior there seem to be no writing achievements that cannot be equally attained by speech. If writing as well as speech distinguish the human species from other nervous system organisms, it is speech that, chronologically, has been developed—before writing—into an instrument of education, social organization, and coordinated human interactions.[13] And even when writing was developed as an instrument of religious power, social organization and human interaction, speech was not abandoned. I am not trying to defend, with this argument, the Western logocentric tradition that Derrida (*De la grammatologie*) worked so hard to debunk. I am suggesting that although contemporary linguistic science was founded on the experience of suppressing writing from its field of inquiry in favor of speech, it does not necessarily mean that writing in the West was never preferred over speech; I am suggesting that it was a sign of a superior level of culture and a true measure of civilization. The Renaissance philosophy of writing, prior to and during the colonization process, bears witness to the fact that the value of speech over writing in Plato and the subsidiary role attributed to writing in Aristotle (and in our time by Saussure) was inverted during the late European Renaissance (Goldberg; Mignolo, "Renaissance Theory," "Nebrija in the New World"), and it was this inversion that justified the missionaries' perception of Amerindian semiotic interactions.

Nebrija's Pharmakon and the Prince's Glory

The emphasis that Renaissance philosophy of language put on writing over speech might not present any particular interest to a person who still believes today that writing and particularly alphabetic writing put Western civilization on a superior level in relation to other civilizations of the world. José de Acosta's beliefs, which authorized his hierarchical arrangement of cultures according to their writing systems, were still at work in the seminal article by Goody and Watt ("The Consequences of Literacy") as well as in the popular book by Ong (*Orality and Literacy*).[14] Elio Antonio de Nebrija (1444-1522) is one example among many that can be selected to illustrate a shift in the Renaissance philosophy of language that clearly indicates both a discontinuity with the classical tradition (and more specifically with Plato's evaluation of speech over writing and with Aristotle's belief that writing was a speech surrogate [see Dubois, *Mythe et langage; L'imaginaire* 49-76]), and the beginning of an ideological construction that was a trustworthy companion of colonial expansion from the sixteenth to the eighteenth centuries (and that is still with us today).

To write as we pronounce and to pronounce as we write were Nebrija's axioms regarding phonetics and orthography (*Gramática castellana* 1 [*Castilian Grammar*], x; *Reglas de orthographía*, second principle). A theory of the letter that is at the same time a theory of writing is presented in the description of the parts into which grammars are divided (*Introductiones; Gramática*). Nebrija began his grammars and, at a later date, his rules for Castilian orthography in *Reglas de orthographía en la lengua castellana* (*Rules for Spelling in the Castilian Language*) by devoting several paragraphs to the letters. It is assumed in every case that the invention of the alphabet was one of the greatest achievements of human civilization. This is one reason why Nebrija was constantly looking into the history of writing and the invention of the letters in order to support his assertion. Below is an example, from the *Gramática castellana*, of the merger between the significance of the letter and its origin and history:

> Among all the things that human beings discovered through experience, or that were shown to us by divine revelation in order to polish and embellish human life, nothing was more necessary, nor benefited us more, than the invention of letters. Such letters, which by a common consent and the silent conspiracy of all nations have been accepted, have been invented—according to those who wrote about antiquity—by the Assyrians; with the exception of Gelio, who attributed the invention of letters to Mercury in Egypt. (Book 1, ii)[15]

In his *Reglas de orthographía en la lengua castellana,* "composed by the Master Antonio de Lebrixa" ("compuestas por el maestro Antonio de Lebrixa"), he states:

> Among all the things that human beings discovered through experience, or that were shown to us by divine revelation in order to polish and embellish human life, nothing was more necessary, nor benefited us more, than the invention of letters. It seems that this invention originated from the fact that before letters were discovered, images were used to represent the things which people wanted to record, such as the figure of the right hand stretched out which meant generosity, and the closed fist which meant avarice, and the ear denoted memory; knees meant mercy; a coiled snake indicated the year, and so on. But since this business was endless and very confusing, the first inventor of letters—whoever that was—looked at the number of different voices in his language, and made as many figures or letters; by means of these figures, when placed in a certain order, he represented all the words he wished, as much for his memory as for speaking with those who were not present and those who were about to come. *Thus the letter is nothing more than a trace or figure by means of which the voice is represented.* (Book 1, ii; emphasis added)[16]

The quotation shows, on the one hand, that Nebrija persevered in his theory of the letter for over twenty-five years; on the other hand, it shows the semiotic context in which the letter was conceptualized. While the letter was conceived in relation to the voice, the signs enumerated beforehand were conceived in relation to their meaning (e.g., the ear to signify memory, which, of course, is meaningful in the context of an oral tradition).

The celebration and history of the letter was followed by Nebrija's pharmakon (Derrida, "La pharmacie de Platon" 69-198) since, once the letter was defined as the representation of the voice, he became concerned with correcting and maintaining the complicity between both. A successful cure for the inconsistencies between sound and letter, for example, as well as a successful preventive remedy depends on the grammarian's success in taming the letter. Otherwise, speakers would pronounce in one way and write in another, which, according to Nebrija, is just the opposite of the reasons for inventing the letters. Therefore, Nebrija's reasoning states an a priori need to explain a long and complex historical development (e.g., the letters were invented to represent the voice) and he forces himself to assert the need for a remedy that will prevent the deterioration and subsequent disintegration of the language (e.g., the control of the voice by means of letters).

Why Nebrija was so concerned about the complicity between the letter and the voice is clear in his prologue to the *Gramática castellana*, so often quoted in the context of "language companion of the empire" ("la lengua compañera del imperio" [Asensio]). Why the Mendicant or Jesuit friars writing grammars of Amerindian languages would follow Nebrija's example is clear at the technical level, not at the ideological one. If, on the one hand, Latin and Castilian grammars were taken as models for writing grammars of Amerindian languages, the programs underlying Nebrija's grammars did not coincide, necessarily, with the friars' program and ideologies.

A glance at Amerindian language grammars written by Castilian friars during the sixteenth and seventeenth centuries shows that the majority of the grammars began with a discussion of the letters and by identifying those letters that Amerindian languages did not have. The common concern with identifying the missing letters indicates that celebrating the invention of writing and finding its origin was no longer an issue. The new preoccupations suggest that the letter has been promoted to an ontological dimension that attributed to it a clear priority over the voice. The Classical tradition has been inverted and the letter no longer had the ancillary dimension attributed to it by Aristotle (*De Interpretatione*), but had become the voice in itself. Without acknowledging the discontinuity of the Classical tradition during the encounter with Amerindian languages we would not be able to understand the common expression "this language lacks such and such letters" ("esta lengua carece de tales letras") if indeed the person who made such an assertion was not presupposing that the letter is not located in the voice, but "outside" of it. The Jesuit Horacio Carochi, in his well-known *Arte de la lengua mexicana* (1645), begins his work by noting that the Mexican language lacks seven letters (Chapter I, i) and, in the next section, urges those learning the language to pronounce it correctly (Chapter I, ii). There is an understandable contradiction, but contradiction nonetheless, between the assertion that a language lacks a given number of letters in relation to an alphabet created for a nonrelated language and the urge to pronounce it correctly. Indeed, Amerindian languages did not necessarily lack letters, but implied different ones, namely those that were not within the sound system of the Romance languages. But, after all, the friars' program consisted of taming (Nebrija and Carochi used the word "reducir") the Amerindian languages and not in analyzing the connivance between picto-ideographic writing and speech, which was of a different kind than that between speech and alphabetic writing.[17] I am making this observation with the intention of understanding the interrelation between Renaissance theories of writing and the colonization of the native languages and not—of course—with the intention of criticizing Father Carochi.

Thus far I have analyzed the complicity between the letter and the voice. It is the interrelation between the letter and the writing of history that now requires our attention. The letter was not only necessary to tame the voice, but also to record the past, which is, at the same time, a way of building the territory. Hence, the conspiracy between the letter and the Prince's glories. This is one of the reasons why in 1517 Nebrija composed, in Alcalá de Henares, his *Reglas de orthographía en la lengua castellana.*

The first two paragraphs of the prologue celebrate, once more, the great achievement of humankind with the invention of letters but, this time, goes beyond just grammatical considerations:

> The past days, when your worship submitted the History of the Illustrious King John the Second to Arnao Guillén for printing, I informed you that the reason for which we had been using letters in Castilian was for the most part corrupt. I am not saying now that old words should be replaced by new ones, since this would mean corrupting books, as opposed to reforming them; rather I say that these days no one writes our language purely, due to the lack of some letters which we pronounce but do not write, and others, on the contrary, which we write but do not pronounce. ("Prólogo o Prefación," *Reglas de orthographía*)[18]

In the next paragraph Nebrija argues in favor of the glory and eternity of all "the Princes of our century." The reason for Nebrija's argument is that if they, the Princes, were so ambitious for fame as those from antiquity, they would not overlook the complicity between the letters, the writing of history and their own glory. One of the examples, among many, that may help us to understand the logic and semantic connections between the letter and the glory of the Princes, is as follows:

> For Palamedes in the Trojan War did not win as much renown in organizing battles, giving the passwords, passing on his surname, assigning the watches and vigils, in discovering weights and measures, *as in the invention of four letters: the Greek y, and three more aspirated letters: ch, ph, th....* ("Prólogo o Prefación," *Reglas de orthographía;* emphasis added)[19]

From the letter to the glory of the Prince there is indeed a great gap, which is large enough to frame, precisely, the idea of civilization and to marginalize the barbarians. The latter are those who do not know Latin letters but also, and perhaps more importantly, those who do not have letters at all.

Oratory in "Traditional" Societies

As we have seen, Sahagún held the speeches of the Mexicans in high esteem, both for their delivery as well as for their moral content. Because of these two factors, he labelled the book in which he collected a sample of Mexican speeches "Rhetoric and Moral Philosophy." Sahagún was rather silent about Mexican writing systems. He might not have been interested in bringing out the fact that the Mexicans were accomplishing by means of oral discourses what the Spaniards (as well as other European states during the sixteenth century) were accomplishing by means of writing. Since rhetoric was the discourse in which the rules and examples for the production of oral and public discourses (oratory) were established, it could be concluded that Sahagún did not collect rhetorical discourses (with the exception of the two examples just quoted), but oratorial (formal) discourses used in public affairs and in education. Although he recognized the beauty and sophisticated value of the speeches (the rhetorical *elocutio*), he was mute regarding their pragmatic values and functions (the rhetorical action in public, or *actio*). The *actio*, however, is implied in Sahagún's description of the situation in which the discourse was pronounced, but nothing was said about the significance of oral discourse in Mexico culture. The discourses collected by Sahagún can be seen, from the point of view of the rhetorical *actio* and the social function of oratory, as forms of social control and socialization.

As forms of social control, the discourses established a direct and privileged form of communication between the leaders and the gods, a form of communication that was not open to all members of the community. Formalized speech existed in which leaders addressed the people. In a society in which literacy was not widespread and the written records were in the hand of the leaders, massive communication was performed by speech and speech was the main vehicle of social control. Formalized speech was also one of the main instruments of socialization. Where no textbooks exist, education has to be achieved through oral discourse. Thus, it should be clear now why *huehuetlatolli* was used by the Amerindians to name a formal discursive genre in which knowledge was transmitted and education accomplished: the respect of the elder as repository of knowledge and emanation of wisdom. Although in the European Middle Ages the cult of the elder was still practiced (Maravall, "La idea del saber" 220), alphabetic writing and the cult of the book took the place—during the Renaissance—of the "men of wisdom." It was perhaps difficult for an educated Spaniard during the sixteenth century to draw a parallel between "the man of wisdom' ("el hombre sabio") and *huehuetlatolli* (those who have the wisdom of the word; *huehue*=elder+*tlatolli*=word or discourse). Moreover, socialization and social control emerged not only in what was being said but in the manner of saying it. Thus, the emphasis placed in the previous quoted speeches from the father to his son and from the mother to her daughter on the manners in which speech should be delivered and its relation to the position of the body were not only rhetorical advices but also social norms.

The Spanish missionaries and men of letters who studied or described Amerindian cultures had a disadvantage in relation to a present observer. It would have been difficult, if not impossible, for the missionaries to detach themselves from their own system of beliefs and to observe themselves describing the Amerindians. The distance between the missionaries' description of the Amerindians in the sixteenth century and the descriptions that humanists or social scientists can provide nowadays of the missionaries describing the Amerindians during the sixteenth century facilitates the understanding of the missionaries in a way that they could not have understood themselves. It would have been impossible for Sahagún, for instance, to think that Greco-Latin oratorial examples and rhetorical treatises were not the yardstick to measure Mexican discourse and to praise them as far as they approached the model, but rather that Mexican discourses were equivalent examples to what had been the experience of the Greek sophists or of Aristotle when he attempted a written formalization of oral discourses in his *Rhetoric*. In other words, Sahagún was not in a position to examine critically the Greco-Roman tradition from the experience of the formalized oral discourse among the Mexican leaders, parents, and elders. He had no other choice than to evaluate Mexican discourses from the perspective of the Greco-Roman tradition.[20]

Oral Discursive Genres

There is, finally, the question of genre related to the question of speech. The question of genre was related to the lack of (alphabetic) writing. In fact, how could someone manage to understand genres in oral communication when that person had been educated in a literate tradition in which, by the late fifteenth and early sixteenth centuries, the question of genre in rhetoric and poetic was so developed, and all its development was on the basis of written practices? Despite the recognition that the Amerindians had their way of recording the past, the true question of genre remained implicit for a long time. It came to the foreground quite recently, when Angel María Garibay published his *Historia de la literatura nahuatl* (*History of Nahuatl Literature*) and confronted the difficulties of organizing Nahuatl literature following the classification of genre in the Western tradition. Historians and missionaries during the sixteenth century had more important worries than the question of genres. As a consequence, the documentation about Amerindian categories of discourse classification was not easy to find in sixteenth- and early seventeenth-century source material. At any rate, there are three aspects in particular that should be kept in mind in relation to the topic under consideration:

1. The first aspect relates to discourse classification when speech is the main source of preservation, organization, and transmission of knowledge, ethics, and education, and when speech is also used in the sphere of pleasure and entertainment (a sphere of human communication that could be compared to Western poetry or literature). Although I will limit myself to historiography, poetry, and rhetoric (three of the major discursive categories during the Renaissance) and their equivalents in Amerindian cultures, the whole sphere of linguistic interactions in both traditions could be examined from the same perspective. León-Portilla (*Toltecayotl*) has provided, in the domain of Nahuatl culture, a reconstruction of Nahuatl vocabulary for genre classification both in the domain of conservation and transmission of the past as well as in the domain of rhythmic discourse related to music and narrative prose ("Nahuatl Literature"). Such a reconstruction, seen in the context of research done on folklore genres and the ethnography of

speaking, shows that the organization of sophisticated discourse classification and generic categories does not depend on writing, nor is writing a necessary condition for lasting discursive patterns. When a graphic system is not in place to fix discourses whose form has become an example of a given genre, human memory fulfills the function of ink and paper. Based on the premise of the reflective capacity of humans, which allows us to be at once participants and observers of our own actions and interactions, it is possible to assume that the members of any human community will concoct a vocabulary to describe their own discursive practices (Dundes; Ben-Amos 215-242). The difficulty at this level, however, is to fall into the trap of the distinction between "literature" and "folklore," one of the consequences related to the celebration of the letter and to the downgrading of speech as a valid form of education, verbal creativity (Western literature), knowledge (Western science), and wisdom (Western philosophy). If we accept that human discursive practice presupposes human observation and descriptions of their own semiotic interactions (or verbal behavior, to use a different jargon), then oral interactions would be inconceivable without a conceptualization (description and observation) by those who engage in them (practitioners, participants). Both oral interactions and their conceptualization constitute orality. The same principle applies to written interactions and their conceptualization by those who engage in them. Both alphabetic written interactions and their conceptualization constitute literacy (Mignolo, "(Re)modeling the Letter").[21]

2. The second aspect relates to discourse classification when the introduction of the alphabet made it possible either to fix pre-Conquest oral composition or allowed Amerindians to adapt the alphabet to their own oral and written traditions (e.g., *Popol Vuh, Anales de Solola*, etc.) or to mix their own with Western genres. Arzápalo Marín has advanced the hypothesis that the well-known mixed genre labelled "Reportorio de los tiempos," very popular in fifteenth- and sixteenth-century Europe, was influential in the organization of the *Books of Chilam Balam*. Furthermore, once the alphabet had been adapted by Amerindian communities, it did not necessarily mean that they would value writing in the same way that Western culture did. Tedlock ("Introduction" and *The*

◄ - - - - ▶ Implication
◄———————▶ Contrary
◄═══════▶ Contradictory

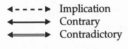

Level of semiotic interactions

oral interactions ◄—▶ written interactions

ORALITY { } LITERACY

conceptualization of ◄—▶ conceptualization of
oral interactions written interactions

Level of conceptualization
of semiotic interactions

Figure 2.

Spoken Word) has shown, for the case of the *Popol Vuh*, that oral transmission is still the preferred performance among the literate Maya-Quiché of Guatemala. The hybrid cultural production emerging from the blending of the endurance of preconquest Amerindian with Western discursive practices illustrates what I have called elsewhere "colonial semiosis" (Mignolo, "Colonial Situations"). Based on what has been said in the previous paragraph, the foundation of colonial semiosis could be outlined in a simplified version of the well-known semiotic square (see Fig. 2).

The sixteenth-century philosophy of writing celebrating the letter provided the foundation for a philosophy of written discourse that reemerged (in the twentieth century) in the "consequences of literacy" and the "grand divide," depicting oral and literate cultures (Goody and Watt, "The Consequences of Literacy"; Ong). The belief in the power of writing to transform (and implicitly upgrade) consciousness (Ong) was responsible for the image of the "grand divide" and it was, in the twentieth century, a rational articulation of the implicit judgment of sixteenth-century missionaries and men of letters when they were confronted with societies whose members were deprived of letters. The ethnographic works done on the genres of speech in non-Western communities (Scollon and Scollon; Calame-Griaule; Bauman and Sherzer; Gossen, "To Speak") has shown that orality is the equivalent, not a precursor, of literacy (Fig. 2).

3. The third aspect relates to the endurance of oral discourse for pleasure, entertainment, or transmission of knowledge in present-day Amerindian communities (Bricker; Gossen, "Chamula Genres," "To Speak," *Chamulas*), which has not only made it possible to study the contexts of verbal interaction but to understand as well both the sophistication in verbal behavior without alphabetic writing and the fact that discourse categorization is not only possible but also necessary. Bricker analyzed the ethnography of some traditional Mayan speech genres and disclosed a complex system of discourse classification that she divided between formal and informal speech (perhaps the primary and secondary systems, in Bakhtin's genres [Bakhtin; Mignolo, "Semiosis"]). Gossen did a similar job among the Chamulas, analyzing their own taxonomy of verbal behavior and evaluation of their own discursive genres ("Chamula Genres"). The result of his analysis shows three large areas of linguistic behavior represented in Figure 3.

Each discursive configuration (like the formal and informal categories in Bricker's reconstruction of Mayan speech genres) is comprised of a high number of discursive types. "Pure or true speech," for example, is comprised of types such as "new or recent words" and "ancient words," "true recent narratives" (tales, genealogies), "ancient narratives" (accounts of the distant past); "games," "ritual speech," and "frivolous languages." Furthermore, discursive configurations and discursive types are bound to the cosmological pattern. Thus, while the "ancient word" belongs to the first, second, and third creation according to the four ages of the world, the "new or recent word" belongs to the fourth creation, which is the one in which the Chamulas are living. Gossen has surmised that there is a correlation between linguistic behavior, style, and cosmological order and has found that "heat" is a basic metaphor that functions as the canon of Chamula criticism of all their kinds of speech performances:

Controlled heat symbolizes order in both a diachronic and synchronic sense. Language is but one of several symbolic domains which Chamulas think and talk about in terms of heat metaphors. (*Chamulas in the World of the Sun* 89)

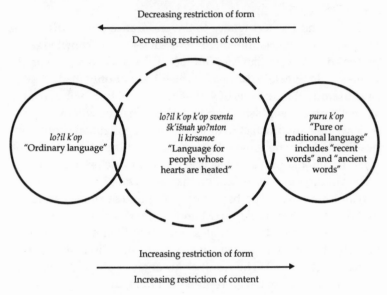

Figure 3. A simplified scheme of Chamula's discursive configuration. Diagram by Gary Gossen, "Chamula Genres." Reproduced by permission of the American Folklore Society from the Journal of American Folklore *84: 331 (Jan.-March 1971). Not for further reproduction.*

The "heat" metaphor (as in "to speak with a heated heart"), applies not only to language but to other domains of social interactions, as well as thoughts, religion, ethics, and cosmology. Gossen argues that

brings us to the fact that oral tradition is primarily concerned with norms and limits of permitted variation within them. In this sense, Chamula oral tradition is a more or less invariant expressive system that provides information which helps people to deal with more or less invariant aspects of the social system. It therefore is fitting and consistent that the primary invariable aspect of Chamula cosmos—the sun deity—should provide a native metalanguage for talking about some of the invariable canons of language use. ("To Speak" 412)

Because the term "metalanguage" has been discredited in academic circles since 1974, it would be preferable to talk about the uses of language to describe and evaluate the uses of language; or of the descriptions and evaluations speakers made of their own verbal behavior (semiotic interactions, to use another jargon). The point I am trying to make is that if this complexity of linguistic behavior and of its categorization and evaluation could be perceived and understood today among the Chamulas, it is conceivable that the oratorial pieces collected by Sahagún under the name of "Rhetoric and Moral Philosophy" were pieces of a larger puzzle that the Franciscans who worked in close connection with the first generation of Mexicans after the conquest (the Jesuits arrived as late as 1572) were unable to understand. And it could also be surmised that if a marginal community, like the Chamulas, survived and maintained their own patterns of verbal behavior, the Aztecs in Mexico-Tenochtitlan, at the height of their economic and political power, most likely had a complex system of categorization and evaluation of their speech whose understanding might still escape humanists and social scientists for whom the letter is a necessary condition for cultural development (see, however, León-Portilla, *Toltecayotl;* "Nahuatl Literature"). While such might be the case for today's humanists, it certainly was the case for many of the Spaniards (as well as for those educated in the ideology of the letter) who devoted their talents to understanding people without letters.

Concluding Remarks: Speech, Interpretation of Cultures, and the Denial of Coevalness

In the last chapter of Vargas Llosa's *El hablador (The Storyteller)*, the narrator comments on what is for him a remarkable achievement of Saúl Zuratas (his Peruvian Jewish friend who became a Machiguenga storyteller) in the following manner:

Becoming a storyteller was adding what appeared
impossible to what was merely improbable. Going back in
time from trousers and tie to a loincloth and tattoos, from
Spanish to the agglutinative crackling of Machiguenga, from
reason to magic and from monotheistic religion or Western
agnosticism to pagan animism, is a feat hard to swallow,
though still possible, with a certain effort of imagination.
The rest of the story, however, confronts me only with
darkness, and the harder I try to see through it, the more
impenetrable it becomes. (244)

The denial of coevalness (Fabian) is still at work in Vargas
Llosa's conception of what a storyteller and an oral based-society
would be, as it was in Carpentier's *Los pasos perdidos* (*The Lost Steps*)
when he equated his hero-narrator's displacement in space with
going back in time. For writers such as Vargas Llosa and Carpentier,
firmly planted in the chirographic tradition, the idea of civilization
is related to writing, to languages that have been "alphabetized"
and are no longer agglutinative, to reason instead of magic, to
cloth covering the body, to monotheistic religions. Instead, for a
Caribbean writer of the West Indies, such as Bratwhaite, the opposite view seems to be more relevant. Thus, in writing about oral
expressions in the Anglophone-speaking Caribbean and in group-
ing his essays under the title of *History of the Voice*, Bratwhaite
opened the doors to a denial of the denial of coevalness: "history,"
a discursive genre (historical narrative) as well as a discursive configuration (historiography) (Mignolo, "El metatexto"), tangled up
with alphabetic writing, is the activity responsible for writing the
history of the "voice," whose limitations to record the past have
been pointed out by those who invented history and historiography in the context of alphabetic writing. If noticing the lack of
letters in the sixteenth century contributed to the construction of
Amerindian images, its legacy in the twentieth century shows that
we are still immersed in the ideology and philosophy of writing
that prevented Spanish missionaries and men of "letters" to understand that their own "lack" of a Mexica writing system could have
been more than a good reason to be perceived as "barbarians" or
"illiterates."

Notes

1. Here I develop further some of the issues addressed in my 1989 essay "Literacy and Colonization: The New World Experience." I would like to point out from the start that although I am using the expression "New World" I am giving it a meaning somewhat different from the original one. Since we know today that the fourth part of the world was not "younger" than the three already known amid several civilizations developed around the Mediterranean Sea, the expression "New World" could be used to refer to the encounter of people from different "Old Worlds," each unaware of the existence of the other. I use "New World" to refer to new and transforming societies and cultures emerging from the cultural encounters between people from what until the end of the fifteenth century was known as "Europe" and people from what until the end of the fifteenth century was conceived as a regional territory, such as "Anáhuac" or "Tahuantinsuyu."

2. English translations of quotations throughout this essay are by Noel Fallows. "... que carecen de literal locución que responda a su lenguaje como responde a la nuestra la lengua latina finalmente, que carezcan de ejercicio y estudio de las letras, y estos tales se dicen ser bárbaros *secundum quid*, conviene a saber, según alguna parte o calidad que les falta para no ser bárbaros, porque en lo demás pueden ser sabios y polidos, y carecer de ferocidad, extrañez y aspereza y porque los ingleses carecían de ejercicio de letras, Beda venerable, que era inglés, porque sus ingleses no fuesen reputados de bárbaros, tradujo las artes liberales en la lengua inglesa, según cuenta su historia, y también Sancto Tomás lo refiere sobre el primero de la Política, lección primera."

3. I am using the term "Renaissance" in the general sense (not limited to the arts) of a change of mentality to which the expansion of the Spanish empire contributed in no small proportion (Maravall, *Estudios* 2: 35-216; Kristeller 1-87; Batllori).

4. "Pero es de advertir que aunque tenían diversas figuras y caracteres con que escribían las cosas, no era tan suficientemente como nuestra escritura, que sin discrepar, por las mismas palabras, refíriese cada uno lo que estaba escrito: sólo concordaban en los conceptos: pero para tener memoria entera de las palabras y traza de los parlamentos que hacían los oradores, y de los muchos cantares que tenían, que todos sabían sin discrepar palabra, los cuales componían los mismos oradores, aunque los figuraban con sus caracteres, pero para conservarlos por las mismas palabras que los dijeron sus oradores y poetas, había cada día ejercicio dello en los colegios de los mozos principales que habían de ser sucesores a éstos y con la continua repetición se les quedaba en la memoria, sin discrepar palabra, tomando las oraciones más famosas que en cada tiempo se hacían, por método, para imponer a los mozos que habían de ser retóricos; y de esta manera se conservaron muchos parlamentos, sin discrepar palabra, de gente en gente, *hasta que vinieron los españoles, que en nuestra letra escribieron muchas oraciones y cantares que yo vi, y así se han conservado.* Y con esto queda respondido a la última pregunta de cómo era posible tener esta memoria de las palabras."

5. The Spanish version of this expression reads: "Todas las naciones, por *barbaras, y de bajo metal que hayan sido...*"

6. "Todas las naciones, *por bárbaras y de bajo metal* que hayan sido, han puesto

los ojos en los sabios y poderosos para persuadir, y en los hombres eminentes en las virtudes morales, y en los diestros y valientes en los ejercicios bélicos, y más en los de su generación que en los de las otras. Hay de esto tantos ejemplos entre los griegos y latinos, españoles, franceses e italianos, que están los libros llenos de esta materia. Esto mismo se usaba en esta nación indiana, y más principalmente entre los mexicanos, entre los cuales, los sabios retóricos, y virtuosos, y esforzados, eran tenidos en mucho; y de éstos elegían para pontífices, para señores, y principales y capitanes por de baja suerte que fuesen. Estos regían las repúblicas y guiaban los ejércitos, y presidían los templos. Fueron, cierto, en estas cosas extremados, devotísimos para con sus dioses, celosísimos de sus repúblicas, entre sí muy urbanos; para con sus enemigos, muy crueles; para con los suyos, humanos y severos; *y pienso que por estas virtudes alcanzaron el imperio, aunque les duró poco, y ahora todo lo han perdido, como verá claro el que cotejase lo contenido en este libro con la vida que ahora tienen. La causa de esto no la digo por estar muy clara."*

7. "... no las hemos sabido romancear con la dulzura y suavidad que en su lengua estos naturales las usaban, atendiendo más a decir lisa y distintamente la sentencia de la doctrina, que la elegancia del lenguaje con que entre ellos se platicaba; porque confieso que en decir su razón estas gentes, así en contar sus bienes como en referir sus males, son aventajadísimos retóricos, no porque ellos hayan oído ningún precepto retórico de los que enseña Quintiliano, ni de los que da Cicerón en sus particiones, sino por serlo ellos naturalmente y tan elocuentes que les es muy fácil decir cualquier cosa que quieren; ... *Por las dichas pláticas y avisos dados podrán colegir los que con buenas entrañas quisieren considerarlo, que estas pobres gentes e indios naturales de México, Tetzcuco, Tlaxcalla y sus comarcas, alcanzaban y sentían, por natural razón y más unos que otros, como vemos entre otras gentes, que no todas tienen una misma habilidad o discreción...."*

8. "Una de las cosas, que mayor confusión causan en una República, y que más desatinados trae a los Hombres, que quieren tratar sus causas, es la poca puntualidad que hay, en considerar sus Historias; porque si Historia es una Narración de cosas acaecidas, y verdaderas, y los que las vieron, y supieron, no las dejaron por memoria, será fuerza al que después de acaecidas, quiere escribirlas, que vaya a ciegas en el tratarlas, o que en cotejar las varias que se dicen, gaste la vida, y quede al fin de ella, sin haber sacado la verdad, en limpio. Esto (o casi esto) es lo que pasa, en esta Historia de la Nueva-España; porque *como los Moradores Antiguos de ella, no tenían Letras, ni las conocían, así tampoco, no las Historiaban."*

9. Nahuatl specialists have studied these authors in relation to the *huehuetlatolli* in a precolonial context: Garibay; García Quintana; Sullivan; Abbot; for their significance in colonial and postcolonial culture see Mignolo and Ebacher.

10. "Examinando el problema con detención, no hallo más respuesta que la de la existencia de dos fondos documentales, ambos procedentes de Olmos. *El primero sería de elementos recogidos de personas populares, o sea de la gente menor*, y ese quedaría aprovechado tanto por el mismo Olmos en su *Gramática*, como por Juan Bautista en su edición. *El segundo repertorio sería el que se tomó de labios de gente principal, perteneciente a la nobleza y el sacerdocio, única que pudo informar sobre estas materias.* Y esta colección es la que tuvo y aprovechó Sahagún para su obra, incorporándola en su libro VI."

11. "y cuando hablares, no te apresurarás en el hablar, no con desasosiego, sino

poco a poco y sosegadamente; cuando hablares, no alzarás la voz no hablarás muy bajo, sino con mediano sonido, no adelgazarás mucho tu voz cuando hablares ni cuando saludares, ni hablarás por las narices, sino que tu palabra sea honesta y de buen sonido, y la voz mediana; no seas curiosa en tus palabras."

12. "Conviene que hables con mucho sosiego; ni hables apresuradamente, ni con desasosiego, ni alces la voz, porque no se diga de ti que eres vocinglero y desentonado, o bobo o alocado o rústico; tendrás un tono moderado, ni bajo ni alto en hablar, y sea suave y blanda tu palabra."

13. An argument could be made to sustain that we human beings "do not have speech" but that we "are speech." This principle cannot be easily reconciled with the "instrumentalist" view of speech because they have always been presented as either/or positions. I perceive a complementary rather that a contradictory relation between them. At one level it is possible to say that "we human beings are speech," taking speech as one of the features that distinguishes different species of living nervous systems. At another level, it seems quite obvious that human beings have turned speech into an instrument of human semiotic interactions including the organization and transmission of knowledge and education, the organization of society, the expression of agreements and disagreements, the control of people, and the exercise of social power.

14. Goody has modified somewhat the position taken in this early article in recent publications; see *The Interface between the Written and the Oral*. For criticism of this early thesis see also Scribner and Cole; Street.

15. "[E]ntre todas las cosas que por experiencia los ombres hallaron, o por revelación divina nos fueron demostradas para polir & adornar la vida umana, ninguna otra fue tan necessaria, ni que maiores provechos nos acarreasse, que la invención delas letras. Las cuales, *assi como por un consentimiento & callada conspiración de todas las naciones fueron recebidas*, assí la invencion de aquellas todos los que escrivieron delas antigüedades dan alos assirios, sacando Gelio, el cual haze invention delas letras a Mercurio en Egipto."

16. "Entre todas las cosas que por experiencia los ombres hallaron, o por revelación divina les fueron demostradas para polir & adornar la vida humana, ninguna otra fue tan necessaria, ni que maiores provechos nos acarreasse, que la invencion delas letras. La qual parece que (ouo) origen de aquello que ante que las letras fuessen halladas, por imagines representauan las cosas de que querían dexar memoria: como por la figura de la mano diestra tendida significavan la liberalidad, & y por la mesma cerrada, la avaricia, por la oreja, la memoria; por las rodillas, la misericordia; por vna culebra enroscada, el año, & assi delas otras cosas. Mas por que este negocio era infinito & muy confuso, el primero inuentor de letras—quien quiera que fue—miro quantas differentias de bozes avia en su lengua, & tantas figuras de letras hizo; por las quales, puestas en cierta orden, represento todas la palabras que quiso, assi para su memoria, como para hablar con los absentes & los que estan por venir. *Assí que no es otra cosa la letra, sino traço o figura por la qual se representa la boz.*"

17. Thus the question of the notion of "to read." In Nahuatl, for instance, *amoxitoa* can be translated as "to read." The word comes from *amoxtli* (a kind of tree that flourished in the lake of Mexico) and *toa* (a verb that could be translated as "to narrate" or "to tell"). The members of a culture without letters tell or narrate what they

see written on a solid surface, although it does not necessarily read in the sense we attribute to this word today. Eugenio Coseriu pointed out to me that the case is similar in Latin: *legere* means basically "to discern." The synonymity between "to discern" and "to read" came about when the use of the verb was restricted and applied to "discerning" the written words.

18. "Los dias passados, quando vuestra merced entrego a Arnao Guillen la Historia del muy esclarescido Rey don Juan el Segundo para que la imprimiesse, le dixe que esta razon de letras que agora teniamos en el uso del castellano, por la mayor parte estava corrompida. No digo oi agora que las palabras antiguas se oviesen de reformar en otras nuevas, por que esto seria corromper los libros, y no emendallos; mas digo que el dia de oi ninguno puramente escrive nuestra lengua, por falta de algunas letras que pronunciamos y no escrevimos, y otras, por el contrario, que escrevimos y no pronunciamos."

19. "Por que, ni Palamedes en la guerra de Troja gano tanto nombre en ordenar las batallas, en dar las señas, en comunicar el apellido, en repartir las raondas y vellas, en hallar los pesos y medidas, *quanta en la invencion de quatro letras: la y griega, y tres que se aspiran: ch, ph, th . . . ."*

20. While this kind of perspective is understandable in the sixteenth century, its persistence in the twentieth century is more troublesome (Abbot). It suggests that in the realm of linguistic behavior, as well as in other aspects of the colonization, sixteenth-century perspectives (or images) of the Amerindian are still alive and well in the twentieth century.

21. Isidore of Seville used the word *literatio* to refer to the domain of alphabetic written practices and conceptualization [*Etymologiae* (I, iii, 1)].

Works Cited

Abbot, Don Paul. "The Ancient Word: Rhetoric in Aztec Culture." *Rhetorica* 5 (1987): 251-264.

Acosta, José de. *Historia natural y moral de las Indias.* 1590. Ed. and intro. E. O'Gorman. Mexico City: Fondo de Cultura Económica, 1961.

Arzápalo Marín, Ramón. "The Indian Book in Colonial Yucatan." Paper presented at the conference "The Book in the Americas," John Carter Brown Library 1987. Ed. J. Mathes and N. Fiering. Conference proceedings, forthcoming.

Asensio, Eugenio. "La lengua compañera del imperio: historia de una idea de Nebrija en España y Portugal." *Revista de Filología Española* 43 (1960): 399-413.

Bakhtin, Mikhail. "El problema de los géneros discursivos." *Estética de la creación verbal.* Trans. T. Bubnova. Mexico City: Siglo XXI, 1982.

Batllori, Miguel. *Humanismo y renacimiento: Estudios hispano-europeos.* Barcelona: Ariel, 1987.

Bauman, Richard, and Joel Sherzer, eds. *Exploration in the Ethnography of Speaking.* Cambridge: Cambridge Univ. Press, 1974.

Ben-Amos, Dan. "Analytical Categories and Ethnic Genres." *Folklore Genres.* Ed. Dan Ben-Amos. Austin: Univ. of Texas Press, 1976. 215-242.

Bloch, Maurice, ed. *Political Language and Oratory in Traditional Society.* London: Academic Press, 1975.

Bratwhaite, Edward. *History of the Voice: The Development of Nation Language in Anglophone Caribbean Poetry*. London: New Beacon, 1984.

Bricker, Victoria. "The Ethnographic Context of Some Traditional Mayan Speech Genres." *Exploration in the Ethnography of Speaking*. Ed. R. Bauman and J. Sherzer. Cambridge: Cambridge Univ. Press, 1974. 369-387.

Calame-Griaule, Genevieve. *Ethnologie et language: La parole chez le Dogon*. Paris: Gallimard, 1965.

Carochi, Horacio. *Arte de la lengua mexicana con la declaración de los adverbios della*. Mexico City: Juan Ruyz, 1645.

Carpentier, Alejo. *The Lost Steps*. 1953. Trans. Harriet de Onis. New York: Knopf, 1956.

Chartier, Roger. "Distinction et divulgation: la civilité et ses livres." *Lectures et lecteurs dans la France d'Ancien Regime*. Paris: Editions du Seuil, 1987.

Derrida, Jacques. *De la grammatologie*. Paris: Minuit, 1967.

———. "La pharmacie de Platon." *La dissemination*. Paris: du Seuil, 1972. 69-198.

Dibble, C. E., and A. J. O. Anderson, eds. "Book VI. Rhetoric and Moral Philosophy." *Florentine Codex*. Santa Fe, N.M.: School of American Research, 1969. Part 7.

Dubois, Claude-Gilbert. *L'imaginarie de la Renaissance*. Paris: Presses Universitaires de France, 1985.

———. *Mythe et langage au seizieme siècle*. Paris: Editions Ducros, 1970.

Dundes, Alan. "Metafolklore and Oral Literary Criticism." *The Monist* 50.4 (1966): 505-516.

Fabian, Johannes. *Time and the Other: How Anthropology Makes Its Object*. New York: Columbia Univ. Press, 1983.

García Pelayo, Manuel. "Las culturas del libro." *Revista de Occidente* 24.25 (1965): 45-70.

García Quintana, Josefina. "Exhortación de un padre a su hijo." Trans. Andrés de Olmos. *Estudios de Cultura Nahuatl* 11 (1974): 137-182.

Garibay, Angel María. *Historia de la literatura nahuatl*. Mexico City: Porrúa, 1954.

Goldberg, Jonathan. *Writing Matters: From the Hands of the English Renaissance*. Stanford: Stanford Univ. Press, 1990.

Goody, Jack, and Ian Watt. "The Consequences of Literacy." *Comparative Studies in Society and History* 5 (1963): 304-345.

———. *The Interface between the Written and the Oral*. Cambridge: Cambridge Univ. Press, 1987.

Gossen, Gary. "Chamula Genres of Verbal Behavior." *Toward New Perspectives in Folklore*. Ed. A. Paredes and R. Bauman. Austin: Univ. of Texas Press, 1972. 145-167.

———. "To Speak with a Heated Heart: Chamula Canons of Style and Good Performance." *Exploration in the Ethnography of Speaking*. Ed. R. Bauman and J. Sherzer. Cambridge: Cambridge Univ. Press, 1974: 389-413.

———. *Chamulas in the World of the Sun: Time and Space in a Maya Oral Tradition*. Cambridge: Harvard Univ. Press, 1974.

Gumbrecht, Hans Ulrich. "The Body Versus the Printing Press: Media in the Early Modern Period, Mentalities in the Reign of Castile, and Another History of Literary Forms." *Poetics* 14.3/4 (1985): 209-227.

Icazbalceta, Joaquín García. *Nueva colección de documentos para la historia de México. Códice Franciscano. Siglo XVI*. Mexico City: Editorial Salvador Chávez Hayhoe, 1941.

Isidoro de Sevilla, San (540-626). *Etimologías*. Versión castellana total, por vez primera, e introducciones particulares de don Luis Cortés y Góngora. Madrid: Biblioteca de Autores Cristianos, 1951.

Juan Bautista, Fray. *Advertencias para los confessores de los naturales compvestas por el padre fray Joan Baptista*. Mexico City: En el Convento de Sanctiago Tlatilulco, por M. Ocharte, 1600.

Kristeller, Paul Oskar. *Renaissance Thought and the Arts*. Princeton: Princeton Univ. Press, 1990.

Las Casas, Bartolomé de. *Apologética historia sumaria*. ca. 1555. Ed. E. O'Gorman. 2 vols. Mexico City: Universidad Nacional Autónoma de México, 1967.

León-Portilla, Miguel. "Nahuatl Literature." *Literature. Supplement to the Handbook of Middle American Indians*. Ed. M. Edmonson. Austin: Univ. of Texas Press, 1985. 7-43.

————. *Toltecayotl: Aspectos de la cultura nahuatl*. Mexico City: Fondo de Cultura Económica, 1980.

Maravall, José Antonio. "La idea del saber en una sociedad estática." *Cuadernos Hispanoamericanos* 197 (1966): 324-350 and 198 (1966): 533-557. Rpt. in *Estudios de historia del pensamiento español*. Madrid: Ediciones Cultura Hispánica, 1967. 203-260.

————. *Estudios de historia del pensamiento español: La época del Renacimiento*. Madrid: Ediciones Cultura Hispánica, 1984.

Mignolo, Walter D. "Literacy and Colonization: The New World Experience." *1492-1992: Re/Discovering Colonial Writing*. Ed. René Jara and Nicholas Spadaccini. Hispanic Issues 4. Minneapolis: Prisma Institute, 1989. 51-95.

————. "Colonial Situations, Geographical Discourses and Territorial Representations: Toward a Diatopical Understanding of Colonial Semiosis." *Dispositio* 36-38 (1989): 93-140.

————. "El metatexto historiográfico y la historiografía indiana." *Modern Language Notes* 94 (1981): 358-402.

————. "Nebrija in the New World: The Question of the Letter, the Discontinuity of the Classical Tradition and the Colonization of the Native Languages." *L'Homme. Revue française d'anthropologie* 122-124 (1992): 187-209 (special issue devoted to *La ré-decouverte de l'Amerique*. Ed. C. Bernand and S. Gruzinski. Forthcoming). A Spanish version in *Primer Symposium de Filología y Literatura Iberoamericana*. Ed. C. Mora. Seville: Universidad de Sevilla: 1991. 171-199.

————. "(Re)modeling the Letter: Literacy and Literature at the Intersection of Semiotics and Literary Studies." *On Semiotic Modeling*. Ed. M. Anderson and F. Merrell. The Hague: Mouton, 1991. 357-394.

————. "Renaissance Theory of Writing, Missionary Discourse and the Colonization of Native Languages." Report presented at the symposium The Colonization of Languages, Visual and Verbal. Univ. of Pennsylvania: Latin American Center, December 1988. Forthcoming in *Comparative Studies in History and Society* 34.2 (1992).

———. "Semiosis, Coherence and Universes of Meaning." Paper presented at the conference Text and Discourse Coherence, Urbino, 1984. Rpt. in *Text and Discourse Connectedness*. Ed. M. E. Conte, J. S. Petofi, and E. Sozer. Philadelphia: John Benjamin, 1989. 483-505.

———. "Signs and Their Transmission: The Question of the Book in the New World" (1987). Proceedings of the conference The Book in the Americas (forthcoming).

Mignolo, Walter D., and Colleen Ebacher. "Alfabetización y literatura: los *huehuetlatolli* como ejemplo de semiosis colonial." *Actas del XXII congreso de literatura Iberoamericana*. Ed. J. Ortega. Forthcoming.

Mottahedeh, Roy P. *The Mantle of the Prophet: Religion and Politics in Iran*. New York: Simon and Schuster, 1985.

Nebrija, Elio Antonio de. *Gramática de la lengua castellana*. 1492. Ed. I. G. González-Llubera. London: Oxford Univ. Press, 1926.

———. *Introductiones latinae*. 1481. Rpt. in *Introductiones in latinam grammaticen*. Granada, 1540.

———. *Reglas de orthographía en la lengua castellana*. Alcalá de Henares, 1517. Ed. I. G. González-Llubera. London: Oxford Univ. Press, 1926.

Ong, Walter. *Orality and Literacy: The Technologizing of the Word*. New York: Methuen, 1982.

Pedersen, Johannes. *The Arabic Book*. Ed. R. Hillenbrand. Trans. G. French. Princeton: Princeton Univ. Press, 1984.

Sahagún, Bernardino de. *Florentine Codex*. ca. 1578. Ed. C. Dibble and A. J. O. Anderson. Book 6, "Rhetoric and Moral Philosophy." Santa Fe, N.M.: School of American Research, 1969.

———. *Historia general de las cosas de Nueva España*. Mexico City: Porrúa, 1956.

Sandoval, Francisco B. "La relación de la conquista de México en la Historia de Fray Diego Durán." *Estudios de historiografía de la Nueva España*. Ed. Díaz-Thomé. Mexico City: El Colegio de México, 1945. 80-83.

Scollon, Roland, and Suzanne Scollon. *Linguistic Convergence: An Ethnography of Speaking at Fort Chipewyan*. New York: Academic Press, 1979.

Scribner, Silvia, and Michael Cole. *The Psychology of Literacy*. Cambridge: Harvard Univ. Press, 1981.

Street, Brian. *Literacy in Theory and Practice*. Cambridge: Cambridge Univ. Press, 1985.

Sullivan, Thelma. "The Rhetorical Orations, or *Huehuetlatolli*, collected by Sahagún." *Sixteenth Century Mexico City: The Work of Sahagún*. Ed. M. Edmonson. Albuquerque: Univ. of New Mexico City Press, 1974. 79-110.

Tedlock, Dennis. "Introduction." *Popol Vuh: The Definitive Edition of the Mayan Book of the Dawn of Life and the Glories of Gods and Kings*. Trans. Dennis Tedlock. New York: Simon and Schuster, 1985.

———. *The Spoken Word and the Art of Interpretation*. Philadelphia: Univ. of Pennsylvania Press, 1983.

Torquemada, Fray Juan de. *Monarquía indiana*. 1615. Mexico City: Universidad Nacional Autónoma de México, 1975.

Vargas Llosa, Mario. *El hablador*. Barcelona: Seix Barral, 1987. Engl. trans. *The Storyteller*. Trans. Helen Lane. New York: Farrar, Straus & Giroux, 1989.

Chapter 11

Colonial Reform or Utopia?
Guaman Poma's Empire of the Four Parts of the World[1]

Rolena Adorno

Introduction

The project *Amerindian Images* asks us to consider how our present assumptions shape our understanding of the Indian of the past. Over the years I have observed three recurrent themes that deserve continual scrutiny and correction. I shall sketch them quickly in the paragraphs that follow.

The first of these critical challenges has been to overcome not only the monolithic image of the Indian but also to get beyond stereotypical notions of the *relations* of Indians and Europeans, which can be reduced to what the editors of this volume call the "paradigm of polarity." In an earlier volume in the Hispanic Issues series, I challenged that model in a piece on the subject position of intermediacy, taking the case of the *mestizo* chronicler Don Fernando de Alva Ixtlilxochitl ("Arms, Letters"). Such bilingual, bicultural subjects of indigenous American heritage, called in the records of colonial administration *"indios ladinos,"* help widen our understanding of European/Amerindian relations, as I hope to demonstrate below.[2]

A second general impression emerges when we move into

the seventeenth century and consider the cases just mentioned, that is, the first writings of cultural (if not racial) *mestizos*. Here the confrontational polarity is absorbed into a single subject and portraits of lost kingdoms emerge. More poignant than the conquistadors' recollections of great cities once seen, these are the long laments, by writers of Amerindian heritage, that we have come to call utopian. El Inca Garcilaso's famous phrase, recalling the Tawantinsuyu that was "destroyed before it came to be known," fixes dramatically the image of a utopia, a kingdom of the sun, that would warm the imaginations of European writers of the seventeenth century as well as our own today. The *mestizo* writers from the 1580s to the 1650s convey to us that sense of utopian idealism by dreaming the heavy dreams of loss. Projects oriented toward the future also have been called utopian, and my reconsideration of a well-known one (Guaman Poma's "empire of the four parts of the world") has led to the present reflection.[3]

Still a third commonplace that haunts our imaginings about the colonial past, related more indirectly to the Indian, is the specter of state and inquisitorial censorship. Creating the impression of *criollo* society as cut off from intellectual developments in Europe, censorship is thought to have made impossible the informed understanding of European intellectual culture on the part of even the most elite members of the native societies.

These, then, are the assumptions that are regularly reinforced and need to be questioned. Of course, it would be wrong to deny the oppositional character of colonial society, the sustained Amerindian lament over kingdoms lost, or the official attempts to control the circulation of books and ideas. What I challenge is not the correctness of these fundamental notions but rather their categorical nature. They need to be mitigated by information that can lead to new insights and understandings about how the colonial world worked. In order to reconsider the issues outlined above, I shall take up the fascinating but little-known history of colonial reform in Peru of the second half of the sixteenth century. Three well-known figures command our attention: Fray Bartolomé de Las Casas, the viceroy Francisco de Toledo, and the Andean writer (an *indio ladino* from the colonizers' viewpoint) Felipe Guaman Poma de Ayala.

In a very real sense, there are three different considerations to discuss: Las Casas's lifelong advocacy for colonial reform on behalf of the Indians, which culminated in his proposal for the Inca restoration; the efforts of Andean lords in the 1560s and 1570s to seek full restitution from the Spaniards and offer to purchase their lost autonomy; and, finally, some five decades later, collaborative efforts to renew and build upon those earlier traditions, as evidenced by the testimony of Guaman Poma. As I hope to show here, Guaman Poma's case was not unique and arising out of nowhere. It is, instead, simply the best-known surviving example of a type of collaboration between sympathetic clergy and other reformers and native Andeans in the decades when the viceregal regime was imposing its enduring patterns on the Andes.

Las Casas and the *Caciques'* Counteroffer

One of the great policy battles of Las Casas's long reformist career was his struggle to end *encomienda*. He argued that the *encomienda*, that is, the royal grants by which peoples and lands were deeded to conquistadors and others, had originated on the island Hispaniola without royal permission (Las Casas 5: 513). In order to counteract its effects, Las Casas attacked it as an institution, from 1535 onward until his death in 1566, through the principles and practices of Christian restitution of ill-got goods (Lohmann Villena 35, 41, 42). These he put into a "guide to confessors of those who now or in the past have been in charge of the Indians of the Indies of the Ocean Sea." Written in the late 1540s, it was one of the tracts he published in Seville in 1552-1553.[4] In 1560, the first archbishop of Lima, Fray Jerónimo de Loaysa, wrote another guide to confessors of Spaniards; it was based explicitly on Las Casas's earlier work (Lohmann Villena 52). The idea behind both was that *encomenderos*, and all those who benefited from them, from their relatives and heirs to merchants and priests, were liable to perform acts of restitution to the Indians upon their deaths. This meant returning the fruits of earthly gain to the native Andeans from whom this wealth had been taken.

Las Casas's attack on the *encomienda* system took a new turn in 1554-1555, when the *encomenderos* of Peru presented the prospective King Philip II with a remarkable offer: They would buy the perpetual rights to the use of the lands and native peoples of Peru from the king of Spain (Wagner and Parish 212). In 1556, after Philip had begun his reign, he was in terrible financial straits and accepted the proposal. Fortunately, it took the Council of the Indies more than two years to appoint a commission to oversee the sale (Wagner and Parish 216-217). In the interim, Las Casas and Domingo de Santo Tomás, through their Dominican colleagues in Peru, organized the lords of Peru (*kurakas*) and received powers of attorney from them.[5] In 1560, Las Casas and Domingo de Santo Tomás presented Philip with an offer more remarkable than that of the *encomenderos:* The *kurakas* would buy their own freedom, paying whatever sum the *encomenderos* had offered, if it could be verified, plus one hundred thousand ducats more (Las Casas 5: 465-468; Wagner and Parish 218-219, 287). Las Casas had presented the idea earlier, when in 1556 he had urged Philip not to accept the *encomenderos'* offer to buy Peru (Las Casas 5: 453-460; Wagner and Parish 217, 284). Offering twenty reasons why the new king should resist so tempting an opportunity, Las Casas had suggested to Philip that he should put at liberty, and make restitution to, the native lords of Peru; they then would purchase their own liberty and give more than the millions that the *encomenderos'* agent Ribera had offered to pay (Las Casas 5: 459; Wagner and Parish 217).

On the occasion of the 1560 counteroffer, and in order to sweeten the pie, Las Casas and Santo Tomás were authorized to throw in the "hidden treasures of the ancestors," that is, the Inca tomb treasures and the rights to the wealth of the mines (Las Casas 5: 468; Wagner and Parish 291). The mines in particular would offer the crown an ongoing source of revenue, in contrast to the *encomenderos'* offer by which, Las Casas and Santo Tomás reminded the king, he would lose all claim to sovereignty and effective control over Peru (Las Casas 5: 466). More importantly, the Dominicans argued, Philip would have to relinquish any control over the sacred charge, given by the popes to the Catholic Kings, to bring the Gospel to these new-found peoples (5: 466). Las Casas and his colleagues effectively won this struggle; Philip sold minor posts only, but no *encomiendas*. Las Casas's ten-year battle on perpetuity was ended (Wagner and Parish 220).

Soon afterward, however, a new and equally disturbing issue, already hinted at, surfaced full-blown: The discovery of Inca tomb treasures, particularly in the northern coastal areas of Peru (Lohmann Villena 66). Who owned these magnificent riches? Even the conviction that the wars of conquest had been just did not provide an answer that favored the conquerors. This debate brought the eighty-year-old Las Casas (see Parish and Weidman 385) to write his last great works, and they were devoted to the theme of the restoration of Inca rule: the treatise in Latin on the tomb treasures (1562) and the *Tratado de las doce dudas* (*Treatise of the Twelve Doubts* [1564]) in Spanish. Las Casas presented his Latin treatise and its Castilian sequel to Philip as his last will and codicil, in other words, as his enduring and final gift to his king. Apart from the specific Peruvian problems addressed, these works were meant to stand as general and lasting guides to Philip on the management of his empire (Wagner and Parish 231-233).

In 1977, I discovered that Guaman Poma quoted and paraphrased the *Doce dudas* in his important chapter of moral and spiritual considerations in the *Primer nueva corónica y buen gobierno* ("Andean View" 129-130). However, there was much more to the relationship between this final work of Las Casas and that of Guaman Poma than I had seen at the time. Only recently have I become aware of this, thanks to conversations with the great Las Casas scholar, the historian and biographer Helen Rand Parish. On reading my arguments, she quickly understood that Las Casas was not merely a literary source for Guaman Poma, but a model, and that Guaman Poma surpassed the lessons that his readings of Las Casas had taught him. Upon reexamining Guaman Poma's work, I have found overwhelming evidence that supports that insight, which in effect places Guaman Poma in a wider circle of reform activity.

The very fact that Guaman Poma read Las Casas suggests that there existed a wider circle of reformers. Guaman Poma never mentioned Las Casas by name; it is possible that he did not know it even though he had access to manuscript copies of his works. (The viceroy Toledo commonly referred to Las Casas in his letters only as "chiapa," an abbreviated and not-too-respectful version of "el obispo de Chiapa.") Of the Dominican and Franciscan reformers Guaman Poma names, the most prominent are the first archbishop of Lima, the Franciscan friar Jerónimo de Loaysa, and the Dominican friar and bishop of Charcas, Domingo de Santo Tomás (477, 926, 1089). Both were contemporaries of Las Casas and worked with him. Nevertheless, Guaman Poma's two references to Dominicans as great learned men suggests that his relationship to them was a literary one (660, 926). He did not, for example, name the Dominicans among his favorite religious orders. Indeed, his pictorial emblem of the order is a picture showing a Dominican friar abusing an Andean woman who is seated on the ground, weaving, with an infant on her back (659). The Dominicans whom Guaman Poma admired were preachers and writers. Since he was fond in particular of Franciscans and Jesuits, it is possible he came to know Las Casas's works through them, rather than through members of the Dominican order. In the 1570s, the viceroy Toledo assured the king that "the works of chiapa were the heart of most of the friars of this kingdom" (Levillier 4: 442).

In addition to Guaman Poma's reelaboration of Las Casas's arguments favoring the rights of all peoples to their own sovereignty (Principles 1 and 2), the other six of Las Casas's principles in the *Doce dudas* presented two more clusters of ideas of great importance in Guaman Poma's thinking about Andean affairs. First, the only right granted to the Catholic Kings by the pope had been to evangelize, not to conquer, subdue, or rule the native populations. Second, the conquests had been illegal (Wagner and Parish 234). The conquests had not conformed to principles of a just war as accepted by Las Casas, namely, the right to defend one's own sovereignty when threatened, to recover that which had been unjustly taken, or to punish an enemy for harm received from him (Las Casas 5: 505). Here it is important to state that for Las Casas there existed no just title of war in the Indies, according to the above criteria, but that, according to them, he recognized as just the war of the reconquest of Spain from the Muslims (Las Casas 5: 459). By all these eight principles, Las Casas argued in the *Doce dudas*, the only way by which the king could save his soul was to make restitution to the Incas and their descendants and, furthermore, restore the Incas as legitimate lords in their own lands (Las

Casas 5: 531). The king of Spain would be "universal lord," being served annually in recognition of this universal hegemony with an allotment of payment and treasures from the Inca (Las Casas 5: 434-435).

The small part of Las Casas's final program for reform that I had seen in Guaman Poma's "considerations" in 1977 was noteworthy at the time, mostly because it was well known that Las Casas's works had been suppressed in Peru by the viceroy Toledo in 1573, seven years after the death of Las Casas (Levillier 4: 442; 5: 312). There was, however, significant evidence in the 1560s and 1570s of Las Casas's works and ideas being circulated and implemented. Before his death, these consisted in the powers of attorney granted to him and other reforming clerics by *kurakas* to press their suits for restitution and liberty at court (Hanke, "Festón" 204-208; Espinoza Soriano; Ugarte y Ugarte; Murra). Afterward, this reform effort was continued in the confessional guides that led to pledges by numerous *encomenderos* to make restitution to the Andeans (Lohmann Villena 50-86). While the success of this later effort cannot be ascertained, the pressure for such acts of restitution is evidenced in the surviving documents from the 1560s. Guaman Poma's writing activity, however, comes later. Even if we take him at his word that he spent twenty or thirty years writing his book, this takes us back to the mid-1580s at the earliest. To find the link between Guaman Poma's activities and the earlier attempts at reform, we turn to the period 1569-1581, the time of the administration of the viceroy Francisco de Toledo.

Guaman Poma and the Tenure of the Viceroy Toledo

The *kurakas'* 1560 counteroffer and Las Casas's bold move demanding Inca restoration were met head on a few years after Las Casas's death by the viceroy Toledo. With the weight of arguments on the side of Inca restoration, the viceroy took as his task an inquiry into Inca history and the legitimacy of Inca rule (Hanke, *History* 1: 87-101). In the 1560s, the grandsons of Huayna Capac Inca, Titu Cussi Yupanqui and his younger brother Tupac Amaru, were alive and Titu Cussi was ruling over the neo-Inca state of Vilcabamba.[6] An analysis of Toledo's regime answers at least two and probably three pertinent questions in this inquiry.

First, Toledo gives ample testimony to the persistence of Las Casas's influence among his colleagues in Peru after the latter's death (Levillier 4: 442, 462; 5: 312, 405). The powerful arguments in favor of returning to Inca rule could *not* be countered by trying once again to prove the right to Spanish rule. As Helen Rand Parish has made clear, they had to be answered by proving the illegitimacy of the Incas.[7] The bulk of the evidence gathered in Toledo's inquiries of 1570-1572 indicated that the Incas had been Johnny-come-latelys on the scene and that they were not considered, by contemporary native witnesses, to have been legitimate rulers (see Hanke, *History* 1: 89-93 for the summary of the documents). Therefore, the threat to Spanish rule, as posed by the surviving members of the Inca dynasty, was diminished (Hemming 412).

Second, Toledo's urgency to prove the illegitimacy of the Incas stemmed from what he saw as the dangerous influence of Las Casas's followers, Dominicans and others, for whom Las Casas's ideas and books were "the heart of most of the friars of Peru" (Levillier 4: 442). Toledo had Las Casas's books suppressed in line with a royal mandate that all books that had been published without royal sanction were to be withdrawn from circulation. Philip was willing to have excommunicated anyone who had Las Casas's books, and Toledo wanted special punishments for those who were guilty of their possession because he considered the ordinary sanctions to be insufficient restraints (Zimmerman 105; Levillier 4: 462).

Finally, Toledo's tenure as viceroy gives us the link between Guaman Poma's personal experience in the 1560s and the source of his knowledge of the Lascasian programs at the time. Circumstantial and textual evidence suggests that he formed part of the entourage that conducted the viceroy's personal inspection tour of Huamanga (454). His precise recollection of the names of the officials who had been in charge forty years earlier, as well as his account of the inspection tour, lend credibility to his claims (Cook ix; Guaman Poma 454, 455).[8] Guaman Poma's description of Toledo's arrival in Cuzco (447), his intimate knowledge (302) and praise for many of the laws promulgated by Toledo (287, 448, 449, 598,

951, 966, 967, 989), as well as his condemnation of the execution of Tupac Amaru (452, 461, 950, 951) and the *reducciones* effected by Toledo (965), all signal his vivid recollection of Toledo's times (450, 452, 1044, 1056, 1058, 1076). Guaman Poma's overall assessment was that Toledo had been an administrator of great ability (951) who had nevertheless done great harm to the Andean people (965).

With the above considerations in mind, we can begin to piece together seemingly unrelated events: Las Casas's 1560 counteroffer and his 1564 arguments about Inca restoration; Toledo's 1570-1572 inquiries into Inca history that concluded that the Incas were usurpers and tyrants; Toledo's 1571 execution of the Inca prince Tupac Amaru; and, finally, Guaman Poma's grand scheme of 1613-1615 for the creation of the universal monarchy of the Spanish king, reigning over the sovereign and autonomous kingdoms of the "four parts of the world."

A New Commonwealth of Nations: Colonial Reform or Utopia?

Guaman Poma's account of Andean history and his proposals for colonial reform are the subjects announced in the title of his *Nueva corónica y buen gobierno*. Guaman Poma tells the ancient and modern history of Peru precisely because his project is oriented toward the future. Briefly, the major claims he makes on the basis of the history he narrates are: first, that the *encomienda* system was illegal because Tawantinsuyu had not been conquered in a just war ("there was no conquest," is Guaman Poma's [564] way of putting it); second, because the war of conquest had been unjust and violated natural, divine, and human law, the Spanish were bound by their religion to make restitution for lands and wealth taken and dominion exercised (572, 573, 741); third and finally, the king of Spain would preside over all the world, which would be divided into four great autonomous monarchies, representing Europe, Africa, the world of the Ottoman Turk, and the Indies, the last of which would be headed by Guaman Poma's princely son (963). This last notion, which may seem to be preposterous, reveals the boldness and originality of Guaman Poma's thought at the same time as it clears up a doubt about his famous apparent ambivalence on the great debate about the legitimacy of the Incas.

Based on the Andean cosmological model of a quadripartite division of space organized around a center, Guaman Poma's new global design of four imperial divisions headed by a universal monarch reiterates (and has been studied for) its placement of European elements in an Andean scheme (Ossio; Wachtel, "Pensamiento"). However, inasmuch as Guaman Poma illustrates the Andean paradigm (the four realms of Chinchaysuyu, Antisuyu, Collasuyu, and Condesuyu, with the Inca at center) in a map he calls "map of the World and Kingdom of the Indies" ("mapamundi y reino de las Indias"), he suggests the synthetic nature of his conception. It is the synthetic character of the construct that we shall pursue here.[9]

Guaman Poma's offer of his son as "king of the Indies" is in effect the repetition, but with a twist, of Las Casas's bids for the Inca restoration as presented in the *Tratado de las doce dudas*. On one hand, the presentation of a new candidate effectively replaces the departed Inca princes, the last of whom had been executed in 1571 by Toledo. Second, this new prince, as described by Guaman Poma, represents both the Inca dynasty and a more ancient one. Guaman Poma offers his son as a great-grandson of Tupac Inca Yupanqui and as an heir to the Yarovilca dynasty of Allauca Huanuco. Apart from the self-serving character of the nomination, Guaman Poma presents the only reasonable alternative to prior proposals: a replacement for Las Casas's last Incas and one who fulfills Toledo's criteria for ancient, authentic, and just rule in the Andes.

This dual descent is crucial on both counts. Though not restored to power, Guaman Poma knew that the Inca descendants, such as Don Melchior Carlos Inca, who was sent to Spain (exiled, says Guaman Poma), were honored by the Spanish monarch (753, 754, 948).[10] So Guaman Poma made the claim of being the grandson of Tupac Inca Yupanqui himself (754), as well as harking back to the prestige of his Yarovilca heritage. Sizing up the contemporary situation, Guaman Poma's offer of his son of dual dynastic lineage effectively reiterates, on one hand, one of the conditions of the 1560 counteroffer and similar efforts made by groups of *kurakas* in the years immediately following. In January 1562, hundreds of

Andean lords met outside Lima to grant powers of attorney to Domingo de Santo Tomás, Jerónimo de Loaysa, and Bartolomé de Las Casas, among other trusted persons, in order to advocate for the restitution of all the lands, properties, and possessions that had been taken from the Andean lords by the Spaniards (Murra xviii-xix). In October and November 1562, the *kurakas* of Chucuito and Arequipa respectively, with the help of Domingo de Santo Tomás, demanded an end to *encomienda*, full restitution of lands and properties usurped by the Spaniards, and rewards and liberties for their services rendered to the king (Ugarte y Ugarte). Apart from these precedents, about which Guaman Poma surely knew, his proposal also reiterates Las Casas's 1564 proposal for the Inca restoration. In other words, Guaman Poma's proposal takes into account and combines initiatives made decades earlier on behalf of the Inca and non-Inca leaderships respectively.

When Guaman Poma remarked in his account of Toledo's regime that the mere fact that the Incas had ruled for 1500 years should be sufficient to consider them bona fide rulers in spite of the fact that they had not descended from the dynasties of the preceding ages (455), he put to the service of a European logic the complex and symbolic chronologies that were part of his Andean heritage. Recorded not only by him but by European chroniclers as well, this indigenous Andean paradigm was coordinated by Guaman Poma with Western notions of temporality (see Ossio 191-197; Wachtel, "Pensamiento" 202-209, on Andean cosmology). In other words, Guaman Poma utilized his complex understanding of Andean time-space (see Wachtel, "Pensamiento" 182-195) to mitigate any and all dangerous arguments about Andean tyranny and also to conceptualize the opening of the ancient cosmology toward the future (Wachtel, "Pensamiento" 194).

Guaman Poma's organizing schemes of space and time integrate historical movement and universal structures not by the conversion of one dimension into the other, but rather by their convergence (Wachtel, "Pensamiento" 194). Space and time correspond in a one-for-one manner only at one point, in Cuzco, with the Incas, which left the system open in the extreme. If the fifth element, the Inca age, was the result of a history in Guaman Poma's scheme (Wachtel, "Pensamiento" 194), the presentation of the Spanish king as "universal monarch" could well be fit into the traditional Andean paradigm, offered by Guaman Poma, which had placed the Inca at the temporal center.

How are the prince of the Indies and the Spanish monarch articulated into Guaman Poma's vision of a universal empire that would include Philip III as "monarca del mundo"? Guaman Poma's proposal consists of a commonwealth of nations of various sovereignties of Christian and non-Christian kingdoms (963). The notion of incorporating non-Christian princes into a world in which all would have their place and dominions is not a utopian fantasy. Again, as in the case of princely dual descent, the idea has links to earlier efforts to restore Andean rule. On one hand, we see traces of the specific proposal made in the *kurakas'* counter-offer in 1560. On the other, we note the application of principles taken from the *Tratado de las doce dudas* about the rights of all peoples to sovereignty in their own lands, their not being Christian in no way disqualifying them from the exercise of this natural right (Principles 1 and 2).

When Guaman Poma used these principles to make his claims for the return of Andean rule to the Andes, he understood their full significance for all the lands and peoples of the world. Thus, he argued that, in this universal order, the "monarca del mundo," the Spanish king, would have no specific jurisdiction as do regular kings and emperors. Rather, he would have beneath him crowned kings, who would be "salaried" in the monarch's court "for the grandeur of the universal world of all the nations and types of persons: Indians, blacks and Spanish Christians, Turks, Jews, the Moors of the world. Consideration for the greatness of His Majesty the king" (963). Here we see how Guaman Poma coordinated the ancient Andean model with ideas that came from more recent sources. I suspect that letters like the one cited below circulated among reformers in Peru.

In 1555, Las Casas had written urgently to the royal confessor, the Dominican Bartolomé Carranza de Miranda, who was with the king in London (Wagner and Parish 213-215; Las Casas 5: 430-450). There he had suggested that the Inca should be restored, and that Philip should receive an annual royal salary for undertaking the conversion of the Indians. This would be like the single great jewel that the King of Tunis gave the emperor every year. Significant is his notion that the Spanish king should be recognized as "supreme prince and emperor over many kings," whose task it should be to protect and conserve the "liberty, dominions and dignities and rights and reasonable ancient laws" of the native lords (Las Casas 5: 444-445). The notion that the king of Spain should give up immediate jurisdiction over the Indies and restore native autonomy was put into practice in the creation of the 1560 counteroffer and *kurakas'* similar efforts from 1559 to 1564 to combat the *encomienda*.

It is fair to say that Guaman Poma presented his program fully aware of the rejection of the counteroffer and similar efforts of Andean lords to restore their freedom of a half century before. The acknowledgment that he knew about the 1560 counteroffer, as proposed by Las Casas and Domingo de Santo Tomás to the Council of the Indies in 1560, is found at the end of Guaman Poma's account of the execution of Tupac Amaru by Toledo. His concluding reflection states: "O, arrogant Christians, who have been responsible for the loss of His Majesty's wealth, of the millions that the city gave and the hidden treasures of his ancestors and all the mines and wealth! His Majesty has lost all this because Francisco de Toledo wanted to be a greater lord and king. Don't be like him!" (452).

Although Guaman Poma claimed that Tupac Amaru had offered Toledo, in return for his life, "his obeisance to the Spanish king, or millions in gold and silver, hidden treasures of his ancestors, or that he would reveal to him great mines and riches and would serve him all his life" (454), he here conflates the 1560 counteroffer with Tupac Amaru's response to his brief captivity in which no such offer was made. In fact, Tupac Amaru had resisted all of Toledo's attempts at diplomacy, refusing to see the envoy Oviedo on his mission of July-October 1571, and ignoring his subsequent ultimatum (Hemming 420-421). When Toledo learned of the murder of his last emissary to Vilcabamba, the prominent Atilano de Anaya, he determined to invade Vilcabamba and put an end to the Incas (Hemming 422-423). There is no mention, by the chroniclers of these events, that Tupac Amaru offered a ransom after his capture, even though the expedition to find him had produced great booty in gold and silver in the discovery of an Inca storehouse (Hemming 437). Therefore, Guaman Poma's reference to the wealth lost as "millions," "hidden treasures of the ancestors," and the wealth of the mines, comes straight from the counteroffer presented by Las Casas and Domingo de Santo Tomás.

The king of Spain definitively lost all this not when he refused to consider the counteroffer, but rather when Toledo had the last Inca executed, thereby closing the door to any idea of the restoration of the reigning Inca line. In two senses, then, Guaman Poma reveals that Toledo "wanted to be a greater lord and king," first, by executing a sovereign as though he were himself one and, second, by usurping Philip II's prerogative to keep open the prospect of acceptance of the counteroffer. In his appeal to Philip II's son, Philip III, Guaman Poma brings up anew the notion of Andean restoration and the commonwealth of nations. Since the era of Toledo and attacks on Inca legitimacy had taken place and the last direct descendants of Huayna Capac were gone, the presentation of a candidate who could be seen either as an Inca descendant or as the heir of an older, more authentic dynasty, is quite logical.

This design for a world monarchy had respected medieval origins. Dante may be cited as the thinker who went farther than any other of his time in "breaking with the old ideal of a unified Christian commonwealth controlled in both its branches by a revealed tradition of thought and action": "Dante in short extends the principle of the autonomy of the State, already partially admitted by Christian Aristotelians like St. Thomas, to an absolute degree" (Morrall 102). Subsequently, thinkers such as Marsilio, More, and Torquemada helped bring to an end "the distinctive political role which Western Europe had conceded to the Church... since the conversion of Constantine" (Morrall 118, 120-121, 133). By mid-sixteenth century, the basic medieval political idea of a Christian commonwealth with its coordinated secular and religious branches had fallen away: "The explicitly accepted religious fragmentation of western Christendom in the sixteenth century was the final proclamation that the old ideal was dead and with it the medieval world" (Morrall 136).

In America, the notion of a universal empire appeared in the fourth and fifth *Cartas de relación* (1524-1526) of Hernán Cortés to the emperor Charles V. Speaking of conquests made and those to come, such as the conquest of the Chichimecas in the north,

Cortés opined that there would remain no area "superfluous" in the world and Charles would be "monarca del mundo" (Frankl 459, 461).[11] Taken together, the Franciscan worldwide vision of the conversion of all peoples, Erasmian and imperialist dreams of a universal empire, along with Cortés's own dreams of the conquest of Cathay—"an empire which he himself would help to found by pressing on from Mexico, across the Pacific to the East"—furnished Cortés with a vision of a "world empire subject to a Charles V who would become 'monarch of the universe'" (Elliott 39-40).

Apart from freshly minted ideas about universal monarchies, inspired by the discovery of the Americas, Guaman Poma found his European model in Las Casas's *Doce dudas*. More like Dante, insofar as his idea of a commonwealth of nations left implicit the possibility of non-Christian members (Morrall 102), and quite unlike Cortés, for whom a universal Spanish monarchy implied conquests and Christianization everywhere, Las Casas's idea as further developed by Guaman Poma specifically made room for the non-Christian world. This is the Andean contribution to the new model. The discovery of Lascasian reformist ideas in the proposals on sovereignty put forth by Guaman Poma does not diminish the native elements in his conceptualization but rather strengthens them. What Guaman Poma has done is to reelaborate a traditional Andean form of jurisdiction and administration in line with the serious proposals presented to the present Spanish king's predecessor regarding colonial reform and Andean restoration. His achievement is, first, to have updated the Andean model of rule by placing it on a worldwide grid and, second, to have updated the Las Casas-Domingo de Santo Tomás counteroffer and the Las Casas proposal for the Inca restoration by presenting a new candidate and by emphasizing that it would be a model incorporating all Christian and non-Christian peoples. What is utopian about this proposal from our perspective, that is, our knowledge that it was never realized, surely was not so from that of reformers (Guaman Poma could not have been alone) who continued to work for justice and reform in the Andes.

What makes Guaman Poma's conceptualization of a commonwealth of nations noteworthy is the place that he assigns to Christian Europe within his universal scheme. Guaman Poma's emphasis on other cultural and religious traditions ("Moors, Turks, Jews") corresponds to a larger legal and ethical view of the world taken from—and extending—Las Casas's most advanced arguments on the topic. However, the Lascasian principles regarding the rights of all peoples, Christians and non-Christians, to dominion in their own lands serves Guaman Poma in a slightly different way. If, for the European reformer, it was forwarded to embrace the Americas into a wider world, Guaman Poma employed it to advance a view that would place Christian Europe among the non-Christian empires and peoples of the world, and clearly not as a "first among equals." Here we adopt Juan Ossio's (179-181) analysis of Guaman Poma's universal scheme that identifies "the king of the Christians" and "the king of the Moors" with the traditional Andean category of *Hurin* (the positionally inferior element) and the "king of the Indies" and the "king of Guinea" (Africa) with the positionally superior category of *Hanan*. In this vision of the world, Christian Europe loses its preeminence and even the Spanish "monarca del mundo" plays a symbolic, rather than jurisdictional, role.

The uniqueness of Guaman Poma's formulation is underscored by comparisons with similar works of the time. A Franciscan friar, Juan de Silva, published in 1613 and 1621 in Madrid works that gave a role to Philip III not unlike the one Guaman Poma gave him. His *Advertencias importantes acerca del buen gobierno y administración de las Indas, assí en lo espiritual como en lo temporal (Important Admonishments Regarding the Good Government and Administration of the Indies, in Spiritual as Well as in Temporal Matters)* integrated the legacy of the peaceful conversion of the Indians of the missionary friars, specifically Las Casas, with official Spanish messianism (Milhou 423). Advocating the peaceful conversion of the natives and inveighing against their exploitation through forced labor, de Silva insisted that the peaceful conversion of the peoples of the "southern continent" was far more important than the recovery of Jerusalem. However, the project of universal conversion proposed by de Silva had no place in Guaman Poma's vision of "the grandeur of the universal world of all the nations and types of persons: Indians, blacks and Spanish Christians, Turks, Jews, the Moors of the world" (963).

A final question that arises about the thinking of an intermediate figure such as Guaman Poma is the degree to which we have wanted to see native intervention in the early colonial period according to a certain model of the retention of "native purity." This almost inevitably imposes an outdated, antiquated if not archaic character on native thinkers and activists, which significant cases show us not to be true. Prophetic, revitalist movements such as Taki Unquy, which preached the return of the Andean gods and the defeat of the Europeans, were characterized precisely by the mixing of European with native elements.[12] The adaptation of European colonial arguments and attitudes is far removed from the servile assimilation of external models or the external manipulation of native desires and needs. The powers of attorney granted to Las Casas and Domingo de Santo Tomás and others by the *kurakas* of Peru in the early 1560s stand as strong evidence to the contrary. Furthermore, they clearly reveal the breadth of the reform movement at mid-century and the degree of friar-native collaboration involved. The enormous activity that could produce the powers of attorney and the counteroffer can only be imagined through these limited scraps of evidence. In the same way, Guaman Poma's testimony is not a "freak case," but rather offers a significant glimpse at the vigor with which reform activity was pursued by the collective efforts of members of colonizing and colonized communities.

Confession, Restitution, and Social Justice

What is the evidence that suggests that Guaman Poma is best seen in light of a wider movement? We must seek the answer in the character of his arguments, because he does not describe such activity as such. For instance, he mentions only one fellow Andean—but this one at great length and repeatedly—who worked defending the Indians.[13] Apart from his insistence on having "disciples" whom he taught to read and write, his own general claims about spending twenty to thirty years defending his people and writing (he saw the two projects as one) are always given as if he had been acting alone. Nevertheless, Guaman Poma's relationship to the larger arena is evident in the prominence he grants to the theme of restitution and his association of it with the first archbishop of Lima, Fray Jerónimo de Loaysa. Guaman Poma's equation of the Christian principle of restitution with social justice as well as spiritual salvation provides the clues to his activity and probable collaborators.

Two significant documents of this type found in Peru were an anonymous confessional guide for "confessors who had to work with lords of Indians and other persons," from the period 1555-1560, and Loaysa's previously mentioned "Avisos para confesores" ("Advices to Confessors" [1560]), which was officially approved by the Second Provincial Council of Lima in 1567-1568 (Lohmann Villena 51, 57). Their vitality through the seventeenth century is evidenced by their incorporation into the 1668 work of the bishop of Quito, Alonso Peña Montenegro, the *Itinerario para párrocos de Indios en que se tratan las materias más particulares tocantes a ellos para su buena administración* (*Itinerary for Priests Tending to Indians Which Deals with the Most Particular Matters Concerning Them and Their Good Administration*) (Lopétegui 575). Both the anonymous guide and Loaysa's "Avisos" proceed, station by station and group by group, through the ranks of colonial society: *encomenderos*, their wives and heirs, their majordomos, conquistadors, tradesmen, and merchants (Barinaga 565-570; Lopétegui 575-581).

These Peruvian documents clearly reveal the impact of Las Casas's 1552 guide to confessors, "approved by four masters of theology," including Bartolomé Miranda de Carranza and Melchor Cano. Las Casas's guide was concerned with three types of persons: those who had been conquistadores; those who currently held Indians in *repartimiento* and those merchants who made money from the Indians, particularly those who sold arms and provisions to Spanish soldiers (Las Casas 5: 235). The twelve rules of Las Casas's *confesionario* constituted his "fiery farewell to Chiapa" as he decided to go back to Spain in 1546 (Wagner and Parish 166). Employing the time-honored doctrine of restitution, which had been accepted for hundreds of years, the controversial character of Las Casas's argument was its application to all the colonizing inhabitants of the postconquest Indies; the basis of his *confesionario* was that all war and gain by Spaniards in the Indies at the expense of the Indians had been unlawful (Wagner and Parish 167-168).

More than fifty years later, Guaman Poma's principal reform argument was precisely the same: the colonizers were duty-bound to return all their ill-gotten gains to the Andeans. Guaman Poma presented the topic of restitution again and again at key points in his work.[14] In fact, his organization of the *Buen Gobierno* (*Good Government*) may be intended to correspond to the systematic, group-by-group treatment of the confessional guides. He demanded restitution of the same social groups as those singled out in the *confesionarios: encomenderos*, miners, majordomos. Guaman Poma's emphasis particularly on *encomenderos* and miners and their heirs (532, 540, 573) represents a comprehensive and consistent application of the respected principles of Las Casas and Loaysa to the effect that all these individuals were obligated to make restitution to the Indians. Guaman Poma's threat first and last (369, 1087) was that those Spaniards who did not perform appropriate and complete acts of restitution would go to hell. Here he made his own the particular arguments of Las Casas in the *Tratado de las doce dudas* (Las Casas 5: 529).

What is unique in Guaman Poma is that he explicitly moves it from a religious argument to a moral and ethical one not tied to Christianity per se. He gives the example of Pontius Pilate's execution of Jesus Christ and notes that although Pilate was not Christian ("he was Jewish," says Guaman Poma), he confessed and made restitution (1087). Guaman Poma's efforts to shame the Christians by holding up the examples of other religious and cultural traditions is done not merely for the drama of the contrast. It corresponds to that wider view of the world of his as described in the preceding section.

Whose War Is Just?

If Guaman Poma argued for full restitution of "life, honor, and wealth" to the Andeans and the restoration of Andean autonomy as well, it was based on his denial of the Spanish right to currently held *encomiendas*, which was grounded in turn on arguments about the illegality of the conquests and the peaceful and voluntary acceptance of Spanish rule by the Andeans. Here again, Guaman Poma gives a startling twist to Las Casas's arguments of the same type. Las Casas had argued that the conquests had been illegal (the general argument of the "Avisos para confesores" and Principles 7 and 8 of the *Doce dudas*) and that the only hypothetical alternative to a justified Spanish rule would have been the peaceful and voluntary submission of the natives. Guaman Poma turns the two around, arguing that his father, along with the three other lords of the four divisions of the empire (*suyus*), had accepted the Spanish emissaries of Charles V (the Pizarro invading party). Therefore, there had been no war, just or unjust, and the imposition of the *encomienda* system had been entirely without justification (377, 378, 564). By making his first claim, he dispensed with the need to argue the other two.

The reasonable reader would still ask: Why did Guaman Poma present such an argument denying the military conquest? Actually, the extent of Inca resistance has only recently been revealed.[15] At the time, the impression given by Guaman Poma squares with the available evidence. Many of the early published accounts of the war conveyed the idea that the Incas had succumbed without a struggle. Of the eyewitness accounts, Francisco de Xerez and Cristóbal de Mena estimated the Andean dead on that first encounter at Cajamarca between 6,000 and 8,000 (Hemming 551).[16] Las Casas, most likely based on these sources, offers the same numbers in the *Doce dudas*. Guaman Poma's account of the massacre declares that the Andeans "died like ants": "so many Indian people died it was impossible to count them" (388).

In 1535, other eyewitness veterans and writers of Cajamarca, Jauja, and Cuzco also returned to Spain, ending their narratives with the fall of Cuzco; Juan Ruiz de Arce, Pedro Sancho, Diego de Trujillo, and Miguel de Estete belong to this group. As Hemming (140) observes, all the eyewitnesses who left a good record of the first years of the conquest terminated their narratives in 1535, with the result that the "history of the Conquest suffers seriously from the resulting hiatus" (140).[17] All in all, these early published accounts conveyed the notion of a swift and complete conquest, before the Quito campaign and the siege of Cuzco by Manco Inca, and before the Incas' ability to hold out for so long at Vilcabamba could have been imagined. From the sixteenth-century historiographic perspective, the notion that Peru was conquered without a great military conquest, conveyed by the early chroniclers and repeated by Las Casas in his *Doce dudas* (5: 531) and Guaman Poma in his *Nueva corónica* (388), was neither novel nor surprising.

Guaman Poma effectively ended the conquest where some of the earlier chroniclers did, with the first shipment of gold to Castile after Cajamarca (393). He described the remainder of the violence as the simple lawlessness of armed and unruly men and the Spaniards' rebellion against their own king.[18] According to Guaman Poma, the first Spaniards conquered Peru with two words: " 'Don't be afraid. I'm the Inca.' They said this shouting to the Indians, who fled with fear. Thus, they did not conquer with arms or spilling of blood or great labor" (397).

On the other hand, Guaman Poma does grant that a just war occurred in Peru in the 1530s. It was the one waged by Manco Inca against the Spaniards in the second half of the 1530s. Elected as king by his captains, Guaman Poma writes, Manco Inca defended himself against the murder of Andean lords, the taking of women and girls "before their very eyes" and many other offenses (401). These crimes have a familiar ring, and they correspond to the causes for a just war as outlined by Las Casas in the *Doce dudas*. There the Dominican had declared that the Spaniards had usurped control of Cuzco when the Incas had only defended themselves; the Spaniards' actions were rapine and plundering, not just war, for they had taken everything by force and against the will of the owners in their very presence (Las Casas 5: 531). Henceforth until the day of judgment, Las Casas declared, the Inca kings and commoners too had every right to make war against the Spanish for injuries suffered (Las Casas 5: 507, 508). It is this right of just war that Guaman Poma attributed to Manco Inca.

Guaman Poma portrayed the actions of Manco Inca and after him Quis Quis Inca as just acts of self-defense which occurred after the peaceful Inca submission to Spanish rule (401, 408). Defeated not by arms but by a miraculous vision of Santiago, Guaman Poma asserts, Manco Inca retired to Vilcabamba, leaving "the kingdom and crown and royal fringe and weapons to the lord king and emperor, our lord don Carlos of glorious memory who is in heaven and his son don Felipe II who is in heaven and his son don Felipe III, our lord and king" (408). Guaman Poma's principle arguments about there having been no just Spanish war of conquest was based not on one historical episode but rather two (see Adorno, "Andean View" 130, *Cronista* 94-95): the diplomatic submission of the four *suyus* at Tumbes and Manco Inca's relinquishment of royal command as he fled to Vilcabamba. Both events are important for they make the murders of Atahuallpa and Manco Inca's son Tupac Amaru illegal in exactly the same manner, that is, as gratuitous crimes committed against the already acquiescent. According to Guaman Poma's argument, the peaceful submission at Tumbes in 1532 and its reiteration by Manco Inca in 1539 now leave no other course open to the Spanish king except to effect an Andean/Inca restoration.

Here we come full circle to the recommendation for the universal monarchy and the princely, autonomous realms envisioned by Guaman Poma. Built on a solid body of work and adapted to local circumstances, his proposal reveals several things: first, the vitality with which Las Casas's proposals were considered decades after his death by like-minded colonial reformers; second, their articulation with principles of Andean thought and worldview; third, the innovations by which the guiding principles of these diverse traditions were woven together to face new problems in new circumstances. In Guaman Poma's view, Christianity is present but not predominant. His "empire of the four parts of the world" advocates the separation of secular and religious jurisdictions, and it does so through respected principles of traditional Andean thought and explicit reference to Las Casas's positions on dominion and sovereignty that reach back to Thomas Aquinas.

Conclusions

The conclusions we can reach from such cases are clear: First, this type of reforming resistance moves us beyond the liberal interpretations that concentrate on the initial defeat of the Amerindian peoples and their states. Second, the strictly monolithic view of Spaniards versus Indians gives way to networks of interrelationship that produced not only collaboration with the colonial regime but also efforts to oppose it. The final great arguments of Las Casas were executed not on behalf of the natives of Spanish America but with their collaboration. Beyond the pathos of the first phase of European/Amerindian actions, we witness a second phase, characterized by resistance and based on knowing the debates of imperial domination and incorporating as well as rejecting elements of them into new formulations. The themes of utopia and loss are augmented by those of persistent and energetic struggle. Finally, the commonplaces about literary suppression and censure are once again opened to revision. We need to learn again the lessons that Irving A. Leonard, in *Books of the Brave*, taught some forty years ago about the ways in which the royal edicts and orders, and Inquisitorial scrutiny, were circumvented in the book trade. Clearly the circulation of ideas deemed dangerous by the Councils of Castile and the Indies could not be suppressed.

Although the viceroy Toledo had appreciated Philip II's warning about the need to keep an eye on friars who thought they could intervene in affairs of state (Hanke, *History* 1: 87-88), and Toledo suggested that special punishments were required to deter friars from reading Las Casas's works, it was demonstrably impossible for Toledo or his successors to control the circulation and promulgation of ideas whose goal was the return of Andean hegemony over Peru. The strenuous battle that Toledo waged against the ideas of the potential Inca restoration is a testimony to the vitality of those ideas, not only as presented by Las Casas but as advocated by his colleagues and followers in the 1570s in Peru. Guaman Poma's writing to the king in 1615, suggesting to Philip III a new version of the ideas that Philip II had rejected, reveals that Toledo's vehemence against Las Casas's recommendations for colonial reform—even in the decade after the Dominican's death—had been well-placed. Guaman Poma's work stands as testimony to the fact that the powerful ideas of reform could not be easily destroyed. Furthermore, his case represents far more than an isolated instance or a single "phase" in the history of European-*criollo*/Amerindian relations pertinent to the articulation of theological principles with demands for social justice. One of the rewards of studying his remarkable and difficult book is to understand that he offers a glimpse at the foundational period of persistent Latin American traditions whose legacy leads us, in the twentieth century, to the lives and writings of present-day reformers such as the Peruvian priest and theologian of liberation Gustavo Gutiérrez.

Notes

1. This study is dedicated to Helen Rand Parish, who has made me read again texts that I thought I knew.

2. The blanket term *indio ladino* was applied to those indigenous Amerindians who had at least partially mastered the language of the colonizers. Their skills were employed in the negotiations of Church and state officials with the native populations. Often serving as interpreters on tours of inspection of local communities, in the Church, and as domestic servants, *indios ladinos* included men and women from every rank and station in native society. Spanish-speaking black slaves were called *negros ladinos* (see Adorno, "Images").

3. Julio Ortega's approach to ideas of prospective utopias in Spanish America is the best I've found. Emphasizing the difference from classical and humanist models, he insists upon the concreteness and, simultaneously, the unreal character of New World utopias that "fuse temporalities and explore a promised land" ("Prólogo" 13; see also *Crítica* 15-29).

4. Having circulated from hand to hand since 1546, these instructions were ordered sequestered by a decree of November 28, 1548. In Mexico, the Franciscan friar Toribio de Benavente Motolinía gladly took up the task of collecting them (Wagner and Parish 171). Ginés de Sepúlveda called the work "scandalous and diabolical." Although Las Casas never so stated himself, his enemies accused him of denying the king's title to the Indies and of thus committing lese majesty (Wagner and Parish 172). All this notwithstanding, Las Casas had the "Avisos" published in Seville in 1552 (Lohmann Villena 41).

5. This document is published in Hanke, "Festón" 204-208.

6. Titu Cussi Yupanqui in 1570 dictated his memoirs to Fray Marcos García, leaving an important Inca testimony of the conquest and in particular his arguments that the Spaniards had betrayed his father Manco Inca, whose siege of Cuzco in 1536 and second "rebellion" of 1538-1539 had placed Spanish rule in doubt.

7. In her introduction to *The Only Way*, Helen Rand Parish makes this important point in contrast to earlier characterizations of Toledo's project as proving the right to Spanish rule (see, for example, Hanke, *History* 1: 87-89). Like Parish, Hemming (421) sees the debate as hinging on the Incas' moral, historical, and legal right to rule Peru, with Toledo's being convinced by the inquiries he had commissioned that they had none.

8. In addition, Guaman Poma's reference to the 1557 *visita* of Huamanga by Damián de la Bandera, of whom he draws a portrait, suggests his early acquaintance with these systematic efforts at census taking (411, 454; Jiménez de la Espada 1: 176-180).

9. The quadripartite division of the world was an honored tradition in medieval European cosmography as it was in the Andes. In maps of 1110 onward, Jerusalem occupied the center, the "umbilicus mundi" of this sacred geography. An explicitly quadripartite division is found in the thirteenth-century Ebstorf (Ger-

many) map in which the inhabited world is inscribed on the crucified and resurrected body of Christ, in which head, feet, and hands occupy the four cardinal directions and the navel of Christ is the center of the world (Milhou 406-407; Bettex 30-31). Such notions were not definitively discarded until the discoveries of the second half of the fifteenth century (Milhou 405). However, myths of a New Jerusalem and of the Center (geographical, spiritual, political, and mythic), tied to notions of the chosen people, the chosen monarch, continued to be important through the seventeenth century (Milhou 412-426). The symbolism of the Center and New Jerusalem were of particular importance in geographical exegesis and in architecture in the Spain of the Renaissance and baroque (Milhou 415).

10. The Inca heirs of Sayri Tupac and Paullu Inca, who had collaborated with the Spanish, prospered, in contrast to the heirs of Manco Inca (Hemming 472-473). However, Melchior Carlos Inca's penchant for high living and trouble led the viceroy Luis de Velasco to want to send him to Spain. Melchior Carlos obliged, by making his own request to go to Spain; it was readily granted when his father-in-law was arrested in Cuzco on charges of conspiracy. A co-conspirator, García de Solís Portocarrero, was arrested and beheaded in Cuzco (Hemming 462-463).

11. To be sure, the notion of the universal dominion of the Spanish monarch had its antecedents in the writings of Pedro López de Ayala in the fourteenth century and in Juan de Mena, among others. However, only one treatise, that of the Spanish theologian Juan de Torquemada of 1467-1468, gives it the Aristotelian-Thomist foundation expressed by Cortés that there be nothing "superfluous on earth" (Frankl 463).

12. See the documents published by Millones and the studies of Cock and Doyle, Millones, Ossio, Pease, Stern, Wachtel, and Yaranga Valderrama on the culturally hybrid character of this sixteenth-century resistance movement.

13. The only such reforming activist whom Guaman Poma mentions is Cristóbal de León, a former disciple of his, whose efforts to defend his Indians brought him affronts, punishments, and exile (498, 499, 500, 501, 502, 572, 694, 704, 745, 944, 951, 990). Exiled in 1611 (944) and 1612 (502), his difficulties with a local priest brought him to grief. At the end, he refers to one Cristóbal de León who usurped privileges he did not have (1107, 1119), but this is not likely to be his former student, whom he had identified as the son, a *segunda persona*, of the lord of the *ayllu* Oma Pacha (499).

14. Guaman Poma demands restitution from the Spanish at the conclusion of his history of the Andes and the Incas, just before he commences his account of the Spanish conquest (369). In the section of the *Buen Gobierno* (*Good Government*) devoted to the archbishops and bishops of Peru, he cites Loaysa's acts of restitution upon his death (477). In the chapters on miners and majordomos (532, 540) as well as in the "prologues" to the chapters on *encomenderos* and the cities and provinces of Peru (573, 1086, 1087), he repeatedly demands the return of Andean possessions, property, and wealth.

15. The second rebellion of 1538-1539, which was the "last effort on a national scale to dislodge the invaders" was not recorded by any single chronicler at the time; Hemming recently reconstructed the events of this insurrection from the disperse public records (255, 584).

16. The Cristóbal de Mena and Francisco de Xerez accounts, published in 1534

after Cajamarca and their early return to Spain at the end of 1533, became best-sellers and were translated into other European languages (Hemming 90). "Post-Renaissance Europe, writes Hemming (90), "was dazzled by the discovery and sudden conquest of an unimagined empire of such brilliance."

17. Among eyewitness accounts, Pedro Pizarro provides the only exception; he continued his narrative well beyond the events of 1535 (Hemming 140).

18. On the first count, Guaman Poma described the uprising as a time when "there was neither the God of the Christians, the king of Spain, nor justice" (391). The Spaniards, the Chancas, Chachapoyas, and Huancas were robbing and looting (391, 397). He next described the murder of the Inca captain Quizu Yupanqui by Luis de Avalos de Ayala in Lima: "And thus the Inca who had not defended himself in any city was conquered" (395). As it happened, however, Quizu Yupanqui's army, marching north from Cuzco, had succeeded in annihilating almost all of the Spanish between Cuzco and the sea. Upon attacking Lima, he was slaughtered by the Spaniards (Hemming 206-207, 212).

Works Cited

Adorno, Rolena. "Arms, Letters, and the Native Mexican Historian." *1492-1992: Re/Discovering Colonial Writing*. Ed. René Jara and Nicholas Spadaccini. Hispanic Issues 4. Minneapolis: Prisma Institute, 1989. 201-224.

——. *Cronista y príncipe: La obra de Don Felipe Guamán Poma de Ayala*. Lima: Pontificia Universidad Católica del Perú, 1989.

——. "Felipe Guamán Poma de Ayala: An Andean View of the Peruvian Vice-royalty, 1565-1615." *Journal de la Société des Américanistes* 65 (1978): 121-143.

——. "Images of *Indios Ladinos* in Early Colonial Peru." *Transatlantic Encounters: Europeans and Andeans in the Sixteenth Century*. Ed. Kenneth J. Andrien and Rolena Adorno. Berkeley: Univ. of California Press, 1991. 232-270.

Barinaga, Augusto. "Documento nuevo sobre casos morales de Indias." *Missionalia hispánica* 12.36 (1955). 565-570.

Bettex, Albert. *The Discovery of the World: The Great Explorers and the Worlds They Found* . . . . New York: Simon and Schuster, 1960.

Cock, Guillermo, and Mary Eileen Doyle. "Del culto solar a la clandestinidad de Inti y Punchao." *Historia y cultura* 12 (1979): 51-73.

Cook, Noble David. "Introducción." *Tasa de la visita general de Francisco de Toledo*. Ed. Noble David Cook. Lima: Universidad Nacional de San Marcos, 1975. ix-xxvii.

Elliott, J. H. "The Mental World of Hernán Cortés." *Spain and Its World (1500-1700): Selected Essays*. By J. H. Elliott. New Haven and London: Yale Univ. Press, 1989. 27-41.

Espinosa Soriano, Waldemar. "Los huancas aliados de la conquista: tres informaciones inéditas sobre la participación indígena en la conquista del Perú, 1558, 1560 y 1561." *Anales Científicos de la Universidad del Centro del Perú* (Huancayo, Peru) 1 (1971-1972): 9-47.

Frankl, Víctor. "Imperio particular e Imperio universal en las *Cartas de Relación* de Hernán Cortés." *Cuadernos Hispanoamericanos* 165 (1963): 443-482.

Guaman Poma de Ayala, Felipe. *Primer nueva corónica y buen gobierno*. 1615. Ed. John V. Murra, Rolena Adorno, and Jorge L. Urioste. Crónicas de América 29 a, b, c. Madrid: Historia 16, 1987.

Gutiérrez, Gustavo. *Dios o el oro en las Indias (siglo XVI)*. Lima: Instituto Bartolomé de Las Casas y Centro de Estudios y Publicaciones, 1989.

———. *En busca de los pobres de Jesucristo*. Lima: Centro de Estudios y Publicaciones e Instituto Bartolomé de Las Casas, 1988.

———. *A Theology of Liberation*. 1971. Trans. Sister Caridad Inda and John Eagleson. Maryknoll, N.Y.: Orbis Books, 1988.

Hanke, Lewis. "Un festón de documentos lascasianos." *Revista Cubana* 16 (July-December 1941): 150-211.

———, ed. *History of Latin American Civilization: Sources and Interpretations*. 2 vols. Boston: Little Brown, 1967.

Hemming, John. *The Conquest of the Incas*. San Diego, New York, London: Harcourt Brace Jovanovich, 1970.

Jiménez de la Espada, Marcos, comp. *Relaciones geográficas de Indias*. Biblioteca de Autores Españoles 183. Madrid: Atlas, 1965.

Las Casas, Fray Bartolomé de. "Aquí se contienen unos avisos y reglas para los confesores." 1552. *Obras escogidas de Fray Bartolomé de las Casas* 5. Ed. Juan Pérez de Tudela Bueso. Biblioteca de Autores Españoles 110. Madrid: Atlas, 1958. 235-249.

———. "Carta al maestro fray Bartolomé Carranza de Miranda." *Obras escogidas de Fray Bartolomé de las Casas*, V. Ed. Juan Pérez de Tudela Bueso. Biblioteca de Autores Españoles 110. Madrid: Atlas, 1958. 430-450.

———. *Los tesoros del Perú*. 1562. Trans. Angel Losada. Madrid: Consejo Superior de Investigaciones Científicas, 1958.

———. "Memorial del obispo fray Bartolomé de las Casas y fray Domingo de Santo Tomás." 1560. *Obras escogidas de Fray Bartolomé de las Casas*, V. Ed. Juan Pérez de Tudela Bueso. Biblioteca de Autores Españoles 110. Madrid: Atlas, 1958. 465-469.

———. "Memorial-sumario a Felipe II." 1556. *Obras escogidas de Fray Bartolomé de las Casas*, V. Ed. Juan Pérez de Tudela Bueso. Biblioteca de Autores Españoles 110. Madrid: Atlas, 1958. 453-460.

———. *Tratado de las doce dudas*. 1564. *Obras escogidas de Fray Bartolomé de las Casas*, V. Ed. Juan Pérez de Tudela Bueso. Biblioteca de Autores Españoles 110. Madrid: Atlas, 1958. 478-536.

Leonard, Irving A. *Books of the Brave: Being an Account of Books and of Men in the Spanish Conquest and Settlement of the Sixteenth-Century New World*. Cambridge: Harvard Univ. Press, 1949.

Levillier, Roberto. *Gobernantes del Peru: Cartas y papeles, siglo XVI*. 14 vols. Madrid: Juan Pueyo, 1921-1926.

Lohmann Villena, Guillermo. "La restitución por conquistadores y encomenderos: un aspecto de la incidencia lascasiana en el Perú." *Estudios lascasianos: IV centenario de la muerte de Fray Bartolomé de las Casas (1566-1966)*. Seville: Escuela de Estudios Hispanoamericanos, 1966. 21-89.

Lopétegui, B. "Apuros en los confesionarios." *Missionalia hispánica* 2.6 (1945): 575-581.

Milhou, Alain. *Colón y su mentalidad mesiánica en el ambiente franciscanista español.* Cuadernos Colombinos 11. Valladolid: La Casa-Museo de Colón y Seminario Americanista de la Universidad de Valladolid, 1983.

Millones, Luis. "Nuevos aspectos del Taki Onqoy." *Ideología mesiánica del mundo andino.* Ed. Juan M. Ossio A. Lima: Biblioteca de Antropología, 1973. 97-101.

——. "Un movimiento nativista del siglo XVI: El Taki Onqoy." *Revista peruana de cultura* 3: 134-140.

Millones, Luis, comp. *El retorno de las huacas: estudios y documentos del siglo XVI.* Lima: Instituto de Estudios Peruanos y Sociedad Peruana de Psicoanálisis, 1990.

Morrall, John B. *Political Thought in Medieval Times.* Medieval Academy Reprints for Teaching 7. Toronto: Univ. of Toronto Press and Medieval Academy of America, 1980.

Murra, John V. "Waman Puma, etnógrafo del mundo andino." *El primer nueva corónica y buen gobierno.* By Felipe Guamán Poma de Ayala. Ed. John V. Murra and Rolena Adorno. Quechua translations by Jorge L. Urioste. Colección América Nuestra 31. Mexico City: Siglo XXI, 1980. xiii-xix.

Ortega, Julio. *Crítica de la identidad: la pregunta por el Perú en su literatura.* Mexico City: Fondo de Cultura Económica, 1988.

——. "Prólogo." *La utopía incaica: Primera parte de los Comentarios reales.* Barcelona: Salvat, 1972. 13-20.

Ossio A., Juan M. "Guamán Poma: Nueva corónica o carta al rey: Un intento de aproximación a las categorías del pensamiento del mundo andino." *Ideología mesiánica del mundo andino.* 155-213.

Parish, Helen Rand, ed. *Bartolomé de Las Casas: The Only Way.* Trans. Francis Patrick Sullivan. Mahway, N.J.: Paulist Press, 1992.

Parish, Helen Rand, with Harold E. Weidman. "The Correct Birthdate of Bartolomé de las Casas." *Hispanic American Historical Review* 56.3 (1976): 385-403.

Pease, Franklin. "Felipe Guamán Poma de Ayala: Mitos andinos e historia occidental." *Caravelle* 37 (1981): 19-36.

——. "Las versiones del mito de Inkarrí." *Revista de la Universidad Católica* 2 (1977): 25-41.

Peña Montenegro, Alonso. *Itinerario para párrocos de Indios en que se tratan las materias más particulares tocantes a ellos para su buena administración.* Antwerp: Henrico y Cornelio Verdussen, 1668.

Silva, Juan de. *Advertencias importantes, acerca del buen govierno, y administración de las Indias, assí en lo espiritual, como en lo temporal.* Madrid: Viuda de F. Correa Montenegro, 1621.

Stern, Steve J. *Peru's Indian Peoples and the Challenge of Spanish Conquest: Huamanga to 1640.* Madison: Univ. of Wisconsin Press, 1982.

Titu Cussi Yupanqui, Diego de Castro. "Ynstrucción del Ynga ... tocante a los negocios que con Su Magestad, en su nombre, por su poder a de tratar." 1570. Ed. Luis Millones. Lima: El Virrey, 1985.

Ugarte y Ugarte, Eduardo L. "Los caciques de Chucuito y Arequipa contra la perpetuidad de la encomienda (1562)." *Hombre y mundo* 1 (1966): 30-50.

Wachtel, Nathan. "Pensamiento salvaje y aculturación." *Sociedad e ideología: ensayos de historia y antropología andinas.* By Nathan Wachtel. Lima: Instituto de Estudios Peruanos, 1973. 165-228.

————. *Los vencidos: los indios del Perú frente a la española (1530-1570)*. Trans. Antonio Escohotado. Madrid: Alianza, 1976.

Wagner, Henry Raup, with Helen Rand Parish. *The Life and Writings of Bartolomé de las Casas*. Albuquerque: Univ. of New Mexico Press, 1967.

Yaranga Valderrama, Abdón. "Taki Onqo ou la vision des vaincus au XVIe siècle." *Les Mentalités dans la Péninsule Ibérique et en Amérique Latine aux XVIe et XVIIe siècles: Histoire et problématique. Actes du XIIIe Congrès de la Société des Hispanistes Français de l'Enseignement Supérieur.* Tours, 1977.

Zimmerman, Arthur Franklin. *Francisco de Toledo: Fifth Viceroy of Peru, 1569-1581*. Caldwell, Idaho: Caxton Printers, 1938.

Chapter 12

Amerindian Image and Utopian Project
Motolinía and Millenarian Discourse

Georges Baudot

(translated by Donna Buhl LeGrand)

The discursive treatment of the Amerindian image, when related to utopian projects of a political-spiritual kind such as the one that is forged and expressed by the first Franciscan missionaries in Mexico, must first be considered in its historical roots. That is, one must contemplate the antiquity of such discourse and its most evident sources. This is not mandated by a previous investigation of possible influences of certain ideological nuclei that might be traced in this discourse, but because only in this manner will the totality of the process and the mechanisms of production of this image become totally understandable to us. In this case, the example offered by the text of one of the "first twelve" missionaries in Mexico, Fray Toribio de Benavente, called Motolinía—in Nahuatl, the poor, unfortunate one, an obvious imitation of the *Poverello* of Assisi— is paradigmatic of the metahistorical construction of an original Amerindian image. For this reason it is necessary to recall from the outset some of those particulars of the "ethnographic" vision that, since the thirteenth century, had structured for some Franciscans the contemplation of other cultural discourses produced by groups of people alien to the thinking and feeling of Western Europe. In this case the Franciscans translate a certain way of conceptualizing their mission in faraway and unknown regions, that is, in strange worlds built upon alterity.

By 1247, a religious Franciscan by the name of Fray Juan del Piano Carpini had written an early, important work that translated this vocation by elaborating an image of the Other that was organized according to utopian criteria. Let us recall rapidly that in 1245 the Council of Lyon and the Supreme Pontiff Innocent VI had charged him to undertake an expedition toward the gates of the Far East and, in particular, toward the Khanian territories of the Volga in order to evaluate the possibilities of converting the Mongols and the peoples of the Asia of Genghis Khan to Christianity. The goal was to accelerate the End of Times and to put in motion the program indicated in the text of the Book of the Apocalypse. Piano Carpini's *Historia Mongolorum*, written upon the conclusion of his mission and his return to Lyon, was, perhaps, the first Franciscan "ethnographic" chronicle that attempted to offer an image of Mongolian society following certain apocalyptic criteria and organized by a certain metahistorical vision. In other words, we have here a millennial Utopia bringing forth an original image of the "Other" fuzzily sketched according to this Other's hypothetical capacities to be integrated into the universal kingdom of Christ and to becoming a part of eschatological hope. This case was not unique at that time.

Some years later another Franciscan friar, Willem Van Ruysbroeck, dedicated the years between 1253 and 1256 to an extensive voyage through the Far East. He arrived in Qaraqorum, visiting the court of the great Khan Mongke, and upon his return, wrote a very valuable "ethnographic" text, the *Itinerarium ad partes orientales*, which, in important ways, shared the same type of discourse as the predecessor's text (see Bergeron). Evidently the utopian background was more or less the same. A political end filled with eschatological hope guided these careful descriptions of Mongolian societies that were analyzed in order to facilitate and, hopefully, accelerate the Christianization of the Asia of Genghis Khan. The program was political: the idea was to surround and lay siege to the Muslim Mediterranean in order to crush Islam, liberate the Holy Land, and allow for the founding of the New Jerusalem and the coming of the millennial Kingdom, a presage to the Last Judgment. It is clear that these works demonstrated some caution with respect to the degree of difficulty of the project, but the proposed image of Mongolian society and its humanity was intimately related to the a priori discursive organization of this metahistorical vision.

Throughout the fourteenth and fifteenth centuries, the urgency of converting Mongolians and Jews and the need to insert the Asia of Genghis Khan into the millennial perspective of global Christianization underlay the "ethnographic" image of Others and lay the foundations of what, at that time, was a wavering consciousness of the plurality of cultures. But, within the limits of this essay, it behooves us to turn our eyes toward America and, concretely, toward Mexico and Motolinía. For America, upon being discovered and conquered, was going to offer the most revealing signs of providential predestination. After all, the routes to Asia would be closed to the utopian dreams of the Franciscans upon the definite conversion to Islam of the western regions of the ancient empire of Genghis Khan in the years 1334-1353, thereby redirecting their eschatological hope toward the western sea routes in order to give human destiny a happy ending.

This is not the place to examine the millennial and Joachimite ideology of the first missionaries in Mexico, a theme which is covered in other studies (Phelan; Baudot, *Utopía* and *La pugna*), nor to insist on the visionary millenarianism of Fray Toribio de Benavente Motolinía, also well documented (Baudot, *Utopía* 247-386; Motolinía, *Historia* 7-89). Rather, we will now attempt to see how the images of the Amerindians are formed in his discourse and how the latter determines the former. Following the illustrative example of his "Mongolist" predecessors—Fray Juan del Piano Carpini and Willem Van Ruysbroeck—Fray Toribio, the "Mexicanist," will strive for an original and novel Amerindian image (in contrast to the image forged by his contemporary conquistadors and discoverers) that proposes another way of representing the native peoples at that time. In that precise historic moment, this representation of the Amerindian certainly establishes serious difficulties for the European worldview. Did those new people have a place within the Christian view of history? Initially, it seemed necessary to scrutinize the image of the Amerindian in order to harmonize it with the prophesies of the Scriptures.

When America entered into the language of Europe and into the apparatus of its signifieds, its codes, and its symbols, the image of Amerindian people must have received, above all, a deliberate treatment, even more so after the continental conquest that had revealed surprising images of a developed urban phenomenon and of a high degree of social, legislative, cosmogonic, and ritual sophistication. How were the urban societies of Central Mexico or of the Andean Altiplano to be placed in the catalog of human varieties? We know clearly that at first simplistic images were forged, especially concerning all that had to do with the bloody liturgies of the Mexicans, and that the Amerindian world could be conceptualized as a remote part of the universe, covered by fathomless designs of the Divine Providence who seemed to have thereby reserved one last hidden corner for the empire of Satan. But this image of the Amerindian, who was explained as a creature dominated by the devil of the Christians and who originated in a concept of alterity founded upon absolute rejection, was excessively simplistic and was a response to the intellectual confusion of the time.

Within thirty-some years, more or less from 1523, when the Flemish Seraphic friars arrived, to 1555 when Motolinía wrote the last of his letters (on November 20), a large part of the Amerindian discourse that had structured the social, cultural, religious, or literary discourse of the pre-Columbian universe became clear to these Franciscan missionaries. In 1533, upon command of Sebastián Ramírez de Fuenleal, the president of the Second Audiencia of Mexico, and of the Seraphic custodian, Fray Martín de Valencia, they began systematic investigations into the so-called Amerindian antiquities or relics which, from Fray Andrés de Olmos to Fray Bernardino de Sahagún, were to offer all of the thematic elements that would rationally save those peoples and would justify their complete inclusion into the history of humankind. We are acquainted with that slow and careful inquiry that, through the delicate deciphering of pictographic codes, through formulas of indigenous communication (orality, written and drawn symbols, codified representations, etc.) and all those documents that express the Amerindian message, reveals the complicated mechanisms of its own particular way of understanding the world (Baudot, *Utopía* and *La pugna*).

We also know that Motolinía was the heart and driving force of this undertaking, which would provide many of the elements that would shape his image of the Amerindian. But we will see that, at times, the Amerindian image claimed by the millenarian project or ideology was frequently not in consonance with the results of "ethnographic" research. But let us examine this carefully. The Franciscans—beginning with Fray Andrés de Olmos down to Motolinía and others—had to produce an image of the Amerindian in accordance with the monogenetic view of the Scriptures, which did not contemplate the presence of these people on earth. This is the source of the confusion in their attempt to elaborate this missing link in the chain of humankind.

Let us recall the words of Fray Gerónimo de Mendieta when he evoked the solutions proposed by Fray Andrés de Olmos, who was the first to construct an image of the Amerindian:

> The said Father Olmos was of the opinion that in one of three times, or from one of three places, came the ancestors from whom these Indians descend. Either they came from the land of Babylon at the time of the division of languages at the tower built by Noah's sons; or they came after that, from the land of Shechem in the time of Jacob, when some of them fled and left that land; or in the time when the sons of Israel entered the promised land and conquered it and drove out the Canaanites, Amorites and Jebusites.... (Mendieta, book 2, chap. 32, vol. 1, 159)[1]

But even for Mendieta, who wrote some sixty years after Olmos, the issue was a difficult one and was not satisfactorily resolved:

> ...Also some could say that they came during the captivities and dispersions of the children of Israel or the last time that Jerusalem was destroyed during the times of the Roman emperors Titus and Vespasian. But because none of these opinions are right or have a foundation upon which to affirm one over the other, it is best to leave the matter uncertain

and each person can believe what he pleases. (Mendieta,
book 2, chap. 32, vol. 1, 159)[2]

In fact, this aspect of the Amerindian image, that is, its crucial
mythical-historical foundation in the "dispersions" of the children
of Israel as evoked by Mendieta, provided an interesting hint in situating the origin of the Amerindians. Searching for an obligatory
biblical affiliation will have very good fortune, in time giving way
to an intense interest in the topic. This trajectory is well known.

At the beginning of the seventeenth century, the Dominican
Gregorio García in his *Origen de los Indios del Nuevo Mundo e Indias Occidentales* (*Origin of the Indians of the New World and West
Indies* [Valencia, 1607]), proposed that the Amerindians were the
descendants of the ten lost tribes of Israel. Gregorio García did not
proceed to elaborate this image of the American aborigine in a fantastic manner, but rather did so by a coherent process of reasoning
within his own system of logic. As a matter of fact, ever since 1538
the Supreme Pontiff Paul III had proclaimed the authentic humanity of the Amerindians in the papal bull *Sublimis Deus*, recognizing
their full capacity to be integrated into human destiny and to receive the biblical message; the idea was to find an unquestionable
filiation with Adam and Eve. The second postulate (according to
the very words of Gregorio García) was that the population of the
so-called West Indies could not have come from anywhere other
than the three parts of the known world: Europe, Asia, or Africa.
After calling upon the authority of Aristotle, Seneca, the prophet
Isaiah, and St. Jerome, and considering and discussing the possible
Carthaginian origins of the Amerindians, Gregorio García ended
up choosing the seductive explanation offered by the fortunes of
those ten tribes, providentially lost by history in the times of the
captivity of Israel under the rule of King Shalmaneser of Assyria.
The author added that the foundation for such opinion was the
character, nature, and customs of the Amerindians, which showed
amazing similarities to those of the Jews (book 2, chap. 1).

In reality, this could not improve the image of the American
Indians at a time when the Inquisition was fiercely pursuing the
Jews and converts who had succeeded in crossing over to Amer-
ica and requiring proof of "purity of blood." But it is certain that

the hypothesis had some definite success. Already in the previous century, Fray Diego Durán had entertained the idea:

> ... another elderly Indian asked what news I had of the departure of Topiltzin (Quetzalcoatl) and began to relate to me Chapter 14 of Exodus.... And as I saw that he had read what I had and knowing how the story was going to end, I didn't ask him much so that he wouldn't tell me the whole story of the Exodus, and all about the punishment of the children of Israel and the serpents for murmuring against God and Moses, which I already knew about.... (Durán 2: 233)[3]

Fray Pedro de los Ríos in the *Códice Vaticanus A* had advanced the same idea (*A*, vol. 3, fig. 13, 36-37). In the seventeenth century and a few years after the publication of the work of Gregorio García, the well-known *mestizo* historian Fernando de Alva Ixtlilxochitl would once again be inspired by this filiation in order to strive for a harmonious integration of the pre-Columbian history of Mexico into universal history. The early times of Mesoamerica were made to coincide with the creation of Genesis and to incorporate biblical narratives such as the flood, the building of the Tower of Babel, Goliath the Philistine, with elements of his pre-Columbian sources, thus succeeding in situating the origin of the Chichimecas in this Judeo-Christian tradition:

> ... according to their histories, the first king that they had was called Chichimecatl, who was the one who brought them to this new world which they populated; because of this it can be inferred that they left Tarsus and were part of the group who was divided in Babylon ... and with their king, who wandered with them throughout the world, they came to this land.... (Alva Ixtlilxochitl, 1: 417)[4]

The prosperity of such interpretations of the origins of the Amerindians was so long-lived that it even lasted until the nineteenth century and to such a degree that Edward King, Lord Kingsborough, would squander his large fortune in order to publish in 1848 the beautiful *Antiquities of Mexico* whose principal end was to demonstrate the Hebrew origin of the Amerindian populations.

As we have been able to prove by way of these rapid reflections and quotations, the image of the Amerindian elaborated by the Europeans as they confronted the Amerindians' past—as well as their origin and the location of their past in the framework of a Christian worldview—once more came to be an image-reflection, an image of diminished and diluted alterity, because it was necessary to reduce the Other to recognizable and conceivable categories. It did not seem possible to attribute to this Other an independent, original, and exclusively American history. Rather, that history had to be related somehow to the historic development of the Old World and included in a common historic plot. The doubt that imposed itself on all imaginations was the exact locus of the Amerindians' past, whether it was related to biblical or Classical antiquity. But in Motolinía's century doubts about the authentic identity of these Amerindians did not flourish within any truly American discourse.

If representing the Amerindians in their insertion into humankind's past was so problematic, one must ask oneself why it was not possible to attempt to forge an image within the future of such humanity. Why not replace that reduced image of the American aborigine with a new image, forged by Christian and eschatological hope, making those people providential instruments of humanity's final salvation? Seeing them as the basis of the future of humanity, as a base for the apocalyptic construction that flows into the Final Judgment, would be a new and novel way of integrating them into scriptural discourse. Reserving this crucial role for the Amerindians completely changes their image, as it is painted in the vivid colors of a prophetic and fundamentally optimistic ideology. Such is the case even if, quite frequently, this image is contradicted by the facts produced by the ethnographic research of the very same Franciscans who concur in the elaboration of two cognitive discourses—the ethnographic and the millenarian—at the same time and within the same ambiguity.

Motolinía inaugurates, with vigorous style and visionary conviction, a new family of images in which the Amerindian is a providential and potential convert who, above all, possesses the signs and takes on the most precious symbols of millenarian hope. A reading of the most important texts of Motolinía in this respect is what interests us here. First, one must consider the *Historia de los Indios de la Nueva España* (*History of the Indians of New Spain*), which was conceptualized and written with urgency toward the end of 1540 and at the beginning of 1541 from rough drafts of more important works in order to produce renewed images of the Amerindians for a dignitary such as the Count of Benavente (Motolinía, *Historia* 71-76). Then there is Motolinía's correspondence, as it is known today, in which at times the representation of the Amerindians is expressed with extraordinary vehemence according to some highly interiorized spiritual convictions. Yet, in this discussion, it does not seem productive to turn to Motolinía's *Memoriales*, for they were provisional and fragile texts, preparatory rough drafts and work notes that, in contrast to *Historia de los Indios de la Nueva España*, were not for public consumption.

The apocalyptic connotation is evident in the choice of terms that express the paradigmatic image of the Amerindian. In this way we find a long series of metaphorical representations based on a specific bestiary belonging to the eschatological texts of the European Middle Ages: "sheep," "little birds," etc., used to translate the meekness and fragility of those who had to be, above all else, protected. On the other hand, Spanish colonists as well as the public officials of the Crown were classified as "carnivorous, hungry wolves"; representations of "mosquitoes" and "locusts" are also found (that is, the third and tenth plagues of Egypt). These images belong to the correspondence of Fray Toribio and increase as time goes on. Without overwhelming ourselves with a list of examples, let us see how the image of the Amerindian used in his letter to Charles V on May 15, 1550, evokes the extreme poverty of the American native (Motolinía, *Epistolario;* Baudot, *Utopía* 322-327):

> ... It would be well for Your Majesty to understand that these Indians are in the most extreme state of poverty ... because if others enter their houses they will see that they and everything in them and all that they wear is so sparse and so base that they wouldn't even know what kind of price to assign them. ... [5]

The tone and lexicon change drastically a little more than five years later in the last letter that we have of Fray Toribio, from November 20, 1555 (Motolinía, *Epistolario;* Baudot, *La pugna* 86-96):

> ...the lamb is not yet weaned from his mother and does
> not yet have wool and already they want to shear him, and I
> pray to God that they wouldn't harm him...or even...what
> will become of these miserable Indians, subjected to so many
> wolves and so many who order them around by beating
> them....⁶

In that letter Motolinía emphasizes once again the general theme
that organizes these images: Amerindian poverty, a crucial poverty, as we shall see, in the ideological apparatus that underlies
the Seraphic project:

> ...Or, if it were possible for Your Highness to see the vanity
> and the excess of some and the misery of others; they
> request from the naked for the one that is well-dressed, from
> the hungry for the one that is full and from the poor for the
> one that is rich. If Your Highness were to see the extreme
> poverty.... (Motolinía, *Epistolario* 89)⁷

Here poverty is not only proof of the state of the Amerindians
after the Conquest but also a more important classification that
they could boast of to their Franciscan missionaries. This poverty was the fundamental evangelical poverty that constituted the
base of the Seraphic adventure from the times of the founder,
the *Poverello* of Assisi, who made *Donna Povertà* the source of liberty and the motor of redemptive hope. Here poverty seems to
be the highest virtue of an Amerindian conceptualized exclusively
as *macehualli*, that is, as "deserving," as a "man of the humble
people who deserves," and whose indigenousness is a promise
of the eternal kingdom. In the *Historia de los Indios de la Nueva
España* the program is clear when Fray Toribio compares the Indians to the Spaniards. Let us recall this well-known paragraph:

> ...These Indians have almost none of the hindrances that
> prevent them from gaining heaven, of the many that we
> Spaniards have and that overwhelm us, because their lives
> are satisfied with very little, so little that they barely have
> enough to wear and eat. Their food is very poor and the
> same with their clothing. Most of them don't even have a
> clean mat on which to sleep.... They sleep with their pitiful
> blankets and upon waking they are prepared to serve God,
> and if they want to discipline themselves, they don't have

any obstruction or embarrassment about getting dressed and undressed.... Their mattresses are the hard soil, without any covering; if anything, they have a broken mat, and for a pillow, only a rock or piece of board, and many don't have a pillow, only the bare ground. Their houses are very small, some covered with only a very low roof, some made of straw, some like the cell of that saint, the Abbot Hilary, which seem more like graves than houses.... (Motolinía, *Historia* 188-189)[8]

The insistence upon the essential poverty of the Amerindians is complemented by another insistence upon their humility and meekness, which is represented by so many images in the Franciscan texts and of which Motolinía gives examples and guidelines that later find numerous followers. Humility takes on characteristics of smallness, of innocence, and is translated almost immediately by the Seraphic pens as "little birds" or "little sheep," images with a strong apocalyptic connotation. For example, the letter from Fray Pedro Xuárez de Escobar to Philip II on April 1, 1579, said:

... All of these Indians are like little birds in their nests, whose wings haven't grown nor will they grow in order for them to learn to fly by themselves, but rather need their watchful parents who come to the nest with food.... (Cuevas, no. 58, 311)[9]

Motolinía will turn preferentially to the image of the sheep:

... They are patient, long-suffering, meek like sheep. I don't remember ever seeing them hold a grudge; humble and obedient to all, not out of necessity but voluntarily, they only know how to serve and work.... They have much patience and are long-suffering during illness ... they eat and drink without making much noise. Without resentment or animosity, they spend their time and their lives, and they go out to look for food to sustain their lives and no more.... (Motolinía, *Historia* 189)[10]

It would be appropriate to emphasize, in passing, that at times this intent on the part of the Friars Minor to reduce the Amerindians at all costs verges on the ridiculous and that it could even show hints of a disturbing segregation. The same Fray Gerónimo de Mendieta, perhaps the most convinced and fervent of Motolinía's disciples, is the one who, more than anyone else, produces these interpretations in their revealing way. Thus, the Amerindians, who were accustomed to a vegetarian and "impoverished" diet, could not have known a diet that included meat because this was the origin of "almost perverse sneezes"! The text says it well upon praising the suitable qualities that were "very favorable for [the] salvation," of those who were "meek, humble, docile, quiet, and peace-loving" and who lose all virtue upon contact with the Spaniards:

> I met the Indians at a time in which I rarely saw them sneeze, and I noticed it for many days, marveling at it. And it was only because they ate what nature provided them to sustain themselves, not more than two or three corn tortillas and some cooked herbs with some chile peppers or pepper, what in Spain we call "pepper from the Indies." The result was that they didn't foster bad humors that needed to be expelled in that way. Now even the children that are still breast-feeding sneeze, getting it from their parents, because they eat meat and the other foods that we Spaniards eat, so they foster thick and abundant humors, like we do, and therefore they sneeze like we sneeze.... (Mendieta, book 4, 167)[11]

This daring formulation of Mendieta, founded upon a "natural" and innocent diet, and in agreement with a poverty that is directly related to innate goodness, is not far from the eighteenth-century image of the *bon sauvage*. Nevertheless, it does not seem precisely appropriate to connect the elaboration of an image of the happy barbarian, belonging to the secularized and rationalist thought of the Enlightenment, with an image of the providential Amerindian, a creature simultaneously simple and mystic, an instrument predestined for the fulfillment of apocalyptic prophecies (Phelan 100-101). Both conceptualizations are based on the same premise: the Amerindian is a "natural" creature who manifests goodness and innate virtues that can be perverted by contact with Others. But the difference is immense, because for Mendieta, and earlier for his teacher Motolinía, the Amerindian has been previously acquainted with a condition and an opportunity in which these dispositions are hidden, or better yet, led astray by the empire of Evil. In particular, for Fray Toribio in the *Historia*, the Amerindian, before the arrival of the Spaniards, is a pitiful caricature of humanity:

> ... This land was a transfer of Hell; it was a sight to see: the dwellers shouting at night, some calling out to the devil, others drunk, others singing and dancing; they played drums, horns, coronets and large shells, especially at the parties for their demons. They had ordinary drinking bouts, the amount of wine that they used and that each one put into his body is incredible. ... It was very pitiful to see men made in the image of God turned into something worse than dumb animals, and what was worse was that they didn't limit themselves to only that sin but they committed many others. ... (Motolinía, *Historia* 125-126)[12]

Regarding the image of the Amerindian forged by the Franciscans, it is clear that if primitive virtue is infused with an enormous predisposition to achieve complete human fulfillment in God—thus enabling the construction of the millennial reign—it inevitably needs the help and education offered by the Franciscan missionaries. The primitive "natural" persons of Jean-Jacques Rousseau are basically creatures who need neither imported education nor any kind of ideological transfusion; in fact just the opposite is true. They must follow the inborn goodness of this nature in order to reach their fulfillment. Motolinía's Amerindians and later Mendieta's are poor, innocent children who may very well represent humanity's infancy but just as surely require an adequate education in the hands of ideal and predestined persons to make the most of their qualities and to construct with them something that transcends their existential being and, from there, their social and historical presence. Of course, the connection between Francis of Assisi and Rousseau is not even minimally direct. Rather, it is diffuse, blurred, and difficult to establish, except with risky episodic proof of conceptual similarities.

Perhaps the generating nucleus of the Amerindian image forged by the millennial Franciscans and Motolinía is founded in the concept of infancy and in a disposition harbored in poverty and in a complete absence of social and material ambition. In this way, the American aborigines are the instruments of the eschatological destiny of humankind through an image that is flattering in appearance, but extremely reductive in reality: "...since they are weak and poor, they have an extreme need for parents and teachers that don't let go of their hands..." or, regarding their indispensable education: "...this almost has to be with the whip in hand, like is done with schoolchildren..." (*Códice Mendieta*, vol. 1, no. 20, 103, 109).[13]

This conception of the Other can come to mean an absolute and strange reduction, carried to a degree that goes beyond a simple paternalism and can even suggest notions of segregation and a differentiation that denies the very human dignity that it attempts to establish or restore:

> ...the talent and ability of the Indians is commonly like that of youth between ten and twelve years old. From this it follows that one can not request more from them nor trust them more than children left to their own free-will.... And here there also arises the need of having those who rule and guide them in spiritual and temporal matters, of being to them like parents who wish and strive for their children's well-being and watch over their wrongs, who, as tutors, can protect them as minors and who, as teachers, can instruct them as children.... And from here one can understand the error of those who believe that it is wrong that clerics or friars *have their Indians whipped even if needed for their well-being and benefit.* And this reveals a lack of knowledge of the Indians, *because they need the whip as much as the bread that they eat, and it is so natural to them that among themselves they aren't accustomed or able to live without it, and they themselves confess that without the whip they are lost, like children....* (*Códice Mendieta*, vol. 2, no. 62, 8-12; emphasis added)[14]

This tremendous reduction of the Other, which places him in a child-like state, incapable of adulthood, in need of humiliating physical punishment ("they need the whip as much as the bread they eat") makes one think of a preparatory, larval stage. The Amerindians will come to know a full and authentic development only in a faraway future in the celestial kingdom for which they are exclusively destined. The text of Mendieta, the maximum spokesman and exponent of conceptions that were, to a certain degree, detailed and organized previously by Motolinía, is clear on this issue:

> ... *they cannot be compared to nor put on the same level as any*
> *peoples known before them, but only to youngsters who have not*
> *yet reached maturity;* and therefore the one who governs
> them does not have any kind of responsibility other than
> that of governing a republic of free children, adopted sons of
> the Heavenly King, who aims to lead them to his kingdom
> and everlasting glory.... (*Códice Mendieta*, vol. 2, no. 62, 8-12;
> emphasis added)[15]

Of course, in light of these statements, the image of the Amerindians ends up being a representation that minimizes them and devalues their human maturity, reduce their identity, and, in the end, discredits their dignity as human beings in spite of the glorious future assigned to them. No matter how one looks at it, the image is one forged a priori by a project, by a program; it is not dictated or structured by an observation, not even by a blind sympathy that only notices virtues and ignores defects. Mendieta has stressed it more than once, delineating the following suggested action:

> ... making ourselves parents of this miserable nation and
> entrusting them to us as if they were (and they actually
> are) children and babies whom we bring up and teach and
> protect and correct, and we save them and make them
> benefit from the Faith and Christian doctrine.... (*Cartas de*
> *Religiosos* 1: 8)[16]

Concerning the topic of Amerindian liberty, the images of "little children," "children," or "boys" who need the guidance of the severe and paternal hand of a "teacher" are in sharp contrast to the image of the "wild animals in the most savage of forests":

> these natural men are purely children, naturally subdued
> and timid, and as a result of having a father and a truly
> Christian and prudent teacher, who loves and corrects them
> like children, and like a teacher instructs and teaches them
> Christian faith and human behavior, this will not be an
> entire province under the hand of a friar but a school of
> children under the hand of their teacher; *because placed in*
> *subjection and obedience, there is no people or nation in the world*

that is more docile than this one when one wants to teach and rule them; while, on the other hand, *there are no wild animals in the jungle more untamable than they are when they are let loose....* (*Cartas de Religiosos* 1, 10; emphasis added)[17]

The image of the Amerindian ends up being shaped by the demands of the anticipated eschatological solutions contemplated by the idea of a reign of a thousand years. Such a reign is situated between the two battles and the two returns of Christ (Rev. 20:4-6). Thus, the image of the Amerindian is subjected to the providential and evangelical poverty of the kingdom of the Holy Spirit as conceived by Joachim of Fiore. For the Friars Minor, the Amerindians' poverty and eternal infancy is a necessary condition, for only in this way can their primacy before God be assured in an eschatological future.

Reading between the lines, one finds that, despite a reductive paternalism, the emerging image of the Amerindian is truly grandiose. The Amerindian becomes, authentically, that absolute Other who is the instrument of salvation of the Old World, blinded by its sins and deafened by the tumults of the new Babylons. Only the Indian of America offers to the Spaniard—that "hungry wolf" involved in the bloody exploitation of the Amerindians— the opportunity to participate in the universal redemption. A crucial ethic and figurative alterity distinguished by its humility, meekness, infantile availability, would therefore permit the Amerindians to fulfill a decisive role in the end of universal history, beyond historical times. In this way the Amerindian will become fully integrated into the Christian worldview. Their metahistorical identity is dependent upon their poverty and childlike condition.

Now in order to achieve this image, Motolinía finds himself obligated to carry out some contortions with the material that the ethnographic and historical research has provided him in the course of his inquiries into the relics of the Amerindians. These undoubtedly form the other side of his discourse and of the Amerindian image that it tries to project. In 1541, upon signing the *Epístola Proemial* to Count Benavente, which heads the *Historia de los Indios de la Nueva España*, and even in his early writings dating back to 1528, he emphasizes the recent implantation of the political and religious domination of the Mexicah (Motolinía, *Historia* 99-102). In that first rough draft, which would serve as the basis for a crucial paragraph of the *Epístola Proemial* drawn up by Fray Toribio in 1528, the relatively modest origin of those who had recently arrived is already stressed:

> The third group are the Mexicans, and everyone says that they are from the generation of the Culhua and their language agrees with it; whether or not it is true, the belief persists that the Culhua were first, and not the Mexica; and *it is said that among these men from Mexico there did not come illustrious lords nor those of distinguished lineage,* although they brought captains and people who led them.... (Motolinía, *Historia* 101)[18]

Twenty-seven years later, in his famous letter to Emperor Charles V from Tlaxcala on January 2, 1555, Motolinía was to give this image its maximum expression, practically branding the Mexicans as usurpers:

> ... to let Your Majesty know, as the principal lord of this New Spain, that when the Spaniards entered it, it had not been many years that it had been part of Mexico or that the Mexicans had been in it and how these same Mexicans had won or *usurped* it through warfare.... (159; emphasis added)[19]

Fray Toribio's firm intent to diminish the historic authenticity of the Mexicah and in particular to debate their political legitimacy is based on the long-term project that the conversion of the Amerindians involved. Here is where the maximum urgency is felt and toward which all of the ideological paths must lead. Because of their past, the Amerindians per se cannot be seen as having the same human rights as the Spaniards or, better still, of Christians in general. The bloody sacrifices of their liturgies are a clear sign of this limitation:

> May Your Majesty be aware of the fact that when the Marquis of Valle entered this land, God our Lord was very offended and the men suffered the cruelest of deaths, and the devil our adversary was well served by the greatest idolatries and cruelest homicides that have ever existed ... and when the Christians entered this New Spain, throughout all the

small towns and provinces in it there were more sacrifices of
dead men than ever before, whom they killed and sacrificed
before their idols, and every day and every hour they
offered human blood to the demons in all places and towns
throughout all this land. . . . (160)[20]

For Fray Toribio, the first and foremost image of the Amerindian is that of Man blinded by the devil, his addicted servant
before the providential arrival of the Europeans. Actually, Motolinía distinguishes two types of Amerindians. On the one hand
are the priests, lords, ruling groups, and leaders of pre-Columbian
society who are at fault for numerous abominations, given to cannibalism and to the most horrible rituals, and on the other hand
are the mass of "low," humble people, the *macehualtin*. When Fray
Toribio highlights the diverse participation in cannibalistic rites, he
clearly specifies the division:

> . . . The other Indians tried to eat the human flesh of those
> who died in the sacrifice, although the principal lords, the
> merchants, and the ministers of the temples commonly ate
> this, *a small bite rarely reached the low people*. . . . (Motolinía,
> *Historia* 127; emphasis added)[21]

On the other hand, as with the selection of rituals that the
Franciscan narrates to the Count of Benavente, he reveals a determined intent to scare the reader and to construct a repulsive
pre-Columbian image of the Amerindian, all the while insisting
on the particular responsibilities of their leaders. The passages
concerning these rituals abound in the "Tratado Primero" of the
Historia; the following are only two of the many examples available:

> . . . One evening during a party in Cuauhtitlan, they raised
> six large trees like masts of ships with their steps, and in this
> cruel vigil, and also on a very cruel day, they cut the throat
> of two slave women at the top of the stairs, before the altar
> of the idols, and there at the peak they skinned their entire
> bodies and their faces, and they took out the shanks of their
> thighs; and in the morning *two Indian leaders* put on their
> skins, and fit them on their faces like masks, and they took
> the shanks in their hands, in each hand its own shank, and

step by step they came down the stairs roaring, so that they seemed like fierce beasts.... (Motolinía, *Historia* 150)[22]

And

> ... This same day another greater and never heard of act of cruelty was being done, and it was that at the top of those six poles that they had raised the evening before the party, they tied and reeled six men captured at war, and down below were more than two thousand boys and men with their bows and arrows, and, as soon as the men who had gone up to tie the captives came down, they rained arrows upon them; and having been pierced by arrows and half dead, some of the others quickly went up to untie them and they let them fall from that height, and from the great blow of the fall, they broke open and all the bones of their bodies were crushed; and later they gave them the third death, sacrificing them and taking out their hearts; and dragging them they moved them from there, and after slicing their throats and cutting their heads off, they gave them to the ministers of the idols; and they carried the bodies like lambs *for the lords and nobles to eat.* ... (Motolinía, *Historia* 151)[23]

This image of a negative, horrible past and of the substantial involvement of political and religious authorities in the production of these monstrosities responds, certainly, to a process that does not belong exclusively to the millennial missionaries. The iconography of the initial encounter with America is full of monstrous beings and, especially, of figures and rituals that were irreconcilable with the tradition of the Old World. In other words, the figures outlined a profound strangeness, a crucial ineffability that translated as a kind of invisibility of the Other before the author or relator. For instance, in Cortés's *Cartas de relación* there is a discussion addressed to Charles V on generalized cannibalism and on the monstrous rituals of human sacrifice, which was probably inspired by the belief of the "satanization" of America. Nevertheless, a rapid analysis of the text shows that Cortés is structuring these materials in order to justify future action. In the same manner, Cortés accuses all Amerindians of being sodomites without providing further explanations: " ... and we have learned and been informed that all of them are sodomites and practice that abominable sin ... " (" ... y hemos sabido y sido informados de cierto que todos son sodomitas y usan aquel abominable pecado ... " [10]). This accusation forms part of the same process of fabrication of negative images destined to permit a discourse of action.

Contrary to the ordinary European view of the conquistadors or discoverers, the image of the Amerindians constructed by the millenarian Franciscans harbors a possibility of understanding that is founded in a prophetic projection toward the future. Perhaps the one who has best expressed it for Mexico is the French Seraphic friar, Fray Jacobo de Tastera, in a revealing letter to the Emperor Charles V, written in 1533. Fray Jacobo explains human sacrifices, as well as the most repugnant and astonishing rituals, by confiding in the future and producing, above all, the image of a humanity that searches desperately for a way to fulfillment and salvation. The words of Jacobo de Tastera about the meaning of the pre-Columbian past and about the eschatological hope that this could imply even in the most concealed of its aberrations is the very essence of this new Amerindian image:

> ... The idolatrous rites and the adoration of their false gods and the ceremonies of diverse kinds of people around their sacrifices, although this is bad, *is born of a natural request, not dormant, that looks for help and does not hit upon the true remedy.* (63) ... [24]

Tastera indicates that this image, constructed by millennial hope, is the strongest and the most decisive of any observation or inquiry into the Amerindian world:

> ... And because of this, when we friars entered this land, *their idolatry did not scare us nor take away our confidence,* but having compassion on their blindness, we had great confidence that all of that *and much more they would do in service to our God, when they met him.* ... (64)[25]

Only within this new semantic framework can the image of the Amerindian take on the positive hues required for the incorporation of the native into the vast metahistorical construct. Thus, the past society of the Amerindian can be evoked through images devoid of hostility and rejection:

... how can they be so incapable with such sumptuous buildings, with so much skill in making delicate things with their hands, silversmiths, painters, merchants, distributors of tributes, art in presiding, distributing by head count, people, services, good speaking manners, and courteousness and style? ... (*Carta de Fray Jacobo de Tastera y de otros religiosos de la orden de San Francisco, al Emperador D. Carlos*, Convent of Rexucingo, May 6, 1533, Facsimile H, *Cartas de Indias* 62-66).[26]

Having returned to their natural condition, freed from "Satanic" political and religious leaders, the Amerindians offer the entire gamut of images that make them acceptable as a construction within the Kingdom of great hope. Poor, humble, docile children needing formation, education, and even the right punishment, the Amerindians are thus human beings capable of material and practical production. The pages dedicated by Fray Toribio to the artistic ability of the Amerindian, especially in chapters 12 and 13 of the "Tratado Tercero" of the *Historia de los Indios*, are, in this respect, eloquent:

... He who teaches man science, that same one provided and gave great talent and ability to these natural Indians to learn all the sciences, arts, and trades that they have taught them, because they have showed them in so little time, that in seeing the trades that take many years to learn in Castile, here by only looking at them and seeing them done do many of them end up being teachers. *They have a keen, calm understanding, not proud nor wasteful like other nations.* ... (Motolinía, *Historia* 353)[27]

These practical abilities reflect the idealized occupations of a utopian, healthy, and simple society based on the discrete exercise of mechanical trades and given, above all, to the preparation for eternal salvation. They form the basis of the last aspect of the Amerindian constructed by Fray Toribio and his Franciscan millenarian associates. One could ask, finally, what was the fate of the metahistorical image of this redeeming Amerindian in the intellectual and imaginary trajectory of modern indigenisms. The latter are often conceived as projects with acknowledged millenarian resonance, although they may also be represented with a tenacious and unacknowledgable bad conscience.

Notes

1. "El dicho P. Olmos tuvo opinión que en uno de tres tiempos, o de una de tres partes, vinieron los pasados de quienes descienden estos indios; o que vinieron de tierra de Babilonia cuando la división de las lenguas sobre la torre que edificaban los hijos de Noé; o que vinieron después, de tierra de Sichen en tiempo de Jacob, cuando dieron a huir algunos y dejaron la tierra; o en el tiempo que los hijos de Israel entraron en la tierra de promisión y la debelaron y echaron de ella a los cananeos, amorreos y jebuseos...."

2. "...También podrían decir otros, que vinieron en las captividades y dispersiones que tuvieron los hijos de Israel, o cuando la última vez fué destruida Jerusalén en tiempos de Tito y Vespasiano, emperadores romanos. Mas porque para ninguna de estas opiniones hay razón ni fundamento por donde se pueda afirmar más lo uno que lo otro, es mejor dejarlo indeciso, y que cada uno tenga en esto lo que más le cuadrare."

3. "...preguntado otro indio viejo la noticia que tenía de la ida de Topiltzín (Quetzalcóatl), me empezó a relatar el capítulo Catorce del Exodo...Y como ví que había leído donde yo y dónde iba a parar, no me dí mucho por preguntarle, porque no me contase el Exodo, de que le sentí tener noticia, y tanta que fue dar en el castigo que tuvieron los hijos de Israel, de las serpientes, por la murmuración contra Dios y Moisés...."

4. "...según parece en sus historias, el primer rey que tuvieron se llamaba Chichimécatl, que fue el que los trujo a este nuevo mundo en donde poblaron, el cual, según se colige, salió de la Gran Tartaria, y fueron de los de la división de Babilonia...y éste su rey, como anduviese con ellos discurriendo por la mayor parte del mundo, llegaron a esta tierra...."

5. "...Bien sería que V. Mag. entendiese que estos yndios están en el extremo de la pobreça...porque si entrar en sus casas allarán que ellas y todo lo que en ellas tienen y lo que traen vestido, es tan poco y tan vil, que apenas sabrán que preçio le poner...."

6. "...está el cordero a los pechos de la madre que aún no tiene lana y ya le quieren tresquilar, y plugiese a Dios que no fuesse desollar..." [or even] "...que será de los miserables yndios, estando subjetos a tantos lobos e a tantos que los manden a palos...."

7. "...O, si fuese posible que V. A. viese la vanidad y superfluidad de los unos y la miseria de los otros; piden al desnudo para él muy vestido, al hambriento para el harto y al pobre para el rico! Si viese V. A. su extremada pobreza...."

8. "...Estos indios cuasi no tienen estorbo que les impida para ganar el cielo, de los muchos que los españoles tenemos y nos tienen sumidos, porque su vida se contenta con muy poco, y tan poco, que apenas tienen con qué se vestir ni alimentar. Su comida es muy paupérrima, y lo mismo es el vestido. Para dormir la mayor parte de ellos aún no alcanzan una estera sana....Con su pobre manta se acuestan, y en despertando están aparejados para servir a Dios, y si se quieren disciplinar, no tienen estorbo ni embarazo de vestirse y desnudarse....Sus colchones es la dura tierra, sin ropa ninguna; cuando mucho tienen una estera rota, y por cabecera una piedra o un pedazo de madero, y muchos ninguna cabecera, sino la tierra desnuda, sus casas son muy pequeñas, algunas cubiertas de un solo terrado muy bajo, algu-

nas de paja, otras como la celda de aquel santo abad Hilarión, que más parecen sepultura que no casa...."

9. "...Son todos aquestos indios como unos pajaritos en los nidos, a quién no les han crecido las alas ni crecerán para saber por sí volar, sino que siempre tienen necesidad que sus padres cuidadosos les acudan con el cebo y alimento a los nidos...."

10. "...Son pacientes, sufridos sobre manera, mansos como ovejas. Nunca me acuerdo de haberlos visto guardar injuria; humildes, a todos obedientes, ya de necesidad, ya de voluntad, no saben sino servir y trabajar.... Es mucha la paciencia y sufrimiento que en las enfermedades tienen... comen y beben sin mucho ruido ni vozes. Sin rencillas ni enemistades pasan su tiempo y vida, y salen a buscar el mantenimiento a la vida humana necesario, y no más...."

11. "Yo los conocí en un tiempo, que por maravilla hallaran indio que le vieran estornudar, y lo noté por espacio de muchos días, maravillándome de ello. Y era porque sólo comían lo que naturaleza había menester para sustentarse, no más que dos o tres tortillas de maíz y unas yerbezuelas cocidas con un poco de ají o chile, que en España llaman pimienta de las Indias. De suerte que no criaban humores superfluos, que tuviesen necesidad de expelerlos por aquella vía. Ahora estornudan hasta los niños de teta, recibiéndolo de sus padres, porque comen carne y las demás viandas que nosotros los españoles comemos, con lo cual crían humores gruesos y superfluos, como nosotros los criamos, y por tanto estornudan como nosotros estornudamos...."

12. "...Era esta tierra un traslado del infierno; ver los moradores de ella de noche dar voces, unos llamando al demonio, otros borrachos, otros cantando y bailando; tañían atabales, bocinas, cornetas y caracoles grandes, en especial en las fiestas de sus demonios. Las beoderas que hacían muy ordinarias, es increíble el vino que en ellas gastaban, y lo que cada uno en el cuerpo metía.... Era cosa de grandísima lástima ver los hombres criados a la imagen de Dios vueltos peores que brutos animales; y lo que peor era, que no quedaban en aquel solo pecado, más cometían otros muchos...."

13. "...por ser débiles y párvulos tienen extrema necesidad de padres y maestros que no los dejen de la mano..."; "...esto ha de ser casi con el azote en la mano, como se hace con los niños del escuela...."

14. "...Que el talento y capacidad de los indios comúnmente es como de mozuelos de hasta diez o doce años. De donde se sigue que no se les ha de pedir más cuadal ni hacer de ellos más confianza que de niños para dejarlos a su albedrío.... Y de aquí también se conoce la necesidad que tienen de que los que los rigen y guían, así en lo espiritual como en o temporal, les sean padres para desearles y procurarles su bien y cuidarles su mal como a hijos, y tutores para ampararlos como a menores, a maestros para enseñarlos como a párvulos.... Y de aquí se colige el error engaño de los que sienten por cosa dura que el clérigo o fraile *haga azotar a los indios que tienen a su cargo, cuando es necesario para su bien y provecho. Y esto es falta de conocimiento de la calidad de los indios, porque les es tanto menester el azote como el pan de la boca, y tan natural, que entre sí no se hallan ni pueden vivir sin ello, e ellos mismos lo confiesan que en faltándoles el azote como niños son perdidos...."*

15. "...*a ninguna manera de gentes antes de ellos conocidas se pueden equiparar o igualar, sino a sólos los mozuelos que aún no han llegado a perfecta edad; y así no habría*

de hacer otra cuenta el que los gobierna, sino que gobierna una república de muchachos libres, hijos por adopción del Rey Celestial, para encaminárselos a su reino y
gloria perdurable...."

16. "... haciéndonos padres desta mísera nación y encomendándonoslos como
a hijos y niños chiquitos para que como a tales (que lo son) los criemos y doc-
trinemos y amparemos y corrijamos, y los conservemos y aprovechemos en la Fe y
policía cristiana...."

17. "... estos naturales son puramente niños, naturalmente subjetos y tímidos,
y así con tener padre y maestro verdadero cristiano y prudente, que los amase como
a hijos y como a tales los corrigiese, y como maestro los enseñase e instruyese en la
fe cristiana y policía humana, no sería más una provincia entera debajo de la mano
de un religioso, que una escuela de muchachos debajo de la mano de su maestro;
*porque puestos en subjeción y obediencia, no hay gente ni nación en el mundo más dócil que
ésta* para cuanto les quisieren enseñar y mandar; y por el contrario *no hay fieras en
las selvas más indómitas que ellos, puestos en su querer y libertad...."*

18. "... Los terzeros son los Mexicanos, e dellos todos vienen a dezir que son de
la generación de los de Culhúa, y su lengua consiente en ello; séanlo o no, porfíase
que los de Culhúa fueron primero que no ellos, y *destos de México se dize que no
venieron señores principales ni de linaje señalado*, en caso que trayan sus capitanes y
personas que los mandaban...."

19. "será hazer saber a Vuestra Magestad cómo el prinçipal señorío desta Nueva
España cuando los españoles en ella entraron, no había muchos años que estaba
en México o en los mexicanos; y cómo los mismos mexicanos lo habían ganado o
osurpado por guerras...."

20. "Sepa Vuestra Magestad que cuando el Marqués del Valle entró en esta
tierra, Dios Nuestro Señor era muy ofendido, y los honbres padesçían muy cruelí-
simas muertes, y el demonio, nuestro adversario, era muy servido con las mayores
idolatrías y homeçidios más crueles que jamás fueron...Y cuando los christianos
entraron en esta Nueva España, por todos los pueblos y provinçias della había muchos sacrifiçios de honbres muertos, más que nunca, que mataban y sacrificaban
delante de los ídolos; y cada día y cada hora ofreçían a los demonios sangre humana
por todas partes y pueblos de toda esta tierra...."

21. ... Los otros indios procuraban de comer carne humana de los que morían
en el sacrificio, y ésta comían comúnmente los señores principales, y mercaderes,
y los ministros de los templos; *que a la otra gente baja pocas veces les alcanzaba un
bocadillo...."*

22. "...Una víspera de una fiesta en Cuauhtitlán, levantaban seis grandes
árboles como mástiles de naos con sus escaleras; y en esta vigilia cruel, y el día
muy más cruel también, degollaban dos mujeres esclavas en lo alto encima de las
gradas, delante el altar de los ídolos, y allí arriba las desollaban todo el cuerpo y
el rostro, y sacábanles las canillas de los muslos; y el día por la mañana, *dos indios
principales* vestíanse los cueros, y los rostros también como máscaras, y tomaban en
las manos las canillas, en cada mano la suya, y muy paso a paso bajaban bramando,
que parecían bestias encarnizadas...."

23. "... Hacíase este mismo día otra mayor y nunca oída crueldad, y era que en
aquellos seis palos que la víspera de la fiesta habían levantado, en lo alto ataban y
aspaban seis hombres cautivos en la guerra, y estaban debajo a la redonda más de

dos mil muchachos y hombres con sus arcos y flechas, y éstos, en bajándose los que habían subido a los atar a los cautivos, disparaban en ellos las saetas como lluvia; y asaetados y medio muertos, subían de presto a los desatar, y dejábanlos caer de aquella altura, y del gran golpe que daban se quebrantaban y molían los huesos todos del cuerpo; y luego les daban la tercera muerte, sacrificándolos y sacándolos los corazones; y arrastrándolos desviábanlos de allí, y degollábanlos y cortábanles las cabezas, y dábanlas a los ministros de los ídolos; y los cuerpos llevábanlos como carneros *para los comer los señores y principales....*"

24. "... Los ritos de las idolatrías e adoraciones de sus falsos dioses e ceremonias de diversos grados de personas cerca de sus sacrificios que, aunque esto es malo, *naçe de una soliçitud natural no dormida, que busca socorro e no topa con el verdadero remediador....*"

25. "... E por esto nosotros los religiosos quando entramos en esta tierra, *no nos espantó ni desconfió su idolatría,* más aviendo compasión de su çeguedad, tuvimos muy grand confianza que todo aquello e *mucho más harían en serviçio de nuestro Dios, quando le conoçiesen....*"

26. "... ¿cómo se sufre ser incapaces con tanta suntuosidad de edificios, con tanto primor en obrar de manos cosas subtiles, plateros, pintores, mercaderes, repartidores de tributos, arte en presidir, repartir por cabezas gentes, serviçios, crianza de hablar e cortesía y estilo? ..."

27. "... El que enseña al hombre la ciencia, ese mismo proveyó y dio a estos Indios naturales grande ingenio y habilidad para aprender todas las ciencias, artes y oficios que les han enseñado, porque con todos han salido en tan breve tiempo, que en viendo los oficios que en Castilla están muchos años en los deprender, acá en sólo mirarlos y verlos hacer, han muchos quedado maestros. *Tienen el entendimiento vivo, recogido y sosegado, no orgulloso ni derramado como otras naciones....*"

Works Cited

Alva Ixtlilxóchitl, Fernando. *Obras históricas.* Ed. Edmundo O'Gorman. Mexico City: Universidad Nacional Autónoma de México, 1975.

Baudot, Georges. *La pugna franciscana por México.* Mexico City: Alianza and Conaculart, 1990.

———. *Utopía e Historia en Mexico City: Los primeros cronistas de la civilización mexicana (1520-1569).* Trans. Vicente González Loscertales. Madrid: Espasa-Calpe, 1983.

Bergeron, Pierre de. *Voyages faits principalement en Asie dans les XIIe, XIIIe, XIVe et XVe siècles* (Précédés d'une introduction concernant les voyages et les nouvelles découvertes des principaux voyageurs). The Hague: J. Neaulme, 1735.

Cartas de Indias. Madrid: Ministerio de Fomento, 1877.

Cartas de Religiosos de Nueva España: Nueva Colección de Documentos para la historia de México. Ed. Joaquín García Icazbalceta. Vol. 1. Mexico City: Chávez Hayhoe, 1941.

Códice Mendieta: Nueva Colección de Documentos para la historia de México. Ed. Joaquín García Icazbalceta. Vols. 4 and 5. Mexico City: Díaz de León, 1886-1892.

Cortés, Hernán. *Cartas de relación*. Biblioteca de Autores Españoles. Madrid: M. Rivadeneyra, 1877.

Cuevas, Mariano. *Documentos inéditos del siglo XVI para la historia de México*. Gathered and annotated by P. Mariano Cuevas, S.J. Mexico City: Museo Nacional de Arqueología, Historia y Etnología, 1914.

Durán, Fray Diego. *Historia de las Indias de Nueva España e Islas de la Tierra Firme*. 2 vols. Mexico City: Porrúa, 1967.

García, Gregorio. *Origen de los Indios del Nuevo Mundo e Indias Occidentales*. Valencia, 1607.

Motolinía, Fray Toribio de Benavente. *Epistolario*. 1526-1555. Collected directly from the originals, and transcribed by Lic. Javier O. Aragón. Ed. P. Lino Gómez Canedo. Mexico City: Lauel, 1986.

―――. *Historia de los Indios de la Nueva España*. Ed. Georges Baudot. Madrid: Castalia, 1985.

―――. *Memoriales*. Mexico City: Universidad Autónoma de México, Instituto de Investigaciones Históricas, 1971.

Mendieta, Fray Gerónimo de. *Historia eclesiástica indiana*. Mexico City: Chávez Hayhoe, 1945.

Phelan, John L. *The Millennial Kingdom of the Franciscans in the New World*. Berkeley: Univ. of California Press, 1970.

Piano Carpini, Fray Juan de. *Historia Mongolorum*. [See Ruysbroeck below.]

Ríos, Fray Pedro de los. *Códice Vaticano A: Antigüedades de Mexico City: basadas en la recopilación de Lord Kingsborough*. Mexico City: Ed. José Corona Nuñez, 1964-1967.

Ruysbroeck, Willem Van. *Itinerarium ad partes orientales*. English version: *The Journey of William of Rubruck to the Eastern Part of the World*, 1235-1255, as narrated by himself, with two accounts of the earlier journey of John Pian de Carpine. London: Hakluyt Society, 1900.

Chapter 13

The Place of the Translator in the Discourses of Conquest Hernán Cortés's *Cartas de relación* and Roland Joffé's *The Mission*

David E. Johnson

In the Christian West, until today, all strength passes through the interpreter....
—Roland Barthes, *A Lover's Discourse*

*You taught me language; and my profit on't
Is, I know how to curse. The red plague rid you
For learning me your language.*
—The Tempest, *I.ii.363-365,*
qtd. in Greenblatt 569

In "Learning to Curse: Aspects of Linguistic Colonialism in the Sixteenth Century," Stephen Greenblatt cites Caliban's lines to Miranda and writes: "Caliban's retort might be taken as self-indictment: even with the gift of language, his nature is so debased that he can only learn to curse. But the lines refuse to mean this; what we experience instead is a sense of their devastating just-ness" (570).[1] Later in this essay I turn to an analogous scene in Roland Joffé's 1986 film, *The Mission*, that depicts the inculcation of a debased language for the natives. Before taking up the latent ideological pedagogy of *The Mission*, however, I want to consider Greenblatt's point of departure—Antonio de Nebrija's *Gramática de la lengua castellana* (*Grammar of the Castilian Language*)—and then proceed not to the representation of the Other but to Hernán Cortés's strategy of textually displacing the translator/interpreter from the site of intercultural communication. By bringing together Nebrija's *Gramática de la lengua castellana*, Cortés's *Cartas de relación* (*Letters from Mexico*), and Joffé's *The Mission*, this essay hopes to demonstrate the ideologically determined shift from the hegemony of grammar to the grammar of hegemony.

Although Greenblatt does not mention Cortés, he anticipates my reading when he writes: "Again and again in the early accounts, Europeans and Indians, after looking on each other's faces for the first time, converse without the slightest difficulty; indeed the Indians often speak with as great a facility in English or Spanish as the Renaissance gentlemen themselves. There were interpreters, to be sure, but these are frequently credited with linguistic feats that challenge belief" (571). In the *Cartas de relación*, Cortés avoids challenging the credibility of his reader—who ostensibly was to have been Charles V—by eliding the interpreter/translator from his letters. In other words, more fundamental than Bartolomé de Las Casas's objection that the narratives of the Conquest were "intentionally falsified, to make the *conquistadores'* actions appear fairer and more deliberative than they actually were" (qtd. in Greenblatt 571), Cortés falsifies his *place* in the discourse, writing the interpreter out of the communicative structure and situating himself discursively closer to the Amerindian interlocutor.

The move from Cortés's *Cartas de relación* to Joffé's film, *The Mission*, should make clear the political importance of the translator, less as a subjective agency than as a position. We should remark that in the history of the Discovery and Conquest of the New World, a history not yet concluded, the strategic positioning of the translator parallels Westerners' increasing recognition that Amerindian civilizations had languages. At first there was some doubt as to whether or not the Indians spoke; Tzvetan Todorov writes in *The Conquest of America*: "Columbus's failure to recognize the diversity of languages permits him, when he confronts a foreign tongue, only two possible, and complementary, forms of behavior: to acknowledge it as a language but to refuse to believe it is different; or to acknowledge its difference but to refuse to admit it is a language" (30). Initially, then, there was no need for interpreters: rather, the Indians had to be taught to speak. Greenblatt cites Columbus: "I, please Our Lord, will carry off six of them at my departure to Your Highnesses, that they may learn to speak [para que aprendan a hablar]" (562). Once it became apparent the Indians had languages, a recognition that made translators necessary, "the first interpreters," Todorov points out, "were Indians" (98). The introduction of Amerindian interpreters into the structure of discourse problematizes communication for the Spaniards; as we will see, they worry about the translators' reliability. But it is of interest that no Spaniards willingly become translators/interpreters at the outset. The first Spanish translator was Jerónimo de Aguilar, who learned the Maya language out of necessity: approximately eight years before Cortés's expedition he had been shipwrecked and was subsequently enslaved. Cortés's "discovery" of Aguilar sets in motion a process that culminates in *The Mission:* Spanish's linguistic domination of "Latin" America.

But let us move first to the *Gramática de la lengua castellana,* which was perhaps the earliest modern European enunciation of the political relation between grammar and government.

On August 18, 1492, Antonio de Nebrija of the University of Salamanca dedicated the first analytical grammar of a neo-Latin language to Queen Isabella of Spain. The prologue's first sentence articulates the text's fundamental assumption, the relationship between language and institutionalized power: " ... language [*lengua*] was always the companion of empire; they began, grew and flourished together, consequently it follows that they died together as well."[2] Nebrija justifies the *Gramática de la lengua castellana* by explaining its uses to the empire; they are threefold.

First, the *Gramática* will standardize written "novelas o istorias," which will make possible the avoidance of, as Nebrija writes, a "thousand lies and errors" ("mil mentiras [y] errores [100]"); the reduction of Castilian to a standardized art elevates the language to the level of Greek and Latin, to a level of historical permanence and prestige. Second, the *Gramática* will enable Spanish national history; without it, Nebrija explains, "one of two things will necessarily happen: either that your Majesty's acts will perish with the language; or that they [i.e., the royal acts] will wander throughout foreign nations for want of their own house in which to live."[3] Nebrija credits the bishop of Avila with articulating the *Gramática's* third use:

> The third use of my work could be the one which, when in Salamanca I showed it to your Royal Majesty, and you asked how best you could use it, the Very Reverend Father Bishop of Avila seized the opportunity and, responding for me, said that after your Highness puts under your yoke

many barbarous peoples and nations of foreign languages, with their defeat they will need to receive the laws that the conqueror imposes on the conquered and with them, our language; therefore, they could come to know it through *Grammar*.[4]

Taken together, then, the three functions of Nebrija's *Gramática de la lengua castellana* bestow on grammar a political and homogenizing value: in short, the purpose of the *Gramática* is to facilitate the administration of power in the newly united Spain.

Although Nebrija writes of conquered territories and vanquished peoples, his introductory remarks do not anticipate the Discovery and Conquest of the New World; his explicit concern is the maintenance of power in Spain. The *Gramática* proposes to enable the effective governance of Spain by standardizing Castilian. Nebrija implements his agenda by attacking the language of the other academic disciplines, claiming that grammar " ... ha[s] jurisdiction over all other [disciplines] insofar as they [touch] language, which is the instrument of all faculties."[5] Because every enunciation has the potential to inculcate and institutionalize the *good* usage of Spanish, Nebrija establishes grammar as the ground of all pedagogy. He does not, however, privilege grammar as a separate discipline. On the contrary, Nebrija values grammar only to the extent that other disciplines use it; in other words, grammar has no value in and for itself, but because all pedagogy depends on language, grammar effectively determines the possibility of value as such. In other words, every pedagogical practice, regardless of its content, is the site of a language lesson.

That every pedagogy is principally a language lesson evinces the companionship of language and empire. An empire's authority reaches only to the limit that its language structures the thought of the conquered. Empires therefore face the double task of, first, guarding themselves against barbarism, against the fracturing of linguistic homogeneity, and, second, of preserving their authority by maintaining the vanquished in a linguistically subordinate position. Put simply, the conquered must know the language well enough to know the law, but not so masterfully as to make possible criticism of the sort that problematizes the grammar of imperialism. To delimit the possibility of such criticism, colonizing powers create and perpetuate the illusion of linguistic mastery.[6] Antonio de Nebrija grounds the future of Spain's empire on the dissemination of Spanish; he grounds the future of Spanish on grammar, on the *Gramática de la lengua castellana*.

From its "discovery" to the present, Latin America has suffered under the illusion of linguistic mastery produced by two historical world powers: sixteenth-century Spain and twentieth-century United States. In what follows we will read the inscriptions of linguistic domination in Hernán Cortés's *Cartas de relación* and Roland Joffé's film *The Mission*. These two texts frame Latin American history: both were produced in but neither are products of Latin America. Although Cortés wrote his letters from Mexico, they literally bear witness to Spain and to Spanish culture. And yet it remains a curious fact that the *Cartas* mark the canonical beginning of Latin American literary history. In spite of being filmed in Argentina and Colombia, and even though thematically it has nothing to do with North America, *The Mission* attests to the linguistic authority of the United States over the Americas. We will see how each of these texts figures power as a function of communication; we will see how Cortés's *Letters* and Joffé's *The Mission* rhetorically determine linguistic authority by the subtle placement and displacement of the translator.

In *Historia verdadera de la conquista de Nueva España* (*The Conquest of New Spain*), Bernal Díaz del Castillo explains the importance of the translator to Cortés:

> Doña Marina knew the language of Coatzalcoalcos, which is that of Mexico, and she knew the Tabascan language also. This language is common to Tabasco and Yucatan, and Jerónimo de Aguilar spoke it also. These two understood one another well, and Aguilar translated into Castilian for Cortés. This was the great beginning of all our conquests, ... because without Doña Marina we could not have understood the language of New Spain and Mexico. (*The Conquest* 86-87)[7]

In addition to this explicit address, off-hand references to the interpreter/translator fill Bernal Díaz's chronicle; a few examples will suffice:

So through Melchior (. . . who now understood a little Spanish and knew the language of Cozumel very well), all the chiefs were questioned. (59)[8]

Cortés then sent for the Caciques and all the principal men, and for the papa himself, and told them as best he could, through our interpreter . . . (62)[9]

On March 4, 1519, being now blessed with a useful and faithful interpreter, Cortés gave orders . . . (66)[10]

When Cortés saw the Indians drawn up for battle, he told Aguilar the interpreter, who knew their language well, to ask some Indians . . . (69)[11]

The *Historia verdadera de la conquista de Nueva España* cites the interpreter passim. Bernal Díaz's frequent reference to interpreters, however, cannot be explained merely as part of an exercise to limit Cortés's place in the history of the Conquest. Although he spends a good portion of the *Historia* correcting the errors of earlier chroniclers, Díaz does not insinuate the interpreter into Cortés's discourse because of a fifty-year-old bitterness over the lack of favorable royal endowment. On the contrary, Bernal Díaz del Castillo and other chroniclers remark on the presence of interpreters because intercultural communication took place only through them; interpreters/translators occupied the most prominent place in the structure of discourse. They could not easily be overlooked.

Indeed, according to Bernal Díaz, Doña Marina's position as interpreter/translator was so obvious and important that the Indians soon began to call Cortés "Malinche":

> . . . in every town we passed through and in others that had only heard of us, they called Cortés Malinche. . . . The reason why he received this name was that Doña Marina was always with him, especially when he was visited by ambassadors or *Caciques*, and she always spoke to them in the Mexican language. So they gave Cortés the name of "Marina's Captain," which was shortened to Malinche. (172)[12]

Neither *The Florentine Codex* nor Cortés's *Cartas de relación* mention the Indians referring to Cortés in this way. It is possible that the Amerindians, when they said "Malinche," referred not to Cortés, but instead addressed themselves directly to the messenger/interpreter/translator herself as a communicating subject of the discourse. The structure regulating the communication of messages in the *Popol Vuh* suggests that the Maya, for example, do not consider the messenger a mere communicative conduit. To the contrary, messages were relayed in such a way that tagged or cited every mediation; thus the *Popol Vuh* recounts the louse delivering to Hunahpu and Xbalanque a missive from the Xijalbans:

" 'Tell it,' the louse was told next, so then he named his word:
'Boys [Hunahpu and Xbalanque],' your grandmother says:
'Summon them.' A message came for them:
'From Xibalba comes the messenger of One and Seven Death':
'In seven days they are to come here. We'll play ball. Their gaming equipment must come along: rubber ball, yokes, arm guards, kilts. This will make for some excitement here,' say the lords, 'is the word that came from them,' says your grandmother. So your grandmother says you must come. Truly your grandmother cries, she calls out to you to come." (133)[13]

The quotation marks and the discursive tags (e.g. "say the lords," "so your grandmother says,") signal the structural embedding of the message within the apparatus that communicates it. In the *Popol Vuh*, at least, a rigorous literality governs the delivery or communication of messages. Such "rigorous literality" does not imply that no interpretation takes place in the delivery and rearticulations of the message; rather, it means the place of the bearer within the discursive space through which the message passes is preserved. The feeble gestures of Bernal Díaz and other chroniclers toward the translator is the closest Western discourse comes to such rigorous placement or "siting" of the message's courier. The difference is remarkable. On the one hand, the messengers in the *Popol Vuh* become part of the message; the message itself grows to include all the various sites of communication. On the other hand, in the Conquest narratives, the message maintains an integrity unchanged by the various conduits through which it passes; these conduits, regardless of their number or the complexity with which they may have operated, are summed up in phrases like, "... through our interpreter..."

Of Cortés's *Cartas de relación*, only the first, which was not authored by Cortés (see "Introduction," *Letters from Mexico*), liberally cites the role of the interpreter, even if it does so only in the off-hand style Bernal Díaz del Castillo employs. For example:

> While taking the water he began to tell them through the interpreter how he would give them the ornaments he was carrying in exchange for gold... (8)[14]

> Cortés then spoke to them through his interpreters... (11)[15]

> ... the captain spoke with them through his interpreter and also through Jerónimo de Aguilar, who spoke and understood that language very well... (19)[16]

All told, the first letter makes no fewer than nine references to the mediating agency of interpreters. Although the first letter deals very little with Indian encounters, virtually every time there is an intent to communicate cross-culturally the text marks the interpreter's place in the discourse. True, unlike the *Popol Vuh*, once cited, the text subsequently leaves out, forgets, silences the interpreter; but the first letter recognizes the impossibility of beginning—even rhetorically—without the interpreter.

Almost four times as long as the first and written by Cortés himself, the second letter contains accounts of the Spaniards' long and eventful march to Tenochtitlan, their first sighting of the city, the description of Moctezuma's zoo, Cortés's struggle with Pánfilo de Narváez, and finally the Aztecs' expulsion of the Spaniards from Tenochtitlan on *"la noche triste"* ("The Night of Sorrow"). It is filled with Cortés's encounters and negotiations with the Cempoalans, the Tlascalans, and the Aztecs, among others. Missing from the representation of these negotiations, however, is the interpreter. In the lengthy text, Cortés refers to his use of interpreters only four times. Moreover, he does not name the interpreters unambiguously; rather, he refers to his *lenguas*, which literally means his "languages" or his "tongues."[17] In the second letter, Cortés not once employs the word *intérprete* to designate the person or persons who translated for him. Further, he invariably possesses his interpreters: "...I spoke to them with the languages I have" (translation mine).[18]

The point is not that Cortés failed to grasp the importance of interpreters; on the contrary, according to Todorov, "The first important action he [Cortés] initiates...is to find an interpreter" (99). This is because, again according to Todorov, "What Cortés wants from the first is not to capture but to comprehend; it is signs which chiefly interest him, not their referents. His expedition begins with a search for information" (99). Thus, upon arriving in Mexico, Cortés, with a few men, goes ashore: "From there I set off with a few followers to gather information" (*Letters* 52).[19] Todorov continues, "Being thus certain of understanding the language, Cortés neglects no occasion to gather new information," and adds, "He is ready to listen to advice, even if he does not always follow it—since the information needs to be interpreted" (103). Todorov makes the connection between finding a reliable interpreter and the possibility of gathering information, some of which, upon being interpreted, will lead to the fall of the Aztec empire. Spanish makes this connection implicitly in the semantic conjunction of interpreter and information in the word *lengua*.

The semantic identity of "information" and "interpreter" in *lengua* interests us because, despite their (i.e., the Spaniards', Cortés's, and, necessarily, the *lenguas*', or interpreters') obsession for gathering information (i.e., *lengua*), *rhetorically* Cortés could only consider the mediation or intervention of interpreters intolerable. In the representation of the Conquest of New Spain, Cortés admits only three agents at work on Spain's behalf: the one, true (i.e., Christian) God; the king, Charles V; and Cortés himself. The absence of *intérprete* in the *Cartas de relación* bears witness to Cortés's unwillingness to inscribe another "subject" between himself and Amerindian interlocutors; Cortés's choice of *lengua* to convey *intérprete* marks the desire to dehumanize the mediating agency that in fact enabled intercultural communication. As opposed to *intérprete, lengua* is an instrument to be used, to be possessed—perhaps especially when it signifies interpreter. To the extent that *lengua* is a nonsubjective agency, without will or spirit, it remains "faithful." Such faithfulness indexes, on the one hand, translating expertise and, on the other hand, subjective disappearance.

Cortés's "possession" of his *lenguas* appropriates the translating voice to himself, transforming a subjectivity into a mechanism, a mouthpiece. This understanding of the interpreter informs Bernal Díaz del Castillo's remark: "Cortés then spoke eloquently to the Indians *through* our interpreters" (64).[20] Cortés does not speak directly to the Indians. If he spoke eloquently to anyone, it was to the Spaniards. How the interpreters translated Cortés's words, and thus how Cortés spoke to the Indians, would have depended on the interpreters' respective facility with both Spanish and the particular Amerindian language. Effectively, Cortés's oratorical skills bore historical and political as opposed to practical or conquistatorial import. His orations, their eloquence, directed as they were at the conquistadors and, in particular, at the scribes, whose task it was to record the events of the Conquest, serve to communicate and legitimate Cortés's actions to Charles V. Otherwise, Cortés's rhetoric fell on deaf ears; not until he resorted to violence did he realize any authority over Amerindian civilizations.[21]

To the extent Cortés intended to communicate with Charles V, not only were the interpreters structurally irrelevant to the discourse, their mediating presence obscured the letters' purpose, which was to persuade the king that the governor of Cuba, Diego Velázquez, was corrupt and self-serving and that Cortés himself deserved the honor of conquering New Spain in his name. The displacement of the interpreter within *lengua* rhetorically brings communication closer to immediacy, to transparency. At stake in this rhetorical transparency or mastery is Cortés's personal success; or, as Beatriz Pastor writes, "The objective of the *Cartas de relación* is not the plain and faithful narrative of the truth, but the creation of a series of fictional models that appear subordinated to a project for the acquisition of fame, glory, and power" (146; translation mine).[22] Unlike the drawing representing the first encounter between Cortés and Moctezuma, which places Malinche in the center and the two military leaders on the margins (Todorov 101), the *Segunda carta de relación* allows no one to stand in the way when Cortés speaks, for the presence of a translator would displace Cortés's authority from himself to the one who speaks for him, to the one who interprets. Charles V, then, hears only Cortés's voice, his *lengua* (tongue); he receives from Cortés *la lengua* (the information) Cortés has gathered. This information is transparent to Charles V because he and Cortés speak or use the same *lengua* (language, tongue, interpreter).

Obviously this does not mean Cortés refused to use interpreters; as Bernal Díaz del Castillo wrote, the entire expedition depended on them and their reliability. Yet, because *intérprete* suggests unreliability,[23] conjuring as it does the image of a human being repeating in a different language—and thus saying for the first time—what has already been said, Cortés rigorously limits his reference to translators. Textually, his authority does not hinge on an interpreter; unlike other *conquistadores*, Cortés does not narrate scenes of interpretive failure. In the *Historia verdadera de la conquista de Nueva España*, for example, Bernal Díaz recounts a delay in the Grijalva expedition (1518) attributed to unfaithful interpreters:

> We took three prisoners in this skirmish, one of whom was a person of some importance; and Grijalva sent them off to summon the *Cacique* of the town, giving them clearly to understand through the interpreters Julian and Melchior that we pardoned them for what they had done. As a sign of peace, he gave them some green beads to hand to their *Cacique*. They departed but never returned. So we concluded that our interpreters had not repeated what they were told, but the exact opposite. We stayed in the town for three days. (91)[24]

Events of this nature do not befall Cortés for two reasons: (1) he employs at least one Spaniard, Jerónimo de Aguilar, as interpreter; and (2) he admits little or no dependence on interpreters. In other words, on the one hand, the interpreter is culturally bound to Cortés's mission, and, on the other hand, Cortés cannot be deceived by an interpreter because, rhetorically, he does not use one.

Using what amounts to a Machiavellian stratagem, in the second letter to Charles V Cortés highlights his linguistic abilities, his freedom from interpretive subterfuge, at Pánfilo de Narváez's expense: Cortés narrates Narváez's inability to arrest him on Velázquez's authority. Cortés writes that Narváez, having heard Cortés had returned from Tenochtitlan to meet him, "rode out of his camp with eighty horsemen and five hundred foot soldiers.... Thus he came to within one league of where I was, but, as all he knew of my arrival he had from the Indians, when he failed to find me he thought they were deceiving him and he returned to the city" (*Letters* 125).[25] Cortés captures Narváez the following night.

Narváez's initial trust and subsequent blaming of interpreters contrasts tellingly with Cortés's textual distrust of presumably reliable translators. On the way to Tenochtitlan the Spaniards stop at Churultecal; while there, Doña Marina (whom Cortés does not name) alerts Aguilar of a plot to ambush the Spaniards; Aguilar informs Cortés. Upon receiving this information, Cortés writes, "I then seized one of the natives of this city who was passing by and took him aside secretly and questioned him; and he confirmed what the woman and the natives of Tlascalteca had told me. Because of this and because of the signs I had observed...in two hours more than three thousand men were killed" (73).[26] Unlike Narváez, Cortés rhetorically moves away from the interpreters and toward truth. Narváez fails, Cortés intimates, because he depends on potentially false interpreters. Thus, strategically, Cortés elides the interpreter as if between him and Amerindian peoples truth went naked.

In the rhetorically immediate discourse between Cortés and the Indians, the place of the translator is transparent, unobtrusive, nonsubjective. The interpreter does not intervene, does not mediate. Cortés was, perhaps, not the first conqueror to realize the importance of "faithful" interpreters; he was, however, the first to recognize the necessity of writing them off, of not representing their structural necessity.

By the 1750s linguistic superiority and (therefore) political rule in Latin America were marked by the explicit positioning of the translator. Roland Joffé's 1986 film, *The Mission*, depicts the intense struggles between the Jesuits on the one side and the Spanish and Portuguese on the other, for the backs and souls of the Guaraní Indians. Ideologically complex, *The Mission* tells the story of the "conquest" of the Guaraní "above the falls"; it also recounts the historical background of the 1767 expulsion of the Jesuits from the Americas. The issue is the transfer of mission territories from Spain to Portugal. The Jesuits oppose the transfer, which will lead to the enslavement of the Guaraní. The Church ultimately appeases the Spanish and Portuguese crowns; the missions are overrun; the Guaraní enslaved. The Jesuits—save one, played by Jeremy Irons—fight alongside the Guaraní, defending their way of life. For this transgression, those who do not die in the conflicts suffer excommunication.

Yet, in Joffé's film at least, the Jesuits assist in the conquest and the subsequent subjugation of the Guaraní to "Spanish" rule.[27] They work this conquest and subordination in two ways. First, the Jesuits radically alter the lives of the Guaraní: they convert them both spiritually and economically. The Guaraní become farmers; the Jesuits teach them to build cathedrals, to make watches, violins, etc. They write books in Guaraní. They learn to add and subtract.[28]

Second, in spite of conducting everyday life in the Jesuit missions in Guaraní, the Guaraní Indians learned Spanish. But they did not learn it well, and not because, as Don Cabeza in *The Mission* suggests, they were animals, savages. To the contrary, they did not learn Spanish well because they weren't taught it well. Wittingly or not, *The Mission* represents the failure and the success of a defective pedagogy. As we will see, it could not have done otherwise, for in the final analysis, *The Mission* concerns the authority of the speaker, the place whence one speaks, and the effects of linguistic pedagogy.

Initially, it does not appear or sound like *The Mission* touches linguistic problems at all. The film makes use of basically two languages, the privileged one being English, the other Guaraní. There are no subtitles; thus, generally, when Guaraní is spoken, the listener must make sense of it from the context. The ease with which one can watch/listen to *The Mission* without puzzling over the discourse of the Guaraní testifies to their lack of authority in the film: *The Mission* displaces the Guaraní much as the Spaniards displaced the missions.

In its linguistic duality *The Mission* is reminiscent of Joffé's first film, *The Killing Fields* (1984), about the friendship and working relationship between Dith Pran, a Cambodian interpreter and reporter, and Sydney Schanberg, a *New York Times* columnist who was covering the American presence in Cambodia during the last days of the Vietnam War. Although Dith Pran, played by Doctor Haing S. Nygor, does a great deal of work in Cambodian, the film translates none of it. *The Killing Fields* forces its audience to confront the devastation of Cambodia by both the United States Armed Forces and the Khmer Rouge, but it does so through American eyes, through American sympathy and guilt: the film seems to compare, not unfavorably either, Schanberg's struggles of conscience in his Manhattan apartment with Dith Pran's struggles for survival in Cambodia. If there is an oppressor in Cambodia, in Southeast Asia in general, *The Killing Fields* suggests, it is English. The similarity between *The Killing Fields* and *The Mission* indicates to me that linguistic imperialism is one of Joffé's special concerns.

As one might expect from its release in the United States by a major American distributor, English dominates *The Mission*. Unlike the historical situation depicted in *The Killing Fields*, however, in which, if one were to have been in Cambodia in the early 1970s, one would have heard English spoken, English is one language unheard on the borders between Argentina, Brazil, and Paraguay in the mid-eighteenth century. No English-speaking people appear in *The Mission;* all the characters are either Guaraní, Spanish, Portuguese, Italian, or *mestizo*. Within the parameters of the film's fictional space, therefore, English is not to be heard as English; instead, it should sound like the Ur-Romance language, like Latin perhaps. Certainly English does the work of an Ur-Western language in *The Mission:* Europeans, regardless of nationality and political bias, communicate flawlessly. Translators neither mediate their conversations nor mitigate their differences. Furthermore, because North American audiences understand the language of the Europeans, their respective positions cannot be represented as other to the viewers' sensibilities; the language of *The Mission*, its dependence on English, and its manipulation of other languages, makes the audience complicitous with both the physical and spiritual violence enacted upon the other, upon the Guaraní.

But English is not the Ur-Western language, and *The Mission* knows it. Romance languages are not transparent to one another, much less to American ears. *The Mission* subtly demonstrates the mutual opacity of Western discourses by insinuating Latin (on one occasion) and Spanish (three times) into certain scenes. These are not thematically important scenes. In them, Latin and Spanish merely provide the sounds of authenticity. For example, the film uses Latin when it blesses the soldiers who are about to kill the Indians. Here Latin is comprehensible because it is ritual speech accompanied by certain gestures: the bowing of heads, the signing of the cross. *The Mission* treats Spanish more severely, relegating it entirely to the background: a servant tells two Guaraní porters that they are in the wrong room ("están en la habitación equivocada"); a young missionary teaches Guaraní children to subtract; Robert De Niro, hearing cannon and gunshots coming from the direction of the mission, says "to mission, ... to the mission" ("a misión, ... a la misión"). The ellipses indicate the omission of De Niro's lines in Guaraní.

The two instances in which missionaries (played by De Niro and Rolfe Gray) speak Spanish are entirely unremarkable except that neither of the utterances is grammatically correct. De Niro's only Spanish lines "a misión, ... a la misión" omit in their first enunciation the definite article "la"—a la misión: to the mission. No doubt this is a minor oversight but to Spanish speakers it indicates a lack of fluency; it also signals a North American lack of respect for the integrity of other languages. The scene in which Rolfe Gray portrays a young missionary teaching Guaraní children to subtract has far greater significance for the discussion of the proximity of language and empire, for it teaches less the mathematical art of reduction than an inferior relation to Spanish. Again, this is an inconsequential scene that, for non-Spanish-speaking Americans, neither needs to be nor is translated, not because non-Spanish-speaking Americans intuitively understand the scene, but because (apparently) the scene makes no difference to the film's structural or thematic development.

Yet the scene makes a difference; it makes it in the Guaraní, for although the children respond to the missionary in Guaraní, they hear and understand his Spanish. The question they answer, however, "How many stones does he have to take away so that there are six left?" ("¿Cuántas piedras tiene que sacar para que quedan seis?"), if not grammatically impossible, is certainly barbarous. The grammatical structure "para que" requires the succeeding verb ("quedar") be conjugated in the subjunctive mood.[29] The difference, then, is one of a letter, the difference between "quedan" (present indicative) and "queden" (present subjunctive).

The effects of this "defective" pedagogy become apparent when the Guaraní attempt to speak "Spanish" (English): it happens only once and the scene is instructive. The papal envoy has traveled to the mission above the falls, San Carlos, and, in spite of its favorable impression, his conscience (de facto and de jure a letter in his pocket received before he left the great mission of San Miguel) dictates that he recommend relinquishing the mission territories to the Portuguese. Much could be made of the relationship between the ambassador's conscience and the letter from Portugal: upon receiving the letter, the ambassador claims to the missive's courier not to have to open it in order to know what it contains; this is the sign that the letter's spiritual essence, its embodiment, its ciphering, in no way impinges on its expressive essence. Such a letter, such an ex-pressed interiority can be delivered, carried, communicated without involving, without including within itself the fact of its communication.[30] The messengers or bearers remain free of the letter. As we have already noted, this was not the case with messages sent in the *Popol Vuh*. The papal envoy's position, however, does suggest the density of communication, approximating the *Popol Vuh* at the same time it articulates a Western (i.e., European) difference.

The ambassador arrives in the Americas with one express purpose, specifically, to relay the pope's message, to communicate the pope's desire. And, as the envoy tells the Guaraní in San Carlos, the Church—which is to say, the pope—is God's *instrument* (*lengua*, perhaps: tongue, interpreter, language, information) on earth. We see, then, the double incarnation or, better, *embocamiento*[31] of the ambassador's words: God: pope: envoy. The messenger is the message. This is not a nod to Marshall McCluhan; rather, the messenger (the envoy) is the message (the *envoi*) because of the play between envoy, *envoyé, envoyer*, and *envoi*. Despite the scene's structural approximation to scenes in which messages are delivered in the *Popol Vuh*, however, this scene from *The Mission* differs fundamentally: although the envoy invokes God and the pope, he does so rhetorically to legitimate, to authorize his

words, his conscience. No rigorous literality operates here, no citation of God's message, framed by the pope's, conveyed by the
ambassador.[32]

At the mission called San Carlos the problems of delivery and
the authority of one's speech come to the fore. After the arrival
of the envoy, but prior to the delivery of his letter, *The Mission*
stages translation. At opposite ends of a long table sit the tribal
elders or chiefs of the Guaraní and the papal envoy. Between
them sits Father Gabriel (Jeremy Irons). His is the most interesting
and, strangely, most marginal position. Contrary to the representation of the first encounter between Cortés and Moctezuma, in
which Malinche, through whom all discourse passed, occupies
the center and most stable position, not all discourse between the
Guaraní and the pope's emissary must necessarily pass through
Jeremy Irons (Father Gabriel): only the papal ambassador requires
a translator/interpreter; the Guaraní understand Spanish—at least,
they understand *some* Spanish. The scene begins, in fact, by indicating the limitations of Guaraní understanding: Father Gabriel
tells the ambassador that he must speak more clearly, that the
Guaraní do not understand. From this point on, effectively the
papal envoy speaks nary a word directly to the Indians; instead
he addresses his own man, the Spanish translator.[33] It is clear the
Guaraní understand some Spanish: they do not always wait for
the translation before responding. But they always respond in
Guaraní, even though the overall sense of the discourse (of the
film) is conveyed in "Spanish" (English). In other words, decisions
of great significance for Guaraní life are made in Spanish, but the
Guaraní, who because of the language barrier are always outside
the decision-making process, outside the structures of power, have
no one *of their own* to validate the language *for them*. They depend on a foreigner to plead their case, in their place, in a foreign
tongue. Their only "Spanish" intervention is the "king's" heavily
accented, "it's your game, it's your game," spoken as he leaves the
"negotiation" table.

The issue, to be sure, is not, as it was in earlier conquest narratives, the "faithfulness" or "reliability" of the translator. The point
is the cultural shift in the place of the translator. Whereas earlier
the translators were Indians, now they are Spaniards. Whereas be-

fore the Spanish found themselves literally at a loss for words and at the mercy of the translator, now the Guaraní speak no Spanish and ineluctably rely on Spanish benevolence for the preservation of their culture.

The decision to conduct mission life in Guaraní had at least two political-historical consequences: (1) it facilitated the dissemination of Christianity by not alienating the Indians; in other words, the Guaraní gave up a certain system of beliefs, but not their linguistic heritage; and (2) it facilitated the eventual conquest and subjugation of the Guaraní by placing them in an inferior position with respect to Spanish. The young missionary's arithmetic lesson inculcates linguistic inferiority. The missionary, then, does the work not of the devil, as Don Cabeza of *The Mission* claims the Jesuits do, but of imperialism.

Doubtless, the Guaraní children learn to subtract without the subjunctive, but they do not learn Spanish without it. More precisely, they learn a debased Spanish that subordinates them to Spanish eloquence and rule. Linguistic subordination becomes a fact of Guaraní life when, "After the expulsion of the Jesuits, Castilian is imposed as the obligatory and only language" ("A partir de la expulsión de los jesuitas, se impone a los indios la lengua castellana obligatoria y única" [Galeano 36, 44]). The Guaraní refused to vacate the missions; instead they chose and continue to choose to oppose their eloquent oppressors.[34] *The Mission*'s concluding scenes (before the credits) suggest the Guaraní's perseverance: the naked children setting off from the destroyed mission to begin again. Between this concluding scene and the credits, *The Mission* interposes two texts:

> The Indians of South America are still engaged in a struggle to defend their land and culture.

> Many of the priests who, inspired by faith and love, continue to support the rights of the Indians for justice, do so with their lives.

> "The light shines in the darkness and the darkness has not overcome it." John, Chapter 1, Verse 5.

These texts make clear that *The Mission* little concerns the Guaraní Indians. We might ask, for example, to whose culture the text refers when it remarks the Indians' "struggle to defend their land and culture." Implicitly the film identifies mission life and Guaraní culture; yet we know that European missionaries who subdued the Indians imported this culture from Europe and imposed it in the Americas. It would seem, then, that the light shining in the darkness is a Christian one, and the darkness it insistently illuminates is nothing other than indigenous culture.

The semantic ambiguity of these concluding texts serves to make the film ideologically even more complex and the position of the Guaraní ontologically even more precarious. In a film that ostensibly centers on the encounter between Guaraní Indians and Jesuit missionaries, the marginalization of the Guaraní and their culture indicates that in *The Mission* the Guaraní struggle without hope. They do so because, grammatically, hope is a function of the subjunctive.

The paradox of the pedagogical scene in which the young Jesuit teaches arithmetic by employing a grammatical impossibility is that in presenting this scene *The Mission* wittingly or not undermines the Jesuit directive, which was to disseminate the Word of God in the New World. The God the Jesuits introduce to the Guaraní is a Western construct, constituted in and of Western discourse. Such a God, Nietzsche suggests, depends on Western grammar. *The Mission*'s representation of the Jesuits' latent imperialism bears witness to grammatical decadence and, in a certain way, to the death of God. In *The Order of Things*, quoting Nietzsche, Michel Foucault explains: "God is perhaps not so much a region beyond knowledge as something prior to the sentences we speak; and if Western man is inseparable from him, it is not because of some invincible propensity to go beyond the frontiers of experience, but because his language ceaselessly foments him in the shadow of his laws: 'I fear indeed that we shall never rid ourselves of God, since we still believe in grammar''' (298).[35]

Notes

1. Translations of passages from the *Gramática* are my own. Stephen Greenblatt and Tzvetan Todorov cite the first part of this passage; see Greenblatt; Todorov.

2. "siempre la lengua fue compañera del imperio; [y] de tal manera lo siguió, que junta mente comen[z]aron, crecieron [y] florecieron, [y] después junta mente fue la caida de entrambos" (97).

3. "I será necessaria una de dos cosas: o que la memoria de vuestras hazañas perezca con la lengua; o que ande peregrinando por las naciones estrangeras, pues que no tiene propria casa en que pueda morar" (101).

4. "El tercero provecho deste mi trabajo puede ser aquel que, cuando en Salamanca di la muestra de aquesta obra a vuestra real Majestad, [y] me preguntó que para qué podía aprovechar, el mui referendo padre Obispo de Avila me arrebató la respuesta; [y], respondiendo por mí, di[j]o que después que vuestra Alteza metiesse deba[j]o de su jugo muchos pueblos bárbaros [y] naciones de peregrinas lenguas, [y] con el vencimiento aquellos ternían necesidad de recibir las leies quel vencedor pone al vencido [y] con ellas nuestra lengua, entonces por esta mi *Arte* podrían venir en el conocimiento della" (101-102). Earlier Nebrija claimed that his intention in writing the *Gramática* was "... to increase the things of our nation" ("engrandecer las cosas de nuestra nación" [100]).

5. "... tenía jurisdicción sobre todas las demás [facultades] en lo tocante a la lengua, que es el instrumento de todas" ("Introduction" 17).

6. Perhaps no empire had done this so well as the Inca; see Garcilaso de la Vega, book 7, chapters 1-3.

7. "doña Marina sabía la lengua de Guazacualco, que es la propia de Méjico, y sabía la de Tabasco, como Jerónimo Aguilar sabía la de Yucatán y Tabasco, que es toda una. Entendíanse bien, y el Aguilar lo declaraba en castilla a Cortés; fue gran principio para nuestra conquista... porque sin ir doña Marina no podíamos entender la lengua de la Nueva España y Méjico" (*Historia verdadera* 85).

8. "Y con Melchorejo... que entendía ya poca cosa de la lengua de Castilla y sabía muy bien la de Cozumel, se lo preguntó a todos los principales" (66).

9. "Y luego [Cortés] mandó llamar al cacique y a todos los principales, y al mismo papa, y como mejor se pudo dárselo a entender con aquella nuestra lengua..." (67).

10. "En cuatro días del mes de marzo de mill e quinientos y diez y nueve años, habiendo tan buen suceso en llevar buena lengua y fiel, mandó Cortés..." (73).

11. "Y desque Cortés los vio puestos en aquella manera, dijo a Aguilar, la lengua, que entendía bien la de Tabasco, que dijese a unos indios..." (140).

12. "... en todos los pueblos por donde pasamos, [y] en otros donde tenían noticia de nosotros, llamaban a Cortés Malinche.... Y la causa de haberle puesto aqueste nombre es como doña Marina, nuestra lengua, estaba siempre en su compañía, especial cuando venían embajadores o pláticas de caciques, y ella lo declaraba en la lengua mejicana, por esta causa llamaban a Cortés el capitán de Marina, y para más breve le ll[a]maron Malinche" (149).

13. See the *Popol Vuh*, translated by Dennis Tedlock, 133; Professor Tedlock alerted me to this passage in particular and to the structural embedment of messages in the *Popol Vuh* in general. For other examples, see pages 109, 110, 130, 131,

among others. See also the story of how the louse arrives to deliver its message to Hunahpu and Xbalanque (131+); the louse's arrival, its mode of transport, mimics the structural embedding of messages within messages.

14. "y allí comenzó a tomar su agua y a les decir con el dicho faraute que les diesen oro y que les darían de las preseas que llevaban" (16).

15. "El capitán le habló con el intérprete" (19).

16. "el dicho capitán les habló con la lengua y faraute que llevábamos y con el dicho Jerónimo de Aguilar... que entendía muy bien y hablaba la lengua de aquella tierra" (22).

17. *Lengua* also means "information" (see *Cartas* 35) as well as "interpreter."

18. "... *les hablé con las lenguas que yo tengo*" (*Cartas* 103). Pagden translates this sentence, "When the prisoners arrived I questioned them most diligently through my interpreters to learn the truth, and it appeared that the captain had misunderstood them" (*Letters* 149). The italicized part of the sentence corresponds to what I translated in the text proper.

19. "E de allí me fui por la costa con alguna gente para saber *lengua*" (*Cartas* 35; emphasis added).

20. "Y luego mandó traer los dos indios y la india..., y con el indio Melchorejo ..., les habló." The English translation is clearly more ideologically loaded than Bernal Díaz del Castillo's Spanish original.

21. For one example among many: "Only a stone's throw from them appeared a large number of Indians, heavily armed, who with a great shout began to attack us with many javelins and arrows. I began to deliver the formal *requerimiento* through the interpreters who were with me and before a notary, but the longer I spent in admonishing them and requesting peace, the more they pressed us and did us as much harm as they could. Seeing therefore that nothing was to be gained by the *requerimiento* or protestations we began to defend ourselves as best we could.... We fought all day long until an hour before sunset, when they withdrew; with half a dozen guns and five or six harquebuses and forty crossbowmen and with the thirteen horsemen who remained, I had done them much harm without receiving any except from exhaustion and hunger" ("El no dos tiros de piedra dellos asomó mucha cantidad de indios muy armados y con muy gran grita, y comenzaron a pelear con nosotros, tirándonos muchas varas y flechas. E yo les comencé a facer mis requerimientos en forma, con los lenguas que conmigo llevaba, por ante escribano. E cuanto más me paraba a los amonestar y requerir con la paz, tanto más priesa no daban ofendiéndonos cuanto ellos podían. E viendo que no aprovecheban requerimientos ni protestaciones, comenzamos a nos defender como podíamos.... y peleamos con ellos, y ellos con nosotros, todo el día, hasta una hora antes de puesto el sol, que se retrajeron; en que con media docena de tiros de fuego, y con cinco o seis escopetas y cuarenta ballesteros, y con los trece de caballo que me quedaron, les fice mucho daño, sin recibir dellos ninguno más del trabajo y cansancio del pelear y la hambre" [*Letters* 59; *Cartas* 40-41]).

22. See chapter 2, "Hernán Cortés: La ficcionalización de la conquista y la creación del modelo de conquistador," for an excellent discussion of Cortés's *Cartas de relación*.

23. Todorov writes: "We have also seen that the first interpreters are Indians; the latter do not have the entire confidence of the Spaniards, who often wonder if

422 ◆ DAVID E. JOHNSON

the interpreter is accurately transmitting what he is told" (98); Todorov's choice of "transmitting" to describe the interpreter's function is telling; "transmit," its technical sound, connotes mechanicality, functionality; it is almost as if a failure to "transmit" accurately could have been a problem of dirty gears: Todorov cites Gomara, who writes of Cortés's first translator, Melchior, " 'This fellow was uncouth, being a fisherman, and it seemed he knew neither how to speak nor to answer' " (98).

24. "En aquellas escaramuzas prendimos tres indios: el uno dellos era principal. Mandóles el capitán que fuesen a llamar al cacique de aquel pueblo, y se les dió muy bien a entender con las lenguas, Julianillo y Melchorejo, que les perdonaban lo hecho, y les dió cuentas verdes para que les diesen en señal de paz. Se fueron y nunca volvieron, y creímos que los indios Julianillo Y Melchorejo no les debieron de decir lo que les mandaron, sino al revés. Estuvimos en aquel pueblo tres días" (35-36).

25. "salió al campo con ochenta de caballo y quinientos peones, . . . y llegó casi una legua de donde yo estaba; y como lo que de mi ida sabía era por lengua de los indios y no me halló, creyó que le burlaban y volvióse a su aposento" (*Cartas* 85).

26. "yo tuve uno de los naturales de la dicha ciudad, que por allí andaba, y le aparté secretamente, . . . y le interrogué, y confirmó con lo que la india y los naturales de Tascaltecal me habían dicho, e así por esto como por las señales que para ello había . . . en dos horas murieron más de tres mil hombres" (49).

27. For a discussion of the historical context of Joffé's *The Mission*, see Llanos and Sánchez.

28. I do not mean the Guaraní were unable to add and subtract prior to the missionaries' arrival; I refer to a specific scene in *The Mission* to which I shall return shortly.

29. Dr. Margarita Vargas of the University of Buffalo first directed my attention to this scene in *The Mission*.

30. The papal envoy's claim that he need not read the letter to know what it contains is not unlike the cinematic practice of reading letters in the voice not of the reader or receiver of the message, nor in the voice of the postman who delivered it, but in the voice of the sender as if the text, the fact of writing, in no way mediates the presence of the writer, of the writer's voice. For a recent example of a film, ironically about writing, that reads letters in the voice of the sender/author, see *Henry and June* (directed by Philip Kauffman, 1990).

31. I will allow myself the neologism. *Embocamiento* would be the Spanish word for literally being-in-the-mouth; to have a sense of this as a communicative structure, see the *Popol Vuh* (Tedlock translation) 131-133.

32. Yet the ambassador's "invocation" of God and the pope maintains a phonetic proximity to the *embocamiento* mentioned above. Both the English "to invoke" and the Spanish "invocar" derive from the Latin *invocare*. Moreover, the Spanish "invocar" sounds like "embocar": to put into the mouth. Thus , when the ambassador "calls upon" or "summons" (invokes, *invoca*) God and the pope, he figuratively makes them present to the interlocutors, which is to say he brings them forth from his mouth: in Spanish, *desembocar*. We see, then, that the language of invocation is literally the bringing forth of the other, to be present and to commu-

nicate his or her message in our place. The one who invokes is merely the courier, the messenger, of the word residing, as the *Popol Vuh* explains, in its belly:

"My word is contained in my belly..." said the falcon.
"So name it," they said to the falcon, and then he vomited a big snake.
"Speak up," they said next to the snake,
"Yes," he said next, then he vomited the toad. (132)

This scene from the *Popol Vuh* represents the beginning of the *desembocamiento* of the message to be delivered to Hunahpu and Xbalanque; the scene begins with the toad suggesting to the louse that the louse will arrive faster if it permits the toad to swallow it; a snake repeats this gesture with the toad and the falcon does the same with the snake. Upon arriving at the boys, the falcon spits up the snake; the snake spits up the toad; and the toad gives up the louse, who then delivers the message. It should be clear that the structure of communication articulated in this scene parallels exactly the structure of citation in the *Popol Vuh* discussed above. The falcon arrives at the boys (Hunahpu and Xbalanque) with a message, but rather than simply conveying the message as if it were his own, the falcon makes present to the boys the snake, and so on until the louse appears with the message.

33. It is interesting that the camera angles reify the cultural tie between the missionary (Jeremy Irons) and the ambassador. In the scene I am describing, the cameras typically show the Guaraní full-face, as if they are being seen from the ambassador's end of the table. The missionary, who sits between the Guaraní and the envoy, is most often shown in profile, and generally from the perspective of the ambassador, as if he stood to the side—on the side—of the missionary.

34. Michel de Certeau writes of their continuing struggle in "The Politics of Silence: The Long March of the Indians"; see *Heterologies*, 225-233.

35. Foucault, *The Order of Things*. Perhaps the displacement of the translator, like the strategy used by Cortés and described earlier in this essay, prevails in the discourses of the United States. Although Foucault's text was published in French and was titled *Les Mots et les choses*, the English translation referred to above lists no translator.

Works Cited

Barthes, Roland. *A Lover's Discourse.* Trans. Richard Howard. New York: Hill and Wang, 1978.

Certeau, Michel de. *Heterologies.* Trans. Brian Massumi. Minneapolis: Univ. of Minnesota Press, 1986.

Cortés, Hernán. *Cartas de relación de la conquista de México.* 7th ed. Madrid: Espasa-Calpe, 1982.

———. *Letters from Mexico.* Trans. and ed. Anthony Pagden. New Haven: Yale Univ. Press, 1986.

Díaz del Castillo, Bernal. *The Conquest of New Spain.* Trans. J. M. Cohen. New York: Penguin, 1963.

———. *Historia verdadera de la conquista de Nueva España.* 8th ed. Colección Austral. Madrid: Espasa-Calpe, 1989.

Foucault, Michel. *The Order of Things: An Archaeology of the Human Sciences*. New York: Vintage, 1970.

Galeano, Eduardo. *Memoria del fuego. Vol. 2. Las caras y las máscaras*. Mexico City: Siglo XXI, 1984.

——. *Memory of Fire: Faces and Masks*. Trans. Cedric Belfrage. New York: Pantheon, 1987.

Garcilaso de la Vega, El Inca. *Royal Commentaries of the Incas and General History of Peru*. Trans. Harold V. Livermore. Austin: Univ. of Texas Press, 1966.

Greenblatt, Stephen J. "Learning to Curse: Aspects of Linguistic Colonialism in the Sixteenth Century." *First Images of America*. Ed. Fredi Chiapelli et al. Vol. 2. Berkeley: Univ. of California Press, 1976.

Llanos, Bernardita, and Francisco J. Sánchez. "La Guerra de 1754: Sensibilidades y géneros literarios de la victoria imperial-criolla y la derrota indígena." *Ideologies and Literature*. New series 2.2 (1987): 77-107.

Nebrija, Antonio de. *Gramática de la lengua castellana*. Ed. Antonio Quilis. Madrid: Editora Nacional, 1980.

Pastor, Beatriz. *Discursos narrativos de la conquista: mitificación y emergencia*. Hanover, N.H.: Ediciones del Norte, 1980.

Popol Vuh. Trans. Dennis Tedlock. New York: Simon and Schuster, 1985.

Shakespeare, William. *The Tempest*. Ed. Frank Kermode. Cambridge: Methuen, 1954.

Todorov, Tzvetan. *The Conquest of America: The Question of the Other*. Trans. Richard Howard. New York: Harper & Row, 1984.

Chapter 14

Other-Fashioning: The Discourse of Empire and Nation in Lope de Vega's *El nuevo mundo descubierto por Cristóbal Colón*

Allen Carey-Webb

If, as in the case of the Indians, the entire republic, by common consent of all the subjects, does not wish to hear us, but retain the rituals of their lands, where there had never been Christians, in such a case we cannot wage war against them.

—Bartolomé de Las Casas

They were as close to me as a reflection in the mirror; I could touch them, but I could not understand them.

—Claude Lévi-Strauss

Once the liminality of the nation-space is established, and its "difference" is turned from the boundary 'outside' to its finitude "within," the threat of cultural difference is no longer a problem of "other" people. It becomes a question of the otherness of the people-as-one.

—Homi Bhabha

During the sixteenth century Spain had the largest and most imposing empire of any European power since Rome. From the Philippines to Africa, from Italy to Peru, it was, in fact, the first imperium on which "the sun never set." Spain was at the forefront of developing and expanding European nations, a model for dominion abroad and absolutism at home. On the peninsula the sixteenth-century agenda included the unification of the Spanish states, the expulsion of the last Moorish rulers, the use of the Inquisition as an instrument of the monarchy, the development of an elaborate system of taxation, and the creation of the most sophisticated state bureaucracy of the age. Nonetheless, absolutism was never complete. Spanish society was conflictive and heterogeneous, with competing centers of economic and political power, and religious, ethnic, class, and gender disparities.

The tensions of the age are present in the works of Lope de Vega, and his *comedia* entitled *El nuevo mundo descubierto por Cristóbal Colón* is exemplary in its diversity and epic proportions. Looking back across the century, the play (written between 1598 and 1603) stages the voyage of Columbus and the momentous "discovery" of the "New World." In addition to Columbus, its major figure, the drama depicts Ferdinand and Isabella, the king of Portugal, Spanish dukes, a Moorish king and his court, a group of allegorical figures including Religion, Providence, and Idolatry, the Devil himself, pilots, greedy sailors, a friar, and, most fascinating of all, Lope's version of native Caribbean islanders. The indigenous people are granted a third of the play's dialogue and include chiefs, princesses, and commoners. The Indians are represented as a fully established *Other* society—in their own setting, with their own social hierarchy, responding as a group and as individuals to contact with Columbus and his men.

The attention given by some social theorists in recent years to the issue of alterity, or "Otherness," has not been extended to Lope's *El nuevo mundo*.[1] Yet this play, contemporaneous with active Spanish colonization of Mesoamerica, is at least as relevant to understanding Spanish perceptions of Columbus, conquest, and Native Americans as an explorer's diary, conquistador's letter, or contemporary scholar's "ethnography." Moreover, since accounts of the first explorers had been available for decades, and fifty years had passed since the famous debate between Bartolomé de Las Casas and Ginés de Sepúlveda on the justness of war against the Indians, Lope's play is a critical site for investigating the development and reproduction of Spanish attitudes toward "New World" peoples. J. H. Elliott writes, "If Spain was a pioneer among the bureaucratic states of modern Europe, it was also a pioneer among the European colonial powers, and I believe that the implications of this pioneering role for both Spanish and European history have scarcely begun to be considered" (xiii). *El nuevo mundo*, then, allows us to consider the construction of identity of both colonized and colonizer during the formative period of European nation and empire.

While Lope's perceptions of Native Americans are drawn, in part, from the accounts of explorers and colonists, his "sources" do not provide transparent "truth" about the native peoples. These accounts, like the play itself, are "framed" in Spanish, European, and Western terms. The portraits of *indios* in *El nuevo mundo* are highly dependent on the complex history of *Spanish* and *European* religious, social, political, and rhetorical practices. It could hardly be otherwise, given the terrible fate of the Caribbean islanders, and neither their self-descriptions nor direct or indirect translations of their voices were available.[2] Michel de Certeau in his critique of Montaigne's essay "Of Cannibals," argues that there is a mutual and interactive validation between the Other's voice and dominant discourse when the voice of the Other is "framed":

> On the one hand, the frame is necessary to assure the
> strangeness of the picture. On the other, it draws upon
> the representation for the possibility of transforming itself:
> the discourse that sets off in search of the Other with
> the impossible task of saying the truth returns from afar
> with the authority to speak in the name of the Other and
> command belief. (69)

The presence of the constructed voice of the Other in *El nuevo mundo* does add validity to the frame; the portrait of the Indians enhances Columbus's "accomplishment."

Nevertheless, the established view of Lope de Vega as consistently orthodox and highly nationalistic has led scholars of his work to miss the conflictive, disruptive, or even subversive ideas found in his writing, and to fail to consider the mechanisms by which such ideas may be contained, controlled, or framed. Walter Cohen argues that putting the history of the nation on stage and representing different and latently conflictive voices establishes the possibility of evaluation and judgment of national action.[3] Cohen distinguishes Spanish and English historical drama, suggesting that, for the Spanish, external conflicts are of critical importance:

> In England the enemy is within and the subject is conflict.
> Spain is the opposite: the English define themselves
> by what they are, the Spanish by what they are not.

> All appearances to the contrary, the Hispanic nation is internally harmonious; it has exported its problems. The late-sixteenth-century Golden Age national history play, regardless of its temporal or geographic setting, tends to emphasize the struggle between Catholic Spain and its infidel, external foes. (226-277)

The depiction on the dramatic stage of people of another culture before, during, and after Columbus's arrival in *El nuevo mundo* stages a dialogic situation, and when the radical Other is incorporated into European discourse destabilizing, even subversive, possibilities arise. Native American difference can suggest the relativism of cultural formations, the historical and contingent nature of knowledge and power. The effort to describe the Indian can lead to a "linguistic impotence" that may "open up new spaces in the colonial construction of reality" (Jara and Spadaccini 16).

I treat *El nuevo mundo*, then, as internally conflictive, intertextually assembled, and socially, historically, and politically imbedded. In its fabrication of a colonized Other the play is an instance of colonial discourse, described by Homi Bhabha in pivotal terms as "an apparatus that turns on the recognition and disavowal of racial/cultural/historical differences" and "a form of governmentality that in marking out a 'subject nation,' appropriates, directs and dominates its various spheres of activity" ("The Other" 154). While the recognition of *difference* between Spaniard and Indian in the play tends to highlight Indian inferiority and justify systems of colonial administration and instruction, in *El nuevo mundo* it is the complex "disavowal" of difference that most fundamentally marks the treatment of Native Americans. Even as forms of *likeness* may establish grounds for claims against empire or its "excesses," such claims are both *in* and *on* Spanish terms. Indeed, likeness between Spaniard and *indio* in this play is crucial to the appropriating, directing, and dominating activities of national as well as colonial government and power.

Generic Conventions

El nuevo mundo is a *comedia*, and the requirements of the genre have a powerful influence on the portrayal of Native Americans in the text. As a popular form, the *comedia* tends to make the Other comprehensible; it naturalizes, "de-exoticizes." The *indio* in *El nuevo mundo* speaks Spanish and even refers to Greek mythology. As the centripetal forces of generic convention pull the Other toward the self, the identity of the constructed Native American subject almost seems to merge with that of the traditional Spanish hero.

Thus it is not surprising that the male Native American figures have many of the traits of the *comedia*'s well-bred *caballero*. Dulcanquellín, the Indian chief/king, is eloquent in his efforts before the arrival of the Spanish to persuade a maiden, Tacuana, to love him, and despite having won her in battle, he is respectful of her wishes to postpone their wedding. After a long catalogue of the mineral, fauna, and floral wealth of his kingdom, he tells Tacuana, "It is a fortunate and beautiful land, but so much greater is my affection that there is nothing so rich that can compare with it" (358).[4] Values from the pastoral tradition are attributed to Dulcanquellín: a genteel eloquence, a pride in his country, and respect for wishes of the object of amorous affection.[5] Tacuana's husband, Tapirazu, is every inch the wronged, yet honorable, Spanish nobleman. Valiant, noble, and dedicated to Tacuana, he risks his life by entering Dulcanquellín's court alone, and ignoring the advice of his frightened warriors, he challenges Dulcanquellín to duel.

The Native American characters in the play are motivated by the classic emotions of the Spanish and European stage. Even the moment that the *indios* are most opposed to the Spanish, their violent rebellion near the end of the play, has its roots in a stereotypically Spanish situation: jealousy and rage over deception by a rival suitor. Dulcanquellín and Tapirazu join forces to seek revenge for what they perceive as chicanery of one of the Spanish colonists, Terrazas, with whom Tacuana has an amorous relationship. These actions construct the *indio* male as a familiar character, one Lope's audience would respect, and even admire.[6]

Moor and Indian

The representation of the Native Americans in *El nuevo mundo* draws in part on the stereotypical presentation of another "nonbeliever" and a common figure in Spanish writing, the Moor. In a recent discussion of the image of the Moor in sixteenth-century Spanish literature Israel Burshatin observes that,

> Depictions fall between two extremes. On the "vilifying" side, Moors are hateful dogs, miserly, treacherous, lazy and overreaching. On the "idealizing" side, the men are noble, loyal, heroic, courtly—they even mirror the virtues that Christian knights aspire to—while the women are endowed with singular beauty and discretion. (117)

The duality evident in the treatment of the Moor is also present in the description of the Indians met by Columbus. We have already seen *indios* as "Christian noblemen" within the *comedia*, yet certain aspects of the "vilifying" extreme can also be found in *El nuevo mundo*. Though the Native Americans are never referred to as dogs, they are called "animales rudos" (rude animals) by Friar Buyle when he first sees them looking at the enormous cross erected by the Spaniards (366), and referred to as "bárbaros bueyes" (barbarous cattle) by the Spaniard Terrazas (369). Nevertheless, the Indians are never presented as "miserly," "overreaching," or particularly "lazy." To the extent that they might possibly be seen as "treacherous," in their rebellion at the end of the play, they are clearly reacting to a deception practiced by the Spaniards Columbus leaves behind when he returns to Spain.

One reason that *El nuevo mundo* itself is such a fascinating textual fragment in the genealogy of Spanish perceptions of the Other is that in one text it includes scenes with the "traditional Other," the Moorish enemies, and scenes with the "new Other," Native American colonial subjects. The coincidence in 1492 of the expulsion of the Moors from the peninsula and the discovery of the New World links Moor and *indio* together in Spanish national history and consciousness, a point underscored by the presence of Moors in a play about Columbus. Moreover, the well-established traditions of Christian Spain's struggle against the Moors were carried over to the campaigns in the Americas. Criticizing Todorov for failing to consider the influences of Spanish history on contemporary Renaissance views of Native Americans, Roberto González-Echevarría points out,

The Spaniards had "prepared" themselves for this complex military, political, and social event [the American conquest] in the wars of reconquest against the Arabs. These wars, which lasted for eight centuries and culminated when the Catholic Kings took Granada in 1492, had been very much like the campaigns Cortés waged against Moctezuma.... The kind of holy war the Spaniards waged against the Indians was a reflection of the holy war the Arabs led against the Spaniards, with Santiago as the counterpart of Mohammed. The polemics of how to treat a different culture that had been defeated did not begin with Montesino's sermon but in recently conquered Granada.... (285)

The relevance of the experience with the Moors to the conquest, administration, and imagination of Spanish relations with the New World cannot be overemphasized. Edward Said's important study of "Orientalism," the complex interpenetration of knowledge and the practices of colonial domination, does not treat Spain, yet European imagination and domination of the Other has important roots in the history of Spanish/Arab conflict and, subsequently, in the Spanish empire.

In *El nuevo mundo* itself two key aspects are common to both the Moors and *indios:* (1) an immoral sensuality, which among the Moors is decadence and among the Indians licentiousness, and (2) a weakness of military tactics: among the Moors and the Native Americans there is passivity until the time for effective action has passed. In the scenes of the Moorish court in the Alhambra, the king of Granada is more interested in amorous dalliance with his courtesan than in preparing for battle against the Spaniards. Both Moorish and Indian women are portrayed as sensuously motivated, full of "el fuego de amor" (fire of love). When it comes to serious conflict, both Indians and Moors are passive until it is too late. The Moors surrender without a fight, and the Indians finally revolt, but quickly give in when the miraculous rising up of a cross convinces them of the truth of Christianity. Both of these traits, passivity and sensuousness, can be linked not only to racist stereotypes of the Moor, but to already coded gender identities as well.

Society, Literacy, and Domination

Spanish social distinctions are part of Lope's construction of the internal order of Native American society in *El nuevo mundo*. The aristocratic demeanor of Dulcanquellín, Tapirazu, and Tacuana is differentiated from Palca, Aute, and the common people. Dulcanquellín explains to the Spaniard Terrazas that even though he himself may be able to understand the new religion and even be convinced to follow it, it cannot be expected that the masses will go along or even be reasonable: "That there is nothing more fierce and indomitable than the common people and the will of the vulgar" (375).[7] This attitude toward the "masses" was probably familiar to the Spanish audience, though the potential for revolt it implies is distanced by placing it in the mouth of an *indio*. Nonetheless, one effect of casting established social differences into the New World is that these differences are universalized and, hence, naturalized for the peninsular audience.

Social distinctions are transferred to the relationship between Spaniard and *indio* in part through European attitudes toward literacy. There are two comic scenes in the third act where Aute, an untrustworthy *indio* commoner, is portrayed as baffled and frightened by the power of writing. Put to work delivering messages for the newly established Spanish settlements, Aute is discovered to have eaten oranges entrusted to him. Aute believes the message paper he was carrying "watched" him and spoke to the friar, revealing his theft. Later, while stealing olives, Aute hides the accompanying written message in a tree so it will not "see" what he does, and is found out again. As in Shakespeare's *Romeo and Juliet* when Romeo and Mercutio taunt Capulet's illiterate servant, the scene achieves a comic effect by playing on the "lower class" person's lack of education and ignorance of the written word. In the nascent colonial economy pictured in *El nuevo mundo*, literacy is a powerful weapon of social reproduction and social control. The *indio* is foolish, untrustworthy, a danger to the goods of the European, and needful of a proper education.

At stake in these "speaking paper" or "talking book"[8] scenes is the ability, through writing, to dominate a social and a commercial interaction. The indigenous people are portrayed as unable to comprehend an impersonal system; the *indio* needs the Spaniard (as the peasant needs the aristocrat) to bring about "rational" exchange. While the Native American's illiteracy, like that of the Spanish peasant, is taken as an indication of stupidity, the participation of Native Americans in an oral culture does not mean, of course, that Caribbean islanders did not work within a well-defined or highly complex sign system. Walter D. Mignolo comments:

> It is interesting to point out in connection with the topic of literacy and colonization, first the attribution of "low" degrees of language development to human communities, and second, that human societies were ranked in the chain of being according to their lack of possession of alphabetic writing. (77)

Closely connected to the mission to Christianize the Indians, prejudicial institutions of literacy played a crucial role in the colonial undertaking:

> The Conquest of America was carried out by the first modern state and with the aid of the printing press. Spain's monarchy was a patrimonial bureaucracy that sought to regulate all transactions of power through writing, a symbolic code that replaced the more direct communication of serfs with their lords. A maze of writing mediated the individual and the state, and it was only through writing that the individual attained legitimacy. (González-Echevarría 289)

René Jara and Nicholas Spadaccini assert, "The domination of the New World was ultimately achieved through writing which was the primary vehicle for the establishment, rationalization, and control of the overseas institutions of the Empire" (10). The privileging of literacy in European society is linked then to advancing capitalism, the development of imperial administration, and the rise of the nation state.

The *requerimiento* is the prototypical example of *text* justifying conquest. Informing the Indians that their lands were entrusted by Christ to the pope and thence to the kings of Spain, the document offers freedom from slavery for those Indians who accept Spanish rule. Even though it was entirely incomprehensible to a non-Spanish speaker, reading the document provided sufficient justification for dispossession of land and immediate enslavement of the indigenous people. Las Casas's famous comment on the *requerimiento* was that one does not know "whether to laugh or cry at the absurdity of it" (3: 58). While it may be absurd, in the *requerimiento* we can see "the recognition and disavowal of racial/cultural/ historical differences" that is the basis of colonialist discourse. Indians are different from Spaniards in that they are subjected to the reading of the text; they are presented with a "choice" between slavery and obedience not forced on Spaniards. Yet Indians are assumed to be enough like Spaniards that they can understand the *requerimiento*'s conditions; thus the text incorporates Native Americans and Spaniards into the same discursive space. The construction of Native Americans as like Spaniards "offers" Native Americans a "choice"; however, it is a choice couched entirely in a Spanish vocabulary, and, as Todorov puts it, "it is the Spaniards who determine the rules of the game" (148). While appearing to respect "rights" the *requerimiento*, in fact, takes them away. We can see, perhaps more clearly than Lope or his audience, that Aute's sense that the paper has betrayed him is not farcical after all.

"Understanding," "Sympathy," and "Respect"

Analysis of the belief system and conversion of Lope's *indios* is relevant to an examination of the principal ideological justification for Spanish colonialism, the spread of Catholic Christianity. In *El nuevo mundo* Lope rejects Columbus's belief that Native Americans have no religion and embraces the view that the Christian devil is, in reality, the Indian's God. Thus, even while being "idolatry," Native American religion is actually part of Christianity. The representation of Native Americans as having a "religion" and the representation of that religion as being within the framework of Catholicism establishes a mutual space, creating an important point of likeness between *indio* and Spaniard and making possible what appears to be understanding, sympathy, and respect.

Constructed Native American idolatry is never scathing nor are Indian beliefs ever presented as profoundly strange or foreign. Despite Menéndez y Pelayo's comment that Lope's portrayals of the Indians "provide a contrast between the savage life and that of the European adventurers" (104), what is most remarkable about Indian religion is its comprehensibility. A conversation that takes place between Dulcanquellín and his god, Ongol, in the pagan temple is reminiscent of a previous conversation of Columbus and the allegorical figures of Idolatry and the Devil that took place in Spain. The customs of Lope's *indios* are not abhorrent to Spaniards. In the Indian worship of Ongol there are no evil rites, no unspeakable Conradian atrocities, not even the infamous human sacrifice. Although there is cannibalism, this is not associated with Native American religion nor is it emphasized in the play. Indeed, when Dulcanquellín orders four fat servants cooked to feed the Spanish, the overriding effect is comic, and cultural difference is made a point of light humor.

What *El nuevo mundo* suggests is that the *indios* need not so much to end pagan practices as merely to convert the object of these practices from the Christian devil to the Christian God. Until the climactic scene, the Native Americans are portrayed as "confused." When Dulcanquellín asks Terrazas for an explanation of how it could be that the Caribbean Indian god and "idols" were "thrown out of heaven" by the Spanish god, he receives a lengthy, detailed history of the Christian faith. Dulcanquellín's response elicits sympathy,

> All this seems to me
> very long and complicated.
> Let the father come
> and we will consider the matter at length.
> For since I have given the gold, from which you have made
> what you call a chalice and other vessels,
> I do not deny that I am a lover [of your faith]. (376)[9]

Menéndez y Pelayo in his introduction to the play claims that Lope would not have read Las Casas, but it is clear that Lope is familiar with the argument that the Indian's spiritual equality requires a more sympathetic conversion than that of the sword and/

or the *requerimiento*. Moreover, the Las Casas stance is clearly articulated in the play in a way that appears to be respectful of Indian
culture and history while offering the *option* of Christianity. Dulcanquellín, the Indian king, suggests to Columbus's brother that
a peaceful promulgation of religion would be the most successful
way to win over his people.

> Bartolomé, I believe what you say;
> I fear your God and your arguments;
> But this law and faith that we profess,
> we have it as we received it.
> Our parents who taught it to us here,
> learned it from their grandparents before them...
> Let the people hear mass, and allow
> them to love your Christ and his laws...,
> so that from them could be born without doubt
> the [idea of] casting their idols to the ground,
> For the triumph and glory of God so high,
> so powerful, and strong. (375)[10]

While the Las Casas position for the spiritual equality of Indian and Spaniard raises questions about methods of conversion,
it does not jeopardize the imperative to convert Native Americans,
instruct them in Spanish, and administer them under Spanish law.
The development of understanding, sympathy, and respect for the
constructed Native Americans in the play is based in large part
on their familiarity, the "disavowal of their racial/cultural/historical
difference." The limitation of likeness, its implication in the project
of colonialism despite its *apparent* subversiveness, is fully evident
in the climactic end of *El nuevo mundo*. Despite the persuasive artic-
ulateness of Dulcanquellín's address to Bartolomé, the movement
of the drama undermines tolerance and supports the position of
those who like Ginés de Sepúlveda argued for a holy war against
the *indios*.

Likeness and Control

A value system that subordinates all else to the saving of souls is established early in the play during the allegorical tribunal, with its echoes of Inquisition logic. Idolatry seeks to maintain her pre-existing claim to the "new" land Columbus intends to "discover," and tries to argue that the Spanish, for all their talk about religious motives, are, in fact, only interested in material gain. Idolatry claims that "under the pretext of religion, they seek silver and gold" (351).[11] But this powerful criticism of the conquest, a critique evidenced in the play by the actions of the Spanish sailors and in the court of world opinion in the formation of the Black Legend, is contained and controlled by being placed in the mouth of Idolatry. Religion can reject the claims of Idolatry because, "He who possesses with bad faith never prescribes" (351).[12] Religion's argument establishes the basic moral grounds for the rejection of claims made against the Spaniards.

Because both Indian and Spaniard are in peril when confronted by the absolute demands of the true faith, likeness to the Spaniard ceases to work in the Indian's interest. Likeness between *indio* and Spaniard is subversive only insofar as Spanish custom extends protection or rights to the Spanish citizen. Likeness is thus double-edged, and this is manifest in the ending of the play and turns on the idea that both Spaniard and Native American possess a "will," in the Christian sense of the term. In the last act, the corruption of the Spanish sailors and the ability of the devil to point this corruption out to Dulcanquellín lead the Indians to what appears to be a rational plan, to rebel against the Spanish and tear down their cross. Yet after being assaulted, in a startling *deus ex machina*, the cross miraculously rises up and the Indians cease their resistance, proclaiming the truth of Christianity. Dulcanquellín and the *indios* are won over by a dramatic, unexpected miracle, and it is Dulcanquellín, the Native American king and earlier exponent of Las Casas's philosophy, who makes the strongest assertion that any pretense of peaceful, rational conversion is no longer necessary. As a new convert Dulcanquellín declares, "Without doubt, the Christian religion is true; whoever should say 'no,' let him die" (378).[13] Conversion by miracle moots equality of intellect, "natural rights," and/or military strength, and *El nuevo mundo* underwrites a providential view of history.

There are no limits on the possessor of the true faith who seeks to reproduce this faith in Others; such is Inquisition logic. The contradiction between the spiritual equality of the Indians and their subjugation is resolved: their "spiritual equality" is ordained by the Spanish, who superimpose their own religious system on the indigenous American. Thus the *deus ex machina* ending, with its echoes of the *auto sacramental*, seals identity between Spaniard and *indio*, between colonizer and colonized. The irrelevance of rationality to a miraculous conversion of the will for both *indio* and Spaniard marks their most essential equality. Ironically, equality itself, the basis for the religious mission, is part of the program of subjugation. Thus, the consequences of constructing the colonized Other within one's own religious space are devastating to claims against empire. Since the Indian religion is only a reflection of Spanish Catholicism, moral arguments made by the colonized Other are engulfed by the totalizing framework of the universal faith.[14]

The position that denies the claims of the Other not only offers a powerful ideological weapon against subversion by contact with the Other, but against subversion from "within." It protects against *self*-awareness. For instance, social distinctions are explained by the Indian king, thus diffusing the insulting or subversive effect such an explanation might have in the mouth of a Spaniard. In the context of early seventeenth-century Spain, the real ideological threat is not the voice of any actual Native American, but the questions raised by Spaniards like Las Casas, who interrogate and attempt to "demystify" the official justification of the colonial mission. The Las Casas position can be clearly and sympathetically articulated in a *comedia* with Native American characters but is nevertheless confined and mastered.

The same play that portrays the Indians as intelligent, with souls worth saving, with traits and customs more like the Spanish than different from the Spanish, justifies even the most extreme excesses of colonial conquest, as Dulcanquellín pronounces, "whoever should say 'no,' let him die" ("quien dijere que 'no,' muera"). This position is foreshadowed in the second act when the Indians bow down before the same cross on hearing Spanish gunfire. Since the conversion of the will of the *indio* is so complete that the Native American becomes the spokesperson for the slaughter of nonbelievers, the crime of the Spanish conquest is projected onto its victims. Resistance by the *indio* is reason enough for further victimization. The dramatic structure of the play provides an emotional justification to Lope's audience for accepting Dulcanquellín's conclusion. Whereas up until almost the end of the play violence against the natives would have been unthinkable, the insurrection that culminates in the deadly attack on the Spaniards makes retribution on violent and dangerous pagans seem warranted, not only to Dulcanquellín but to the audience.

The rising up of the cross in the last act establishes for Lope's Indians their own sense of guilt for resisting the Spanish and their own recognition of the need for continued subservience to the Spaniard. The Indians speak as a chorus with one voice,

Tacuana: From today I begin to tremble.
Tapirazú: Today pole [of wood] you will become the
scepter of the King of these vassals.
Again, forgive us. (378)[15]

The constructed Indian voice asks for forgiveness, accepting guilt in the crucifixion and submitting to the authority of Christ as well as the Spanish king. Individual guilt is connected to the necessity for a hierarchical authority in the formation of the subject space of the Other. The reaction to the miracle of the cross posits *a desire to be colonized* in the mind of the Native American. The colonizer's desire to colonize perceives its mate, and the Other is constituted as the projection and reflection of that desire. The powerful sexual language associated with the rising up of the cross/pole/scepter is a striking overlay of religious, patriarchal, feudal, and nationalistic images. Various European discourses of power are brought together, and the represented Native American himself pronounces his inferior, submissive position as penitent, vassal, subject, and "female."

Female Desire

Like the photo of the African saluting the French flag analyzed by
Barthes in *Mythologies* (99), the story of Malinche is detached from
historical events, from the "signified," and becomes a symbol, a
"sign," that can be manipulated by colonizing discourse without
pointing to itself as transported or reinvented. A Nahuatl (Aztec)
speaker sold as a slave to the Mayas, Malinche, also known as "Malintzin" to the Indians and "Doña Marina" to the Spanish, was
given to Cortés and became his translator, mistress, and tactical advisor. Generalized as the representative figure of Native American
women under colonialism, her story of female desire for the European colonizer becomes "natural, eternally true" for women of
disparate cultures and historical situations, and what is achieved is
what Barthes calls "the elimination" of "the contingent, historical,
in one word: fabricated, quality of colonialism" (131).[16]

In *El nuevo mundo* we can see how the Malinche story has, even
by the time of Lope, entered what Roland Barthes calls "mythical
speech." Although entirely anachronistic, Malinche is the generative model for the development of the three female Indian
characters met by Columbus and his men in *El nuevo mundo*—
Tecue, Palca, and Tacuana. The play incorporates and modifies the
Malinche model, projecting it backward in time to the very earliest
encounter of Spaniards and Native Americans.

Throughout the play these Indian women act as mediators
between the Spanish conquistadors and Native American males.
Tecue is the first to report on seeing the disembarked Spaniards.
Palca is the first to meet them and describe the innocence of Spanish intentions; her attraction to their bells and mirrors accommo-
dates Dulcanquellín and his court to the Spanish arrival. Palca
readily consorts with a Spaniard, Arana.

While each of the minor Indian female characters resembles
Malinche, Lope borrows most directly from the Malinche story for
the portrayal of Tacuana, the principal *india* character. Like Malinche, Tacuana has been taken from her family by a rival tribe,
turns to the Spanish because of divisions among the Native Americans, gives up her Indian husband in order to become a mistress to
a conquistador, and, finally, leaves her own people to join the camp

of the invaders. The colonial female in *El nuevo mundo* unambiguously desires the Spanish conquistador and Spanish colonialism.
Tacuana makes an elaborate speech of welcome to the Spanish soldiers, inviting them to spread their religion from "Haiti to Chile"
and requesting them to bring their sons to the "New World" so that
they can " . . . marry with our daughters, and mix their blood with
ours that we may all become Spanish" (371).[17] While the significance of the play to the construction of the nation is developed in
the next section, we should note in this passage that nationality is a
matter of blood, of race. Spanish blood does not mix; it transforms,
and the indigenous woman is a willing vessel for the metastasis of
racial, cultural, and national identity.

Tacuana's sexual desire is not portrayed as carefree, "natural," or unreflective along the lines of Rousseau's "noble savage."
Nor is Tacuana's desire a humble submission before the God-like
power of a conquering hero. Instead—and this is what makes it
all the more persuasive as justification for Spanish treatment of indigenous women—Tacuana's effort to become Terrazas's mistress
involves a careful ratiocination and an awareness of the appearance of propriety:

> Enough, for this Spaniard
> is not God, for he does not know
> what I am thinking:
> I am beside myself thinking of his love;
> for with this invented story,
> feigning such reasons,
> I will go to his arms submissively
> so that he may take and carry me off.
> He thinks he is forcing me,
> but love surrenders me without force
> where my grief may rest
> from so much danger. (371-372)[18]

The Malinche model depends on the notion of intelligent submission: knowing full well who the Spanish are and what they

desire, the Indian woman allies herself with the conquerors, opening soul, heart, and body to their designs. The portrayal of a willed submission of the body by the indigenous female supports the usurpation of the body of indigenous men and women into slavery and forced labor in the Spanish New World empire. Tacuana's sexual desire for the Spanish colonizer is linked to Dulcanquellín's desire for Christianity; both legitimate colonialism. Yet Spanish attitudes toward women express themselves in the differences between Dulcanquellín and Tacuana. The woman's desire is portrayed as guided by her intellect but ruled by her body. As a woman she does not occupy a public political space.[19] Because she belongs less to the Indian culture and more to her private need, her desire is traitorous to the nation.

National Identity

Benedict Anderson points to a discrepancy between the relative recentness of nation states and the antiquity of their self-justifications. The discourse of nationalism, which Anderson dates from the end of the eighteenth century, "turns chance into destiny" (19), fabricating connections between people stretching forward and backward through time. European nationalism needs to be understood, he argues, not only on the basis of self-consciously held ideologies but on the large cultural systems that preceded it, the religious community and the dynastic realm. Written at the juncture of imperial power and the coalescing of the modern nation state, *El nuevo mundo* in its depiction of Spain's national history is an embodiment of protonationalist discourse.[20] In retelling a hundred-year-old story of colonial encounter and Spanish accomplishment, *El nuevo mundo* unifies present and past in a Christian and national view of history, fashioning Spanish national identity on the world stage.

El nuevo mundo descubierto por Cristóbal Colón celebrates a saintly national hero.[21] Absolutely confident of the existence of the Indies, Columbus is driven by divine inspiration. The play follows the chronicles of Oviedo and Gómara and the opinion of Las Casas summarized in Todorov's statement that "infinitely more than gold, the spread of Christianity is Columbus's heart's desire" (10).

A comparison to Phaeton, Apollo's overreaching son, by one of Columbus's potential patrons is proved false in the play: throughout Columbus is upright, confident, and faithful. The carefully constructed figure of Columbus is metonymic for both the Spanish state and religion, and it is King Ferdinand himself who proclaims that Columbus was predestined by his name, "Christóbal" (378). Spanish national identity is embodied in this male hero whose nobility, certainty, and discovery and conquest of the "New World" enact the truth of Christian religion and fulfill national destiny.

El nuevo mundo also provides evidence for Anderson's claim that the religious community is closely connected to the rise of national identity. According to Menéndez y Pelayo, throughout the diversity of settings and the telescoping of historical events in El nuevo mundo there is a "unity of the great enterprise, interpreted with an undeniably religious and patriotic sense" (105). Although Columbus appeals to both the Portuguese and English monarchs' desire for material gain, Ferdinand and Isabella are appealed to on a specifically religious basis. The Spanish rulers are not only more moral than their European counterparts, their support of Columbus is motivated by divine will,

> For mourning Jesus
> that he [the Devil] should reign among you
> who shed his blood
> on the cross, death having died,
> He [Christ] orders Ferdinand of Spain,
> Christian and prudent King,
> to send Columbus
> He who will convert you to his faith. (376)[22]

The linkages between religious community and nation state allow the carry-over of self-justifying ideology, and the same ideological system that ensures the divine right of kings also protects the colonial enterprise. This is not surprising since in European history nationalism arises simultaneously with imperialism. Justifications of power that flow from religious community to nation and empire can also work in reverse. While a religious national-

ism insulates colonialism, colonial domination develops and sat-
isfies national pride. Moreover, the state itself owes some of its
ideological and institutional force to the particular history of the
colonial relationship.[23] A genealogy of nationalism must recognize
national identity as discursive, institutional, cultural, and dialectical. "Knowing the Other" solidifies the construction of a Spanish
self; the action of defining the Indian simultaneously participates
in the creation of a Spanish "imagined community."

The construction of national identity in the play is not limited
to Spain. Even in *El nuevo mundo*, written in the early seventeenth
century, there are hints of the development of colonized nationalisms based on European principles. In a fascinating moment a
Spaniard advises the Indian ruler on how to govern his own people. When Dulcanquellín prepares to leave to find Tacuana rather
than attend Catholic mass, Terrazas tells him,

> There, in Spain, we say
> that the kings are the mirror
> where is seen the advice
> that we vassals follow. (374)[24]

The self-fashioning of the Spanish king in the "mirror" of public
opinion is a self-conscious strategy of absolutist politics, something we associate with Charles V (or Louis XIV). Yet Terrazas's
expression is double-edged, risking subversion in the same way
that Machiavelli's *The Prince* risks subversion: the open expression
of the modeling of power denaturalizes it.[25]

In *El nuevo mundo* the glorified, self-conscious conduct of the
king is taught to the would-be colonized ruler, and nationalism
begins its march toward becoming a universal value. Tracing the
founding moments of colonized nationalism back to the time of
Columbus shows a transposition of European national models,
a "marking out of a 'subject nation,'" and it prefigures the difficulties encountered by the anticolonial nationalisms that arise
hundreds of years later. In the disappointing postcolonial experience of many "Third World" nations is evident the tainted history
of adopted nationalism. The construction of "nationalities" as natural and eternal markers of difference serves the interests of elites

in the margins as well as the center. Yet, progressive possibilities are evident too in the interrogation of nationalist structures of identity that cross over and back between colonizer and colonized, between "metropolis" and "periphery." The analysis of the depicted Other in *El nuevo mundo*, its breakdown into constituent parts, reveals not so much the eternal nature of Otherness but the conflictive heterogeneity of the constructed and hegemonic national "self."

Notes

1. An MLA computer search produced references to two articles (Dille, "El descubrimiento," and Weiner). In 1980 a French edition of the play included relevant notes and introduction (Lemartinel). A chapter of Robert Shannon's 1985 Ph.D. dissertation (published in 1989) is the only attempt to treat the play thoroughly. Shannon makes a source-influence study of the relation of specific conquest narratives to three Lope plays: "I hope to identify in the play the sources which Lope has followed in the process of artistic creation and where he has departed from the lead in order to reveal, perhaps, his own personal observation" (8). Shannon believes that Lope drew on the accounts of both Gómara and Oviedo in *El nuevo mundo*, but followed neither one very closely. Shannon's analysis is limited by (1) his interest in Lope's "personal" perspective; (2) his treatment of the Conquest accounts as independent of Spanish discourse and transparently "real," and; (3) his apparent acceptance of the position he ascribes to Lope " ... that the spiritual direction of the Conquest is of far greater importance and will, in the end, triumph and stand as Spain's overwhelming achievement in America" (91-92). Shannon is working on a bilingual critical edition of the play.

On the existence of other plays on Columbus, Glen Dille concludes that, not counting those that make simple allusions, there are only a dozen extant Spanish Golden Age plays on the subject. Dille does not specify how many of the twelve depict Native Americans. Menéndez y Pelayo in his scholarly introduction to the play (1898) calls it "the oldest dramatic production dedicated to the discovery of the New World" (translation mine).

2. While "in two years [after the Arawak rebellion of 1495] through murder, mutilation, or suicide, half of the 250,000 Indians on Haiti were dead," by 1650 in Haiti there simply were no "native informants" still alive (Zinn 4). Accounts by other "natives" from New Spain were not available during Lope's time. Garcilaso de la Vega, el Inca, did not publish *Comentarios reales* until 1609 and Guaman Poma's *Primer nueva corónica y buen gobierno* was not available until 1920.

3. "The audience witnessing a national history play at the public theater comes to feel that its own history is being performed. In a sense, such a belief is a corporatist illusion, especially since the crown's interests were not ultimately national. But it is also a progressive insistence on the right of the populace to judge the ruling class's exercise of state power. In this respect the national history play in the

public theater inherently subverts aristocratic ideology" (221). Reactions to Cohen by Hispanists can be found in Zahareas.

4. All quotations from *El nuevo mundo* are from the *Real Academia* edition. All translations are my own.

5. Shannon compares Dulcanquellín to "an idealized Christian king" and finds him "a symbol of tyranny, egotism, and moral and social corruption" (91). Shannon bases his view on Dulcanquellín's waging war on Haiti, abducting Tacuana, and, at times, showing uncertainty about the Christian faith. The second point may be the most persuasive, though I think Shannon overstates the case. Nonetheless, to the extent that Dulcanquellín is *different*, he differs in ways that suggest his unfitness as a ruler *in idealized Spanish terms*. Shannon's reading provides a more direct justification for Spanish colonialism than a reading that emphasizes likeness and familiarity, and is consistent with the polarities found in the treatment of the Moor.

6. Even in a *comedia* other generic conventions can be influential. The emphasis in *El nuevo mundo* on Christian faith, allegorical character, and miracle echoes the *auto sacramental*. Walter Cohen's argument that the secular *comedia* is a national form, containing the potentially conflictive voices of different social groups and classes does not apply to the *auto*, as he recognizes (379). A vehicle for the teaching of Christian doctrine, the *auto* is thus more monological and less conflictive than the *comedia*. The situation of the pagan Native American in *El nuevo mundo* can be compared to that of the unconverted Jew in *El niño inocente*, a *comedia* also thought to be influenced by the *auto sacramental*. Catherine Swietlicki argues against a straightforward reading of that play as anti-Semitic since she believes Lope authentically recreates the language of the Jewish Other. Nonetheless, according to Swietlicki, there is no question that "Within the metatheatrical *auto* the Jew's words are dominated by the monolithic Christian view..." (219). Like the *comedia* the *auto* "de-exoticizes," accommodating difference to preexistent patterns. In terms of the *auto* the Native American is in a well-known category, that of "nonbeliever." The intention to convert the nonbeliever is a conventional generator of plot, and the conversion to Christianity of the Native Americans is a driving mechanism of *El nuevo mundo*.

7.   "Que no hay cosa más fiera é indomable

         Que el común apellido y voz del vulgo."

8. Henry Louis Gates, Jr., argues that the "talking book" is the signal trope of African-American literature. Issues of literacy are thus critical to both colonial hegemony and counterhegemonic projects.

9.   "Muy largo y intricado y muy difícil

         Todo eso me parece; venga el padre

         Y trataremos con espacio deso;

         Que pues el oro dí, de que habéis hecho

         Lo que cáliz llamáis y otras vasijas,

         No niego que le soy aficionado..."

10.   "Bartolomé, yo creo lo que dices,

Temo tu Dios, y tus razones temo;

Pero esta ley y fe que profesamos,

Como la recibimos, la tenemos.

Nuestros padres, que aquí nos la enseñaron,

Ya de nuestros abuelos la aprendieron...

Deja que oigan esa misa, y deja

Que a tu Cristo y sus leyes aficionen...

Que de ellos mismos naciera sin duda

Dar por el suelo con los mismos ídolos,

En triunfo y gloria de ese Dios tan alto,

Tan poderoso y fuerte."

11.   "So color de religión,

Van a buscar plata y oro."

Prescott uses this line as an epigram in his famous history.

12.   "Quien posee con mala fe,

En ningún tiempo prescribe."

13.   "Sin duda que es verdadera

La cristiana religión;

Quien dijere que no, muera."

14. The attempted control of subversion by a totalizing system is by no means limited to the Spanish. By drawing connections between documents from the Plymouth Colony and Shakespeare's *Henry* plays, Stephen Greenblatt (1988) shows that by recording the potentially disturbing voice of the Other within the discourse of the culture in power, subversive ideas can be contained. In the case of *El nuevo mundo* where the Other is not something recorded in a document of direct contact, but instead is written of years later and in the traditions of a well-established genre, any subversion suggested by an "Other" can be all the more thoroughly neutralized. That the *comedia* functions in this way is acknowledged even by those who criticize a sociological approach to its interpretation. A case in point would be Charlotte Stern's comment that, "In fact, the *comedia* exhibits a remarkable capacity for absorbing and neutralizing dissident views" (11).

15. *Tacuana:*   "Desde hoy comienzo á temballos."

    Tapirazú: "Hoy palo el cetro has de ser

Del Rey de aquestos vasallos,

Danos otra vez perdón."

16. Demythologizing Malinche has been an important undertaking in the critique of colonial discourse. Mexicans have generally considered Malinche an emblem of the betrayal of indigenous values. Octavio Paz, for example, sees Malinche as representative of the violated and seduced mother of the Mexican national per-

sonality. As symbol of the secret conflict of Mexico's past, Paz believes she poses a critical dilemma: she must be, and at the same time cannot be, repudiated (78-79). Todorov makes a rather Eurocentric reading of Malinche by downplaying her role as traitor and celebrating her as "the first example, and thereby the symbol, of the cross-breeding of cultures" (101). Norma Alarcón believes that Paz and others treat Malinche only at the level of the figurative; something we might see as a sort of colonizing of female experience by a male discourse. Alarcón argues that the symbolic system that appropriates Malinche must be ruptured by considering the emotional suffering of a historically specific real-life woman (183). Such an approach emphasizes both Malinche as Native American threatened by Spanish colonialism *and* as woman living under indigenous patriarchy. Alarcón's position underscores the heterogeneity of indigenous peoples; at the very least, for instance, we ought to attempt to differentiate the culture of the various Caribbean islanders Columbus meets from the assorted continental peoples encountered by Cortés. Her attention to the specificity of Malinche's experience urges us to critically reexamine the stories told by Columbus and the many European male colonizers who followed him about Indian women.

Malinche has many counterparts; in North America they include Pocahontas and Sacajawea.

17.   " . . . casar

    Con nuestras hijas, adonde,

    Mezclándose nuestra sangre,

    Seamos todos españoles."

18.   "Basta, que aqueste español

    No es Dios, pues que no conoce

    El pensamiento que traigo,

    Perdida por sus amores;

    Que con aquesta invención

    Fingiendo tales razones;

    Vengo á sus brazos rendida

    Porque así me lleve y robe.

    El piensa que me hace fuerza,

    Y amor sin fuerza me pone

    Donde descanse mi pena

    Que tanto peligro corre."

19. Thus in Jean Franco's recent book on women and national identity in Mexico, she can note that national identity is "a problem of *male* identity" (131).

20. Walter Cohen (219) stresses the efficacy of the national history play in the development of national consciousness.

21. In the writing about Columbus and in the scholarly work that does exist on *El nuevo mundo*, the famous "discoverer's" treatment of the indigenous peoples con-

tinues to be characterized as "pacific" or even as "humane" (Weiner 67). Yet "sailing the ocean blue" entailed more than the hardship and romance of discovery: Columbus himself initiated the New World slave trade, taking five hundred slaves to Spain (two hundred dying en route); the Spanish under Columbus systematically cut off the hands of Indians who didn't produce the gold Columbus imagined was in their possession. Columbus's actions were, of course, a mere prologue to a genocide that consumed 70 million people (Todorov 133).

22.   "Pues condoliéndose Cristo

        De que entre vosotros reine,

        Que le costasteis su sangre

        En la cruz, muerta la muerte,

        Al rey Fernando de España,

        Cristianísimo y prudente,

        Manda a Colón envíe

        Éste que a su fe os convierte."

23. In discussing the development of nationalism, Timothy Brennan notes, "Even though as an ideology it [nationalism] came out of the imperialist countries, these countries were not able to formulate their own national aspirations until the age of exploration. The markets made possible by European imperial penetration motivated the construction of the nation state at home. European nationalism itself was motivated by what Europe was doing in its far flung dominions. The 'national idea,' in other words, flourished in the soil of foreign conquest. Imperial conquest created the conditions for the fall of Europe's universal Christian community, but resupplied Europe with a religious sense of mission and self-identity . . ." (59).

24.   "Allá, en España, decimos

        Que son los reyes espejo

        Donde se mira el consejo

        Que los vasallos seguimos."

25. I refer to *The Prince* in general, though there is a particularly pertinent passage referring to Ferdinand of Aragon as the model of the modern statesman. See also Gómez-Moriana (99).

Works Cited

Alarcón, Norma. "Chicana's Feminist Literature: A Re-Vision through Malintzin/or Malintzin: Putting Flesh Back on the Object." *This Bridge Called My Back*. New York: Kitchen Table, 1983.

Anderson, Benedict. *Imagined Communities: Reflections on the Origin and Spread of Nationalism*. London: Verso, 1983.

Barthes, Roland. *A Barthes Reader*. Ed. Susan Sontag. New York: Hill and Wang, 1982.

Bhabha, Homi K. "Dissemination: Time, Narrative, and the Margins of the Modern Nation." *Nation and Narration.* Ed. Homi Bhabha. London: Routledge, 1990. 291-322.

———. "The Other Question: Difference, Discrimination, and the Discourse of Colonialism." *Literature, Politics and Theory.* London: Methuen, 1986. 148-172.

Brennan, Timothy. "The National Longing for Form." *Nation and Narration.* Ed. Homi Bhabha. London: Routledge, 1990. 44-70.

Burshatin, Israel. "The Moor in the Text: Metaphor, Emblem, and Silence." *"Race," Writing and Difference.* Ed. Henry Lewis Gates, Jr. Chicago: Univ. of Chicago Press, 1985. 117-137.

Certeau, Michel de. *Heterologies: Discourse on the Other.* Trans. Brian Massumi. Univ. of Minnesota Press, 1986.

Cohen, Walter. *Drama of a Nation: Public Theater in Renaissance England and Spain.* Ithaca, N.Y.: Cornell Univ. Press, 1985.

Dille, Glen F. "El descubrimiento y la conquista de América en la comedia del Siglo de Oro." *Hispania* 71 (1988): 492-502.

———. "The Plays of Cervantes, Lope, Calderón and the New World." *LA CHISPA Selected Proceedings.* Ed. Gilbert Paolini. New Orleans: Tulane Univ., 1987. 89-97.

Elliott, J. H. *Spain and Its World: 1500-1700.* New Haven: Yale Univ. Press, 1989.

Franco, Jean. *Plotting Women: Gender and Representation in Mexico.* New York: Columbia Univ. Press, 1989.

Gates, Henry Louis, Jr. *The Signifying Monkey: A Theory of African-American Literary Criticism.* New York: Oxford Univ. Press, 1988.

Gómez-Moriana, Antonio. "Narration in the Chronicles of the New World." *1492-1992: Re/Discovering Colonial Writing.* Ed. René Jara and Nicholas Spadaccini. Hispanic Issues 4. Minneapolis: Prisma Institute, 1989. 97-120.

González-Echevarría, Roberto. "America Conquered." *The Yale Review* 74 (1985): 281-91.

Greenblatt, Stephen. *Renaissance Self-Fashioning: From More to Shakespeare.* Chicago: Univ. of Chicago Press, 1980.

———. *Shakespearean Negotiations: The Circulation of Social Energy in Renaissance England.* Berkeley: Univ. of California Press, 1988.

Jara, René, and Nicholas Spadaccini. "Introduction: Allegorizing the New World." *1492-1992: Re/Discovering Colonial Writing.* Ed. René Jara and Nicholas Spadaccini. Hispanic Issues 4. Minneapolis: Prisma Institute, 1989. 9-50.

Lévi-Strauss, Claude. *Tristes Tropiques.* Trans. John and Doreen Weightman. New York: Atheneum, 1973.

Las Casas, Bartolomé de. *Historia de las Indias.* 3 vols. Mexico City: Fondo de Cultura Económica, 1951.

Menéndez y Pelayo, Marcelino. "Observaciones preliminares." *Obras de Lope de Vega.* Madrid: Real Academia Española, 1900. 11: 11-162.

Mignolo, Walter D. "Literacy and Colonization: The New World Experience." *1492-1992: Re/Discovering Colonial Writing.* Ed. René Jara and Nicholas Spadaccini. Hispanic Issues 4. Minneapolis: Prisma Institute, 1989. 51-96.

Paz, Octavio. *El laberinto de la soledad.* Mexico City: Fondo de Cultura Económica, 1959.

Said, Edward. *Orientalism.* New York: Vintage, 1979.

Shannon, Robert. *Visions of the New World in the Drama of Lope de Vega*. New York: Peter Lang, 1989.

Stern, Charlotte. "Lope de Vega, Propagandist?" *Bulletin of the Comediantes* 34.1 (1982): 1-36.

Swietlicki, Catherine. "Lope's Dialogic Imagination: Writing Other Voices of 'Monolithic' Spain." *Bulletin of the Comediantes* 40.2 (1988): 205-226.

Todorov, Tzvetan. *The Conquest of America: The Question of the Other*. Trans. Richard Howard. New York: Harper & Row, 1984.

Vega Carpio, Lope de. *The Discovery of the New World by Christopher Columbus*. Trans. Frieda Fligelman. Berkeley: Gillick Press, 1940.

———. *El nuevo mundo descubierto por Cristóbal Colón*. Ed. E. J. Lemartinel and C. Minguet. Paris: Presses Universitaires de Lille, 1980.

———. *El nuevo mundo descubierto por Cristóbal Colón*. *Obras de Lope de Vega*. Ed. Marcelino Menéndez y Pelayo. Madrid: Real Academia Española, 1900. 11: 342-380.

Weiner, Jack. "La guerra y la paz espirituales in tres comedias de Lope." *Revista de Estudios Hispánicos* 17 (1983): 65-79.

Zahareas, Anthony N., ed. *Plays and Playhouses in Imperial Decadence*. Minneapolis: Institute for the Study of Ideologies and Literature, 1985.

Zinn, Howard. *A People's History of the United States*. New York: Harper & Row, 1980.

◆ Chapter 15

Authoritarianism in Brazilian Colonial Discourse

Roberto Reis

(translated by José Mauro Zonis)

Parrots of Different Colors

> *I have seen in Portugal some parrots that were taken from here,*
> *of different colors, but so symmetrical that they looked like they*
> *were hand-made.* (206)[1]
>
> —Ambrósio Fernandes Brandão, 1618

The colonial period is one of the least known in Brazilian literary studies.[2] One of the reasons might be a paradigm that is still current among Brazilian historiographic literary studies that emphasize a close reading of texts and/or the specificity of poetic language. As a result of those tendencies, texts such as Father Nóbrega's *Cartas do Brasil* (*Letters from Brazil*) and Jean de Léry's *Viagem à terra do Brasil* (*Travels to Brazil*) are not considered to be "literary" texts.[3] Thus, critics such as José Aderaldo Castello prefer the term "literary manifestations" when dealing with colonial letters, and in his *História concisa* Alfredo Bosi has observed that:

> It is thanks to these direct overviews of the landscape . . . that we capture the primitive conditions of a culture that *only later could count on the phenomena of the word-art.* (Bosi 15; emphasis added)

Confronted with these difficulties, it is clear that a more productive approach would need to consider the broader phenomena
of discursive formations that refer us to the social, the political,
and to an all-encompassing cultural framework. The emphasis on
discourse allows one to capture the ideological unconscious that
underlies the colonial enterprise. In this essay, then, I shall attempt
to discover the traces of an authoritarian pattern in the discourse
produced by the educated elite, which was to leave a definite imprint on the make-up of the colonized Amerindian. At the same
time, I shall deal with the impact of the encounter between the
European and the Amerindian and on the contribution of that encounter to the crisis of meaning in the European baroque (a matter
that has been underscored by Foucault), which precipitates the
emergence of modernity itself.

Their Treasure Is Bird Feathers

> *They are people with beautiful bodies and stature, men and women
> alike, like the people over here, all sun tanned, for they all walk
> naked, young and old, and they cover their private parts with
> absolutely nothing. But they disfigure themselves with paintings.
> They have no beard, because they pull out their hair by the roots as
> soon as they grow. They make holes in their lower lips, their cheeks
> and ears and they hang stones from them. It is their ornament.
> Besides that, they dress in feathers. (161)[4]*
>
> —Hans Staden, 1557

It is well known that the discoveries are a chapter of European
expansion undertaken by the centralized and absolutist modern
state (Novais; Prado) as it sought to expand the trade routes. In
this enterprise the state had an ally in the Church under whose
shield the conquest and colonization were justified.

The contact between the Portuguese and the native Amerindians highlighted the opposition between a monolithic, Christian image of the world and the one that was to emerge from
within and that we recognize today as a response to alterity.
The latter view was to undermine the wholeness and integrity
of European discourse. The first mark of this impact was the exhaustive description of nature (flora, fauna, landscape) on the

part of the early chroniclers. Good examples are the following by Gandavo:

> They called them armadillos, and they are as big as rabbits, and they have a shell like the lobster's or the turtle's, but it is divided into grooves, like plates; they altogether look like an armored horse, they have a tail from the same long shell, the muzzle like the pig's, and their heads are the only thing they stick out of the shell, they have short legs and they live in holes, their meat tastes almost like chicken. This hunt is highly regarded in the land. (49)

> Another fruit grows on big trees, and if these are not planted, they grow on their own; this fruit when it is ripe turns very yellow: they are like long pears, they call them *cajús*, they are very juicy, and on the edge of this fruit there is a nut like a chestnut, and it grows on the edge of the same fruit, which has a peel that is more bitter than bile and when it touches the lips, the bitterness lasts a long time and it blisters the whole mouth; on the other hand, when the nut is baked, it is more tasty than almonds; they have an extremely hot nature. (50)[5]

These examples, which could easily be multiplied, attest to the linguistic impotence of the colonizer and the reader to whom the writing is directed when faced with an unknown reality.

The first chroniclers were even more amazed by certain rituals and habits of the Brazilian Indians: anthropophagy, communal life, nudity, the ritual of *cauim*, polygamy, and childbirth among the Indian women.[6] In the Brazilian context, chroniclers and travelers, like the Catholic missionaries, tended not to distinguish between the diverse Indian cultures, opting instead for the term "savage" or "nations" when they were indiscriminately referring to a multifaceted and polymorphic reality.[7]

A specific instance of linguistic impotence and of the projection of European values may be found in a famous passage by Gandavo in which he refers to the lack of letters—and by extension to other important aspects of European culture:

> The language of these savages is one all over the coast: it lacks three letters—scilicet, the letters F, L, and R are not present, something that can cause amazement because

this way they have no Faith, no Law and no King [*Rei*, in Portuguese], making them live with no Justice or order.... As I said, there is no King, no Justice among them, there is only, in each village, the most important person, like a captain, whom the Indians obey of their own free will and not by force; when this person dies, his son takes his place; he does not do anything but go with them to war and advise them on how to act, but he does not punish them for their mistakes nor does he order anybody to do anything against their will. This important person has three, four wives; the first one is more highly regarded than the others. This is commonly accepted and is a reason for honor. They neither worship anything, nor believe that there is glory to the good and punishment for the bad in another life, they believe that all is over when they die and their souls die with their bodies, and this way they live bestially without concerns, weight, or measurement. (53-54)[8]

This example is one of many showing the extent of the appropriation of the phonological systems of the Amerindians by European alphabetic writing (Mignolo, "Literacy and Colonization," and in this volume; Jara and Spadaccini; Merrim). This statement—with its various implications: religious (lack of faith), juridical (absence of law), and political (lack of a king)—projects an image of Indian society that is opposite the society encompassed within the Portuguese universe. Or, to put it in another way, any form of social organization outside the monarchic and Christian state could not be conceived. Of course the Indian tribes had gods, chiefs, and power structures; what they did not have, if we endorse Pierre Clastres's conclusions, is the notion of State and the coercive power that it could generate. Hence, the Europeans are amazed that the community follows orders of its "own free will and not by force" or that leadership is just another strategy to be used only in time of war. Their astonishment is compounded by the practice of polygamy and by the Indians' lack of belief in an afterlife. Thus their practices were considered to be bestial and excessive as it was preoccupied only with the here and now. Through these discursive mechanisms, the Europeans cancel the identity of the Amerindian and turn their culture into a *tabula rasa*. Thus, the Indian element and the landscape surveyed by the chronicles are used as a prop by the Europeans to reinforce their own ethnocentric vision of the world.

One of the few exceptions to the discourse described above is the work of the Calvinist Jean de Léry (1578), which is praised by Lévi-Strauss for instituting cultural relativism:

> Let us not completely abominate the cruelty of the anthropophagous savages. Among us there are more creatures as abominable, if not more, and more repulsive than those who attack only enemy nations from whom they want revenge. It is not necessary to go to America, nor even leave our country [France], to see such monstrous things. (Léry 204)[9]

Léry's text is constructed in dialogical opposition to that of André Thevet—who had visited Antarctic France—and thus incorporates a certain polysemy and a level of ambiguity that is absent in the texts that have been mentioned here.

Later on, some of the Portuguese chroniclers seem to emphasize the wealth and prodigality of the land—especially the production of sugar—which gives shape to the myth of *ufanismo*, i.e., the exaltation of Brazil's potential for exploitation and commerce. This is clearly seen in the poem "A ilha de Maré" ("The Island of Tide"), from Botelho de Oliveira (c. 1705).[10]

> I have explained the fruit and vegetables,
> That make Portugal envious;
> I have compiled
> What Brazil has to be enviable,
> And to prefer all the land,
> Perfect in itself, four A.A. comprise.
> It has the first A. in the trees
> Always green to the eyes, always joyful;
> It has the first [*sic*] A. in the trees
> In the agreeable temperature, and safe;
> It has the third A. in the cold waters,
> That refresh the chest, and are healthy,

> The fourth A. is the enjoyable sugar,
> Which is the world's most delicate present.
> Therefore the four A.A. are unique
> Trees, Sugar, Waters, Air. (Oliveira 188)

> [In Portuguese, the words tree ('arvoredo'), air ('ar'), water ('água'), and sugar ('açúcar') begin with the letter A].[11]

The image of the cornucopia of the land that provided the opportunity for commercial profit is complemented by another no less important one: the possibility to expand the domain of Christianity in order to achieve the long sought-after desire of universality. This is what I shall develop in the section that follows.

Writing Freely

> *Here few letters are enough because everything is blank pages and there is nothing else but to write freely.* (54)[12]
> —Father Manuel da Nóbrega, 1549

In the letter that the Jesuit Father Manuel da Nóbrega sends to his peers and superiors in 1549 he writes:

> These savages do not worship anything, nor do they know God, only the thunder they call Tupana, as if they were saying a divine thing. So we do not have a more convenient word to bring them to the knowledge of God other than call Him Father Tupana. (62)[13]

Nóbrega is writing freely on the "blank page" that is Indian culture. In appropriating the sign Tupana, he endows it with a Christian reference. Thus Tupana becomes the Christian God who is also the Father, a signifier that afterward will play a crucial role in the Brazilian patriarchal system.

The Jesuits' method of teaching about the faith was based on having Indians learn the words and then their meanings. Such an approach was to fail as the Indians were not attuned to the abstractions of the Christian faith. Hence Anchieta's advice that "there is no better preaching than the sword and the iron stick" (qtd. in

Paiva 26). The Amerindians, according to Nóbrega, relate only to the material world:

> There are very few words to declare well our faith to them, but nevertheless we make them understand as best as we can and some things we declare to them through circumlocutions. They are very attached to sensual things. Many times they ask me if God has a head, and body, and wife, and if He eats, and what He wears, and similar things. (66)[14]

What the Indians will contest is talk of an abstract and bodyless god who does not belong to the physical world. Thus the Jesuits' preaching is compromised not only by the scarcity of words ("few words") and by their way of communicating through "circumlocutions," but also in the semantic aspect: while for the Jesuits God is a pure and absolute spirituality—and does not need to have a concrete reference—the Indians must be able to feel him.

The priests concentrated their efforts on indoctrinating the young and on discrediting native authorities such as the shaman. In another letter also from 1549, Nóbrega registers an encounter with a shaman and his subsequent conversion to Christianity:

> I worked with a wizard, the greatest of this land, whom everybody called to cure their diseases. I asked him in *qua potestate haec faciebat*, if he communicated with God, who created Heaven and Earth and ruled in Heaven, or with the Devil, who was in hell? He answered me shamelessly that he was god and that he was born god and introduced me to someone who he claimed he had given health, and that the god of the heavens was his friend, and appeared to him in the clouds and thunder, and lightning and in many other ways. Seeing such blasphemy, I gathered all the people in the village in a loud voice and I denied and unsaid what he had been saying for a long period of time, with the help of a translator who was there, who loudly repeated what I was telling him with the same feeling I was showing. He was confused. And I made him recant what he had said and I told him to correct his life and that I would pray to God to forgive him. ... Later he asked me to be baptized because he wanted to be a Christian. Now he is one of the preachers. (56)[15]

It is not necessary to stress the "symbolic effectiveness" of the shaman who serves as articulator of meaning in primitive tribes (Lévi-Strauss). The shaman, therefore, is an adversary who must be conquered by the missionaries. It must be recalled, however, that not all the missionaries who were in Brazil completely shared the policies and practices of the Company of Jesus.[16]

Oh! Forest, Whatever Happened to Your Children?

> *[The indians who] survived the carnage, or were reduced to slavery,*
> *or were forced to flee to the forest, upon their return these were*
> *more or less in the same state as when they had left before the*
> *Europeans' arrival. (54)[17]*
>
> —Johann Moritz Rugendas, c. 1835

The question asked by the verse of Bernardo Guimarães that serves as title to this section, and the diagnosis of Rugendas that appears as the epigraph, can be answered only now that anthropology has begun to question the centrality of European culture and now that the theology of liberation movements are reevaluating the role of the Church in Brazil. This can be seen in the recent works of Luiz Felipe Baêta Neves, José Maria de Paiva, and Eduardo Hoornaert, to whom I will now refer, in order to provide continuity to the delineation of authoritarianism in Brazilian colonial discourse.

These authors attempt to characterize the discourse of evangelization and its implicit ideology. When alluding to the Portuguese maritime enterprise, Hoornaert states that it adopted a missionary language that went on to identify the kingdom of Portugal with the kingdom of God and the Conquest with the propagation of the holy Catholic faith (Hoornaert et al. 23-24). He then develops a characterization of the discourse as universalist (knew no boundaries), doctrinal (preach strongly, hurriedly, in a loud voice), and warlike (the Church that evangelized Brazil was a church "on a war footing") (Hoornaert et al. 24-27). The Portuguese kings, he writes in another text, "consider the navigation to America as 'crusades'; the Indians as 'savages' to be converted; and the war against the Indians as a 'holy war,' everything in the best Iberian tradition of conquest and reconquest after the Arab domination" (Hoornaert, *Formação* 32).

Baêta Neves captures the warlike aspect of evangelization in the title of his book—*O combate dos soldados de Cristo na terra dos papagaios* [*The Combat of the Christ's Soldiers in the Parrots' Land*]— which shares some of Hoornaert's ideas. Christianity is endowed with a universal vocation; the mission given to the Jesuits encompasses "a code that is in itself the Truth and the way to the Truth" (Neves, *O combate* 29). Western expansion aims to incorporate territorially and spiritually the newly discovered American people and bring them into the unified Christian kingdom:

> How to admit that God, that a society that came from God, has "loose" regions or regions that were split by factionalism? The Christian God is only one, in spite of his triple constitution (Father, Son, and Holy Spirit), and the Catholic Church restated him against many heresies throughout the Middle Ages—and there was no reason to abandon its position otherwise. Expansion, universality, integration, unity are dear notions to the Western world, which is engaging in its greatest adventure of conquest. (Neves, *O combate* 28)[18]

According to these medieval ideas, God is the first signifier, origin, source, and founder of meaning. Thus everything acquires meaning and a system of identities and hierarchies is established.

We can conclude with Foucault that the world of the sixteenth century is a world of similitudes. The origin of this world, God, gave meaning to it. The world reflects God's presence and suffers God's absence. The encounter with the American aborigine is a violent one. This violence is manifested at the level of the discourse, when the ready-made truths that are part of the vision of the *orbis christianus* are brought to the New World. The imposition of an already crystalized meaning gives to this discursive pattern an authoritarian aspect, because it does not consider the possibility of the existence, among the native inhabitants of America, of other understandings of the world, other meanings, other interpretations, other cultural codes:

> God spread the signs of his presence; they are now in new lands. It is necessary to read these signs to know to what extent the Devil managed to shuffle them. This new way of reading them is not a break with the ancient way of reading;

the comprehension methods are the same. The Holy Book
also did not change—It is immutable.... The Company
of Jesus was founded to spread the Word, especially to
the people who did not know it.... Catechism is, then, a
rationally made effort to conquer men; it is an effort to
highlight the similarities and erase the differences. (Neves,
O combate 44-45)[19]

The need to assimilate the Other comes from observations that
reveal to the Europeans a repugnant behavior on the part of the
Amerindian—behavior such as incest and cannibalism for example. This need confronts problems of communication on cultural
and linguistic levels. In any case, the idea is to model Amerindian
society after the European and this authoritarian response may
be seen in the distribution of Indians into villages where a new
order replaces the order of tribal societies. Under this new system, individuals from different cultures are mixed, thus facilitating
acculturation and mortally desegregating and disarticulating the
savage mind. The results are well known: the native Amerindians
who did not succumb to disease, or who were not decimated by
the euphemistically called "just wars," or were not "saved" by the
Jesuits, took shelter in the forests. The Brazilian Indian population
before the discovery is estimated at 5 million; today it is about two
hundred thousand.

I Shall Convince

> When you serve your masters, do not serve them as those who serve
> men but rather as those who serve God...; because, then, you do
> not serve them as captives, but rather as free men, nor obey them
> as slaves, but rather as sons. You do not serve them as captives,
> but as free men, because God should pay you for your work. (qtd.
> in Cidade 74)[20]
>
> —Father Antonio Vieira

Father Vieira's sermons deserve to be remembered here, even if
briefly, because it is probably through them that the authoritarian
discourse that later will permeate Brazilian culture begins to be articulated. Vieira, in some way, can be considered a spokesman for
the Portuguese state, which was somewhere between the world

of the *orbis christianus* and an incipient bureaucratic apparatus in process of formation. Vieira's speech strikes a balance between some declared high ideals and the petty contingencies of social life (Palacin). Vieira is said to experience the "incompatibility between the colonial system and a just government, and between the demand for freedom (which is in the essence of the human being) and the legal demands of slavery, imposed by the determinations of the colonial policy" (Palacin 11). While Vieira's defense against Indian enslavement is well known, it is also the case that he accepted as legal and moral the servitude of blacks. At this time I shall limit my comments to an examination of Vieira's "Sermon for the Good Success of the Army of Portugal against the Ones of Holland," which was delivered in the city of Bahia when that city was cornered by Dutch troops in 1640.

In his sermon Vieira tries, indirectly, to persuade the audience to join the Portuguese against the invaders, applying passages from Psalm 43 and other biblical texts to the historical situation: the siege of the city. The Jesuit does not perceive, evidently, that the underlying contexts of the Scriptures and the ongoing situation are incompatible. That is, the arguments taken from the psalm only dehistoricize the events of the siege. The preacher orchestrates time and appeals to authority—the authority of the word inscribed in the sacred books—in order to make an impression on the audience: the connection between the city's present misfortune and the word of David ("with such propriety David describes in this psalm *our misfortunes*" [Vieira 17; emphasis mine]) is later followed by the statement "I shall convince" (Vieira 20-21) in which the priest clearly identifies his mission with God's will. This identification had a purpose: to commit the audience to his message.

The religious overtones of Vieira's discourse come through in the epithets used to describe the Dutch: they are called "insolent heretics," "sordid and brutal heretics," "infidels," "excommunicated," "impious" (24-26). The religious battles of Europe are transplanted to the tropics, where the Portuguese and the Dutch contest the commercial routes to the Indies, which had been defined by the pope in the Treaty of Tordesillas, allocating the New World to Spain and Portugal. The sermon stresses that "only the Roman faith we profess is Faith, truthful and yours" (Vieira 25).

The implication seems clear: if the Roman faith is the authentic one, then the listeners have no option but to follow it; if this is the faith of the Portuguese, the audience should embrace the Portuguese cause against the heretic invaders. As we can see, we are talking about religion, but the implicit shift from religion to politics is easily made.

Vieira's reflection, however, goes farther: how can the Lord be angry with his "extremely loyal servants," the Lusitanians, and favor the "excommunicated" Dutch (26)? Thus he addresses the Lord in the following manner: "consider, God of mine—and forgive me if I speak inconsiderately—consider from whom you take away the lands of Brazil and to whom you give them. You take away these lands from the Portuguese, to whom you originally gave them." He adds: "you take away these lands from the same Portuguese whom you chose among all nations of the world to be the conquerors of your Faith" (27, 28).[21]

Elsewhere he writes,

You also take away Brazil from the Portuguese, who conquered these very vast lands, like the very remote ones in the Orient, at the cost of many lives and much blood, for spreading your name and your Faith (for this was the preoccupation of those very Christian kings), rather than increasing and extending their empire. (28)[22]

Vieira dramatizes what would happen should the Dutch achieve victory. The ordered world of the true Christian faith and of Catholic Portugal and its colony Brazil would be replaced by disorder and chaos:

The heretics will enter this church and others, they will destroy the custody in which now you adore the angels, they will take the holy cups and vases and will use them for their nefarious drunkenness, they will drop the statues of the saints from the altars, they will deform them by slashing them, and they will burn them, and the furious and sacrilegious hands will forgive neither the images of Christ crucified, nor those of the Virgin Mary. (Vieira 36)[23]

Using religion to advance an economic and political agenda, Vieira turns into a spokesman for the interests of Portugal and the dominant segments of colonial society. The Jesuit's discourse is authoritarian, situating a historical and political problem in a nonhistorical and divine space, in order to persuade the public: "I shall convince." He closes his text to the circulation of meaning, a meaning that has been frozen by the inescapability of the biblical referent.

Vieira may be viewed as a spokesman for the established social order. Notwithstanding Vieira's sympathies for the Indian, his work can be seen as the beginning of authoritarian discourse in Brazil. This discourse will be consolidated during the eighteenth century by poets such as Gonzaga, Basílio da Gama, Silva Alvarenga, and Cláudio Manuel da Costa. In the nineteenth century, the Indian will be mythicized and some black characters emerge with skin as white as ivory and with blue eyes.

The emergence of the Indian in the literary discourse produced by the upper segments of Brazilian society in the nineteenth century is correlative with their disappearance from the physical world and their replacement with African labor. Thus, Romantic Indianism will help to establish the hegemony of an agro-exporting economic group that found in the Amerindian rather than in the Portuguese the heroic and mythical ancestors needed to create a nationalist tradition that was not blemished by miscegenation. It was not by chance that the opposite happened to blacks: their overwhelming presence in the Brazilian daily life of the nineteenth century will correspond to their relative absence or concealment (above all the "whitening" of them) in the literary production of the last century.

Biting Its Own Tail

> Through reports of explorers, travelers, and missionaries, the closed civilization of medieval Europe learned of the existence of so many other cultural, independent and irreducible worlds, and what could superficially seem like literature of amusement . . . ends up, slowly and insensibly, producing a deeper shock in the relativization of values, than the very discovery of the insignificance of our planet, through the heliocentric theory and the affirmation of infinite space, in the seventeenth century. (63)
>
> —Luís Palacin

The New World "difference" that is inscribed in European discourse during the period of colonization will reinforce the notion of a new conception of knowledge and circulation of meaning, marking the beginning of modernity (Foucault; Rama). Thus, a discourse that was initially marked by a authoritarian perspective returns fragmented and imbued with multiple ambiguities.

I have argued that the discourse that was anchored in the *orbis christianus* fractured when it came into contact with the reality that was the New World and that, ultimately, certain authoritarian voices surfaced to grant legitimacy to the socio-political organization imposed upon colonial society. What we saw with Vieira's sermon is, in many ways, still emblematic and fits within a canonical scheme that envisions sermons, chronicles, and other cultural products as vehicles of official culture—the latter understood as conservative, "mass"-oriented, urban, and guided. This is precisely Maravall's thesis regarding the culture of crisis of the Spanish and European baroque and, curiously enough, is applicable to Brazilian cultural development:

> The desired direction to impress on those groups bearing the brunt of this operation undoubtedly pointed toward the restoration and preservation of values that came from the seigniorial tradition, but in the sixteenth century, the modern and individualist experience undergone by European societies was not in vain. Instruments of greater efficacy would have to be used, instruments capable of influencing individuals who recognized their freedom; a complex regime of social control, organized in the shadow of the absolute monarchy, strove to maintain these individuals actively integrated in a conservative society of traditional privileges. In this way, the society of the seventeenth century—biting its own tail—revealed the grounds of its own crisis: a process of modernization that was contradictorily set in place to preserve inherited structures. (Maravall 263)

Within the framework of this discussion Brazilian colonial discourse shows the establishment of an authoritarian pattern that throughout Brazilian history has tended to obliterate alterity, plurality of meanings, and difference, thus slowing down the inception of modernity and committing dissonant voices to the margins. Parrots of different colors will beautify a Europe that is in crisis, before our ancestors could lock the birds up in cages just to admire how perfect and harmonious their feathers were.

Notes

1. "Tenho visto em Portugal alguns papagaios, que se levaram de cá, de cores diferentes, mas tão compassadas que davam mostra de serem feitas a mão" (Ambrósio Fernandes Brandão, 1618).

2. There are few satisfactory monographic studies dealing with many of the writers of this period. In the existing bibliography one can find some efforts to embrace the colonial output in its totality. The classical work by Sérgio Buarque de Holanda, *Visão do paraíso*, still presents a thematic approach when it traces the "edenic motives" in the chroniclers' and travelers' texts; the works by Luiz Felipe Baêta Neves and José Maria de Paiva, to which I will refer later on, get closer to filling the gap, as they approach evangelization from more comprehensive perspectives. A special mention should be made of the work of Silviano Santiago, which maps the metaphorical chains of the Brazilian colonial discourse, from Caminha and Vieira to Lima Barreto.

3. One of the available sources on the Jesuits in Brazil is Father Serafim Leite. A contemporary reevaluation of the Jesuit enterprise in Brazil may be found in Hoornaert.

4. "São gente bonita de corpo e estatura, homens e mulheres igualmente, como as pessoas daqui; apenas, são queimados de sol, pois andam todos nus, moços e velhos, e nada absolutamente trazem sobre as partes pudendas. Mas se desfiguram com pinturas. Não têm barba, pois arrancam os pelos, com as raízes, tão pronto lhes nascem. Através do lábio inferior, das bochechas e orelhas fazem furos e aí penduram pedras. É o seu ornato. Além disso, ataviam-se com penas."

5. "chamão-lhes tatüs, são tamanhos como coelhos e têm hum casco á maneira da lagosta como de cagado, mas he repartido em muitas juntas como laminas; parecem totalmente hum cavallo armado, têm hum rabo do mesmo casco comprido, o focinho he como de leitão, e não botão mais fora do casco que a cabeça, têm as pernas baixas e críam-se em covas, a carne delles tem o sabor quasi como de galinha. Esta caça he muito estimada na terra."

"Outra fruita se cria numas árvores grandes, estas se não plantão, nascem pelo mato muitas; esta fruita depois de madura he muito amarella: são como peros repinaldos compridos, chamão-lhes cajús, têm muito sumo, e cria-se na ponta desta fruita de fora hum caroço como castanha, e nasce diante da mesma fruita, o qual tem a casca mais amargosa que fel, e se tocarem com ella nos beiços dura muito aquelle amargor e faz empollar toda a boca; pelo contrario este caroço assado, he muito mais gostoso que amendoa; são de sua natureza mui quentes em extremo."

6. Today we have very distinct interpretations of these and other aspects of the Brazilian Indian cultures. Thus, when analyzing Indian society, Florestan Fernandes states that the rituals concerning anthropophagy were sacralizations of the

spirit of bravery and of the desire to preserve the cultural patrimony that was threatened by enemy tribes: "There was neither sadism or disdain for the enemy, but the capturing of courage in him and the restitution of the old peace order" (qtd. in Hoornaert 53). Anthropologist Berta Ribeiro writes: "the Christian morality imposed by the Jesuits on the catechumen, such as the prohibition to marry more than one woman, encountered great resistance. The Tupi societies found by the Portuguese were ruled by older men and women and the elderly. One of the chief's, the warrior's, and the shaman's rewards was the access to young women. The imposition of clothing on the Indians and the attempts against the communal house are explained by the same patterns of sexual morality. The big *maloca* [hut], the economic, political, and ceremonial Indian unity, is immediately affected because, according to the priests, it represents a factor of tribal habit preservation because of its own architectonic projection.... This equalitarian, indivisible, socializing character—and at the same time a place for working, sleeping, eating, resting which was characteristic of the Indian *maloca*—offended the mercantile, puritan, and individualist ideology of the missionaries. The physical atomization of the house affected the social-economic structure and the ceremonial life of its occupants, because of the division of the nuclear families that took shelter in the huts which were given to each couple.... The Jesuit action also tried to eliminate another serious offense to the pudency of the time, which was the ostensive Indian nudity. The Indians were not only dressed in rough clothes (shirts that covered them down to the feet), but they were also deprived of wearing their ornaments which were 'deforming,' according to the view of the Jesuits. That was a way of visually Christianizing them, since the body, mainly its private parts, was the locus of 'sin,' lasciviousness, dissolution, and 'devil's temptations.' The elimination of body ornaments and its coverings obliterated the Indian characteristics and undifferentiated them from the Europeans and, at least, it gave the priests the sensation that they had tamed the Indians. On the other hand, the uncovered genital organs could not be seen by the priest's pudic eyes, much less in sacred places" (Ribeiro 45-46). For a view of the Indian during the Republic, when the Indian Protection Service (predecessor of the current FUNAI, a federal agency that is supposed to protect the Indians) was created, see Gagliardi; for research of the current situation of several Brazilian tribes, see *Povos indígenas do Brasil*, an eighteen-volume work (I had access to volumes 3, 5, and 8), which was coordinated by Carlos Alberto Ricardo and published by the Ecumenical Center of Documentation and Information; for an example of a trial against Indian societies, see *Autos da devassa contra os índios Mura do Rio Madeira e nações do Rio Tocantins (1738-1739)*. For an account of the history of the conquest of Brazilian Indian tribes, see Hemming.

7. By using the term *Indian*, as Júlio Cezar Melatti observes, "the conquerors labelled the most diverse populations, from the north to the south of the American continent. Such populations differed from one another both in the physical aspect and traditions. Members of very distinct societies such as the Incas and the Tupinambás, who spoke completely different languages and had different habits, were included in the same category: Indians. While the former were road and city builders and lived in an empire that was administered by a group of bureaucrats and organized in hierarchized social segments, the latter lived in villages, in straw huts, in a society without social divisions, in which the highest political unity was

probably the village itself. Therefore the American population shared nothing in common that could justify their being denominated by a single term, Indians, except for the fact that they were not Europeans" (Melatti 19-20). The Tupi Indians gave the first chroniclers and missionaries the impression that the Indian world was divided into two big categories: "the world of the ones who spoke their language and practiced their customs and the world of their opposites, the so called Tapuia, which means slave. This division of the Brazilian Indians between Tupi and Tapuia remained for a long time and was used to distinguish the groups who lived on the coast from the ones who lived inland. After the stripping of the hinterland, during the centuries that followed discovery, the Europeans had a more precise idea of the Indian mosaic that inhabited the country" (Ribeiro 19). This uniform image of the Indian, by the way, still exists today in many textbooks of Brazilian history.

8. "a língua deste gentio toda pela Costa he huma: carece de tres letras—silicet, não se acha nella F, nem L, nem R, cousa digna de espanto, porque assi não têm Fé, nem Lei, nem Rei; e desta maneira vivem sem Justiça e desordenadamente.... Não ha como digo entre elles nenhum Rei, nem Justiça, sómente em cada aldêa tem hum principal que he como capitão, ao qual obedecem por vontade e não por força; morrendo este principal fica seu filho no mesmo lugar; não serve doutra cousa se não de ir com elles a guerra, e conselha-los como se hão de haver na peleja, mas não castiga seus erros nem manda sobrelles cousa alguma contra sua vontade. Este principal tem tres, quatro mulheres, a primeira tem em mais conta, e faz della mais caso que das outras. Isto tem por estado e por honra. Não adorão cousa alguma nem têm para si que ha na outra vida gloria pera os bons, e pena pera os maos, tudo cuidão que se acaba nesta e que as almas fenecem com os corpos, e assi vivem bestialmente sem ter conta, nem peso, nem medida." A slight variation of this passage may be found in contemporaries such as Sousa, Brandão, and Friar Salvador.

9. "não abominemos portanto demasiado a crueldade dos selvagens antropófagos. Existem entre nós criaturas tão abomináveis, se não mais, e mais detestáveis do que aquelas que só investem contra nações inimigas de que têm vingança a tomar. Não é preciso ir à América, nem mesmo sair de nosso país [a França], para ver coisas tão monstruosas."

10. Slowly, sugar will appear in the travelers' narratives: already referred to in the *Tratado descritivo do Brasil em 1587* ("from these mills, more than one hundred and twenty thousand arrobas [1,767 short tons] of sugar leave Bahia during each year" [Sousa 162]), stressed by Brandônio in *Diálogos das grandezas do Brasil*, from 1618 ("sugar is the main thing that makes Brazil noble and rich" [Brandão 126]) until it occupied a prominent position in Antonil's monograph (c. 1709), *Cultura e opulência do Brasil*, truly a manual of the sugar mill owner. The myth of *ufanismo* [attitude of exaltation of Brazil's potential] and the prodigality of the land will deeply crease the Brazilian cultural discourse. After the first impressions, Brazil was more important as an object of colonial exploitation: "all of Brazil produces profits to the income of His Majesty without any expenses, which is what should be appreciated" (Brandão 138). On the other hand, by 1835, Rugendas acknowledged the war of extermination against the Indians and the disastrous effects of the contact with the Europeans (Rugendas 54); Charles Ribeyrolles (c. 1859) noted that the Indians wandered through the forests and did not constitute a labor force, while the blacks

were "truly workers of the great Brazilian empire" (Ribeyrolles 82 and 86); naturalists such as Spix and Martius (c. 1817-1820), Guido Boggiani (1894) or Karl von
den Steinen (c. 1886), would elaborate more "scientific" studies about the remaining
native population.

11. "Tenho explicado as fruitas, e legumes,

Que dão a Portugal muitos ciumes;

Tenho recopilado

O que o Brasil contem para invejado,

E para preferir a toda a terra,

Em si perfeitos quatro A.A. encerra.

Tem o primeiro A, nos arvoredos

Sempre verdes aos olhos, sempre ledos;

Tem o primeiro [sic] A. nos arvoredos

Na temperie agradaveis, e seguros;

Tem o terceiro A. nas agoas frias,

Que refrescam o peito, e são sadias;

O quarto A. no açúcar deleitoso,

Que é do Mundo o regalo mais mimoso.

São pois os quatro A.A. por singulares

Arvoredos, Açúcar, Agoas, Ares."

12. "Cá poucas letras bastam, porque é tudo papel branco e não há mais que
escrever á vontade."

13. "esta gentilidade a nenhuma coisa adora, nem conhecem a Deus, sòmente
aos trovões chamam Tupana, que é como quem diz coisa divina. E assim, nós não
temos outro vocábulo mais conveniente para os trazer ao conhecimento de Deus,
que chamar-lhe Pai Tupana."

14. "têm mui poucos vocábulos para lhes poder bem declarar a nossa fé, mas
contudo damos-lha a entender o melhor que podemos e algumas coisas lhes declaramos por rodeios. Estão muito apegados com as coisas sensuais. Muitas vezes me
perguntam se Deus tem cabeça, e corpo, e mulher, e se come, e de que se veste, e
outras coisas semelhantes."

15. "trabalhei por me ver com um feiticeiro, o maior desta terra, o qual todos
mandam chamar para curar as suas enfermidades. Perguntei-lhe in qua potestate
haec faciebat, se tinha comunicação com Deus, que fez o Céu e a terra e reinava
nos Céus, ou com o demônio, que estava nos infernos? Respondeu-me com pouca
vergonha que ele era deus e que havia nascido deus e apresentou-me ali um a
quem dizia ter dado saúde, e que o Deus dos Céus era seu amigo, e lhe apare-
cia em nuvens e trovões, e em relâmpagos, e em outras coisas muitas. Trabalhei,
vendo tão grande blasfêmia, por ajuntar toda a Aldeia com altas vozes aos quais
desenganei e contradisse o que ele dizia, por muito espaço de tempo, com um
bom língua, que ali tinha, o qual falava o que eu lhe dizia em alta voz com sinais
de grandes sentimentos que eu mostrava. Viu-se ele confuso. E fiz que se des-

dissesse do que tinha dito e emendasse a sua vida e que eu rogaria a Deus que lhe perdoasse.... Depois me pediu este que eu o bautizasse que queria ser cristão. E agora é um dos catecúmenos."

16. Names such as Gonçalo Leite, Miguel Garcia, or Luís da Grã, in spite of not having the stature of a Las Casas, rose up against various aspects of evangelization (Hoornaert 59-60). Yet, because I want to emphasize the order of the discourse, I find it worthwhile to point out that scholars such as Father Serafim Leite basically repeated the same posture stressed above, proving that the position of Nóbrega was the one that definitely passed on to the pantheon of the official historiography. Writing about three centuries later, Serafim Leite endorsed both the ideology that underlay the work of the Jesuits and the ideology of the chroniclers. After quoting the famous passage "with neither Faith, nor Law, nor King," he comments: "but if it is philologically deficient, it characterizes well the situation of the Indians upon the arrival of the Jesuits. They had neither an external cult, nor a positive written law, nor a hereditary authority, but only rudiments of religion and of unwritten law; and they did not have a true chief, except on the occasions of war.... If a king had existed, that alone could have brought more resistance to the colonization, but if he converted, by example, all the people would have been converted as well.... It was necessary to destroy in each one [Indian] the centuries-old weight of his own psychology, accustomed to anthropophagies, polygamies, and other carnal vices, as well as to gluttony, particularly drunkenness, along with his intermittent nomadism" (Leite, *História da Companhia de Jesus no Brasil* 6).

17. "O que sobreviveu à carnificina, ou foi reduzido à escravidão ou forçado a fugir para a floresta, aí voltando, mais ou menos ao mesmo estado de que saíra pouco antes da chegada dos europeus."

18. "como admitir que Deus, que uma sociedade vinda de Deus, tenha regiões 'soltas' ou cindidas pelo faccionalismo? O Deus cristão é um só, apesar de sua tríplice constituição (Pai, Filho e Espírito Santo), e a Igreja Católica o reafirmara contra muitas heresias no correr da Idade Média—e não havia porque abandonar sua posição pelo contrário. Expansão, universalidade, integração, unidade são noções caras a um Ocidente que se lança à sua maior aventura de conquista."

19. "Deus espargiu os sinais de sua presença; eles agora estão em terras novas. É preciso ler estas marcas e saber até que ponto o demônio conseguiu embaralhá-las. Essa nova leitura não é uma ruptura com as antigas formas de ler; os métodos de compreensão são os mesmos. O Livro Sagrado também não mudou—Ele é imutável....A Companhia de Jesus foi fundada para difundir a Palavra especialmente a povos que não A conheciam....A catequese é, então, um esforço racionalmente feito para conquistar homens; é um esforço para acentuar a semelhança e apagar as diferenças."

20. "...quando servis a vossos senhores, não os sirvais, como quem serve a homens, senão como quem serve a Deus...porque então não servis como cativos, senão como livres, nem obedeceis como escravos, senão como filhos. Não servis como cativos, senão como livres, porque Deus vos há de pagar o vosso trabalho...."

21. "considerai, Deus meu—e perdoai-me se falo inconsideradamente—considerai a quem tirais as terras do Brasil e a quem as dais. Tirais estas terras aos portugueses, a quem no princípio as destes;" "tirais estas terras àqueles mesmos

portugueses a quem escolhestes entre todas as nações do mundo para conquistadores de vossa Fé."

22. "tirais também o Brasil aos portugueses, que assim estas terras vastíssimas,
como as remotíssimas do Oriente, as conquistaram à custa de tantas vidas e tanto
sangue, mais por dilatar vosso nome e vossa Fé (que esse era o zelo daqueles
cristianíssimos reis), que por amplificar e estender seu império."

23. "entrarão os hereges nesta igreja e nas outras; arrebentarão essa custódia;
em que agora estais adorado dos anjos; tomarão os cálices e vasos sagrados, e aplicá-
los-ão a suas nefandas embriaguezes; derrubarão dos altares os vultos e estátuas
dos santos, deformá-las-ão a cutiladas, e metê-las-ão no fogo; e não perdoarão as
mãos furiosas e sacrílegas, nem às imagens tremendas de Cristo crucificado, nem
às da Virgem Maria."

Works Cited

Antonil, André João. *Cultura e opulência do Brasil*. São Paulo: Nacional, 1967.

*Autos da devassa contra os índios Mura do Rio Madeira e nações do Rio Tocantins (1738-
1739)*. Manaus/Brasília: Fundação Universidade do Amazonas/INL, 1986.

Boggiani, Guido. *Os caduveos*. Belo Horizonte: Itatiaia; São Paulo: EDUSP, 1975.

Bosi, Alfredo. *História concisa da literatura brasileira*. 2nd ed. São Paulo: Cultrix, 1976.

Brandão, Ambrósio Fernandes. *Diálogo das grandezas do Brasil*. São Paulo: Melhora-
mentos, 1977.

Castello, José Aderaldo. *Manifestações literárias do período colonial*. 3rd ed. São Paulo:
Cultrix, 1978.

Cidade, Hernani, ed. *Padre Antonio Vieira: Sermões pregados no Brazil, II*. Vol. 3. Lisbon:
Agência Geral das Colônias, 1940.

Clastres, Pierre. *A sociedade contra o Estado*. 2nd ed. Rio de Janeiro: Francisco Alves,
1982.

Foucault, Michel. *The Order of Things: An Archeology of the Human Sciences*. London:
Tavistock, 1970.

Gagliardi, José Mauro. *O indígena e a República*. São Paulo: Hucitec/EDUSP, 1989.

Gandavo, Pero de Magalhães. *Tratado da terra do Brasil—História da província de Santa
Cruz*. Belo Horizonte: Itatiaia; São Paulo: EDUSP, 1980.

Guimarães, Bernardo. *Poesias completas*. Rio de Janeiro: INL, 1959.

Hemming, John. *Red Gold*. Cambridge: Harvard Univ. Press, 1978.

Holanda, Sérgio Buarque de. *Visão do paraíso*. Rio de Janeiro: José Olympio, 1959.

Hoornaert, Eduardo. *Formação do catolicismo brasileiro, 1550-1800*. Petrópolis: Vozes,
1974.

Hoornaert, Eduardo, et al. *História da Igreja no Brasil (primeira época)*. Petrópolis:
Vozes, 1977.

Jara, René, and Nicholas Spadaccini. "Introduction." *1492-1992: Re/Discovering Colonial Writing*. Hispanic Issues 4. Minneapolis: Prisma Institute, 1989. 9-49.

Leite, Padre Serafim. *Cartas dos primeiros jesuítas do Brasil*. Vol. 2. São Paulo: Comissão
do Quarto Centenário, 1957.

———. *História da Companhia de Jesus no Brasil*. Lisbon: Portugalia, 1938.

Léry, Jean de. *Viagem à terra do Brasil*. Belo Horizonte: Itatiaia; São Paulo: EDUSP, 1980.

Lévi-Strauss, Claude. "A eficácia simbólica." *Antropologia estrutural*. Rio de Janeiro: Tempo Brasileiro, 1975. 215-36.

Maravall, José Antonio. *Culture of the Baroque*. Trans. Terry Cochran. Minneapolis: Univ. of Minnesota Press, 1986.

Melatti, Julio Cezar. *Índios do Brasil*. 3rd ed. São Paulo: Hucitec, 1980.

Merrim, Stephanie. "The Apprehension of the New in Nature and Culture: Fernández de Oviedo's *Sumario*." *1492-1992: Re/Discovering Colonial Writing*. 165-199.

Mignolo, Walter. "Literacy and Colonization: The New World Experience." *1492-1992: Re/Discovering Colonial Writing*. Ed. Nicholas Spadaccini and René Jara. Hispanic Issues 4. Minneapolis: Prisma Institute, 1989. 51-96.

Neves, Luiz Felipe Baêta. *O combate dos soldados de Cristo na terra dos papagaios*. Rio de Janeiro: Forense-Universitária, 1978.

Nóbrega, Padre Manuel da. *Cartas do Brasil e mais escritos*. Coimbra: Universidade de Coimbra, 1955.

Novais, Fernando A. "O Brasil nos quadros do antigo sistema colonial." *Brasil em perspectiva*. Multiple authors. São Paulo: Difusão Européia do Livro, 1968. 53-71.

Oliveira, Botelho de. *Música do Parnaso—A ilha de Maré*. Rio de Janeiro: Alvaro Pinto, 1929.

Paiva, José Maria de. *Colonização e catequese, 1549-1600*. São Paulo: Autores Associados/Cortez, 1982.

Palacin, Luís. *Vieira e a visão trágica do Barroco*. São Paulo: Hucitec; Brasília: INL, 1986.

Prado, Jr., Caio. *Formação do Brasil contemporâneo*. 16th ed. São Paulo: Brasiliense, 1979.

Rama, Angel. *A cidade das letras*. São Paulo: Brasiliense, 1985.

Ribeiro, Berta. *O índio na história do Brasil*. São Paulo: Global, 1983.

Ribeyrolles, Charles. *Brasil pitoresco*. 2 vols. Belo Horizonte: Itatiaia; São Paulo: EDUSP, 1980.

Ricardo, Carlos Alberto, org. *Povos indígenas do Brasil*. São Paulo: CEDI, 1983 (vol. 3); 1981 (vol. 5); 1985 (vol. 8).

Rugendas, Johann Moritz. *Viagem pitoresca através do Brasil*. 6th ed. São Paulo: Martins, 1967.

Salvador, Frei Vicente do. *História do Brasil, 1500-1627*. Belo Horizonte: Itatiaia; São Paulo: EDUSP, 1982.

Santiago, Silviano. "A palavra de Deus." *Barroco* 3 (1971): 7-13.

———. Paper presented at CEHILA. Mimeo, 1977.

Sousa, Gabriel Soares de. *Tratado descritivo do Brasil em 1587*. 4th ed. São Paulo: Nacional/EDUSP, 1971.

Spix, Johann Baptist von, and Karl Friedrich Philipp von Martius. *Viagem pelo Brasil, 1817-1820*. 4th ed. 3 vols. Belo Horizonte: Itatiaia; São Paulo: EDUSP, 1981.

Staden, Hans. *Duas viagens ao Brasil*. Belo Horizonte: Itatiaia; São Paulo: EDUSP, 1974.

Steinen, Karl von den. *O Brasil central*. São Paulo: Nacional, 1942.

Vieira, Padre Antonio. *Sermões e cartas*. 5th ed. Rio de Janeiro: Agir, 1968.

Chapter 16

Sor Juana Inés de la Cruz; or, The Snares of (Con)(tra)di(c)tion

Elena Feder

> *I want to know how God created this world.*
> *I am not interested in this or that phenomenon,*
> *in the spectrum of this or that element;*
> *I want to know his thoughts; the rest are details.*
> —Albert Einstein

> *¡Oh infeliz altura, expuesta a tantos riesgos!*
> *¡Oh signo que te ponen por blanco de la envidia*
> *y por objeto de la contradicción!*
> —Sor Juana Inés de la Cruz[1]

In her *Respuesta a Sor Filotea de la Cruz* (*Reply to Sor Philothea*), Sor Juana states: "And in truth I have never written except against my will and when forced to and then only to please others; not only without gratifying pleasure but with actual repugnance." She later adds, "I do not remember ever writing anything for my own pleasure except a scrap of paper they call *The Dream*" (*Respuesta* 4: 444, 471).[2] By calling *Primero Sueño* (2: 325-359)[3]—one of the most complex poems ever written in Spanish—a "papelillo" and by singling it out in her only explicitly autobiographical narrative, Sor Juana is clearly calling attention to a relationship between the two works. Although critics have noted this relationship, its implications have not yet been fully explored.[4]

This essay proposes to take a closer look at such implications by means of a detailed reading of the formal and thematic aspects central to *Primero Sueño* (*First Dream*), a reading mediated both by the autobiographical references in the *Respuesta*, as well as by the historical context surrounding the two works. My purpose is to show that what binds them together is the feminine specificity of their author's perspective on the vicissitudes of writing for and as woman, and to understand from this perspective the distinction Sor Juana makes between writing "for [one's own] pleasure" and writing "when forced to and then only to please others." A gender-historical focus will also help us to understand the (con)(tra)di(c)tions she has embodied: woman and intellectual, woman and poet, woman and playwright, nun, musician and scientist, but woman nonetheless. Her work with and against ("con y contra") dictions, traditions, and contradictions marked her as a dangerous writer and as a threat to the social order, making her escape from the "fires of persecution, the chalice of torment" (*Respuesta* 4: 458) increasingly more problematic.

My reading of *Primero Sueño* reestablishes the disguised relationship between Sor Juana's biographical "I" and literary "I," to date misunderstood in the reception of the poem. Because such a relationship goes beyond a comfortable adequation and fixation of its terms, necessarily marked by historical specificities of subject and author, my position is a strategic one. It is informed by the desire to underscore certain biographical referents in her texts that have been consistently ignored and that I find inseparable from the work of the exceptionally talented nun who earned, if not the power, at least the ambiguous glory of Tenth Muse of America.[5]

To insist on foregrounding the explicitly gendered voice of Sor Juana's texts is not, as we will see, to impose a reading extraneous to them. As the epithet Tenth Muse indicates, and as a close look at the pictorial representations of her image discloses the seal of "Woman" was not only bestowed on Sor Juana by others, it was carried by her as the mark of distinction of her body and as the emblem of difference of her soul—a soul that lived to soar to the limits of the imagination in *Primero Sueño*, only to break under the weight of censorship two years before her body exhaled its last breath. By returning this important aspect of her life and work to the central place it historically occupied, we will be in a better position to understand the gender-specific strategies Sor Juana found necessary to adopt and adapt in her constant efforts to whittle away censorship in its multiple guises—from overt and covert condemnation to self-censorship—strategies to which she resorted ingeniously and astutely, often with razor-sharp wit.[6]

Although both works are radically different—the *Respuesta* is an autobiographical essay in epistolary form and *Primero Sueño* a monumental baroque poem—they are thematically and conceptually inseparable. As artistic manifesto and autobiographical testimony, both are hybrids that break with the limitations of those literary genres in order to accommodate their author's unique perspective: that of a scholarly woman without economic means who, given the limited number of spaces available to her in the corrupt, reactionary, and quite fanatically religious society of late seventeenth-century New Spain, sought the protection of convent life as a means to satisfy her curiosity and insatiable thirst for knowledge.[7]

The determination with which she carved a social place for her singular self has led many to see her, albeit anachronistically, as the first feminist of America.[8] Throughout her life, Sor Juana struggled virtually alone, having "nothing but a mute book as a teacher, an unfeeling inkwell as fellow student" ("teniendo sólo por maestro un libro mudo, por condiscípulo un tintero insensible" [Reply 217; Respuesta 4: 450-451]). Although she never gave up trying to understand the social and psychological problems a woman faced when her "natural inclination" ("natural impulso") compelled her to write,[9] it was not until the latter years of her life, when she wrote the Sueño and the Respuesta, that she felt the need to lighten the burden of that isolation historically specific to her gender and focus her increasingly acrimonious gaze on the structure and systemic functioning of the institutions that interfered with her project.

While the Sueño dissects Western culture's ontological and epistemological foundations and formations, the Respuesta opens a window to a world where the secular roots of today's Americas were germinating as well. They showcase the efforts of a tenacious woman struggling to remain loyal to her vocation and passion, while at the same time fighting the intolerance and petty tyranny of "learned men" ("varones doctos") of lesser talent but greater power. Little did it matter that she had, as she bitterly remarks, "four superficial degrees" even though "my sex, age, and especially my life oppose it" (Reply 209).[10]

The Respuesta closes the cycle of the polemic that began with the publication of the Carta Atenagórica (Athenagoric Letter), a name that the bishop of Puebla, Manuel Fernández de Santa Cruz, had ironically given to Sor Juana's text in order to insinuate a connection between her and Athena, goddess of wisdom and war (*Obras Completas* 4: 412-439).[11] The bishop published the *Carta* without Sor Juana's knowledge[12] together with his own critique, which he signed with the pseudonym of Sor Filotea de la Cruz (*Carta de Sor Filotea de la Cruz, Obras Completas* 4: 694-697).[13]

Under the guise of a friendly reprimand and a seductive if badly intentioned exhortation to abandon her preference for the profane and turn instead to divine matters, "Filotea's" mordant insinuations represented a dangerous threat.[14] For behind Fernández de Santa Cruz lurked the ominous figure of the new archbishop of México, the Jesuit Francisco Aguiar y Seijas, whose well-known misogyny went beyond absurdity itself,[15] and behind the archbishop, the implacable machine of the Inquisition (Benassy-Berling 46). Sor Juana had stepped on the toes of the Jesuit boys' network protected by the institution of the Church—a dangerous thing to do for any woman, regardless of her personal opinions and beliefs.[16]

Sor Juana understood the stakes very well.[17] Rather than remaining silent, a possibility she seriously considered, she chose to put her cards on the table and make her defense public: to expose the hypocrisy of the bishop's *Admonishment* and of the institution that attempted to silence her. The *Respuesta*'s massive critique is a veritable *tour de force* of linguistic dis-figuration. Not only does it defend a woman's right to deal with profane and scientific themes whenever she feels so disposed, but it astutely establishes the validity of such intellectual enterprise by appealing precisely to arguments of a theological nature. The human intellect, whether male or female, is by nature potentially divine, because knowledge comes from divine grace. Since divine law is more valid and eternal than any law drafted and instituted by men, she implies, it is to God that women should appeal for justice.

Sor Juana's *Carta* was a bold rebuttal of a sermon by the polemical and celebrated Jesuit preacher Antonio Vieira, which dealt with the exegeses of Christ's Sermon on the Mount as recorded by St. Augustine, St. Thomas Aquinas, and St. John Chrysostom. In other words, not only was its subject as "edifying" as those the bishop/Filotea advised her to undertake, it also encompassed no less than the most crucial and discussed aspects of ecclesiastical dogma, abstracted in no less than one of the most important theological debates of the day: the attempt to determine whether Christ's sermon showed his preferential love for humanity.[18]

Sor Juana was quick to notice the contradiction and to expose its censoring casuistry. "Though it comes *in the guise of* counsel," she states early in her *Respuesta*,

> it will be for me equivalent to a precept, since I take no
> little comfort in the thought that my obedience seems to
> have anticipated your pastoral suggestion, as if at your
> direction, as may be inferred from the subject and the *proofs*
> of the Letter itself. I well recognize that your very sage
> advice does not apply to *it*, but to all those writings of mine
> which you will have seen on human subjects. (*Reply* 208;
> emphasis added)[19]

The bishop's *Admonishment* backfired in other ways as well. Typified by his Filotea's own incapacity to discern between "intriguing" and "edifying sciences" (the core of the accusation aimed at Sor Juana), the studied simplicity of his/her style revealed his/its own limitations (Cruz, *Admonishment* 202; Cruz, *Sueño* 696). While the bishop's intention was to curb Sor Juana's desire to participate effectively in the important theological debates of her time, the required simple-mindedness of a woman's discourse resulted in a Filotea with a limited capacity to reason. The unfortunate result of the masking was that the enunciation ends up affirming, twice and duplicitously, that sacred matters are beyond the "subtleties of nature" ("sutilezas de la naturaleza") of *every* woman—a point Sor Juana also picked up and responded to sarcastically.

Not only does she argue for protecting the rights and benefits of, at the least, private study for women,[20] she also claims equal access to sacred texts solely on the basis of merit: "the interpretation of Holy Scripture should be forbidden not only to women, considered so very inept, but to men, who merely by virtue of being men consider themselves sages, unless they are very learned and virtuous, with receptive and properly trained minds."[21] Those "of an arrogant, restless, and overbearing turn of mind, who"—like Vieira and the bishop—"are partial to new interpretations of the

Law (where precisely they are to be rejected), would benefit more from ignorance than from knowledge" (*Reply* 230).[22]

A sincere believer, Sor Juana was not overly concerned with earthly threats, especially when they were based on ignorance or willful misuse of power. In her value system, divine justice was backed by absolute truth. Earthly justice was a personal matter, negotiated with one's God in the privacy of the heart: "when I reflect on all this, here by myself" ("cuando esto considero acá a mis solas" [*Reply* 206; *Respuesta* 4: 441]). Sor Juana's ideal God was not, as we will also see in *Primero Sueño*, one to demand blind faith and unconditional obedience from disempowered and unthinking subjects. God had instilled in her a boundless love of truth ("me ha hecho Dios la merced de darme grandísimo amor a la verdad" [*Reply* 210; *Respuesta* 4: 444]), and with that love the freedom and responsibility of ethical integrity: "A special favor, this, for which I recognize my indebtedness to Him . . . , a special way of making me ashamed and embarrassed, for it is an almost exquisite type of punishment to make me, knowing myself as I do, be my own judge, deliver my own sentence" (*Reply* 206).[23] In the last instance, that belief was her best protection against the injustices perpetrated by the lost ecclesiastical sheep of the time.

Her critique of Vieira, in many ways more doctrinaire and traditional than his sermon, is based on an appeal to God's higher authority. Quoting in Latin directly from the Scriptures—"Why dost thou declare my justices, and take my covenant in thy mouth?" ([Ps. 49:16] *Reply* 208; *Respuesta* 4: 443)—she will prove definitely that those who judge her are the ones guilty of the greater sin. In a difficult balancing act of self-protection and self-defense, she will reiterate the sincerity of her devotion to the institution to which she also belonged, not because she respected its values and procedures, which she thought corrupt, but rather because she believed in its potential for greater justice:

> If [our Holy Mother Church] with her most holy authority does not forbid my [setting forth my views], why should others forbid it? Was holding an opinion contrary to Vieira an act of boldness on my part, and not His Paternity's holding one opposing the three holy Church Fathers? Is not my mind, such as it is, as free as his, considering their

common origin? Is his opinion one of the revealed precepts of Holy Faith, that we should have to believe it blindly? (*Reply* 237)[24]

This two-step movement, keeping one eye on her goals and another watchful of potential dangers, is the strongest characteristic of Sor Juana's work. An effect of censorship and repression, her intended dialogism also accounts for her sharper wit. While in the *Respuesta* she takes the institutions of learning, and especially the Church, to task, in the *Carta* and in the *Sueño* she also puts her own discursive talents to the test. Although at first sight the *Carta* might look like one those texts that Sor Juana wrote "only to please others," we cannot fail to notice the epistemophilic pleasure permeating that text, especially since it was not even intended for publication. The pleasure of engaging in theological argumentation—"the goal I aspired to" ("el fin al que aspiraba")—must have been all the greater when she allowed herself the freedom to question ideas and interpretations that she considered grounded in a faulty understanding of theology, the "style of the Queen of all Sciences"—a faulty understanding, that is, not only of her concepts, but particularly of the laws of rhetoric, which Sor Juana considered true and immutable (*Reply* 212; *Respuesta* 4: 447).

Sor Juana's strongest criticism of Vieira is precisely to have forgotten the spirit while playing with the letter of the law. She reads "the sermons of an excellent orator," she tells us in her *Carta Atenagórica,* "at times praising his basic propositions, at other times dissenting, but always surprising myself at the sight of his unequalled cunning ["ingenio"], for he stands out even more for the second than for the first."[25] In other words, Vieira's sin is to have disguised a weakness in the conceptual base of his argument— what in the *Dream* she calls Man's "flimsy foundations" ("flaco fundamento" [l. 688])—with a cunning (ab)use of the flowers of oratory.[26]

Practicing what she preached, Sor Juana's own rhetorical style is impeccable. For example, grounded in the classical tradition of oratory, the *Reply* makes use of the "formulas of affected modesty" and "self-abasement," which the manuals advised adopting from the outset as a means of capturing the audience's attention *(captatio benevolentiae)* (Perelmuter, "Estructura" 153). However, her vows of humility and obedience are but the icing on a bitter cake. They are so excessive and elaborate that they end up parodying the rules of oratory. Caught between a rock and a hard place, rather than following Vieira's example, her choice was either to remain silent and obediently please the Bishop, or to mark her silences and please herself. While, in itself, silence "explains a great deal by its insistence on not explaining" ("explica mucho con el énfasis de no explicar"), it can be made to speak by means of "some brief label... to enable one to understand what it is intended to mean" ("ponerle algún breve rótulo para que se entienda lo que se pretende que el silencio diga" [*Reply* 207; *Respuesta* 4: 441]).[27]

Silence and obedience. Paradoxical imposition on the word forces the act of writing, by nature public, to remain on the threshold between darkness and light. The context in which the *Carta* was published demonstrates that this paradox was the result of concrete social impositions extraneous to the creative act itself.

Given her own insistence that the words flowing from her pen are the product of a voice that foregrounds its femininity, and given that her dual condition of woman and writer are at the heart of the polemic that led to the *Respuesta*, we cannot but ask ourselves what Sor Juana's intention was when she directed her readers from the framework of her intellectual apologia back to the only "trifle" ("papelillo") she had written for her own pleasure. The temporal relation between these two works is not at all clear. We do not know the exact date of composition of *Primero Sueño*. Sor Juana must have written it before the *Respuesta*, for she refers to the poem in the past tense in spite of the fact that it was published for the first time in 1692, that is, over a year after her defense.[28] Was the delay due to self-censorship? Or was it due to the external pressures to abandon her writing, which came down on her with particular intensity after the publication of the *Carta* in 1690? If in her *Respuesta* Sor Juana makes public the difficulties that her creative talent ("ingenio") caused her because she was a woman, how are these difficulties manifested in her *Sueño*? What, for instance, does the erudite defense of her intellect before the growing ecclesiastical attack tell us about a poem that, at least at first sight, seems to inscribe itself within the mystical tradition?

Georgina Sabat-Rivers, who has consistently studied Sor Juana's work, considers *Primero Sueño* a "synthesis of her intellectual life, her search for a comprehensive vision of physical, physiological and psychological realities" ("Prologue," Cruz, *Obras selectas* 16). My reading of this hermetic poem adds to the list the ways in which Sor Juana's personal experience translates also into a historical and philosophical vision of a world divided unequally along gender lines. The poem reenacts this division and the conflicts it (en)genders, by re-presenting an unequal and violent war of the sexes where the real and symbolic losers are almost invariably women. A deeply rooted and unjust division of power emerges from her analysis of culture, Language (*langue*) being not only the glue that holds it together, but also the realm of its potential undoing.

Sor Juana's interest in gender issues did not start with the *Sueño*. The work of her earlier years allows for a chronological division into two divergent but complementary positions. While in the first she criticizes the superficial vanity of her contemporaries, the second reflects a mature if impassioned criticism of society itself: its contradictory impositions turn women into both its innocent victims and unconscious accomplices. The sonnet that begins "Al que ingrato me deja, busco amante" and her celebrated "Sátira filosófica" ("Philosophical Satire") mark the difference between these two periods.[29] The radical shift was the effect of a lesson learned from personal experience. The "Sátira filosófica"—which begins "Foolish are you men who wrongly fault women" ("Hombres necios que acusáis / a la mujer sin razón")—was composed in 1666, that is, during the scandal brought about by her sister's decision to live outside the bonds of marriage with Francisco Villena, after her husband walked out on her and her two children.[30]

Primero Sueño, fruit of her intellectual, artistic, and spiritual maturity, is the culmination of this trajectory. Sublating the opposition between the previous two periods, instead of criticizing the weakness of women, Sor Juana comes to see vanity as the effect rather than the cause of repression, as a mask that, like a marked silence that "says a great deal without saying," activates while concealing a powerful weapon of resistance. *Primero Sueño* will adopt this strategy and will take it to the limit of its aesthetic and existential possibilities.³¹ Around and about the discursive arabesques strung together by the poem, Sor Juana will inscribe an alternative vision of history, pointing a guiding beam of light in the direction of the obscured and silenced underside of the dominant one. As with the beam of light projected at the opening of the poem from the lighthouse of Alexandria—a pagan marvel devalued by subsequent rewritings of history—her guiding pen will illuminate the absented presence of woman as active social subject, both in the society of her time as well as throughout history.

To this end, Sor Juana turns the literary and mystic *topos* of the journey of the soul into a metaphor for the mechanics of repression and the resistance it is met with. Ultimately, her aim is to understand and expose the ways in which culture functions to neutralize the transgression that the search for knowledge represents when the seekers are women. *Primero Sueño* is an attempt to conceptualize and systematize the social and psychic mechanisms responsible for their subordination, as well as the objective and subjective, institutional and affective consequences of their daily practice.

As if to prove, both to herself and the world, that sexual prejudices have no foundation, Sor Juana enlists in the battle of letters armed with the baroque style of immense formal complexity against which the most ambitious pens of the day measured themselves and, with *Primero Sueño*, demonstrates a complete control over its limits and possibilities. In her hands, the complexity of baroque syntax and argument become the weapon-mask that would enable her to evade censorship and avoid being silenced. Like the *Respuesta*, the *Sueño* is not only an indictment of her accusers and an ardent defense of the right of women to occupy the place they deserve in history, it is also a deployment of the erudition that gives Sor Juana the right to occupy her own.³² Both works display not only her profound knowledge of history but also her familiarity with the forms of hegemonic discourse, the one, by a sophisticated handling of baroque euphuistic poetry, the other through the elegant scholastic logic of the argument. An enormous number of references to classical, popular, and theological texts, which she cites in the original, complement her masterly dominion over language.

I will not analyze all the discursive spaces with which *Primero Sueño* speculates.[33] Its complexity makes such an undertaking impossible within the confines of an essay. Suffice it to say that Sor Juana weaves into this compendium of human knowledge practically all the fundamental ideas of her day. Not only does she establish a philosophical dialogue between them, but she also considers their implications and measures their importance in terms of gender issues. Even though in her book Sabat-Rivers does not pay attention to this last aspect, she does not exaggerate when she tells us that "no other poem presents the same amount of new and old themes belonging to the philosophy and science of the day in that systematic and conscious way of enclosing everything—mythology, scientific yearnings, and the human desire for knowledge—within a poem that will tell the story of that scientific yearning in its negative-positive aspect of both frustration and success" (151)—frustrations and pleasures, we might add, of the creative effort that have a specific meaning when the hand holding the pen belongs to a woman.

The *Sueño* inscribes itself, historically and formally, in the space of rupture where two powerful epistemological currents of the time coexist and confront one another: scholastic tradition, bulwark of the Counter-Reformation, and Renaissance humanism, which reached Sor Juana through the filter of Florentine neo-Platonism, especially in its hermetic aspect which can be traced back to Egypt.[34] The laws regulating this space of rupture and encounter are conceptualized dialectically in the poem. Sor Juana is careful not to attribute an instrumental order to history. She breaks with the cause-effect relation regularly imposed on facts, which she knew results in the valorization of one current at the expense of the other. Her use of the baroque's specular logic with historical, social, and political aims is more appropriate to her epistemological framings. It makes possible the simultaneous appearance of distinct facts and signs, especially those in opposition and/or contradiction, and allows her to maintain the multiple significations to which facts have been subjected in the course of their historical development. Most of all, it facilitates a strategy of resistance that depends on its ability to disguise autobiographical referents under multiple levels of signifiers.

This discursive strategy begins with the opening of the poem. As sleep takes over the body, leaving the soul free to speculate on the possibility of reaching heights denied to matter, a play of light and shadow fuses and diffuses places, objects, concepts, and symbols. In this imaginary world, wonders of the pagan world appear side by side with biblical icons. Sor Juana gives her own interpretation to this spatial relationship. In her value system, the lighthouse of Alexandria, the pyramids of Egypt, and the tower of Babel symbolize a part of humanity's historical trajectory that, together with icons of the state and Church, are illuminated by divine Light. Nonetheless, pagan icons are also capable of casting light of their own, as is the case with the lighthouse of Alexandria, which illuminates the pyramids. Furthermore, the multidirectional play of light that opens the poem frees the creative imagination from the limited vision of a single perspective. It suggests as well that transgressing geographical, historical, or ideological barriers might lead to more fertile terrain for the attainment of knowledge.

By means of the displacement and condensation of pagan and Christian signs, Sor Juana conceptualizes historical moments of transition and reconstellation as spaces of contact, spaces where hegemonic traditions confront material and ideological changes and where contradictory and potentially antagonistic positions are negotiated. Through instrumental logic, such negotiations result in the (re)construction of signifieds at the expense of silencing one of two or more realities in conflict.[35] The baroque's specular logic, on the contrary, makes possible the simultaneous representation of opposite signs, without covering over the bipolarity and instability of the signifier/signified dyad.

Sabat-Rivers reminds us that the pyramids had already a "certain ambiguous meaning, somewhere between glorious and pagan," which oscillated between "solely human wonders or authentically divine miracles, pre-Christian revelations of Truth" (139; translation mine). Sor Juana inscribes their multiple connotations into the poem, highlighting the (am)bi-valence and power struggle that surface during such moments of encounter between different cultures. She establishes, for instance, a metonymical relation between the Egyptian and biblical heritage. The pyramids of Egypt and the tower of Babel are, respectively, icons of an ideal and a failure of language, hieroglyphs and babble symbolizing both the universality of the human potential to reach unexpected heights, and the disenchantment ("desengaño") that is the price of the failure of that ambition.

Although this type of polarity is a *topos* of the baroque, Sor Juana resorts to it in order to justify beforehand the "disproportionate pride" ("desproporcionanada soberbia") that will lead her soul to undertake an equally risky discursive journey. Her discursive adventure ultimately succeeds because her writing does not eliminate the polysemy of the dissimilar objects and places she associates. Instead, it maintains several connotative levels by means of the displacement of signifiers that, because they range from immediate denotations and/or autobiographical connotations to their multiform historical, philosophical, and ideological or religious representationality, are of a wide spectrum.

At the formal level, a new signified is produced from the displacement of a signifier onto other referents, each signified more abstract than the previous one, until a new and unexpected meaning for the poem as a whole emerges. For example, just as the pyramids and the tower of Babel are willfully materialized manifestations of the human spirit ("especies son del alma intencionales"), and just as their very materiality represents their aspiration to reach the Heavens, "just so" ("así"), Sor Juana claims, "the human mind, / like ardent flame toward Heaven / pyramidally pointed" ("la humana mente / su figura trasunta [va más allá] / y a la Causa Primera siempre aspira [ll. 403-408]). In other words, the history of the human spirit, scripted on/by the objects it has created, is not only a measure and reflection of its potential but also of the ultimately unbridgeable distance separating it from the First Cause, the Heavens, and absolute Truth.

Sor Juana's dialectical approach is deceptively simple. The laws and mechanisms governing *the encounter* of the human and the divine are an indispensable part of our historical legacy. Their structure must be recognized, analyzed, and elucidated before change can be possible. For instance, the traditional valorizing of one history at the expense of another must be questioned because of the interestedness of the choice. Ultimately, Sor Juana's tactics are intimately connected to the desire to (re)open a space within that monument to the human spirit for a history systematically silenced by the forces controlling social discourse: that history of resistance lived, and in some manner documented, by the women who came before her.

In his exhaustive study of Sor Juana, Octavio Paz notes her daily struggle to overcome the external and internal pressures to silence her.[36] Speaking of the poem, however, he excludes categorically the possibility that the soul's frustrations might be a direct consequence of being a woman. Erasing the gender specificity of the subject of the enunciation, "the protagonist," Paz insists, "has no name, age, or gender: it is the human soul":

> Not until the last words of the last line ("the world was filled with light, and I awakened") do we learn that the soul is Sor Juana's. This information in no way alters the impersonality of the poem; Sor Juana had said again and again, "Souls have no gender." The impersonality accentuates the allegorical and exemplary nature of the poem: it does not tell us a story, in the strict sense of the word "story," but unfolds before us a a model, a synthetic archetype. Personality and individuality have been carefully excluded: the poem is simultaneously allegory and confession. (366)

As Perelmuter's reading of the poem has shown ("Situación" 185-191), and as we will see later, Paz is wrong in insisting that all the autobiographical references are suppressed until the last line. Furthermore, as with other critics, the elements that according to him serve as a motor-function to the *Sueño* lead to an aporia: the poem is simultaneously "allegorical and exemplary" and a "confession"; the night when the *Sueño* unfolds, simultaneously unique and emblematic of many such nights that Sor Juana must have spent searching for knowledge by candlelight; the subject of speech, both personal or feminine and impersonal or neutral; her sex, simultaneously reality and "pretense"—all is a pretense that "naturally . . . breaks down at the end."

Built on oxymorons, the above argument, as well as the whole passage from which it is taken, is among the most tense and forced ones in Paz's study. Curiously, it is also the place where the most important (con)(tra)di(c)tion of the poem, sexual difference, (dis)appears. Paz minimizes the importance of the autobiographical references to the subject of speech, obscuring at the same time the feminine specificity of the subject of the enunciation. By differentiating contextually between them, he turns the purported gender neutrality into a momentary escape from the undesirable feminine "nature" of the author. For Paz, the soul becomes impersonal, neutral, emblematic, and eternal when it finally manages to free itself from the snares of sexual difference, that is, when this difference becomes what Luce Irigaray has called "in-difference."

In *Plotting Women*, Jean Franco also insists on the neutrality of the soul, but with aims that are diametrically opposed to those of Paz. For her, it is another example of the flexibility of Sor Juana's voice to assume a variety of enunciative positions: "a symbolic mobility that enabled her to change her gender, class, and race" (29). It should be remembered, however, that the gender mobility of the subject of speech does not necessarily alter the gender specificity of the subject of the enunciation.[37] Sor Juana not only insists on inscribing her gender(ed) perspective in the poem, she wants to put into question, unmask, and reject the mechanisms whereby the value and importance of the feminine are constantly diminished and denied. Her aim is to underscore that, in Heaven's books, a soul's value is not contingent upon gender. Even if souls are not gendered at the origin, Sor Juana suggests, the body that envelopes them on earth—one of those "intentional species of the soul" ("especies [que] son del alma intencionales" [l. 403])—is indelibly marked by experience, society, and history. As in the case of the pagan/divine duality, souls are not originally subjected to the structural silencing that ensues from gendering. The ability to imagine subjectivity as occupying a multiplicity of generic positions does not eliminate either the specificity of these positions nor the meanings we assign to the experience that makes them possible, a differential experience historically assigned to anatomical differences.

Blinded by his insistence on neutralizing Sor Juana's gender, Paz makes another important interpretative error. He sees the poem as breaking with the traditional genre of dreams of anabasis—expeditions to the world of the spirit, carried out with the help of a guide with whom the pilgrim identifies spiritually or intellectually. Although Paz is correct in noting that not a single supernatural agent intervenes to guide the soul and instruct her in her journey, he is mistaken when he claims that "in Sor Juana's dream there is no dead grandfather, no Pimander, no Virgil or Beatrice, no Cosmiel" (366). Sor Juana's rupture with the genre consists rather in the fact that she chooses as guide not one god or other well-known patriarchal ancestor, but rather several female historical and mythological subjects belonging to the forgotten and buried cultural tradition, which she seeks to recuperate by re-marking their silences. As she states in the *Respuesta,*

> I also confess that..., although, as I have said, I did not need models [*ejemplares*], all in all I was greatly assisted by the many that I have read in both divine and human letters. For I see a Deborah handing down laws, both military and political, and governing a nation that counted many a learned man. I see a most wise Queen of Sheba, so learned that she dared to challenge with enigmas the wisdom of the wisest. Rather than being reprimanded for her actions, she became the judge of the unbelieving. I see so many women so highly renowned... in sum, the whole throng of women who earned the names of Grecian, of muse, of sybil and oracle; for all of them were learned women, known, celebrated, and venerated as such by the ancients.... (4: 460-462; translation mine)

Sor Juana's eclectic reading, forced on her by cloistered isolation, had the advantage of allowing for an unrestricted exploration of worlds that the books themselves opened to her. Electa Arenal notes, for example, that Sor Juana mentions some forty-two names of women in the *Respuesta*, ranging from her contemporaries to women in mythology, Antiquity, the Bible, literature, and real life (177-178). Models for her work, they will now become illustrious guides in the journey of her soul. Her most bitter complaint is that women's cultural heritage has been swept under the grids of history, a "harm" (*daño*) that could have been "eliminated if there were older women of learning, as Saint Paul desires, and instruction were passed down from one group to another, as is the case with needlework and other traditional activities" (*Reply* 233; *Respuesta* 4: 465).[38] In *Primero Sueño*, Sor Juana reclaims her birthright and sets out to (re)form and (re)constitute the apocryphal constellation by (re)establishing a continuity torn asunder by dominant culture. It is her successful evasion of the ecclesiastical panopticon, a pleasurable journey into the self with a guarded eye turned toward the center. It is not only an allegorical representation of her Other history, but also of the ways in which Western discourse has functioned to erase women's contribution from the final print of dominant culture.

Notable for that apparent absence that has fooled so many critics, the presence of women in the poem is also made possible by the feminization of the classical and popular traditions on which Sor Juana draws as she weaves her narrative.[39] As with the silenced chorus of birds at the beginning of the poem, whose tenuous but insistent echoes turn into a loud battle cry at the end, voice and body are given to a variety of other women. The poem thus stages an immemorial battle between two factions of unequal power: one feminine, the other masculine. As with the other confrontations of opposites—resolved, as mentioned earlier, through a semiotic operation that preserves the visibility of both sides of the conflict— each encounter represents a symbolic link in the chain of conflict between the sexes that accounts for the formal development of the poem. The visible rem(a)inder is not the defeat of the feminine side, but rather its resignation.

In spite of the obstacles she finds on her way, the soul does not resign herself until the end. As she begins her incursion into the "silent domain" of night ("imperio silencioso" [l. 20]), she observes a struggle between the ascending shadow "pretending to climb the Stars" ("escalar pretendiendo las Estrellas" [l. 4]) and the latter. The "proud" ("altiva" [l. 3]) shadow engages "dreadfully" ("pavorosa") in a "gloomy war" ("tenebrosa guerra" [l. 7]). The double meaning of these words—"altiva" (proud and/or ascendant), "pavorosa" (cause and/or effect of terror), "tenebrosa" (gloomy and/or terrifying), and "pretendiendo" (intentionally and/or pretending)— maintains the (am)bi-valence of this warlike transgression. The words connote, on the one hand, an antagonistic relationship between darkness and light and, on the other, the contradictory feelings of terror and aesthetic pleasure experienced before the "beautiful lights" ("las luces bellas") of the Stars. The ambiguity and double meaning of the adverb ("pavorosamente") reflect semantically a double movement of retreat and counterattack, such as that felt before committing a "sacrilege," a sacrilege such as the one Sor Juana's soul is also on the verge of committing by breaking into the temple of knowledge, forbidden to her because of her gender.

The important dichotomy between night and day opens and closes the poem and lets loose a constant play of light and shadow—that violent *chiaroscuro* noticed by Dámaso Alonso (Cruz, *Obras Selectas* 16). In their plenitude, both night and day cover over contradictions, eradicate differences. By contrast, during sunset or sunrise, moments of transition between night and day, antagonisms and conflicts rise to the surface.

Liminal spaces are revelatory. The fall of night hides but at the same time exposes the unequal struggle between darkness and light. The Stars and the Heavens need to prove neither themselves nor their entitlement to a place in the hierarchy: they are "exempt always, always scintillating" ("exentas siempre, siempre rutilantes" [l. 6]). Sor Juana capitalizes "Stars" and "Heavens" in order to connote the official nature of their title, the source of their power. In the case of darkness, on the other hand, neither the shadow nor the chorus of birds found at the gate of night (ll. 21-24) is capitalized. This apparently innocuous distinction reproduces the power imbalance between femininity and masculinity, repeated at different levels in the poem.

The silent chorus revealed by the incipient darkness defends itself against the light while the latter tries, paradoxically, to obscure and silence their voices. The turbulent "flock" ("turba" [l. 66]) appeals to strategies of resistance and adaptation characteristic of subordinate groups and withdraws in silent protest. The nightbirds, Sor Juana suggests, are not vanquished due to cowardice or ineptitude, but rather to the terrifying strength of their enemies. The memory of the "insult" ("escarnio" [l. 52]) and the "offensive way/form" ("forma sí afrentosa" [l. 43]) with which the "sad intercadent song of the stunned flock" ("triste són intercadente / de la asombrada[40] la turba temerosa" [ll. 65-66]) had been silenced, give an epic as well as an ethical sense to their fight. By seeing it from the perspective of its victims and by giving them the recognition they deserve for their courageous resistance, Sor Juana rescues their history from oblivion with a sense of compassion, restoring justice and dignity to their struggle.[41]

Sor Juana gives transhistoric reasons to justify not only the terror of the birds, but also the "pavor" felt and occasioned by other silenced women whose voices she will also recuperate from cultural amnesia later in the poem. The nightbirds turn out to be mythological women, metamorphosed and silenced by force, punished for daring to contravene an established authoritarian order. They recoil incapacitated, unable to break through the imperious will of the threatening though seductive finger of Harpocrates, Egyptian god of silence (ll. 73-76).[42] Among them are the "daring Sisters" ("atrevidas Hermanas"), Minias's three daughters who, as a "terrible punishment" ("tremendo castigo"), were turned into bats after being driven mad for refusing to participate in the cult Bacchus had demanded of them. Sor Juana calls them "hardworking" ("oficiosas"), in recognition of their cultural labor that Bacchus had unhesitatingly destroyed: "whose home was turned to barren field ... and thread to vine and weed" ("su casa / campo vieron volver, sus telas hierba" [Harss 37-39; ll. 39-52]).

The theme of women's contribution to culture, as well as the violent attack to which they are subjected as a consequence of such daring, is introduced with the rape of Nyctimene, another nightbird protected by the silenced chorus. Turned into an owl as punishment for her father's incestuous relations with her, the metamorphosed girl, Sor Juana says, loses her courage and withdraws "shamed" ("avergonzada" [ll. 25-27]). The passive voice of the verb indicates simultaneously an admission of guilt and a consequence of her father's incestuous desire. The conceit is reminiscent of the famous opening lines of the "Sátira filosófica" ("Philosophical Satire"), where Sor Juana criticizes men for faulting women for effects of which they are the cause.

Metamorphosis functions as disguise as well. It helps to establish an important connection between Nyctimene and Minerva, learned goddess of wisdom and war and, by extension, with Sor Juana herself. Turning the unjust punishment in her favor, the "sacrilegious" ("sacrílega") Nyctimene "lies in ambush" ("acecha") at Minerva's temple, waiting to avail herself in whichever way possible—through "doors," "clairbuoyes," and "cracks"—of the fruits of the goddesses knowledge. By sucking the olive oil from the "sacred lamps" ("faroles sacros"), "shining" ("lucientes") with "perennial flame," the transgressor steals, recuperates, and is nurtured by the fruits of the goddess's apocryphal knowledge, forcefully appropriated by dominant culture (ll. 25-38). Sor Juana describes this type of forceful appropriation in similar terms in the *Respuesta:* "At the topmost point of temples, figures of the Winds and of Fame are commonly placed as ornaments; to protect them from the birds, they cover them all over with barbs. This sounds like a defense; in fact it is an obligatory adjunct" (*Reply* 220).[43]

Sabat-Rivers observes that "more than a visual image of darkness" the description of the nightbird's chorus yields "a paradoxical auditive image of silence" (*Sueño* 132). This synaesthetic image of changing personae and intermittent cadences functions, like Echo's voice, as a background to, in this case, a listening Narcissus, their ethereal, perennial, and urgent voices teaching the journeying soul other ways of seeing and hearing.

If knowledge is transgression, in the clothes of a woman it becomes either an illicit act or a sin, depending on the institutions that control access to it. Represented at this stage of the *Sueño* by the forces guarding Minerva's temple, the exclusionary power of guardian institutions obliges the transgressor to resort to strategies of resistance that place her outside patriarchal law. As Sor Juana most likely knew, the mythological olive tree, whose oil the owl steals, was emblematic of Minerva's victory over Poseidon. The warring goddess planted the tree during a dispute with Poseidon over the ownership of Attica as a way of establishing her rights over that territory. At this stage of the *Dream*, both Minerva's and Nyctimene's ingeniousness and tenacity function as models of survival for the soul, once more connecting her, and them, to the invisible edifice constructed throughout history by those "so many women so highly renowned" ("tantas y tan insignes mujeres") Sor Juana names in the *Respuesta* (4: 460-461).

Not all the victims that the soul finds in her journey are women. When the characters are men, however, their punishment is invariably the consequence of a lack of solidarity with the cause of women. In general terms, their crime consists of either trying to intrude into a world that values the wishes and opinions of women

(Actaeon) or of interfering with the desires of a goddess in favor of a god (Ascalaphus).

Playing again with metaphors of light and darkness, Sor Juana refers to Actaeon as "once upon a time enlightened monarch" ("monarca en otro tiempo esclarecido" [ll. 113-122]), now a hunter devoured by his own hounds. According to the myth, this happened after Artemis turned him into a stag for having dared to lay eyes on her naked body. As did Sor Juana after finding marriage repugnant, the goddess had made strict vows of chastity. And Ascalaphus, once "Pluto's prattling spy" ("parlero/ministro de Plutón un tiempo" [Harss, l. 51; ll. 53-54]), was turned into an owl by Demeter for revealing that her daughter Persephone, violently kidnapped by the god, had eaten pomegranates. By this act, the chaste maiden was condemned, despite her divine mother's unrelenting struggle to save her, to spending six months every year in her kidnapper's subterranean kingdom.

The theme of Persephone's abduction and Demeter's betrayal will reappear later in the poem, where Sor Juana indirectly contrasts the behavior of Ascalaphus and Arethusa. Transformed into a fountain, this time in order to avoid being raped, Arethusa's "useful curiosity" ("útil curiosidad" [l. 723]) helps rather than hinders Demeter's search. As in the case of Nyctimene, with "crystal clear" direction ("curso dirige cristalino" [l. 714]) she flows "through lands once bounteous" ("campañas hermosas"), penetrating the "frightful caverns / sunk in horrendous abyss" ("las cavernas pavorosas / del abismo tremendo" [Harss, ll. 705-708; ll. 714-718]) of Pluto's reign, until she finds his wedding bed, now sadly shared by his triple-faced wife ("tálamo ya de su triforme esposa"), and guides Demeter to the encounter with her lost daughter (ll. 712-729). It is significant that this passage—where resistance to the patriarchal order is defined in terms of a complicity between women, and where the mother/daughter relationship is valued above the bonds of matrimony imposed by an insensitive god against the will of both—should follow the temporary defeat of Sor Juana's soul (ll. 709-711) and should precede her recovery.

Much has been written about the soul's defeat. Scholars have coincided in placing it at the center of the poem, presenting it also as the failure of the intuitive faculty to attain knowledge.[44] While the narrative centrality of the moment is obvious, the soul's defeat is not so clear. It is apparent that she loses the battle, but not the war. The soul, Sor Juana suggests, is struck down by the blinding light of an implacable Sun whom she surreptitiously accuses of a lack of compassion—for punishing indiscriminately both the strong and the less fortunate who had placed their trust in him—and of insensitivity to the consequences of his peerless power. Disregarding the power imbalance, the Sun punishes, by flogging with his rays, those who, "unsuspicious," once dared to but now cry for having attempted to look his blinding power in the face ("que fuerzas desiguales / despreciando, castigan rayo a rayo / el confiado, antes atrevido / y ya llorado ensayo" [ll. 462-465]).[45] This accusation, which comes close to heresy, is also an appeal to divine pity and tolerance as well as to a sense of justice.

Furthermore, the defeat of the soul is not due, as has been claimed, to a failure of the intuition (by a curious coincidence, a category of knowledge generally and almost exclusively attributed to women) but rather, as Sor Juana herself underscores, to a failure of the method that the intellectual faculty ("entendimiento" [l. 469]) had employed so far as it tried to participate, like the mystics (albeit with different means), in the knowledge of the divine.

In the opening epigraph to this essay, Einstein articulates his life project in more contemporary terms than Sor Juana, but the goals are the same: to study God's book, nature, as well as the book of civilization, and to reach beyond the confines of human knowledge until the eternal laws of the universe are deciphered—a heroic and ambitious attempt that, for women, as Sor Juana discovered, led to envy, silence, self-mortification, and even to an early death.

When she began *Primero Sueño*, Sor Juana was still confident that the intellective and intuitive faculties had the potential of conceptualizing, and maybe of realizing, alternative options. After her soul is blinded by the power of the Sun, and "the simplest part remained obscure / of Nature's works closest at hand" ("aun la más fácil parte no entendía / de los más manüales / efectos naturales" [Harss, ll. 696-697; ll. 709-711]), Sor Juana looks for help elsewhere: in other "manuals," in other discursive systems. This is when she remembers the wickedness of Pluto and Ascalaphus, finds solace in the relief of Demeter's sorrow by Arethusa's generosity, and realizes that the latter learned to overcome the obstacles in her path by keeping a clear eye on her goal (ll. 712-714). This is also where she outlines the new strategy that will ensure the success of her journey.

Constructing a conceit around the common reflection on the ephemeral beauty of a flower, Sor Juana redefines vanity, which she calls "a feminine art" ("industria femenil" [l. 753]), and realizes its potential as the ultimate tool of resistance available to the weak; to those who under the feigned veil of a "translucent complexion" "turn the deadliest poison / to even deadlier effect" ("el más activo / veneno, hace dos veces ser nocivo / en el velo aparente / de la que finge tez resplandeciente" [Harss, ll. 752-753; ll. 753-756]). Why is a woman's frailty, she asks, like a flower, "in ivory... circumscribed" ("por qué ebúrnea figura / circunscribe su frágil hermosura" [Harss, ll. 726-727; ll. 731-732])? Why does she dress in colors delicate yet strong (like ivory), "exhale... amber" (sighs, that solidify in the air)? And, most importantly, how, in spite (or because) of the manner of her dress ("lightest clad / in flimsiest garment" ("el leve, si más bello / ropaje" [Harss, ll. 731-732; ll. 737-738]), does she have the power to "explain" to the wind (l. 738) how she wishes to reproduce and succeeds in doing so?

What is at stake here is precisely reproduction: the (parthenogenetical) reproduction of women's knowledge, of tradition, of self. As in the case of the immaculate conception—suggested by "the broken bud's white seal" of "Venus's sweet wound" ("que— roto del capullo el blanco sello—/de dulce herida de la Cipria Diosa" [ll. 742-743]), its blood scattered by the directed wind— reproduction takes place here without the participation or interference of men. Unlike men painters who assign one shade to every flower ("el que la colora / candor al alba, púrpura al aurora" [l. 745-746]), Sor Juana's flowers multiply with the wind as daughters ("multiplica hija" [ll. 739-740]) of "mixed" and complex shadings.

Armed with the above insights, the soul then returns to the matter at hand. Not being a mystic, Sor Juana knows that the distance separating her from the First Cause is unbridgeable. If language "recoils in fear" ("se espeluza" [l. 765]) when asked to explain even a "single object" ("un objeto solo" [l. 757]), let alone a "segregated species" ("especie segregada" [l. 761]), why should we expect words to flow fearlessly, like Arethusa's waters, when thought's "timid (tímido el pensamiento [l. 758]) discursive tools crumble, like a "coward" ("cobarde el discurso se desvía") by the sheer size of the "terrifyingly immense machine" ("espantosa máquina inmensa") in the laws of Nature under investigation (ll. 760-780)?

After other such tribulations, the soul concludes that her defeat has been the result and condition of epistemological limitations, which are historically determined, rather than to a fault or lack intrinsic to her being. Now free to explore a more promising epistemological frame, she resorts to rational scientific analysis, introduced with the Renaissance, and develops discursive strategies that will allow her to explore the limits and possibilities of its historical (dis)encounter with scholasticism.

Applying the scientific method, she will question the Renaissance belief in the unlimited potential of science—amazing observation, the consequences of which we are only now beginning to grasp—while, without abandoning her scholastic training, recognizing as well that, given the magnitude and complexity of the totality of knowledge, it is impossible that one person alone, "forcibly cramming the vast overflow / of objects into a tiny vessel" ("ciñiendo con violencia lo difuso / de objeto tanto, a tan pequeño vaso" [Trueblood, ll. 568-569; ll. 557-558]) could comprehend it all.

To reach the heights of sacred theology, she writes in the *Respuesta*, "it is necessary to ascend the steps of human arts and sciences, for how can one who has not mastered the style of the ancillary branches of learning hope to understand that of the queen of them all?" (*Reply* 213).[46] If that is the case for theology, how can human "intellectual eyes," regardless of how "perspicacious" and "beautiful" ("perspicaces y bellos" [ll. 440-441]) they might be, hope to reach the same heights as the First Cause itself?

Octavio Paz has correctly rejected the interpretation that inserts the poem within the mystical tradition. According to him, the theme of the *Sueño* is the "inverse of revelation." The poem is, he tells us however, "the first example of an attitude—the solitary soul confronting the universe—that later, beginning with Romanticism, would be the spiritual axis of Western poetry" (367).[47] Such an interpretation of the genre's singularity imposes an anachronistic meaning on the poem. By ascribing a proto-existentialism to her, it ignores Sor Juana's insistence that she would not have chosen solitude had she had a choice. It also implies that the refusal of mystical experience is equivalent to a denial of the existence of God. The fact is that to seek a new epistemological framework for the apprehension of reality does not imply a belief that sign systems are capable of representing the intuition of the ineffable.

The theme of the poem would be "the inverse of revelation" only in the religious sense of this experience. In the context of Renaissance rationalism, however, the revelation that follows the encounter of the soul with the First Cause is of another kind. Sor Juana toys with the possibility of reaching a balance between religion, whose immutable truths were unquestionable at the time, and scientific reason, whose methods promised a more correct *approximation* to the truth. As we have seen, Sor Juana believed that the human spirit has the ability to come close to the First Cause because it is everyone's origin and *telos*, regardless of earth-bound differences. But to come close is not the same as to transcend. To transcend implies a denial of the distance separating words from things, sign from referent, representation from the real—a distance language is forever condemned to try to bridge.

It is the knowledge of this impossibility that keeps Sor Juana, scientist, philosopher, and poet, from falling into the dangerous mysticism that the Church itself feared as heretical. She is not interested in either denying or affirming the possibility of a mystical experience. Like the scientist who changes the lens of a microscope in order to get closer to her object of vision, she simply transplants a religious *topos* to a different framework and experiments with the outcome. The soul's journey would have ended in failure only if the poem were the testimony of a failed mystical experience. If, on the contrary, we read it as a philosophical experiment, it becomes evident that instead of scripting the desire to immerse oneself in an orgasmic loss of consciousness until the body transcends its materiality, the poem tells the tale of a traveler who is interested in transcending the horizon of the heretofore imaginable with the help of her intuitive and intellective faculties, intuition *and* reason, in order to get closer to an understanding of the universal laws of divine creation.

The other kind of transcendence ascribed to the poem is that of the femininity of its author. In mystic writings, gender becomes problematic when the experience of uniting the profane with the sacred is appropriated and/or written by women. When the author is a man, the danger diminishes considerably. In his *Noche Oscura* (*Dark Night*) for instance, San Juan de la Cruz has no problem describing the union of spirit and matter with the divine presence in explicitly sexual terms: "oh! night, you who joined woman and man in love, she transformed into her lover" (¡oh noche que juntaste / amado con amada, / amada en el amado transformada! [139]).

San Juan resolves the problem of sexual difference by transcending it. The imaginary gain of his mystical experience is a polymorphous and unstable sexuality where masculinity is transcended to make room for an androgynous subject: the male poet becomes Christ's feminized beloved. The instability of the dreamer's gender is produced and reproduced by the untranslatable phonetic and semantic play of the word "trans-forma-da," which contains the vowels and consonants that literally shape the words "amado" and "amada" (beloved).

In the *Sueño*, the senses, both semantic and generic, also become diffuse, but under a more elaborate disguise and with very different ends. The subject of speech slides into subject positions traditionally associated with either masculinity or femininity, but their specificity is never eliminated: one never becomes the other. Although she shows that gender difference, and especially its differential value, is an effect of instituted social practices propped up by discursive constructions, Sor Juana preserves the conceptual and material barriers separating both positions. While her deconstructive strategy brings out the frictions and contradictions of sexual difference, the specular logic of the baroque allows her to stretch this difference to the limit, turning the world on its head, so to speak, until it is seen as but a historical construct and an effect of language and, as such, susceptible to change.

By trans-forming the epistemological parameters defining the mystical understanding of transcendence, Sor Juana performs for literature what until then was possible only through a mystical experience. She not only creates a subject of enunciation that supersedes that of the *Dark Night*, she takes advantage of one of the few discursive avenues at the disposal of women in her day in order to transform a fundamentally religious experience into an intellectual one. At a time when, as Arenal has pointed out, "smart women were seen as precocious children (*monjita, damita*)" and "women who wrote autobiographies were supposed to be making total confessions" (176), her deference to the Holy Church did not go so far as to settle for the only subject position at the disposal of women, a position of nonbeing, or to comply with the "holy ignorance" that was expected of them. *First Dream* is not a confession, as Paz has suggested, but an accusation and a denunciation of those who, by confusing human with divine power, turn the latter into a travesty.

The soul's defeat is rather a disenchantment ("desengaño"), an inevitable step in the difficult spiritual, artistic, and intellectual exploration that signals the beginning of an epistemological crisis. At this critical moment, stunned by her (mis)encounter with the First Cause, the soul, instead of losing her powers of observation, momentarily steps outside the pre-Renaissance episteme and comes to the conclusion that her confusion is due rather to the failure of the "categories" of thought that order reality. Categories are, Sor Juana writes, a product of artifice ("artificiosas") *and* a metaphysical reduction ("reducción metafísica") of the universal laws of Nature (ll. 581-588), which humanity has yet to understand. Without a connecting thread, the elements that compose the conceptual structure that gave it meaning fall apart. With impeccable and innovative intellectual integrity, Sor Juana brackets in this manner the totalizing and rigid vision of the Counter-Reformation.

The fundamental difference between epistemological crisis and mystic transcendence explains the movement of retreat, reconsideration, and reconstitution that follows the frustrated journey of the imagination. It also puts into a different perspective the limited reality to which Sor Juana cannot help but awaken, a reality that had motivated her desire to explore other alternatives in the first place.

More than a defeat, the images depicting the soul's reaction to the "vision of non vision," as Paz calls it (367), denote astonishment and confusion. For even at the worst moment, Sor Juana tells us, "from the confusion of species it embraced," the soul "formed a picture of disordered chaos" ("inordinado caos retrataba / de confusas especies que abrazaba" [Trueblood, ll. 561-562; ll. 550-551]). Momentarily stunned by chaos, which she never stops recording ("retrataba") however, the soul decides that in order to understand the logic of creation she must begin from the beginning.

Replacing the deductive method with the inductive, she will analyze the parts of the crumbled building one by one and order them according to categories more adequate to what, since Foucault, we would call the new discursive formation she is about to articulate. As she recovers the confidence in her own imagination, "fuerza imaginativa" (l. 643), the soul starts to order things according to genus and species, though assigning a different value to the established Aristotelian categories (ll. 575-599). She also realizes that the difficulty in deciphering the laws of creation is not due to their incomprehensibility, inaccessibility, or resistance to being known. Instead, "all of creation" ("todo lo crïado" [l. 445]) offers itself to the soul's eyes as "an immense assemblage, / ... / though holding out to sight / some chance to be taken in" ("un inmenso agregado, / ... [que] a la vista quiso manifiesto / dar señas de posible" [Trueblood, ll. 457-460; ll. 446-448]). Forced to face its own limitations, the understanding had ceded terrain to the vision of nonvision, a temporary blindness that would lead to greater insight.

Sor Juana suggests that, instead of accepting the offer of "all of creation" and following its clues, the terrorized soul "turned coward and drew back" ("retrocedió cobarde" [Trueblood, l. 464; l. 453]). Later in the poem, she will refer to cowardice again, stating clearly that it is rather an effect of fear, significantly, both of failure and success. "Stunned" ("asombrado" [l. 767]) maybe too quickly, "timid thinking" ("tímido el pensamiento" [l. 758]) "refuses" to valiantly participate in "the contest" for knowledge, "turning its back" on the challenge because "it fears comprehending badly, or never or too late" ("da las espaldas al entendimiento, / y asombrado el discurso se espeluza / del difícil certamen que rehusa / acometer valiente, / porque teme—cobarde— / comphenderlo o mal, o nunca, o tarde" [ll. 764-769]). Terror and cowardice, two sides of the same coin, she suggests, are the biggest obstacles to knowledge: point zero, the limit of consciousness. Therein clash the desire for knowledge and the terror of transgressing limits imposed on the spirit, consciously or unconsciously, by others or by oneself. Years before, Sor Juana had written in a ballad: "there are neither enclosures nor prisons for the soul, because she is only confined by those she constructs herself."⁴⁸ With time she would come to see things with a lesser feeling of omnipotence and with a greater sense of the difficulty of overcoming restrictions imposed by the socio-symbolic order on individual freedom. When she introduces the figure of Phaethon into the poem, for instance, she will say that "more than fear" ("más que temor"), cowardice is a healthier response, the result of lessons learned from the example of those less fortunate transgressors who have been chastised for their daring ("ejemplos de escarmiento" [l. 791]).

Like the women she saw earlier in the poem, the soul does not surrender either. Instead, she continues to search amid the ruins of the "inordinate chaos" (l. 550) for her mislaid voice. Although her sight is encumbered by the excessive number of objects ("entorpecida / con la sobra de objetos" [ll. 450-451]), the intellective faculty does not give up. She recovers from her confusion "by degrees" ("por grados" [l. 513]) and resumes her journey. This time following different signposts, she first takes refuge in the darkness, a space once filled with memories of pain and terror, which now serves to give her new strength. Without deviating from the Thomist principles of cognition, Sor Juana underscores the relation between the essences of night and shadow, shadow being the indeterminate space between light and darkness and, metonymically, between sense and nonsense. Due to that sympathetic relation, the soul appeals to the shadow's "pious mediat[ion]" (piadosa medianera) to recover her vision. The shaded soul,

> appeals to that same shade which formerly
> had been a shadowy obstacle to the sight,

against the light's offenses,

. . .

so the shadow, merciful mediator,
now serving as an instrument
to bring about the eyes' recovery
their gradual restoration,
so that, unfalteringly,
reliably, they may discharge their task.

(Trueblood 184)[49]

A liminal space is once more the appropriate "instrument" for laying out the scheme that will eventually help Sor Juana to displace Man from the central place he has occupied in history, making possible the (re)valorization of the now visible place occupied by Woman.

From the ruins of the once enormous epistemological edifice emerges a small and still malformed "embryo": the germ of a new conceptual construction that will give different (pregnant?) meanings to the search and will return to the soul her voice, silenced by force and fright. "The soul . . . pull[ed] her attention back," not yet knowing how to find the silenced speech within herself, terror "allowing her scarcely more / than a rudimentary embryo" (Trueblood 184-185).[50]

For the rest of the poem, this embryonic concept will grow as if in a laboratory dish ("pequeño vaso" [1: 558]), developing in stages that correspond to the hierarchical order of the universal Chain of Being, but with a twist. The soul methodically revises the medieval scheme of things inherited by the Renaissance, beginning with the mineral kingdom, going on to the vegetal and the animal, and ending up with Man whom she calls the most powerful "hinge" ever imagined ("bisagra . . . de mayor portento / que discurre el humano entendimiento" [ll. 690-691]). As with the other links ("engarces") conforming the Universal Chain, however, the central place Man occupies turns out to be an effect of artificial appearances and correspondences. As Sor Juana says in the *Respuesta*, the Chain is held together "by means of variations and occult connections . . . [so]

that they *appear* correlated and bound together with marvelous concert and bonding" (emphasis added).[51] Appearances, she has always insisted, are deceptive.

Diverging from the Renaissance's unquestioned belief in the unlimited potential of Man, Sor Juana sees him as a "connecting hinge" ("bisagra engarzadora" [l. 659]): one that not only joins but also limits, hooks, locks together, sutures. As with Nebuchadnezzar's "eminent statue" with whom she compares Man (Harss, ll. 671-673; l. 684), this "portent" has a head of gold and "feet of crumbled clay" (fábrica portentosa / que, cuanto más altiva al cielo toca, / sella el polvo la bocca [Harss, ll. 672-673; ll. 678-679]). Sor Juana inverts the values of the hierarchy and suggests that a system that privileges one extreme, calling it "noble" (l. 624), to the detriment of the lower levels, which serve it as base and support, is not only unjust; it is also unstable. Sor Juana questions in this manner not only the right that men feel to "boundless pride" but by gendering the generalized use of the noun "man," which pretends to be applicable to both genders equally; she also extends the roots of the paradigm she has been deciphering to language itself.

A similar inversion of values is applied in the *Respuesta* when Sor Juana conceives of frying eggs in the same terms as any other scientific experiment. There she implies that when direct observation and empirical deduction are applied equally to every surrounding phenomenon, unexpected results and discoveries of great importance can take place—that is, if no a priori hierarchization is imposed on them. "What could I not tell you, my Lady," she says half in jest, "of the secrets of Nature which I have discovered in cooking!" (225). She then jabbingly asks Sor Filotea "what is there for us women to know, if not bits of kitchen philosophy?" (226). Finally taking the hierarchical inversion to its logical extreme: "If Aristotle had been a cook," she insists, "he would have written much more" (226). By contrast, Sor Juana "[studied] everything God had created, all of it being my letters, and all this universal chain of being my book" (224).[52] Everything that God created, no matter how insignificant, carries the imprint of divine wisdom. Hierarchization, ordering according to categories, and imposing a structure and value judgment on that order, is a man-made perversion of the purpose of creation.

In the *Sueño*, Sor Juana also displaces the value of the links of the chain by feminizing the privileged spaces they occupy. Nature, she reminds us, is "the second productive cause" (God is the first). Like a beneficent mother, not only does she support the hierarchical order built on and out of her body, but gives it life and nurtures it. For example, the "inanimate beings" (the mineral kingdom) are the "least favored, / but still cherished" ("menos favorecido / sino más desvalido" [Harss, ll. 607-608; ll. 620-623]). Instead of the "bisagra engarzadora," the soul now privileges Tethys—ambitious mother of Achilles, daughter of Oceanus—described as a generous, efficient, and extremely intelligent mother.

Tethys's participation marks the moment in which the new "series" or structure replaces the hierarchical order of the great chain. Goddess of the waters, she reigns here over all of nature. As with the fish, who at nightfall were protected by the oceans, "asleep / in the oozy beds / of their cavernous dark" bosom ("lamosos / ... oscuros senos cavernosos" [ll. 90-91]), every link forming the Universal Chain is nurtured by her generosity. By means of a recurring metaphor of suckling, the ocean, primal source of all life, is represented as the undiscriminating, generous, and protective mother. Once more, the "attractive" Tethys gives birth to a new understanding, her "primo-genital," or first-born, and nurtures it with the "natural ... most sweet nourishment" flowing from her "fertile maternal breasts," thus helping Sor Juana's method to "pass on to the most noble hierarchy" (ll. 617-632). The soul moves on, again with the guidance of a feminine mythic model.[53]

The fluidity of this primo-genital method of evaluation and selection demands an open, process-oriented approach. The soul realizes that the new structure is also one more of those "species intended by the soul" ("especies [que] son del alma intentionales" [ll. 403-408]). It consists of mutable forms whose usefulness and value depend on the place they occupy within a discursive formation at specific times. That is, a formation that is not rigid and predetermined, because it is composed of different substances. The method used to decipher its economy is once more based on the example of Tethys who is:

> engaged in the combined
> and contrary operation
> whereby, fourfold, it attracts
> and, diligently, now selects
> its needs, now superfluity expels,
> and from abundance, only
> substance to its use converts.
>   (Harss, ll. 617-23)[54]

Reproductions protect appearances and hide the truth. Getting closer to the substance of things, "with a following wind on a milky sea" ("viento en popa y mar en leche"), as she says in the *Respuesta* (*Reply* 218; *Respuesta* 4: 452), the soul is now ready to embark fully on the new stage of her formal, intellectual, and aesthetic project. The imaginative faculty ("bold phantasy") chooses from among the ruins those elements that, although of maybe lesser "form," "more minor" or "lower," are definitely more sensitive and of "greater beauty" and thus are capable of presenting a "fair[er]" challenge to the Sun. This realization represents Sor Juana's greatest transgression and affront to the established order:

> then, this form once examined,
> to scrutinize another form, more beautiful—
> one that possesses feeling
> (and, what is more, equipped with powers
> of apprehending through imagination)
> grounds for legitimate complaint—
> if not indeed for claiming insult—
> on the part of the brightest star
> that sparkles, yet lacks all feeling,
> however magnificent its brilliant light—
> for the lowest tiniest creature
> surpasses even the loftiest of stars,
> arousing envy.
>   (Trueblood, ll. 650-662)[55]

The inversion of values is now complete. The Sun, most "lú-cida ... Estrella," is transformed into "inanimate" matter. He is also unfeeling. This time its "proud ... sparkles" ("resplandores") shine, but with anger. At the opening of the poem we saw how the Stars fought against the ascending movement of the shadow because its unfurling threatened to reveal the contradictions veiled by their light (ll. 1-12). In the above lines, Sor Juana tells us explicitly that the reason for their attack was envy, a point she also will stress in the *Respuesta:* "Oh singularity, set up as a target for envy and an object of contradiction! Any eminence, be it in dignity, nobility, wealth, beauty, learning, is subject to this penalty, but most implacably subject to it is eminence of mind" (*Reply* 221; *Respuesta* 4: 455).[56]

The intelligent are the most vulnerable, because the greater their understanding, "the more modest and long-suffering, and the less prone they are to defend" themselves (455). Modesty and silence, long-suffering daughters of understanding, are indicators of wisdom. Cowardice in the face of envy comes from having learned the potential consequences of a confrontation with the brute force of "wealth and power" [455]. In contrast to Sor Juana, the aim of those who abuse their power is not to arrive at truth and justice, but rather to protect their own interest and the institutions that guarantee it.

The only solution to this well-known problem, Sor Juana suggests, is to continue to displace, methodically and insistently, the kingdom of the Sun from the center. Success in this enterprise can come only from learning the ways in which the human versions of the First Cause function—stories, myths, monuments, rhetoric, etc.: to unmask its distortions, to fight it in its own territory, with equal weapons and in the name of a higher justice. The soul's model at this stage of the journey is the figure of Phaethon.

Sor Juana's identification with the Sun's bold son is straight-forward: "pernicious model beckoning / wings to repeated flight" ("Tipo es, antes, modelo: / ejemplar pernicioso / que alas engendra a repetido vuelo" [Harss, ll. 801-802; ll. 803-805]). "By Phaethon's feat inspired" (Harss, l. 787), she inserts the second autobiographical reference into the poem. Hers is also an effort, she tells us, where "a pathway summoning it to dare; / once treading this, no punishment can deter / the spirit bent upon a fresh attempt / (*I* mean a thrust of new ambition)" ("abiertas sendas al atrevimiento, / que una ya vez trilladas, no hay castigo / que intento baste a remover segundo / [segunda ambición, *digo*]"; Trueblood 191, ll. 803-806; ll. 793-796), emphasis mine.[57]

Like Juana Inés, Phaethon was the bastard son of an absent father and of a mother who raised him without his help. Apollo had abandoned him at birth, not seeing him until several years later, when, following his mother's advice, the ambitious young man went to find him in order to demand the rights befitting the son of such an illustrious father. Applying a sorjuanesque strategy—"finding in terror itself a spur / to prick up courage" ("Del mismo terror haciendo halago / que al valor lisonjea" [Trueblood 191, ll. 818-819; ll. 807-808])—Phaethon asks to ride the luminous carriage driven daily by his father around the planet. In what Sor Juana qualifies as an irresponsible and cowardly gesture coming from a father, Apollo acquiesces: "the laureate showed a great deal of cowardice before conceding, for at least he could have struggled somewhat harder" ("demasiada acusaba cobardía / el lauro antes de ceder, que en la lid dura / haber siquiera entrado" [ll. 783-785]).

"Brave example" ("ejemplar osado" [l. 786]), Phaethon pays for his "daring" (l. 793) with his life. The classic emblem of a poet's daring search for immortality through art, he ends up, like Sor Juana herself, by "his name / in ruin immortalized" ("su nombre eternizar en su rüina" [Harss, 799-800; l. 802]).[58] Making still more evident the parallel with her own life, Sor Juana uses Phaethon as a model also for the appropriation and trans-formation of the dominant language, now in ruins. Paying attention to its most minute and apparently innocuous details in order to rescue what is worthy of glory, with the same "ambitious desire" ("ánimo ambicioso") as Phaethon, the soul "spells old glories with the letters found in the rubble" ("las glorias deletrea entre los caracteres del estrago" [ll. 809-810]).

Phaethon's defeat represents an important lesson for all those whose wings have been "engendered" (l. 805) by his example. The point is not to follow to the letter the example of a hero whose body was destroyed by *hubris* before his spirit could make sense of the experience—just as it was not a matter of copying the mystic model, whose corporeal language does not leave recuperable traces. What is needed is to create a new language: to "spell old glories" in ways that will make it possible to overcome the gender division of signification, without silencing the voices at the margins of discourse that supposedly threaten to contaminate the purported purity of its truth.

Sor Juana will insist in the *Respuesta* that their silence is due to women's exclusion from the educational system and to the lack of access of young women to the knowledge of older women teachers.[59] In the *Dream*, she infers that their exclusion becomes effective and is perpetuated by means of explicit and implicit forms of repression, as for example, official censorship, calculated indifference, and, as a last resort, public punishment:

> Either the punishment should not be known
> so that the crime would never become contagious,
> a politic silence covering up instead,
> with a statesman's circumspection,
> all record of the proceedings;
> or let a show of ignorance prevail,
> or the insolent excess
> meet its just deserts by secret sentence
> without the noxious example
> ever reaching public notice.
>
> (Trueblood 200)[60]

Excessively insolent,[61] then, Phaethon threatens to contaminate an order administered according to arbitrary norms and without popular consensus. Power protects itself more by censorship than by repression (see Foucault). It is better served by a disappeared person than by a martyr; by that which is ignored ("lo ignorado") than by what is learned from suffering ("lo escarmentado" [ll. 817-826]). Over three hundred years before René Girard noticed the symbolic importance of contamination as well as the dangers it presents to the survival of culture,[62] and equally as many before Derrida observed the same process in the mode of functioning of writing itself (Derrida, *Dissemination*), Sor Juana reached the same conclusions. When she analyzes the relation between dominant discourse and its margins, she uses an almost identical conceptual paradigm, describing it in astonishingly similar terms. The dissemination of alternative experiences, she writes, is the greatest threat to the hegemonic order,

> for broadcasting makes the wickedness
> of the greatest crime all the greater
> till it threatens a widespread epidemic,
> while, left in unknown isolation,
> repetition is far less likely
> than if broadcast to all as a would-be lesson.
> (Trueblood 191)[63]

Sor Juana was not alone in recognizing the transgressive power of language, and especially of its dissemination's "contaminating" potential. As is evident from his *Admonishment*, the Bishop also knew that the appropriation of language from the margins is dangerous only when it is allowed to reach the ears of others, in other words, when it is not denied the constitutive potential of interpellation. "It is true," he/she slyly cajoles Sor Juana, "that Saint Paul says that women should not teach; but he does not dictate that they should not study in order to know; because all he wanted was to avoid the risk of arrogance for our sex, always prone to vanity" ("Carta de Sor Filotea de la Cruz," *Apuntes* 66).

The polarization between center and margin is exacerbated as the cycle of the poem draws to a close. Here, Sor Juana divides the planet into two opposing halves ("antípoda[s] opuest[as]" [l. 890]) and has night and day reigning separately, joined, however, by a dividing line that becomes progressively more unstable and conflicted, and where a series of images of struggle abound (ll. 888-894). While before nightfall the moon occupied the orb separating the Stars from the darkened earth (ll. 12-19), before day arrives it is Venus, the Morning Star, who occupies this transition space.

Sor Juana inverts the goddess's negative association with vanity, referring to her positively as gentle and timid, an appeasing ("apacible") though daring Queen, whose "beautiful forehead, [is] crowned with early morning lights" (ll. 904-905). Significantly, she is a star that is both a masculine ("el hermoso / apacible lucero" [l. 897]) and feminine signifier, "precursor," of the sun ("bella precursora / signífera del Sol" [ll. 917-918]). The Sun, on the other hand, is once more described as a threatening "Father of the burning Light" ("Padre de la Luz ardiente" [l. 887]).

Dawn, Aurora, also appears after Venus and occupies an equally poli-valent space. Although significantly called "tyrannical usurper / of the empire of daylight" ("tirana usurpadora / del imperio del día," Cruz, *Admonishment* 194; ll. 911-912), she wears "a laurel crown of countless shadows" ("negro laurel de sombras mil ceñía" [l. 9133]) on her forehead. Neither light nor shadow, she not only assumes the function that darkness had at the beginning, but also takes on the substantial properties of water.[64] In this manner, Aurora transgresses the natural element with which she was typically associated in the scholastic conception of the four elements, to end up related, metonymically, to Tethys and Arethusa.[65]

Once more, the confusion and trans-substantiation of elements occurs during one of those cognitive (un)suturing moments that serve as links to the poem. In Dusk's undetermined space, we again see a fight between opposites who are marked by unstable gender differences. Sor Juana resorts here to her knowledge of astronomy to depict the rotation of the Earth with respect to the Sun and uses an ostensibly martial lexicon to insert this physical phenomenon into the general symbolism of the poem.

After defeating Night with great difficulty, Aurora confronts the Sun as an "amazon arrayed in countless lights / (her armor against the night), beautiful though bold, valiant although tearful" (Trueblood).[66] In typical fashion, the Sun responds to her timorous valor with disproportionate strength, "the fiery planet / who was busy marshaling his troops / of glimmering novices / reserving glowing veterans, more robust, to fill the rearguard— / against the tyrannical usurper..." (Cruz, *Admonishment* 194).[67]

The war to stop the arrival of day is fully unleashed with this encounter. Aurora advances from the East ("en el Oriente tremolo estandarte"), to take on the Sun's army by the rearguard (ll. 918-9). She is preceded by the "soft yet bellicose clarions of the birds / (skillful, if artless)" ("bélicos clarines de las aves / (die-stros, aunque sin arte"), who, in contrast to the silent chorus barely heard at nightfall, advance here to the sound of "loud trumpets" (ll. 918-923).[68]

Notwithstanding, Aurora "cowardly as tyrants always are, and beset [literally, pregnant] by timorous misgivings" ("como tirana al fin, cobarde, de recelos medrosos embarazada," Cruz, *Admon-ishment* 194; ll. 924-926), vainly (in both senses of the word) tries to "flaunt" her forces while, at the same time, shielding them from his "stabbing brightness" with her "fatal cloak" (ll. 927-930). Unable to resist the blazing power of the Sun, the hosts under Aurora's command—as terrorized and blinded as the soul was af-ter her own encounter with the strongest Light—retreat forming "black squadrons" ("escuadrones negros") and seek refuge in the opposed hemisphere (ll. 936-958). There, under the protection of Dusk, they will rest, heal their wounds, and wait to recover their strength. In that indeterminate space between light and shadow, they will be joined by the voices of other fugitive contingents of women whose memories flow silently along cavernous deep rivers, harnessed and stymied by dominant culture.

The conceptual game that closes the poem inverts again its partial versions of history. Although at first sight it seems that success belongs to the Sun's hosts, Dawn's defeat is not all that clear. Unlike Phaethon, but like the soul, the feminine hosts, de-termined not to give up despite their overwhelming subjection, overcome their initial defeat and rise from the ruins of battle in expectation of the next round. Sor Juana describes their obstinate "courage" ("aliento") with a blend of compassion and admira-tion, and crowns them for their rebellion and their determination (ll. 961-966). "In defeat / and ruin recovering her force," the deter-mined Aurora "once again installed / her rebel throne, restored / to westard rule over / the dark half of the globe / forsaken by the Sun" (Harss, ll. 960-966).[69]

After they beat the Sun at his job of putting things in their place, Venus and Aurora are reduced to a position of inferior-ity due to the privilege that Day, regardless of how limited its space may be, lends to the Sun. The latter's unequal victory is not all that clear either. Sor Juana represents it, not without a touch of irony, by means of a metaphor both textual and textile that feminizes him. The Sun rules by covering over with his "beautiful...golden skein" ("dorada...madeja hermosa" [l. 968]) every possible contrast, limiting the operation of every sense and faculty other than the "external," which had earlier been devalued by Sor Juana.[70] But the surfaces his "judicious light" ("luz judiciosa") colors ("ilustraba... / repartiendo / a las cosas visibles sus colores"), are drawn upon what Sor Juana here stubbornly calls, "our Hemisphere" ("nuestro Hemisferio" [ll. 967-973]).

The Sun, as it is currently interpreted by the Church, is capable of administering justice only in a superficial and limited manner. By privileging the external senses, of less value than the internal, he blocks the capacity to observe and apprehend Truth at all its levels. With blind but definitive authority, his light sweeps the historical war of the sexes under the Earth's illuminated carpet, returning order to a world disordered by the contradictions that dawn and dusk had brought to the surface. Intuition, fantasy, and the imagination, the mothers of creativity and art, on the other hand, make it possible to visualize the multiple sides of the (con)(tra)di(c)tions eradicated by dominant culture. Their work is erased by the so-called illuminated world into which Sor Juana wakes up.

The privileged position that the internal senses occupy in Sor Juana's conceptual system makes it difficult to understand why she has insistently been compared to Descartes (Sabat Rivers 15). For the French philosopher consciousness and reason are the main instruments for capturing truth, the only way to conquer the instability of illusion and dreams and their interference with the real.[71] Although she shares his objectives, the road Sor Juana follows is less direct and a great deal more difficult. Not only does it require elements that belong to the realm of reason or to understanding, but it is most benefited by others such as intuition, fantasy, and the imagination. Although both thinkers start from the same Thomist-Aristotelian premises, they arrive at opposite conclusions. While for Descartes, reality is equally confusing while asleep as while awake—day perceptions "no more real than the illusions of my dreams" (non plus vrais que les illusions de mes songes)—for Sor Juana dreams clear up thoughts obscured by day. Descartes's conclusion was his famous *Cogito ergo sum*, which centers the individual and makes consciousness the only means for arriving at the truth. Sor Juana, on the other hand, never stopped believing that in order to apprehend reality it is necessary to appeal to more than one of the qualities or states of the soul, and especially to dreams. As she tells Filotea, "even my sleep was not free from this constant activity of my brain. In fact, it seems to go on during sleep with all the more freedom and lack of restraint, putting together the separate images it has carried over from waking hours with greater clarity and tranquility, debating with itself, composing verses..., including certain thoughts and subtleties I have arrived at more easily while asleep than while awake..." (*Reply* 226).[72]

The unconscious, then, mirror of a negotiated social imaginary, was for Sor Juana one of the most revealing of those states. Descartes would not have understood the baroque. His style was logical and followed carefully constructed linear arguments. Sor Juana, on the contrary, moved with equal ease in and between both forms of access to reality. That is why she considered the baroque an ideal discursive strategy.

Unlike Vieira, however, Sor Juana did not sacrifice meaning to form. She played with language, experimented with its limits and contradictions, stretched it to the points where meaning threatened to disappear, and then, as if by magic, managed to produce a word, the right word, the concept and conceit that once more could give meaning to things: her own meanings. This must have been the reason why such a difficult aesthetic and philosophical exercise gave her so much pleasure.

A great deal has also been written about Góngora's baroque influence on *Primero Sueño*.[73] Nonetheless, the differences between these two great poets are more substantial than the similarities. As Jean Franco points out, Sor Juana breaks with this literary father by disguising with phantasy the "secular productive process" that Góngora had liberated (31-32). Octavio Paz also asserts that the "Andalusian poet does not put reality into question: he transfigures it. The Mexican poet's resolve is to describe a reality which, by definition, is not visible.... Góngora: verbal transfiguration of the reality perceived by the senses; Sor Juana: discourse on a reality perceived, not by the senses, but by the soul" (470). If we add to these differences the political focus of the poem, we notice that Góngora doesn't exploit the baroque's potential as weapon of resistance to the extent that Sor Juana does. Her object is to transform a hostile reality, to imagine alternatives, and to find linguistic structures that will re-present them adequately. Góngora's project is aesthetic: he plays with language in order to produce luminous metaphors and his relation to reality is not nearly as problematic: reality offers the material and the artist imitates and plays with it. Sor Juana's project is as much aesthetic as it is political; her search as much intellectual as ethical, her relationship to language as lucid as it is functional. Her purpose is not to paint reality with "falsely colored syllogisms" ("falsos silogismos de colores"),[74] but rather to try to understand and re-produce it in all its complexity. This singular vision is Sor Juana's greatest contribution to the baroque (and probably to our understanding of postmodernism).

Her work was published in several editions during her lifetime and her name exceeded the horizons of New Spain. However, despite her talent and well-deserved fame, she never received the recognition she deserved. Armed with an intellectual precocity that eventually led her to explore territories that were considered out of bonds for women, she transformed dominant literary forms and used them to display her erudition. Her mastery of language and her resistance to occupying the subject position that Barbara Johnson has called "sujet supposée simple" have led critics, since the beginning of her public life to only a few years ago, to speak constantly of the "virility" and "masculinity" of her language.

Due to the perceived immiscibility of her erudition and her sex, already at the court of the viceroy and vicereine of Mancera, where she lived before entering the convent, she was subjected to an intense and minute interrogation by the most learned men of the day. In this century, Emilio Abreu Gómez, in one of the first few serious studies of her work, ends up making the same mistakes despite his sensitivity to her circumstances. "She must have suffered in the midst of that frivolous society," he writes, "her pride and sensibility regularly broken.... Add to this crisis a certain sexual abnormality that certain circumstances allow us to assume." In order to demonstrate this "abnormality," he looks for evidence in the physical traits her portraits reveal to him: "Her very figure, notwithstanding the beauty of her face, announces a certain rigidity—the thickness of her eyebrows and the rictus of her lips—that fits perfectly the characteristics of a viriloid nature." Abreu Gómez is as bothered by Sor Juana's "unnatural" predilection for solitude and her rejection of marriage as others who wrote about her three hundred years earlier. He finds her abnormality everywhere: "one notices it in her actions, [which betray] rather than feminine reflexes, virile impulses, such as reason, and her character..., of viriloid nature." "Her nature," he concludes, "reveals an introverted being. It is possible that she was, in reality, a hysteric.... [She was] sexually, potentially at least..., abnormal, a freak" ("Introduction," Cruz, *Poesías completas* 40-41).

I have spent this much time presenting the attitude of Abreu Gómez because he represents more the rule than the exception in the reception of Sor Juana's work. Barring some of the better earlier feminist readings, Sabat Rivers's study, and Paz's important book (limited, however, when it comes to his sensitivity to gender issues), critics have generally missed its complexity. Studies like Ludwig Pfandl's, for instance, also an oversimplification of Freud's ideas, conclude that Sor Juana was the victim of a defective nature and a deformed childhood due to her father's total absence and what he considered her mother's indifferent and licentious presence (188-189). Thus, the fact that the body of a woman could contain a mind like Sor Juana's has been seen as an aberration of nature; her vocation, as indicative of a sexually pathological inclination; her life and letters, as an anomaly. While Freud studied pathology to understand normality, his followers, disguised as literary critics, read Sor Juana's complex lucidity as pathological.

The intensity and persistence of the efforts to relegate Sor Juana to the margins of normality only reflect the magnitude of her perceived threat to the patriarchal order. With few recent exceptions, such as those already mentioned, from her first biographer to the present the methods used have been the same: to box her in a badly understood singularity and to turn her into a sacred monster. Not only have her critics contributed to minimizing the historical potential of her transgressions, like her contemporaries had done, but, by categorizing her work in ways that impaired her reputation, they have tried to contain her within the most narrow bonds of another institution, that of literature. Called the Tenth Muse, she has continued to be punished for daring to live up to the name.

As we have seen, regardless of his general sensitivity to the historical conditions affecting Sor Juana's life and work, not even Paz manages to escape the badly veiled misogyny of those critics. His main error, however, consists in his application of the instrumental logic that privileges a syntagmatic reading of the poem at the expense of the baroque architectonics Sor Juana constructed precisely to work around that linearity. As she herself had stated in the *Respuesta*, "the logician's sentence proceeds in a straight line, taking the shortest way, while the rhetorician's moves in a curve, taking the longest, but ... the two end up at the same point" (216).[75] His desire to situate her in modernity, moreover, is counterproductive. It isolates her and has her speaking in a solitary and atemporal voice, condemning her to share in the destiny of those other women who Sor Juana had tried to rescue from oblivion in order to reintegrate their voices into the dominant patriarchal culture. Sor Juana might not have been either obsessively devout or a mystic—like so many other women of the time who, lacking other options, resorted to convent life in order to escape an oppressive reality.[76] But there is no doubt that she was a sincere believer. There is no evidence to the contrary.

Although, as we would say today, the center of the poem is an absent center, that absence is only momentary, in no way definitive. Unless we read the word "man" literally, as it seems that Sor Juana did in her *Sueño*, it is a mistake and an anachronism to assert, as Paz does, that in the poem "her world lacks a center and man feels lost in its uninhabited spaces." (383) Sor Juana does not belong to the episteme that shares the post-Nietzschean vision of the death of God, the absence of a center. Her Christian universe is real and God is synonymous with meaning and truth. Although the counterposing of opposites, the fluidity of her metaphors, and other baroque (de)formations seem to invite such interpretation, the baroque was such a dominant style in the culture of the time, that it is possible to speak of a baroque of the State (see Maravall and Moraña). It is important to remember, however, that although this observation points to the mutual implication of the baroque form (despite its dominant logocentric structure) with the scantily centralized power of the empire, it does not explain the differences in application.

Three years after the attack that began with the publication of the *Carta Atenagórica*, Sor Juana was finally defeated. She abandoned literature, gave away her books, took apart the chemistry lab she had in her room, and devoted herself completely to the only existence for which society rewarded women: self-sacrifice and total dedication to the needs and demands of others. Abandoning her solitude, she obediently devoted herself to the arduous and demanding labors of the convent. No longer under the protection of viceroys and vicereines, weak and vulnerable, she died after contracting the plague, not having taken any precautions while obsessively caring for its victims. Would it be an exaggeration to consider her death the only kind of suicide available to a religious person in her day? The last thing she wrote before her death was her confession, which she significantly signed with her own blood: "I, the worst of the world" ("Yo la peor del mundo"). "Juana Inés de la Cruz" (4: 523).[77]

I would like to insist before closing that although it is important to underscore the negative aspects that her feminine condition introduced into her life, it is also necessary to appreciate the legacy of strategies of resistance and adaptation we find in her writing. After all, Sor Juana chose convent life in order to escape from the restrictions and impositions of worldly life. In the name of knowledge, she knew how to benefit from as many connections and alliances as her circumstances would allow. During her short stay at court, she not only managed to obtain the necessary dowry money to enter the convent and live comfortably there for the rest of her days, but she also continued to enjoy the protection of many of the illustrious people she had met there. She was a close friend of the viceroys and vicereines of Mexico, whom she showered with poems (for which she was surely well remunerated) on every possible occasion: births, birthdays, and even casual visits to the convent. Although we can almost be sure she did not write them "for pleasure," it is obvious that the gratitude she expresses in them must have had some foundation.

Moreover, her recognition of the power that some women had in the kingdom often helped her change circumstances in her favor. The importance Sor Juana gives to protection is an indication that she well understood how their society functioned. It is no accident that the attack of the Church authorities should begin only after the death of her friend and protector, the "beautiful, divine Elvira" of Toledo, Countess of Galve, Vicereine of New Spain. It is one of those unfortunate coincidences of history that her death should overlap with the arrival of the Archbishop, probably one of the most misogynist men to ever set foot on the continent.

Sor Juana's work foreshadows one of the most effective and resistant conclusions of contemporary feminists, the radical insistence that the personal is political, to which she adds her singular perspective on the ways in which the private and the public (dis)join one another. This essay set out to follow her own ingenious indications of the ways in which she establishes a parallel between her own daily existence and the real and symbolic role she has played together with other women in the history of ideas. As we have seen, however, Sor Juana's original contribution in the *Respuesta* and in *Primero Sueño* is not restricted to her insistence that the topic of women deserves equally far-reaching philosophical and intellectual consideration. Her boundless curiosity and her encyclopaedic knowledge link her equally to the greatest thinkers in history with whom her pen dialogued in the silence of the night. To forget this fact would be to repeat the encapsulation and segregation her work has suffered due to her difference.

Sor Juana never negates her femininity. On the contrary, she carries it proudly, even if marked by suffering, resentment, and, finally, resignation. It governs her way of relating to the world and gives a special meaning to her artistic vocation. It might be a mark of contradiction, but doesn't she say that the best road to truth is a "pleasurable" play of (con)(tra)di(c)tions, with and simultaneously against dictions and traditions?

Notes

1. This epigraph is part of a longer quotation. See footnote 56 for the Spanish text and page 506 for the English translation.

2. "Y, a la verdad, yo nunca he escrito sino violentada y forzada y sólo por dar gusto a otros; no sólo sin complacencia, sino con positiva repugnancia.... [And] no me acuerdo haber escrito por mi gusto sino es un papelillo que llaman *El Sueño*"

(translation mine). When not my own, passages in English will be followed by a page reference to Allan Trueblood's translation, *Reply to Sor Philothea*, in *A Sor Juana Anthology*.

3. When not my own, the English is either from the excellent translation by Luis Harss, "Sor Juana's Dream," or from Allan Trueblood's translation, as indicated in the text.

4. See Reyes (371).

5. See Stephanie Merrim, ed., *Feminist Perspectives*. In this excellent and long overdue collection, Merrim proposes a rereading aimed "to awaken the feminine in Sor Juana criticism, to 'restore' Sor Juana as a woman writer and as a woman writing" (21).

6. Both the *Respuesta* and the *Primero Sueño* may be said to contain lessons on how to utter the unutterable, that is, lessons on the use of rhetoric to evade censorship. For an informed rhetorical analysis of the radical strategies of which the poet availed herself in order to disguise her own voice, Rosa Perelmuter Pérez, "Estructura" and "Situación."

7. In contrast, her good friend Carlos de Sigüenza y Góngora was nominated professor of astrology and mathematics at the Real y Pontífica Universidad, in spite of his earlier rebelliousness that had led to his expulsion from the Jesuit order.

8. See works by Hiriart, Castañeda, and Arroyo, who sees the *Respuesta* as "the first manifesto of women's spiritual liberation." Tempting as it may be, this judgment is anachronistic and may even be detrimental to furthering our understanding of the interconnectedness of dominant culture with women's histories or, for that matter, with the everyday practices and traditions of learning, which, as we will see, Sor Juana herself privileged. The historian Asunción Lavrin has done pioneering work in this area. See, for example, "In Search of the Colonial Woman"; "Women and Religion"; "Female Religious"; as well as her "Unlike Sor Juana?"

9. A "natural" impulse that came not from birth, however, but from learning: "from my first glimmers of reason, my inclination to letters was of such power and vehemence" ("desde que me rayó la primera luz de la razón, fue tan vehemente y poderosa la inclinación a las letras") (*Reply* 210; *Respuesta* 4: 444).

10. "repugnándolo el sexo, la edad y sobre todo las costumbres..., cuatro bachillerías superficiales" (*Respuesta* 4: 443-444).

11. This text was later published as "Crisis de un sermón" in *Segundo tomo de las obras de Sor Juana Inez de la Cruz* (Seville, 1692).

12. "One who had the Letter printed so completely without my knowledge, gave it a title, underwrote the expense..." (... porque quien hizo imprimir la Carta tan sin noticia mía, quien la intituló, quien la costeó... (*Reply* 208; *Respuesta* 4: 442).

13. See Trueblood's translation in *Admonishment: The Letter of Sor Philothea de la Cruz*, included in his anthology, 199-203. Philothea means "lover of God." See Dorothy Schons's reference to the textual precedents of this name in "Some Obscure Points" (154, n. 31).

14. "It is a pity that so great a mind should stoop to lowly earthbound knowledge and not desire to probe into what transpires in heaven. But once it does lower itself to ground level, may it not descend further still and ponder what goes on in hell!" ("Lástima que un tan gran entendimiento, de tal manera se abata a las rateras noticias de la tierra, que no desee penetrar lo que pasa en el Cielo; y ya que se

humille al suelo, que no baje más abajo, considerando lo que pasa en el Infierno" [*Admonishment* 202; *Carta de Sor Filotea* 4: 696]).

15. His biographer tells us that he "believed in the importance of guarding his eyes to preserve his chastity; he made sure that women not visit him except under the most urgent of circumstances, and even then, when their visits were necessary, he refused to look at their faces... various times we heard him say that if he found out that any woman had entered his house, he would order the bricks upon which they had stepped to be removed.

"And this horror, and aversion to women, lasted his whole life, as he consistently preached against his female visitors and their finery.... He considered it a great gift from God that he was nearsighted" (José Lezamis, *Breve relación de la vida y muerte del Doctor D. Francisco de Aguiar y Seyxas* [México, 1699], qtd. in Schons 144.

16. Like Vieira, the bishop and archbishop belonged to the Jesuit order.

17. "...no son aquellos que con declarado odio y malevolencia me han perseguido, sino los que amándome y deseando mi bien..., me han mortificado y atormentado más que los otros, con aquel: *No conviene a la santa ignorancia que deben, este estudio; se ha de perder, se ha de desvanecer en tanta altura con su misma perspicacia y agudeza*" (452). Sor Juana uses as a warning Juan Díaz de Arce's regret that the contribution of at least two nuns, whose names Sor Juana notes he does not mention, was lost to the Church because of its inability to understand that their writings were interpretations of the Scriptures into the vernacular. She also reminds her reader that, as a consequence, Arce had come to the conclusion that "it is not only proper but most useful and necessary for women, and especially for nuns, to study sacred texts" ("que es que no sólo es lícito, pero utilísimo y necesario a las mujeres el estudio de las sagradas letras, y mucho más a las monjas") [*Reply* 238; *Respuesta* 4: 469]).

18. This was not the first time Sor Juana was preoccupied with the complexities of this question. It also lies at the heart of her *Divino Narciso*. Stephanie Merrim, who interestingly also connects this work to the *Respuesta*, sees Sor Juana as "equating her situation with that of Christ, as one whose superiority inspires incomprehension and hatred" ("Narciso *desdoblado*" 115).

19. "...recibo en mi alma vuestra santísima amonestación..., que aunque *viene en traje de* consejo, tendrá para mí sustancia de precepto; con no pequeño consuelo de que aun antes parece que prevenía mi obediencia vuestra pastoral insinuación, como a vuestra dirección, inferido del asunto y *pruebas de la misma Carta*. Bien conozco que no cae sobre ella vuestra cuerdísima advertencia, sino sobre lo mucho que habréis visto de asuntos humanos que he escrito" (*Respuesta* 4: 443).

20. "el estudiar, escribir y enseñar privadamente, no sólo les es lícito, pero muy provechoso y útil" (*Reply* 231; *Respuesta* 4: 462).

21. "Y esto es tan justo que no sólo a las mujeres que por tan ineptas están tenidas, sino a los hombres, que con sólo serlo piensan que son sabios, se había de prohibir la interpretación de las Sagradas Letras" (*Respuesta* 4: 462).

22. "de ánimos arrogantes, inquietos y soberbios, amigos de novedades en la Ley (que es quien las rehusa)" ..."más daño les hace el saber que les hiciera el ignorar" (*Respuesta* 4: 462-463).

23. "Especial favor de que conozco ser su deudora...que es más primoroso

medio de castigar hacer que yo misma, con mi conocimiento, sea el juez que me sentencie y condene mi ingratitud" (*Respuesta* 4: 441).

24. "Pues si ella, con su santísima autoridad, no me lo prohibe, ¿por qué me lo han de prohibir otros? Llevar una opinión contraria de Vieyra fue en mí atrevimiento, y no lo fue en su Paternidad llevarla contra los tres Santos Padres de la Iglesia? Mi entendimiento tal cual ¿no es tan libre como el suyo, pues viene de un solar? ¿Es alguno de los principios de la Santa Fe, revelados, su opinión, para que le hayamos de creer a ojos cerrados?" (*Respuesta* 4: 468)

25. "alabando algunas veces sus fundamentos, otras disintiendo, y siempre admirándome de su sinigual ingenio, que aun sobresale más en lo segundo que en lo primero" (4: 412).

26. As a young woman, Sor Juana tells us, she cut her hair when her ability to learn Latin did not meet her own expectations, "knowledge being the more desired ornament" (... que era más apetecible adorno [las noticias], *Reply* 212; *Respuesta* 4: 446).

27. For example, Perelmuter points out that "the bishop had recriminated her for her excessive profane erudition. If she were now to answer with a similar display of erudition to that of the *Carta Atenagórica*, by ordering her proofs in accordance with scholastic argumentation and by assuming a formal and polemical tone, the result would have been counterproductive. It would be emphasizing precisely what, for her, was advantageous to deemphasize. This explains Sor Juana's partial dissimulation of the formal or judicial aspects of her *Respuesta* (that is, that it had been composed as a defense of her intellectual rights), and her concealment of the identity of the *oratio* under the disguise of confidences expected from the [literary genre] of the familiar letter" ("La estructura retórica" 151; translation mine).

28. First published in *Segundo Volumen de las obras de Sor Juana Inés de la Cruz* as "First Dream, that thus did Mother Juana Inés de la Cruz entitle and compose it, imitating Góngora" ("Primero Sueño", que así intituló y compuso la Madre Juana Inés de la Cruz, imitando a Góngora").

29. *Obras Completas*, 2: 289 and 228, respectively. Electa Arenal sees the "Sátira filosófica" as "the culmination and refinement of a theme used and abused for several centuries..., that sums up one of the debates between misogynists and philogynists so popular in that period" (172). Arenal refers us also to Pilar de Oñate's work, *El feminismo en la literatura española*, where the reader can find several poems in this tradition that precede the "Sátira." Other references that relate the "Sátira" to the *Sueño* can be found in Méndez Plancarte's edition, *Obras completas* 1: 488-492.

30. "The connection is made by Salazar Mallén, who perceives at this time (1666) a change in Sor Juana's attitude to the plight of women, which culminated in her decision to enter a convent for the first time one year later (*Apuntes* 44-46).

31. For a psychoanalytical explanation of the ambiguous use of masks, see Joan Rivière and Luce Irigaray. For an important discussion of this concept applied to the context of the practice of mysticism during colonial times, see Franco.

32. In a parallel fashion, Arenal sees the *Respuesta* as "a demonstration of her mental virtuosity, a portrait of the origins and development of her intellectual passion and of the suffering it caused, a defense of the education and intellectual life of women,... a protest against ecclesiastic—and all kinds of—stupidity and repression" (176).

33. Sabat-Rivers's book traces carefully the large number of *loci classici*, and biblical, literary, and popular traditions to which Sor Juana refers as well as the singular ways in which she modifies them.

34. This current of thought, traceable to the early years of the Christian era, developed independently of the Church. It came to Sor Juana by way of the works of Athanasius Kircher, a German Jesuit, whom she cites in the *Reply* (450), and from Hermes Trimegistus, the alleged author of *Corpus Hermeticum*, "legendary priest and magician from Ancient Egypt." Hermes is also a figure from Phoenician mythology. Carrier of the word, like Christ, he was advisor to Chronos and the son of Uranus and Gaia.

35. For the theoretical basis of this discussion, see the chapter on "Suture," in Silverman.

36. "The complement to *First Dream* is the *Response:* a prose version of the same theme, the search for knowledge but over a lifetime, not in the course of a single night" (366).

37. Although a great deal more research needs to be done to understand this specificity, it is once more emerging as axiomatic from recent studies undertaken by feminist theorists who have started to focus once again on women authors, examples of which are Merrim's edition of Sor Juana and Franco's *Plotting Women*.

38. "si hubiera ancianas doctas como quiere San Pablo, y de unas en otras fuese sucediendo el magisterio como sucede en el de hacer labores y lo demás que es costumbre."

39. Sabat-Rivers traces the thematic development of classical and popular images and topics that appear in the poem, but makes no note of their feminization. She catalogues six variants of dreams: the dream as healing the body; romantic dream, which brings repose from amorous tribulations; dream as the illusion of love; mystic dream; dream as death, and as lived reality (dream within a dream); and dreams that teach us how to live on earth in preparation for eternal life (51-53). Sor Juana includes all of the above variants and transforms them. In her conclusion, for example, she privileges the last topic and demystifies it. For her, life on earth is as important as eternal life. This version of the tradition can be traced back to Scipio's dream, the *Somnium Scipionis* narrated by Cicero in his *De republica*, and to Seneca's *Hercules furens*. For a detailed study see Sabat-Rivers (23-28).

40. The play on the word "a-sombra-da"—surprised, stunned, but also shaded—links, metonymically, birds, soul, and shadow, and is untranslatable.

41. The reference to birds establishes another link with Hermes Trimegistus, who, as Sabat-Rivers has noted, had "invented the hieroglyphs that were considered mystical birds of the universe in Florence" (16; translation mine), an important link because of the reference to writing. The relationship between word and time, Hermes and Harpocrates, is one of the subtexts active in the poem. Sor Juana might well be using the birds as emblematic of another writing, one inscribed in another place and another time, with different tools through different media, as, for example, the commemorative flower arrangements, such as the one for which she composed her *Neptuno Alegórico*. This type of overdetermination of the sign is typical of the baroque, especially in its mannerist and conceptist aspects favored by Sor Juana.

42. We find here another level of inversion and simultaneity of the positions

held by the contraries. In reference to Harpocrates, son of Isis and Neptune in some mythological versions, Paz tells us that Sor Juana was fascinated by the figure of Harpocrates which she connected to Neptune's by means of a singular syncretism of the figure of silence, "Because he is the god of the waters, whose children, fish, are mute, as Horace said: O mutis quoque piscibus / donatura cygni, si libeat, sonum (Oh, to the mute fish, if you so wished, you could give the song of swans)." As Paz notes, the metonymical relation changes the tempestuous and unpredictable Neptune into a hermetic and silent god (160).

43. "Suelen en la eminencia de los templos colocarse por adorno unas figuras de los Vientos y de la Fama, y por defenderlas de las aves, las llenan todas de púas; defensa parece y no es sino propiedad forzosa" (*Respuesta* 4: 454). Sabat-Rivers notes the classic connection between the owl and this goddess, which she also links to both the popular and literary traditions: "Góngora had referred to the oil as squeezed out of Minerva (*Soledad* I, 1.834). The owl is also Minerva's bird. Sor Juana combines these ideas with a common superstition and masterfully develops a new mythological concept," which is to establish a link with the myth of Phaethon, emblem of the limits of human daring in the search of knowledge (132), a theme which Sor Juana will fully develop later in the poem.

44. It is the sixth of the twelve parts into which Méndez Plancarte divides the poem: ll. 412-559. For Sabat Rivers the defeat of the intuition occurs in ll. 412-494.

45. My discussion on the Sun, not only as origin and *telos* of the universe (as in either scholastism or Renaissance humanism), but also as the invisible and enigmatic metaphor of the power at the center of every patriarchal structure, is based on an application of Jacques Derrida's insights in "White Mythology."

46. "dirigiendo siempre..., los pasos de mi estudio a la cumbre de la Sagrada Teología; pareciéndome preciso, para llegar a ella, subir por los escalones de las ciencias y artes humanas; porque ¿cómo entenderá el estilo de la Reina de las Ciencias quien aun no sabe el de las ancilas?" (*Respuesta* 4: 447).

47. The interpretation that Paz rejects had begun with her first biographer, Father Diego P. Calleja. Paz is not the only one to assert that Sor Juana's work prefigures the aesthetic and literary project of modernity. Benassy-Berling agrees with him as well. For Arenal, it foreshadows the ideas of the Enlightment.

48.   "Para el alma no hay encierro
          ni prisiones que la impidan,
          porque sólo la aprisionan
          las que se forma ella misma." ("Ala misma señora [la condesa de Galve], en ocasión de cumplir años," *Obras completas* 2: 120-123)

49.   "y a la tiniebla misma, que antes era
          tenebroso a la vista impedimento,
          de los agravios de la luz apela

          ...

          sirviendo ya—piadosa medianera—
          la sombra de instrumento

para que recobrados por grados habiliten,
porque después constante
su operación más firmes ejerciten." (ll. 504-515)

50.   "...el Alma,...

la atención recogió, que derramada
en diversidad tanta, aun no sabía
recobrarse a sí misma del espanto
que portentoso había
su discurso calmado,
permitiéndole apenas
de un concepto confuso
el informe embrión que, mal formado,
inordinado caos retrataba
de confusas especies que abrazaba." (ll. 540-549)

51. "por variaciones y ocultos engarces...de manera que *parece* se corresponden y están unidas con admirable trabazón y concierto." Sor Juana connects this concept to its syncretic and hermetic background in the sentence that follows. "This is the chain," she writes, "that the ancients pretended emerged from Jupiter's mouth, on which all things were strung and linked together. So much is demonstrated by the Reverend Father Athanasius Kircher in his curious book *De Magnete* [On the Magnet]. All things proceed from God, who is at once the center and the circumference from which all existing lines proceed and at which all end up" (Es la cadena que fingieron los antiguos que salía de la boca de Júpiter, de donde pendían todas las cosas eslabonadas unas con otras. Así lo demuestra el R. P. Atanasio Quinqueiro en su curioso libro *De Magnete*. Todas las cosas salen de Dios, que es el centro a un tiempo y la circunferencia de donde salen y donde paran todas las líneas criadas) (*Reply* 216; *Respuesta* 450).

52. "Qué os pudiera contar, Señora, de los secretos naturales que he descubierto estando guisando?"..."¿qué podemos saber las mujeres sino filosofías de cocina?"..."Si Aristóteles hubiera guisado, mucho más hubiera escrito"..."estudiaba en todas las cosas que Dios crió, sirviéndome ellas de letras, y de libro toda esta máquina universal."

53. It is important to note that the earth is feminized by Sor Juana for its maternal rather than its sexual attributes.

54.   "de cuatro adornada operaciones

de contrarias acciones,
ya atrae, ya segrega diligente
lo que no serle juzga conveniente,
ya lo superfluo expele, y de la copia
la substancia más útil hace propia." (ll. 633-637)

55.   "forma inculcar más bella
(de sentido adornada,
y aun más que de sentido, de aprehensiva
fuerza imaginativa), que justa puede ocasionar querella
—cuando afrenta no sea—
de la que más lucida centellea
inanimada Estrella,
bien que soberbios brille resplandores
—que hasta a los Astros puede superiores,
aun la menor criatura, aun la más baja,
ocasionar envidia, hacer ventaja—" (ll. 640-651)

56. "¡Oh signo que te ponen por blanco de la envidia y por objeto de la contradicción! Cualquiera eminencia, ya sea de dignidad, ya de nobleza, ya de riqueza, ya de hermosura, ya de ciencia, padece esta pensión; pero la que con más rigor la experimenta es la del entendimiento."

57. Sabat-Rivers notes that "instead of failing definitively, Phaethon becomes a symbol of those who dare, time and again, to attempt the same feat despite repeated failures" (81).

58. Jean Franco also notices this aspect of the relation between Sor Juana and Phaethon (36-37).

59. "Lo que sí pudiera ser descargo mío es el sumo trabajo no sólo en carecer de maestro, sino de condiscípulos con quienes conferir y ejercitar lo estudiado, teniendo sólo por maestro un libro mudo, por condiscípulo un tintero insensible" (833+).

60.   "O el castigo jamás se publicara,
porque nunca el delito se intentara:
político silencio [por razones de estado] antes rompiera
los autos del proceso—circunspecto estadista—;
o en fingida ignorancia simulara
o con secreta pena castigara
el insolente exceso." (ll. 811-819)

61. The untranslatable play with the word "in-sol-ente," "sol" meaning sun and "ente" being, mirrors Phaethon's action and his desire to be the sun, his father.

62. See especially *Violence and the Sacred; Things Hidden since the Foundation of the World;* and *The Scapegoat.*

63.   "sin que a popular vista [del pueblo]
el ejemplar nocivo propusiera:
que del mayor delito la malicia
peligra en la noticia,
contagio dilatado transcendiendo;

porque singular culpa sólo siendo,

[si fuera no regla sino excepción]

dejara más remota a lo ignorado

su ejecución, que no a lo escarmentado." (ll. 819-826; emphasis mine)

64. She occupies "the place of the element water," as Sabat-Rivers notes (*El "Sueño"* 98), without giving up her relation to fire and, therefore, to the sky.

65. The choice of Aurora or Eos, a mythological figure, is truly a stroke of genius on Sor Juana's part. An *Encyclopaedia of Mythology* tells us that "it was she who brought the first glimmer of day to men. Every morning at dawn she slipped from the couch of her husband, Tithonus, and emerging from the ocean [the kingdom of Tethys], rose into the sky." Did Sor Juana know that she was originally represented as accompanying her brother Helios [the Sun] during the daily journey? Dawn and Dusk also open and close the circle circumscribing the rotation of the Earth. Sor Juana's reference to Aurora's old husband—"del viejo Tithón la bella esposa"— is more direct but somewhat more difficult to figure out. Venus—mentioned by Sor Juana a few lines before, had made Aurora fall in love with Tithonus. Wishing that this love should last for eternity, Aurora asked Zeus/Jupiter for her husband's immortality but forgot to also ask for his eternal youth. Tithonus grew old despite the efforts of his wife, leaving her no other recourse than to lock him up in a room where, alone and impotent, he remained until the gods took pity on him and turned him into a grasshopper. What did Sor Juana want to convey with this reference? Is it possible that Tithonus might symbolize a patriarchal order that is ages-old and in the process of disintegration? Does Aurora represent the tired voice of a heretofore well-meaning devoted wife announcing, if not a new era, at least another option to that order's decrepitude? These important questions must remain in the realm of speculation for now.

66.   "amazona de luces mil vestida

contra la noche armada, hermosa si atrevida

valiente aunque llorosa." (ll. 899-902)

67.   "tropas reclutando

de bisoñas vislumbres

—las más robustas, veteranas lumbres

para la retaguardia reservando." (ll. 907-910)

68. "Trompetas sonorosos." We note the use of a masculine adjective to qualify a feminine noun, untranslatable into English.

69.   "y—en su mismo despeño recobrada

esforzando el aliento en la rüina—

en la mitad del globo que ha dejado

el Sol desamparada,

segunda vez rebelde determina

mirarse coronada." (ll. 961-966)

70. For a detailed description of the theory of humors and animal spirits, natural and vital, see Paz (487-491).

71. "Et enfin, considérant que toutes les mêmes pensées, que nous avons étant éveillés, nous peuvent aussi venir quand nous dourmons, sans qu'il y en ait aucune, pour lors, qui soit vraie, je me résolus de feindre que toutes les choses que m'étaient jamais entrées dans l'esprit, n'étaient non plus vraies que les illusions de mes songes" *(Discours* 85).

72. "ni aun el sueño se libró de este continuo movimiento de mi imaginativa; antes suele obrar en él más libre y desembarazada, confiriendo con mayor claridad y sosiego las especies que he conservado del día, arguyendo, haciendo versos... y... algunas delgadezas que he alcanzado dormida mejor que despierta..." *(Respuesta* 4: 460).

73. See, for example, Eunice Joiner Gates; Méndez Plancarte, *El sueño;* and José Pascual Buxó. Sor Juana herself acknowledges the influence in her subtitle of the poem.

74. Sonnet 145, *Obras completas* 2: 277. Cruz, *Admonishment* 94–95. This sonnet can also be read as Sor Juana's critique of baroque aestheticism.

75. "la oración del lógico anda como la línea recta, por el camino más breve, y la del retórico se mueve, como la corva, por el más largo, pero van a un mismo punto los dos" (450).

76. Asunción Lavrin, "Unlike Sor Juana?" For a general insight into the vicissitudes of woman's spirituality, see Giles.

77. See also "Protesta que, rubricada con su sangre, hizo de su fe y amor a Dios la Madre Juana Inés de la Cruz al tiempo de abandonar los estudios humanos, para proseguir, desembarazada de este afecto, en el camino de la perfección," *Obras completas* 4: 518.

Works Cited

Abreu Gómez, Emilio. *Semblanza de Sor Juana*. Mexico City: Ediciones Letras de México, 1938.

Arenal, Electa. "The Convent as Catalyst for Autonomy." *Women in Hispanic Literature*. Ed. Beth Miller. Berkeley: Univ. of California Press, 1983.

Arroyo, Anita. *Razón y pasión de Sor Juana*. Mexico City: Editorial Porrua, 1971.

Benassy-Berling, Marie-Cecile. *Humanisme et religion chez Sor Juana Inés de la Cruz: La femme et la culture au XVIIe siècle*. Paris: Editions Hispaniques/Sorbonne, 1982.

Calleja, Diego P. *Vida de Sor Juana*. Ed. Emilio Abreu Gómez. Mexico City: Antigua Librería Robredo, 1936.

Castañeda, Carlos E. "Sor Juana Inés de la Cruz, primera feminista de América." *Universidad de Antioquía* 1.26 (1951): 701-717.

Cruz, San Juan de la. *Renaissance and Baroque Poetry of Spain*. Ed. Elías Rivers. New York: Dell, 1966.

Cruz, Sor Juana Inés de la. *Admonishment: The Letter of Sor Philothea de la Cruz: A Sor Juana Anthology*. Ed. and trans. Allan Trueblood. Cambridge and London: Harvard Univ. Press, 1988.

————. *Carta de Sor Filotea de la Cruz: Obras completas de Sor Juana Inés de la Cruz.* Vol. 4. Ed. Alberto G. Salceda. Mexico City: Fondo de Cultura Económica, 1957.

————. *Obras selectas.* Ed. Dámaso Alonso. Barcelona: Noguer, 1976.

————. *Poesías completas.* Ed. Ermilo Abreu Gómez. Mexico City: Botas, 1940.

————. "Reply to Sor Philothea." *A Sor Juana Anthology.*

————. "*Respuesta* a Sor Filotea de la Cruz." *Obras completas.* Vol. 4. Ed. Alfonso Méndez Plancarte. Mexico City: Fondo de Cultura Económica, 1951-1957.

————. *Segundo volumen de las obras de Sor Juana Inés de la Cruz.* Seville, 1692.

————. *Sor Juana's Dream.* Trans. Luis Harss. New York: Lumen, 1986.

————. *El sueño.* Ed. Alfonso Méndez Plancarte. Mexico City: Imprenta Universitaria, 1951.

Descartes, René. *Discours de la methode.* Ed. Etienne Gilson. Paris: Vrin, 1961.

Derrida, Jacques. *Dissemination.* Trans. Barbara Johnson. Chicago: Univ. of Chicago Press, 1981.

————. "White Mythology: Metaphor in the Text of Philosophy." Trans. Alan Bass. *Margins of Philosophy.* Chicago: Univ. of Chicago Press, 1982. 207-272.

Foucault, Michel. *The History of Sexuality.* Vol. 1. New York: Random House, 1978.

Franco, Jean. *Plotting Women.* New York: Columbia Univ. Press, 1989.

Giles, Mary E., ed. *The Feminist Mystic: And Other Essays on Women and Spirituality.* New York: Crossroad, 1985.

Girard, René. *The Scapegoat.* Baltimore: Johns Hopkins Univ. Press, 1986.

————. *Things Hidden since the Foundation of the World.* Trans. Michael Meeter and Stephen Bann. Stanford: Stanford Univ. Press, 1987.

————. *Violence and the Sacred.* Trans. Patrick Gregory. Baltimore: Johns Hopkins Univ. Press, 1977.

Hiriart, Rosario. "La primera feminista de América." *Américas* 25 (1973): 2-7.

Irigaray, Luce. *This Sex Which Is Not One.* Trans. Catherine Porter, with Carolyn Burke. Ithaca, N.Y.: Cornell Univ. Press, 1985.

Johnson, Barbara. Paper presented at Gender at the Crossroads Conference, Stanford Univ., March 9-10, 1990.

Joiner Gates, Eunice. "Reminiscences of Góngora in the Works of Sor Juana Inés de la Cruz." *P.M.L.A.* 54 (1939): 1041-1058.

Lavrin, Asunción. "Female Religious." *Cities and Society in Colonial America.* Ed. Louise S. Hoberman and Susan M. Socolow. Albuquerque: Univ. of New Mexico Press, 1986. 23-59.

————. "In Search of the Colonial Woman in Mexico: The Seventeenth and Eighteenth Centuries." *Latin American Women: Historical Perspectives.* Westport, Conn.: Greenwood Press, 1978. 165-195.

————. "Unlike Sor Juana? The Model Nun in the Religious Literature of Colonial Mexico." *Feminist Perspectives on Sor Juana.* Ed. Stephanie Merrim. Detroit: Wayne State Univ. Press, 1991. 61-85.

————. "Women and Religion in Spanish America." *Women and Religion in America.* Ed. Rosemary Radford Ruether and Rosemary Skinner Keller. Vol. 2. San Francisco: Harper & Row, 1983. 42-78.

Maravall, José Antonio. "Un esquema conceptual de la cultura barroca." *Cuadernos Hispanoamericanos* 273 (1973): 423-461.

Merrim, Stephanie. "Narciso *desdoblado:* Narcissistic Stratagems in *El Divino Narciso* and the *Respuesta a sor Filotea de la Cruz." Bulletin of Hispanic Studies* 64.2 (April 1987): 111-117.

———, ed. *Feminist Perspectives on Sor Juana Inés de la Cruz.* Detroit: Wayne State Univ. Press, 1991.

Moraña, Mabel. "Barroco y conciencia criolla en Hispanoamérica." Lecture at Stanford Univ., March 23, 1988.

Oñate, Pilar de. *El feminismo en la literatura española.* Madrid: Espasa-Calpe, 1935.

Pascual Buxó, José. *Góngora en la poesía novohispana.* Mexico City: Universidad Nacional Autónoma de México, Centro de Estudios Literarios, 1960.

Paz, Octavio. *Sor Juana, or the Traps of Faith.* Trans. Margaret Sayers Peden. Cambridge: Harvard Univ. Press, 1988.

Perelmuter Pérez, Rosa. "La estructura retórica de la *Respuesta a Sor Filotea. Hispanic Review* 51. 2 (Spring 1983): 147-158.

———. "La situación enunciativa del *Primero Sueño." Revista Canadiense de Estudios Hispánicos* 11 (1986): 185-191.

Pfandl, Ludwig. *Sor Juana Inés de la Cruz: La décima musa de México, su vida, su poesía, su psique.* Trans. J. A. Ortega y Medina. Mexico City: Universidad Nacional Autónoma de México, 1963.

Reyes, Alfonso. *Letras de la Nueva España. Obras Completas,* 12. Mexico City: Fondo de Cultura Económica, 1960.

Rivière, Joan. "Womanliness as Masquerade." *Formations of Fantasy.* Ed. Stephen Heath. London: RKP, 1986.

Sabat-Rivers, Georgina. *El Sueño de Sor Juana Inés de la Cruz: Tradiciones literarias y originalidad.* London: Tamesis Books, 1976.

Salazar Mallén, Rubén. *Apuntes para una biografía de Sor Juana Inés de la Cruz.* 3rd ed. Mexico City: Universidad Nacional Autónoma de México, 1981.

Schons, Dorothy. "Some Obscure Points in the Life of Sor Juana Inés de la Cruz." *Modern Philology* 24.2 (November 1926): 141-162.

Silverman, Kaja. *The Subject of Semiotics.* New York: Oxford Univ. Press, 1983.

◆ Chapter 17

The Indian as Image and as Symbolic Structure: Bartolomé Arzáns's *Historia de la Villa Imperial de Potosí*

Leonardo García Pabón

Introduction: Indians in Potosí

From 1545, the year the Indian Huallpa discovered the Mountain of Potosí, where the Imperial City of Potosí would be founded, until its days of decadence and abandon at the end of the eighteenth century, Potosí carried the mark of the indigenous in its history. As the necessary labor force for the mining industry, the Indians had become an essential part of social life in Potosí by the time the Imperial City reached its apex as the most important center for silver production in the viceroyalty of Peru between 1577 and 1604. The participation of the Indians in the history of Potosí was subject to the tensions imposed by a double system of domination. On the one hand, from the perspective of integration into the colonial system, there was an accentuation of the extreme conditions of the relationship with the colonial state, which was one of exploitation. On the other hand, the Indian workers, or *mitayos,* found ways to maintain their vision of the world, their otherness, and to prevent total alienation by Spanish civilization.

In the eighteenth century these conditions, among others, were summarized, in an extraordinary fashion by Bartolomé Arzáns

(1676-1736), a *criollo* [1] from Potosí. His monumental work, *Historia de la Villa Imperial de Potosí* (*History of the Imperial City of Potosí*), comprised a portrait of more than two centuries of colonial life. This text is more than a chronicle or a history, as Arzáns tried to include all possible aspects of Potosí's life, especially those that could give transcendental meaning to the initial greatness and the later decadence of the city. In this comprehensive view he could not help but recognize the Indian not only as an actor in the making of history, but also as the producer of a vision of the world that could explain that history differently and, sometimes, even better than could Christian ideology: the worldview supposedly in charge of resolving the contradictions of material life with the doctrine of a one and only God.

This would not have been possible in a context other than that of Potosí, a city that developed a special dynamic, due to the opulence of daily life, the levity of its behavior, its arrogance, its eagerness for autonomy, the quantity and diversity of peoples in its territory, and the thirst for wealth that infected its inhabitants. The unlimited exploitation of silver in one privileged place, the Mountain, created a large concentration of labor in the city, forcing Spanish, *mestizos, criollos*, Indians, blacks, and foreigners to live and work together more closely than in other areas. The Indians were undoubtedly the largest group in Potosí, but with them arrived other and quite different social groups. For example, there were large groups of idle Spaniards looking for fortune, the remnants of armies that fought during the Conquest and the internal wars such as the one between Pizarro and Almagro. These groups of vagabond soldiers preferred Charcas, the region of present-day Bolivia where Potosí was located, as the place for their wandering, probably because it was a region removed from Lima's control (Lockhart 143). As time passed, these vagabonds and other Spanish groups gave rise to the formation of the most decisive social stratum in the city's political life: the *criollo*.

A crucible of peoples and cultures of that age and one of the most diversified centers of population and customs, "Potosí, naturally, took the lead in this: its cosmopolitan atmosphere, the transient population, the shaking rhythm of the miners' famous "cobdicia," its propensity for envy and revenge, all contributed to give the city an atmosphere of an imminent mutiny. Deaths, fights, robberies, frauds, love quarrels, disregard for the authorities, upheavals, and effronteries abounded in complaints to the central arbiters in Lima or in the Metropolis" (Barnadas 159).[2] The bloody encounters between the *vicuñas* (*criollos* and people from Andalucía) and the *vascongados* (people from the Basque country) that tormented Potosí in the first decades of the seventeenth century are an example of Potosí's turbulence. This continuous and frequently violent interaction yielded a vision of the world characteristic of the Charcas zone, which years later would be the basis for the independence of Bolivia.

Part of that vision can be traced in the work of Arzáns, especially in those aspects that relate to the formation of the *criollos'* ideology with the introduction of traits from indigenous culture. Since the Indians were an important part of Potosí's history, their place in the *Historia*'s pages is preponderant. Although it would be difficult to affirm the existence of a purely Indian voice or a purely Indian mentality in Arzáns's work, which is clearly determined by his own *criollo* condition, it is possible to see narrative processes in which his vision of the city's history is modified by the inscription of the indigenous. Arzáns's procedure of representation follows two paths: first, the Indians as actors and participants in the historical events of Potosí (working in the mines, participating in the city's holidays, creating new relationships among themselves and with Spaniards); and second, the incorporation of the Indians' beliefs and mythical world into Arzáns's narration (which, necessarily, would modify his own vision of the world). In the following pages I will pursue the second path, perhaps the more ideological, through the inscription in Arzáns's text of two symbols that contain a mythical conception of time: water as an element of change in historical cycles; and the Silver Mountain, Potosí's emblem, as a key inscription of time. But first let us briefly examine the first aspect, in order to provide a frame of reference for the second.

Indian Miners and Warrior Values

The Indians are permanent characters in the *Historia*. As Hanke ("Bartolomé Arzáns") has noted, for Arzáns it was clear that "without Indians, there are no Indias" (lxxiii). The characterization of the Indians in the *Historia* usually indicates a positive evaluation of their traditions and values. To understand this evaluation more fully, I will mention three aspects of the positive representation of the Indian: as victim, as an equal to others, and as a warrior.

The Indian as Victim

Under this heading may be grouped Arzáns's comments on the treatment of *mitayo* Indians (those subjected to forced labor in the mines by the *mita* system). The *mita* was the hub in the exploitation of the Indians by the Spaniards. It is striking that the *mita* in Potosí was an institution created by the miners of the city,[3] to which the Crown only had to grant legality (Barnadas 266-272). Despite the efforts of friars and legislators, the *mita* could not be eradicated until the period of Independence.

Arzáns did not express a definite position about the *mita*, but vacillated between feelings of justice and compassion, and the need to continue silver production to maintain the economy of the city (2: 189). He came to believe that the *mita* could be abolished, but only if the economy in the region could be diversified, thereby halting silver production. However, his sympathy was always with the Indians. Arzáns describes the *mitayos* in the following terms:

It is a great shame to see them set out for this city, leaving behind their towns and homes every year in payment of this *mita*. What demonstrations of feeling they make, what weeping, what sobs of the women and cries of the children are heard when one says his goodbyes in those fields and villages! In order not to see themselves in these straits many families have disappeared from their houses and lands without ever being heard from again, having gone into unknown, pagan lands, and many have taken their lives with their own hands, fleeing from their masters who would summon them to the *mita*. It certainly is a great shame the miserable servitude to which these unfortunate natives have arrived, not through just war made against them, particularly in this Peruvian region, which they themselves were giving openly and freely as friends, and the first conquerors after seeing them submissive made them slaves

and treated them worse than if they were, and if any war
were made against them, it was very unjust, whereby there
cannot be dominion over the vanquished nor could the
conqueror acquire it, for which this unjust and incorrect title
cannot be given them, for which one cannot call him lord
but rather tyrant. (trans. Marilyn Miller)[4]

The Indian as an Equal to Others

Even though the polemic on the status of the Indian as an equal
human being had been settled by Las Casas long before the eighteenth century, in practice the Indian was still considered an
inferior being. This happened because the anthropological view
that prevailed in defining the relationship between social groups,
that is, Spanish ethnocentrism, was never eliminated (Barnadas
165). For the Spaniards, the Indians were lascivious, lazy, and
drunkards. The image of an inferior Indian implied the image
of a superior European, even to other Potosinians, such as the
criollo or the foreigner; it pervaded all government acts, as well as
social and political events. This image also justified the exploitation of the Indians, creating a rich Potosí from the free labor of
thousands of *mitayos*. It is true that a powerful group of miners existed in Potosí (because of its impressive wealth), but the human
contingent by which this wealth was accumulated was no less
impressive.[5]

Arzáns's position on the status of the Indian is much more
clearly defined. The Indians were human beings equal to Europeans: "The complete contempt with which [the Spaniards] regard
and treat the humble Indians is indescribable, their brothers being of the same species (however much it pain them), and what is
more, sons one and the other of the same God the Father" (1: 12).[6]
In his view, the Indians in many cases were even better than the
Spaniards themselves: " . . . commonly those of this Peruvian reign
have outstanding skill, clear understanding, and general application, so that one finds (with great regret from the Spaniards) that
the Indians have elevated themselves in the exercise of all offices,
not only those of industry but also those of art" (1: 20).[7]

The Indian as a Warrior

The fortitude in defending what was theirs and the courage in attempting to gain new space in their private and social lives are aspects of the Indians' character that caused admiration in Arzáns. In the first pages of the *Historia*, he relates that in the same year of the discovery of the Mountain, the Indians from Cantumarca, a town near Potosí, challenged the Spaniards. By not keeping their promise to treat the Indians well and pay for their work, the Spaniards provoked an Indian rebellion.

> And so the Indian captain (whose name was Chaqui Ctari, which is interpreted foot of the viper) standing full of ire and rage told him: "Say to those enemies of ours, thieves of gold and silver, bearded and without honor, that if we had known that they were people without piety and who do not keep treaties, from the point we learned that they were in the mountain of Porco we would have made war against them, and casting them away from there, we would not have allowed them to enter where we were nor take the silver from Potosí." (1: 39)[8]

For the Indians, the Spaniards' offense was a moral one; that is why in their declaration of war they sought reparation. In general, in the *Historia* the Indian is described as a figure of goodwill, natural and pacific; the sole cause of his transformation into a warlike being was the moral offense of the Spaniards.

The same logic prevails in the story told by Arzáns about the Indian Agustín Quespi. This Indian is distinguished for not fearing anyone; on the contrary he is feared by almost everyone (3: 201). His strength and fortitude are such that nobody dares to challenge him, not even Spanish justice: "He became so feared in the Mountain that even the bravest Spaniard would avoid a confrontation with him, and the overseers and chief justice of mines experienced fierce resistance when they would go to apprehend him for complaints of the Azogueros [the owners of the mines] that he was making personal profit from their mines." Although Agustín reacts violently to others provocations, his nature is rather peaceful: "This Indian Agustín was not offensive in usual labors ... " (3: 201).[9]

The figure of the Indian as a rebel seems to have originated in a historical archetype that gives meaning to this behavior: the image of Atahuallpa. Arzáns points out that "even in these times he is held in high regard by the Indians, as they demonstrate when they see portraits of him" (1: 99).[10] The writer underscores the Indians' fear, at the mere mention of Atahuallpa's name. The Indians' reverence for the dead Inca can be fully appreciated in the *Tragedia del fin de Atahuallpa*, a play that Arzáns claims was performed in Potosí for holiday occasions, from the sixteenth century on (1: 98). This *mise-en-scène* of Atahuallpa's death modifies the outcome of the historical event and has the king of Spain punishing Pizarro for killing the Inca.[11]

In the play Atahuallpa is seen as a very courageous king, even to the point of cruelty, but one who could not use his courage to defeat the Spaniards (1: 28-29). Atahuallpa represents, then, the courageous Indian, but in his courage there was a terrible moment of weakness that caused the ruin of the Inca kingdom. The Inca's fortitude and fierceness are portrayed as both present and absent traits, becoming therefore ambiguous. For this reason the Indians see in these traits a symbol of their tragedy and, at the same time, the only point of access to an understanding and restoration of their history. Why was a powerful emperor, whose mere name inspired fear among his subordinates, unable to accomplish the essential mission of defending his empire? This question probably could not be answered, but it generated the feeling from which the Indians began to recover an image of themselves as a courageous people despite their apparent weakness, a people unjustly dominated. They began to understand that the Inca defeat was not a matter of a lack of courage, but one of an ethical imbalance, represented by the Spaniards' deceit. For them the defeat was acceptable; the cowardice of killing a nobleman could not be accepted, and much less justified. As a result, they considered Atahuallpa's death (not his defeat) unjustifiable and changed the ending of the play. For this reason, they contraposed the unlimited power of the Spaniards with their own measured fortitude, to be used by them only when it was absolutely necessary. In this way, they tried to restore their culture and reinstate their ethical vision. It would seem that in the memory of Atahuallpa, as it is narrated by Arzáns, the Indians saw not only a deed from the past and an affirmation of their culture, but also an ethical and political lesson: to know how to use power, keep calm, and place pacifism and justice above all.

In conclusion, the descriptions of the Indians, as protagonists of Arzáns's narrations and of Potosí's history, as inscribed in his text, provide, in effect, a positive image. The Potosinian writer seems to find in them an important referent of the city's history. This favorable attitude toward the Indians allowed him to inscribe their voices in his text. That inscription goes beyond what is explicit in order to represent their conception of the world. Perhaps this is why the Indian voices betray the explicit narrator, officially declared Christian in the introduction to the book (1: cclxxxiii-cclxxxv). By including oral tradition with the historical facts in the narration of daily life in Potosí, the meaning of important symbols in Arzáns's narration acquires a tint that clearly comes from non-Christian Andean thought.

Andean Symbols in Arzáns's Work

Where does the indigenous voice that is registered in Arzáns's text come from? Among the few references to his personal life, Arzáns highlights having a *ladino* Indian, Pablo Huancani, as "compadre" (a godfather relationship) (2: 393). This Indian was likely one of his most important sources of information about life, feelings, and oral tradition. In his search for historical data, Arzáns used many different people in the city as sources of information. Thus, he makes constant reference to witnesses of events included in his *Historia*, which indicates that oral testimony was one of his preferred sources of data.

The importance of oral transmission in Potosí can be seen in the fact that Arzáns's work, not published until our century, was largely known through oral accounts in Potosí. In reference to this subject, Vicente Cañete's testimony is illuminating. He arrived in Potosí at the end of the eighteenth century intending to write a history of the city, but from the perspective of an enlightened scholar. He found several "stories" circulating as part of Potosí's history, which came from Arzáns. As a learned scholar, Cañete judged them to be false (Cañete 11).[12] It is also important to recall that—

from the only extensive document that exists about Arzáns's life, the report by his student Ortega y Velasco (Introduction xxxvi-xxxviii)—parts of the *Historia* were read in churches as motifs for preaching and sermons. In other words, oral communication was very much part of Arzáns's profile as an Andean writer.

We can assume that the oral tradition in the Andean region in the eighteenth century had the same political and cultural power and reach that is recognized today in ethnic groups such as the Aymaras from the north of Potosí. The conquered not only had a vision of the Conquest, which was maintained and transmitted for centuries, but also possessed a vision that was—and still is—a system of thought for the survival of their cultures in a world that permanently tried to alienate them. The Indians appealed to their strong conception of the world, trying to reinterpret the colonial relationships in order to survive in the midst of that oppressive regime.

The previously mentioned case of the Aymaras, one of the ethnic groups affected by Potosí's *mita*, shed light on the organization of Andean indigenous thought. Tristan Platt ("Entre 'ch'axwa'" 116) points out that the relationship between Aymara *ayllu* (community) and Inca kingdom was an agreement of reciprocity, of exchange of "goods" for service. The relationship between Aymara society and the Inca state was not one of simple domination or submission. The Aymara tributes were paid for certain benefits that the Inca state provided. Something was given in order to receive something, but more importantly, in this way the indigenous peoples could maintain a certain cultural identity that was not directly threatened, because it did not enter into the margins of the agreement of reciprocity. Under this mentality they tried to live with the Spaniards (and later with the Republic), but facing the colonial regime, which was based, not on reciprocity, but on imposition, they had to reduce and adapt these imposed relationships to their own terms, in order to keep their political and cultural ideology alive. The Aymaras initiated a "creative transference of Andean cultural categories to the new socioeconomic structure that was developing among the besieged ethnic groups. Confronted with a plethora of new cultural forms proceeding from overseas, under the shadow of a conquering violence, the Aymara people hastened to scrutinize the practices authorized by the new Spanish 'falcon' [the symbol of Inca empire], to interpret them in terms of their own intellectual tradition, and intervene actively and strategically in the colonial society based on the results of their analysis" (Platt 116).[13] Platt suggests that the Aymaras understood perfectly the system that dominated them, so that they could mask, under a feigned adoption of those forms of social power, their Andean conception of society and history.

This attitude permeated Indian life in Potosí. The indigenous appropriation of activities such as architecture and painting shows the creation of spaces of cultural expression, by means of which they kept their tradition alive within the imposed Spanish social system. In architecture, the fruits of this activity would be seen in the seventeenth and eighteenth centuries with the creation of the "*mestizo* baroque" in the highland of Bolivia and Peru (Mesa and Gisbert 36). Something similar happens in the writing of the period.

When Arzáns gives an account of the finding of Indian deities and the Indian explanation of their significance, or when he tells stories about the Indians' sexual sins, or when he describes the life of an Indian sorceress, although his intention is to condemn those activities—an attitude continually assumed by the chroniclers since the beginning of the Conquest, as in the cases of Acosta and Sahagún (Adorno)—he reveals that the ideology that informs those accounts is opposed to the Christian ideology of the official narrator. Furthermore, upon reconstructing the major ideological structure of the *Historia* it becomes apparent that his conception of history is closer to Andean thought than to the Christian conception. This can be seen through an analysis of two important symbols contained in Arzáns's text: the water and the Mountain.

Vital Liquids

The predominant symbolic element in the *Historia* connected to liquids: flooding, droughts, rivers of blood, artificial lakes, drownings in the lagoon of Tarapaya, and inundated mines. Liquids repeatedly appear in the scenery of Potosí, and the city appears darkened by waters and torrents and by blood and tears. But the liquid quality does not appear without a purpose; its participation has a precise function established according to a textual code, whose best examples were the *azotes* (scourges) of Potosí.

Arzáns divides the first part of his *Historia* into three cycles that span the years 1545 to 1650. Each one of these cycles ends with a cataclysmic event that marks God's rage at the continued increase of the sins of the Potosinians. Arzáns calls the ends of these cycles the three *azotes* (scourges) of Potosí. The first one is the spilling of blood originated by the war between the *vicuñas* and the *vascongados;* the second one, the flooding of the city, due to the collapse of a dike in one of the artificial lakes of the miners' *ingenios* (mills); and the third, the devaluation of the currency, coined in Potosí, when a counterfeit is discovered.

The *azotes* are set forth in association with liquids. In the first case, the blood spilled in Potosí because of the war between the Vicuñas and the Vascongados symbolizes the loss of a vital liquid: the blood of all Potosinians. Arzáns writes:

> Not only were these civil wars carried out against the Vascongados (the motive they took for starting them), but also against all other rational beings that dwelled in this unfortunate City, of all ages and sexes, of all states and characteristics, for the twelve nationalities that inhabit it would tear each other to pieces, and in the same manner the Indians. (1: 321-322)[14]

In the second case, the miners have accumulated water in artificial lakes in order to move their mills. One day, the walls of the lake of Caricari collapse and the overflowed water inundates the city, causing great damage to all the inhabitants: "This was the second destruction of Potosí for its sins, and (as Méndez and Acosta say) it was the most lamentable..." (2: 14).[15] Arzáns narrates in detail the substantial losses in money and goods that affected all social levels, without exception.

The third case, that of the money, was also a vital loss. Metaphorically, money is the vital liquid of the economy. One can speak of it in terms of *liquidez* (cash flow). It is also usually said that money circulates, a clear metaphorical reference to the blood in the human body. When it is discovered in 1651 that the coin made in Potosí has a false part and that a percentage of the silver used in the mint is being pilfered by the Potosinians, the Controller ("Visitador") Nestarés Marín orders the devaluation of the currency.[16] More than the loss of wealth, it implies the discovery of an inherent malignancy: since the silver coin was the city's emblem of honor and source of pride, we can understand how the devaluation was symbolically and socially degrading for all residents of Potosí.

This last *azote* touches the very heart of Potosí's existence. Thus, Arzáns foresees the end of the city:

> [God] put in the ground (the proper place of the feet) the treasures and splendors of its inhabitants, being such this fall that until now it hasn't been able to raise itself . . . so that overwhelmed and without strength this City can hardly say now: "I am the greatest in riches," but rather, "I was, and my excessive pride has reduced me to a state of great disfavor." (2: 123)[17]

The three *azotes* point, then, to the loss of vital liquids, which have been "spilled" and "wasted." A vital liquid has run out of its channel (the water from the lake; the blood from the body; the coins from the economy) and has been lost beyond recovery, thus leading to the weakening of Potosí's social body. From this perspective, the history of Potosí is the history of a slow wasting away, a slow erosion that can be understood either as the decrease of silver in the Mountain, and therefore as the impoverishment of the mines, or symbolically as the loss of indigenous vitality.

In effect, the depletion of the silver symbolizes a vital loss that can be completely understood only from the Indian point of view. If, on the one hand, silver functions as the basic element for commercial exchange in the society of Potosí, the relation of silver to feminine principles, on the other hand, is essential to Andean thought. Rostorowski explains, from a myth told by Calancha (*Crónica moralizada*), the triple sexual and social division in the Andean region as Collana (gold-elder man), Payan (silver-woman), and Layao (copper-man or little brother) (147). If we recall that women are also elements of exchange in the formation of kindred relations, the association is unmistakable.[18] In other words, if, from Western civilization's perspective, using the silver as a mercantile element causes the loss of its value, which ends in the devaluation of the silver coin, in the frame of Andean thought, that slow waste by circulation would be a waste of the feminine principle, and therefore, a loss of indigenous fertility. As the silver is spent and wasted as money, the capacity for regeneration and vitality in the city is symbolically lost. This is why the divine *azotes* (scourges) come as losses of vital liquids, which Arzáns associates with the economic and moral fall of Potosí.

The mediation of liquids as instruments of punishment allows another interpretation, which comes again from Andean myths. We must now investigate the symbolism of water, more than that of blood or silver.

Water and Doubles

Water has a very important meaning in Andean thought: mediation and division. The main divider in the highland area of Collasuyo (the region to the south of Lake Titicaca) is the water line that goes from Lake Titicaca to the salt lick at the north of Potosí. This aquatic dividing line runs parallel to the volcanic chain in the western Andes. The water and the fire associated with these mountains are divisor elements[19] and, therefore, related with what is double and/or divided.

In the work of Arzáns, this relationship can be seen in two short stories about homosexuality. The first one refers to two indigenous homosexual couples, one of men and the other of women. In the story, God punishes these Indians by killing them with a thunderbolt in the Arenal, a place near Potosí, while they are engaged in their sexual activity. When the people of the city arrive at the Arenal, they are found " ... in the same form as when they were committing this grave sin, but their bones were made pieces and smoke was coming out their bodies" (1: 129).[20] This story already presents several key elements of Andean thought: the ideas of double and mirror; the duality that duplicates itself and configures the four parts of the Inca empire; and the destruction by lightning, characteristic of Illapa,[21] the god associated with the double.

The other story about homosexuality is taken from Calancha. It is the biblical narrative of Sodom and Gomorrah, adapted to a native environment. Arzáns relates that the Indians in the town of Ancoanco (close to Lake Titicaca) had fallen into the practice of sodomy. The Church decides to abandon any further attempt to evangelize there and only one cleric remains in the town. One night the cleric leaves the town, and upon returning finds only two ponds filled with fish of "some human likeness" and a very bad smell. Only one ten-year-old girl had been saved, protected by the Virgin Mary from destruction of the town by fire.

The transformation of the Sodomites into fish and the reduction of the town to ponds indicate an association with zooanthropomorphic Andean gods related to water and sexuality. Likewise, the location of Ancoanco is significant because it is close to Lake Titicaca, a very important place of worship to the water deities. In fact, Copacabana, a god with a human face and a fish-like body, was venerated in a sacred town (later called Copacabana) located on the shores of Lake Titicaca.

Calancha and Torres describe this god with these words:

This idol had no more form than a human face, was deprived of feet and hands, the face ugly and the body like a fish. They worshipped this god as the god of the lake, as the creator of its fishes and as the god of all sensuality. (1: 139)[22]

In her research on Andean iconography, Teresa Gisbert has shown that the image of the Andean siren originated from this "idol" by accepting traits of the siren of the European baroque. This symbol then spread throughout the entire highland region, including Potosí. An illustrative representation of this image can be found, for example, in the portal of the church of San Lorenzo (*Iconografía* 51-60), in which the Virgin is opposed to the siren's sensuality, which was associated, by analogy, with Copacabana. As a consequence the duality Virgin/siren became Virgin/Copacabana. The siren was to replace Copacabana in the iconography of the time, acquiring Andean attributes such as the *charango* (the little Indian guitar).

In Arzáns's plotting of the stories, the relationship between Copacabana and sodomy is established through the emphasis on sensuality and the transformation of human beings into fish. In contrast, the girl who is saved from fire and the Virgin who protects her speak of an inactive sexual condition. Thus, the Christian aim of opposing purity to sensuality, which could be done only by repressing sensuality and sexuality, materialize in Arzáns's story as the stigma of a bad smell.

For now I am interested less in the confrontation—to which I will return later—than in the fact that the nucleus of both stories is the subject of the double. The idea of homosexuality brings with it a mirroring dimension: two identical beings—and not only similar, as a man/woman couple would be—meet and unite. In the story of Ancoanco, the two ponds are located symmetrically next to the road: "The two marshes like filthy ponds rested at an equal distance from the highway" (1: 129).[23] Even the name Ancoanco is a repetition of itself. This concept of the double is basic to Andean thought. It is, for example, the starting point for the thetradivision, the system of spatial division in the Inca empire.[24] Rostorowski shows how that doubleness works for the configuration of the Andean gods. She explains that particularly male gods usually have pairs of attributes (22-24). Tunupa, for example, is the god of lightning and of lava, that is to say, with a celestial attribute and an earthly one. From these binary oppositions, it is possible to extract an important concept in the ideology of some ethnic groups in the southern part of the Andes: the concept of mirror, as studied by Tristan Platt ("Symetries"), who shows that for the Macha, an ethnic group located north of Potosí, their thought is structured following the model of perfection provided by the human body:

> The ritual repetition *yanantín* [that which is united in one category] can be interpreted as an attempt to assimilate the couple to the perfect duality provided by the model of the human body. Following this interpretation, it would be more exact to say that men and women should be *yanantín* more than to say that *yanantín* means man-and-woman: these should actualize this perfect union, the one of the two halves of the human body. (1096)

Thus, perfection is produced—as in the human body—by the union of two symmetrical sides, as reflected by a mirror: the left is united to the right and vice versa. If the body is already double, its inverted image in the mirror would give the thetradivision of the Andean space. Doubles and mirrors constitute, then, the pattern of the Andean universe. It is not strange that twins should be considered perfect, and therefore, that the union of twins would be the perfect and divine union.

The emergence of doubles marks the opening of an ideal space, original and harmonious, as the pattern for perfection. In the story of Ancoanco we can see that, under the apparent condemnation of the Andean religious system, there is a regression to the old gods (fishes and doubles). It is as if Christian repression had forced the Andean deities to return to an earlier state in their formation, to the doubleness of the original period of the constitution of those deities.

We can see that water has a broad and multiple significance: the division of space and the creation of doubles, and images of sexuality associated with the mirror (the water in lakes and rivers). But in Arzáns's text, these meanings have an ambiguous function. Despite its association with the Christian god, as an instrument of punishment, the function of water in Arzáns's stories points toward the Andean vision. One of the most remarkable functions of water as an Andean symbol is to reverse the direction established by Christian ideology. In spatial terms, the falling water (flooding, spilled blood) of negative characteristics is opposed to the water springing up from under the earth (lakes, rivers) with productive, fertile, and sexual forces distinctive of the Andean world. This means that the water that represents destruction coming from the Christian god is transformed into the Andean water of sensuality and doubleness. But this opposition can be better appreciated in another type of confrontation: the mountain gods versus the Virgin Mary.

The Mountain as a God

We have seen that life in Potosí revolved around the exploitation of silver, the mineral that seemed to "grow" from the entrails of the rich mountain. This determined the great importance of its symbolic dimension. Without doubt, one aspect of that symbolization came from the conception of mountains in the Andean world. As is known, many mountains are associated with gods, or the mountains themselves are considered to be gods. This animism was favored by the disappearance of the Inca. The religious system imposed by the latter was fiercely combated by Christianity, allowing the resurgence of older religions that had not yet been banished completely (Wachtel, *La vision* 131). For example, the custom of creating sacred places in the mountains for the *huacas* (deities and spirits with connotations of vital and generative strengths [Rostorowski 9-10]) is one of the habits that the Spaniard—not very successfully—tried most to eradicate.

If we read the chroniclers who gathered the oral traditions about the Mountain of Potosí, we can see that this area is assigned from the moment of its discovery to the category of marvelous space. The term used most often was "beautiful," sometimes followed by the designation "perfect." Calancha describes it in the following manner: "Here God created the most beautiful mountain, the richest mountain which lies on earth..." (1676).[25] And Garcilaso says: "The summit of the mountain is round, it is beautiful to the sight because it stands alone; nature so adorned it so that it might be as famous throughout the world as today it is" (2: 279).[26]

Arzáns provides a version, taken from the oral tradition, where the perception of the Mountain as a deity is explicit. For Arzáns the discovery of the Mountain occurred much earlier than the arrival of the Spaniards:

> [The Inca Huayna Cápac] before taking leave [of Porco] saw our famous Mountain, and astonished with its grandeur and beauty said (speaking with members of his court): "This one without doubt will have in its bowels much silver"... (1: 27)[27]

The Inca gives the order to start the exploitation of the Mountain, but when the mining work is to begin a great clamor is heard in the sky and a voice says:

> "Do not take the silver from this Mountain, because it is for other owners"... Speaking of the case in their own tongue, [the Indians] upon the sound of this loud speech said "Potocsi," which means *it gave a loud clamor* and from this was later derived (corrupting a letter) the name of Potosí. (1: 27)[28]

In this narrative the topics of Andean sacredness and Christian ideology are mixed. The ideological consequence implicit in the message carried by the voice is that the silver is for the Spanish empire. But it also shows that the Mountain is marked from its discovery as a space of extraordinary and/or sacred manifestations.

The narrative of the discovery of an image inside the Mountain is still more explicit about the Mountain's sacred value for the Indians:

> They took [the statue] outside and causing a great stir among themselves, the Indians began their customary and diabolic interpretations, and then there was a great cry and clamor, and then the natives and the diviners were saying that that was the Mountain of Potosi and that the Spaniards already had taken from it its head, as they had done with the Incas and all their goods. (1: 160)[29]

The association is clear: the Mountain of Potosí is a god and its origin dates back to the time of the Incas. As all Andean deities— and Arzáns's narrative treatment proves it—the Mountain presents several attributes that cannot be ordered in a single category. Arzáns describes the Mountain in the following terms:

> The famous, always supreme, exquisite and everlasting Mountain of Potosi, the singular work of the power of God, unique miracle of nature, perfect and permanent wonder of the world, joy of mortals, emperor of the mountains, king of the hills, prince of all [the] minerals, lord of 5,000 Indians (who extract from it its entrails); bugle which resounds in all the sphere, army enlisted against the enemies of the faith, rampart which impedes their designs, castle and formidable weapon whose bullets destroy them, attraction of men, magnet of their wills, base of all treasures, ornament of the sacred temples, coin with which heaven is bought, monster of wealth, body of earth and soul of silver ... to whom the painters run and paint in figures and hieroglyphs of a venerable ancient with white hair and a long beard, seated on the throne of his well-appointed mansion, arrayed in precious robes of silver, the temples of his imperial crown encircled in triumphant laurel, scepter in the right hand, in the left a rod of silver. (1: 3) ... [30]

This description, flattering in its baroque images, speaks of a male god, but one whose meaning is ambiguous. On the one hand, the allegoric images that describe the Mountain as an omnipotent being, as a pagan god, are opposed to the image of that old man that closes the description and who reminds us of the Christian god. This image suggests a constant element of the way in which Andean and Western religions mixed: behind the Western deity there is in reality an Andean god.[31]

The affiliation Mountain-masculinity-god is clearly marked in this complex manner of describing the Mountain. Other attributes of the Mountain have to do with fertility, which is more of a feminine trait. In the interior of the mines, the silver is generated[32] and veins appear and disappear mysteriously in different years. Arzáns assigns these events to God's will (1: 108, 1: 117, 1: 125, 1: 142). In the same way he registers the popular belief that one must enter the mine chewing coca leaves to avoid the loss of the mineral (2: 268). This means that silver must be *cultivated* with ceremonies and its abundance is dependent on the will of the Mountain. Somehow the Mountain acquires traits from the Pacha Mama, the earth deity.

Furthermore, the relationship femininity/Mountain can be better explained by the confrontation Virgin/Mountain. Besides the images related to Andean religion, the Mountain also produces images of Christian lineage, as crosses and a representation of the Virgin (1: 130). In effect, when Arzáns writes about the finding of a Virgin's face carved in stone inside the Mountain, he explains that devotion to her increased notably at that moment. As an immediate measure an altar of the Virgin of the Conception (which suggests once more the subject of fertility) was placed in the interior of the mine, in the *cruceros*[33] of the tunnels, the place where she was found for the first time. Some time later this became a general practice in all mines:[34]

> From the moment in which this image was found, the devotion of the Indians and miners grew in such a manner that in all the mines already discovered and in those which would later be discovered, they hung within the crossbeams the image or our Lady of the Conception.... (1: 131)[35]

Another aspect that must be underlined is the conversion of an Andean male deity into a Christian feminine deity, by the iconographic incorporation of the Virgin into the Mountain (see Figure 1). As Gisbert has shown, during that period of time, several paintings were produced, which transformed the Mountain by wrapping it in the Virgin's cloak or by incorporating the Virgin inside the Mountain (*Iconografía* 17-22). Furthermore, the association Virgin-Mountain was promoted by some religious orders to reinforce the substitution of Andean gods with Christian images. This is proven by the texts of the Augustinian friars Calancha and Ramos Gavilán (19).

In the Mountain, the masculine side seems to have a clear Andean affiliation and representation, while the feminine side, also part of the Andean representation, is opposed to and displaced by the Spanish tradition. If one realizes that Potosí is in *Urcu*, male territory, the apparition of the Virgin can only be seen as an upsetting of Andean religious balance.[36] The Christian system imposed by the feminine representation of the Virgin breaks the masculine harmony of the Mountain gods. This will have important consequences in the formation of the ideology of the *criollo*.[37]

Thus the Mountain is another complex element in Arzáns's symbolization. It maintains ambiguous and double attributes, usually framed in Western images as the old man or the Virgin, but hides within itself Andean gods and meanings.[38] This characterization of the Mountain coincides perfectly with the description of Andean deities of the mountains made by anthropologists. Berthelot, explaining the exploitation of mines during the Incan empire, affirms that each mine was the encounter between high deities of the Mountain and low deities from the earth, between the *Urcusuyo* and the *Umasuyo*, the masculine and the feminine facets (980-1014). And Martínez shows how complex these gods can be, embracing not only masculinity and femininity, but also a double ambiguity in creative and conservative aspects (86). Martínez concludes that the mountains are deities that assume different roles according to contextual needs and show facets that are conditioned by historical situations. Is not this the exact description of the Mountain of Potosí? Sometimes it provides silver and sometimes it does not; the mineral veins appear and suddenly

Figure 1. Pachamama of the Virgin-Mountain of Potosí.
Painting by an anonymous artist, sixteenth century.
Photo courtesy of Teresa Gisbert.

disappear; its richness is denied to the Incas but is offered to the Spaniards; according to its will, there are times of splendor and times of destruction in Potosí. It would seem that the Mountain has in its hands the times and destiny of Potosí.

The Mountain as the Inscription of Time

The conception of the Mountain as a deity has crucial importance in the *Historia* because it illustrates Arzáns's vision of historical time. To better understand this aspect, we can consider, in his own words, a second image found in the mines:

> It had the head of a toad, one human arm and the other of a cow, the body could not be distinguished for its poor form, although Captain Pedro Méndez (as an eyewitness) affirms that it was in the manner of the shell of a turtle, and this (he says) was over the back and the sides, and that across the belly it was without form and smooth as a slab, and that it had not feet but only (in the place where it should have them) two unequal hooves. (1: 160)[39]

The narrator adds that the Indians found a "cord knotted at intervals formed of one and the same stone" and that the older Indians' explanation was that "their ancestors might have put it their, because each knot in that tie of stone was said to signify a large number of years."[40] Arzáns completes this explanation by saying that according to the Indians each knot was *pachac,* which means the number 100. His calculation postulates that the image had been placed there two thousand years earlier.

Clearly this image is an intermediate being between nature and humankind, and it could be classified with Copacabana. It gives the impression of being in a state of pregnancy where different creatures, animals and men, are blending or detaching themselves, as at the entrance or exit of chaos. On the other hand, the word *pachac* amplifies its semantic spectrum when associated with *pacha,* a word with extensive meaning in the Aymara language. The most important meaning is related to time,[41] but as Bouysse-Cassagne and Harris (18-34) explain, following Bertonio's dictionary (1612), that concept is quite complex. They mention the following meanings of *pacha:* (1) totality and abundance; (2) the coming of a new time or cycle; and (3) the special relationship between opposite worlds, such as the upper and the lower ones.

Following these three meanings, Bouysse-Cassagne and Harris mark three moments of the development of time in Aymara thought: first, the age of *Taypi*, the time of the origin and creation of men and ethnic groups. This is the time of Tunupa, god of fire and water, of lightning and rain. Second, the age of *Puruma*, time for differentiating and limiting the wild from the cultural space. And third, the age of *Awqa*, which is the time of *Pacha Kuti*, the time of the change of cycle (18-21). In spatial terms these cycles have a centripetal bearing. First, this refers to the legend of Tunupa, who came out from a central point (Lake Titicaca) to divide space and expand his cult. Then comes *Puruma* time, with the marking of territories and meanings and the establishment of frontiers for dominated territory. Finally the time of war arrives when the territorial marks are displaced and/or disappear, the time in which another cycle is initiated.

Returning to Arzáns's *Historia*, we can see that the meanings of *Pacha* are related to general aspects of Arzáns's organization of history in Potosí. The first meaning may clearly be associated with the periods of richness of the mines in Potosí. The second is related to the idea of cycle, which is apparent in Arzáns's translation of *Pachac* as one hundred years, a century, which is in Western culture the equivalent of a cycle. It is also connected with the history of Potosí, which Arzáns understands as one of consecutive cycles. The third meaning is also associated with the idea of the cycle. After a period in which opposed forces cannot live together, another time follows where coexistence is possible by a system of alternations. In the transition from one period to another, a *Pacha Kuti*, which is a change of cycle, occurs. This expression has also the meaning of "war time." In Potosí, as Arzáns narrates, one of the permanent subjects is war, to the extent that he thought of calling his work *Guerras civiles y casos memorables de Potosí* (*Civil Wars and Memorable Cases in Potosí*). The history of Potosí seems to be exactly the transition from one time to another, manifested through a permanent malaise, a nocturnal and rainy background, and a time of war and blood. This is symbolized in those figures found in the Mountain, representing intermediate status between a nondifferentiated stage of existence and a stage of defined beings.

This suggests that historical time as well as the cyclic punishments of Potosí are somehow related to things coming from the Mountain's interior, like the silver or the images found there. The Mountain becomes the producer of the symbols of time in the *Historia*, and therefore the historical time of Potosí is defined following the Andean conception of time.

It is interesting to see that the three stages of Andean time are present in the history of Potosí. If we accept Bouysse-Cassagne and Harris's idea of a *Taypi* that is "a potential microcosm that would give meaning to time and space, and from which the different ethnic groups would have spread" (20), then Potosí looks like a *Taypi*. The city that emerges from Arzáns's pages, especially in the first part of his *Historia*, is a microcosm of the Spanish colony. With extraordinary clairvoyance, Arzáns calls his city an "orbe abreviado" ("abbreviated orb"). In Potosí are represented all Spanish nationalities and all the ethnic Indian groups from the north of Cuzco to the south of Potosí. Furthermore, it is the cradle of a new society. But in the eighteenth century, when Arzáns writes his book, that Potosí-taypi is lost and one senses the end of a cycle. Potosí's tragedy is that its consolidation and expansion were fragmentary and never completed. Its *Taypi* age was never accomplished. On the contrary, Arzáns feels that the *Awqa* time has arrived, the Pacha Kuti of war and the time for a change of cycle. From this *Awqa* Arzáns tries to recover the memory of the original *Taypi*: the glorious lost Potosí.

In addition to this, however, we can see that the dominant setting in the *Historia* is the *Puruma*, the time when wild and civilized zones are in the process of demarcation, when the limits between nature and humankind, light and darkness, are not totally defined because of the lack of a completed *Taypi*. That is why Potosí lives in an atmosphere of shadows, the general domain of *Puruma*, "basically a moment of diffuse light, like the one at dusk when the sky darkens" (Bouysse-Cassagne and Harris 22). This can be translated in social terms as an epoch of "stateless society" (Potosí, the land of easy riches, the mining territory without law or order). *Puruma* is the wild space; here are privileged the summits, the border zones between the sky and the earth (Bouysse-Cassagne and Harris 25). Such is the case with the Mountain that, until the arrival of the Spaniards, was an uninhabitable, wild place. In effect, Potosí, time and space of *Puruma*, is marked by the signs of gods living in the peaks, especially the gods of lightning and rain such as Illapa, deities who manifest themselves continually in Potosí. One should also remember that in Andean thought the marks of these gods are related to the idea of the double. Those who are touched by lightning have divided lips; the lightning engenders twins (Bouysse-Cassagne 25), and, as we have seen, this has a direct relation with the stories of homosexuality.

One might ask which of these three temporal constructs best defines Potosí. "Abbreviated orb," "stateless society," or "war time?" The extraordinary thing in Arzáns's text is that all three cycles function simultaneously. These cycles that should unfold in time are condensed in one mythical space: Potosí. So Arzáns's Potosí becomes a privileged symbol, the key to an Andean explanation of colonial history. The *Historia* ciphers a series of processes whose explanation is to be found in the forms of Andean symbolism that the text absorbs as part of its narration. This means that the "final" explanation is ciphered in the Mountain, the symbol of Potosí's history.

If the punishments and cycles in Potosí are determined from the Mountain, if the essential ambiguity of Potosí—richness and poverty, confusion and destruction, the masculine and the feminine faces—is found in the symbolization of the Mountain, and if the *Taypi* (origin-water-mountain), *Awqa* (war-change and end of a cycle), and *Puruma* (limits and shadows) are superimposed in Potosí's history, one realizes that Arzáns is using a mythical conception of time and space as the underlying structure of history in Potosí. From this point of view, the Mountain is something more than a god belonging to the Andean culture and recovered by the *Historia;* it is a structural complex, constructed on an Andean base with Western elements, in which the meaning of the history of Potosí is ciphered. As a system impossible to exhaust, the Mountain continuously absorbs Andean and Christian symbols. In it the masculine and the feminine side, the *huaca* and the Virgin, the Indians and the Spaniards, the upper and the lower worlds, are mixed; in it traditional limits are lost; and in it there is a clue to the new future configuration of the cultures and the untamed.

If the Mountain became a sort of fetish for the residents of Potosí because it was the provider of well-being and the only means for subsistence, this feeling was augmented by the sacred magnitude it held for the Indians. Step by step the attributes proceeding from religious Indian thought and the attributes that the activity of exploitation provided would merge in the image of the Mountain. Arzáns clearly reflects this accumulation of meanings in the Mountain. As a result the Mountain became the very complex symbol that we have extracted from his narrative. The ways in which he describes it, along with the stories of Andean and Christian gods that appeared in the interior of the Mountain, are part of a privileged portrait of the Mountain. But the breadth of Arzáns's narrative is such that, even without his realizing it, the symbolic aspects of the Mountain acquire such importance that they become the inner system of ideological organization of historical time in Potosí. In essence, the Mountain is not only the origin of Potosí's economy, but the origin of time and life in the Imperial City.

Conclusion

I have been guided by the certainty that Arzáns, although shaped by Christian ideology, had to break with this mold to give a more coherent summary of the course of history in Potosí, one of the main goals of his work. The break became manifest in images and symbols that were close to his life and experience, yet not necessarily explicit as an ideology: myths and beliefs in Potosí, with their patently Andean roots. This process was facilitated by the sympathetic and positive evaluation of the Indians included in Arzáns's writing. His open love for his country (Potosí) included its inhabitants, among whom he counted the Indians. If he did not treat the Indians with the same importance he assigns to the *criollos*, it is certainly with more understanding than did other Spanish or *criollo* people of the same city. The Indians for Arzáns were important actors in Potosí's history, and not only as labor, but particularly in terms of the form that their culture would give to the mining city.

This understanding of the Indians in their historical role (for

Arzáns, social history was made out of particular stories) allowed him to inscribe in his text facts, narratives, traditions, beliefs, and myths whose origins are found in Andean narrative. The blending of this narrative with Western discourse of written history, and the Christian orientation, produced a narrative that is very difficult to frame in any of the original discourses. The points of intersection can be seen in those symbols that function as allegory and/or explanation of the history of Potosí. In this sense, the water and the Mountain are paradigms of how the different visions of the world that feed the *Historia* are fused.

However, it should not be forgotten that the cause of this transformation is a violent alteration of cultural processes. The brutal violence of the first part of the Conquest was followed by a violent acculturation that had effects in the Indian communities as well as for the *criollos*, who somehow began to feel excluded from cultural and historical development. In the case of Potosí, this violent confrontation was obvious in the exploitation of the mining force, but can also be seen in the opposition of the Christian deity to the Andean one. This confrontation is seen and understood by Arzáns through a mediating element, water, which is taken from the Andean thought and used as the mobile element that reflects the interaction of Christian and Andean mythical forces in the history of Potosí.

One of the major consequences of this confrontation is the emergence of the concept of the double in Arzáns's work, whose origin can be traced in the Andean tradition. This concept is an important element of his narrative, because it serves as an abstract and general pattern for characters,[42] stories, and his mythical explanation of the history of Potosí. One of its textual materializations is the Mountain as origin and controller of time.

From this perspective, Arzáns's vision of the world is an interpretation of the colonial system, neither purely Indian nor purely Christian, but a reformulation in terms of Andean thought. This prompted Arzáns to recreate the history of Potosí in his own *textual* and *ideological* terms. The *Historia* is more than the mere history of a colonial mining city; it is the story of the history of Potosí, a mythical Andean city.

Notes

1. To avoid confusion with the word "creole" in English, I use the Spanish term *criollo*, which refers to those born in the New World from Spanish parents.

2. "Potosí, naturalmente, se llevaba la palma en esto: su cosmopolitismo, la población flotante, el ritmo trepidante que imponía la famosa 'cobdicia' minera, las envidias, las venganzas, todo contribuía a dar a la Villa un ambiente de perpetuo motín larvado. Muertes, pendencias, robos, estafas, querellas amorosas, desplantes contra la autoridad, 'bullicios' y 'atrevimientos' afloran una y otra vez en las quejas a las instancias centrales limeñas o metropolitanas."

3. Although it has been said that the *Mita* was a creation of the Inca, this assertion is inexact. One cannot deny the existence of work in the mines of the Incas, which was obligatory and rotational as it was later in the colonial *Mita*. But this should be understood in the frame of relationships of reciprocity which the indigenous community maintained with the Inca state, and not as the system of inhumane exploitation which the Spaniards implemented. The conclusion of Berthelot about the system of work in the Inca empire is striking in this regard: "Thus one finds oneself in the presence of coherent ideological system, in which the Inca's work in the mines is no longer seen as violence or exploitation in the eyes of the Indians; rather it assumes the form of a traditional obligation of reciprocity and of a duty of a religious character . . ." (1011; translation mine).

4. " . . . es una de las grandes lástimas el verlos salir para esta Villa dejando sus provincias y casas cada año al entero de esta mita. ¡Qué de demostraciones de sentimientos no hacen, qué de llantos, alaridos de mujeres y gritos de sus hijos no se oyen al despedirse por aquellos campos y poblados! Por no verse en este trance muchas familias se han desaparecido de sus casas y tierras sin que jamás se haya sabido de ellas por entrarse en las incógnitas tierras de infieles, y muchos se han quitado la vida con sus propias manos huyendo de sus gobernadores al convocarlos para la dicha mita. Ello ciertamente es grandísima lástima la miserable servidumbre a que han llegado estos desventurados naturales, no por guerra justa que les hiciesen, particularmente en este reino peruano, que ellos se les fueron dando por amigos llana y libremente, y los primeros conquistadores luego que los vieron rendidos los hicieron esclavos y los trataron peor que si realmente lo fueran; y si les hicieran alguna guerra fue muy injusta, por donde no puede haber señorío sobre el vencido ni el vencedor lo pudo adquirir, porque el injusto y mal título no se le puede dar, por el cual no se puede ese tal llamar señor sino tirano" (2: 189). Translations of quotations from Arzáns are by Marilyn Miller.

5. For a current study of the *Mita* in Potosi, see Cole; for data on the production of silver, see Abecia and López Beltrán; on labor in Potosí, the studies of Bakewell and Tandeter; and on the impact of the *Mita* in the rural communities, see Sánchez-Albornoz (69-154). The work of Buechler on Potosí in the eighteenth century is also of interest.

6. "No es decible el sumo desprecio con que [españoles] miran y tratan a los humildes indios, siendo de una misma especie hermanos suyos (y aunque les pese), y lo que es más, hijos unos y otros de un padre Dios."

7. " . . . comúnmente los de este peruano reino son de muy rara habilidad, claro entendimiento y general aplicación, pues se experimenta (con gran sentimiento de

los españoles) el que los indios se hayan alzado con el ejercicio de todos los oficios, no sólo los mecánicos mas también los del arte" (Introduction xxxvi-xxxviii). The humanitarian position of Arzáns was clear and explicit: Indians are equal to Spaniards and capable of doing the most specialized and difficult jobs. Looking at these statements and the ethic that follows from them, it is not surprising that powerful people who believed they were affected by Arzáns's position tried to suppress his book.

8. "Y así el indio capitán (cuyo nombre era Chaqui Ctari, que se interpreta *pie de víbora*) puesto en pie lleno de ira y rabia le dijo: 'Decid a esos enemigos nuestros, ladrones de oro y plata, barbudos sin palabra, que si hubiéramos sabido que era gente sin piedad y que no cumplen los tratos, desde que supimos que estaban en el cerro de Porco les hubiéramos hecho guerra, y echándolos de allí no les permitiéramos entrar donde estabamos ni sacar la plata del Potocsí.'"

9. "Hízose tan temido en el Cerro que el más bravo español huía de su encuentro y los veedores y alcalde mayor de minas experimentaron fieras resistencias cuando iban aprenderlo por quejas de los azogueros que decían les disfrutaban las labores. ... No era nocivo este indio Agustín en las labores corrientes...."

10. "hasta en este tiempo es tenido en mucho de los indios como lo demuestran cuando ven sus retratos."

11. This is the version in Quechua recovered by Jesús Lara (*Tragedia*), which seems to be the most faithful to the tradition. Gisbert (*Esquema*) notes that the change to Quechua occurred in the eighteenth century as part of the indigenous fervor of that period. For a detailed study of this work, see Wachtel (*La vision*). See also Bredow for an account of its present representation.

12. Before the writing of the *Historia*, Arzáns offered a similar history in a short text called *Anales de la Villa Imperial de Potosí*. The *Anales* were widely circulated in Potosí and the popular Potosinian traditions were cited within. This book was one of the sources used by Ricardo Palma to write his *Tradiciones peruanas*.

13. "Los aymaras consiguieron una 'transferencia creativa de las categorías culturales andinas hacia la nueva estructura socio-económica que se iba levantando en torno a los grupos étnicos asediados. Confrontado con una plétora de nuevas formas culturales procedentes de Ultramar bajo la sombra de la violencia 'conquistadora,' los aymara se lanzaron a desmenuzar las prácticas autorizadas por el nuevo 'halcón' [el símbolo del imperio incaico español, interpretarlas en términos de su propia tradición intelectual, e intervenir activa y estratégicamente en la sociedad colonial en base a los resultados de sus análisis."

14. "No sólo fueron estas civiles guerras contra los vascongados (motivo que tomaron para emprenderlas), mas también unos contra otros todo género de viviente racional que moraba en esta desventurada Villa, de todas edades y sexos, de todos estados y calidades, pues de 12 naciones que la habitaban, las unas contra las otras despedazaban, y de la misma manera los indios."

15. "Esta fue la segunda destrucción de Potosí por sus pecados, y (como dicen Méndez y Acosta) fue la más lamentable...."

16. Cañete y Domínguez explains thus the alteration of the coin:

No fue difícil a los Mercaderes de Platas, por la mucha mano que tenían en estos negocios, el corromper a los Ensayadores y demás oficiales de la Casa, para alterar la ley de la moneda, en perjuicio de la confianza pública.... Para la averiguación, castigo y remedio de estos daños fue nombrado por visitador y Presidente de Charcas, Don Francisco Nestarés Marín, el año de 1649, comenzó luego a practicar su comisión.... (161)

Vázquez, Mesa, and Gisbert add:

Nestarés hizo en 1651 la rebaja de la misma moneda, convirtiendo los pesos de ocho reales en pesos de cuatro reales. Esta medida que fue una verdadera catástrofe económica para todo el Alto Perú y especialmente para los potosinos causó honda consternación y gran animosidad en contra suya. (162)

17. "[Dios] puso en los suelos (propio lugar de los pies) los tesoros y pompas de sus vecinos y demás moradores, siendo tal esta caída que hasta hoy no se ha podido levantar... conque agobiada y sin fuerzas no puede ya casi decir esta Villa: 'Yo soy la grande en riquezas,' sino: 'Yo fui, y mis soberbias me han puesto ahora por los suelos.' "

18. Studying the principle of reciprocity in distinct societies, Lévi-Strauss (84) showed that women could be treated as goods of exchange, because they were "le supreme cadeau." The system of exchange concludes in the matrimonial relationship, where the great gift of the woman is given. Lévi-Strauss emphasizes that "the fundamental trait of marriage, considered to be a form of exchange appeared, in a particularly clear manner, in the case of dualistic organizations" (*Les structures élémentaires* 84), which is the case in the Andean societies (translation mine).

19. This dividing line was definitely a geographic, social, and religious limit. Along this line lived the Urus, a group that the Aymaras considered savage. Obviously this social group demarcated the difference between the savage and the civilized (Wachtel, "Hommes d'eau" 1125-1159). On the other hand, Gisbert shows that this water line runs parallel to the trajectory of the god Tunupa, whose steps are marked by the volcanoes of the region (*Iconografía* 35-46).

20. " ... en la misma forma que cuando cometían tan grave culpa, pero hechos pedazos los huesos y saliendo humo de sus cuerpos."

21. Illapa is the god of lightning in the southern Andes. His name and iconography are associated with St. James by way of the element thunder/musket fire. The qualities of this god are particularly ambiguous. Sometimes he is confused with Tunupa, a god who was also associated with rain, lightning, and fire. Illapa is a god of various faces; hence, the missionaries invented three Illapas (Intiyllapa, Yllapa and Chuquilla) in order to explain the Christian trinity (Rostorowski 39-42).

22. "Este ídolo no tenía más figura que un rostro humano, destronado de pies y manos, el rostro feo y el cuerpo como pez. A éste adoraban por dios de su laguna, por creador de sus peces y dios de sus sensualidades" (Calancha and Torres 1: 139).

23. "Quedaron solamente al igual del camino real las dos ciénagas a modo de lagunillas asquerosas."

24. This is one of the basic concepts in the organization of the Andean vision of the world. Murra (191) argued for an incorporation of Andean data in the studies of dual social organization (see Lévi-Strauss, *Anthropologie;* Zuidema). Those facts are another verification that systems of duality dominate in the Andean, Incan, and pre-Incan cultures. In this regard, one of the most innovative studies was that of

Zuidema. Explaining the organization of the Ceques in the Inca empire, Zuidema makes the following observation:

By combination of the two forms of organization, an organization was achieved that consisted of two territorial moieties, which were each divided into four territorial groups, which were each subdivided into two nonterritorial moieties. This type of organization was the same as that found in the third representation of the organization of Cuzco. (113)

Another example is the study of Silverblatt (*Moon* 20) on political hierarchies and gender in the Andes, which is based on that duality:

The racial relations into which Andean women and men were born highlighted gender as a frame to organize life. Chains of women paralleled by chains of men formed the kinship channels along which flowed rights to the use of community resources. Women and men acted in, grasped, and interpreted the world around them as if it were divided into the interdependent sphere of gender.

25. "Aquí crió Dios el cerro más precioso; el más opulento monte que pisa el mundo...."

26. "Lo alto del cerro es redondo, es hermoso a la vista porque es solo; hermoséolo la naturaleza para que fuese tan famoso en el mundo como hoy lo es" (2: 239).

27. "[El inga Huayna Ccápac (sic)] antes de partirse [de Porco] vio nuestro famoso Cerro, y admirado de su grandeza y hermosura dijo (hablando con los de su corte): 'Este sin duda tendrá en sus entrañas mucha plata....'"

28. "'No saquéis la plata de este Cerro, porque es para otros dueños'...Refiriendo [los indios] el caso en su idioma, al llegar a la palabra estruendo dijeron 'Potocsi' que quiere decir *dio un gran estruendo*, y de aquí se derivó después (corrompiendo una letra) el nombre de Potosí."

29. "Sacáronla afuera [la estatua], y moviéndose un gran alboroto entre los indios comenzaron sus acostumbradas y diabólicas interpretaciones, y luego un llanto y vocerío, pues como simples y agoreros decían que aquel era el Cerro de Potosí y que ya los españoles le habían quitado la cabeza, como lo habían hecho con sus ingas y todas sus cosas."

30. "El famoso, siempre máximo, riquísimo e inacabable Cerro de Potosí; singular obra del poder de Dios; único milagro de la naturaleza; perfecta y permanente maravilla del mundo; alegría de los mortales, emperador de los montes, rey de los cerros, príncipe de todos [los] minerales; señor de 5,000 indios (que le sacan las entrañas); clarín que resuena en todo el orbe; ejército pagado contra los enemigos de la fe; muralla que impide sus designios; castillo y formidable pieza cuyas balas los destruye; atractivo de los hombres; imán de sus voluntades; basa de todos los tesoros; adorno de los sagrados templos; moneda con que se compra el cielo; monstruo de riqueza; cuerpo de tierra y alma de plata...a quien corren los pinceles y pintan en figura y hieroglífico de un venerable viejo con cana y luenga barba, sentado en el cetro de su bien formada máquina, adornado de preciosos vestidos de plata, ceñidas sus sienes de imperial corona rodeada de triunfador laurel, cetro en la diestra mano, en la siniestra una barra de plata...."

31. Current anthropological studies also show this. For example, Gabriel Martínez analyses the image of Qollka Mallku, a god represented by a mountain in Isluga, to the north of Chile and near Potosí, which could be confused with the apostle St. James. Teresa Gisbert (*Iconografía* 23-26) similarly describes the association between Tata Sabaya, an Andean deity, and St. Martin of Tours. And Wachtel analyzes this same figure, with the same characteristics, in the zone of Chipaya (cited by Martínez 97).

32. Berthelot (1008) says that the metals of the mines were associated with the gods who propitiated them, the same as fruits of the earth. Hence, "chaque mine a son idole particulière, sa *huaca*" (1008).

33. A *crucero* is defined by García de Llanos as "the site where a mining tunnel meets a vein, whether it crosses it or not, and whether it continues the tunnel or not" ("la parte donde cualquier socavon coge una veta, que la cruce que no, y que pase el socavon mas adelante o no pase...") (26).

34. This may even be considered the origin of one of the most deeply rooted mining traditions in Bolivia, which is related to the themes of sexuality and fertility. It deals with the rituals related to the character/deity called el *Tío* (the Uncle), a small figure of clay whose image is similar to Priapo. El *Tío* is considered an ambiguous being who can favor or punish miners. For this reason, these miners bring offerings in the form of alcohol, cigars, and coca leaves when they enter the mines. The figure of el *Tío* is placed in the *cruceros* of the mines, in the place that previously belonged to the image of the Virgin. It would seem that el *Tío* at some moment in Andean history substituted for the Virgin as protector of the mines. This substitution is so direct that it cannot fail to draw our attention: to the purity of the Virgin is opposed the phallic and sexual character of el *Tío*. On the other hand, in the city of Oruro, a mining city near Potosí, a Carnival is celebrated every year. This festival is the celebration of the Virgin of the Mullein, patron of miners. Among the ritual dances performed, the most important is the *Diablada* (bedeviled). This dance represents the devils that leave the mines and confront the angels. Upon being vanquished, they declare themselves servants of the Virgin. It would seem that with the passage of time, the role of the Virgin has been relegated more toward the exterior of the mines, while their interior has recuperated the characteristics of Andean thought, and this has been identified with the devil—the denominator that Christianity always has imposed on the Andean gods. (For an outline of the relationships between *Tío*, Carnival, and mask, see Gisbert, "Introducción al estudio de la máscara" 10). The role of el *Tío* in the social and ideological formation of the miners is of great importance. One may even note its symbolic importance in the total development of American history, as René Jara does, seeing in the transition of the Virgin to the phallic *Tío* an indication that America was historically "prepared to define itself" (*Perfil historiográfico* 9-10).

35. "Desde el punto en que fue hallada esta imagen, creció la devoción de los indios y mineros en tanta manera, que en todas las minas descubiertas y la que en adelante se descubriera, colocaron dentro de los cruceros la imagen de la Concepción de Nuestra Señora...."

36. The Aymaras divide the space of the high plains into a masculine and feminine world. *Urcusuyo* represents the masculine, associated with mountains and war, while *Umasuyu* represents the plains, the feminine, the liquid. Bouysse, studying

the lists of the *mitayos* who arrived in Potosí, has classified the region of Potosí as belonging to the *Caracaras*, an *Urcu*, or masculine ethnic group (1059).

37. For the implications and importance of the double in Arzáns's *Historia*, as well as the implications of the Virgin and the Mountain in the formation of the ideology of the *criollo* in the eighteenth century, see García Pabón.

38. Against the idea of religious syncretism, today one is more likely to think that behind the Christian gods many native beliefs were maintained. Silverblatt discusses the social and/or political function of these gods: "Andeanized Santiagos encouraged resistance but it was a resistance contained within the boundaries of colonial power relations. The hispanified mountain gods/nativized saints embodied the didactic memories of colonized history, memories that spoke of ethical distinction and violations of morality" ("Political Memories" 191).

39. "Tenía la cabeza de sapo, un brazo de gente y el otro de vaca, el cuerpo no se distinguía por lo mal formado, aunque el capitán Pedro Méndez (como testigo de vista) afirma que era a manera de una concha de tortuga, y esto (dice) era por la parte del lomo y de los lados, y que por la barriga estaba sin ninguna forma liso como una tabla, y que no tenía pies mas solamente (en el lugar donde los pudiera tener) dos pezoncillos desiguales" (1: 160).

40. "cordel anudado a trechos formado de la misma piedra" ... "lo pondrían sus antepasados, porque cada nudo en aquel lazo de piedra decía significar una cuenta grande de años."

41. Bertonio translates *pacha* as "time, ancient time, heaven, earth, and hell." For *pacahacutic* he gives "time of war" (242).

42. For a more thorough development of this topic, see García Pabón.

Works Cited

Abecia Baldivieso, Valentín. *Mitayos de Potosí: En una economía sumergida*. Barcelona: Técnicos Editores Asociados, 1988.

Adorno, Rolena. "Literary Production and Suppression: Reading and Writing about Amerindians in Colonial Spanish America." *Dispositio* 11.28-29 (1986): 1-25.

Arzáns de Orsúa y Vela, Bartolomé. *Anales de la Villa Imperial de Potosí*. La Paz: Ministerio de Educación y Cultura, 1970.

———. *Historia de la Villa Imperial de Potosí*. 3 vols. Providence: Brown Univ. Press, 1965.

Bakewell, Peter. *Miners of the Red Mountain: Indian Labor in Potosi, 1545-1650*. Albuquerque: Univ. of New Mexico Press, 1984.

Barnadas, Josep M. *Charcas: Orígenes históricos de una sociedad colonial: Charcas en el siglo XVII*. La Paz: CIPCA, 1988.

Berthelot, Jean. "L'explotation des Métaux Précieux au temps des Incas." *Annales* 33 (1978): 980-1014.

Bertonio, Ludovico. *Vocabulario de la lengua aymara*. 1612. Cochabamba: Centro de Estudios de la Realidad Económica y Social, Instituto Francés de Estudios Andinos y Museo de Etnografía y Folclore, 1984.

Bouysse-Cassagne, Thérèse. "L'espace Aymara: Urco et Uma." *Annales* 33 (1978): 1057-1079.

————, and Olivia Harris. "Pacha: En torno al pensamiento aymara." *Tres reflexiones sobre el pensamiento andino*. La Paz: Historia Boliviana, 1987. 11-60.

Bredow, Luis. "La escena de la muerte del Inca." *Hipótesis* 23-24 (1987): 319-329.

Buechler, Rose Marie. *Gobierno, minería y sociedad. Potosí y el "Renacimiento" Borbónico 1776-1810*. 2 vols. La Paz: Biblioteca Minera Boliviana, 1989.

Calancha, Antonio de la. *Crónica moralizada*. Ed. Ignacio Prado Pastor. Lima: n.p., 1960.

Calancha, Antonio de la, and Bernardo de Torres. *Crónicas Agustinianas del Perú*. Ed. Manuel Merino. 2 vols. Madrid: Consejo Superior de Investigaciones Científicas, 1972.

Cañete y Domínguez, Pedro Vicente. *Guía histórica, geográfica, física, política, civil y legal del gobierno o intendencia de la provincia de Potosí*. Potosí: Editorial Potosí, 1952.

Cole, Jeffrey A. *The Potosí Mita, 1573-1700: Compulsory Indian Labor in the Andes*. Stanford: Stanford Univ. Press, 1985.

Garcilaso de la Vega, Inca. *Obras completas*. 4 vols. Madrid: Ediciones Atlas, 1960.

García de Llanos. *Diccionario y maneras de hablar que se usan en las minas y sus labores en los ingenios y beneficios de los metales*. 1609. La Paz: Museo de Etnografía y Folklore, 1983.

García Pabón, Leonardo. *Espacio andino, escritura colonial y pensamiento andino: La historia de Potosí en la narrativa de Bartolomé Arzáns*. Diss. Univ. of Minnesota, 1990. Ann Arbor: University Microfilms, 1990.

Gisbert, Teresa. *Esquema de literatura virreinal en Bolivia*. La Paz: Facultad de Filosofía y Letras, 1968.

————. *Iconografía y mitos indígenas en el arte*. La Paz: Editorial Gisbert, 1980.

————. "Introducción al estudio de la máscara." *Arte Popular en Bolivia*. La Paz: Instituto Boliviano de Cultura e Instituto Andino de Artes Populares, 1988. 5-14.

Hanke, Lewis. "Bartolomé Arzáns de Orsúa y Vela, y las opiniones sobre indios en su 'Historia de la Villa Imperial de Potosí.'" *XXXVI Congreso Internacional de Americanistas: Actas y memorias*. Seville, 1966. 4: 131-141.

Hanke, Lewis, and Gunnar Mendoza. Introducción. *Historia de la Villa Imperial de Potosí*. By Bartolomé Arzáns de Orsúa y Vela. 3 vols. Providence: Brown Univ. Press, 1965. 1: xxvii-clxxxi.

Jara, René. "Perfil historiográfico de una escritura colonial." Conference. Ohio State Univ. Columbus, May 1990.

Lévi-Strauss, Claude. *Anthropologie structurale*. Paris: Plon, 1958.

————. *Les structures élémentaires de la parenté*. Paris: Presses Universitaires de France, 1949.

Lockhart, James. *Spanish Peru 1532-1560: A Colonial Society*. Madison: Univ. of Wisconsin Press, 1968.

López Beltrán, Clara. *Estructura económica de una sociedad colonial: Charcas en el siglo XVII*. La Paz: Centro de Estudios de la Realidad Económica y Social, 1988.

Martínez, Gabriel. "Los dioses de los cerros en los Andes." *Journal de la societé des Americanistes* 69 (1983): 85-115.

Mesa, José de, and Teresa Gisbert. *Contribuciones al estudio de la arquitectura andina*. La Paz: Academia Nacional de Ciencias, 1966.

Murra, John. *Formaciones económicas y políticas del mundo andino*. Lima: Instituto de Estudios Peruanos, 1975.

Ortega y Velasco, Bernabé Antonio de. "Informe remitido al Consejo de Indias por Bartolomé Antonio de Ortega y Velasco, vecino de la Villa Imperial de Potosí, en cuanto a una historia escrita de la fundación de aquella Villa." Lewis Hanke and Gunnar Mendoza. Introducción. *Historia de la Villa Imperial de Potosí* xxxvi-xxxviii. Originally published in *Historia de la Compañía de Jesús* VIII, primera parte. Ed. Pastells. 265-266.

Palma, Ricardo. *Tradiciones peruanas*. Ed. Lucilo Ortiz. Buenos Aires: Ediciones Troquel, 1963.

Platt, Tristan. "Entre 'ch'axwa' y 'muxsa': Para una historia del pensamiento político aymara." *Tres reflexiones sobre el pensamiento andino*. La Paz: Historia Boliviana, 1987. 61-132.

———. "Symetries en miroir: Le concept de Yanantin chez le Macha de Bolivie." *Annales* 33 (1978): 1081-1107.

Rostorowski de Díaz Canseco, María. *Estructuras andinas del poder: Ideología religiosa y política*. Lima: Instituto de Estudios Peruanos, 1983.

Sánchez-Albornoz, Nicolás. *Indios y tributos en el Alto Perú*. Lima: Instituto de Estudios Peruanos, 1978.

Silverblatt, Irene. *Moon, Sun, and Witches: Gender Ideologies and Class in Inca and Colonial Peru*. Princeton: Princeton Univ. Press, 1987.

———. "Political Memories and Colonizing Symbols: Santiago and the Mountain Gods of Colonial Perú." *Rethinking History and Myth: Indigenous South America Perspectives in the Past*. Ed. Jonathan Hill. Chicago: Univ. of Illinois Press, 1988. 174-194.

Tandeter, Enrique. "Trabajo forzado y trabajo libre en el Potosí colonial tardío." *CEDES* 3 (1980) 6: 3-40.

Tragedia del fin de Atawallpa. Trans. and ed. Jesús Lara. Cochabamba: Imprenta Universitaria, 1957.

Vázquez Machicado, Humberto, José de Mesa, and Teresa Gisbert. *Manual de Historia de Bolivia*. La Paz: Editorial Gisbert, 1983.

Wachtel, Nathan. "Hommes d'eau: Le probleme Uru (XVI-XVII siècles)." *Annales* 33 (1978): 1127-1159.

———. *La vision de vaincus: Les indiens du Pérou devant la conquête espagnole 1530-1570*. Paris: Gallimard, 1971.

Zuidema, R. Tom. *The Ceque System of Cuzco: The Social Organization of the Capital of the Inca*. Trans. Eva M. Hooykaas. Leiden: E. J. Brill, 1964.

◆ Chapter 18

Images of America in Eighteenth-Century Spanish Comedy

Bernardita Llanos

In the popular Spanish heroic comedy of the early eighteenth century the Conquest of America is related to the issue of evangelization. At the same time, two images of the Amerindian emerged: the image of the wild man—in contrast to the superior nature of the Spaniard—and that of the Noble Savage who was imbued with the European virtues of decorum, spirituality, and intelligence (White 186+; López Baralt 452-453).

The image of the Amerindian as both noble and wild are two different aspects of the European representation of native subjects. These tropes produced two different attitudes: one of extermination and another of conversion and redemption (White 194). The metaphor of the Noble Savage enters the discourse of the Conquest through the spiritual subjugation of the Amerindian, a subjugation that entails an acceptance of imperial power. The wild men, on the other hand, are those who persist in their cultural differentiation against the rules of the conquerors. Thus their pacification is produced through violence.

The heroic comedy of the eighteenth century undertakes a defense of the Conquest that echoes the position staked out by Ginés de Sepúlveda in his famous debate with Las Casas. Let us recall that Sepúlveda had interpreted Aristotle to justify the inferior status of the Indian as a "natural slave." Such inferiority was attributed to a lack of rationality as seen in their sexual promiscuity and ritual sacrifices. The Amerindians' sexual and religious practices are highlighted in the discourse of the heroic comedy of the eighteenth century as motives for Cortés's Conquest. The reduction of native cultures is thus tied to the Enlightenment project of fostering a new political ideal: the Nation. Cortés is portrayed as a crusader fighting evil in un-Christianized lands.

The heroic drama *Apostolado en Indias y martirio de un cacique* (*Apostolate in the Indies and Martyrdom of a Chieftain*) written by the Toledan playwright Eusebio Vela during his stay in Mexico is one of the earliest pieces to focus on this issue. The play was performed in 1732 for the entertainment of an audience of Spanish and Creole elites, including the viceroy (see Spell and Monteverde, "Introduction" in Vela xvi). Vela takes events from Mexico's history following the chronicles of Motolonía, Mendieta, Torquemada, and Vetancurt (xx). In his play, the military campaign led by Cortés acquires epic dimensions as it entails the spiritual conquest of the Indians.

Cortés's army is stationed in Tlascala, awaiting the arrival of the twelve Franciscan missionaries sent by Charles V to propagate the faith among the conquered. In the beginning of act 1, Cortés delivers a public address to the Cacique Axotencalt—future traitor and infanticide—in which he legitimizes his own military triumph as God's will:

> Famous Axotencalt,
> I already see my desires fulfilled,
> because the main reason
> for the triumph that I have achieved
> was a desire to exalt
> the true Faith in these domains,
> extending its mysteries
> to the most remote Indians,
> who, ignorant of such goodness,
> adore false gods;

> and to achieve my zeal,
> my lord Charles V
> sends an apostle,
> who in imitation of Christ's apostolate
> will instruct you in the Faith,
> not with the overly careful rigor
> which you have experienced
> until now; because,
> they will gently oblige you,
> and rendered will conquer you;
> thus, tell the *caciques*
> to gather their sons,
> so that we can all go and welcome
> them together. (3-4)[1]

The epic hero explains his war mission as the propagation of a divine truth guided according to a providentialist plan. This sacred and just war will lead the savages to abandon their barbarous beliefs and adopt the true faith. From the perspective of the victor, such an argument presupposes that the domination initiated by Cortés is needed for the transformation of monstrous and abnormal creatures into "free" collaborators (López Baralt 456). This discursive strategy institutionalizes war as a way to build a new society representing the interests of both the Crown and the Church.

In Vela's play, the Franciscan order, led by Friar Martin, becomes a model for a rigid and disciplinary morality based on vows of poverty and frugality. Those constraints are broken only by the appetite of the *gracioso*, Friar Mendrugo. The Franciscans' journey to the Indies serves as a contrast to the journeys of the *indianos* who are generally Spanish commoners who go to America in search of wealth. In his first sermon to the multitude who welcomes him, Friar Martin defines his mission:

> My dear and beloved sons,
> do not think that I have come

to these kingdoms for the silver
hidden in its mines;
nor to pretend
to improve my fortune, being
here more comfortable,
for I come only to look after your own good,
from which my own is born at the same time,
without seeking more wealth
than this sackcloth I
wear; for to eat, I appeal to
Providence, which cannot desert me,
for my God takes care of that,
that the riches of the land
stay here when we die,
and good deeds serve
as a ladder to heaven;
these are to solicit you and
reduce you to truth
and enlighten you, for until now
the Devil has blinded you,
making you idolize
perverse gods. (11-21)[2]

Friar Martin's sermon condemning indigenous rituals and idolatry is staged to make an impression on the multitudes and to highlight the image of Cortés as "Heroic Conqueror of saintly zeal" ("Conquistador Heroico de santo celo encendido"). Cortés himself underscores the respective, complementary functions of the missionary and the soldier in the enterprise of the Conquest and colonization. Referring to the Franciscans he says:

... though very pious soldiers,
for they militate under
Christ's great ensign,

carrying his flag
to kingdoms overseas
they come, not like us
dressed in strong steel,
but barefoot and ragged,
being the cilicium the coat
and patience the shield
the band a girdled rope,
feathers their thoughts,
the breastplate a sackcloak
the clean steel discipline;
their words are their shots
and what they might not reach
in stubborn chests
and at the strike of their words
the indolents might not soften,
with the strikes of this sword
(which are thunderbolts sent by God to
America, irritated by your perverse rites),
I will proudly annihilate. (4-5)[3]

Religion here is complemented by war while Cortés's virtue as a martial hero is defined in terms of his victories on the battlefield against the non-Christian natives. Cortés is thus portrayed as a patriotic figure at a time when heroes are needed to foster the Enlightenment project.

The arrival of the Franciscans in the New World was to initiate a phase of the Conquest marked by alphabetic writing (Mignolo). In the case of Vela, the arrival of the missionaries is semantized according to enlightened ideals that view education as an activity controlled by the state based on a model of indoctrination (Godzich and Spadaccini 16-21). Thus, the missionaries' paternalism complements the warlike figure of Cortés. In Vela's play, the new nobility promoted by the missionaries is based on the ideals of asceticism and military power as means of defending Christ's cause. In addition to the exclusion of those aspects of indigenous culture—such as human sacrifices and idolatry—considered to be alien to civilization, there is the repression of the natives' understanding of their own material environment. The use of Spanish as a dominant language demanded a rejection of native cultures so that the civilizing process could begin unconstrained, from a *tabula rasa* (López Baralt 448).

The battle between the Spaniards and the Indians adheres to a biblical pattern. The struggle of the Catholic soldiers is symbolically related to the proselytizing efforts of the first Christians and many of their successes and failures are presented as the result of God's or Satan's actions. Thus, Cristóbal (son of the Cacique Axotencalt) is shown as being the "chosen" one who follows God's will. The intolerance displayed by the Spaniards toward native culture is assumed by the new convert for whom the native culture is tantamount to falsehood and moral ruin. In this manner Cristóbal rejects his father's authority, beliefs, and teachings and accepts the moral authority and legitimacy of the Catholic Church. This change brings about the child's confrontation with his father and his ultimate martyrdom. The boy's holiness begins to manifest itself when he destroys the images of his native gods and replaces them with that of the Virgin Mary (Nuestra Señora), to whom he prays guarded by two angels. Cristóbal's life as a saint will manifest itself the day his father attempts to destroy an image of the Virgin. From that moment on, the tension between them increases until the final burning of the boy at the hands of his father, Axotencatl.

The figure of Cortés, the man of war, is placed strategically in the play to support the boy's deeds of sainthood and martyrdom. His exemplary justice is carried out through the public dismemberment of the Indian leader's body. Such punishment was meant to exemplify the eradication of evil through the application of pain and was meant to be a lesson to the entire community.[4] This episode is also linked to the stories regarding the martyrdom of saints (Caro Baroja, *Teatro popular* 83). The ending of *Apostolado en Indias y martirio de un cacique* conforms to the lesson of Christian doctrine and to the values of imperial Spain: Cristóbal's mother, Mihuazochil, is to marry Iztlizuchil, a paradigm of the loyal chieftain.

In *Hernán Cortés triunfante en Tlascala* (*Hernán Cortés Triumphant in Tlascala* [1780]) by Agustín Cordero, we find a defense of the Conquest within a more enlightened perspective. Thus, while some of the spectacular elements remain, a scientific conception of war frames the old values of courage and heroism. War is now controlled according to laws, and the military man is a professional who performs his tasks with scientific mastery. Cortés has been turned into a general who articulates the sensibility of the enlightened leader who bases his rule on pragmatism and discipline (508). In this sense, Cordero seems to follow Prussian absolutism, which based the power of the state on the efficiency of a strong army (Sánchez Diana 519).

Unlike the Spaniards, who have adopted modern habits and thinking, the Indians continue to adhere to traditional values and behavior. The new model of warfare adopted by the Spaniards is underscored in the following lines of the play:

> ... In the marked battlefield
> the artillery defends
> the sides: the left flank
> is defended by Pedro Albarado;
> in the middle there is Olid; to the right
> Montejo; the Cempoalas,
> in reserve, when they see
> the horses advance
> will show no mercy.
> With the reserved troop
> I will go everywhere.
> To arms, friends, to arms,
> each one to his post.... (23)[5]

While the Tlascaltecas function within a belief system based on tradition, the Spaniards rely on a modern, scientific conception of warfare based on prudence. With the aid of all human and technical resources, victory is viewed as a predictable and controllable event and war as a military science (McClelland 513). The aim is to display Spanish valor and is thus connected to the enlightened military policies of the age as embodied by the Prussian philosopher King Frederick II.[6] Cordero's play seems to imply that the victories achieved by the Spanish troops with only five hundred men attest to their intellectual superiority, to their knowledge of military science, and to their diplomatic skills that allowed them to make alliances with those Indian people who opposed Aztec hegemony. Such is the case with the Cempoala warriors whose chieftain decided to join the imperial forces in the fight against Moctezuma's tyranny.

Cordero's strategy in showing the disunity and disarray among the native populations is to set the stage for the intervention of an enlightened state that would convert chaos into order. The nationalist thesis of the Conquest is clear: the New World needs the intervention of an enlightened reorganization of society. In opposition to Moctezuma's oppressive power Cortés proposes tolerance and discipline and, as a politician, he defends social institutions and individual rights within the confines imposed by a conception of power as promoted by enlightened despotism.

The Amerindian prophesies announcing the imminent destruction of their world are used to lend legitimacy to the Spanish invasion. Such is the case with the neoclassical tragedy *Atahuallpa* (1784) written by Cristóbal María Cortés, who uses the intervention of fate to account for the Amerindian defeat. In this play, god Viracocha's omen, recorded in the will of the last Inca, also predicts the end of the world. This dramatic device reinforces the legitimation of the Conquest through the myths and beliefs of the defeated. Therefore, the Conquest is not an exterior force, but rather an inevitable event, predicted by the Amerindian divinities. The Spanish view of such a body of knowledge encompasses two seemingly contradictory perspectives: on the one hand, Amerindian religious practices are seen as superstitious and deformed and in need of the corrective power of evangelization; on the other, they are viewed as elements that will benefit the imperial cause.

From Cordero's ideological perspective, the Conquest is justified as a rational enterprise whose goal is to expand Catholicism and civilization to the rest of the world. Moreover, the Conquest is legitimized and placed in opposition to the so-called Black Legend and its charges of fanaticism and brutality. Enlightened despotism, as shown in Cordero's play, makes of the Spanish nation the first hegemonic and modern world power, supported by a strong army and an absolutist monarchy.

Both *Apostolado en Indias y martirio de un cacique* and *Hernán Cortés triunfante en Tlascala* coincide in a reevaluation of the Conquest from an eighteenth-century perspective in order to portray Spain as a civilizing colonial power. Cortés is the protagonist of the glorious achievements of a powerful nation, which expands its faith through one of its most famous soldiers. The New World and its entrance into European history is presented as the deed of one Spanish hero, who, under the directions of a modern state, executes previously designed military plans. Thus, there is an attempt to account for the rationality of this mission and its relationship with state policies. The legitimation of the military as well as the cultural domination of the New World is expressed as a new and national crusade for the propagation of Christianity.

The concern with Spain as a colonizing power pervades eighteenth-century theater not only in the heroic genre, but also in what has been called the "minor theater." In this dramatic form, America is portrayed as the space of wasteful riches, where Spaniards become laughable anti-heroes. The grotesque figure of the *indiano*, who accounts for the contact between the metropolis and the colonies by means of interest and profit, becomes the sign of a hyperbolic, mercantile attitude that manifests itself in the relentless accumulation of wealth. Consequently, the *indiano*'s stories awake scornful reactions among various social groups, all of whom reject his opportunism and pretensions of honor. Unlike the pretentious *indiano* who embodies all that is undesirable in Spanish society, the *majos* and *majas*—those masculine and feminine social types born from the lower classes—become the embodiment of popular and untainted Spanish values that include not only grace, bravery, boldness, and passion, but also the right to be vulgar, insolent, and aggressive (Caro Baroja, *Temas castizos* 20).

One of the most important features of the *indiano* is his predilection for lying. The *indiano embustero*, or the liar, is a recognizable

stocktype who constantly lies in order to gain admiration or favors from his listeners. Quite often he is an *indiano escarmentado*,
that is, he is unmasked by means of a moral lesson. In some situations he is an *indiano galán* (gallant gentleman) who falls in love
with all women, though he prefers wealthy Spaniards and Creoles. A recurrent theme in the *indiano*'s adventure is the voyage by
sea, which is one of the recognized avenues to attain *medro*, or a
life of privilege. The perils and efforts that every *indiano* must endure in his transoceanic journey to America and back to Spain form
the background of his discourse. Thus, the *indiano* is free to create
his own stories, since his adventures in the New World have no
referent in the Old.

One of the main features of the plot of comic plays dealing with
the *indiano escarmentado* is the introduction of a mythical world
devoid of hardship, labor, and scarcity. The overseas riches can
be gathered from the cornucopia available to those who travel
in search of adventure. According to this vision, America is the
paradise of wealth, an Eden before the Fall, in which the *indiano*
becomes the owner of castles and slaves. The Indies are the world
of a thousand marvels, where gold, money, and jewels are readily
obtainable. The exuberance of the geography, the greatness of its
rivers, and its fertile vegetation are inexhaustible sources of wealth
in the *indiano*'s imagination. The witness who has seen and experienced these events becomes another, constructing a new social
identity through exaggeration and hyperbole. Thus, the *indiano*
negates his obscure and humble origins. No one can accurately
know the past that he has recreated into a landscape of adventures
leading to the accumulation of wealth.

Nobody knows what the *indiano* has actually done in his long
stay overseas. His identity is marked by his experiences in the Indies and his return to the metropolis is motivated by a desire for
social mobility. Hence, the distrust of society toward the *indiano*,
and the ensuing confrontation of his discourse with those of other
segments of the social body. That confrontation molds two opposing discourses and interpretations of reality: that of the *indiano*,
which is a literary construction made up of marvelous and exotic
wonders of the New World experience, and the traditional and
popular discourse that affirms the "true" Spanish worldview. The

latter is based on the idea of social origin, according to which the individual's position in society is marked by birth. The *indiano's* attempt to move up the social latter thus involves a transgression and, therefore, is contested by the system.

A good example of the attitudes of the lower classes toward the *indiano* may be found in the anonymous "sainete" *La marquesa fingida y robo del indiano* (*The Fake Marchioness and the Robbing of the Indiano* [1772]). The first scene opens with a group of *majos* and *majas* dancing on a *tablao* (dance floor), singing and playing the castanets in the outskirts of the court. Paca, one of the *majas*, has just learned of the arrival of a rich *indiano* who has a weakness for women. She decides to assume the role of a marchioness in order to rob the *indiano* of his money. Paca gets hold of expensive dresses, reserves a room at an inn, and orders a costly dinner for her alleged husband the marquis who comes from Peru. The *indiano* is astounded by the opulence of the Spanish capital and by the beauty and charm of its women who dazzle him with their speech:

> What spacious streets!
> What supreme factories!
> What a crowd! What superior
> coaches! How beautiful the
> ladies are! What a natural
> air they all have!
> What grace! And, what I most
> admire is how
> attractive they are
> with their sweet tongues,
> for, at the moment I hear them
> I melt like butter.
> Well now, I will go to the Prado,
> for it is there where they show off
> the most—as I have been told—gracefulness,
> elegance, resolution, and gentility. (8)[7]

This type of *indiano* goes to the capital in search of a position at court. Aware of his wealth, he seeks to befriend the aristocracy and even aspires to marry into the upper ranks. In the process of doing so, he squanders the fortune made in America. The *indiano's* wealth is suspect in the sense that the origin of his riches cannot be traced. Let us recall that in a society of orders and estates, how one earns money and makes a living is a sign of one's social origin and upbringing. Thus, any connection to manual labor and retail commerce disqualifies one from a life of privilege. This position, which is reflected in the attitudes of popular types such as *majos* and *majas* toward the *indiano*, is a traditional one and runs counter to the official position of the enlightened State that promoted the importance of education and the learning of certain artisanal activities with the aim of stimulating industry. The *maja's* robbery of the laughable *indiano* may be seen as a corrective move on the part of the populace, which continues to identify with the values of the nobility. It must also be remembered that this conflict is staged within the framework of a popular comic genre that enjoys immense popularity during the eighteenth century. *Sainetes* and *tonadillas* usually end with a moral that reaffirms the values of a society based on a strict hierarchy in which individuals have a specific role and function. According to Serge Salaün, each minor dramatic piece implies a moral project where verbal humor works as the natural sanction of a conventional ethics and a rigid conformism (253, 258). Economic and social ascent are allowed only within the strict confines of the segment to which one belongs.

The introduction of the character of the *indiano* allows the playwright to break with the conventional realism of the comedy of manners. The articulation of a discourse of the unknown and of the marvelous introduces a tension between the present of the characters and the creation of a myth with which the characters identify in their desire to profit and to climb the social ladder. The play's audience is fascinated by the wonders found on the other side of the Atlantic, a fascination that will soon collide with the realities of everyday life. The *indiano's* narration cannot be true, and this impossibility is what brings it to a moral closure. The *indiano* will be punished for lying and for pretending to be what he is not.

The third part of *El soldado fanfarrón* (*The Boasting Soldier*

[1795?]), a *sainete* by Juan Ignacio González del Castillo and the anonymous *sainete* entitled *El indiano embustero* (*The Lying Indiano* [1755]) highlight the figure of the *indiano* as a liar. In the latter play, the *indiano* promises his friends and family to shower them with gifts:

> I will give you lots of expensive gifts
> because my trunks are filled
> with topazes and diamonds
> of such great beauty
> that the smallest (and you may see)
> weighs an *arroba* and a half. (27)[8]

As an interesting deviation from the convention, this *indiano* introduces the origin of his wealth and explains its sources. He tells of his efforts and of the hard work he has had to endure in order to acquire his possessions. The voyage, the storms, and the shipwreck have been part of his adventure at the sea. Nevertheless, when he recalls the perils and reflects on the miracle of being alive, he assumes the traits of a demi-god:

> I will paint it
> with hands, body and ears.
> The sea roared, the wind neighed,
> when the gulf between the waves
> had already swallowed us:
> but I drank the sea, and up to Cádiz
> we all arrived by land. (29)[9]

One can imagine how the *indiano* was portrayed in a staged performance. The actor would surely have resorted to kinetic signs, underscoring the insufficiency of verbal language to communicate his experiences in the marvelous world of the Indies. What makes this play unusual is that the *indiano* is presented as being conscious of his lies. Moreover, at the end of the play, his world is exposed when his poverty becomes apparent beneath the opulence of his rented clothes. The statement that attempts to cover up the unmasking—that his clothes will arrive in the year ninety—provokes laughter and allows the audience to share in a moral that highlights the revelation of truth and the debunking of lies.

The representation of the *indiano* in eighteenth-century minor theater functions as a signpost for a transgression that will not be allowed within the national ideals of the Enlightenment. The condemnation of the *indiano* in the minor theater has its counterpart in the exaltation of enlightened heroism, which is the basic subject of heroic comedy. Thus, the annihilation of the presumptuous *indiano* and the glorification of Cortés—the courageous conqueror—are images that attest to the creation of a value system directed toward the achievement of national cohesion and productivity, the erasing of foreign influences, and the projection of the enlightened values of industry, rationality, and initiative.

Notes

1.   "Ya, famoso Axotencalt,
        veo mis deseos cumplidos,
        pues el motivo primero
        del triunfo que he conseguido,
        fue el deseo de ensalzar
        la fe en aquestos dominios,
        extendiendo sus misterios
        en los más remotos indios,
        que ignorantes de tal bien
        adoran dioses mentidos;
        y para lograr mi celo,
        ya mi señor Carlos Quinto
        envía un apostolado,
        que a imitación del de Cristo
        os instruyan en la fe,
        no con el rigor prolijo
        que habéis experimentado
        hasta aquí; porque, benignos,
        os obligarán afables,
        y os conquistarán rendidos;

y así avisa a los caciques
que convoquen a los hijos,
porque a recibirlos vamos
todos juntos al camino."

2.   "Hijos y queridos míos,
no entendáis que a aqueste reino
he pasado por la plata
que encierran sus minas dentro;
ni menos por pretender
mejorar fortuna, siendo
aquí más acomodado,
porque solamente vengo
a mirar por vuestro bien,
pues de él nace el mío a un tiempo,
sin pretender más riqueza
que este sayal que poseo
para vestir; que comer,
a la providencia apelo,
que ésta no puede faltar,
que mi Dios se encarga de eso,
que los bienes de la tierra
se quedan acá en muriendo,
y las buenas obras sirven
de escala para ir al cielo;
éstas son solicitar
reduciros a lo cierto
y alumbraros, que hasta aquí
el Demonio os tiene ciegos,
haciéndoos que idolatréis
en los ídolos perversos
  . . ."

3.   ". . . aunque soldados, muy píos,
pues que militan debajo
del grande alférez de Cristo,
que a tremolar su bandera,
en reinos ultramarinos

viene, no como nosotros,
de acero fuerte vestidos,
sino descalzos y rotos,
siendo la cota el cilicio,
y el escudo la paciencia,
la banda un cordel ceñido,
las plumas sus pensamientos,
el peto un sayal, el limpio
acero la disciplina;
sus palabras son los tiros,
y lo que ellos no alcanzaren
en pechos empedernidos,
y al golpe de sus palabras
no se ablandaren remisos,
con los golpes de esta espada
(que es rayo que ha despedido
Dios a América, irritado
de vuestros perversos ritos),
destrozaré, aniquilando
almas, soberbio."

4. In his book *Discipline and Punish: The Birth of the Prison*, Michel Foucault starts the first chapter about the body sentenced to torture precisely with the public spectacle of the punishment of Damiens, the regicide killed in 1757. The view of the corporal torment passes through different stages which go from peeling off the skin and putting burning oil in the wounds to dismemberment by four horses (3). The body, according to Foucault, was the target of judicial repression; its torture, mutilation, and scars belonged to the ceremony of punishment understood as public spectacle, which glorifies the power of justice as violence (8-9).

5. "... En el campo demarcado
la artillería resguarda,
los costados: la ala izquierda
Pedro Albarado manda;
el centro Olid: la derecha;
Montejo: los Cempoalas
en el retén, cuando vean,
que los caballos avanzan,
a nadie darán cuartel.
Con la Tropa reservada

yo acudiré a todas partes.

Al arma, Amigos, al arma,

cada uno su puesto ocupe.... "

6. He became the eighteenth-century symbol of the enlightened monarch who combined military discipline and humanity (Sánchez Diana 12). During the century he exemplified real absolutism, where the king represented the beginning and end of the nation, and where the monarchy was inalienable and the emanation of all states (519). Prussia based its power on a strong army, in charge of the defense of the territory, and on a bureaucratic machinery that controlled domestic policy with the participation of the nobility. The Prussian state, according to Sánchez Diana, regulated life between the quarter and royal decrees, with a sovereign who declared himself to be in the service of the nation, joining the pedagogical enlightened ideal with the figure of despot (519 and 521). The glory of this monarchy rested on its moral politics, its sense of duty, work, honesty, and sacrifice; its king had understood the real mission of the throne (521-522). Where Prussian influence excelled in Spain was in its army, an institution that needed renovation and modernization. Thus, the Spanish army was reformed according to Frederick's military conquests and new offensive strategies (528). In this sense, Cordero participates in the enforcement of the new military spirit that viewed heroism as a calculated skill subject to discipline and training. Thus, war and the Spanish victory are understood as a scientific and rational endeavor, where a body of rules and practices were designed in a coordinated fashion.

7.   ¡Qué calles tan espaciosas!

         ¡qué fábricas tan supremas!

         ¡qué gentío! ¡qué carrozas

         tan superiores! ¡qué aires

         tan natural todas llevan!

         ¡qué gracejo! Y, sobre todo,

         lo que más me lisonjea

         es lo atractivas que son

         con lo dulce de su lengua,

         pues, al punto que las oigo,

         me hago todo una manteca.

         Ahora bien, yo voy al Prado,

         pues es donde más ostentan

         —según me han dicho—el donaire,

         garbo, brío y gentileza."

8.   "Yo os daré mucho y muy rico,

         porque ahí mis cofres se llenan

         de topacios y diamantes

de tanta hermosa grandeza
que le menor (y puede verse)
pesará su arroba y media."

9.   "Voy a pintarlo
con manos, cuerpo y orejas.
Bramó el mar, relinchó el aire,
cuando el golfo entre las crespas
ya sorbidos nos tenía:
más bebí el mar, y hasta Cádiz
llegamos todos por tierra."

Works Cited

Caro Baroja, Julio. *Teatro popular y magia*. Madrid: Revista de Occidente, 1974.
———. *Temas castizos*. Madrid: Ediciones Istmo, 1980.
Cordero, Agustín. *Hernán Cortés triunfante en Tlascala*. Cádiz: Imprenta Don Luis de Luque y Leiva, 1780.
Cortés, Cristóbal María. *Atahuallpa*. Madrid: Don Antonio de Sancha, 1784.
"El indiano embustero." *El indiano en el teatro menor español del setecientos*. Ed. Daisy Ripodas. Madrid: Atlas, 1986. 23-32.
Foucault, Michel. *Discipline and Punish*. Trans. Alan Sheridan. New York: Pantheon, 1977.
Godzich, Wlad, and Nicholas Spadaccini. "From Discourse to Institution." *The Institutionalization of Literature in Spain*. Ed. Wlad Godzich and Nicholas Spadaccini. Hispanic Issues 1. Minneapolis: Prisma Institute, 1987. 9-38.
González del Castillo, Juan Ignacio. "El soldado fanfarrón." *El indiano en el teatro menor español del setecientos*. Ed. Daisy Ripodas. Madrid: Atlas, 1986. 223-236.
"La marquesa fingida y el robo del indiano." *El indiano en el teatro menor español del setecientos*. Ed. Daisy Ripodas. Madrid: Atlas, 1986. 77-90.
López Baralt, Mercedes. "La iconografía política de América: El mito fundacional en las imágenes católica, protestante y nativa." *Nueva Revista de Filología Hispánica* 32.2 (1985): 448-461.
McClelland, Ivy L. *Spanish Drama of Pathos*. 2 vols. Liverpool: Liverpool Univ. Press, 1970.
Mignolo, Walter. "Literacy and Colonization: The New World Experience." *1492-1992: Re/Discovering Colonial Writing*. Ed. René Jara and Nicholas Spadaccini. Hispanic Issues 4. Minneapolis: Prisma Institute, 1989. 51-96.
Salaün, Serge. "El 'género chico' o los mecanismos de un pacto cultural." *El teatro menor en España a partir del siglo XVI*. Madrid: Consejo Superior de Investigaciones Científicas, 1983. 251-261.
Sánchez Diana, José María. "El despotismo ilustrado de Federico El Grande y su influencia en España." *Arbor* 100 (1954): 518-543.

Vela, Eusebio. *Apostolado en Indias y martirio de un cacique. Tres comedias.* Ed. Jefferson Rea Spell and Francisco Monteverde. Mexico City: Imprenta Universitaria, 1948. 3-84.

White, Hayden. "The Noble Savage Theme as Fetish." *Tropics of Discourse: Essays in Cultural Criticism.* Baltimore: Johns Hopkins Univ. Press, 1978. 183-196.

Chapter 19

Humboldt and the Reinvention of America

Mary Louise Pratt

It was in 1799 that Alexander von Humboldt and Aimé Bonpland secured permission from the Spanish Crown to travel freely throughout the interior of its American colonies. Their trip lasted from 1799 to 1804, during which time they journeyed widely in South America, Mexico, and the United States. Bonpland returned to South America in 1814 and remained there for the rest of his days (he "went native" in Paraguay, in fact). Humboldt remained in Europe and, between 1807 and 1834, published some thirty volumes based on his travels. These writings (or at least some of them) played a key role in the discursive and ideological reinvention of Spanish America that took place on both sides of the Atlantic at the turn of the century. As Spain's hegemony crumbled, a process of reimagining America was necessary both to the commercial classes of Europe, poised to extend themselves into the region, and to the *criollo* elites (persons of Spanish descent born in the Americas) as they sought forms of legitimation and self-understanding for the new republics. Humboldt's writings on America represent an influential voice in a transatlantic dialogue that is the subject of this essay.[1]

Expansion and Interiors

From a global perspective, Humboldt's American travels and his writings correspond to a particular juncture in European capitalist expansion. The famous South Sea explorations of Cook and Bougainville in the 1760s and 1770s marked the last great maritime phase in European exploration. Cook discovered and mapped the shores of the last uncharted continent, Australia. At the end of the eighteenth century, the emphasis shifted to internal, inland exploration, probably for the first time since the conquest of Peru and the search for El Dorado. Humboldt registers the change of momentum in a preface: "It is not by sailing along the coast," he says, "that we can discover the direction of the chains of mountains, and their geological constitution, the climate of each one...and so on." His English translator aestheticizes the point: "In general, sea-expeditions have a certain monotony which arises from the necessity of continually speaking of navigation in a technical language.... The history of journeys by land in distant regions is far more calculated to incite general interest" (*Personal Narrative* 1: vii).

The economic momentum for interior exploration was clear. As industrialization accelerated production in Europe, demands for markets and raw materials intensified; European capitalists sought more direct trade abroad without local competition and local middlemen; a vast, Euro-centered appropriation and transformation of the planet began to get underway. Throughout the nineteenth century, the exploration and description of continental interiors was an activity of central importance to this expansionist process, both instrumentally (e.g., mapmaking, documentation, initial contacts) and ideologically. As in earlier expansionist moments, travel writing was a chief vehicle for creating knowledge and forms of understanding that, in the theatrical sense, "produced" the expansionist project for the European imagination. Immensely popular throughout the nineteenth century, travel books did not simply present European readers with stable, canonical representations, anchored in coherent, consistent ideological systems. Rather, the internal variety of travel writing, even about a single region, was an important part of its popular appeal and its ideological workings. So, as I hope to show below, Humboldt's discourse on America must be heard in dialogue with contemporaneous writings by others.

It was of course in Great Britain that capital was accumulating and production was outpacing markets most rapidly. And it was from Great Britain that the chief initiatives for inland exploration came. In the acquisitive dreams of England's Protestant bourgeoisie, the nakedness of all the world would soon be modestly draped in British textiles. In 1788 the Society for the Discovery of the Interior Parts of Africa was formed and began exploration of the Niger. Alexander von Humboldt, then nineteen years of age, immediately became a member. Over the next thirty years the society sent out such famous explorer-writers as Mungo Park, Richard Denham, and Richard and John Lander. (Park was one of Humboldt's personal heroes.) The interior of Southern Africa simultaneously underwent a mini-invasion of explorer-writers, starting with the naturalists Anders Sparrman and the Franco-Brazilian Le Vaillant. British military interventions followed in 1802 and 1806. North Africa was treated to Napoleon's incursion in 1797, the event that obliged Humboldt and Bonpland to transfer their itinerary from Africa to the Americas.

Pressure likewise had been building up in Spain's American empire, whose interior had been officially closed to foreigners for many years. The carte blanche granted to Humboldt and Bonpland by the Spanish Crown was a response to intense economic interests and to the demands of powerful European scientific and diplomatic communities as well. And again exploration came hand in hand with invasion: on the heels of Humboldt came the British, who invaded La Plata in 1806 and again in 1807. (These were the same British generals, in fact, who had invaded South Africa a year before). In the decades that followed, South America's interior was "opened up" by an influx of North European traveler-writers in much the same way Africa's was.

Science and Planetary Consciousness

While Cook's sea expeditions may have closed a chapter in the history of travel, they opened a chapter in the history of travel writing—a chapter that Humboldt lived out to an extreme. It was above all the writings from the Cook expeditions that consolidated scientific discourse as a dominant mode in the literature of travel and exploration. By the 1790s, European writing about the non-European world was clearly becoming polarized. At one extreme there was science, represented in travel accounts and innumerable volumes of taxonomic natural history, and, at the other, there was sentiment, represented in travel accounts, novels, and romantic poetry of the sublime. (One recognizes in this polarization the two faces of emerging bourgeois hegemony, the splitting off of subjective and objective forms of authority, of the private and public spheres.) Humboldt was born into these dynamics, and they played themselves out in a telling fashion in his work. This point is highlighted by the contrast between Humboldt and his direct predecessor in South America, the French scientist Charles de La Condamine. At the initiative of the European scientific community, La Condamine had led an international expedition in 1735 to measure the exact length of a degree at the equator. As with Humboldt, securing permission for the journey from the Spanish Crown was an astonishing achievement, which could be attained only through the disinterested name of science and through delicate diplomacy. There the similarity ends, however.

La Condamine's expedition completed its mission, but it is most remembered for its human drama rather than its scientific achievements. The explorers suffered many disasters, and as they straggled back to Europe ten years after their departure, they brought with them not specimens of plants, but hair-raising tales of espionage, intrigue, murder, sickness, suffering, and love. These were tales in a mode eighteenth-century Europeans readily recognized—narratives of hardship, suffering, and survival that had been the staple of travel writing since the sixteenth century. The poetics of this "literature of survival" called for an Aristotelian balance between instruction and amusement, the latter provided by the excitement and exoticism of the narrative, the former by moral dramas of salvation and redemption as well as by descriptive appendices about customs, flora, and fauna. In his own report to the Paris Academy of Sciences in 1745, La Condamine readily adopted this old, prescientific configuration. For Humboldt sixty years later, no possibility could have been more remote. In fact, in a preface he explicitly referred to this kind of writing as belonging to a "former age." Though La Condamine's project was a scientific one, in the 1740s there did not yet exist a general discursive authority specifically anchored in science; for Humboldt in 1800 this form of authority was already a strong imperative.

Between La Condamine and Humboldt, then, lies Cook, the rise of scientific travel writing in Europe, and the emergence of science as a normative form of knowledge. Humboldt invested hugely in this development. Most of his life's work was devoted to what he referred to as "the great problem of the physical description of the globe." Of the thirty volumes that resulted from his American travels, most are taxonomic botanical and zoological treatises—on equinoctial plants, a couple of volumes dedicated exclusively to mimosas, some physical atlases, and some works of comparative zoology and anatomy—plus the ecologically based demographic description of the famed *Political Essay*. Indeed, so committed was Humboldt to the project of descriptive science that he expressed an overt mistrust of narrative forms. For many years he refused to write a narrative account of his American journey, and one suspects it was the competing voices of later travelers that finally persuaded him to undertake his *Personal Narrative* in 1814. Despite its popular success, he abandoned the project five years later after painfully completing three volumes and destroying the manuscript of the fourth.

It is of course the totalizing and stabilizing power of descriptive, classificatory science that appealed to Humboldt and his scientific peers and that trivialized narrative for them. In a narrative mode, one person tells only one small story and treads on a unique and narrow path across the face of the earth. The great descriptive categories of taxonomic science, on the other hand, effortlessly blanket the globe, naming everything, subsuming everything into a set of systems of classification, which, as Humboldt hoped, would ultimately express the underlying unity and harmony of the cosmos. (The last decades of his life were dedicated to an encyclopedic *magnum opus* called *Cosmos*.)

Clearly the "great problem of the physical description of the globe" as it emerged in late eighteenth-century Europe was by no means independent of the great projects of commercial and political expansion that Europe was articulating simultaneously on a global scale. Whatever else they were to be, Europe's descriptive taxonomies, like its museums, botanical gardens, and natural history collections, were symbolic forms of planetary appropriation, articulations of an emergent "planetary consciousness" through which, to paraphrase Daniel Defert, Europe came to see itself as a "planetary process" rather than simply a region of the world. (One notes that the term "descriptive power" is used to discuss and evaluate such systems.) Despite their anchor in the nonsocial world, then, scientific writings like Humboldt's must also be seen as "statistical," in the etymological sense (e.g., the German term *Staatistik*) linked to statecraft. Geography and natural science are, among other things, discursive apparatuses through which states define and represent territory. It is no coincidence that description of landscapes became an important signifying practice in the midst of struggles to found the first bourgeois republics in the Americas and Europe. And it is no coincidence that Humboldt's descriptions of landscapes were appropriated over and over again by Spanish American *criollo* writers in the decades following independence.

The connection with state-building, clearest in Humboldt's *Political Essay*, underscores the political and class dimensions of the rise of science. As mentioned above, by the late eighteenth century, the complementary discourses of science and sentiment had taken root as central ideological formations of an emerging bourgeois hegemony. As Norbert Elias has shown, they constitute the bourgeois challenge to the ideologies of courtly life. In the latter, personal value lies in the purity of one's (noble) blood rather than the depths of one's (bourgeois) soul. The external world is read through categories of hierarchy and privilege rather than (bourgeois) classificatory description. Humboldt occupies a unique position with respect to this dialogue between courtly and bourgeois hegemony. He was a bourgeois who was raised at the court of Frederick II, where his father was chamberlain to the Imperial Prince. In his student years, Humboldt enjoyed the role of court radical, choosing with his brother Wilhelm to frequent the salons of the Jewish intelligentsia in Berlin rather than those of the German nobility. When he met Simón Bolívar in Paris, Humboldt expressed strong support for the American revolutions, as he had for the French. Yet all his life he wavered between keeping and discarding the courtly *von* his father had won in 1738. It was precisely the combination of Humboldt's courtly connections with his technical expertise as a mineralogist and mining inspector that secured him the confidence of the Spanish Crown.

A New Columbus

While seeming to take the project of descriptive science to its encyclopedic extreme, Humboldt was always uncomfortable with its spiritual and aesthetic impoverishment and its inevitable tedium. Recognizing the extent to which scientific observation had influenced travel writing, he says, "I am afraid the temptation will not be great to follow the course of travellers who are incumbered with scientific instruments and collections"—like himself ("Preface," *Personal Narrative*). Alongside his scientific treatises on the Americas, Humboldt experimented with nonspecialized forms of writing in which he sought to mitigate the dullness of scientific detail by meshing it with the aesthetic, while still seeking to preserve the authority of science over the "merely personal." Both his first and last works on the Americas were such experiments, and they were the widest read of his works during his lifetime. It is on these nonspecialized writings that I will focus in what follows.

His first experiment is *Views of Nature* (1806), a book based on a series of lectures Humboldt gave in Berlin on his return and considerably expanded in its 1826 and 1849 editions. *Views of Nature* is an innovative book in which Humboldt tries to blend scientific description with the romantic discourse of the sublime, producing what he called "the aesthetic mode of treating subjects of Natural History" ("Preface"). His goal is to reproduce in the reader "that enjoyment which a sensitive mind receives from the immediate contemplation of nature" ("Preface"). South America is declared a privileged site for "Nature's ancient communion with the spiritual life of man." "Nowhere," says Humboldt, "Does she more deeply impress us with a sense of her greatness, nowhere does she speak to us more forcibly than in the tropical world" (154). In attempting to represent this greatness and communion, Humboldt is

convinced that the vividness of aesthetic description can be complemented and intensified by science's revelations of the "occult
forces" that make Nature work. It is an exercise he finds "fraught
with difficulties in execution," however. The first essay in the collection, the famous one "On Steppes and Deserts," opens with a
hypothetical traveler's turning his eyes away from the cultivated
littoral zones of Venezuela toward the *llanos* (plains) of the interior:

> When the traveller turns from the Alpine valleys of Caracas,
> and the island-studded lake of Tacarigua, whose waters
> reflect the forms of the neighboring bananas,—when he
> leaves the fields verdant with the light and tender green
> of the Tahitian sugar cane, or the sombre shade of the
> cacao groves,—his eye rests in the south on Steppes, whose
> seeming elevations disappear in the distant horizon.... He
> suddenly finds himself on the dreary margin of a treeless
> waste. (3)

Humboldt sets about making this wasteland come marvelously
alive for his readers. Here is a fine example of his aesthetic/scientific
style:

> Scarcely is the surface of the earth moistened before the
> teeming Steppe becomes covered with Kylligniae, with the
> many-panicled Paspalum, and a variety of grasses. Excited
> by the power of light, the herbaceous Mimosa unfolds its
> dormant, drooping leaves, hailing, as it were, the rising sun
> in chorus with the matin song of the birds and the opening
> flowers of aquatics. Horses and oxen, buoyant with life and
> enjoyment, roam over and crop the plains. The luxuriant
> grass hides the beautifully spotted Jaguar, who, lurking in
> safe concealment, and carefully measuring the extent of
> the leap, darts, like the Asiatic tiger, with a cat-like bound
> on his passing prey. (16)

Alive these *llanos* surely are, but conspicuously devoid of people. Social fantasies of harmony, industry, absence of alienation
are projected onto the nonhuman world (birds in matin song,
plants greeting the sun, and so forth), but people are absent. Their
traces are there: the horse and oxen have arrived through some
human intervention. But the hypothetical European traveler is
the only person mentioned in these "melancholy and sacred soli-

tudes." Indeed, the absence of people becomes essential to Humboldt's vision of the Americas. It is this very absence, Humboldt argues, that "allowed freer scope for the forces of nature to develop themselves" (*Views of Nature* 12). Thus people and place tend to mutually exclude one another, and Humboldt's eye depopulates and dehistoricizes the American landscape even as it celebrates its grandeur and variety.

Humboldt's effort to fuse science and aesthetics was to have many imitators. Though innovative, in other ways, his posture typifies what I referred to earlier as a European "planetary consciousness" emerging in this period. Natural science subsumes the world as nature, and specifically *not* as history. "Man" might occupy the center of the universe in Europe, but not in the rest of the world, as the Europeans saw it. History would only be admitted into the picture when evolutionary thinking allowed it to be subsumed as nature. Likewise, the aestheticization here is detached from a historical human subject, a potential implicit in the aesthetics of the sublime. The hypothetical traveler-observer is the only remaining vestige of the narrative of travel and of historicity.

At the same time, Humboldt's discourse represents a recurrence of a strategy shared by a variety of the first "inventors of America." It is the strategy of portraying America as a primal world of nature; an Other who is not an Enemy; a space containing plants and creatures (some of them human), not organized by societies and economies; a space whose only history is that which is about to begin; an unstructured space to be portrayed in a discourse of accumulation, a catalogue, then structured and historicized. Humboldt's hypothetical traveler is a new Columbus who this time lands and heads inland to repeat Columbus's founding gesture. In fact, Columbus is often directly alluded to. In *Views of Nature*, the essay on the Orinoco, for instance, begins with the view of a hypothetical mariner who "on approaching nearer to the granitic shores of Guiana . . . sees before him the wide mouth of a mighty river, which gushes forth like a shoreless sea" (206). The allusion to Columbus's encounter with the Orinoco during his third voyage is clear. It is not without reason that Humboldt is so frequently applauded as the "rediscoverer" of America (see Stoetzer). After applauding, however, one must inquire what it means to relive Columbus's primal gesture after three centuries of Spanish colonial rule.

The project of reinvention prevails in Humboldt's *Personal Narrative*. Here too Nature is the spectacle; colonial society, and with it historicity, is either backstage or altogether offstage. One might expect the social and human fabric of Spanish America to show through more clearly in a day-to-day narrative. After all, Humboldt's movements were completely embedded in and dependent on the colonial infrastructure. Yet this infrastructure appears in his narrative only incidentally. The missions, hospitals, farms, outposts, and villages he stayed in are mentioned but almost never portrayed; the same is true for their inhabitants, be they Spanish missionaries, *criollo* settlers, or the slaves and indigenous laborers who guided and transported the party and its equipment. Consider the following passage:

> The farmers, with the aid of their slaves, opened a path across the woods to the first fall of the Rio Juagua; and on the 10th of September, we made our excursion to the Cuchivano.... When the cornice was so narrow, that we could find no place for our feet, we descended into the torrent, crossed it by fording or on the shoulders of a slave, and climbed to the opposite wall.... The farther we advanced, the thicker the vegetation became. In several places the roots of the trees had burst the calcareous rock, by inserting themselves into the clefts that separate the beds. We had some trouble to carry the plants we gathered at every step. The cannas, the heliconias with fine purple flowers, the costuses, and other plants of the family of the amomyms, here attain eight or ten feet in height, and their fresh and tender verdure, their silky splendor, and the extraordinary development of the parenchuma, form a striking contrast with the brown color of the arborescent ferns, the foliage of which is so delicately shaped. The Indians made incisions with their large knives in the trunks of the trees, and fixed our attention on those beautiful red and golden yellow woods, which will one day be sought for by our turners and cabinet makers. (*Personal Narrative* 3: 73-74)

Critics are right to praise this Humboldtian style for its vividness and for its valorization of the American landscape in the face of longstanding European indifference. Moreover, they are correct in recognizing in Humboldt a key antecedent for the tradition of the *real maravilloso* (in the passage quoted above, contemporary readers cannot help but hear the voice of Alejo Carpentier's *Los pasos perdidos* [*The Lost Steps*]). At the same time, one must notice the place of the social world in Humboldt's discursive project. Conspicuously, in the passage quoted above, America's inhabitants come alive only in the service of the Europeans. The one initiative they are seen to take on their own is to point out exploitable resources to the Europeans, as if eager to facilitate the industrial appropriation of their environment. Indeed their gesture seems to trigger one of Humboldt's relatively rare allusions in these books to the designs of European capital. Meanwhile, any sense of these inhabitants as masters of an economy or ecology of their own is absent.

In sum, Humboldt's "aesthetic mode of treating subjects of natural history" reenacts an America in a primal state from which it will now, depending on which way you look at it, rise to the glory of civilization or fall into the corruption of civilization. What did it mean to revive this strategy on the eve of Spanish American independence and the eve of a new phase of European intervention? Humboldt and his hypothetical travelers were staking out for Europeans a new beginning of history in South America, a new point of origin for a future that starts now, and that will rework that "savage terrain." In one of his prefaces Humboldt alludes to this future:

> If then some pages of my book are snatched from oblivion, the inhabitant of the banks of the Orinoco will behold with ecstasy, that populous cities enriched by commerce, and fertile fields cultivated by the hands of freemen, adorn those very spots, where, at the time of my travels, I found only impenetrable forests, and inundated lands. (*Personal Narrative* 1: li)

In keeping with Humboldt's practice, the transformed vision of America is again rendered as a landscape seen by a hypothetical witness. Between Humboldt and that future observer, however, there lies a chain of events from which Humboldt explicitly excludes himself. His self-presentation throughout these writings is resolutely noninterventionist, resolutely innocent. One must recognize a mystification here. Yet, as I shall be discussing below, it was this very mystification that made Humboldt's writings usable to *criollo* intellectuals seeking to decolonize their culture while retaining European-based values and white supremacy.

The Transculturation of Humboldt

Andrés Bello's "Silva a la agricultura en la zona torrida" ("Ode to Agriculture in the Torrid Zone," 1825) is only one of many Spanish American texts that has roots in the writings of Humboldt. As a young student in Caracas, we know Bello met Humboldt and Bonpland, accompanied them on some of their local expeditions, and was inspired by their project. Years later, writing in celebration of Spanish American independence, Bello repeats Humboldt's gesture of (re) discovery in the opening of his famous "Silva." "Hail, oh, fertile zone" ("Salve, fecunda zona"), he begins, approaching like Humboldt's hypothetical traveler, for the first time. There follows a rhapsodic catalogue of America's native riches, from grapes to grain, sugar cane, cochineal dye, prickly pear cactus (*nopales*), tobacco, yucca, cotton, breadfruit, and so forth. The same discourse of accumulation is found, the same rhapsodic tone, the same vision of the flourishing primal world. The echo of Columbus is perhaps even more pronounced than in Humboldt.

With respect to the reinvention of America, Bello spoke from a different position than that of Humboldt and his European disciples, however. As a *criollo* intellectual, Bello's project in the "Silva" was a decolonizing one. He was seeking new forms of self-representation for the new republics, a discourse that would anchor self-understanding and legitimation in the present and project the new societies into the future. (His "Silva" was written as part of a three-part epic titled *America* which, like Humboldt's totalizing *Cosmos*, was never completed.)

As a *criollo* man of letters, Bello followed a complicated course in the search for a decolonized literate culture. On the one hand, he was committed to European-based letters in contrast to indigenous "barbarism" and rural provincialism. On the other hand, he saw the need for Americanist self-affirmation in the face of a new wave of European interventionism. One of Bello's responses was to "transculturate" (to borrow the term from Fernando Ortiz and Angel Rama[2]) certain European paradigms and play them against other European paradigms. Thus, while Bello initially repeats Humboldt's gesture of rediscovery in the "silva," he repeats it *only as a gesture*. After some sixty lines of accumulative botanical rhapsody, the poem abruptly changes key. It becomes an exhortation to the inhabitants of the new republics to populate the empty landscape, reject the enervating evils of the cities in favor of a simple country life: "Oh, young nations, oh, raise to the astonished west your heads newly crowned with laurels! Honor the country, honor the simple life of the laborer and his frugal fulfillment (ll. 351-355)."[3] The future, barely glimpsed by Humboldt, becomes the subject of Bello's text. To articulate that future, Bello takes up another European paradigm, the pastoral. A particular debt to Virgil's *Georgics* in the second part of the poem has been noted, a debt significant enough to inspire Menéndez y Pelayo to reclaim Bello as "the most Virgilian of our poets" (qtd. in Hespelt et al. 113). Bello's pastoral retains the aestheticizing posture of Humboldt's writings, but substitutes the focus on nature and the visual with a moral and civic mission. Bello evokes Humboldt only to set him aside and go on to something else. Other key texts of the period do the same. Both Echeverría's *La cautiva* and Sarmiento's *Facundo* open with unmistakably Humboldtian landscapes, and both, having appropriated Humboldt's gesture of rediscovery *as a gesture*, move into other discursive formations.

The English Interventionists

Surrounded by Humboldt, Virgil, and Menéndez y Pelayo, should one conclude that Bello's decolonizing project is nothing but an exercise in alienation? Perhaps. Yet it is also important to recognize the experimentalism of his text and of the moment of its writing. Theorists of transculturation identify *selection* and *invention* as the two central processes by which peripheries incorporate culture from the metropolis, processes whose experimentalism and innovation are ignored by theories of acculturation (see Rama). Both selection and invention are clearly at work in Bello's "Silva," trans-culturating European materials into a decolonizing vision that in important respects contests the hegemonizing vision of Europe. *La cautiva* and *Facundo* can likewise be seen as distinctively *criollo* experiments in search of a decolonized lettered culture.

To make this point clear, one need only examine other writings on Spanish America with which Spanish American writers, and Humboldt, were in dialogue. For by the 1820s, another very different discourse on Spanish America was echoing Bello in London and Humboldt in Paris. As colonial travel restrictions gave way after 1810, dozens of travelers, mainly British, flooded into Spanish America, and dozens of them wrote travel books. Quite possibly it was this wave of travel books that moved Humboldt to belatedly undertake his own *Personal Narrative*. Bello continuously read and reviewed these writers for Spanish American readers (see his *Repertorio Americano*) and occasionally (though very selectively) translated excerpts.

As Jean Franco has shown, these Independence-era British visitors for the most part traveled and wrote explicitly as the advance scouts for European capital. Engineers, mineralogists, breeders, agronomists were sent to pinpoint resources, contact and contract with local elites, report on potential ventures, labor conditions, and transportation, and so forth. They developed a discourse directly expressive of their mission. As Franco discusses, this wave of traveler-writers often sought out a consciously anti-aesthetic stance in their writings, introducing economic, interventionist rhetorics that were almost absent in the writings of Humboldt and his aesthetic-scientific disciples. Consider, for instance, this vision of the Andes in an 1827 account by the English mining engineer Joseph Andrews:

> Gazing on the nearest chain and its towering summits, Don Thomas and myself erected airy castles on their huge sides. We excavated rich veins of ore, we erected furnaces for smelting, we saw in imagination a crowd of workmen moving like busy insects along the eminences, and fancied the wild and vast region peopled by the energies of Britons from a distance of nine or ten thousand miles. (qtd. in Franco 133)

Similarly John Mawe in 1815 attempts to describe the "wild and romantic" scenery he encounters in La Plata, but finds he cannot, and only manages to exclaim, "What a scene for an enterprising agriculturalist! At present all is neglected" (121). Charles Cochrane, a Briton whose ambition is to take over Colombian pearl fishing, sees in the American landscape a dormant machine waiting to be cranked into activity:

> In that country there is every facility for enterprise, and every prospect of success: man alone is wanting to set the whole machine in motion, which is now inactive but which, with capital and industry, may be rendered productive of certain advantage and ultimate wealth. (1: vii)

The contrast with Humboldt's vibrant panoramas could scarcely be greater. Almost obsessively in these writings, American nature was recast as the future object of European exploitation. The Humboldtian exoticism and romantic rhetoric were explicitly set aside in favor of a modernizing, industrializing vision. Humboldt's writings were often singled out for criticism on the grounds that they were "too scientific, and entered into too few details to become fit for general perusal," as one 1825 writer put it (Stevenson 1: vii). The prospect of European intervention occupies the center, not the margins, of this discourse, and the speakers celebrate rather than mystify their role in that process. In direct contrast with Humboldt (and Bello), primal nature is seen as problematic, or even ugly, its very primalness a sign of human neglect. Charles Brand in 1828 finds the pampas "barren and inhospitable" (57), though he repeatedly encounters beauty in scenes of indigenous labor. "It was beautiful," he says, when two mule trains met on a trail, "to see the peons keeping their own troops separate from each other" (208). For the Frenchman Gaspar Mollien (1824), primal nature is either uninteresting or indecipherable, while beauty is to be found in domesticated landscapes reminiscent of Europe:

> After traversing a very thick wood, we kept continually on the ascent till we arrived at a spot from which a prospect truly magnificent burst upon our view: the whole province of Maraquita lay before us, its mountains appearing from the place where we stood, but as insignificant hillocks: we

could however distinguish the white houses of Maraquita. Much nearer to us lay the town of Honda, the walls of which are washed by the Magdalena, whose verdant banks impart peculiar beauty to the surrounding landscape. One would have supposed it to have been the Seine meandering through the rich meadows of Normandy. This beautiful sight however soon vanished as I again struck into the wood.... (57)

Criollo society, at the margins of Humboldt's discourse, is dwelt on at length by this capitalist vanguard, often in a highly negative light. Though the elites are frequently praised for their hospitality and their aristocratic way of life, *criollo* society in general is almost obsessively indicted for indolence in failing to develop the resources surrounding it. "While nature has been profuse in her blessings," says John Mawe, "the inhabitants have been neglectful in improvement of them" (32). Notes Mollien, "The greater proportion of the lands lie fallow; they would, however, produce considerable crops, if the inhabitants were less indifferent. No encouragement can rouse them from their indolent habits and usual routine" (89). According to John Miers, "The people out of the villages, although living on the most fertile ground, and having nothing to do, never cultivate the smallest spot" (30). The *criollos'* failure is diagnosed as the refusal not simply to work, but also to rationalize production, to specialize and maximize. The Europeans are struck by the absence of enclosures and fences, the failure to separate weeds from crops, the indifference to diversifying crops, the failure (particularly irksome to John Mawe) to "preserve the breed" in dogs, horses, even themselves.

With equal vigor the *criollos*, especially in the provinces, are criticized for failing to develop modern habits of consumption. Though enthusiasm is often expressed for the picturesqueness of provincial society, traveler after discomfited traveler complains of *criollo* indifference to the virtues of comfort, efficiency, cleanliness, variety, and taste. John Mawe can scarcely conceive, let alone tolerate, a society whose members by choice lived on a diet of beef and *mate*. Accommodations are found disgustingly crude, horses hard to come by, delays unbearably long. Traveler after traveler is shocked by the "filthy habits" they encountered in the populace. Arriving in Lima, Charles Brand is disgusted by the *Limeña* women who are "slovenly and dirty" and "never wear stays"; their men likewise are "dirty and indolent to an amazing degree" (182). John Miers registers the same impression in the Argentine interior: "Such are the filthy habits of these people, that none of them ever think of washing their faces, and very few ever wash or repair their garments: once put on, they remain in wear day and night until they rot" (31). Equally horrifying for some is the sharing of food plates, cooking pots, drinking vessels, and beds. Occasionally, contradictions make their way to the surface. On the pampas, Miers is at least slightly puzzled that people exert themselves minimally yet "are notwithstanding healthy, robust, muscular and athletic" (32). Charles Brand is moved by the egalitarianism of pampa society ("Living as free and independent as the wind, they cannot and will not acknowledge the superiority of any fellow mortal") but finds it "strange withal that they should be so dirty and indolent; the women in particular... are disgustingly so. Comfort they have no idea of..." (74-75).

If the American landscape was to be transformed from a wilderness into a scene of industry and efficiency, its colonial population had to be transformed from an indolent, undifferentiated mass lacking appetite, hierarchy, and taste, into two things: waged labor and a market for metropolitan consumer goods. Bello, in his call for humble farmers unafraid of hard work, clearly shared the British critique of traditional provincial society that had failed to seize hold of its environment. At the same time, neither salaried labor nor consumerism had any place in Bello's call for a frugal, simple life on the land. Bello's preindustrial, pastoral outlook must be seen not simply as nostalgic or reactionary, but as a dialogic response to the commodifying, expansionist vision of the English engineers. An urban man of letters, Bello looked to Europe for alternatives to such a vision and transculturated Virgil and Humboldt for his purposes. The noticeable omission of minerals from Bello's song of praise of America is perhaps symptomatic of his decolonizing intent: mining (as Humboldt well knew) was the great magnet for foreign capital and the locus of neocolonial designs.

Reinventing Europe

Bello's "Silva," then, enters a transatlantic dialogue initiated by Humboldt and carried on by many writers on both sides of the ocean throughout the independence period. It is a dialogue in which very diverse voices are engaged in what I have referred to as "reinvention of America." For Spanish American writers in particular, it was a highly experimental moment in which the transculturation of European paradigms was of fundamental importance. Lest it be thought that only America was at stake in this dialogue, I propose to end by briefly discussing a text in which Europe is reinvented by a Spanish American traveler. I refer to the Argentine writer Domingo Faustino Sarmiento's account of his travels to Europe in 1845-1847, *Viajes por Europa, Africa i América.*

Given the long association of travel writing with Europeans and European expansionism, it is not surprising that Sarmiento found his own authority as a travel writer problematic. For any writer, says Sarmiento in his preface, interesting travel books are difficult to write now that "civilized life reproduces everywhere the same characteristics" (2).[4]

> The difficulty is even greater if the traveler comes from a less advanced society to learn about a more advanced one. Then one senses the inability to observe, for lack of the necessary spiritual preparation, which leaves the eye blurry and myopic because of the breadth of the vistas and the multiplicity of objects found therein. (22)[5]

As an example of this backwardness, he cites his own inability to perceive in factories anything more than inexplicable piles of machinery. Were his own text to be compared to those of great European travel writers like Chateaubriand, Lamartine, Dumas, or Jacquemont, he concludes, "I would be the first to abandon the pen" (6).[6]

Despite this elaborate disclaimer, which again must be read as a gesture, Sarmiento does go on to write his travel account, with no evidence of the crippling of spirit he ascribes to himself in this preface. Instead, he in effect takes up the question before him: In the Age of Independence, how does the American man of letters position himself with respect to Europe? The opening chapter of the account presents a fascinating episode dedicated to answering that question, at least in the realm of the symbolic. The narrative opens with Sarmiento's ship leaving Valparaíso bound for Montevideo and then Europe. As if reflecting Sarmiento's difficulties in getting his text off the ground, the ship is immediately becalmed for four days just off the Chilean coast. This nonevent, decidedly out of keeping with standard travel-book rhetoric, takes place alongside an island called Más-a-fuera ("Farther out").

Though "farther out" from civilization, this island has a history that links it firmly to Europe and European literary tradition. Más-a-fuera is one of the Juan Fernández Islands where the Scotsman Alexander Selkirk was marooned for many years at the end of the seventeenth century. Selkirk and his story later became famous as Defoe's model for *Robinson Crusoe*. Mindful of this precedent, Sarmiento and some companions use the occasion to orchestrate, and revise, the Crusoe experience for themselves. They decide to spend a day on the island of Más-a-fuera. They are astonished to find it is already inhabited by four North American castaways who live there, in Sarmiento's words, "without care for the morrow, free from all subjection, and beyond the reach of the vicissitudes of civilized life" (9).[7] As this language suggests, Sarmiento's account of life on Más-a-fuera retains some of the utopian spirit of Defoe's *Crusoe*. He depicts a masculinist paradise with many of the features of Bello's humble pastoral vision. In keeping with the times, it is also a republican paradise; there are no enslaved Fridays, and the prevailing hierarchy is that of father-son.[8] The gentlemanly ethos of *Crusoe* prevails: the men amuse themselves by organizing a day's hunt of the wild goats that teem the island. (Crusoe, as we recall, captured and bred these goats; the original Selkirk, on the other hand, recounted dancing with them for want of human company.) As the account proceeds, however, Sarmiento gradually demystifies the utopian paradigm. The four men, it turns out, are unhappy and divided among themselves—leading Sarmiento to conclude that "discord is a condition of our existence, even where there are neither governments nor women" (22).[9]

As with the original Crusoe story, Sarmiento's Más-a-fuera episode lends itself to an allegorical reading. In this case, what is allegorized are Sarmiento's own complex relations to European, North American, and Argentine cultures. On Sarmiento's all-important scale of civilization, he finds the inhabitants of Más-a-fuera "farther out" than himself, but not as far out as some inhabitants of the Argentine interior. Noting that the stranded North Americans, like Crusoe, have been able to maintain an accurate calendar, Sarmiento is reminded of the time the populace of one of Argentina's provincial capitals discovered from a passing traveler that they had somehow lost track of a day. For going on a year, so it was told, they had been "fasting on Thursday, hearing mass on Saturday, and working on Sunday" (14).[10] (Even marooned, it seems, Anglo-Americans can keep a grip on rationalized time while the colonial provinces cannot.)

Allegorically, this anecdote and the whole Más-a-fuera episode enable Sarmiento to situate himself with respect to the multiple cultural referents that impinge upon him. With respect to Europe, Sarmiento is slightly "más afuera." At the same time, his marginality has an affirmative dimension: the transculturated Crusoe episode makes the gesture that contemporary terminology now calls magical realism. Facing the metropolis, the decolonizing writer seems to say, "Your fictions (*Robinson Crusoe*) are my realities (Más-a-fuera); your past is my present; your exoticism (a world outside of clock time) is my everyday life (the Argentine interior)." Only after so situating himself does Sarmiento begin to take on the travel writer's role as cultural mediator. His journey proceeds, in effect, only when the cultural mediation can proceed.

It is entirely in keeping with this gesture that once in Paris, Sarmiento represents himself as a discoverer—the discoverer of an exact analogue of what Humboldt found in the equinoctial regions. Paris was a bulging cornucopia, a place of endless, exotic variety and plenty. What Humboldt found in the jungles and pampas, Sarmiento found in the shops of the Rue Vivienne, the collections of the Jardin des Plantes, the museums, galleries, bookstores, and restaurants. Sarmiento's catalogue-laden descriptions of Paris reproduce Humboldt's discourse of accumulation and its posture of innocent wonderment. The naturalist is ironically rediscovered in the urban *flaneur*. Sarmiento dwells at length on the joys of the *flaneur*, whose privilege, as Sarmiento describes it, uncannily resembles that of the natural scientist:

In Paris, *flaneur* is such a holy and respectable thing, such a privileged practice that no one dares to interrupt it. The *flaneur* has the right to stick his nose everywhere.... If you stop in front of a grill in the wall and look at it with attention, another enthusiast will stop to see what it is you are looking at; a third arrives, and if there are eight gathered, the passersby stop, the street is obstructed, a herd. (117)[11]

Like Humboldt the naturalist,

The *flaneur* also pursues something, which he himself does not know; he searches, looks, examines, passes on, goes gently, takes turns, walks, and at last arrives ... sometimes at the banks of the Seine, others at the boulevard, most often at the Palais Royal. (116)[12]

In a parodic, transculturating gesture, then, Sarmiento refocuses the (preindustrial) Humboldtian descriptive discourse back on its own context of origin: the capitalist metropolis. It is the Humboldtian paradigm minus one dimension, however: the dimension of appropriation. An alienated figure, the *flaneur* does not buy, collect samples, classify, erect totalizing schema, or fancy transforming what he saw. He does react, however, and Sarmiento, the *arch-flaneur*, reacted to the spectacle of the *flaneurs* by asking a very American and a very republican question: "Is this really the people who made the revolutions of 1789 and 1830? Impossible!" (112)[13] A smug statement for a South American to make, and on the eve of 1848, a resoundingly prophetic one.

Notes

1. For an extended treatment of this subject, see Pratt, *Imperial Eyes*, chaps. 6-8. The present essay first appeared in Spanish as "Humboldt y la reinvención de América," *Nuevo Texto Crítico* 1 (1987): 35-53.

2. This term originally coined by the Cuban sociologist Fernando Ortiz in the 1940s has recently been reintroduced into Latin American literary studies by Angel Rama, notably in his *Transculturación narrativa*.

3.   "¡Oh, jóvenes naciones, que ceñida

alzáis sobre el atónito occidente

de tempranos laureles la cabeza!

honrad el campo, honrad la simple vida

del labrador, y su frugal llaneza."

4. "la vida civilizada reproduce en todas partes los mismos caracteres."

5. "Mayor se hace la dificultad, si el viajero sale de las sociedades menos adelantadas, para darse cuenta de otras que lo son más. Entonces se siente la incapacidad de observar, por falta de la necessaria preparación de espíritu, que deja turbio i miope el ojo, a causa de lo dilatado de las vistas, i la multiplicidad de los objetos que en ellas se encierran."

6. "yo sería el primero en abandonar la pluma."

7. "sin preocuparse por el mañana, libres de toda sujeción, y fuera del alcance de las vicisitudes de la vida civilizada."

8. I am indebted here to Elizabeth Garrel's work on generational concepts in Sarmiento's *Facundo*. See E. Garrels, "Layo y Edipo" and "Sarmiento ante la cuestión de la mujer."

9. "la discordia es una condición de nuestra existencia, aunque no haya gobierno ni mujeres."

10. "ayunando el jueves, oyendo misa el sábado i trabajando el domingo."

11. "Es cosa tan santa i respetable en Paris el *flaneur*, es una función tan privilegiada que nadie osa interrumpir a otro. El *flaneur* tiene derecho de meter sus narices por todas partes.... Si Ud. se para delante de una grieta de la muralla i la mira con atención, no falta un aficionado que se detiene a ver qué está Ud. mirando; sobreviene un tercero, i si hai ocho reunidos, todos los paseantes se detienen, hai obstrucción en la calle, *atropamiento*."

12. "El *flaneur* persigue también una cosa, que él mismo no sabe lo que es; busca, mira, examina, pasa adelante, va dulcemente, hace rodeos, marcha, i llega al fin... a veces a orillas del Sena, al boulevard otras, al Palais Royal con más frecuencia."

13. "¿Este es, en efecto, el pueblo que ha hecho las revoluciones de 1789 i 1830? ¡Imposible!"

Works Cited

Bello, Andrés. *Repertorio Americano. Obras Completas de Andrés Bello*. Vols. 19-20. Caracas: Ministerio de Educación, 1957.

Brand, Lieutenant Charles. *Journal of a Voyage to Peru: A Passage across the Cordillera of the Andes in the Winter of 1827*. London: Henry Colburn, 1828.

Carpentier, Alejo. *Los pasos perdidos*. 14th ed. Mexico City: Compañía General de Ediciones, 1973.

Cochrane, Captain Charles Stuart. *Journal of a Residence and Travels in Colombia during the Years 1823 and 24*. 2 vols. London: Henry Colburn, 1825.

Defert, Daniel. "La collecte du monde: pour une étude des récits de voyages du XVIe au XVIIIe siècle." *Collections Passion*. Neuchatel: Musée d'Ethnographie, 1982.

Echeverría, Esteban. *La cautiva. El matadero*. Ed. Juan Carlos Pellegrini. Buenos Aires: Huemul, 1965.

Elias, Norbert. *The History of Manners*. 1939. Trans. Edmund Jephcott. New York: Pantheon, 1978.

Franco, Jean. "Un viaje poco romántico: viajeros británicos hacia Sudamérica, 1818-28." *Escritura* 7 (1979): 129-142.

Garrels, E. "Layo y Edipo: padres, hijos y el problema de la autoridad en el *Facundo*." *La Torre* 2.7 (1988): 505-526.

———. "Sarmiento ante la cuestión de la mujer: desde 1839 hasta el *Facundo*." Berkeley: Univ. of California Press (forthcoming).

Hespelt, A., et al. *An Anthology of Spanish American Literature*. New York: Appleton-Century Crofts, 1946.

Humboldt, Alexander von. *Cosmos: A Sketch of a Physical Description of the Universe*. Trans. E. C. Otte. New York: n.p., 1870.

———. *Personal Narrative of Travels to the Equinoctial Regions of the New Continent, 1799-1804*. Trans. Helen Maria Williams. London: Longman, 1822. (See also the translation by Thomasina Ross, 1851.)

———. *Political Essay on the Kingdom of New Spain*. Trans. John Black. London: Longman, 1822.

———. *Views of Nature or Contemplations on the Sublime Phenomena of Creation*. Trans. E. C. Otte and Henry G. Bohn. London: Henry G. Bohn, 1850.

La Condamine, Charles de. *A Succinct Abridgement of a Voyage Made within the Inland Parts of South America*. London: E. Withers, 1748.

Mawe, John. *Travels in the Interior of Brazil, Particularly in the Gold and Diamond Districts*. Philadelphia: M. Carey, 1816.

Miers, John. *Travels in Chile and La Plata*. London: Baldwin, Cradock and Joy, 1826.

Mollien, Gaspar. *Travels in the Republic of Colombia in the Years 1822 and 23*. London: C. Knight, 1824.

Pratt, Mary Louise. *Imperial Eyes: Travel Writing and Transculturation*. London and New York: Routledge, 1992.

Rama, Angel. *Transculturación narrativa*. Mexico City: Fondo de Cultura Económica, 1982.

Sarmiento, Domingo Faustino. *Viajes por Europa, Africa i América*. Obras de D. F. Sarmiento. Vol. 5. Paris: Belin Hermanos, 1909.

Stevenson, W. B. *An Historical and Descriptive Narrative of 20 Years Residence in South America*. 3 vols. London: Hurst, Robinson and Co., 1825.

Stoetzer, Carlos. "Humboldt: redescubridor del Nuevo Mundo." *The Americas* 11.6 (1959): n.p.

◆ Chapter 20

Atahuallpa Inca: Axial Figure in the Encounter of Two Worlds

Marta Bermúdez-Gallegos

Atahuallpa was the last Inca in power before the Spanish arrival and for this reason the colonial imaginary presents Atahuallpa as the point of intersection of the two worlds that participate in the drama of colonization. One might say that all discourses making up the network of colonial culture seem to converge in ambiguity in the portrayal of Atahuallpa's *persona*. In this essay I plan to show how three different interpretative traditions within colonial discourses make the illegitimate child of Huayna Capac either an active protagonist of civilization or of barbarism depending on the point of view of the enunciating producer(s). To prove my point I will establish an active dialogue among Garcilaso de la Vega Inca's *Comentarios reales* (*Royal Commentaries*), "El rescate de Atahuallpa" ("Atahuallpa's Ransom"), a popular Hispanic ballad of the Potosí and La Paz area of Bolivia, and *Tragedia del fin de Atahuallpa* (*Tragedy of the End of Atahuallpa*), a traditional Quechua play of southern Peru and Bolivia, composed in verse.[1] My focus will be the semiotization of the incidents that lead to the polemical configuration of Atahuallpa in order to uncover the discursive patterns in each representation of his character. Although there does not seem to be a consensus on the portrayal of the Inca in the hegemonic discourse of the chronicles, there is even less agreement in their *criollo, mestizo*, and Amerindian counterparts.² Popular traditions from both worlds only bequeath greater obscurity.

Marginality in Colonial Discourse

The literature of the Conquest is composed of genres imported by Spanish soldiers. Among them are the ballad and the chronicle, which promote the discourse of the warrior, chivalric psychology, and the utopian representation of reality. This initial hegemonic literature acquires marginal characteristics, first because in the case of the ballads they originate in orality and, second, because both chronicles and ballads are composed within the colonial situation. The peripheral character of those texts underscores the presence of fissures that, though not perceptible at first sight, are ultimately apprehended by the reader. The gaps derived from these "indeterminate spaces," as Wolfgang Iser would have it, allow the reader a more active participation in the construction of meaning.³

The Spanish version of Atahuallpa's fate has survived in ballads and other songs, while the indigenous view prevails in the Indian dramatic tradition as well as in song. The latter's autochthonous efforts, preserved through orality, constituted an attempt to resist colonization by maintaining their native language and their own representation of events. On the other hand, colonialist readings of the events of the Conquest have produced devastating results for the Amerindian imaginary. The purpose of my reading is to elucidate the image of Atahuallpa by filling those gaps generated both by autochthonous texts and by official historiography.⁴

Atahuallpa: A Case of Colonial Semantization

Atahuallpa was a key figure for both Amerindians and Spaniards alike. Popular tradition captures his singularity and sings to the complexity of his existence for Latin America by showing the injustices committed by and against him. Garcilaso de la Vega Inca, a humanist scholar of *mestizo* origin, wrote the *Comentarios reales* (*Royal Commentaries*), a hybrid chronicle of the conquest of Peru in which the reader can detect the tensions derived from the depictions of Huayna Capac's illegitimate son. That is, one cannot help but perceive how Garcilaso narrates the events of the encounter of the two cultures in the most rigorous of logocentric traditions.

Let us recall that Atahuallpa was fooled by the invader as he was led to believe that his life would be spared in exchange for gold. Instead, the Inca leader was executed in Cajamarca on Saturday, November 16, 1532. Atahuallpa's execution and betrayal are the central themes of a ballad, "El rescate de Atahuallpa" ("Atahuallpa's Ransom"), collected by Ciro Bayo in the area of Upper Peru.

> Atabaliba is imprisoned,
> imprisoned in his own jail;
> he's gathering the treasures
> that he will render to the Spaniard.
> He doesn't count like a Christian,
> but rather with cotton beads.
> He runs out of cotton beads
> but does not run out of treasures.
> The Indians who bring him treasures
> give him the full account:
> "This metal is the silver
> that was stripped from Potosí.
> This metal is gold
> from the holy Temple of the Sun.
> These are the pearls the seas
> threw up on our shores.
> These stones are the emeralds
> given up by the kingdom of Quito.
> These crimson rubies . . ."
> "These . . . I do not want
> for they are the drops of blood
> that my brother shed." (translation mine)[5]

This song is a direct descendant of medieval Hispanic tradition and it seems that its formulaic patterns go back to the ballad called "Fernan Gonzales, Imprisoned" (Durán 700 I 461). The oral tradition brought by the conquistador appears as a series of plurivocal texts open for active readings. The heteroglossic quality of the traditional ballad (*romance*) makes manifest a diachronic mutation of codes that allows the reader to fill the textual blanks. That is, the reader decodes those mutations by referring to parallel discourses.

"El rescate de Atahuallpa" is a ballad consisting of three semantic segments divided according to the different voices interacting in the text. The narrative voice, in the third person singular, narrates the episode that introduces and frames the poem. The voice of the speaker is directed toward an "other," in the Bakhtinian sense, as it unfolds a silent expectation that awaits a response. The answer can be achieved by establishing an internal and external dialogue with concurrent discourses of the same event.

The significant aspect of the *romance* as a cultural text[6] is the manner in which the basic voice manipulates an ubiquitous point of view that allows the interaction of two fictitious speakers who relate the final objective: the message. The interaction, which takes the form of quotidian speech practice, suggests an encounter between text and interlocutor. The encounter becomes an active force in a system of signs through which ideology intersects, leaving room for various interpretations.[7] The manipulation of the point of view allows the speaker greater credibility. Through the use of demonstrative adjectives (*este/esta; estos/estas*), the speaker enacts participation in the action as he appears close to the objects described. The game of perspective and the resulting dialogization are typical recourses of the traditional Hispanic ballad. We see that the singular masculine adjective, *este* ("this"), and the plural feminine *estas* ("these") are repeated consecutively. Through the use of the masculine plural adjective, *estos* (related to the rubies), there is a change in point of view and the enunciating voice becomes that of Atahuallpa.

The speaker's ubiquitous perspective provokes the need for a detailed research of the context. The ubiquity of the first voice in the ballad generates the openness of the text. The fictitious voice of the Inca vassals connotes recrimination: "it is the silver stripped from Potosí" ("es la plata que al Potosí se arrancó") and "from the holy Temple of the Sun" ("del santo templo del sol"). The virulent tone of the last verse leads me to date this song in the post-Conquest settlement period, despite the fact that the moment of enunciation recreates the events connected to Atahuallpa's incarceration and death.[8]

The poem closes with an accusatory tone that inspires Atahuallpa's feelings of guilt. The Inca's remorse arises from the betrayal of his half-brother Huascar Inca. Let us recall that when Atahuallpa's treachery took place, before the Spanish arrival, Huascar was the legitimate heir to the crown, according to Garcilaso's version. The Inca's account of the betrayal has pretty much become the official story. In the ballad when the Inca is offered "los bermejos rubíes" ("crimson rubies"), he rejects them because they are "las gotas de sangre/que mi hermano derramó" ("the drops of blood that my brother shed").

Although the ballad is typical within its genre, it acquires a uniqueness that can only stem from its marginality. The appropriation of the hegemonic discursive genre by popular culture to tell an Amerindian tale is quite a remarkable trait in transculturation. The particularity of this song is brought about by the colonial context from which it emerges. The distinct American historical (colonialist) conjuncture provides the tension that can only result in peripheral discourses. The gaps emerging from the tangential nature of the enunciation must be filled with concurrent texts pertaining to the circuits that enact the network of colonial culture. Garcilaso's chronicle provides an ideal interaction for the enactment of Atahuallpa's conflictive *persona* because of its own unfulfilled abstruseness. This is how Garcilaso describes the incarceration incident: "Atahuallpa the Inca, seeing himself a prisoner and in iron chains, tried to negotiate to free himself from them; he promised that if they freed him, he would cover with gold and silver vessels the floor of the great room that held him prisoner" (3: 56).[9] As one can see, Garcilaso situates the reader in the first moment of negotiation between the Amerindian leader and the Spaniards, coinciding with the beginning of the ballad. Both ballad and chronicle select Atahuallpa as their subject because he reiterates the conflictive nature of the event. The Indian chief is a key figure because he personifies the binary oppositions that become the axis of colonialist semantization. Atahuallpa's representation, then, arises at the margin of European monolithic discourse: power/subservience; victim/victimizer; traitor/betrayed.

Treason as the Pivot of Colonial Semiosis

The central plot of all three texts is the betrayal of Cajamarca, which is the point of convergence for the encounter between two different cultures. The violence derived from the meeting must be observed in light of the *Comentarios reales* as they expose the intricacies of Atahuallpa's relationship with his half-brother, Huascar Inca. The treason to which the last verse of the ballad refers is that against Huascar.

Contrasted to the oral traditions, Garcilaso's discourse brings to light a new series of binary oppositions denoting his Western heritage. Writing vs. orality, reason vs. irrationality, loyalty vs. disloyalty, blood purity vs. impurity of blood become the centers of description of Atahuallpa and his participation in the events that frame the arrival of the bearded white men ("viracochas"). Although as a *mestizo* chronicle, the *Comentarios reales* contribute to the deconstruction of hegemonic discourse, Garcilaso's interpretative mode relies on his own forging of an "other," very much in the tradition of "civilization and barbarism" constructed by European logocentric discourse.

Garcilaso builds upon a game of logic when structuring fable and metaphor as a strategy for storytelling. The irrationality of circumstances, hazards, and fate creates a chain of events that determine the Amerindians' behavior as they help the Spaniards gain power. On the other hand, Garcilaso follows the rules of verisimilitude when he integrates into the official story the fabulous origin of the Inca empire, a story in which the arrival of white men ("viracochas") is predicted. Orality, which Garcilaso shares with his ancestors, is the source and foundation on which he empowers his discourse, while reason and European erudition, united with native orality, facilitate Garcilaso's twofold program: (1) the promotion of that aspect of his culture that has been demeaned by the conqueror and, (2) the granting of respectability and reliability to oral discourse in a society where the written word was given considerably greater credibility.[10] The fusion of two interpretative systems legitimizes orality in the eyes of Garcilaso's European public.

There is another set of binary oppositions that prevail within Garcilaso's value system. Benevolence, justice, and knowledge opposed to violence, injustice, and ignorance reveal Garcilaso's construction of alterity as he assigns negative values to both the Spaniards and those natives who do not belong to the Inca lineage. Depending on the circumstances, Garcilaso either minimizes or exaggerates Atahuallpa's culpability, pointing to his disloyalty toward Huascar or to the victimization of other cultures during his illegitimate reign. In the ballad, however, treachery and guilt prevail as the song suggests both Atahuallpa's blame and the justice of his victimization.

The ballad emphasizes ambivalence and contradiction as integral elements in history. The *romancero* tradition makes possible the reiteration of the ambiguous message by thousands of voices and variations, allowing for a dialogue between past and present. In order to clarify the significance of "El rescate de Atahuallpa" within the Hispanic tradition of balladry, a hermeneutical look at Garcilaso's axial element in his discourse provides the reader with a duplicate image of the context from which it emerges and illuminates the manner in which the narrative desecrates the secret relationships between the two worlds.

Garcilaso's *Comentarios reales* as a Polyphonic Text

The polyphonic quality of Garcilaso's text allows for a debunking of the monolithic language of previous historical accounts. Earlier official versions of the encounter undermine the superimposition of a political rhetoric that falsifies Amerindian culture at all levels. Garcilaso's voice, the voice of the ubiquitous first speaker in the *romance*, and the Quechua oral tradition constitute the expression of the colonial subject who searches for truth in the past, seeking to find the word that opposes the elimination of its self-identity. The inquiry by the colonial subject is not contentious or belligerent. Rather, it develops independently from the hegemonic versions.

As an acculturated *mestizo*, Garcilaso breaks through the limits of official discourse through the use of erudition, building from that position a linguistic mode of emancipation. In its popular expression, the ballad displays its freedom through multiple voices that will relay its message in diverse spaces and times. The Quechua dramatic tradition, on the other hand, lives on as a form of resistance, declaring its own distinct, almost mythical version of the events.

While the ballad is a completely ambiguous (and open) text, Garcilaso's chronicle and the Quechua oral dramatic tradition make up conflicting discourses in their mode of informing. When Garcilaso tells the story of the Huascar/Atahuallpa relationship, he indirectly blames their father. Garcilaso infers that Huayna Capac was guilty of breaking Inca tradition. If the old Inca had not violated the sacred laws of his heritage, his children would never have been exposed to betrayal, thus leaving the empire intact.

Atahuallpa had his brother Huascar assassinated because the latter was the legitimate heir of the empire. Huayna Capac was legitimately married to Mama Ocllo, Huascar's mother, while Atahuallpa was born out of an adulterous relationship with a concubine from Quito. Garcilaso, through a slanted look at the story, allows the reader to discover Huayna Capac's treachery to the sacred Inca laws: "because of his qualities of body and soul his father loved him (Atahuallpa) tenderly, and he always felt him within; he wanted to leave him his whole empire, but since he couldn't deprive his first child, Huascar Inca, the legitimate heir, he attempted against the canon and statute of all his ancestors to take away from him [Huascar] at least the reign of Quitu, with some shade and appearance of justice" (1: 348).[11] Using irony, "con algunos colores y apariencias de justicia" ("with some shade and appearance of justice"), Garcilaso points out Huayna Capac's "unnatural" decision of favoring one son over the other.

During one of Huayna Capac's long visits in Quito, Huascar was called and made to promise that he would desecrate the law of Manco Capac, the first Inca, by acceding to his progenitor's desires: "he was thoroughly delighted to obey his father, the Inca, in this and in anything else he was asked to do.... (1: 349)[12] Garcilaso favors Huascar, and he points to Huayna Capac's original betrayal by violating tradition as the beginning of the two brother's struggle for power. After his father's death, Huascar, dissatisfied with his inheritance, trusting that the Inca conventions still ruled, summoned his brother.[13] The Inca heir made Atahuallpa promise two things: (1) not to continue conquering further north and (2) that he should recognize him as lord and be his vassal (1: 374).[14] According to Garcilaso, "Atahuallpa received this message with all the submission and humility that he could feign" (1: 374)[15] and he is said to have astutely responded that he would always be his unconditional vassal and that he would not only not continue to augment his territory but would, in fact, " strip himself of it and would live as a private individual in his court just like any of his relatives, serving his prince and lord in peace and in war, and everything that was asked of him" (1: 374).[16]

Garcilaso obviously points out that in the struggle for power Huascar and Atahuallpa function within two very different ethical codes and the chronicle favors the first of the two in a religious way.[17] While Huascar is from Cuzco (and so is Garcilaso) and a legitimate son of Inca, he remains faithful to Inca rules. In turn, Atahuallpa is from Quito, an illegitimate child, and he betrays his brother's trust: "Both brothers were very happy with this, the one quite unaware of the machinations and treason that were being enacted against him to take away both his life and his empire, the other diligent and cunning, immersed in the treason to assure his enjoyment of both life and empire" (1: 375).[18] Atahuallpa not only breaches the promises to his brother but, according to Garcilaso, he also profanes the Inca code of honor by deceiving his people. Atahuallpa camouflaged his army as a royal entourage and gave his people an inaccurate proclamation of what he was about to do. He gathered "more than thirty thousand warriors, most of them select veterans left to him by his father, with experienced and famous captains whom he always brought along with him" (1: 375).[19] The tension grows in the narration as Garcilaso, far from having an objective point of view, ascertains that Atahuallpa's treachery is absolutely intolerable from the Inca cultural standpoint. Garcilaso makes sure that the reader will have a clear idea of the ethical impropriety in Atahuallpa's behavior and how his people interpreted his blunder: "Huascar Inca, trusting his brother's words, and even more his own long experience that among those Indians there was respect and loyalty as vassals to the Inca, and even more toward relatives and siblings..." (1: 375).[20] Atahuallpa's totally unexpected disloyalty, according to Garcilaso, resulted in Huascar's defeat and execution. Without resorting to deceit, in Garcilaso's opinion, Atahuallpa would have never prevailed: "Atahuallpa Inca used shrewdness and cunning by dissimulation and deceit and simulating against his brother because he was not powerful enough to wage war against him openly. He attempted and expected more of deceit than of his own strength. If he found his brother, Huascar Inca, unsuspecting, he would win the contest; if he gave him warning to get ready, he would lose" (1: 375-376).[21] Garcilaso's discourse becomes quite descriptive of Atahuallpa's cruelty and rage as he stormed against all of those "hundreds of thousands" who could have been of royal lineage. In spite of the carnage, some managed to escape the genocide. Among those survivors were the narrator's mother and uncle, who are used in the narrative to guarantee the reader that the account is trustworthy:

> ... All of the ones missing were boys and girls, children less than ten or eleven years old; one of those girls was my mother and there was a brother of hers named don Francisco Huallpa Tupac Inca Yupanqui, whom I knew, and who has written me after I arrived here in Spain; and of their account that I heard many times comes all this calamity and plague that I'm narrating; besides them I met a few others who escaped that misery. I met two *auquis*, which means princes; they were the children of Huayna Capac; one was named Paullu, who was already an adult when that calamity occurred and of whom the Spaniards make mention in their accounts. The other one was called Titu, and he was of legitimate lineage.... (1: 380-381)[22]

From this part of the text the reader infers that the power struggle and the betrayal of Inca law are the ultimate causes of the loss of the empire. When the sacred rules of the Amerindian's religious system were violated, the outcome could only be fatal. Garcilaso's providential interpretation of the events becomes coherent within the Judeo-Christian cognitive system. The same case in a biblical context, i.e., the violation of God's wishes and commands, would also have a catastrophic outcome for the guilty subjects. The use of a rational development of events allows Garcilaso as the narrator to validate a hypothesis based in the fantastic mythological origin of Inca tradition. The reader's horizon of expectations is satisfied with the verisimilitude of the narration because the narrator has interpreted the events from the European religious perspective. The reader is also able to notice the paradox: concurrent Western religious thought is just as irrational as the Amerindian beliefs of the time.

Civilization and Barbarism

Tension arises between the narrator's message, which intends to bring light into the real story, and the logocentric interpretation used by Garcilaso. For instance, his manner of establishing that the source of the betrayal lies in the legitimacy of blood lineage could easily find parallels within the Western interpretative system. Garcilaso constructs a discourse built upon the opposition between "civilization and barbarism." Every aspect of his own genealogy is presented as positive while everything that does not correspond to it is presented as negative.

The portrayal of Atahuallpa adheres to a line of reasoning that has its roots in sameness as a formulating model. Garcilaso invests his text with the ability to be "a narrative of space" (Certeau 67) and uses socio- and ethnocultural boundaries in order to make his representation of the "other" credible. Atahuallpa is located in a "no-place," Quito, in opposition to Cuzco, where the legitimate Inca heirs live, including Garcilaso himself. Thus it is in describing the "non-Incas" (the Quiteños, the Spaniards, or other Amerindian cultures of the area) that Garcilaso's text constructs a place of its own.

After Garcilaso describes the massacre of the royal family, he resorts to his uncle's voice to discard the last possibility of Inca lineage in Atahuallpa's blood. During the burial of one of Atahuallpa's presumed children, Garcilaso asks his uncle the reason for his joy instead of grief at the death of Don Francisco: " Inca, how can we rejoice at the death of Don Francisco being that he is such a close relative?" (2: 383).[23] Garcilaso's uncle denies Atahuallpa's Inca heritage, arguing that he was not a legitimate child of Huayna Capac. The justification for Atahuallpa's betrayal is found in the underlying accusation of adultery: Huayna Capac had also been deceived by Atahuallpa's mother, who is ultimately to blame for the fall of the Inca empire.

In Garcilaso's discourse the reader has to play a primordial role in capturing the true feelings, motivation, and ideology underlying the text. The true artifice in the construction of Garcilaso's subtlety, however, must be discovered in the contrast of Atahuallpa with the Spaniards. Garcilaso's strategy begins with the description of Atahuallpa Inca as a tyrant: "He rejoiced at thinking that with his cruelty and tyranny he was securing his empire; how careless and nonchalant to imagine that through those same [strategies], foreigners were going to strip him of it; at a time as prosperous and favorable as was promised, they knocked at his door to plunder his throne and take his life and his empire; those people were the Spaniards" (3: 17).[24] Irony emerges upon the realization that Atahuallpa's euphoria is going to dissipate as a result of the more effective, technical cruelty of the Spaniards. Further into the narration the Spaniards are presented as having an insatiable thirst for riches and reputation at the same time that their deeds hint at some noble lineage : "they were so eager to discover new lands, and others more and more pristine, that even though they were so rich and prosperous, not completely content with what they possessed . . . they returned again to new conquests with greater zeal, so that they would accomplish in deeds that would immortalize their names" (3: 17).[25] Pizarro and his cohorts are endowed with "noble blood" ("muy noble sangre"). Thus we see how Almagro's lineage is defined: "his lineage is not known, but his works, so great and generous, say that he was very noble" (3: 17).[26] Garcilaso, no doubt, is relying on the complicity and the historical knowledge of the reader to fill the gaps that irony leaves behind. The seventeenth century had already witnessed the bloodshed resulting from the Conquest and civil wars in Peru.

When Atahuallpa is contrasted to the Spaniards, the narration turns into an ironic game manipulated by Garcilaso. It is a game of mirrors that humanizes Atahuallpa, who now emerges as a victim: "Atahuallpa, Inca, as we will later see; and it is right to tell of his good attributes with which he was endowed by nature, those that he used at that time with these Spaniards and many others that later we will recognize regarding his ingenuity, discretion, and cleverness..." (3: 41).[27] When the violence of the Spanish Conquest is juxtaposed to that of Atahuallpa, the latter's ferocity appears more humane. At this point the chronicler has achieved the major purpose in writing, which is an unending dialogue between the European worldview and the reality of the Amerindian world.

The Tragedy of Atahuallpa

Atahuallpa's final days are dramatized in an ancient play that deals with the arrival of the Spaniards in Peru.[28] In this play, Atahuallpa is portrayed in a very favorable light. His name is spelled *Ataw*, meaning glory and martial honor, and *wallpa*, from the verb *wallpay*, which means to create. The name is divided in the text in order to underscore its noble, royal meaning. The plot is very similar in the three different available versions of the texts. One of them, known as the *Chayanta Codex*, begins with a dialogue between Atahuallpa and the princesses Cora Chimpu and Coyllur Tika. The monarch appears deeply troubled by a dream in which he has seen his father, the Sun god, eclipsed by a deep, shadowing smoke, while the Andes burned in a scarlet fire and a *huaca* (oracle) brings him the omen of an inexpressible event. Atahuallpa fears that his country will be invaded by iron warriors who will rob him of his power. In a monologue Atahuallpa remembers his ancestor, Manco Capac, the first Inca, and invokes the god Viracocha, who had been the first to see the iron men and knew that they were coming to invade. He declares solemnly that he is the son of Huayna Capac and vows to "let a hundred blood lakes run, with the help of the Sun god, to throw the iron men out of his kingdom" (7).[29] Atahuallpa later finds out from Huaya Huisa, the supreme priest, that the bearded enemies from the sea have arrived.

The description of the Spaniards brings a definite difference to the configuration of colonial discourse:

> They wear three-pointed horns
> just like the *tarukas*
> and their hair
> is sprinkled with white flour,
> and on their mandibles they boast
> blazing red beards,
> similar to long strands of wool
> and they carry in their hands
> extraordinary iron slings
> whose occult power
> is to vomit flaming fire
> rather than launching stones.[30]

The portrayal of the Spaniard seen for the first time as a total alien denotes complete confusion and anxiety on the part of the speaker. The civilization/barbarism dichotomy used by Garcilaso seems to be secondary to the tone of bewilderment that characterizes the play.

Huascar appears in the play as a first cousin of the thirteenth Inca and as a royal emissary to the first encounter with the Spaniards. As such, he becomes a victim of communication: since the Spaniards speak an "incomprehensible dialect" ("un dialecto incomprensible" [26]), the written piece of paper (*chala*) that Pizarro gives to Huascar and the latter takes back to Atahuallpa cannot be deciphered. Huascar then takes the note back to Pizarro, who harangues him with an aggressive and arrogant response: "Understand, you barbarian, and know that this note is the royal command of my lord, the King of Spain."[31] The manner of describing the note reinforces the baffling cross-cultural experience that the arrival of the Spaniards was for the Amerindian:

> Seen from this side
> it is a swarm of ants.
> Viewed from this other angle
> and they seem to me like the footprints

left by the birds
on the muddy banks of the river.
Seen this way it looks like *tarukas*
turned up-side down
with their feet up in the air.
And if we only look at it this way
it resembles the llamas
with their heads hanging low
and *taruka* horns.
Who could possibly understand this?[32]

The written order from the king was to apprehend Atahuallpa and take him back to Spain. The Quechua tragedy makes mention of Atahuallpa's betrayal of Huascar only once during the play. Pizarro through his interpreter, Felipillo, recalls that betrayal to Atahuallpa: "In the same manner that you humiliated your brother, Huascar Inca, you will succumb to me" (29).[33] Remarkably, the only one who perceives Atahuallpa's behavior toward Huascar as treason is a Spaniard.

The outcome of the play is essentially the same in all three known manuscripts. Pizarro kills Atahuallpa brutally in front of everyone. The captain, then, returns to his country, where he is to be sentenced by the king (who is a personification of Spain) for having killed such a great monarch. The conquistador invokes Jehovah and the Virgin Mary and confesses the horrible crime that he committed in Peru. Pizarro is struck dead and Almagro is ordered by the king to confirm his death and to cremate his remains together with his family and possessions. The most interesting aspects of the play are its religious search for justice and its proselytizing function. The idea of the play is to present the "true" facts and have the invaders answer to divine justice.

The dialogue that emerges between the chronicle and other discourses such as the ballad and the Quechua dramatic tradition stirs up several messages. First, the language that characterizes the discourse of the Conquest is defined by the need to create an "enemy." Second, both the Spanish chronicles and the Hispanic oral tradition resort to the dialectics of civilization and barbarism as a narratological device. As opposed to these, the native Amerindian tradition configures a discourse of bafflement and insists on a different version of the "truth." The dialectic of civilization and barbarism does not remain constant in Western texts since the enemy, the barbarian, can manifest himself in many different ways.

We have seen how Garcilaso constructs enemy subjects when trying to represent the Inca empire as Utopia. Yet, since the Incas were also colonizers, what we have, in essence, is the antithesis of Utopia. Garcilaso's discourse is thus filled with contradictions that can only stem from his desire to construct "others." With the purpose of explaining Atahuallpa's betrayal as the real reason behind the fall of the empire, Garcilaso needs to create enemy-subjects out of other Amerindians. Garcilaso's line of reasoning can only guide him to the conclusion that Atahuallpa betrayed Huascar and his people because he was not of real Inca lineage. When Atahuallpa is contrasted to the Spaniards, Garcilaso must make him into a victim in order to emphasize the brutality and barbarism of the conquistadors. Despite Garcilaso's logocentric worldview, his need to communicate another version of history results in a deconstruction of the previous narratives of the Conquest.

As in the case of Garcilaso's text, the uniqueness of the ballad also lies in its open discourse, allowing it to interact with other concurrent texts. In the ballad the dichotomy of Atahuallpa's image is quite apparent. The ubiquitous perspective allows the reader (or the listener) of the lyrics to question history. The openness of this particular ballad, "El rescate de Atahuallpa," maintains a suspenseful doubt about the underlying truth surrounding the complexity of a historical figure who constitutes the semantization of imperialism in the Americas.[34] Finally, the play portrays Atahuallpa as a great man with supernatural virtues who was victimized and deceived to the bewilderment of his people. Victim and victimizer, Atahuallpa represents the essence of the colonial conjuncture in a process that reclaims, for its natural existence, the polarization between winners and losers. Remarkably, Garcilaso's *Comentarios reales* are also the scene of a struggle between orality and literacy. In "writing" orality, Garcilaso legitimizes the Amerindian tradition of storytelling as a form of memory. The *mestizo* scholar includes orality as a trustworthy source within the logocentric discourse of hegemony. The need to legitimize orality within the Western interpretive tradition[35] establishes an ambiguity that is a sign of colonial marginality. Furthermore, this ambivalence, which is present in the three texts commented above, constructs a *mestizo* world through the merging of different realities channelled both through the Spanish and native oral traditions, thus generating tensions in the margins of the discourse structured by colonialism, opening up worlds that construct a *mestizaje* (racial and cultural) of their own.

Notes

1. This essay is part of a broader project soon to be completed as a book. Many of the ideas that I propose here, but from different perspectives, have been part of two previous articles: "Diálogos de traición" and "Oralidad y escritura." For the Quechua "tragedy" I used Jesús Lara's bilingual edition, in which Lara provides a brief history of the "Chayanta" manuscript, which collects the oral dramatic encounter in folkloric representations around different areas of Bolivia. Some of the versions, such as the one in Charcas, near Potosí, used both Spanish and Quechua (the actors playing the conquistadors speak only Spanish and the ones playing the Incas speak Quechua) while others are performed only in Quechua and all actors use the native language. Lara places the origin of the tragedy in the sixteenth century and attests to the fact that the Quechua used appears in its original form without traces of Spanish influence. The date and place of the codex, however, are "Chayanta, March 25, 1871." See Lara 17-33.

2. Two articles published recently deal with the incident of Atahuallpa's encounter with "the book." Both MacCormack and Seed present an excellent account of the different interpretations by chroniclers, both hegemonic and counter-hegemonic, of Atahuallpa's behavior when confronted with the assailant's technology.

3. See Iser; Mary Gossy, in her reading of women in Golden Age texts, perceives a similar phenomenon, which she calls "the untold." Gossy examines how gaps in narrative by traditional reading strategies reflect the treatment of women and women's bodies, making of the gap a fetishized feminine object.

4. The notion of gaps coincides with what Gérard Genette calls "paralipsis." Genette indicates that the element that is missing has been avoided consciously or unconsciously in the selection process. The concept of paralipsis allows for a reestablishment of those elements whose essence lingers in the marginal text's tangent. Ideologically, these elements have been omitted by hegemony but the lack is active and perceptible because it always leaves a trace that is felt and needs to be filled by the reader.

5.　Atabaliba está preso, está preso en su prisión;

juntando está los tesoros que ha de dar al español.

No cuenta como el cristiano, sino en cuentas de algodón.

El algodón se le acaba, pero los tesoros, no.

Los indios que se los traen le hacen la relación.

—"Este metal es la plata que al Potosí se arrancó.

Este metal es el oro del santo templo del sol.

Estas las perlas que el mar en la playa vomitó.

Estas piedras, esmeraldas que el reino de Quito dió.

Estos bermejos rubíes . . . "—"Estos no los quiero yo,

que son las gotas de sangre que mi hermano derramó."

Bayo does not offer much information about this ballad. He only assigns author-ship to a "milonguero" (a singer) from La Paz, Bolivia. Given the issues raised in this study, precision regarding authorship or date is not important for our purpose. The values of the song lie in its study as a cultural text. As far as the background of the *romance*, see Bermúdez-Gallegos, "Diálogos de traición."

6. The term "cultural text" is used as in Lotman (304).

7. Here we must again refer to Lotman (18) in order to reflect the polycultural aspect of the geosocial context in which the text is formulated. Lotman warns that not every text is considered as "cultural" but that there are other texts that culture does not claim, a sort of "anti-texts," which are censured by the canon. I believe that such could be the case of the folkloric text because in a culture that is heavily oriented toward writing (as is the case of Western hegemonic discourse in the An-dean area), folklore plays an inferior role. Folklore, as well as other oral forms, has not received sufficient attention until recently within our discipline.

8. The most notorious exploitation of the Potosí mines occurred during the second half of the sixteenth century and in the seventeenth century. For a detailed version of the exploitation of the Potosí mines in Upper Peru and a description of the hostile, uninhabitable conditions under which the Amerindian workers were forced to labor, see Acosta.

9. "El inca Atahualpa, viéndose preso en cadenas de hierro, trató de su rescate por verse fuera de ellas; prometió porque le soltasen cubrir de vasijas de plata y oro el suelo de una gran sala donde estaba preso. . . . "

10. At this point, Garcilaso subverts Renaissance precepts. Personal experimen-tation, as the foundation of observation, was the most trustworthy documentation for the scholar of the times. Garcilaso, meanwhile, accepts that what is heard is just as accurate and valuable as what is seen. In his mother's culture, orality is the only way that memory is registered; therefore, he validates the indigenous method of recording history. As one can see, oral history is another point of intersection of interpretative traditions.

11. "por estos dotes del cuerpo y del Animo lo amó su padre [a Atahuallpa] tiernamente, y siempre lo traía consigo; quisiera dejarle en herencia todo su impe-rio, mas no pudiendo quitar el derecho al primogénito y heredero legítimo que

era Huascar Inca, procuró contra el fuero y estatuto de todos sus antepasados quitarle siquiera el reino del Quitu, con algunos colores y apariencias de justicia y restitución."

12. "holgaba en extremo de obedecer al Inca su padre en aquello y en cualquiera otra cosa que fuese servido mandarle. . . . "

13. Huascar realizes that the part of the territory that belongs to him has very little room for growth while the northern part of the empire has still many areas left for expansion. Consequently, he fears that Atahuallpa will be the one who will conquer the remaining cultures that surround Quito, thus becoming the most powerful ruler.

14. "la otra que ante todas cosas le había de reconocer vasallaje y ser su feudatario."

15. "Este recaudo recibió Atahuallpa con toda la sumisión y humildad que pudo fingir. . . . "

16. "se desposeería de él y se lo renunciaría, y viviría privadamente en su corte como cualquiera de sus deudos, sirviéndole en paz y en guerra como debía a su príncipe y señor en todo lo que mandase."

17. One must not forget that the Inca empire was a theocracy. The traditions and the laws of the reign could not be separated from its religion. It is interesting to observe how Garcilaso indirectly adopts the religion as his and accepts the tradition as part of his double life.

18. "Con esto quedaron ambos hermanos muy contentos, el uno muy ajeno de imaginar la máquina y traición que contra él se armaba para quitarle la vida y el imperio, y el otro muy diligente y cauteloso, metido en el mayor golfo de ella para no dejar gozar de lo uno ni de lo otro."

19. " . . . más de treinta mil hombres de guerra, que los más de ellos eran de la gente veterana y escogida que su padre le dejó, con capitanes experimentados y famosos que siempre traía consigo."

20. "Huascar Inca, fiado en las palabras de su hermano, y mucho más en la experiencia tan larga que entre aquellos indios había del respeto y lealtad que al Inca tenían sus vasallos, cuanto más sus parientes y hermanos. . . . "

21. "Atahuallpa Inca usó de aquella astucia y cautela de ir disfrazado y disimulado contra su hermano porque no era poderoso para hacerle la guerra al descubierto. Pretendió y esperó más en el engaño que no en sus fuerzas; porque hallando descuidado al rey Huáscar, como le halló, ganaba el juego, y dándole lugar que se apercibiese lo perdía."

22. " . . . Todos los que así faltaron fueron niños y niñas, muchachos y muchachas de diez a once años abajo; una de ellas fue mi madre y un hermano suyo, llamado don Francisco Huallpa Tupac Inca Yupanqui, que yo conocí, que después que estoy en España me ha escrito; y de la relación que muchas veces les oí es todo lo que de esta calamidad y plaga voy diciendo; sin ellos conocí otros pocos que escaparon de aquella miseria. Conocí dos *auquis*, que quiere decir infantes; eran hijos de Huayna Capac, el uno llamado Paullu, que era ya hombre en aquella calamidad, de quien las historias de los españoles hacen mención. El otro se llamaba Titu, era de los legítimos en sangre . . . " (380-381). Here is the beginning of another set of ambivalences and betrayals that I deal with in another part of my project. Paullu and Titu are two very contradictory historical figures in the Conquest and settlement of

Peru. Paullu collaborated with the Spaniards and won a privileged place with the invader. Titu united with the resistance forces at Vilcabamba and was executed. As we can tell, Garcilaso stresses ironically that Paullu is part of Spanish "history."

23. "Inca, ¿Cómo nos hemos de holgar de la muerte de don Francisco siendo tan pariente nuestro?"

24. "tan contento y ufano de pensar que con sus crueldades y tiranías iba asegurando su imperio, cuan ajeno y descuidado de imaginar que mediante ellas mismas se lo habían de quitar muy presto gentes extrañas, no conocidas, que en tiempo tan próspero y favorable como él se prometía llamaron a su puerta para derribarle de su trono y quitarle la vida y el imperio, que fueron los españoles."

25. "andaban tan ganosos de descubrir nuevas tierras, y otras más y más nuevas, que aunque muchos de ellos estaban ricos y prósperos, no contentos con lo que poseían ... volvían de nuevo a nuevas conquistas y mayores afanes, para salir con mayores hazañas que eternizasen sus famosos nombres."

26. "no se sabe de qué linaje, más sus obras tan hazañosas y generosas dicen que fue nobilísimo."

27. "El Inca Atahuallpa, como adelante veremos; séanos lícito decir sus buenas partes de que le dotó naturaleza, y sean las que al presente usó con estos españoles y otras muchas que adelante veremos de su buen ingenio, discreción y habilidad ... " (3: 41).

28. It is believed that the *Chayanta Codex* manuscript presents the most trustworthy of all versions of the ancient play about the arrival of the Europeans to Peru. Jesús Lara also refers to two manuscripts, the San Pedro and the Santa Lucia, which present *mestizo* versions of the tradition. The three manuscripts do not vary in the essential elements of the story nor the way they portray Atahuallpa. The three versions do differ in the language and some of the characters. The San Pedro and the Santa Lucia versions include Spanish dialogue in the lines spoken by the Spanish characters and Felipillo, the interpreter, as well as some elements that were added in more recent versions. Also, in the Santa Lucia manuscript, the devil appears in Atahuallpa's premonitory dream about the arrival of "the bearded invader." The demon attempts to tantalize the Amerindian chief into submitting to the enemy and his lines are emitted in Spanish. The Chayanta manuscript, however, is composed in traditional Quechua verse (free verse, not like the Castilian verse of the same period) with no dialectological influences from the Spanish nor of later informational intrusions by modern transcribers.

The translation from Lara's Spanish version is mine. The tragedy is believed to have been composed in the Quito region. The original *runasimi*, or Quechua from the Chinchay Suyu, is the dialect used in the transcription of the *Chayanta Codex*. The accounts of the event stemming from this region seem to be favorable to the image of Atahuallpa (such as Guaman Poma de Ayala's) and not so favorable when portraying Huascar. The southern accounts, from Cuzco and Upper Peru (among them Garcilaso's) tend to be quite negative toward Atahuallpa.

29. " ... hacer correr lagos de sangre hasta arrojar a los hombres de hierro con la ayuda del Sol, su padre."

30.   "Llevan tres cuernos puntiagudos

    igual que las tarukas.

y tienen los cabellos

con blanca harina polvoreados,

y en las mandíbulas ostentan

barbas del todo rojas, semejantes

a largas vedijas de lana,

y llevan en las manos

hondas de hierro extraordinarias,

cuyo poder oculto

en vez de lanzar piedras

vomita fuego llameante." (34)

31. "Entended, bárbaro, y sabed que este papel es la real orden de mi Señor el rey de España."

32.   Vista de este costado

es un hervidero de hormigas.

La miro de este otro costado

y se me antojan las huellas que dejan

las patas de los pájaros

en las lodosas orillas del río.

Vista así, se parece a las tarukas

puestas con la cabeza abajo

y las patas arriba.

Y si solo así la miramos

es semejante a llamas cabizbajas

y cuernos de taruka.

Quién comprender esto pudiera." (35)

33. "Del mismo modo que en tus manos humillaste a tu hermano el Inca Waskar, asimismo ante mi te doblegarás."

34. On this subject see also the excellent study on the Inca Garcilaso by Susana Jakfalvi-Leiva (107-111).

35. On Garcilaso and the Renaissance philosophy of language, see Zamora.

Works Cited

Acosta, José de. *Historia natural y moral de las Indias*. Ed. Edmundo O'Gorman. Mexico City: Universidad Nacional Autónoma de México, 1940.

Bakhtin, Mikhail. *The Dialogic Imagination*. Ed. Michael Holquist. Austin: Univ. of Texas Press, 1988.

———. *Problems of Dostoevsky's Poetics*. Ed. and Trans. Caryl Emerson. Theory and History of Literature 8. Minneapolis: Univ. of Minnesota Press, 1984.

Bayo, Ciro. *Romancerillo del Plata*. Buenos Aires: Ediciones Popular, 1945.

Bermúdez-Gallegos, Marta. "Diálogos de traición y de muerte: 'El rescate de Atahuallpa' y *Los comentarios reales* del Inca Garcilaso." *Romance Languages Annual*, 1991. Forthcoming.

———. "Oralidad y escritura: Atawallpa, traidor o traicionado?" *Revista de Crítica Latinoamericana*. Forthcoming.

Certeau, Michel de. "Of Cannibals." *Heterologies*. Minneapolis: Univ. of Minnesota Press, 1989.

Durán, Agustín, ed. *Romancero General o Colección de romances castellanos anteriores al siglo XVIII*. Vol. 1. Madrid: Imprenta de los sucesores de Hernando, 1921.

Garcilaso de la Vega, El Inca. *Los Comentarios reales*. Vols. 133, 134. Madrid: Biblioteca de Autores Españoles, 1960.

Genette, Gérard. *Narrative Discourse: An Essay in Method*. Trans. Jane E. Lewin. Ithaca, N.Y.: Cornell Univ. Press, 1980.

Gossy, Mary. *The Untold Story: Women and Theory in Golden Age Texts*. Ann Arbor: Univ. of Michigan Press, 1989.

Iser, Wolfgang. *The Act of Reading: A Theory of Aesthetic Response*. Baltimore: Johns Hopkins Univ. Press, 1978.

Jakfalvi-Leiva, Susana. *Traducción, escritura y violencia colonizadora: un estudio de la obra del Inca Garcilaso*. Syracuse: Maxwell School of Citizenship and Public Affairs, 1984.

Lotman, Juri. "Sign Mechanism of Culture." *Semiotica* 12.4 (1974): 304.

Lara, Jesús, ed. *Tragedia del fin de Atawallpa: Atau Wallpaj p'uchukakuynimpa wankan*. Bilingual edition. Trans. Jesús Lara. Buenos Aires: Biblioteca de Cultura Popular. Ediciones del Sol, 1989.

MacCormack, Sabine. "Atahuallpa and the Book." *Dispositio* 14.36-38 (1989): 141-168.

Seed, Patricia. "Failing to Marvel." *Latin American Research Review* 26.1 (1991): 7-32.

Zamora, Margarita. *Language, Authority and Indigenous History in the* Comentarios Reales de los Incas. Cambridge: Cambridge Univ. Press, 1988.

◆ Chapter 21

Art and Resistance in the Andean World

Teresa Gisbert

(translated by Laura Giefer)

The Persistence of Andean Culture

The encounter between the native Andean peoples and the Spaniards was to favor the invaders, for the Inca empire, which had previously dominated the entire region, was in the midst of a civil war. The ethnic lords of the south supported Huascar, whose court was in Cuzco,[1] while his half brother, Atahuallpa, dominated the north. The Spaniards met Atahuallpa in Cajamarca, and it was there that they killed him.

Atahuallpa's death was not mourned by Huascar's sympathizers, who saw in the conquistadors a handful of men with whom an agreement could be reached. Such was the "Herod-like" attitude of Paullo and Sairi Tupac (Gisbert, "Toynbee" 372), while others such as Manco II and Tupac Amaru I, who were against the invaders, had a zealous attitude.

As Renaissance men who were inspired by Machiavellian political theories, the conquistadors also resorted to pacts and concessions in order to obtain the loyalty of the indigenous leaders. An example is the case of Moroco and Coysara, leaders of Caracara and Chayanta (in the region of Potosí, Bolivia) at the time of the invasion, when both were in Cuzco as members of the Council of Huascar (Espinoza). The same Coysara was later to command the troops that attacked Gonzalo Pizarro and his men in Cochabamba, eventually accepting surrender as the only possible option. In the battle against Pizarro, Coysara had been joined by Aymoro, chief of the Yamparaes (region of Chuquisaca, Bolivia), and it is this leader who vacated the city of Chuquisaca so that the Spaniards could establish there the capital of the Audiencia of Charcas. The Spaniards could also count among their collaborators the Guarachi family (see Aguirre; Espinoza), which claimed to have preceded the Incas and even Manco Capac himself. We must emphasize once again that the Spaniards also met with strong resistance, as was the case with the commanders of the Pacajes and the Urus.

With the death of the Inca leader Tupac Amaru I, Viceroy Francisco de Toledo was to put an end to this collaboration. The requirement of forced labor in the mines through the *mita* system in addition to the already established institution of *encomiendas* allowed him to place socioeconomic control of the territory into the hands of the Castilians. Even the collaborator Coysara, who headed an important confederation (Charcas, Caracaras, Chuis, and Chichas) was forced to accept the transfer of the capital of Charca from Sacaca to Chayanta. This move not only diminished Coysara's influence, but also had the effect of undermining an important ancestral center of power. The viceroy had taken those steps deliberately and had consulted with a group of advisers who could lend legitimacy to his actions with their expert counsel. Among them were the Jesuit naturalist José de Acosta, the jurists Juan de Matienzo and Hernando de Santillan, and the historian Pedro Sarmiento de Gamboa, among others. Juan Polo de Ondegardo, who was interested in Indian "antiquities," can also be considered a member of this group.

The measures of control taken by the viceroy were effected through careful scrutiny as different types of surveys were made and the "juridical" situation of Indian communities was assessed. Thus, Sarmiento de Gamboa's *Historia Indica* (finished in 1572) supplied important data about Collasuyo and other regions dominated by the Incas. The viceroy and his advisers were also aware of the importance of religion and indigenous beliefs, which they sought to eliminate, going so far as to obliterate all images of ancient Amerindian myths as represented in the *keros*, or wooden vessels used for libations.[2] One of Toledo's provisions reads as follows: "And so said inhabitants also worship certain species of birds and animals, and for said purpose they paint and carve them into *mates*, drinking vessels made of wood and silver, and onto the doorways of their homes, and they weave them into frontals and canopies for their altars and paint them on the walls of their churches. I ordain and mandate that you efface and remove any such images that you may find on their doors and that you also prohibit the weaving of these images into the clothing that they wear, paying especial attention to this as well" (Gisbert, Arze, and Cajías 10-11).[3]

While Toledo was successful in asserting control in the socio-political sphere—as expressed in the establishment of the *mita* system and in urban planning of Indian villages—his attempted prohibitions in the area of culture and ideas were to meet with considerable resistance. Flores Ochoa has shown that *keros* wood cups continued being painted with scenes from ancient myths; an example is the festival of Coyllourite represented on a *kero* from the Orihuela collection, presently in the Archaeological Museum of Cuzco (30+). There are also many other examples attesting to this resistance: the Indian gods, such as the Inca Sun or the Puma, characteristic of the Pucara and Tihuanaco cultures, have survived in the baroque décor of the temples. While some textiles incorporated new designs (such as in Tarabuco, where baroque floral ornamentation and horses were inserted), others did not. Actually, some weavings exist with representations of ancient mythical beings, such as birds with various heads and animals with transparent bodies that reveal another being within. The latter can be found in the textiles of Leque and Potolo (Jalka), which follow an aesthetic typical of cultures as ancient as Paracas. The survival of this art was also assured by certain patterns of composition such as the representation of anthropomorphic beings who are endowed with some of the features of the puma, the condor, and the serpent. Such is the case with the pottery of Tihuanaco and Chavin and is repeated in the textiles of Sacaca, Leque, and Potolo (Gisbert, Arze, and Cajías 11-12).

We can see, then, that the "Ordinance" of Viceroy Toledo had little effect in this area. The same can be said of similar prohibitions stated by the Dominican Friar Juan Meléndez in his *Tesoros verdaderos de las Indias* (*The True Treasures of the Indies*): "[Indians should have] taken from their eyes not only all that which was an openly worshipped idol... and thereby it has been decreed that not only not in churches, but in no place, public or secret, in the Indian communities... may be painted... terrestrial, flying, or marine animals, especially of certain species.... And therefore it has been decreed... that the sun, the moon and the stars not be painted, thus taking away from them the possibility of returning to their ancient deliriums and absurdities" (2: 62).[4]

The lack of compliance with these types of decrees and ordinances may be attributed to the fact that, after years of an active campaign to eradicate idolatry under Toledo, the religious pressures began to recede. On the other hand, it became difficult to control the indigenous people who were knowledgeable about the mechanisms of the new society. One must remember that they were the artisans in charge of weaving, painting, carving, and building, providing a large labor force that was more responsive to its traditional leaders than to the architects and clerics—both Creoles and Spanish—who served as their mentors.

The latent native culture tried to assert itself through the arts, using churches and Christian imagery. The baroque's fondness of the strange, the eccentric, and the exotic was receptive to Andean suns, moons, monkeys, and pumas in the same way that it accepted Hermes, Diana, Hercules, and other elements of the Greco-Roman world (see Mesa and Gisbert 259+). In any case, there were authors who advocated some tolerance toward the religious practices of the Amerindians in order to harness their faith and steer it in the direction of the true Christian God.

Such is the case of the Jesuit José de Acosta whose "Procuranda Indorum Salute" says: "And I think it is in no way desirable to destroy the temples that hold their idols, so upon seeing that their temples are respected, those people will remove from their hearts all error, and upon knowing the true God and adoring him, they will assemble in places that are familiar to them" (502).[5] Some Augustinian monks, above all those born in the Andes, like Antonio de la Calancha and Alonso Ramos Gavilán, try to equate Christian dogma with ancient myths. Ramos Gavilán in his *Historia del célebre santuario de Nuestra Señora de Copacabana* (*History of the Famous Shrine of our Lady of Copacabana* [1621]) says that "just as the sun casts its rays over the earth making it a mother so that it may benefit humankind, so God deposits his rays in Mary, also making her a mother in order to benefit humankind."[6] In this literary simile an identification is established between God and the Sun, impregnator of Mary-Pachamama (Gisbert, *Iconografía* 31).

By the middle of the seventeenth century, less than one hundred years after the arrival of the viceroy Francisco de Toledo, Andean ideology had become embedded in the artistic fabric of the colonial society. This can be seen beyond the doorways and *keros* into the living world of folklore, in the world of literature, in dances, and in theater. This type of cultural syncretism can be seen, for instance, in the representation of mermaids; in the inclusion of an Inca in a painting of the Wise Men who journeyed to Bethlehem; in a procession of angels whose names are taken from atmospheric and celestial phenomena and who struggle with demons; and, finally, in the representation of Atahuallpa's death and of scenes characteristic of Inca epic. These artistic manifestations of a pre-Hispanic, partially submerged culture and values, persist until today.

The Cultural Route of the *Mita*

When one looks at the social, economic, and political map of the Andean world of the eighteenth century, one realizes that the changes that took place brought with them corresponding changes in the cultural realm. The ample territory that had been under the jurisdiction of the viceroyalty of Peru was reduced in 1716 when the viceroyalty of New Granada was created, bringing with it the Audiencia of Quito. The Audiencia of Lima and Charcas remained under the jurisdiction of the viceroy of Peru. In fact Charcas, which would later form the Republic of Bolivia, was to depend upon Peru until 1776.

These jurisdictional demarcations were related to commercial routes, and labor forces and these new arrangements were to have a profound impact on the communication and, thus, the permanence of that culture. By establishing the *mita*, Toledo obliged sixteen provinces, from Cuzco to Potosí, to work in the mines of this metropolis. For three centuries there was constant migration of indigenous people who, working in the mines processing minerals and in the maintenance areas of the artificial lagoons that supplied water for the grinding of minerals, shared the penuries of work in the imperial city. These native Amerindians resided in their respective parishes, which were organized according to different ethnic groups: the Lupacas of Lake Titicaca had the St. Martin parish; the Carangas that of St. Lorenzo; the Quillacas, led by their chief Guarachi, controlled the market area, or *Ccatu*. Thus the entire Indian nation, which composed the Collasuyo (the southern part of the Inca empire) gathered together in Potosí, and this migration frequently transmitted cultural forms through textiles and *keros* glasses. Similarly in the theater, the portrayal of "the Magi," which is performed in present-day Cuzco and San Pedro de Cacha, corresponds to the tradition of Potosí created by *mita* workers, or *mitayos*, upon returning to their places of origin.[7] In view of the realities of Potosí that were characterized by the convergence of native Amerindians from various parts of the Southern Andean area, it is not possible to distinguish between Cuzco and Potosí, or to omit the peoples along the route, just as it is not possible to study the plastic arts without considering a parallel and similar phenomenon in theater arts.

Drama as Transmitter of a New Ideology

Just as the formal representation of certain myths reproduces itself in the baroque décor of temple portals, a verbal tradition appears in the festival, in which both dialogue and theatrical representation play a very important role, not only by entertaining and highlighting certain events, but also by transmitting ideas. Such is the case, for example, with the eclogue entitled "El Dios Pan" ("The God *Pan*"), written by Diego Mejía de Fernangil in the mountainous region of Andamarca (Oruro, Bolivia) when the Brotherhood of the Holiest Sacrament was established in the city of Potosí between 1607 and 1621 (Vargas Ugarte 8). In this work the Christian shepherd Melibeo attempts to convert his pagan friend Damón by taking him to a festival in Potosí. The wonder and delight that the festival produces in Damón is cause for him to become Christian, and Mejía puts into the mouth of the pagan shepherd expressions such as these:

> I would remain here for a century
> If this would always be here
> But, my dear friend, I leave ready
> (the God *Pan* as my witness) for baptism
> and subject myself as slave to this *Pan*.
> (Vargas Ugarte 69; emphasis added)[8]

It is obvious that *Pan* (Bread) alludes to the Eucharist and that this God will replace the pagan *Pan* (bread) that is worshipped by Damón, the idolatrous country shepherd. Following the customary practice of Mannerism of the time, Mejía de Fernangil cloaks the idolatry of this Andean shepherd in the robes of Greco-Roman gods. However, beneath this euphemism lies a clear reference to pre-Hispanic gods, whose veneration was still in force. This can be seen in Melibeo's description of the god adored by Damón, which seems to allude to a pre-Columbian idol and to the festival of Taqui Oncoy.[9]

> ... Your Pan
> is a sinister, imagined, monster,
> an absurd pretense,
> a God without spirit,
> a counterfeit form
> which has never existed,
> he is the apparent nonsense
> of a blind and ignorant people
> who offer incense

with festive and boundless joy

to a trunk or a mute stone

(Vargas Ugarte 49).[10]

This is not the only time that Andean idolatry is cloaked in classical language by Mannerist and baroque writers. Fernando de Valverde also does so in his work *El santuario de Nuestra Señora de Copacabana* (*The Shrine of Our Lady of Copacabana* [Lima, 1641]), where satyrs, nymphs, cupids, and Venus circulate about Ilabe, Copacabana, and Tiquina as if it were the most natural thing in the world. Nor is there a lack of mermaids emerging from Lake Titicaca, an event that coincides with an old Indian tradition of the fish-women with whom Tunupa, god of the Collas sinned (Gisbert, *Iconografía* 46-47).

Mejía attempts to portray the Eucharist as the Sun, creating the identification God=Sun, Christ=Sun of Justice, an identification evidenced in various pictorial representations of the Trinity (Gisbert, *Iconografía* 89, fig. 24) and that is also suggested by the Augustinian Ramos Gavilán. When Melibeo explains to Damón the hieroglyphics that adorn the diverse altars, he says: "Oh, great Sun of Justice. Blessed Christ!/Oh great God Pan to whom I sing. How you shine your light/upon your children and keep it hidden from those strangers!"[11]

The work's language tells us that it is not directed to the indigenous population, but to a society that needed to coexist with them and for whom idolatry was a loathsome phenomenon. For those enlightened Spaniards and Creoles who were acquainted with the gods of classical antiquity, a comparison with classical mythology made coexistence much easier. The eclogue about the God Pan establishes a dialectical bridge between two very ideologically distant societies—the indigenous and the European—initiating a process that made coexistence, if not complete integration, possible. Of course, we are talking about an urban mentality, for in the countryside around the same date, eradication of idolatry proceeded in a drastic fashion. For their part, the indigenous people expressed themselves, not in the pedantic language of their conquerors, but in Quechua. They did so both in religious dramas and in those that exalted their ancient glories. One might say that Quechua was for the native people of the Andean region a language used to express resistance to the values of the conquerors.

Toward the end of the eighteenth century, Indian ideology is expressed along political lines in a concrete frontal attack in the uprising of 1781. As had been the case in the mid-sixteenth century, we again find traces of two different positions of the Amerindians toward the Spaniards: an accommodating, Herod-like one, and a contesting will. The actions based on the former were to ensure the survival of Spanish domination in Peru for a few more decades. That domination would end with the independence attained by Creoles, aided by *mestizos* and by part of the indigenous population.

The Festival

In order to understand colonial society it is necessary to understand the significance of the festival, that is, the series of performances that normally took place during the course of a week. Occasions for festivals were a particular saint's day, the ascension of a new king to the throne, a celebration in honor of the viceroys, and other similar activities. The festival par excellence was that of Corpus Christi. During these festivals there were morning processions and parades as well as nocturnal parades, called *mascaradas* (masquerades) in which different groups entered dressed as Incas, Ethiopians, mythological characters, Spanish kings, and the like. Festivals also comprised formal theatrical performances that were given in coliseums and playhouses when the subject matter of the play was secular and in church atriums or plazas when the themes were religious. The same custom applied for plays in the indigenous language. Finally, festivals incorporated bull fights, stick and hoop games, and fireworks. Out of this ensemble, of special interest are the masquerades and street performances, which are linked to the great mass of indigenous people, and popular religious festivals.

Theater in the form of sacred drama, loa, or eclogue was an integral part of these festivals. In the masquerades loas were recited, and during the processions sacred dramas and mystery plays were performed. The literary component was embellished with dances, masks, triumphal arches, chariots, and street altars, before which people usually danced and recited dialogue.

The above-mentioned eclogue of Diego Mejía de Fernangil, "*El Dios Pan*," alludes to the showiness of the festival, whose wonder produces the following conversion. Thus Damón says:

> I am astonished and filled with wonder, Melibeo,
>
> since what I see, with my own eyes
>
> seems to me passing fancy or illusion;
>
> windows, balconies, and terraces
>
> are glorified with displays
>
> of rare excellence, for darkness
>
> there are candles, there are carpets,
>
> there are tapestries from Cairo and
>
> taffeta from Granada;
>
> ... then the gold,
>
> pearls, silver, and treasure that I behold
>
> showered and bestowed upon the spacious plaza,
>
> dazzle, disturb, and baffle me ...
>
> (Vargas Ugarte 52-53)[12]

Arzáns de Orsúa y Vela relates so many "masquerades" that it would take too long to record; however, worthy of mention is one presented in honor of the Archbishop Diego Rubio Morcillo de Auñón when he passed through Potosí on his way to Lima upon being named viceroy. During the evening masquerade (Arzáns 3: 50), all in verse and dialogue written by the Augustinian Juan de la Torre, there was a chariot with a young man playing the part of an "Indian princess" singing praises to His Most Illustrious One, followed by the entry of two small boys representing Europe and America. The chronicler Arzáns says: "in the middle of the loa that was being sung a small Indian boy, in the fashion of those who work the mines, emerged from the mouth of the cave in Potosí." When the coach set off at the end of the performance, those playing other roles, like "the Sun, the Moon and the Planets, all on horseback and richly adorned," followed and "finally one of the Incas or the King of Peru departed with his princesses by way of some scaffolding."[13]

The indigenous component of the festivals was so pronounced and so integral to the form that it was to survive in contemporary festivities such as the "Gran Poder de la Paz" ("Grand Power of La Paz"; see Albo and Preiswerk) and the Carnival of Oruro (see Gisbert, "La máscara").

Few societies have so efficiently used audio-visual means to disseminate ideas and to create an almost permanent evasion. The festival allows the individual momentarily to forget the penuries of the hard and inequitable life that is typical of an intensely stratified society.

Sacred Drama and Painting

A few years ago, in the church of Santa Barbara in the town of Ilabe (near Puno, Peru) José de Mesa and I found an anonymous painting, dated 1680, which portrayed the "Epiphany" or "The Adoration of the Magi" (see *Historia de la pintura cuzqueña*). This work, which was probably by an indigenous painter, depicts an Inca as one of the three Wise Men, thus introducing an indigenous element as a modifier of a Christian composition. The painter seems to have been acquainted with the Indian leaders' garments, for the Wise Man in the painting wears clothing similar to that worn by the Indian leaders of Inca ancestry who are shown as having taken part in the famous "Procession of Cuzco" around 1680.[14]

This canvas has an antecedent in another painting dealing with the theme of the "Epiphany" found in the town of Juli. This painting is the work of the Flemish Jesuit Diego de la Puente (1586-1663)—who was active in Peru from 1620 until his death—and portrays an Inca in very inappropriate apparel. Recently, a third painting with the same characteristics has been found in Arequipa. These paintings are related to Guaman Poma de Ayala's *Nueva corónica y buen gobierno*, which tells us that "in the time of Sinchi Roca Inca, the infant Jesus was born to the ever Blessed Virgin in Bethlehem, where he was adored by the three kings of the three

*Figure 1. Anonymous canvas dated 1680 found in a church in Ilabe
(Province of Puno, Peru). Representation of the Epiphany in which one
of the Wise Men is an Inca. Photo by Teresa Gisbert.*

nations that God put on earth: the Indian Melchor, the Spaniard Baltasar, and the African Gaspar...." (Guaman Poma de Ayala 1: 72).[15] It is clear that Guaman Poma's three kings are identified with the three nations of his world—Spaniards, Blacks, and Indians, thus breaking with the traditional model that spoke of three continents—Europe, Asia, and Africa.

In 1988 Margot Beyersdorff published *La adoración de los Reyes Magos* (*The Adoration of the Magi*), a drama based on a colonial tradition, which is still performed today in the San Blas district of Cuzco on January 6. The work, which is based on a text by Father Palomino, takes into account the existence of another altered and very short drama that was performed in Cacha, a town relatively close to Cuzco on the road to Collasuyo. Traditionally, it is believed that this dramatization was brought from Potosí by the *mita* workers (Beyersdorff 24). It is known that these performances were common in Potosí, a fact alluded to by El Inca Garcilaso de la Vega, who writes that a *Diálogo de la Fe* (*Dialogue of Faith*) was represented there with more than 12,000 Indians in attendance (2: 83). In both *The Adoration of the Magi* and in the *Dialogue of the Faith*, one of the kings is indigenous, and in the text from Cuzco only the Indian King (in this case Gaspar) speaks in Quechua, thereby affirming his ethnic origin.

There is an evident parallel between theater and the plastic arts, in the sense that integration is shown. One must keep in mind that for Christians, Jesus's accessibility to the Wise Men, who come from the three parts of the ancient world, means that his message is not only directed to the Jewish population to which Christ belonged, but to all of humanity. For the American world, however, that humanity is not represented by the three continents, but by the three constituent races within human society. This dramatization, which takes place in Cuzco, includes a street cavalcade accompanied by songs in which Herod stations himself on a balcony (which carried his name before being demolished). In Cacha the performance ends with a race by the Three Kings, which predicts whether the coming year will be good or bad.

Theater, Dances, and Processions in Honor of the Virgin

Related to this type of festival, there is a work dedicated to the Virgin of Guadalupe written in Potosí in 1600 by a Hieronymite monk called Diego de Ocaña, who came to America to promote devotion to the Virgin's image. Diego de Ocaña was also an artist who painted the Virgin of Guadalupe everywhere he went: Lima, Potosí, and Chuquisaca. He had been the illuminator of choir manuscripts in the Convent of Guadalupe in Cáceres, Spain, and consequently his pictorial work demonstrates great archaism (Mesa and Gisbert, *Holguin* 37+). His most famous image is the one found in Chuquisaca (today Sucre), a very Byzantine version mounted on a silver plate and covered with jewels.

Ocaña was a confident man of the world, as attested to by his observations regarding feminine graces in his chronicle (*Un viaje fascinante por la América Hispana del siglo XVI* (*A Fascinating Voyage through Sixteenth-Century Hispanic America*) dealing with Chile, Peru, and Bolivia. His 1601 play *Comedia de Nuestra Señora de Guadalupe y sus milagros*, (*Comedy of Our Lady of Guadalupe and Her Miracles*) does not preserve unity of time, as it spans various

Figure 2. The adoration of the Magi in the city of Cuzco.
Photo courtesy of Beyersdorff.

centuries between the initial part, which recounts the Moorish invasion of Spain and the consequent concealment of the Virgin of Guadalupe's image, and the discovery of the painting after the Reconquest. The allusion to America is brief and circumstantial. At the end the author allows a liberated captive to express himself in this manner:

> And you Imperial City
> of Potosí on this occasion
> you may with reason
> judge your fortune equal
> to that of Spain, since you also
> have the treasure which she already has;
> from whom have the hope
> that great wealth will come to you. (*Comedia* 114)[16]

Except for this allusion, there is little reference to America. Yet, in the manner of Spanish theater of the same period, there are chivalrous dialogues referring to King Rodrigo's love for Florinda, daughter of the nobleman who facilitated the Moors' entry into Spain:

> KING:
> And I have come to such an extreme
> that with your iciness I burn myself.
>
> FLORINDA:
> It's certainly a terrible case.
> But what fault has Florinda
> if her iciness burns you?
>
> KING:
> That the Heavens made you so lovely
> With eyes that make
> love itself prostrate before you. (*Comedia* 39)[17]

In this play there emerges a criticism of royal authority and the court, under the pretext of a celebration of the Virgin of Guadalupe. Such a criticism is conveyed through a buffoon named Crisanto, who speaks truths about the abuse of power that would not be admitted by Spanish courtiers. The two brief dialogues transcribed below illustrate such a revelation:

> KING:
> Am I very evil?
>
> LOCO:
> Well . . . quite a bit
> I gather it from what you do.
> Do you know what they say at court?
> that you are such a grand villain
> that there is no one who can bear you.
>
> •
>
> CRISANTO (addressing the king):
> Listen, beware:
> your star, your fate, or your destiny
> incline you to want only
> Florinda who is woman;
> King, that which she most
> intensely despises here is you;
> you adore her; for by force
> you make her like you.
> For you are king, despite myself,
> whether justly or unjustly,
> rightly or against the law,
> steering toward your pleasure you can make, Sir,
> a king who is very just to all. (*Comedia* 33)[18]

In these lines one notices the public questioning of hierarchically established values and the view that the king can distort justice to his liking. Thus this play, which is composed and represented for an audience made up of Amerindians, Creoles, and assimilated Spaniards is in a position to question the values and hierarchies of the empire. In explaining the details of the festival in honor of the Virgin of Guadalupe, Ocaña also talks about an apparently jocular procession representing Jews, despite the fact that Jews usually do not figure in masquerades and festivals. His description is as follows: "more than seventy Extremaduran men entered the church, all dressed as Jews in disguises and colored breeches, which greatly entertained the public, and they brought a Jewish bride.... Before her they sang a couple of tunes... and later the Jews danced in such a way that, when they finished, people were aching with laughter"[19] (Ocaña, *Un viaje* 330). This burlesque performance, which took place in the morning, is part of the intolerant and racial attitude of the period toward Jews and other minorities. Ocaña further relates that in the afternoon another one of his works was represented and that "the image was carried to the plaza, where there was a theater; and there a comedy, based on the same story of Our Lady and her Miracles, was presented by strolling players" (330).[20] With the comedy concluded the procession continued.

Over the next few days there took place a medieval joust, which consisted of threading a quoit with a lance from a galloping horse. The lady for whom they ran the joust was the Virgin Mary. This game was cause for the triumphal chariots to enter the plaza; Ocaña describes them as follows: "at the approach of a street they answered with a couplet of hornpipes from the triumphal chariot, pulled by four horses being flogged by a savage who ran alongside. It is worth noting that behind the savage came four ladies representing Mercy, Peace, Justice, and Truth" (*Viaje* 333),[21] followed by four evangelists on horseback and the Church's doctors of divinity. These entourages were also represented in paintings such as those of Jesús de Machaca, Guaqui, and Achocalla in the area around Lake Titicaca. These are complex and difficult paintings to understand nowadays, although their symbolism was clearly accessible to the average individual of the time, since they were repeated innumerable times at festivals. The theme of the "savage," representative of primitive people, and in this case synonymous with Native Americans, is repeated on other days.

Such is the case with "El salvaje de Tarapaya" ("The Savage of Tarapaya"), who appeared in the valley bordering the city of Potosí dressed in tree moss. (This type of character has disappeared from the Bolivian folkloric festivals but can still be seen close to Cuzco in the festival of Paucartambo, which is celebrated July 16 in honor of the Virgin of Carmen). Other "savages" came with him, supporting a huge rock inside of which was the Inca, "monarca y rey de los indios" ("monarch and king of the Indians"). They left the rock in the plaza, which was then entered by all the Indians of the Potosí provinces, dressed in their own garments and carrying the Inca insignia: a staff with feathers and on top of it an image of the Sun. Before them was placed a lady on horseback representing Faith, who asked that the Sun be removed and that a cross be put in its place. Ocaña mentions a dialogue between these characters, which, unfortunately, he does not record. Finally, there is a struggle between the demon and the Church, a theme of great importance to which I shall return later. Today there is little left of the festival as described by Ocaña, except for the procession and the rogations sung in Quechua on September 8. Recently there has been a reinstatement of folkloric dances in the procession, following the model of the ancient masquerade.

Some of these dramatic pieces in praise of the Virgin were written in Spain so that they might be formally represented in a theater or playhouse; such seems to be the case of the *Aurora de Copacabana* (*Aurora of Copacabana*) a work by Pedro Calderón de la Barca published in Madrid in 1672. The play is written with complete accuracy so that one cannot doubt that Calderón was well informed. His source seems to have been Alonso Ramos Gavilán's *Historia del célebre santuario de Nuestra Señora de Copacabana* (*History of the Celebrated Shrine of Our Lady of Miracles of Copacabana* [1621]), or *Coronica Moralizada del orden de San Agustín en el Perú* (*Chronicle of the Order of St. Augustine in Peru* [1638]), by Augustinian chronicler Antonio de la Calancha, who later writes about the same theme. Possibly he was familiar with the books of these Augustinians through Aguirre, an influential friar of the same order who exalted the Virgin in Madrid, where he served as confessor to Viceroy

Mancera when the latter returned from Peru after finishing his tenure. Calderón had contact with people who were interested in Peru, as in the case of Mollinedo y Angulo, parish priest of the Almudena in Madrid, who later became bishop of Cuzco (from 1664 to 1699), and who gave his approval to the *Tercera parte de comedias del célebre poeta español, Don Pedro Calderón de la Barca,* in the 1687 edition (*Third Collection of Plays by the Celebrated Spanish Poet Don Pedro Calderón de la Barca*). Mollinedo praises Calderón in the following terms: "and being the author so esteemed and applauded in most nations of the world ... any approval or censorship of mine will be quite short; I can only say that I would like to be listening to him continually, because the effectiveness of his argument and his spoken language lead to great consideration" (Gisbert and Mesa 234).[22]

Prior to this work other plays had appeared that had an American theme; such was the case with the *Trilogía de los Pizarros* (*Trilogy of the Pizarros*) and *Amazonas de las Indias* (*Amazons of the Indies*) by Tirso de Molina. It is likely that Calderón's work was performed in America since the companies of roving players had works from the Spanish theater in their repertoire. Thus, around 1620, Gabriel del Río, who performed both in Lima and in Potosí, had in his company repertoire works by Lope de Vega, Tirso de Molina, and Jiménez del Enciso (Gisbert, *Esquema* 62).

The *Aurora of Copacabana* fits within Calderón's dramatic patterns despite the intervention of Indian characters such as the sculptor Tito Yupanqui, who expresses himself with the arrogance characteristic of Spanish noblemen when the Virgin he has sculpted is criticized. The Spanish gold gilder says that he must help him:

> ... Friend
> what I gather from seeing it
> is that your zeal is good
> but your skill is not.
>
> ...

The Indian responds:

... That

is none of your business. (430)[23]

Naturally, idolatry appears in the work, and a metaphor is used to balance out the Inca Sun with a new Sun. This new Sun is represented by a young man who announces that the Creator is invisible and that he was already known before the arrival of the Spaniards, thanks to a holy preacher. Calderón alludes to the legend of Tunupa, a mythical character from Collao who went about the villages preaching goodness. He was an emissary of Viracocha, the creator god and previous Sun. The youth who announces this, just like Segismundo of *La vida es sueño* (*Life Is a Dream*), hides in the bowels of a cliff until the day that he announces the Good News rising as the new Sun. This character is both necessary and ambiguous in the context of the play.

The rocky height situated in Lake Titicaca was, according to indigenous myths, the birthplace of the Sun, and from it emerged Manco Capac, the first Inca and supposedly the son of the Sun God. Calderón describes the sacred precipice as follows:

> there rests that lofty cliff
> that was for a time
> the temple of the Sun, its peak being
> where the diabolic drive
> made believe that the Sun God
> could give over his son, so that
> he might command, govern, and rule them. (222)[24]

Opposite the island was the idol of Copacabana, god of the lake, with a human face and the body of a fish. Calderón alludes to him in the following terms:

> They called the superior idol
> Faubro, which means
> holy month; and while heaven

does not reveal to us the enigma,
it is useless that we now
reflect upon its etymology. (222)[25]

Faubro refers to February, a month replete with rains and water, as the month dedicated to the Virgin of Copacabana, whose feast day is February 2 and who is the one who defeats the lacustrine idol. Apparently the work was commissioned by the clerics who came from Peru, like Aguirre. It was difficult to translate to baroque verse a myth so complex as that of Copacabana, Viracocha, and the Sun, which even today is not fully explained. Except for the part that refers to the statue of the Virgin and the brief scenes about the Conquest, the play was barely accessible to either a Spanish or an American audience. What is important is that a playwright of Calderón's fame has broached the subject.

There was so much interest in the theme in question that another play dedicated to the Virgin of Copacabana was written in America, this time from the perspective of Cuzco. Originally written in Quechua, it is entitled *Usca Páucar* (see Cid and Martí) and takes place in Cuzco and Copacabana. The protagonist is a poor man, practically a beggar, who sells his soul to the devil in exchange for wealth and love. The devil attempts to collect his dues, and the Virgin of Copacabana rescues the protagonist.

The indigenous elements are very few. We can mention Choque Apu, the father of Cori Ttica, who is loved by Usca Páucar. Apu means "Lord of the highest rank." The name Choque Apu is common in the region surrounding Lake Titicaca. Given the transcendence and durability of both the dialogues and dances of demons in the indigenous festivals, the appearance of a drove of demons headed by Lucifer, who figures under the name of Yunca, is significant. In Aymara *Nina* means fire and *Yunca* means man of the underworld.

The work *El pobre más rico* (*The Richest Poor Man*) by Gabriel Centeno de Osma, priest of the Bethlehem parish in Cuzco, was written in Quechua and is similar to *Usca Páucar* (Cid and Martí). Here again the protagonist relinquishes his soul to the devil, in this case named Nina Quiru (Quiruas are also men of the underworld). In this work there is a somewhat prolonged intervention by an angel who argues with the devil, while in "Usca Páucar" the angel only announces Mary's goodness. Both works, written in Quechua, attest to the popularity of this theater in Cuzco, a theater that attracted even the famous Juan Espinoza Medrano (see Sánchez 3: 114+).

These two works, in honor of the Virgin, must also have been part of street performances, accompanied by procession and dance. Regrettably, today only the written testimony of the two Quechua dramas remains. Another dramatic piece of the same type, of which we have only written allusions, is a play composed in the Aymara language by a Jesuit so that it might be performed in the village of Juli, a town situated on the shore of Lake Titicaca (Gisbert, *Esquema* 37). Its theme was based on Genesis 3:15: "I will put enmities between you and the woman and she herself will shatter your head." As indicated by the Virgin's struggle with the serpent, we deduce that the theme of this text is that of the Virgin of Copacabana, who vanquishes the regional idol: the fish-serpent with the human head.

Angels and Demons

Without a doubt, one of the most influential sacred themes is the struggle between St. Michael and the Demons, which has given rise to the famous "Diablada" ("Dance of Demons") performed in Oruro today. The dance, which originally accompanied a previous theatrical performance, has by now almost disappeared. Two versions remain: the "Relato" by Goitia, collected by Julia Elena Fortún (9-11), and a dialogue recovered by Ulises Pelaez, who later published a modern adaptation (Pelaez). These two pieces have old precedents. One of the oldest dates from 1601, and in it the devil appears during the festivals that took place in Potosí in honor of the Virgin of Guadalupe (Ocaña, *Un viaje fascinante* 337+). Lucifer enters on horseback with a letter that is read publicly indicating that Proserpine, the goddess of the Underworld who looks like a siren, is the most beautiful of the goddesses. The missive carried by the devil says the following:

To the obscure dungeon of these infernal caverns (where I
have my royal throne of torment, with the nobility of the
angelic nature that with me descended in the middle of
Lake Styx, ablaze with spirited flames of sulphur...) news
arrived which obliges me to leave this fiery inferno: and it
is that a gentleman on horseback, who claims to represent
the Church, is in the plaza in order to joust on behalf of
Mary.... can a prince such as myself defend Proserpine on
this occasion? For only she is worthy of vassalage because
of her beauty and splendor. (337)[26]

The challenge is accepted in a letter from a panel of judges that
reads:

We received your letter, Prince of Darkness, in which
we have seen your old pride and how you...and those
of your kingdom are constructors of lies. They lied to
you...(because) the competition is not for or against Mary,
but rather in her honor and glory and for greater rejoicing
during her festival.... And so we give you permission to
enter the plaza. (338)[27]

At the end of duel, the judges render their verdict in the following communication: "In the Imperial City of Potosí, of the
kingdoms of Peru, on the thirtieth day of September in the year
1601, we find according to the statutes of the competition that we
must and do declare the Tartarean Prince to be prisoner of the Most
Serene Queen of the Angels, Our Lady the Holy Virgin Mary, who
is represented in the image of Guadalupe."[28] These texts give us
an idea of the nature of these "dialogues" that were part of processions that were accompanied by chariots, fireworks, masquerades,
and dances.

Before the competition begins, a meal is served to the atten-
dants and then, after artillery fire and sulphur rockets are exploded, "many demons enter the plaza on swift horses, all with
black clothes and blazing fire.... Then comes out... a triumphal
chariot, drawn by four serpents, which were being flogged by a
devil, and above the seat where the demon was seated there was
an image of hell.... On top of the chariot, at its four corners, were
four statues of four famous heretics who wrote against he virgin-
ity of Our Lady.... on the right side was seated Proserpine, with a

face and hands that were lovely and fair; her hair was black... and from the waist down she had the shape of a serpent and with her tail she surrounded the chariot" (*Viaje* 338-340).[29]

This image of the infernal goddess was indebted to Greco-Roman mythology, and is later transformed—as in the case of Calderón's *El valle de la zarzuela* (*The Valley of Zarzuela* [Gisbert and Mesa 236]) into the figure of "guilt." Like Proserpine, the infernal goddess will be identified with the mermaid. Thus in the baroque the mermaid is equal to: woman-fish, woman-serpent, goddess of the underworld (Proserpina), and guilt (sin).

The Andean painting common in Bolivia between 1680 and 1730 portrays many triumphal chariots where the figure of the mermaid-serpent surrounds with her tail the lower part of the chariot. Well known are the examples of the Jesús de Machaca, which was painted by Juan Ramos, and those of the Church of Guaqui attributed to the same painter (Mesa and Gisbert, *Holguin* 86+).

Let us recall that in his description of the festival of Guadalupe the chronicler Ocaña tells that when the devil hears the name of Jesus Christ, he falls down and that "the other devils fled mounted on their horses... and the triumphal chariot began to fire so many rockets and to cast so much fire that... everything was engulfed by fire and in such a way that within a quarter of an hour the firing of rocketry did not cease for even a moment... which seemed that all of hell was in the plaza.... Once the fire was extinguished, there remained all the workings of the shattered chariot converted into ashes" (*Viaje* 342-343).[30] Finally a chain was thrown about the neck of the "Tartarean Prince," he was lifted up to the altar where the Virgin was, and he was tied at her feet.

The Presence of the Past

One might ask oneself: What remains of all this? The closest resemblance may be seen in the present-day festival in honor of the Virgin of Carmen, which is celebrated in the town of Paucartambo located on the edge of the jungle near Cuzco. In this festival I was able to see a battle in which devils participate but are somewhat subjected to the Virgin. Although a small bibliographic reference to this festival exists (Villasante 197+), in order to capture the whole of its complexity and splendor, one must witness the festivities. Many dance ensembles perform in Paucartambo; I will limit my comments to the aforementioned battle.

Paucartambo is a village that, from an urban point of view, goes back to the eighteenth century. One approaches it along a stone bridge that carries the name of King Charles III. The church, in unusual fashion, does not rise up above the plaza but rather points to the end of the main street, which begins from one of the two existing plazas. The houses have two levels, the higher of which is approached not from the patio but by way of an exterior staircase from the street itself. The day of the festival the balconies are occupied in such a way that the town becomes a great theater whose backdrop is the church. Some events take place in the plazas, but all the theater ensembles end at the doorway of the church, where they offer their praises and present their best dances.

Of the many groups that gather, three are of special interest to us: the *Collas*, the *Chunchos*, and the *Saqras*, or Demons. The *Collas* come from the shores of Lake Titicaca and, according to tradition, were the ones who carried the image of the Virgin to Paucartambo. They represent the Aymara villages from the south, which formed the Collasuyo in the Incan empire. They have a mayor, a young woman ("imilla"), and the dancers come in two groups with their respective captains who represent Anan and Urin. They carry cloth caps and masks woven from alpaca wool, which cover their faces (Gisbert, "La mascara"). The group brings a llama weighed down with goods gathered from the land. The *Collas* install themselves in one of the plazas, where they receive new members with an initiation ceremony of feigned lashes.

The traditional enemies of the *Collas* arrive a little later. They are the *Chunchos*, who come from the jungle that went under the name Antisuyo and was part of the Inca empire. Entering on horseback, they wear feather headdresses and carry parrots in their hands; accompanying them are *kusillos*, or "monkeys," who almost always officiate as buffoons. The *Chunchos* establish themselves separate from the *Collas* with whom they enter into fruitless dialogues, which produce a battle. The *Chunchos* slay all the *Collas*, one by one, leaving their remains scattered on the ground. At this moment the

Figure 3. The Collas *in the festival of Paucartambo.*
Photo by Teresa Gisbert.

Saqras appear with flaming chariots they supposedly use to carry the dead *Collas* down to the Underworld.

We are without doubt witnessing a performance that today relies mainly on mime and that recalls the traditional battle between the people of the jungle and those of the highlands. These conflicts precede the conquest of the Incas and even after that conquest the Christianized *Collas* were to retain the fear of an incursion by the *Chunchos* of the jungle. The appearance of the demons gives a Christian touch to the ancestral battle.

There are eight *Saqras*, or devils, who also have their dance; there is a leader who is equated with Lucifer and seven demons who represent the seven deadly sins. Although the recorded dialogue of this group has been lost in the Paucartambo representations, it is still conserved in Bolivia. In any case, the masks remain in order to identify the demons. Thus Gluttony wears the mask of a boar; Pride that of a rooster; Envy that of a dog; and Lust— as happens in Oruro (Bolivia)—is a feminine devil. The costumes, which are similar to those of the *seises* (children who sing at reli-

Figure 4. The Saqras, *or demons, dancing at the entrance of the Church of Paucartambo. In the foreground there is the guide who is wearing the mask of a pig. Photo by Teresa Gisbert.*

gious festivities), can still be seen in the Corpus Christi procession in Toledo (Spain). The conservation of the customs representing the seven deadly sins indicate that we are dealing with one of the most ancient devil dances ("Diablada").

Paucartambo is the only place where demons still carry chariots of fire as occurs, along with the recorded variants, in the performances that took place in Potosí in 1601. Likewise, the demons, who are present in the procession of the Virgin of Carmen, are wounded or killed during the celebration. This occurs on the following day when the demons take possession of the rooftops of houses, indulging in countless dangerous pirouettes until the arrival of the Virgin, who, passing down the street, wounds them with her presence, causing them to shrink in fear, to cover their faces, and to fall from balconies and rooftops until they vanish completely. It is an episode of "mime" that provides a special effect to the procession, above all due to the element of danger arising from a spectacle that is produced from rooftops.

Figure 5. The procession of the Virgin of Carmen in Paucartambo. The Saqras *are on the roof while the public is accommodated on the balconies. Photo by Teresa Gisbert.*

Another remnant of this tradition is the "Diablada" of Oruro, which today is a spectacular dance performed at the carnival "Entrance" in different types of masquerades, the same ones customarily seen in the previously mentioned festival of "Gran Poder" ("Great Power") in La Paz, Bolivia. The "Diablada" of Oruro is presented on the Sunday of the Holy Trinity, before a painted image representing a God with three faces, two of which have been erased.[31]

The groups of devils in Oruro and La Paz, like those in Puno, are dressed in Roman attire, with breastplate and metallic overskirt. The major demons also wear capes. The metal utilized was silver or silver-zinc alloy (today silver thread is embroidered over pasteboard and fabric). It is the same vestment worn by St. Michael the archangel in colonial paintings. The mask has evolved from a simple devil mask covered with snakes and toads to the present-day mask that resembles those of the Far East. In some of the old surviving representations, devils have three faces, in apparent parody of the Trinity.

What today remains only in the form of dance was in past years fundamentally a sacred drama. What has been conserved is available in two versions, one recorded by J. E. Fortún in 1953 from the dancer Zenón Goitia, who still remembered a short text named "The Story," which had two principal demons—Lucifer and Satan—along with the Angel and a chorus of devils. The second text, which was recorded by a writer from Oruro named Ulises Pelaez (Fortún 12+), seems to have a first act that comes from the same original recalled by Goitia.

Goitia's text:

> LUCIFER: "I, Lucifer, elegant prince of these rebellious angels, am the powerful star of the heavens, who has enraged the Supreme Being with my pride. Today I suffer my arrogance. . . . I am mounting up world upon world, because for me the world is nothing, and the entire world is my abode. Don't you know that with my golden fangs I devour the maggots of the earth that penetrate the wealthy mines of gold and silver." (qtd. in Fortún 9)[32]

Pelaez's text:

> LUCIFER: "I, Lucifer, elegant prince of the rebellious angels, who in the heavens wanted to shine as a luminous star; that with my pride I enraged the Supreme Maker, I suffer my arrogance. . . . I come tempting, through the centuries, healthy and dying men! Inciting evil is my duty! I am an entity superior to all, since time and the universe are nothing to me!" (qtd. in Fortún 12-13)[33]

The dialogues are similar except for Goitia's allusion to the mines. The first act, in which each character is identified, transpires among Lucifer, Satan, St. Michael, and the choir of demons. The dual characterization of Lucifer and Satan is somewhat strange, although one officiates as king and the other (Satan) as captain of the militia of demons. In the second act, which is registered only in the Pelaez version, the battle begins. The choir of angels (which has disappeared from today's dance) says, referring to Lucifer: "Tie him to a rock in the depths of Hell." At that moment

Figure 6. Luzbel (the Devil) of the "Diablada" dance in Oruro.
Photo by Teresa Gisbert.

Figure 7. The Archangel St. Michael in a seventeenth-century canvas, found in the Convento de la Concepción of Lima, Peru. Photo by Teresa Gisbert.

Figure 8. The Archangel St. Michael, without a mask, in the festivities of "Gran Poder" in La Paz, Bolivia. Photo by Teresa Gisbert.

St. Michael intervenes with a greater punishment, saying: "Oh, Holy Seraphim, leave them be! Both Lucifer and Satan, along with their entire entourage of demons, will be judged before the temple of the Virgin of Socavón, patron saint of the miners of Oruro" (qtd. in Fortún 15).[34] In the third act, which takes place on the doorsteps of the church, the Angel calls each demon by name: Pride, Avarice, etc., covering the seven deadly sins. In their turn, each of the sins describes his own characteristics in the following manner:

> LUST: "Here is Lust. Arr Arrr [grunts]. Lust consists of a filthy appetite of carnal desires, respects neither chastity nor purity; encompasses the desire to possess innocence and vice.... Oh wretched me, I experience great torment with my unsatisfied desire. Let me go to the depths where crime and iniquity dwell... Now let me go... Arr Arrr."
>
> ANGEL: "Christians. Against Lust?"
>
> THE PEOPLE: "Chastity." (qtd. in Fortún 18)[35]

Pelaez has undoubtedly altered Goitia's text from the beginning of the century, although not significantly. However, the work as we know it today is but a pale reflection of the sacred baroque comedy from which it came. Pelaez also went on to create a new version for the theater, introducing a miner and a lusty maidservant (China Supay), who is the only personalized demon remaining in today's dance, with the exception of Lucifer and Satan.

Amerindian History and Theater:
The Tragedy of Atahuallpa

The permanence of Amerindian culture can be seen in various artistic constructions that over the centuries have defied obliteration and loss of memory. Much has been written about the *Tragedia del fin de Atahuallpa*, which was edited by Jesús Lara[36] and which is performed in Oruro on Sunday morning during Carnival time (Wachtel; Gisbert, *Esquema* 40+). It is usually part of the "Dance" of the Incas and, despite its attractiveness, it is rarely performed.

The tradition to which this work belongs is worth reviewing. In his *Comentarios reales*, Garcilaso de la Vega writes:

Figure 9. Scene from the reenactment of the "Death of Atahuallpa,"
which takes place in Oruro the Sunday before Lent.
In the foreground is Pizarro. Photo by Teresa Gisbert.

Figure 10. Scene from the "Death of Atahuallpa"
showing the Inca's court. Photo by Teresa Gisbert.

The Amautas, who were philosophers, did not lack ability to compose comedies and tragedies, which on solemn feast days were performed before their kings and the nobility who attended court. The performers were not commoners but were Incas and of noble rank... so that the *autos* [sacramental features] of the tragedies would be properly performed; their plots always dealt with military matters, with triumphs and victories, with the exploits and grandeur of kings.... Also in the account of Blas Valera it is read that "the days of the triumphs which they call *hailli*... there were great dances, great performances of battles, comedies, tragedies and other similar events...." (2: 79)[37]

Of course those performances differed greatly from those of the Spanish and colonial theaters, as they drew upon their pre-Hispanic tradition by using masks and by adapting the dialogue of native languages. Even in our days the *Tragedia del fin de Atahuallpa* retains some characters, such as the king of Spain and Columbus, who wear masks while the text is recited in Quechua.

In addition to the aforementioned testimony of Garcilaso and Blas Valera, there is also the account of the historian Arzáns, who tells that in the feasts honoring Santiago and the Virgin, in 1554, eight comedies were produced, the first four of which were famous and very well received. He describes those comedies as follows:

One dealt with the origin of the Incan monarchs of Peru, in which was represented in a very life-like fashion the way and manner with which the aristocrats and the learned people of Cuzco introduced the very distinguished Manco Capac,... the ten provinces that he secured and colonized with arms.... The second dealt with the triumphs of Huayna Capac, eleventh Inca of Peru, which he attained at the expense of the three nations: from the Changas, the Highlanders, and the Lord of the Coyas... a battle which took place face to face in the fields of Hatuncolla.... The third tragedy was about Cusi Huascar, twelfth Inca of Peru,... the uprising of his brother Atahuallpa,... the imprisonment and disgraceful treatment to which they subjected the unfortunate Cusi Huascar; the tyrannies that the usurper [Atahuallpa] registered in Cuzco.... The fourth dealt with the collapse of the Inca empire; the Spaniards' entry into Peru was represented; the unjust imprisonment of Atahuallpa, ... the tyrannies and the indignities imposed by Spaniards upon the Indians, ... and the death they gave [to Atahuallpa] in Cajamarca. (1: 98)

Arzáns comments: "These comedies were very special and famous, not only due to the expense of their special effects, or the propriety of their costumes and the novelty of their tales, but also for the elegance of their mixed verse, which combined the Castilian with the Indian language" (Arzáns 1: 98).[38] Without a doubt this tetralogy is aimed at a public composed largely of *mita* workers living in Potosí. Thus, Manco Capac is exalted; the principal events of Inca history are distilled in the figure Huayna Capac, whose memory was still alive among the indigenous people; and Atahuallpa is shown as a usurper and as murderer of his brother in order to emphasize his flaw and the tragic consequences of his actions.

One wonders how works that were so politically dangerous could survive until the end of the colonial period. Yet such was the case. According to Arzáns's testimony, the four comedies were again staged in 1590 on the occasion of the inauguration of the church of the Society of Jesus. The plays are again mentioned in 1641 in the following terms:

four comedies were performed, the last of them, a new work by our poet-historian Juan Sobrino, was entitled *Prosperidad y ruina de los Ingas del Peru* [*The Rise and Fall of the Incas of Peru*]. In it their origin in Cuzco was represented and how from there those powerful monarchs went on to take possession of most of these extensive kingdoms. ... There was also represented the entry into and discovery of Peru by the Marquis Don Francisco Pizarro along with the motive for the civil wars. ... Also represented was the great wealth of the Inca Kings; the tragic death of Huascar Inca and of the illegitimate Atahuallpa; and lastly the complete destruction of those monarchs ... the arrival of the Viceroy Francisco de Toledo. (Arzáns 2: 86)

The play also recalls in detail the events of the death of the last Inca, Tupac Amaru, whose decapitation was ordered by the viceroy Francisco de Toledo. The chronicler adds: "This comedy was much applauded, as much for its novelty as for the reliable and previously unheard of events that were depicted in it. For the Indians it was an emotional event and they screamed with satisfaction (Arzáns 2: 86).[39]

This tale allows us to see that these four early comedies had been altered over the course of a century, incorporating the Incas of Vilcabamba. Apparently three of the works were traditional, while Juan Sobrino had glossed the fourth one. Of the four comedies presented in 1554 only the fourth, whose theme was the death of Atahuallpa, survives. This work survived in the rural areas and was preserved for us in a Quechua transcription. Arzáns notes that this work was performed in Potosí in the sixteenth century in Spanish and Quechua, but Jesús Lara makes available a text in which Spaniards are silenced and their mute speeches are "translated" by Felipillo. This indicates that we go from a bilingual audience to a purely indigenous and rural one.

Lara finds four manuscripts: those of St. Peter of Buenavista, St. Lucia, Challanta, and Toco. In the first two texts, which seem to derive from a common original, the characters express themselves in Castilian and Quechua,[40] while the texts of Chayanta and Toco are in Quechua only. Lara considers the Chayanta manuscript, dated 1871, to be authentic, and he assumes that Chayanta's work is that described by Arzáns. I believe that it is a transcription from the end of the eighteenth century with evident alterations and that it is tied to the great indigenous rebellion of 1781.

The Chayanta manuscript contains certain anachronisms that allow one to infer the period from which it belongs. This may be gathered from descriptions such as that in which the Indians describe the Spaniards:

> they wear three-pointed horns
> just like the *tarukas*
> and their hair
> is sprinkled with white flour,
> and on their mandibles they boast
> blazing red beards. (qtd. in Lara 87)[41]

The description corresponds to the three-cornered hat and powdered wig characteristic of eighteenth-century masculine attire and not of the period of the Conquest. In the St. Lucia text, Atahuallpa proves to be the brother of Tupac Amaru and Tupac Catari, leaders of the 1781 rebellion, which indicates that these works were used as political propaganda. In the Chayanta manuscript, Spain not only reproaches Pizarro, but the latter dies instantaneously and his remains are burned by Almagro. This allusion is further evidence that the play belongs to the eighteenth century, for we know that sixteenth-century Spaniards were not given to incinerating the bodies of the deceased.

> ALMAGRO:
> My sole lord and master
> is now certainly dead.
>
> SPAIN:
> Carry him away if this is so
> go and deliver him unto the flames
> ...
> Of this infamous warrior
> nothing shall remain
> this is all that I ordain. (qtd. in Lara 147)[42]

This work is invaluable, and it is the first of its kind to be found in Bolivia. It is a testimonial piece that differs from Spanish plays in view of the active role that the chorus plays in it. The lines that follow demonstrate the active role of the chorus, which expresses the indigenous admiration for writing:

> WAYLLA WISA:
> Who knows what this tender ear
>   of corn [*chala*] will say.
> It is possible that
> I will never come to know it.
> Seen from this side
> it is a swarm of ants.
> Viewed from this other angle

they seem to me like the footprints
left by the birds
on the muddy shores of the river....

Who could possibly understand this.
No, no it is impossible for me
to grasp it my Lord. (qtd. in Lara 79)[43]

The Chayanta drama, already very well known, can be summarized as follows: Atahuallpa tells the *ñustas* (princesses) a dream that has disturbed him. The Sun God covered himself with black smoke, and a divine spirit (*huaca*) announced to him the arrival of warriors dressed in iron. The princess Cora Chimpu suggests that he ask the priest to interpret his dream. Atahuallpa orders the soothsayer Waylla Wisa to sleep in the room of gold so that he might interpret the dream. In the meanwhile, he invokes the Sun God and Viracocha. Awakening, the soothsayer confirms the arrival of the bearded men.

In the second part there is a meeting between Almagro and Waylla Wisa. The latter asks why the red-bearded men invade. In answering, Almagro moves his lips, and the translator, Felipillo, says that they have been invaded by the most powerful Lord of the earth. Here Bishop Vicente de Valverde intervenes, indicating that they come to teach about the true God. He proceeds to hand over to the soothsayer a letter intended for the Inca; it is a letter that they cannot read and that they describe as an "ear of maize" (*chala*).

The Inca of Vilcabamba, Sairi Tupac, and the generals of Atahuallpa, Chalcochima and Quizquiz, intervene in the drama. There is an absurd dialogue between Sairi Tupac (who officiates as emissary) and Pizarro. Finally, in the third act, Pizarro bursts into Atahuallpa's palace and with the movement of his lips translated by Felipillo he orders the Inca to follow him to Barcelona. Atahuallpa surrenders, and the chorus begins its lamentations. While his son Inca Churin requests to die with Atahuallpa, the latter takes leave of his people and curses Pizarro. His fate is cast. Valverde tries to convince him to obey but the Inca does not understand. Pizarro then proceeds to thrust his sword into Atahuallpa. As a corollary of the events, the king of Spain appears on the scene to eulogize the Inca and to condemn Pizarro. It is also worth noticing that in the Oruro performance Columbus is usually included in the cast of characters.

It is well known that Atahuallpa was garotted to death, so that his fate in this play, in which he lies dead by Pizarro's sword, shows alterations characteristic of the popular tradition. There are also paintings that show him decapitated. Thus, the cause of death is changed in both cases. This transformation may be related to the myth of Inkarri in which the Inca loses his head. The reunification of the head and the body signifies both the resurrection of the Inca and the reconstitution of the empire. In both the painting and the drama there is a longing for the return of the Inca empire and a desire that the invader be punished. On the other hand, there are deliberate chronological displacements such as the introduction of Sairi Tupac as a messenger for Atahuallpa, a juxtaposition that is explained by the friendship of Sairi Tupac with the Spaniards. This play embodies the ideology of the vanquished that today is kept alive not so much in the drama itself as in the dance of the Incas, which represents the triumph of resistance in the history of the Amerindian.

Corollary

Art is an instrument of transformation in that it converts history into myth and symbol. By means of artistic expression—be it in architecture, painting, or drama—the remnants of pre-Columbian culture are preserved; Amerindian desires are expressed; symbols, which are not part of the reality of daily life, are crafted; and historical events are modified through myth. Atahuallpa did not die by the sword, nor were the Incas present alongside the Wise Men at the birth of Christ, nor did demons intervene in the battle between the *Chunchos* and the *Collas*. Yet there is something of history, one's own and someone else's, which operating through syncretism allows for the survival of ancient cultures through artistic expression. Thus the pre-Columbian world survives in the twentieth century just as it managed to survive during the difficult days of the conquest and colonization.

Notes

1. In the declaration surrounding the ascendance of Colque Guarache in the year 1575, Humiro, the cacique of Moromoro (to the north of Potosí), says: "To the sixth question this witness [Humiro] says that he was the servant of Guayna Capac...and saw that one day the said Inca summoned the said Inca Colque Guarachi, and as a sign of friendship...he gave him three shirts" ("A la sexta pregunta dijo que este testigo [Humiro] era criado del dicho Guayna Capac...e vió que un dia el dicho Inga llamó ante sí al dicho Colque Guarachi Inga, y en señal de amistad...le dio tres camisetas" [Espinoza, 1981, 242]). The same relationship was maintained with Huascar, the legitimate heir.

2. The *keros* were wooden vases with incisions full of colored resins forming drawings and scenes. They were used in pairs for libations.

3. "y por cuanto dichos naturales también adoran algún género de aves e animales, y para el dicho efecto los pintan e labran en los mates que hacen para beber de palo y de plata, y en las puertas de sus casas y los tejen en los frontales, doseles de los altares, e los pintan en las paredes de las Iglesias. Ordeno y mando que los que hallareis los hagais raer y quitar de las puertas donde los tuvieren y prohibireis que tampoco los tejan en la ropa que visten, poniendo también sobre esto especial cuidado."

4. "quitarles de los ojos todo aquello que no solo manifiestamente fué ídolo adorado...y así se tiene mandado que no solo en las iglesias, sino en ninguna parte, ni pública ni secreta de los pueblos de indios...se pinte...ni animales terrestres, volátiles, ni marinos, especialmente algunos de ellos...." He adds: "y así se tiene mandado...que no se pinte el sol, la luna y las estrellas, por quitarles ocasión de volver a sus antiguos delirios y disparates."

5. "Y pienso que no conviene de ninguna manera destruir los templos que tienen sus ídolos, para que viendo esas gentes que respetan sus templos, depongan de su corazón el error, y conociendo al dios verdadero y adorandolo concurran a los lugares que les son familiares."

6. "así como el Sol derrama sus rayos en la tierra haciéndola madre, para que beneficie al hombre, así Dios deposita sus rayos en María, haciéndola también madre, para beneficiar al hombre."

7. According to Beyersdorff the altered drama came from a tradition associated with Potosí and was represented in San Pedro de Cacha. Encouraged by this, a priest named Palomino had it reinstated in Cuzco (24).

8.   "...yo estuviera

un siglo aquí, si hubiera siempre aquesto.

Pero me voy muy dispuesto, caro amigo

(el Dios pan es testigo) a bautizarme

y a este Pan entregarme por esclavo."

9. I have reordered the verse keeping the consonance, which is not respected in Vargas Ugarte's transcription. While it is evident that the manuscript has been altered, I have been faithful to the wording.

10. " ... El Pan vuestro
es un monstruo siniestro,
imaginado
es un disparatado
fingimiento
es Dios sin ser aliento,
es un fingido bulto,
que nunca ha sido,
es aparente disparate
de gente ciega y ruda
que a un tronco o piedra muda
ofrece incienso con fiesta
y con inmenso regocijo."

11. "Oh gran Sol de Justicia ¡Cristo Santo!
Oh gran Dios Pan que canto ¡Como alumbras
tus hijos y deslumbras los ajenos!"

12. "Suspenso y asombrado, o Melibeo,
estoy, pues lo que veo, con mis ojos
me parecen antojos o ilusiones;
ventanas y balcones y terrados
estan glorificados con presencias
de rara excelencias para sombras
ai velas, ai alfombras, hay cairinos
tapetes; granadinos tafetanes;
... pues el oro
perlas plata y tesoro que esparecido
columbro y repartido en la ancha plaza,
me ofusca, turba y embaraza ... "

13. "a la mitad de aquella Loa cantada salió de la bocamina de aquel Cerro [de Potosí] un indiecillo a la propiedad de cuando labran las minas ... el Sol, la Luna y los Planetas, todos en caballos con ricos aderezos," y "por último iba en unas andas uno de los Ingas o Rey del Perú con sus coyas."

14. One of the canvasses of the Corpus Christi procession shows the portrait of the adolescent King Charles II (Mesa and Gisbert [1 : 177; 2: fig. 236]).

15. "en tiempo de Sinci Roca Inca, nació Niño Jesús en Belén, parió Santa siempre Virgen a donde fue adorado de los tres reyes de tres naciones que Dios puso en el mundo; Melchor indio, Baltasar español, Gaspar negro. ... "

16. "Y tu Villa Imperial
     de Potosí con razón
     puedes en esta ocasión
     juzgar tu ventura igual
     a España, pues también tienes
     el tesoro que ella alcanza;
     de quien ten cierta esperanza
     que te vendrán grandes bienes."

17. REY:
     "Y he llegado a tanto extremo
     que con tu hielo me quemo."

     FLORINDA:
     "Por cierto caso terrible
     ¿Qué culpa tiene Florinda
     de que sus hielos te abrasen?"

     REY:
     "Hacerte el cielo tan linda
     darte esos ojos que hacen
     que el mismo amor se te rinda."

18. REY:
     "¿Soy muy malo?"

     LOCO:
     "Así ... de porte
     Por lo que haceis lo saco
     ¿Sabéis que dicen en corte?
     que sois tan grande bellaco
     que no hay quien os soporte."

     CRISANTO (dirigiéndose al Rey):
     "Escucha, advierte:
     tu estrella, tu hado o tu suerte
     te inclina solo a querer
     a Florinda que es mujer:
     tú, rey la cosa mas fuerte.
     Ella te desdeña aquí:
     tu la adoras; pues por fuerza

> haz que su gusto tuerza.
>
> Pues eres rey, pese a mí
>
> en caso justo o injusto,
>
> con razón o contra ley,
>
> enderezando a tu gusto,
>
> puede hacer, señor un rey
>
> que sea a todos muy justo."

19. "entraron en la Iglesia mas de sesenta hombres de Extremadura, con un disfraz que entretuvieron mucho al pueblo, vestidos todos de judíos, con martingalas coloradas y trajeron una novia judía. . . . Delante de la novia cantaron un par de tonadas . . . y despues bailaron los judíos de suerte que, cuando acabaron, tenían la gente los cuerpos quebradas de risa."

20. "Llevose la imagen a la plaza, donde estaba un teatro; y allí se representó una comedia de la misma historia de Ntra. Sra. y de sus milagros, la cual representaron unos faranduleros." The author adds: "Esta comedia también fue propio trabajo mío."

21. "respondieron a la boca de una calle con una copla de chirimías que vanían en un carro triunfal, el cual tiraban cuatro caballos, a los cuales venía azotando un salvaje. Es de notar que detras del salvaje venían cuatro damas representando la Misericordia, la Paz, la Justicia y la Verdad."

22. "y siendo el Autor, tan estimado y aplaudido en las mas Naciones del Mundo . . . cualquier aprobación, o censura mía quedará muy corta, solo se decir, que continuamente le quisiera estar oyendo, porque la eficacia de sus razones, y lenguaje en el hablar, cede a toda ponderación."

23.   " . . . Amigo

> lo que he sacado de verla,
>
> es que vuestro celo es bueno
>
> mas la habilidad no es buena.
>
> . . .
>
> Responde el indio:
>
> . . . Eso
>
> no corre de vuestra cuenta."

24.   "Yace aquella peña altiva

> que adoratorio del Sol
>
> fue un tiempo, por ser su cima
>
> donde diabólico impulso
>
> hizo creer que el Sol podía
>
> dar a su hijo para que
>
> los mande, gobierne y rija."

25. "Faubro al ídolo llamaron
superior; que significa
mes santo; y mientras el cielo
no nos revele el enigma,
ocioso es que discurramos
ahora su etimología."

26. "Al oscuro calabozo de estas cavernas infernales (donde tengo mi real silla de tormento, con la nobleza de la naturaleza angélica que conmigo descendió, en medio del lago Estigio, ardiendo en vivas llamas de azufre...) llegó ahora una nueva... que me obliga a dejar el fogoso averno: y es, que un caballero que se intula de la Iglesia, está en esta plaza para poder correr lanzas en competencia de María... podrá un príncipe como yo defender en esta ocasión a Proserpina: pues a ella sola se debe dar vasallaje de hermosura y belleza...."

27. "Vuestra carta recibimos, príncipe de las Tinieblas, en la cual habemos echado de ver vuestra antigua soberbia y como vos y los de vuestro reino sois autores de mentira. Os mintieron... (porque) no es en competencia de María ni contra ella, sino para honra y gloria suya, y para mas regocijo de su fiesta... Y así os damos licencia para que entreis en la plaza."

28. "En la Villa Imperial de Potosí, de los reinos del Perú, en 30 días del mes de septiembre de 1601 años, fallamos según los fueros de la sortija, que debemos declarar y declaramos al Príncipe tartáreo por prisionero de la Serenísima reina de los ángeles la Virgen María Señora Nuestra, en cuya imagen de Guadalupe es representada."

29. "muchos demonios en caballos muy ligeros, todos con ropas negras y llamas de fuego." "Salió luego... un carro triunfal, el cual tiraban cuatro sierpes, a las cuales iba un demonio azotando, y por encima de la silla donde venía sentado este demonio... venía una boca de infierno.... Encima del carro, a las cuatro esquinas, venían cuatro estatuas, de cuatro famosos herejes que escribieron contra la virginidad de nuestra Señora.... en la mano derecha venía sentada Proserpina, el rostro y manos muy blanco y hermoso, el cabello negro... y del medio cuerpo para abajo de sierpe y con la cola rodeaba el carro."

30. "los demás demonios huyeron montados en sus caballos... y el carro triunfal comenzó a disparar tantos cohetes y echaer tanto fuego de sí que... todo se convirtió en fuego y de tal manera que en un cuatro de hora no cesó en un punto de disparar cohetería... que no parecía sino que todo el infierno estaba en la plaza.... Acabado el fuego quedo toda aquella máquina del carro deshecha y convertida en ceniza."

31. There are two complete versions of this image, one in the Museo de Arte de Lima (see Gisbert, *Iconografía*, fig. 85) and another in the Museo Charcas of Sucre.

32. LUZBEL: "Yo Luzbel, elegante príncipe de estos ángeles rebeldes, en las alturas soy el astro poderoso, que por mi soberbia encolericé al Supremo, hoy padezco mi altivez... vengo amontonando mundo sobre mundo, porque el mundo para mí no es nada y todo el mundo es mi morada, no sabéis que devoro con mis colmillos de oro, a los gusanillos de la tierra que penetran en las ricas minas de oro y plata...."

33. LUZBEL: "Yo Luzbel, elegante príncipe de los ángeles rebeldes, que en las alturas quise brillar cual astro luminoso; que por mi soberbia encolericé al Supremo Hacedor, hoy padezco mi altivez. ¡Vengo tentando, a traves de los siglos, al hombre sano y moribundo!... ¡Incitar al mal es mi deber! ¡Soy ente superior a todos, ya que el tiempo y el universo no son nada para mí!"

34. "Dejad ¡oh benditos serafines! Ambos, Lucifer y Satanás, con toda su corte de demonios serán juzgados ante el templo de la Virgen del Socavón, la Patrona de los mineros de Oruro."

35. LUJURIA: "Aquí está la Lujurio. Arrr Arrr. La lujuria consiste en el apetito inmundo de los deseos carnales, no respeta castidad ni pureza; abarca el deseo de poseer la inocencia, y el vicio.... Oh desgraciado de mí tengo suficiente tormento con mi deseo no satisfecho. Dejadme ir a las profundas simas donde moran el crimen y la iniquidad... Dejadme ya... Arrr Arrr.

ANGEL: "Cristianos ¿Contra Lujuria?

PUEBLO: "Castidad.

36. See also Wachtel; Gisbert, *Esquema* 40+. There exists another version of this text written in Quechua (see Meneses Morales).

37. "No les faltaba habilidad a los Amautas, que eran los filósofos, para componer comedias y tragedias, que en días de fiestas solemnes representaban delante de sus reyes y de los señores que asistían en la corte. Los representantes no eran viles sino Incas y gente noble... porque los autos de las tragedias se representasen al propio; cuyos argumentos siempre eran de hechos militares, de triunfos y victorias, de las hazañas y grandezas de los reyes...." También en la relación de Blas Valera se lee como en "los días de los triunfos que llaman el hailli... había grandes bailes y danzas, grandes representaciones batallas, de comedias, tragedias y otras cosas semejantes...."

38. "Fue la una el origen de los monarcas Ingas del Perú, en que muy al vivo se representó el modo y manera con que los señores y sabios del Cuzco introdujeron al felicísimo manco Capac... las 10 provincias que con las armas sujetó.... La segunda fué de los triunfos de Huayna Capac, 11 Inga del Perú los cuales consiguió de las tres naciones: changas, montañeses y del señor de los Collas... batalla que se dió de poder a poder en los campos de Hatuncolla... Fué la tercera de las tragedias de Cusi huascar, 12º Inga del Perú... el levantamiento de Atahuallpa hermano suyo... prisión e indignos tratamientos que al infeliz cusi Huascar le hicieron; tiranías que el usurpador (Atahuallpa) hizo en el Cuzco... La cuarta fue la ruina del Imperio Inga: representose la entrada de los españoles al Perú; prisión injusta que hicieron de Atahuallpa... tiranías y lástimas que ejecutaron los españoles en los indios... y muerte que le dieron (a Atahuallpa) en Cajamarca." ..."Fueron estas comedias muy especiales y famosas, no solo por lo costoso de sus tramoyas, propiedad de trajes y novedad de historias, sino también por la elegancia del verso mixto del idioma castellano con el indiano."

39. "representáronse cuatro comedias, siendo la última de ellas nueva... Fué su autor nuestro poeta historador Juan Sobrino intitulándola 'Prosperidad y ruina de los Ingas del Perú': Representose en ella su origen cuando (como cuentan las historias) lo tuvieron en el Cuzco y de allí aquellos poderosos monarcas se fueron enseñoreando de la mayor descubrimiento del Perú por el Marqués Don Francisco

Pizarro y el motivo de las guerras civiles.... Representose asímismo la gran riqueza que tuvieron aquellos reyes Incas, trágica muerte de Huascar Inga y el bastardo Atahuallpa y ultimamente la ruina y acabamiento de estos monarcas... la venida del Virrey Francisco de Toledo."

"Fue muy aplaudida esta comedia tanto por lo nuevo de ella cuanto por los verdaderos e inauditos sucesos que en ella se representaron. Para los indios fue de mucho sentimiento levantando grandes alaridos conforme se declaraban."

40. Unfortunately Lara does not publish all of them. The two editions derive from the text of Chayanta.

41. "Llevan tres cuernos puntiagudos

igual que las tarukas

y tienen los cabellos

con blanca harina polvoreados,

y en las mandíbulas ostentan

barbas del todo rojas... "

42. ALMAGRO:

"Mi noble y único señor

ciertamente está muerto ya."

ESPAÑA:

"Lleváoslo si es así

id y entregadlo al fuego

...

De este guerrero infame

no debe quedar nada

esto es cuanto yo ordeno."

43. WAYLLA WISA:

"Quien sabe que dirá esta chala

es posible que nunca

llegue a saberlo yo.

Vista e este costado

es un hervidero de hormigas

la mire de este otro costado

y se me antojan las huellas que dejan

las patas de los pájaros

en las lodosas orillas del río.

...

Quien comprender esto pudiera.
No, no me es imposible
mi señor penetrarlo."

Works Cited

Acosta, José de. *Obras*. Ed. Padre Francisco Mateos. Biblioteca de Autores Españoles. Madrid: Atlas, 1954.

Albo, Xavier, and Matías Preiswerk. *Los señores del Gran Poder*. La Paz: Centro de Teología Popular, Taller de Observaciones, 1986.

Aguirre, Marta de. "Los caciques Guarache." *Estudios Bolivianos en Homenaje a Gunnar Mendoza*. La Paz, 1978.

Arzáns de Orsúa y Vela, Bartolomé. *Historia de la Villa Imperial de Potosí*. 1736. Ed. Lewis Hanke and Gunnar Mendoza. 3 vols. Providence: Brown Univ. Press, 1965.

Beyersdorff, Margot. *La adoración de los Reyes Magos: Vigencia del teatro religioso español en el Perú*. Cuzco: Centro de Estudios Rurales Andinos "Bartolomé de las Casas," 1988.

Calancha, Antonio de la. *Coronica Moralizada del orden de San Agustín en el Peru*. 1638. Ed. and transcribed Ignacio Prado Pastor. 6 vols. Lima: Universidad Nacional Mayor de San Marcos, 1974.

Calderón de la Barca, Pedro. *La Aurora de Copacabana*. *Dramas*. *Obras Completas*. Madrid: Aguilar, 1945.

———. *La vida es sueño*. Ed. José María García Martín. Madrid: Castalia, 1983.

Cid Pérez, José, and Dolores Martí de Cid, eds. *Teatro indoamericano colonial*. Madrid: Aguilar, 1973.

Espinoza, Waldemar. "El reino Quillaca azanazque, siglos XV y XVI." *Revista del Museo Nacional* 45 (1981): 175-274.

Flores Ochoa, Jorge. *El Cuzco, resistencia y continuidad*. Cuzco: Editorial Andina, 1990.

Fortún, Julia Elena. *La danza de los diablos*. La Paz: Ministerio de Educación y Bellas Artes, 1961.

Garcilaso de la Vega, El Inca. *Comentarios reales de los Incas*. Ed. César Pacheco Vélez. Lima: Ediciones del Centenario, Banco de Crédito del Perú, 1985.

Gisbert, Teresa. *Esquema de literatura virreinal*. La Paz: UMSA, 1968.

———. *Iconografía y mitos indígenas en el arte*. La Paz: Editorial Gisbert, 1980.

———. "La máscara y el Carnaval de Oruro." *Encuentro* 5 (1989): 23-30.

———. "Toynbee y la civilización Andina." *Historiografía y bibliografía americanistas* 16.3 (1972): 357-376.

Gisbert, Teresa, Silvia Arze, and Marta Cajías. *Arte textil y mundo andino*. La Paz: Editorial Gisbert, 1987.

Gisbert, Teresa, and José de Mesa. *Arquitectura andina*. La Paz: Embajada de España en Bolivia, 1985.

Guaman Poma de Ayala, Felipe. *Primer nueva coronica y buen gobierno*. 1613. Ed. John V. Murra and Rolena Adorno. 3 vols. Mexico City: Siglo XXI, 1980.

Lara, Jesús. *Tragedia del fin de Atahuallpa*. Cochabamba: Imprenta Universitaria, 1957. Rpt. Cochabamba: Amigos del libro, 1989.

Menéndez, Fray Juan. *Tesoros verdaderos de las Indias*. Raúl Porras Barrenechea. *Los cronistas del Perú (1528-1650) y otros ensayos*. Ed. Franklin Pease. Lima: Banco de Crédito del Perú, 1986. 679.

Meneses Morales, Teodoro. *La muerte de Atahuallpa*. Lima: Universidad de San Marcos, 1987.

Mesa, José de, and Teresa Gisbert. *Historia de la pintura cuzqueña*. Lima: Fundación A. N. Wiese, Banco Wiese, 1982.

———. *Holguin y la pintura altoperuana del Virreinato*. 2nd ed. La Paz: Editorial Gisbert, 1977.

Ocaña, Diego de. *Comedia de Nuestra Señora de Guadalupe y sus milagros*. 1601. La Paz: Ed. Gisbert, 1957.

———. *Un viaje fascinante por la América Hispana del siglo XVI*. Madrid: Ed. Alvarez, 1969.

Pelaez, Ulises. "La lucha entre el bien y el mal." *Arte popular en Bolivia*. La Paz: Instituto Boliviano de Cultura, 1988.

Ramos Gavilán, Alonso. *Historia del célebre santuario de Nuestra Señora de Copacabana*. Lima, 1621. La Paz, 1969.

Sánchez, Luis Alberto. *La literatura peruana*. 5 vols. Asunción, 1951.

Sarmiento de Gamboa, Pedro. *Historia Indica*. 1572. *Obras completas del Inca Garcilaso de la Vega*. Madrid: Ediciones Atlas, 1960.

Valverde, Fernando de. *El santuario de Nuestra Señora de Copacabana*. Lima, 1641.

Vargas Ugarte, Rubén. *De nuestro antiguo teatro*. Lima: C. Milla Batres, 1974.

Villasante, Segundo. *Paucartambo provincia Folklórica*. Mamacha Carmen. Cuzco: Editorial León, 1979.

Wachtel, Nathan. *Los vencidos: Los indios del Perú frente a la conquista española*. Trans. Antonio Escohotado. Madrid: Alianza, 1976.

Chapter 22

Saer's Fictional Representation of the Amerindian in the Context of Modern Historiography

Amaryll Chanady

> *Without Europeans, I feel, all our past would have been washed away, like the scuff-marks of fishermen on the beach outside our town.* (18)
>
> —V. S. Naipaul, *A Bend in the River*

The Latin American novelistic production of the past few decades has contributed to the rereading, rewriting, and demystification of history and has thus frequently challenged hegemonic interpretations. Some of the most notable examples are Alejo Carpentier's *El arpa y la sombra* (*The Harp and the Shadow*), in which the Cuban author analyzes the economic discourse characterizing Columbus's reports of the New World and questions the evangelizing motivation of the Conquest, and Gabriel García Márquez's *El general en su laberinto* (*The General in His Labyrinth*), which demythologizes the figure of Simón Bolívar. One recent novel belonging to this category of historiographic fictions, Juan José Saer's *El entenado* (*The Adopted Son, or Stepson* [1983]), recreates an episode surrounding Juan Díaz de Solís's ill-fated expedition to the Río de la Plata region in 1515, in which the pilot major and a small landing party were killed by the indigenous inhabitants. In his highly fictionalized narrative, based on very limited documented information, Saer describes the ten-year sojourn of a fifteen-year-old cabin boy among the members of the Colastiné tribe (the captivity of a white person by Amerindians has been a common motif almost since the time of the Conquest) and his problematic reinsertion in Spanish society after being "rescued" by his countrymen.

Unlike many other recent historiographic fictions, however, *El entenado* does not appear to be a subversive reinterpretation of official axiological systems and discursive practices. On the contrary, the story, related by an autodiegetic narrator (the cabin boy) who recounts his experiences several decades after his voyage to the New World, contains many familiar stereotypes about the Amerindian, presented in a seemingly nonproblematic manner. A rapid perusal of a number of colonial and later writings enables us to consider Saer's portrait of the Amerindian partially as a distilled amalgam of several specific textual sources. The description of anthropophagia and other practices corresponds to a great extent to Staden's ethnographic account; the portrayal of the tribe as lacking culture, government, and religion echoes Columbus's initial observations; and the details of the annual orgy, in which all manner of sexual encounter is practiced in a state of inebriation, reminds us of Acosta's condemnation of indigenous lubricity and perversion.[1]

Rather than merely reveling in the intertextuality of Saer's text and perusing its affiliations with particular textual sources, I propose to examine why such a novel is written in our time, and what a contextualization of it with respect to more recent discourses in the areas of historiography, especially ethnographic historiography, and also to a certain extent philosophy, psychoanalysis, and general cultural studies, reveals concerning not only our conceptualization of the Amerindian, but also our critical reappraisal of past paradigms. How can we interpret Saer's gesture of writing a fictional autobiography of a sixteenth-century cabin boy in the New World who recounts his story with all the prejudices of his time?

In his short story entitled "Pierre Menard, Author of the *Quixote*" ("Pierre Menard, autor del Quijote"), Jorge Luis Borges explains that there are basically three ways of rewriting in the present a few pages of Cervantes's novel that would be identical to the original: simply copying it; immersing oneself in the culture of the early seventeenth century to the point where a perfect recreation of the Spanish masterpiece is possible; and recreating the text from a twentieth-century perspective ("to go on being Pierre Menard and reach the *Quixote* through the experiences of Pierre Menard," 419) in an endeavor not only of archaeological reconstruction, but also of radical recontextualization, in which expressions already existing three centuries earlier now acquire an entirely different meaning. The result, according to Borges's narrator, is that "Cervantes's text and Menard's are verbally identical, but the second is almost infinitely richer" (421). Don Quijote's preference of arms over letters in Menard's text can thus be explained in various ways: the subordination of the author to the hero's psychology, the transcription of the original, the influence of Nietzsche, or Menard's "resigned or ironical habit of propagating ideas which were the strict reverse of those he preferred" (421). As for the self-evident statement that history is the mother of truth, it no longer means, as in the seventeenth century, that truth can be arrived at through the study of the record of past events (considered as unproblematical reality), but that history, a human symbolical construction, provides the parameters for our conceptualization of reality, which is thus itself a creation of the human mind (422). The result of Menard's rewriting is an invitation to adopt a new technique of reading, by which older texts are enriched by a recontextualization in a later time period.

Saer's novel, written in modern Spanish in spite of its thematization of a sixteenth-century autobiographical narrator and its function as an obvious palimpsest of early ethnographic texts and chronicles, renders our task of understanding and situating the author's enterprise, partially akin to Menard's, more obviously necessary, if not exactly easier. The style, as well as patent discursive and textual affinities with certain twentieth-century symbolic productions, such as Sartre's existentialist writings, which are also an obvious intertext of *El entenado*, constitute an indication of the manner in which the novel should be interpreted—not merely as a fictitious recreation of an imaginary sixteenth-century autobiography, but as a Menardian endeavor to problematize past cultural and discursive practices and recontextualize them within the present. On the surface, the novel seems a perfect illustration of Fredric Jameson's definition of postmodernism as the "random cannibalization of all the styles of the past" (65-66), provided we replace the word "styles" by "discourses," and an example of a radical destruction of a sense of history, since Saer dwells on a few key themes such as otherness, anthropophagia, the uncertainty of reality and fictionalization, without giving many historical or ethnographic details, so that the novel does not always seem to be situated in any specific geographical location or historical period. Instead of a historiographic fiction (or historiographic metafiction, to use Linda Hutcheon's term), the novel appears to be a postmodern "historiophagous"[2] fiction in which texts are systematically decontextualized, reassembled in a heterogeneous collage, and reworked in a homogeneous style, in order to constitute a Borgesian distillation of the global text, more in the sense of *Historia universal de la infamia* than in that of Menard's *Quijote*. However, this would be a superficial reading of the novel, since its complexities warrant a deeper investigation.

> *With the death of some gods, the birth of others always follows. To the death of the god "reality," who had the scientist as his preacher, there has corresponded the appearance of the sect of écriture, which has the écrivain as its high priest.* (144)
> —Luiz Costa Lima, Control of the Imaginary

The Saussurian legacy has been partly responsible for the emphasis on the formal construction of language, the systematization of the study of language that was to render possible modern linguistics, the widespread theorization concerning semiotic systems in general, and the application of concepts and methodological tools developed in the area of linguistics and semiotics to other disciplines, such as literary theory, anthropology, sociology, and history. Even the field of literary writing has been increasingly constituted by texts that not only experiment with language and foreground conventions by exaggerating or subverting them, but also thematize aspects of production and reception such as the act of writing and reading, and discuss literary codes, techniques, traditions, and forms in what has started to appear as a rather tedious and repetitive metadiscourse. Already in 1968, John Barth ironically chided his reader for perusing yet another specimen of metafiction, of which Barth is, of course, one of the major practitioners (*Lost in the Funhouse*). In his critical writings, he even claimed that since nothing new can be invented in fiction, our possibilities of innovation being exhausted, the "literature of replenishment" must be built upon the rereading, reinterpretation, and rewriting of previous works ("The Literature of Replenishment").

With the proliferation of metafiction written by "postmodern" authors such as Barth, Nabokov, Calvino, and Fowles, a plethora of critical and theoretical essays and monographs has appeared on the new metafiction, variously called narcissistic narrative, self-conscious literature, or fiction with an autorepresentational dominant.[3] As Henri Lefebvre pointed out in 1968, "discourse on discourse, the second degree" has proliferated in every area, as philosophers write about philosophy, poets about poetry, dramatists about drama, and novelists about the novel (248). According to the French philosopher, metalanguage has replaced language: "an enormous emptiness has been created and signs fill it in" (254). Metalanguage, for Lefebvre, is "the great alibi for masking and forgetting those historical tasks and missions that have not been accomplished, for erasing responsibility, for diffusing a latent guilt, an imprecise feeling of frustration and uneasiness" (254; translation mine).

In the type of investigation newly baptized "metahistory" (some of its concerns were already discussed by philosophers of history),[4] the questions addressed concern not only, as Hayden White remarked, the structure of a specific historical consciousness and the epistemological status of historical explanations, but also the forms of historical representation, since historical narratives are "verbal fictions, the contents of which are as much invented as found and the forms of which have more in common with their counterparts in literature than they have with those in the sciences" ("The Historical Text" 42). A particular historical interpretation can be neither disconfirmed nor negated, as in the case of the sciences, since history, like literature, makes sense of the world "by endowing what originally appears as problematical and mysterious with the aspect of a recognizable, because it is a familiar, form" (61). Drawing on Northrop Frye's ultrastructuralist quadripartite classification of "pre-generic plot-structures" or "mythoi," White explains that historians "emplot" the historical events according to the tragic, comic, romantic, or ironic modes, in order to create a comprehensible story. Since no set of events is inherently comic or tragic, it can be emplotted in different ways according to the ideology of the historian. Gibbon, for example, displays an ironic attitude in his portrayal of the rise and fall of nations, while Hegel encompasses his tragic view of individual destinies within an overall comic conceptualization of universal spiritual progress (that of the *Geist*).

It is in the context of White's emphasis on the ideological signification of historiographical plot-structures and Lefebvre's critical stance with respect to the proliferation of metadiscourse that we can reinterpret the recent histories of the conquest of the New World. One of the most influential and frequently cited, at least in the area of literary and cultural studies, is Tzvetan Todorov's *La conquête de l'Amérique: La question de l'autre* (*The Conquest of America: The Question of the Other*). Inquiring into the reasons for the relatively easy domination of the more numerous Aztecs by the Spaniards, Todorov adds to the traditionally given factors of Moctezuma's vacillating character, internal dissention among the indigenous peoples, Spanish superiority in arms, and lack of resistance of the native inhabitants to germs propagated by the invaders, a fifth explanation based on the importance of the semiotic and communicational dimension. Whereas the Aztecs had developed a complex system of interpreting natural phenomena for divination and explaining events according to the religious calendar, the Spaniards mastered not only the technique of acquiring and interpreting information about the inhabitants, but also that of using language and other sign systems in their strategies of conquest. Todorov explicitly claims that "the specialists of human communication win" (103; translation mine), that the "conquest of information leads to that of the realm" (110; translation mine), and that it "is owing to their mastery of human signs that Cortés maintains control over the ancient Aztec empire" (124; translation mine). Since the Aztecs' symbolic and semiotic practices are less developed that those of the Spaniards, they are not capable of understanding the Other as well as the Spaniards, because the perception of the Other and the symbolic function are intimately linked (163).[5] The Aztecs considered signs as directly emanating from the referent, since they had not learned to understand that language is a system, based on arbitrary signs, that can be used to manipulate the Other (95). With respect to the sacrifice of human idols representing divinities, Todorov explains that the Aztecs literally confused the representative with what he represented, and that this proved the "superiority" of the European forms of symbolization (165). On another occasion, Todorov explains that the existence of a system of writing in a particular culture indicates the evolution of mental structures (86).

Rolena Adorno rightly points out that in spite of Todorov's claim that he lets the sources speak for themselves, the texts he cites are all part of his "sermon" (202), which makes a plea for the respect of the Other in twentieth-century totalitarian regimes and gives no place to the voices of the Amerindian other, except as represented and mediated by European accounts:

> Where we might have expected to hear from the sixteenth-century Amerindian others, these potential subjects slip immediately from sight only to emerge, at the end of the book, as ourselves. Through conquest or under totalitarianism, the speech of the dominated subject is silenced. (205)

She contrasts Todorov's treatment of the Amerindian other with that of Michel de Certeau in *Heterologies*, in which the French historian and ethnologist writes that "the written discourse that cites the speech of the other is not, cannot be, the discourse of the Other. On the contrary, this discourse, in writing the Fable that authorizes it, alters it" (78; qtd. in Adorno 207).[6]

Before returning to the problem of alterity in past and contemporary historical and ethnographic discourses, however, I would like to examine not only the implications of the emphasis on the semiotic function in Todorov's explanation of the conquest of the New World, but also the light shed by "semiotic historiographers" such as Todorov and metahistorians such as Hayden White on Saer's fictional representation of the Amerindian. With respect to the first issue, one could tentatively apply White's theory of pre-generic plot-structures to Todorov's account, with the result that while the fate of the Amerindians is definitely considered as an individual tragedy and reminds us of other such tragedies in the present, Todorov's statement that Cortés was not like Columbus and we are no longer like Cortés (257) suggests that in spite of the existence of totalitarian regimes and the contemporary lack of communication with and respect for nature, a certain element of progress can be discerned. The protoperspectivism that Todorov ascribed to Las Casas has become generalized to the extent that everything is permitted, and this, while leading to the maintenance of certain totalitarian systems justified by the argument of relativism, is presented as yet another stage in the world's moral and cultural development, since Todorov criticizes the rampant "polylogia" (255) in favor of a return to value judgments. What is more significant, however, is that Todorov, who insists on the value of nonviolent communication, considers the triad slavery/colonialism/communication as corresponding to a chronological succession (187) and concomitantly to moral and cultural progress. Whereas he considers Columbus's conception of language analogous in many respects to that of the Aztecs, especially in his consideration of signifiers as standing directly for referents, since he did not realize that language forms a system in which the signifier and signified are arbitrary (34-35), Cortés had a more subtle grasp of the power of language as a tool of persuasion and domination. The Aztecs are thus presented as less developed and belonging to a prior phase of symbolic development rather than simply a different one. Change is inevitable, since culture that attempts to remain identical and stationary manifests an evident death-wish (183). In short, history is seen as progress, albeit with reversals and stagnant periods, while the criterion with which that progress is measured is determined by the Western dominant semiotic paradigm of the past few decades.

In Saer's novel, the traditional dichotomy between the culturally advanced European civilization and the Amerindian peoples who possess neither writing, nor religion, nor politics, nor art is maintained. I will return to this point later on in my essay in my discussion of the (mis)representation of the Other. What is particularly interesting in Saer's fictional representation of the Colastiné tribe is the central reason for the cabin boy's captivity. Since the tribe has no system of writing and since its members are terrified of the dissolution of material reality as well as of themselves, they capture a member of another tribe every year in order to be represented, and thus continue living for another subject. As the narrator explains at the end of his autobiography, the Colastinés believe that objects exist only as perceived and when perceived by human beings, while human beings exist only by virtue of distinguishing between themselves and the objects they perceive around them.[7] The fact that these explanations are obvious references to the theories of philosophers such as Sartre—according to whose phenomenological system consciousness must necessarily be consciousness of something and Being would be indistinct, undifferentiated mass without consciousness to constitute it into discrete entities corresponding to what we call objects—is significant in the sense that it illustrates the superiority of Western intellectual systems in describing the Other. As the narrator points out, the Colastinés are not consciously aware of their attitudes to reality, since, we could add, they have only a spontaneous, prereflexive consciousness that must be discovered, explicated, and theorized by the more advanced foreign observer. I will return to the importance of this aspect later. In any case, it is already significant that the cabin boy, who remains with them for ten years, has the function of representing them, in his case in writing, so that they will not disappear in the general oblivion of conquered peoples.

It is difficult not to consider the description of the tribe and the plot of the novel as allegorical. This dimension hardly seems surprising, in view of the fact that ethnographic writing, to which *El entenado* shows definite resemblances, is in itself frequently allegorical. According to James Clifford, ethnography is

> a performance emplotted by powerful stories. Embodied in
> written reports, these stories simultaneously describe real
> cultural events and make additional, moral, ideological,
> and even cosmological statements. Ethnographic writing is
> allegorical at the level both of its content (what it says about

cultures and their histories) and of its form (what is implied by its mode of textualization). (98)

The final destruction of the tribe by the Spaniards is partly caused, in an obvious analogy to Todorov's account, by its lack of advanced semiotic structures and, more specifically, a system of writing. It is their obsession with immutable material objects, probably rendered necessary by their lack of symbolic systems (although the narrator's existentialist account of their demise provides the explicit reason), which forces them to return to their settlement on the banks of the river, where they will be massacred by the Spaniards. But it is also their need of a witness who will record their life that prevents them from killing the cabin boy and insuring that he will not be able to communicate their geographic location to the Spaniards. Although the absolute annihilation of the tribe, without leaving any material trace, is partly to be explained by the fact that the Amerindians in the Río de la Plata region that Saer fictionalized in his novel did not construct lasting architectural works, his novel is not a compensatory "monument" to a vanished people (Bianciotti 15), but a monument to European ethnographic, historiographical, and literary endeavors, without which, according to the dominant ideology of the past few centuries, little would have remained of the vanquished inhabitants of the New World. The allegorical signification of the novel would thus be summed up succinctly by the quotation taken from Naipaul's *A Bend in the River* and given at the beginning of this section: "Without Europeans, ... all our past would have been washed away..." (18). But the narrator's assertion that he is writing down the story of the Colastinés in their name (114) can be considered not as a solution to the problem, but as a symptom of it.

The importance of external representation in the depiction of the Colastiné tribe, contrasting with the lack of internal means of consignment to memory, forms the subject of a large portion of the novel. And once the cabin boy returns to Spain, successive practices of semiotization occupy the remaining years of his life. His first attempt at representing his experiences in the New World is the verbal account he gives to Father Quesada, who writes down the story in a manuscript entitled *Relación de abandonado*. He then joins a group of traveling comedians, with whom he presents a theatrical version of his experiences to highly appreciative audiences. The Amerindians are portrayed by the women of the troupe, which brings to mind Todorov's semiotic analysis of Sepúlveda's Aristotelian master-slave dichotomization in the 1550 debate with Las Casas, between Indians, children, women, and animals characterized by ferociousness, intemperance, matter, the body, appetite and evil on the one hand, and Spaniards, adults, men, and humans characterized by clemency, temperance, form, the soul, reason, and good on the other (159). In northern Europe, where the difference between the indigenous languages and that of the Spanish comedians is an obstacle, the troupe performs the New World play as a pantomime. A final semiotization of the cabin boy's experiences occurs during the last years of his life, when the aged narrator sets down in writing his experiences of sixty years ago. More than a third of the novel, in fact, is situated in the time period following the cabin boy's return to Spain, where he dedicates his life, after the first seven years of learning how to read and write from Father Quesada and acquiring instruction in the traditional subjects of the time, to representing his New World hosts, a pursuit he deems necessary in view of his debt to the Colastinés. The emphasis on writing is evident in Saer's novel, not only in the thematization of a writing subject, but also in the constant autoreferential comments to the act and context of writing, as well as in the ever-present intertextual references. The cabin boy, who repeats on several occasions that as an orphan he comes from nothing, has constituted a past and an identity for himself through his writing about his encounter with the Amerindians: " ... I understood that if Father Quesada had not taught me to read and write, the only act that could justify my life would have been outside my reach" (99).[8] What was a tragedy for the Colastiné tribe, has become a source of self-definition, purposeful life and material fortune for the homeless and destitute cabin boy. Once again, the New World has provided fortune for the European explorers, and a pretext for a valorizing discourse.

> *Strangely, the stranger inhabits us: he is the hidden face of our*
> *identity. (Etrangement, l'étranger [the foreigner and what is*
> *foreign] nous habite: il est la face cachée de notre identité.) (9)*
> —*Julia Kristeva*, Etrangers à nous-mêmes

Michel de Certeau identified four notions on which the newly emerged scientific discipline of ethnology was based when it became systematized in the eighteenth century: radical alterity of the society studied, orality, spatiality (lack of historical consciousness), and a general lack of (reflective) consciousness that characterized the "primitive" society (*L'écriture*). Since the last is characterized by language "which circulates without knowing which silent rules it obeys" (215; translation mine), an ethnologist is required to articulate these laws and organize the space of the Other in a coherent, scientific discourse. Modern historiography, on the other hand, was based on the notions of writing, temporality, identity, and consciousness. Ethnographic historiography thus always "exiled" orality and replaced the discourse of the Other with its discourse founded on scientifically articulated knowledge. Whereas "primitive" societies could have no reliable history, oral discourse being considered incapable of retaining the past except in a deformed and fragmentary form, the ethnographic historiographer creates the history of the Other and consigns it to permanent record. The Other remains the object of this learned discourse, and, we may add, a pretext for the constitution of the modern scientific subject. Because the goal of the ethnologist is to master knowledge, the radical Other is reduced to familiar categories and conceptualized in terms of the self. An example of this is travel literature, which constitutes, because of frequent depictions of indigenous eroticism, singing, and sacrifice, an "immense complement and displacement of demonology" (244; translation mine).

Saer's Amerindians correspond to the ethnographic historian's portrait of the Other. They lack writing, history, and reflective consciousness and are presented as radically different. Their difference, however, is extrapolated from the same, and thus remains difference, and not alterity, according to the distinction emphasized by the sociologist and ethnologist Francis Affergan, who claims that "quantified alterity" ("l'altérité quantifiée"), or, in other words, difference, is the only object of ethnology (7). As Todorov demonstrated in his analysis of Las Casas's ideal portrait of the Amerindians and Columbus's initial description of them, they were conceptualized in positive terms based on the hegemonic norms of what constituted the perfect Christian. Their different valorization of certain objects, for example, led Columbus to praise what he considered to be their generosity. On the other hand, when they resisted evangelization and assimilation, they were suddenly portrayed as savages. Ever since the Spanish arrival in the New World, and until neo-indigenist authors such as Jose María Arguedas complexified the treatment of the Amerindians, they have been represented either as savages, or as noble savages.

Saer's novel, whose story is set in the sixteenth century, is no exception. The members of the Colastiné tribe are described as healthy, robust, of pleasant appearance, neither too old nor too young (see Columbus's first description of the Amerindian), endowed with great physical endurance, living frugally, peacefully, modestly, and chastely, and setting great store on personal cleanliness; or as savage, anthropophagous subhumans, wallowing in filth and copulating with each other in a drunken stupor without regard for gender, age, or family ties. The lengthy description of their cannibalism, inebriation, and erotic excesses portrays them as bestial beings, entirely governed by instinct—"animal delirium" ("delirio animal" [Saer 43]). Their feverish longing for the human feast is presented in erotic terms such as "desire" ("deseo" [42, 43, 47, 48]), "amorous contemplation" ("contemplación amorosa" [46]), "inexpressible excitement" ("excitación inenarrable" [46]), and "amorous fascination" ("hechizo amoroso" [47]). At the same time they are described as children jumping from one foot to the other, like primates vigorously scratching various parts of their body, and when finally in possession of their portion of meat, like beasts scuttling away to devour their prey without danger of being despoiled by other members of the horde. The cabin boy, like the ethnographic observer, contemplates them from a distance, but not impartially. His explanation of the Colastinés' rapid and frenzied rhythm of eating, their disappearance once in possession of their prey, and their postprandial somnolence are attributed to their sense of shame ("culpa," "vergüenza" [48, 49]), or their feeling of "doubt and confusion" ("duda y confusión" [49]), and thus presented in terms of Christian morality. Once their meal is partly digested, alcohol provides a stimulus for erotic practices including incest, sodomy, fellatio, homosexuality, and onanism. Their excesses eventually convert them into melancholy, enfeebled and pitiful specimens of abject humanity who snivel, play with their excrement, and generally behave like "sick and abandoned children" ("criaturas enfermas y abandonadas" [64]). In spite of the nefarious consequences of their orgies, the members of the tribe feel an irrepressible need every summer to indulge in these activities.[9]

In accordance with the religious background of the captive, this drive is interpreted as the periodical appearance of Satan (66), even though elsewhere it is described as the surfacing of the repressed unconscious (75, 83-84). The explanation of their annual orgiastic explosions as the emergence of bestial drives otherwise submerged by the "water of forgetfulness" ("agua del olvido" [83]) becomes particularly significant in the light of Freud's theories. Roy Schafer, who has analyzed the various psychoanalytical explanations of the development of the human psyche as narratives and emphasized their constructed and thus fictitious nature, retells Freud's "story" as follows:

> One of his primary narrative structures begins with the infant and young child as a beast, otherwise known as the id, and ends with the beast domesticated, tamed by frustration in the course of development in a civilization hostile to its nature. Even though this taming leaves each person with two regulatory structures, the ego and the superego, the protagonist remains in part a beast, the carrier of the indestructible id. The filling in of this narrative structure tells of a lifelong transition: if the innate potential for symbolization is there, and if all goes well, one moves from a condition of frightened and irrational helplessness, lack of self-definition, and domination by fluid or mobile instinctual drives toward a condition of stability, mastery, adaptability, self-definition, rationality, and security. If all does not go well, the inadequately tamed beast must be

accommodated by the formation of pathological structures, such as symptoms and perversions. (26-27)

The Colastinés are frequently described as insecure in their attitude toward reality, obsessed with the fear of instability, and incapable of developing a strong feeling of identity; their lack of self-definition forces them to resort to the services of an outsider who will observe and eventually represent them in a verbal account, and in the case of the cabin boy a written one as well, thus defining them and fixing their identity. They have inadequately tamed the beast within them and therefore indulge in a variety of perversions, which they are unable to avoid. Although this reading of Saer's text does not deny the explicit intertextuality with respect to Sartre's form of existentialism, it does point to an interesting transformation of a traditional paradigm, far less flattering than existential anguish. Whereas Amerindians were considered as not quite human by representatives of the Spanish Church such as Sepúlveda, they are represented in the context of at least one modern psychoanalytic narrative as not having mastered the contradiction between the demands of civilization and their natural drives, and thus as deficient in some respect. As evangelization has become secularized, the devil has been replaced by destructive drives that must be exorcized by a new version of the religious crusade destined to "save" individuals from the negative part of themselves.

Whereas the revelers are depicted as lecherous and inebriated beasts, a radically different portrait is drawn of those who prepare the meat. Described as sober, and tranquil men who partake of a frugal meal of fish and forego the pleasures of alcohol and collective fornication, they appear as ideal examples of human moderation. The terms used in their description (sober, tranquil, simplicity, generous and paternal attitude, discrete satisfaction, pleasure, tenderness, delicacy, generous simplicity, austere, cordial monosyllables; see 50-51) contrast with the negative isotopy (constituted of terms denoting and connoting bestiality, instinct, anger, and lust) characterizing the description of the others. According to the narrator, both groups seem to belong to "two different realities" ("dos realidades distintas" [55; see also 61 and 83]). However, the suffering ex-revelers are themselves eventually converted into paragons of moderation: "Those who had been, in the first days, worse than wild animals, were gradually turned with the passing of time into the most chaste, sober and balanced beings I have ever met during my long life."[10] The stronger members of the tribe protect the weak, scarce goods are equally shared, and all follow the natural rhythm of the seasons, huddling in their shelters during the winter and resuming their normal activity in the summer. The dichotomization is too obvious for the portrayal of the tribe not to be considered as a foregrounding of discursive conventions, just as John Barth's hyper-realistic description of trivial details in *Lost in the Funhouse* immediately appear as a foregrounding of the literary conventions of realistic illusion. The Manichean description of the Colastinés, however, is not as absolute as first appears to be the case. Their refined manners are considered effeminate, their concern for hygiene excessive, irritating, and even maniacal, and their consideration for each other ostentatious and affected (67).

Both the positive and negative portraits are based on prevalent moral paradigms. But the negative one is also conditioned by repressed aspects of the psyche of the European observer. This is made clear when the cabin boy, interrogated by sailors, officials, and priests after his "rescue," realizes that their questions demonstrate a veritable obsession for the lurid details of the tribe's perverse practices (96). Their own unavowed desires and fantasies are thus projected onto the Other, since their religious values and social regulation prohibit their manifestation. The ex-cabin boy's wish for greater tranquillity in the convent in which he spends seven years after his return to Spain apparently demonstrates that he has learned to appreciate the way of life of the Amerindians. But it can also be interpreted according to the official monastic valorization of quiet, modesty, chastity, simplicity, and reclusion, which sheds a different light on the captive's positive description of the simple life of the Colastinés. Their life is thus praised because it conforms to a particular conception of how a good Christian should live.

As I have previously mentioned, the Colastinés are considered deficient in the area of semiotic practices. As Walter D. Mignolo has demonstrated, literacy has always been equated in our society with the development and mastery of an alphabetic system of writing, seen as superior and more advanced than picto-ideographic systems and considered as one of the essential characteristics of civilization. Not only was literacy instrumental in the organization of the empire, but it was used by the *letrado*-humanists as a justification of the Conquest (85). This "tyranny of the alphabet" still conditions present conceptions of language and its function in society, since current scholarship conceives of alphabetic writing as "the end of a linear evolutionary process" (86). This belief characterizes Todorov's study, for example, in which the author equates the development of an alphabetic system of writing with advanced mental structures.

Saer's narrator, not surprisingly, considers the language of the Colastinés as rudimentary ("rudimentario"). The function of the cabin boy is considered to be of utmost importance for the tribe, whose members treat him with great deference, invite him to observe their daily activities and annual orgies, and act out exaggerated, and constantly repeated, roles so that he will remember them after his departure: "They expected of me that I duplicate, like water, the image they gave of themselves, that I repeat their gestures and words, that I represent them in their absence..." (134).[11] The name given to him by the tribe, *def-ghi*, symbolizes language in general, since its meanings, as understood by the cabin boy, vary from idol or icon, to a reflection in water, the person who acts a role, a spy, a public speaker, or a witness (133). The vivid comparison of the Colastinés' desperate facial expression as they attempt to attract the captive's attention with the look of a man helplessly sinking into a swamp (87) takes on a particularly pejorative significance in the light of the hierarchical division between civilized and noncivilized cultures. Not only are the Other's voice and customs saved from oblivion by a more literate and thus more developed society, but the native inhabitants, conscious of their imminent disappearance, without leaving any trace, since they do not have their own system of writing (or even other forms of marking their transient passage in this world, such as architecture, painting, or jewelry), beseech the foreigner to represent them for posterity. The fact that other captives belong to Amerindian tribes does not diminish the implications of the Spanish cabin boy's function.

An even more problematic aspect of the narrator's description of the Colastiné tribe is his explanation of their attitude toward reality. Is it a mere pretext for expounding existential anguish, formulated in accordance with the central theories of Sartre's *Being and Nothingness* and other major works, so that while ostensibly describing the Amerindian, the narrator is describing himself? Should one consider the central preoccupations of *El entenado* to be the apparent lack of solidity of reality in the twentieth century, just as Rolena Adorno considers the goal of Todorov's account of the conquest to be the condemnation of the silencing of the subject in modern totalitarian regimes, and Kristeva's *Etrangers à nous-mêmes* (*Strangers to Ourselves*) can be interpreted as a disquisition on her own situation as a foreigner in French society? While it is not impossible that Sartre's form of existentialism is still perceived as pertinent in 1983, forty years after the publication of *L'être et le néant* (*Being and Nothingness* [1943]), the question remains why Saer chose to represent the Amerindians as partaking of existential anguish. Is it simply an empathic recreation of our conception of what they possibly felt when their world was to be annihilated? Or is it because Sartre's theories correspond to the Western historiographical, ethnological, and philosophical construction of the Amerindian Other?

I have already alluded to the chroniclers' and historiographers' depiction of the New World inhabitants as deficient in the cultural and specifically semiotic domain. But even philosophers integrated this Manichean division of the civilized and the primitive world into their metaphysical edifices. Hegel, for example, explained that it is only normal that Amerindians are annihilated by their contact with the European *Geist* (spirit, genius, intellect), since not only are they physically inferior, as is the fauna of the continent, but also morally and intellectually. Obsequious, lacking dignity, and devoid of intelligence, only those who intermarry with Europeans acquire a certain measure of self-esteem, a higher degree of consciousness, and a desire for autonomy and independence. Lazy and immature, they are like children (see Todorov's analysis of Sepúlveda's axiological system), without thought or superior goals, who are being displaced by more civilized and culturally developed peoples (*Die Vernunft in der Geschichte* [*Reason in History*], 4: 2).[12]

Sartre's *La transcendance de l'Ego: Esquisse d'une description phénoménologique* (*Transcendence of the Ego: An Existentialist Theory of Consciousness*) and *L'être et le néant* (*Being and Nothingness*) provide a distinction that one can use to formulate this dichotomy with all the prestige of modern philosophical trappings and specialized jargon. When he criticized Descartes's notion of the cogito (*Transcendence of the Ego*), Sartre pointed out that one must distinguish between spontaneous, nonreflective doubt (the prereflective cogito), and the deliberate awareness of and reflection upon that doubt, which is the Cartesian cogito. What he calls "non-thetic" or "non-positional" consciousness does not suffice to constitute a genuine self-consciousness or *conscience de soi*, which is positional and thetic since consciousness becomes an object of reflection.

In Saer's novel, the narrator explains that a blind certainty in one's human nature equates one with beasts and that his own constant feeling of "doubt and confusion" during his sojourn in the New World, caused partly by the inhabitants' imprecise language, which contributes to "the taste...of not an infinite, but an unfinished world, an undifferentiated and confused life, blind matter without any plan" (85),[13] is thus not altogether negative. But he is the only one consciously aware of this situation and capable of a sustained, coherent Cartesian reflection on doubt. His explanation that "all these elucubrations were much more painful to them [the Colastinés] than appears when written down, because in spite of living them in flesh and bone, they were not aware of them" (123)[14] corresponds to Sartre's distinction between reflective and nonreflective consciousness. The Colastinés thus represent not the external Other, but the Other of the modern, Cartesian cogito, that consciousness within us that has not yet reached a state of reflective awareness. They stand not for an alternative to European *ratio*, for a genuine Other that we cannot yet apprehend with our conceptual categories, but the Other reduced to perpetually excluded difference, which is defined in opposition to the self-conscious and rational hegemonic center. The Other is thus defined as a more primitive part of ourselves, symbolizing a prior state of intelligence and civilization on the evolutionary ladder of human development. The marginalizing force of such a dichotomization is even more effective than Todorov's distinction between the Aztecs' communication with God and the world and the Spaniards' communication with human beings, but both represent a mode of conceptualization consistent with the basic Manichean paradigm of Western ethnographic historiography.

> *In spite of worthy and indispensable efforts to bring another moment in history alive and to possess it, a clairvoyant history should admit that it never completely escapes from the nature of myth.* (48)
> —Claude Lévi-Strauss,
> Overture to the Raw and the Cooked

Hayden White's study of the forms that historiographical writing have taken does not illustrate an obsession with *écriture* for its own sake, but leads to our consideration of far more problematic questions. When he discusses the implications of Kant's distinction between three different conceptions of the historical process—the eudaemonistic (history as progress), the terroristic (history as degeneration), and the abderitic (history as stasis or repetition)—he emphasizes that for Kant all three conceptions are equally fictive and adds that they "represented to him evidence of the mind's capacity to impose different kinds of formal coherence on the historical process" (*Metahistory* 57). Since there is no scientific and logical reason to justify or reject any one of these conceptions, the ultimate choice, which is aesthetic and ideological, rests with the historian. This realization has led to what White calls an ironic mode of historiography in the twentieth century, which he admits to adopting himself, but against which he also cautions us. Increasingly, historical consciousness has been considered as "a specifically Western prejudice by which the presumed superiority of modern, industrial society can be retroactively substantiated" (*Metahistory* 2). In the final pages of his study, he advocates a transcendence of this ironic perspective and a move away from absolute skepticism and moral agnosticism, a movement that has already been begun by recent philosophers and cultural critics (433-434). White's conclusion reminds us of Todorov's problematization of relativism, which, while it may be considered laudable in Las Casas, has become generalized to the point where it leads the modern world to inaction in the face of morally unacceptable situations.

Without entering into this argument, I would like to point out that the implications of the delegitimization of discourse that gained momentum since Nietzsche needs to be further examined in its implications before we reject the "ironic mode." It is not just a matter of whether we "emplot" history as tragedy, comedy, romance, or irony, but how we construct the events thus emplotted. As Foucault reminded us in *L'archéologie du savoir* (*The Archaeology of Knowledge*), an object of knowledge such as mental illness, for example, is "constituted by the sum of what was said in the group of all the utterances that named it, segmented it, described it, explained it" (45; translation mine). Likewise, Sartre's reflective consciousness, valorized as an attribute of the European in Saer's novel, is a conceptual and discursive creation useful for the constitution of the cultural identity of the center, the dichotomization between center and margin, and the resulting devalorization of the excluded Other.

As Todorov pointed out, the Other in the early chronicles was presented in terms of positive or negative axiological categories. In other words, recognition of their difference did not entail their perception as equal, but as either better (Las Casas) or worse (Sepúlveda). In Saer's novel, as in *Gulliver's Travels*, the non-European incarnates the best and the worst qualities of the traveler's country of origin. But the description of the tribe also relativizes European superiority. Although the values explicitly presented as belonging to the official ideology—"discipline, courage, and love of God, the King, and Work" ("la disciplina, el coraje, y al amor a Dios, al Rey, y al Trabajo" [13])—are only partly observed by the Colastinés, who are extremely disciplined except for their annual orgies and hard-working in order to survive (the narrator calls the village "urbane, hard-working, austere" ("urbano, trabajador, austero" [70]), but have neither religion ("in all these years I never saw the Indians worship anything," "nunca vi en tantos años que esos indios adoraran nada" [65-66]) nor government, their behavior is described in more positive terms (except for the orgies) than that of the Spanish sailors. The latter practice sodomy (15), gambol seminaked, like "animals in a stampede" ("animales en estampida" [16]), on the beach, where they run in all directions or in circles, climb trees like children, and almost attack each other in a heated argument in which each side refuses to listen to the other (18). Furthermore, the cabin boy, in spite of his revulsion when confronted with the Colastinés' cannibalism, perceives the aroma of the roasting flesh as "pleasant" ("agradable"), succumbs to involuntary salivation, and experiences a strong desire to try the "unknown animal" ("ese animal desconocido" [45-46]). His horrified realization that humanity forms only a thin veneer of the human being relativizes the superiority of Europeans; however, it is less effective as a reversal of the traditional perspective on cannibalism than the description of the well-seasoned, slowly sizzling pieces of human flesh as a delicious barbecue with the juices and melted grease dripping onto the embers. When he is rescued by his compatriots ten years later, he has not only forgotten Spanish, but become so used to the Colastinés' ways of life that his perception of everything European has changed. He perceives his countrymen as simple ("un poco simples" [90]), is surprised by the ceremonial dress of the captain (92), and considers as absurd the captain's expectation that the native inhabitants should instinctively recognize his superiority, come to meet him, and submit to his designs: " ... the idea that the Indians might have their own opinion about these plans seemed inconceivable" (94; translation mine).[15] It is interesting that the narrator also describes the Colastinés as incapable of conceiving the possibility that others may not know their language and customs, which he deduces from their expectation that he understand them immediately and know their intentions of adopting him as a witness and observer (132). Rather that a specific indictment of his countrymen, this observation is thus directed at a general trait of human beings.

His initial reaction to the pedagogic efforts of Father Quesada is also negative: "more than Latin, Greek, Hebrew, and the sciences that he taught me, it was difficult to inculcate in me their value and necessity" (99; translation mine).[16] This resistance to traditional humanistic learning is reminiscent of the critical position adopted by Latin American writers at the end of the eighteenth and beginning of the nineteenth centuries with respect to the colonial heritage. According to many intellectuals of that period, the bookish knowledge provided by the Spanish heritage was not adequate for the difficult task of constructing a new society, which required practical knowledge (see Vidal). However, the cabin boy's resistance appears more as a temporary reluctance to become civilized that is finally overcome by Father Quesada, who is presented in positive terms as a man of great wisdom and learning. Moreover, the knowledge he imparts to his young pupil permits the latter to realize the "only act that could justify [his] existence" ("el único acto que podía justificar [su] vida" [99])—namely, writing his autobiography. The questioning of hegemonic values is thus only apparent.

A more significant reversal of perspective occurs after the cabin boy has listened to the debate concerning the human nature of the Amerindians (an obvious reference to actual religious debates of the sixteenth century, such as that between Father Las Casas and Father Sepúlveda) and answered questions about their system of government, private property, hygiene, commerce, music, religion, and dress. Father Quesada's assertion that the inhabitants of the New World are "sons of Adam" ("hijos de Adán" [103]) elicits the silent reflection on the part of the cabin boy that the only real men he had ever met were the Colastinés and that his own countrymen were only considered to be men according to convention. An interminable succession of copious dinners, ostentatious ceremonies, and noisy gatherings characterizes the life of the convent, in sharp contrast to the peaceful life of the American natives. However, this criticism does constitute a questioning of official ideology, since it corresponds to the admonitions of the superior of the convent himself and reflects the condemnation within Spanish society of the excesses of some of its members. The apparent reversal of perspectives is entirely dissolved, moreover, by the description immediately following it of the exaggerated poses that the brothers assume, in an obvious parallel to the Colastinés, for the benefit of the resident portrait painter, who is treated with as much deference as the *defghi* by the tribe. What is thus criticized is not the behavior of Spaniards from an external point of view (that acquired by familiarity with the life-style of the Other), but a specific type of behavior from within, according to religious and moral paradigms that are not questioned, but applied to the Other as well.

Another apparent reversal of perspectives characterizes the ex-cabin boy's disillusionment with the audience's rapture when presented with a theatrical performance based on myths and stereotypes: "More than the cruelty of armies, the indecent plundering of commerce, the moral juggling to justify all kinds of evil,"[17] the success of his comedy illustrated the despicable nature, spiritual emptiness, intellectual mediocrity, and vacuous role playing of his countrymen. But rather than an example of critical distance with respect to hegemonic values, his condemnation reflects the *topoi* of *vanitas vanitatum, la vida es sueño,* and "the world is but a stage," besides the frequent censure of the cruelty of the conquistadors, which does not necessarily invalidate the justification of the evangelization and "civilization" of the New World. The ex-cabin boy's alternative is a quiet life with his adopted children, operating a printing press and writing his autobiography in a room filled with books. Whereas the Colastinés had adopted him (he is their *entenado*) so that he could write their lives, he adopts children so that he can teach them to print the writings of others. The ultimate source of a fulfilling life is thus tranquillity, learning, writing, and propagating written culture, entirely in accordance with the dominant humanistic paradigm. The repetitiousness of his life, with simple, identical meals brought at the same time each day (113), may appear as an indication that some of the values of the Amerindian Other have been adopted by the narrator. But this alternative to the construction of society and technological progress evokes a frequent Western yearning for a return to nature and the simple life, far from the maddening crowd.

With respect to the rites of Catholic religion, the cabin boy's inability to appreciate the significance of "the monotonous noise of words without meaning and the ritual repetition of empty manipulations" (104)[18] is immediately contextualized within a hegemonic perspective, when Father Quesada explains that his pupil "had just entered the world and arrived naked as if he were emerging from [his] mother's womb" (105).[19] The questioning of European values is thus transformed into the description of the incapacity of an uncivilized man (since Amerindian society is not considered as part of the civilized world, and thus not even part of the "world," which is equated with Europe) to comprehend the complexities of modern society. Needless to say, the mastery of the institutions of civilization is presented as a praiseworthy endeavor.

The narrator's praise of the Colastinés' pacific nature, again apparently a problematization of European bellicosity since the tribe considers warriors "irrational creatures" ("criaturas irrazonables" [Saer 115]), is annulled by his explanation that their abhorrence of war is due to their fear of losing their possessions, and that the death of a family member causes less grief than the destruction of a utensil. Just like the Europeans, they consider with great scorn the different practices of other tribes: "Their peculiarities were always a source of mirth . . . everything seemed to the Indians equally inept, useless, and ridiculous. They were in the center of the world; the rest, uncertain and amorphous, on the periphery" (117-118).[20] They gave reality to their formless surroundings as they moved to other areas in their expeditions, and this transitory reality vanished as soon as they left (119). The narrator explains that the extermination of the Amerindians thus has negative consequences for the Spaniards, since the destruction of the people who gave reality to their surroundings, and who were in fact the foundation of reality and can therefore not be considered savages ("Calling them savages is a proof of ignorance; one cannot call beings with such a responsibility savages") (25),[21] plunged everything, including the Spanish soldiers, into nothingness. In spite of the obvious intertextual link with Sartre's existentialism and phenomenology in general, this description of the Colastinés has more far-reaching implications, since it can be considered a reference to the learned European discourses on the Other, human and geographic, which it constituted as an object of knowledge. It can be read as an indirect criticism, like that in *Gulliver's Travels*, of the European practice of considering as universal its own paradigms, as a treatment of the Other as a pretext for further knowledge of the self, and as the reduction of the Other to the same in a projection of schemas elaborated to account for one's own reality. But within the context of the twentieth-century emphasis on the constructed nature of reality the lamentation over the disappearance of reality accompanying that of the Amerindians is not only a criticism of the European destruction of autochthonous peoples, but also evidence of the realization that with their ethnocide a particular reality has disappeared, since their perception and organization of the world constitutes a reality, and is not merely a perspective on a reality considered as objectively there.

All these apparently critical reflections of the narrator on his country's institutions and cultural practices, which are made possible by his sojourn among the Amerindians, turn out to be anchored within his own paradigms. Incapable of understanding radical alterity, or even accepting it, he is also incapable of a complete reappraisal of his own culture. His disillusionment on returning to Spain thus reveals no genuine relativization. However, his negative portrayal of the Colastinés' language and certain cultural practices paradoxically delegitimizes the claim to universality of European cultural and linguistic institutions. His description of their language as "unpredictable, contradictory, without apparent form" ("imprevisible, contradictoria, sin forma aparente" [121]), polysemic and absurd, characterizes the arbitrariness of language in general, which inevitably appears confusing and illogical to those who speak a different language. The example he gives of the word *negh*, meaning continuity, which is used to take leave of someone, is particularly ironic, since in many languages continuity is indicated by such forms of address (*au revoir, auf Wiedersehn*, and even *hasta mañana*). His reference to the fact that the Colastinés consider the custom followed by a neighboring tribe of giving lavish feasts at funerals as absurd and his remark that some of their own customs are equally so demonstrate that he is quite aware of the relativization of values and practices as applied to others. But this realization does not enable him to question seriously his own assumptions.

In spite of the superiority of the Colastinés in certain respects, at least in the narrator's explicit portrayal of their advantage over the Spaniards, the implications of his scriptural construction of the self, made possible by his greater learning and self-consciousness, are that the annihilation of the tribe and the consequences for Europeans represent a further stage in the development of progress. The Amerindians, on the contrary, represent absolute stasis, as the repetitive emphasis of the narrator makes abundantly clear: "Everything repeated itself... the same cloying smiles... the repetition of events in identical order" (77-79). "There was nothing besides... a future promising more repetition than novelty" (86).[22] Although the cabin boy is influenced by the Colastinés obsession with undifferentiated and inconsistent reality, the mature narrator, having benefited from European learning, has acquired the intellectual and discursive tools to reintroduce an order into that reality and systematize it in his consignment of experience to the permanent memory of the text. Progress is of course only possible with the systematization of knowledge, and this is why the novel's Amerindians, semiotically deficient, are condemned to eternal repetition in a vain effort to maintain a sense of permanence. Lévi-Strauss's pessimistic belief in *Tristes tropiques* that human institutions and customs are a "transient efflorescence" ("efflorescence passagère") applies to the Colastiné tribe in Saer's novel more than it does to Spanish culture, whose representatives, unlike humankind portrayed by Lévi-Strauss as contributing toward "the dissolution of an original order and precipitating a powerfully organized matter toward an ever greater inertia which will one day be definitive" (417; translation mine), counteract dissolution with their cultural institutions. His fear of an eventual monoculture existing in a state of entropy in which the transmission of information has eliminated cultural distances, and his sardonic replacement of the term "anthropology" with "entropology," is definitely not that of Saer's narrator.

Notes

1. "...they come together without distinction of age, sex or parentage... everything is permitted with everyone, according to the rules of drunkenness... the virgin is not respected, and neither is the mother... the appetite is whetted even with men...." " "...concurren sin nunguna diferencia de todas edades, sexo y parentesco... todo es lícito contra cualquiera, según las leyes de la borrachera ...no se respeta la doncella, no se tiene cuenta con la madre,...se enciende el apetito aun con los varones..." (Acosta 884-885; translation mine). Compare this with Saer's description, which begins in an almost identical way, and then supplies the details that Acosta refused to give because they offended his sense of "decency" ("pudor"): "They took into consideration neither age, nor sex, nor parentage. A father could penetrate his own daughter of six or seven years of age, a grandson

sodomize his grandfather...." "No tenían en cuenta ni edad ni sexo ni parentesco. Un padre podía penetrar a su propia hija de seis o siete años, un nieto sodomizar a su abuelo..." (59).

2. In "Le travail du non-contemporain: Historiophagie ou historiographie?," Walter Moser distinguishes between Ernst Bloch's interpretation of the German National Socialist appropriation of familiar folk themes, *topoi*, and songs as a heterogeneous amalgam that was most effective in seducing the public, in contrast with the Socialist inability to integrate popular elements and thus gain wider acceptance, and Fredric Jameson's characterization of postmodernism as cannibalization of heterogeneous texts and discourses, decontextualized and thus stripped of historical significance and emotional impact, a strategy Moser calls "historiophagy," which he tentatively compares in a note with the Brazilian *modernismo* movement, especially in its *manifesto antropófago*.

3. Some of the most frequently cited critical and theoretical works dealing with metafiction are as follows: Linda Hutcheon, *Narcissistic Narrative: The Metafictional Paradox*; Patricia Waugh, *Metafiction*; Robert Alter, *Partial Magic: The Novel as a Self-Conscious Genre*; *L'autoreprésentation: le texte et ses miroirs*, special issue of *Texte*, 1982; see also my article entitled "Une métacritique de la méta-littérature: quelques considérations théoriques," *Etudes françaises*.

4. In "The Historical Text as Literary Artifact," White explicitly defines metahistory as an investigation of the structure of historical consciousness, the epistemological nature of historical knowledge, and the forms of historical representation (41). In *Metahistory*, however, the term "metahistory" also refers to the mythical and fictitious component of the historical work: "In short, it is my view that the dominant tropological mode and its attendant linguistic protocol comprise the irreducible 'metahistorical' basis of every historical work" (xi).

5. Beatriz Pastor adds an important qualification to the portrayal of the Spaniards as more capable of understanding the Other. According to her, Cortés's systematization and organization of knowledge about the Aztecs is restricted to what is necessary for his conquest of them: "The laws that are formulated on the basis of that rational presentation are never concerned with the development of autochthonous socio-cultural processes or the full understanding of the new reality as primary objective. Their objective is simply the formulation of an optimum method for the control of that reality and, above all, its integration in the framework of a colonial relationship with the Spanish State" (135).

6. A rapid glance at the texts presented and discussed by Todorov, in fact, confirms that although the subtitle of the work is "The Question of the Other," the selections are comprised exclusively of European accounts of the Other, or non-native compilations of information provided by native informants. As Beatriz Pastor has pointed out, the voices of the Other have been systematically silenced since the Conquest, and only isolated cases of the emergence of nonhegemonic voices, such as the accounts compiled by León-Portilla (although even these are presented by a non-Amerindian mediator) can be found.

7. "The Indians could not put faith in the existence of the tree because they knew that the tree depended on their own existence, but at the same time, since the tree contributed, with its presence, to guaranteeing the existence of the Indians, the Indians could not feel as if they existed completely because they knew that if

existence came to them from the tree, that existence was problematic since the tree seemed to obtain its own existence from that which the Indians gave it" ("Los indios no podían confiar en la existencia del árbol porque sabían que el árbol dependía de la de ellos, pero, al mismo tiempo, como el árbol contribuía, con su presencia, a garantizar la existencia de los indios, los indios no podían sentirse enteramente existentes porque sabían que si la existencia les venía del árbol, esa existencia era problemática ya que el árbol parecía obtener la suya propia de la que los indios le acordaban" [120-121]). The narrator also explains that the Colastinés have no word equivalent to the Spanish *ser* or *estar* (to be) and that the only similar expression in their language is a word meaning *parecer* (to seem) (122). The reference to phenomenology is obvious.

8. "comprendí que si el padre Quesada no me hubiese enseñado a leer y escribir, el único acto que podía justificar mi vida hubiese estado fuera de mi alcance."

9. It is interesting to compare this description with Octavio Paz's discussion of the nature and function of Mexican fiestas in *El laberinto de la soledad* (42-58).

10. "Los que habían sido, en los primeros días, peores que animales feroces se fueron convirtiendo, a medida que pasaba el tiempo, en los seres más castos, sobrios y equilibrados de todos los que me ha tocado encontrar en mi larga vida."

11. "De mí esperaban que duplicara, como el agua, la imagen que daban de sí mismos, que repitiera sus gestos y palabras, que los representara en su ausencia...."

12. I am indebted to my colleague Antonio Gómez-Moriana for the stimulation provided by numerous discussions we have had on this question, which contributed to the elaboration of my reflections on marginalizing discourse in the context of German idealist philosophy.

13. "un sabor...a mundo no infinito sino inacabado, a vida indiferenciada y confusa, a materia ciega y sin plan."

14. "Todas estas elucubraciones eran para ellos mucho más penosas de lo que parecen escritas porque ellos, a pesar de que las vivían en carne y hueso, las ignoraban."

15. "la idea de que los indios pudiesen tener un punto de vista propio sobre esos planes parecía inconcebible."

16. "más que el latín, el griego, el hebreo y las ciencias que me enseñó, fue dificultoso inculcarme su valor y su necesidad."

17. "Más que las crueldades de los ejércitos, la rapiña indecente del comercio, los malabarismos de la moral para justificar todas clase de maldades."

18. "el ruido monótono de palabras sin sentido y la repetición ritual de manipulaciones vacías."

19. "acababa de entrar en el mundo y había llegado desnudo como si estuviese saliendo del vientre de [su] madre."

20. "Sus peculiaridades eran siempre motivo de risa...todo les parecía a los indios igualmente inepto, inútil y ridículo. Ellos estaban en el centro del mundo; el resto, incierto y amorfo, en la periferia."

21. "Llamarlos salvajes es prueba de ignorancia; no se puede llamar salvajes a seres qui soportan tal responsabilidad."

22. "Todo se repetía...Las mismas sonrisas acarameladas...el regreso de los

acontecimientos, en un orden idéntico." "No había más que ... un futuro que anunciaba más repetición que novedad."

Works Cited

Acosta, José de. "Encomiendas. De procuranda indorum salute." *Historiadores de Indias*. Ed. Angeles Masia. Barcelona: Bruguera, 1972. 2: 848-895.

Adorno, Rolena. "Arms, Letters and the Native Historian." *1492-1992: Re/Discovering Colonial Writing*. Ed. René Jara and Nicholas Spadaccini. Hispanic Issues 4. Minneapolis: Prisma Institute, 1989. 201-224.

Affergan, Francis. *Exotisme et altérité: Essai sur les fondements d'une critique de l'anthropologie*. Paris: Presses Universitaires de France, 1987.

Alter, Robert. *Partial Magic: The Novel as a Self-Conscious Genre*. Berkeley: Univ. of California Press, 1975.

Barth, John. "The Literature of Replenishment." *Atlantic Monthly* (Jan. 1980): 65-71.

——. *Lost in the Funhouse*. Garden City, N.Y.: Doubleday, 1968.

Bianciotti, Hector. "Monument pour des Indiens disparus." *Le Monde* (June 12, 1987): 15, 22.

Bloch, Ernst. *Erbschaft dieser Zeit*. Frankfurt a. M.: Suhrkamp, 1960.

Borges, Jorge Luis. "Pierre Menard, Author of the Quixote." *Fantastic Worlds: Myths, Tales, and Stories*. Ed. Eric S. Rabkin. New York: Oxford Univ. Press, 1979. 415-423.

Carpentier, Alejo. *El arca y la sombra*. Mexico City: Siglo XXI, 1979.

Certeau, Michel de. *L'écriture de l'histoire*. Paris: Gallimard, 1975.

——. *Heterologies: Discourses on the Other*. Trans. Brian Massumi. Theory and History of Literature 17. Minneapolis: Univ. of Minnesota Press, 1986.

Chanady, Amaryll. "Une métacritique de la méta-littérature: quelques considérations théoriques." *Etudes françaises* 23.3 (1988): 135-145.

Clifford, James. "On Ethnographic Allegory." *Writing Culture: The Poetics and Politics of Ethnography*. Ed. James Clifford and George E. Marcus. Berkeley and Los Angeles: Univ. of California Press, 1986. 98-121.

Columbus, Christopher (Cristóbal Colón). "Diario de navegación. Primer viaje." *Historiadores de Indias. Antillas y tierra firme*. Ed. Angeles Masiá. Barcelona: Bruguera, 1971. 229-237.

Costa Lima, Luiz. *Control of the Imaginary: Reason and Imagination in Modern Times*. Trans. Ronald W. Sousa. Theory and History of Literature 50. Minneapolis: Univ. of Minnesota Press, 1988.

Foucault, Michel. *L'archéologie du savoir*. Paris: Gallimard, 1969.

Frye, Northrop. *Anatomy of Criticism*. New York: Atheneum, 1965.

García Márquez, Gabriel. *El general en su laberinto*. Buenos Aires: Editorial Sudamericana, 1989.

Gibbon, Edward. *The Decline and Fall of the Roman Empire*. New York: Collier, 1900.

Gómez-Moriana, Antonio. "Narration and Argumentation in the Chronicles of the New World." *1492-1992: Re/Discovering Colonial Writing*. Ed. René Jara and Nicholas Spadaccini. Hispanic Issues 4. Minneapolis: Prisma Institute, 1989. 97-120.

Hegel, G. W. F. *Hegel: Die Vernunft in der Geschichte*. Ed. Johannes Hoffmeister. Hamburg: Felix Meiner Verlag, 1955.

Hutcheon, Linda. "Canadian Historiographic Metafiction." *Essays on Canadian Writing* 30 (1984-1985): 228-238.

———. *Narcissistic Narrative: The Metafictional Paradox*. Waterloo: Wilfred Laurier Univ. Press, 1980.

Jameson, Fredric. "Postmodernism, or The Cultural Logic of Late Capitalism." *New Left Review* 146 (1984): 53-92.

Kant, Immanuel. *On History*. Ed. Lewis White Beck. Indianapolis and New York: Bobbs-Merrill, 1963.

Kristeva, Julia. *Etrangers à nous-mêmes*. Paris: Fayard, 1988.

Lefebvre, Henri. *La vie quotidienne dans le monde moderne*. Paris: Gallimard, Collection Idées, 1968.

Lévi-Strauss, Claude. "Overture to *le Cru et le cuit*." Trans. Joseph H. McMahon. *Structuralism*. Ed. Jacques Ehrmann. New York: Anchor Books, 1970. 31-55.

———. *Tristes tropiques*. Paris: Plon, 1955.

Mignolo, Walter D. "Literacy and Colonization: The New World Experience." *1492-1992: Re/Discovering Colonial Writing*. Ed. René Jara and Nicholas Spadaccini. Hispanic Issues 4. Minneapolis: Prisma Institute, 1989. 51-96.

Moser, Walter. "Le travail du non-contemporain: Historiophagie ou Historiographie?" *Etudes littéraires* 20.2 (1989): 25-41.

Naipaul, V. S. *A Bend in the River*. Harmondsworth: Penguin, 1980.

Pastor, Beatriz. "Silence and Writing: The History of the Conquest." *1492-1992: Re/Discovering Colonial Writing*. Ed. René Jara and Nicholas Spadaccini. Hispanic Issues 4. Minneapolis: Prisma Institute, 1989. 121-163.

Paz, Octavio. *El laberinto de la soledad*. Mexico City: Fondo de Cultura Económica, 1950.

Saer, Juan José. *El entenado*. Mexico City: Folios, 1983.

Sartre, Jean-Paul. *Being and Nothingness*. Trans. Hazel E. Barnes. New York: Washington Square Press, 1966.

———. *Transcendence of the Ego: An Existentialist Theory of Consciousness*. Trans. Forrest Williams and Robert Kirkpatrick. New York: Noonday Press, 1957.

Schafer, Roy. "Narration in the Psychoanalytic Dialogue." *On Narrative*. Ed. W. J. T. Mitchell. Chicago and London: Univ. of Chicago Press, 1981. 25-49.

Todorov, Tzvetan. *La conquête de l'Amérique: La question de l'autre*. Paris: Seuil, 1982.

Vidal, Hernán. *Socio-historia de la literatura colonial hispanoamericana: tres lecturas orgánicas*. Minneapolis: Institute for the Study of Ideologies and Literature, 1984.

Waugh, Patricia. *Metafiction*. New York and London: Methuen, 1984.

White, Hayden. "The Historical Text as Literary Artifact." *The Writing of History: Literary Form and Historical Understanding*. Ed. Robert H. Canary and Henry Kozicki. Madison: Univ. of Wisconsin Press, 1978. 41-62.

———. *Metahistory: The Historical Imagination in Nineteenth-Century Europe*. Baltimore and London: Johns Hopkins Univ. Press, 1973.

Chapter 23
An Image of Hispanic America from the Spain of 1992

Angel López García

(translated by Jennifer M. Lang and Paul Johnston)

The Spanish Conquest of the American continent that began in 1492 is one of those historical topics that seem to leave no room for neutrality. From that year on, arguments both for and against the American enterprise have abounded: beginning with Las Casas's report of genocide in his *Brevísima relación de la destrucción de las Indias* (*Brief Account of the Destruction of the Indies*) and the corresponding exoneration of Ginés de Sepúlveda, and ending with the recent essays by Tvzetan Todorov and Xavier Rubert de Ventós—the former condemning, the latter revealing an absolving nature.

I do not intend to be drawn into this end-of-the-century dispute, which will probably never be resolved with unanimity of opinion. Perhaps the confusion lies in the fact that an attempt has been made to transfer a hermeneutic argument—that is, a disagreement regarding interpretations of events—to the events themselves. This situation turns the American debate into a vast fabric of accounts, not always verified, of victims and atrocities, on one hand, and produces a no less disproportionate list of rules, for the most part never followed, on the other. Was there a discovery, or an invention of America, according to Edmundo O'Gorman's depiction? We will never know. Even Las Casas and Motolinía, both defenders of the Indians, differ radically in their visions of what must be done. According to L. Nicolau d'Olwer, "Las Casas proposes the restoration of extinct Indian monarchies, under the emperor's eminent and distant sovereignty; while Motolinía's political vision anticipates Conde de Aranda's idea by two and one-half centuries, and Iguala's plan by almost three centuries" (26).[1] The fact is that both of them were wrong; what has developed is neither Indian, nor *criollo*, but rather *mestizo*, the verbal multi-race. That is how history is written.

It is clear that many indigenous peoples were exterminated, and it would be wise to state clearly that there is no excuse that can conceal that dreadful tragedy. The echoes of a massacre, which has yet to end in some countries of America, may still be heard. For the sake of truth, we must also realize that throughout history there have been many vanquished peoples, as countless as the stars in the heavens or the sands of the sea: the Vietnamese just two decades ago; the Jews, Ukrainians, and Poles during World War II; the Armenians and Koreans of World War I; and the Zulus before that. We can go further back in time, to the Irish, Apaches, Berbers, and others, until we reach the point where historical memory is lost. Nevertheless, there is no lack of a utilitarian alibi in any of these cases: in order to secure its supremacy over a greater number of territories, the corresponding oppressor (a plenary session of the United Nations could be held among them) imposes the law of survival of the fittest. In the final analysis, it is a simple matter of patience: the wheel of Fortune, which attracted the ancients so much, offers each nation the opportunity to oppress and be oppressed, as evidenced by the recent Gulf War in the Middle East.

We all agree that the Middle Eastern situation was handled poorly, yet we are quick to point out, with greater or lesser doses of cynicism, that nothing can be done. Sometimes, when there exists sufficient distance from the actual events, and, moreover, when testimony of the suffering of the vanquished nation is lacking, the evaluation can even prove to be positive. Such is the case of the annihilation of Carthage at the hands of the Romans, which made it possible for virtually the entire Western world to "benefit" from the dissemination of the culture of Latium.

The problem of the Indian genocide in Hispanic America is a

matter of reason rather than emotion. What matters is not only that our sensitivity is roused in the face of the atrocities related by Las Casas, but, more importantly, we do not understand—not even now—the aim of that genocide. We must not be misled by the ethical debates held by Europeans during the Conquest: what is really being disputed is the lack of *efficiency* of Spanish colonialism. It is quite possible that Nicolás Sánchez-Albornoz is justified in opposing the time-honored thesis regarding the genocide, and that the principal motive behind the indigenous depopulation of the West Indies and Central America should be attributed to epidemics (first smallpox, then measles, and later typhoid fever or *matlazahuatl*). Nevertheless, for these analysts what is important is that, given the lack of a labor force, the colonies were unable to develop a solid capitalist economy, precisely when capitalism was taking off. The same holds true today.

The contrast between the analysis of the extermination of North American Indians by descendents of the pilgrims of the Mayflower and the genocide of those in Central and South America at the hands of the successors of the soldiers who took part in the first expeditions out of Huelva and Cádiz still serves as a reference, well-worn, but no less instructive. Although the efficiency of the former seems to have been superior—to the point of leaving virtually no trace of the natives in the United States— for the mythology propagated by the movie industry and readily accepted in our time, General Custer is still a hero, while Pizarro is viewed as a villain. Mythology is never wrong: Custer is a hero (for capitalism) because he rid the plains of Indians, thus permitting the subsequent immigration of European labor. Pizarro, who, besides killing many Indians, had to resign himself to contemplating the survival of the others in unattainable "reductions" (*reducciones*), which were controlled by the members of religious orders, proves to be somewhat worse than a traitor—he is precisely the scapegoat of this (hi)story.

The polemic surrounding America following the discovery was the contemporary of a transcendental event that conditioned it completely: the invention of the printing press. This fact normally goes unrecognized, but it is of utmost importance. The dissemination of information and testimonies through editions with thousands of copies was to take the question of America out of the hands of the erudite and handed it over indiscriminately to all. The rules of its reception were also new: they were those of mass culture, which was also coming into being at that time. For that reason it was evaluated with the bare and lifeless Manichaeism of a smash-hit soap opera. Some, especially in Spain, believed that America was a continuation of the novels of chivalry; others, mainly in the rest of Europe, were drawn to Ahrimán, which, as we know, would later inspire "Dallas" and "Dynasty." It is useless to insist that both visions were mere comic strips. For the first time, humanity turned history into spectacle and was unwilling to give up its plaything (centuries later specialists would find in this atemporal and noncritical "everydayness" of this vision of history one of the most salient characteristics of mass culture).

The fact is that the American enterprise was also seen in another way—which we will examine carefully—that is, as a sacred play:

Act I: Others were destroyed in order to be assimilated. Such assimilation that would be followed by the abundant wealth characteristic of all colonial systems. It seems that the conquistadors destroyed for the sheer pleasure of destruction; they participated in a satanic diversion that would very soon turn against them, taking away the labor force needed for their agricultural and mining operations in the New World. Consequently, Spain's colonial enterprise proved to be decidedly mediocre, due to the infrastructure that they left behind and the profits that they managed to gain from their colonial experience, an experience which in turn was colonized indirectly by European banking.

Act II: The counter-argument of the champions of the Spaniards' action takes an interesting route: the principal motive behind the American enterprise, they say, was evangelization, and it is based on this assumption that one must evaluate that incredible adventure, one undoubtedly stained by blood and outrageous acts, but positive overall for Christianity. That this kind of argument *a divinis* should clash with the desacralized era in which we have lived since the eighteenth century seems to be the cause of the limited acceptance of that argument outside of Spain and even outside of the most conservative circles within Spain. (It is quite likely that this motive is understood in Islamic countries, for example, but that is another issue).

Act III (dénouement): Whether we like it or not, the fact remains that the Christianization of the indigenous peoples constituted the only official motive for the Spanish Conquest of America, while the desire for wealth undoubtedly motivated most of those who took part in that enterprise. It seems to me that the first step in reaching an understanding of this enterprise with guaranteed success is to acknowledge both positions—the external and the internal—in a straightforward manner.

Rarely in history has a colonial project been undertaken with such an incessant need for ideological justifications. We know that the sovereigns of Spain hastened to legitimize their claim to ownership of the occupied lands by persuading the pope to divide the evangelizing efforts in the new continent between the Portuguese and the Spanish. Each time the Spanish soldiers came to an indigenous village they would read a proclamation (the *requerimiento*) instructing the natives to "convert" and to "pledge loyalty to the King and to His Holiness the Pope." Afterward, and often regardless of the peoples' attitude, the soldiers would proceed to fire their harquebuses at the Indians with utmost serenity, in the same way that the Israelites speared the Philistines in order to take back God's promised land. (This comparison is not gratuitous; it was established by M. Fernández de Enciso at the beginning of the sixteenth century.) Today, the ironic response of certain Indians of what is now Colombia, who called the pope a drunkard for giving away what he did not own and the king a madman for taking it, seems both anthological and full of common sense. However, it is quite likely that things were not seen in this way at the time, and that, regardless of whether or not the Spaniards were right (obviously they were not), and even if the Indians had been able to understand them (for there was not always an interpreter on hand to translate the legal document), the response proved highly troublesome, at least at first, because the *requerimiento* also met with resistance on the Peninsula.

From a contemporary perspective, the sixteenth-century Spanish colonial system seems to be a merciless and hypocritical colonialism: merciless because it placed all of its expansive zeal in finding more and more gold, and hypocritical for concealing this primary motivation in a presumed desire to evangelize. What is interesting is that certain episodes in European history (ancient or contemporary), such as the Crusades, follow identical parameters, and yet enjoy a favorable image among the public, outside of certain circles limited to historians. Moreover, if we bear in mind that the American enterprise was conceived by the Spaniards as an extension of the "crusade" against the Moslem territories in the south of the Iberian Peninsula, it becomes even clearer that, either its description as merciless or hypocritical is unfair, or the benevolence with which the expeditions to the Holy Land are usually received is absurd.

Perhaps everything rests on the question of genres: colonialism and the Crusades were myths while the Conquest of America was a tragedy. The disinherited individuals who enlisted in the ranks of Richard of England's armies went for the spoils, but they were firmly convinced that by killing "infidels" they would be, moreover, self-justified. The adventurers who advanced through Africa in the nineteenth century did not deceive themselves with false hopes regarding the legitimacy of the plunder, but they knew that they possessed the *de facto*, if not moral, justification of the country whose flag they had embraced. For the conquistadors, on the other hand, trapped in a period of transition between two worlds—the medieval world that survived in the automatism of the state, and the modern one that was already emerging in each individual—schizophrenia was unavoidable. Moreover, schizophrenia, like all contradictions between the conscious and the unconscious, at least since Sophocles's *Oedipus*, is found at the origin of tragedy.

When other European nations tried to settle in Hispanic America during the sixteenth century, they carried out a genocide that was similar and that provoked identical remorse. What is interesting is that they were incapable of founding permanent settlements at that time—exemplified by the unsuccessful incursions of the Welsers into Venezuela—and that two centuries went by before that implantation became possible. This is what is interesting about the Spanish case, regardless of ethical considerations.

In our society the mad or crazy are the others: those individuals who deviate from the common pattern and those who are considered as such by accepted convention. The notion that we are all mad and that often people who are committed to mental institutions express more lucid judgment than the sane is, naturally, an ancient cliché. But the weakness of that argument applies to the case of isolated individuals, and not to the case of entire societies. To brand a whole society mad reveals the inability to understand it. The meaning of history always belongs to the conquerors, who, by having conquered, illusively believe that they have understood. Were the Indians mad? This is what the Spaniards believed, and for that reason, when faced with anthropophagy (a rite of communion, and, perhaps, a biological necessity of a diet lacking in mineral salts) or with sodomy (a common practice in Hellenic culture, which the very European sixteenth century was discovering), they reacted with horror and condemned their practitioners to devourment by dogs, according to Las Casas. Were the Spaniards mad? Many Europeans of the time believed so, though it must be stated that not all shared the same opinion. Montaigne, for example, in his chapter entitled "On Cannibals" (1580) limits himself to reproducing condemnation of the conquistadors, and in "Of Coaches" (1588) includes Europeans in general, pointing out their radical inability to understand the New World.

Spanish colonialism of the sixteenth and seventeenth centuries has proven particularly intolerable for Europeans. Moreover, the explanation being given in Spain for this position contains, in my opinion, an error in focus. The so-called Black Legend was perhaps born out of ill will—we will recall Spain's position as the foremost European power of the time—but what is certain is that it persisted until quite recently (it still preoccupied Julián Juderías just a few years ago), due more to a lack of understanding than anything else. The unmitigating condemnation of said colonialism does not respond to the fact that it exhibits—and indeed it does—all traces of colonial plunder. But rather, it responds precisely to the fact that *it was not just colonialism*, for it tried to blend the speculating greed of the individual with the apparent—and for the most part, real—disinterestedness of the state. While the crudest British colonialism in India has found its bard in Rudyard Kipling, the Spanish enterprise can offer only individual exonerations in which proud self-affirmation and the pain of remorse are mixed in the style of so many chroniclers. Hernán Cortés's testament is clear:

> For regarding the natural slaves of said New Spain, whether from war or from ransom, there has been and there are many doubts and opinions regarding whether or not in good conscience they could have been kept and until now it has not been determined, I order that everything that is generally ascertained be for the purpose of relieving [people's] consciences. (*Colección de documentos inéditos* 26: 135-148)[2]

Another case in point is told by Motolinía: while his hands grew tired at the end of each day from hearing confession from the Indians, the hands of the conquistadors suffered from beating them. I do not propose this link between private brutality and public exemplarity as something new in the history of humanity, for all states present themselves as entities endowed with historical justification, including, and perhaps to the greatest extreme, totalitarian regimes. But the motive for the Spanish Crown, in that tenuous boundary that separates the Middle Ages from the modern era, was objectively damaging to its interests, if we view things from the state's perspective. Given that the state was not a medieval but a Renaissance invention and that the Spanish state was precisely its first historical incarnation, we can understand that its attitude regarding America may be considered an unexplained phenomenon (rather than one of madness, as the Europeans of the time believed.)

We will now approach the question from a semiotic perspective. Until 1492 the world was seen as a manifestation of principles that emanated from God and that were capable of reconciling contradictions. If some Christian prince called for a massive slaughter of heretics—as occurred in the case of the Cathari in the south of France—or if some Moslem chief ordered the execution of the Christians in his territory, the morality in force did not make them responsible for their actions, for it was able to offset the apparent evil with the hidden good, through Divine Will. But, beginning in 1492 things began to be seen in a different light: individuals were valued for who they were and for what they did, thereby displacing ethical judgment to the utilitarian plane. The bourgeois ethic advocated by the Reformation separated emotion, for which all individuals were responsible only before themselves, from the sphere of action, which would be measured by its exterior projection, by its capacity to generate "progress." The conquistadors, trapped between the *Zeitgeist* that brought them to action and the absolute truths that tended to halt that action, had no option but the split personality. The legalistic obsession shared by almost all of them, which has attracted the attention of innumerable researchers, arose from an attempt to reconcile this essential disparity between the individual and the whole.

It proved a vain attempt indeed, for the ideology of that society was medieval rather than modern. The sixteenth-century Spanish state, the first state of the modern age, did not resemble a modern state with regard to its relationship to the Indies, but rather, paradoxically, a medieval one, a state constructed in honor of the attainment of a Catholic order in which the very notion of "earthly progress" implied a contradiction. The historian Juan de Mariana considered "the discovery of the West Indies ... to be a marvelous thing and which, out of so many centuries, was reserved for this age" (1: 174);[3] providentialism was the unattackable doctrine of a state with which the utilitarian goals of the conquistadors would inevitably clash.

But if what the conquistadors were doing lacked justification in the eyes of society as a whole, because it entailed all kinds of crimes against the indigenous peoples, it also lacked justification in their own eyes. Where could they turn for alibis? It has not always been noted that the very constitution of Hispanic America implied from the very beginning the seed of its separation from the Peninsula. The distant European state clearly exploited the Indies for the benefit of the Catholic religion, to whose expansion it contributed for two centuries with shipments of metals from the Americas to pay for European religious wars. For this reason the conquistadors tended early on to detach themselves and to form independent clusters that often reproduced the regional confrontations of the Iberian Peninsula (the most famous struggles between peninsular factions were those of the *vicuñas*—Andalusians and Castilians—and the *vascongados*—Basques—in Potosí in 1552).

In spite of the favorable Gulf currents the Spanish colonies

were not established, like the English colonies, to look toward
Europe. Rather, a prudent distance was left between the continents. Moreover, faced with the need to blend personal interest
with certain collective goals, the colonies soon ceased to perceive
themselves as being in solidarity with the Catholic empire overseas. In reality, Lope de Aguirre's revolt against Philip II is just the
submerged tip of an iceberg, that of modern men who tried to establish colonies in nineteenth-century style before their time and
against a state that could not understand them. Gonzalo Pizarro's
revolt in Peru against the New Laws of 1542 must be placed in
the same category, along with other minor episodes such as the
incipient separatism of the second marquis del Valle in Mexico.

The conquistadors were modern men guided by a vision of
the world that anticipated by several centuries, in both positive
and negative ways, that of their compatriots who stayed on the
Peninsula. On one hand, they revealed the curiosity and the desire
to discover new lands so characteristic of newly emerging European science. On the other, they exhibited all of the insensitivity
toward their equals and all the desire for wealth that would later
characterize incipient European capitalism. Finally, they instituted
bourgeois political structures that would not arrive in Spain until
the nationalist movements of the nineteenth century.

In comparison, the Spanish state that had sent them possessed
an unmistakably medieval tonality. In a negative sense, the state
was characterized by anti-progressive inefficiency; in a positive
sense, its policies were much more humanitarian than those that
would bring about the Industrial Revolution. Let us observe the remarkable instructions of government given by the Catholic Kings
to Nicolás de Ovando:

> What you, Friar Nicholas of Ovando, Comendador de Lares
> of the order of Alcántara must do on the isles and *terra firme*
> of the Ocean Sea, where you will be our governor, is the
> following. First, you should pursue with much diligence
> things pertaining to the service of God, and that holy offices
> be performed with the pertinent degree of esteem, order,
> and reverence. *Item:* Since we want the Indians to convert to
> our Holy Catholic Faith, and their souls to be saved ... you
> should endeavor, without forcing them, like the clergy who

are there, to inform and admonish them toward it with
much love, so that they may convert as soon as possible.
(*Colección de documentos inéditos* 21: 13-18)[4]

The conquistadors could not understand this. For them the
conquest and exploitation of new territories came first, while the
evangelization of the indigenous peoples came second, and often as a mere legal cover. For this reason the decrees of Hernán
Cortés, commander-in-chief and governor of New Spain, share no
likeness with the above instructions:

First, I order that any resident or inhabitant of said cities and
towns that there presently are or will be have in his house a
lance and a sword or dagger.... *Item* that any resident who
has been granted Indians (through *repartimiento*) be obliged
to place with them, each year, with every one hundred
Indians obtained through *repartimiento* one thousand
sarmientos.... *Item* that as Catholics and Christians, our
principal intention should be addressed toward the service
and honor of God our Lord...; hence, I order that all of
those people who in this New Spain have Indians obtained
through *repartimiento* that they be obligated to take away
their idols, and to admonish them not to have them from
then on. (*Colección de documentos inéditos* 26: 135-148)[5]

Five centuries of Hispanic America are condensed in these
two anthological references. On one hand, we see the extreme
misunderstanding on the part of the Spanish state, which never
became a colonial power despite having extensively sprinkled the
new world with colonies. On the other, we note the interest of
individuals, who, lacking official colonial direction, established individual colonies, basically forts in the middle of a jungle with
several hundred Indians under their control. Their exclusive preoccupation was defending and enriching themselves while maintaining a legal appearance that allowed them to enjoy the institution of the *encomienda*.

It has often been observed that, while the Anglo-Saxon colonies
of North America progressed slowly, so that at the beginning of the
nineteenth century they still had not crossed the Mississippi, the
Spanish colonies covered the entire continent in only fifty years.
This was the case not only in the south, but also in the north.

For example, on the world map of Diego Ribero (1529), Louisiana and Florida were the land of Garay; the Virginias and the Carolinas the land of Ayllón; and Pennsylvania and New York, that of Esteban Gómez. However, this is not surprising: the Spanish conquistadors were not creating commercial trading posts connected to the Peninsula that had to be secured slowly. Rather, they were creating "their colonies," that is, their personal fiefdoms, isolated among the indigenous lands, maintaining the smallest connection possible with the centers of power created by the state in Mexico-Tenochtitlan and in Lima.

Without realizing it, the conquistadors were vindicating Sir Thomas More, who, in his *Utopia*, had established the basis of modern colonialism upon justifying the appropriation of infertile lands by Utopians coming from a densely populated island, and the concept of "just war" against indigenous peoples who resisted. Two centuries later, Jacob Vanderlint still considered defensible any colonial enterprise that had as its objective "fighting for Territory when we are overpeopled, and want land for them, which our Neighbors have but will not part with on amicable Terms" (in his 1734 essay, revealingly entitled *Money Answers All Things*). There is no doubt that the territorial claims of the United States upon Mexico, which deprived that country of half its territory, obeyed the same spirit, as Thomas Jefferson would have explicitly recognized. In contrast, the Spanish state, after all manner of reservations and tortuous deliberations of theologians and universities, ended by adopting a much more timid policy, inspired in strict scholastic principles, in particular those of Thomas Aquinas.

It is not my intention to pass judgment on the attitudes of anyone. I sincerely believe that all individuals, just as all eras, are the product of particular circumstances and that they can do very little—although they can do something—to avoid their least justifiable acts. What matters more, in my view, is that we understand the reasons why: if society and the state are the expression of the rules of the game determined by individuals, how can we explain the unqualified modernity and Europeanism of the colonialist structures of the conquistadors alongside the medieval ideological stagnation of an already modern state, as Spain was in the sixteenth century?

The reader might imagine that I am making an apology for the aforementioned state; as that is not my intention, I think it appropriate that I quickly clear up a misconception. The Spanish state of the sixteenth century was theocratic, but it had definite vested interests. Every imperial regime needs legitimacy, and Spanish imperialism found this in Catholicism, or to be more precise, in the defense of Catholicism against Islam and Lutheranism. The fact that the "enemies" of Catholicism were also the very ones who threatened the borders of the empire is a coincidence that explains the entire foreign policy of the House of Hapsburg. Directed against the Turks, the Flemish, and the British, it conveniently branded them as both enemies and heretics. Every empire that prides itself as such has acted in this way. For the French empire, inheritor of the Revolution, the Napoleonic Wars were justified as campaigns against intolerance and in favor of truth; for United States imperialism, foreign interventions are said to conform to a desire to thwart the expansion of Communism or, more recently, that of Islamic fundamentalism, now that the former seems to have exhausted itself.

In this sense a perfect symbiosis existed between the Spanish state and its subjects, both of them at once modern and fanatically Catholic. Undoubtedly, difficulties arose when that ideology consequently had to be applied to the American front. According to scholastic ideology, the Indians were not "heretics," but rather "infidels." Moreover, in spite of vacillations by theologians, it seemed clear that the policy that had to be pursued with regard to them was not extermination, but rather preaching and subsequent conversion. The conduct of the inquisitorial tribunal on both sides of the Atlantic is a case in point. While in Spain and the rest of Europe its proceedings were characterized by an extreme cruelty, in the Indies it did not go beyond being a tepid court, which was rarely convened and which, moreover, was forbidden to concern itself with the natives. The Hispanic American Inquisition began proceedings against *criollo* practitioners of Judaism (for instance, the Treviño Martín family [Mexico, 1648]); against Lutherans (such as the Flemish Juan Millar [Lima, 1548]); or against blacks accused of witchcraft (the case of the Mexican black-Indian half-breed [*zambo*] Francisco Rodrígues in 1646 is well known). In other words, the Inquisition persecuted the conquistadors and their followers, but it left the indigenous population alone.

We could express this simplistically by saying that the Spanish state was struggling with a fundamental ambiguity: with respect to Europe, it sought to elevate itself to the position of the champion of Catholicism; with regard to America, that ideology clearly jeopardized its colonial ambitions. When it sided with the religious orders and, through them, with the Indians, it promoted medieval economic, social, and linguistic policies that made enemies of the colonizers. When it attended to the demands of the conquistadors, it behaved like a "modern" state, fully European and colonialist, but also much more inhumane.

What existed in Hispanic America was a spatial coincidence of two worlds with different worldviews: the world of the Europeans, allied with the institutional arm of the state, and the world of the indigenous people, supported by the state's religious/ideological arm. The former, because of the ambiguous position of the arbitrating state, tended irremediably toward dispersion; the latter, necessarily confronted with a state whose ideological convictions they knew to be economically based, fomented the same dispersion. Thus was produced the paradox that, over time, *criollos* and clerics came to concur in their yearnings for independence in spite of the disparity of feelings that inspired them. Any appraisal of Hispanic society that ignores this duality beneath an appearance of uniformity is condemned, in my opinion, to miss the mark. Furthermore, Hispanic America is precisely that: a plurality of groups within the unity of emotional pulsations cemented by the existence of a common foreign enemy. If in the colonial era conquistadors and members of religious orders confronted one another, but both eventually came to rebel against the Spanish state, from the moment of independence on the various Hispanic American nations, having maintained bloody border disputes (such as the one that deprived Bolivia of almost the entire Chaco, or Chile of Eastern Patagonia) have been united in their repudiation of the Anglo-Saxon colossus to the north.

Curiously, both the early conquistadors and the clerics, and later all Hispanic American nations, distinguish themselves by their propensity toward messianic positions. The messianism of the friars has been carefully traced by Jacques Lafaye and has its roots in the providentialist ideology of the Spanish state: The *Historia de las Indias de Nueva España e islas de Tierra Firme (History of the Indies of New Spain and Islands of Tierra Firme)* by the Dominican friar Diego Durán initiated the hypothesis that the Indians were descendents of the emigrating Israelites of the first diaspora of Solomon. As a consequence, the complementary idea that the apostle St. Thomas had preached to the Gentiles *supra Gangem* (according to the *Acta Thomae*) and the identification of him with the Mexican god Quetzalcoatl gain plausibility. In this reckless race of colorful attributions, it should surprise no one that the pious tradition of the apparition of the Virgin Mary in Guadalupe de Tepeyac would result in the transformation of Mexico into the New Jerusalem, the native land of Christians and, simultaneously, of anyone born in Mexico and not in Europe—in other words, of Mexicans, as the erudite Sigüenza y Góngora had designated them.

Yet if the members of religious orders had ended up imbibing the "nationalist" spirit of the conquistadors, the descendents of the latter group came to accept the convenience of being supported by the indigenous communities that the friars had created. Thus it was that when the Mexican priest Miguel Hidalgo rose up in arms in Dolores on September 16, 1810, he did so by exhorting the Indians to add their numbers to the revolutionary movement in these terms: "Will you make the effort required to recover from the hated Spaniards the lands they stole from our ancestors three hundred years ago?" (qtd. in Rama 30).[6] This was a surprising imputation, from the mouth of a descendent of those very Spaniards. And then, curiously, perhaps by contrast, when the Peninsula ordered the hero of the Mexican Revolution to be shot on July 30, 1811, it did so through the office of the Inquisition, accusing him of siding with French liberty, libertinism, and formal heresy; of fomenting Judaism, Lutheranism, Calvinism, rebellion, and schism; and of suspicion of atheism.

I am not saying anything that is not already known. Hispanic American *caudillismo* (political bossism) implicitly carried the old seed of being an end unto itself and only needed an ideological support in order to bear fruit. The evangelization of the New World was from the start an enterprise alien to the European interests of the Spanish state, and it strove to break off ties to the Peninsula. The alliance between the two, although contradictory and the cause of so many imbalances in contemporary Hispanic America, was an accomplished fact. In a 1781 letter to the king, the words of José de Avalos, mayor of Caracas, leave no room for doubt and are worth more than the several volumes of commentary made since then:

> Your Highness: The length of my residence in these Americas... [has] led me to reflect often on the backwardness of its opulent provinces and on the character of the native people. Religion, which ordinarily unites hearts and wills to the state, shows itself to be exceedingly sickly in the Americans...; in such a way that it would not be temerity on my part to state that it is the secular and regular clergy that, while enjoying the protection of immunity, sows the detestable seeds of aversion to obedience and the Throne.... Most of the subjects who have been sent since the Conquest... have acted and act with the desire of, and with an eye to getting rich, and this is a common truth, from the lowliest among them to the greatest... from whom have emanated an immense number of prejudices...; for all Americans harbor, or are born with, an aversion and much ill will toward Spaniards in general; to which should be added that the Spaniards who enter into matrimony and make their homes in these countries are worse than the natives themselves. (Muñoz Oraa 460-462)[7]

The words of Avalos constitute one of the last Spanish texts by which an image of the colonies can be formed. Those that followed came after the independence of the American nations and are founded upon myth: first upon the myth of a lost (and yearned for) paradise, and later upon the myth of a paradise regained. But these are two different paradises.

The Spaniards of the nineteenth century and of the first half of the twentieth dedicated their most productive intellectual energies toward the creation of a false image of themselves and of their overseas experience. The so-called Generation of '98 promoted an alienating ideology with respect to the American question that proclaimed both a patriotic exaltation and a soothing oblivion, which was nothing more than a complement to the former. They held that if the cause of the decline had originated in the abandonment of Castilian virtues and if the solution depended on turning back upon themselves, then it was clear that what was needed was a blotting out of the errors committed in the Indies, a clean slate. But this did not imply any remorse "for what had been done," but rather "because it had been done." Unamuno's message was clear: those who grasp for much end up with little, so let us return to what is ours and cure ourselves of failures and chimeras. The message of Ramón Menéndez Pidal, in which he futilely insisted on transforming Father Bartolomé de Las Casas into a neurotic, was no less revealing.

Spain's decline lasted three centuries, beginning with a century and a half of economic and political collapse, followed by a century and a half of intellectual uneasiness and lack of confidence in its own strengths. But all things come to an end in the lives of nations just as they do in the lives of individuals. The Spain of the second half of the twentieth century, especially democratic Spain, is a completely different country. Passionately oriented toward integration with Europe, exulting (everything is relative) in its economy—and much less so in its culture—post-Franco Spain has discovered its new communitarian El Dorado, which gives the Spanish state confidence in the future, and even a certain self-sufficiency, which it has not known since the sixteenth century.

One has to wonder, with regard to all of this, whether the European myth is compatible with a rebirth of interest in Hispanic America. The greater the efforts expended by the Spanish State to celebrate 1992, the more apparent it is that the public is greeting those efforts neither positively nor negatively, but simply with indifference. The Spain of 1492, which initiated the expeditions to the New World, expelled the Jews in the same year. The Spain of 1992, preparing itself for the festivities of the Quincentennial, is integrating itself—with the *Acta única* (unrestricted circulation of people and goods within the European Community beginning in 1993), monetary union, and new immigration and residency laws—into a fortress called Europe, from which other countries are barred by law. The contradiction remains as operative as it was five centuries ago; at the same time that Spain immerses itself in a seething mix of nations, it proclaims the law of purity of blood within its own borders. The problem is that today's missionaries—intellectuals, writers, and professors—do not seem inclined to give up their share of the booty, their share of the perks that generously rain down from official projects. Whether these take the form of conferences on "Hispanicity" or "Genocide," for example, makes no difference, since in the end they understand nothing. But this, while it is the main issue, is yet another question.

Notes

1. "Las Casas propone restaurar las extintas monarquías indianas, bajo la soberanía eminente y lejana del emperador; en tanto que la visión política de Motolinía se adelanta dos siglos y medio a la idea del conde Aranda y casi tres siglos al plan de Iguala."

2. "Porque acerca de los esclavos naturales de la dicha Nueva España, así de guerra como de rescate, ha habido y hay muchas dudas y opiniones sobre si se han podido tener con buena conciencia o no, y hasta ahora no está determinado, mando que en todo aquello que generalmente se averigüe que en este caso se debe hacer para descargo de las conciencias. . . . "

3. "el descubrimiento de las Indias Occidentales cosa maravillosa y que de tantos siglos estaba reservada para esta edad."

4. "Lo que vos, Fray Nicolás d'Ovando, comendador de Lares, de la Orden de Alcántara abeys de fazer en las islas e tierra firme del Mar Océano, donde abeys de ser nuestro gobernador, es lo siguiente. Primeramente procuraréis con mucha diligencia las cosas del servicio de Dios, e que los oficios devinos se fagan con muncha estimación e orden e rreverencia como conviene. Item: Porque Nos deseamos que los yndios se conviertan a nuestra Sancta Feé Catholica, e sus ánimas se salven . . . ternéys mucho cuidado de procurar, sin les fazer fuerza alguna, como los rreligiosos que allá están los informen e amonesten para ello con muncho amor, de manera que lo más presto que se pueda se conviertan. . . . "

5. "Primeramente, mando que qualquier vezino e morador de las dichas cibdades e villas que agora ay e obiere, tenga en su casa una lanza e una espada o un puñal. . . . Item que qualquier vezino que tobiere indios de repartimiento sea obligado a poner con ellos, en cada un año, con cada cien indios de los que tobiese de repartimiento mil sarmientos. . . . Item que como catholicos e cristianos, nuestra principal intinción ha de ser enderezada al servicio e honra de Dios Nuestro Señor . . . ; por ende mando que todas las personas que en esta Nueva España tobiesen indios de repartimiento, sean obligados de los quitar todos los ídolos que tobiesen, e amonestarlos que de allí adelante no los tengan."

6. "¿Harán ustedes el esfuerzo necesario para recuperar de los odiados españoles las tierras que robaron a nuestros antepasados hace trescientos años?"

7. "Señor: la larga residencia que llevo por estas Américas...me han con-
ducido muchas veces a tender la vista con reflexión por lo dilatado de sus opulentas
provincias y el carácter de los naturales. La religión, que es la que suele unir los corazones y las voluntades con el Estado, se advierte en los americanos sobradamente
achacosa...; de modo que no sería temeridad sentar que el estado eclesiástico secular y regular es seguramente el que, al abrigo de la inmunidad que goza, anima más
la detestable semilla de la aversión contra la subordinación y el trono.... La mayor
parte de los sujetos que han sido destinados desde la Conquista...lo han hecho
y hacen con el deseo y la mira de enriquecerse, y es axioma común desde el más
pequeño hasta el más grande...de que han dimanado y dimanarán inmensidad
de perjuicios...; pues todos los americanos tienen, o nace con ellos una aversión y
ojeriza grande a los españoles en común; a lo que debe añadirse que los españoles
que contraen matrimonio y avecindad en estos países son peores que los mismos
naturales."

Works Cited

*Colección de documentos inéditos relativos al descubrimiento, conquista y organización
   de las antiguas posesiones españolas de Ultramar.* 25 vols. Madrid: Sucesores de
   Rivadeneyra, 1885; 1932.
Durán, Diego. *Historia de las Indias de Nueva España e islas de Tierra Firme.* Mexico
   City: Porrúa, 1967.
Fernández de Enciso, Martín. *Suma de geografía.* Seville, 1919.
Juderías, Julián. *La leyenda negra: estudios acerca del concepto de España en el extranjero.*
   Barcelona: Araluce, 1926.
Lafaye, Jaques. *Quetzalcoatl and Guadalupe: The Formation of Mexican National Con-
   sciousness.* Trans. Benjamin Keen. Chicago: Univ. of Chicago Press, 1976.
Las Casas, Bartolomé de. *Aquí se contiene vna disputa, o controuersia, entre Bartholome
   de las Casas o Casaus y el doctor Ginés de Sepulueda.* Seville: Sebastián Trugillo, 1552.
———. *Brevísima relación de la destrucción de las Indias.* Mexico City: Secretaría de
   Educación Pública, 1945.
Mariana, Juan de. *Historia general de España.* 9 vols. Valencia: B. Monfort, 1783-1796.
Menéndez Pidal, Ramón. *El padre Las Casas: su doble personalidad.* Madrid: Espasa-
   Calpe, 1963.
Montaigne, Michel de. *Complete Works.* Trans. Donald M. Frame. London: H. Hamil-
   ton, 1958.
More, Sir Thomas. *Utopia.* London: Burns, Gates, and Washbourne, 1937.
Motolinía, Toribio. *Historia de los indios de la Nueva España.* Ed. Claudio Esteva.
   Madrid: Historia 16, 1985.
Muñoz Oraa, Emilio. "Pronóstico de la independencia de América, y un proyecto
   de Monarquéas, en 1781." *Revista de Historia de América* 50 (1960): 460-462.
Nicolau d'Olwer, L. *Cronistas de las culturas precolombinas.* Mexico City: Fondo de
   Cultura Económica, 1963.
O'Gorman, Edmundo. *La idea del descubrimiento de América.* Mexico City: Centro de
   Estudios Filosóficos, 1951.

————. *La invención de América*. 2nd ed. Mexico City: Fondo de Cultura Económica, 1977.

Rubert de Ventós, Xavier. *El laberinto de la Hispanidad*. Barcelona: Planeta, 1987.

Sánchez-Albornoz, Nicolás. *Population of Latin America: A History*. Trans. W. A. R. Richardson. Berkeley: Univ. of California Press, 1974.

Todorov, Tzvetan. *The Conquest of America: The Question of the Other*. Trans. Richard Howard. New York: Harper & Row, 1984.

Vanderlint, Jacob. *Money Answers All Things*. Baltimore: Lord Baltimore Press, 1914.

Contributors

Rolena Adorno. Professor of Latin American Literature at Princeton University. She is the author of *Guaman Poma: Writing and Resistance in Colonial Peru* (1986), a critical edition of the *Nueva corónica y buen gobierno*, 3 vols. (with John V. Murra, 1980, 1987), an edited volume *From Oral to Written Expression: Native Andean Chronicles of the Early Colonial Period* (1982), and numerous articles on colonial Spanish American literature, including an essay for volume 1 of the *Cambridge History of Latin American Literature*. She is currently at work on a study of Renaissance humanism in early colonial Mexico.

Manuel Alvar. President of Spain's Real Academia de la Lengua and Professor of Spanish Literature and Linguistics at the Universidad Complutense de Madrid. He has authored and edited more than fifty books, including *El mundo americano de Bernal Díaz del Castillo* (1968); *Juan de Castellanos, tradición española y realidad americana* (1972); an edition of Columbus's *Diario del descubrimiento*, 2 vols. (1976); and *Léxico del mestizaje en Hispanoamérica* (1987).

José J. Arrom. Professor Emeritus of Spanish and Latin American Literature, Yale University. Among his books are *El teatro de*

Hispanoamérica en la época colonial (1956, 1967); *Esquema generacional de las letras hispanoamericanas* (1963, 1977); *Certidumbre de América* (1971, 1980); *Estudios de lexicología antillana* (1980); *Mitología y artes prehispánicas de las Antillas* (1975, 1989); and editions of Hernán Pérez de Oliva, *Historia de la invención de las Indias* (1965); Matías de Bocanegra, *Comedia de San Francisco de Borja* (1976); José de Acosta, *Peregrinación de Bartolomé Lorenzo* (1982); and others.

Georges Baudot. Professor of Latin American Literature and Culture at the University of Toulouse-Le Mirail, France, where he directs its Institut Pluridisciplinaire pour les Etudes sur L'Amérique Latine and the journal *Caravelle*. He has edited Friar Toribio de Benavente, Motolinía, *Historia de los indios de Nueva España* (1985) and has written extensively on the first chroniclers of Mexican civilization. His most recent books are *Utopía e historia en Mexico: Los primeros cronistas de la civilización mexicana 1520-1569* (1983) and *La pugna franciscana por México* (1990).

Marta Bermúdez-Gallegos. Assistant Professor of Spanish American Literature at Rutgers University. She has published several essays on colonial literature and culture and is presently finishing a book on the subject of the essay written for this volume.

Allen Carey-Webb. Assistant Professor of English at Western Michigan University. His areas of interest are postcolonial literature and theory and critical pedagogy. Recent publications have appeared in *American Literary History, College Literature*, and *English Journal*.

Amaryll Chanady. Associate Professor of Comparative Literature at the Université de Montréal. She is the author of *Magical Realism and the Fantastic: Resolved versus Unresolved Antinomy* (1985) and numerous articles on Latin American literature, including "Entre la quête et la métalittérature: Aquin et Cortázar comme représentants du postmoderne excentrique" (*Voix et Images*, 1986), "La thématisation de la marginalisation discursive dans le néo-indigénisme équatorien" and "Exil et littérature haïtienne: un questionnement axiologique," *Parole exclusive, parole exclue, parole transgressive,* ed. A. Gómez-Moriana and C. Poupeney Hart (1990).

Tom Conley. Professor of French at the University of Minnesota and currently on the faculty at Miami University of Ohio. Specializing in problems of text and image in French and comparative literatures, he has published on Montaigne in *Oeuvres et critiques, Modern Language Notes,* and other journals. Work in Hispanic areas includes *Surrealismo documental: lectura de "Tierra sin pan"* (1988) and "Broken Blockage: notas sobre la guerra civil en el cine de Hollywood," *Revista de Occidente* (1987). *Ensayos sobre el cine* is promised to appear through Hyperion editions. His most recent book is *Film Hieroglyphs* (1991).

Elena Feder. Ph.D. candidate in comparative literature at Stanford University, where she also coedits *Stanford Humanities Review*. She works in film theory and testimonial literature and is interested in the manner in which the latter problematizes the issue of authority and authorship.

Leonardo García Pabón. Assistant Professor of Latin American Literature at the University of Oregon. He has written on contemporary poetry, on various facets of Bolivian literature, and on texts from colonial Latin America. His publications include *El paseo de los sentidos: Estudios de literatura boliviana* (1983) and *Pensamiento andino y tradición historiográfica americana en la f(ec)undación de la ciudad colonial: La* Historia de Potosí *de Bartolomé Arzáns (1676-1736),* forthcoming. At present he is working on a *Historical Dictionary of Bolivia* for Scarecrow Press.

Teresa Gisbert. She has taught at the Universidad Católica de Chile, the Universidad Nacional de México, the Ecole des Hautes Etudes Sociales de l'Université de Paris, and the Universidad Mayor de San Andrés in La Paz, Bolivia. She is a specialist on Andean art, textiles, literature, and history, and has received special recognition from the governments of Bolivia (1989), Spain, and France (1989). Her publications include *Esquema de la literatura virreinal* (1968); *Arte textil y mundo andino* (1987); *Historia de la pintura* *cuzqueña* (1962, 1982); and *Historia del arte hispanoamericano* (1985), the latter two in collaboration with José de Mesa.

David Henige. African Studies Bibliographer, University of Wisconsin, Madison. Author of *The Chronology of Oral Tradition* (1974) and *Oral Historiography* (1982) as well as numerous articles in African history, he has recently turned his attention to the study of New World contact population and to the early texts of the Encounter. His most recent book is *In Search of Columbus: The Sources for the First Voyage* (1991).

René Jara. Professor of Spanish American Literature and Chair of the Department of Spanish and Portuguese at the University of Minnesota. He has written on Spanish and Spanish American literature and culture as well as on topics dealing with literary theory and criticism. His most recent books are *Los límites de la representación* (1985); *El revés de la arpillera: Perfil literario de Chile* (1988); *1492-1992: Re/Discovering Colonial Writing* (coedited); and, *La modernidad en litigio* (1990).

David E. Johnson. Received his Ph.D. in English from the State University of New York at Buffalo in 1991. He has essays published or forthcoming in *Arizona Quarterly, Chasqui*, and *The Americas Review*. Presently he is working on the textualization of voice in twentieth-century Latin American narrative and Octavio Paz's cultural criticism.

Miguel León-Portilla. Professor of History at the Universidad Nacional de México and the Colegio de México; he also serves as Mexico's ambassador to UNESCO. He is the author of some forty books on indigenous cultures, including *Visión de los vencidos* (1962; Eng. trans. *The Aztec Account of the Conquest of Mexico*, 1962); *Aztec Thought and Culture* (1963); *Tiempo y realidad en el pensamiento maya* (1973; Eng. trans. *Time and Reality in the Thought of the Maya*, 1973; rpt. 1988); *Toltecayotl: Aspectos de la cultura nahuatl* (1980); *Literaturas de Mesoamérica* (1984); and *Culturas en peligro* (Eng. trans. *Endangered Cultures*, 1990).

Angel López García. Professor of Hispanic Linguistics and Linguistic Theory at the Universidad de Valencia, Spain. He is the author of many books, including *Para una gramática liminar* (1977); *Estudios de lingüística española* (1983); *El rumor de los desarraigados: Conflicto de lenguas en la Península Ibérica* (1985); *Psicolingüística* (1988); and *Fundamentos de lingüística perceptiva* (1989). His latest book, *El sueño hispano ante la encrucijada del racismo contemporáneo* (1991), speculates on the consequences of the encounter between the European and Amerindian worlds.

Santiago López Maguiña. Doctoral candidate in Spanish American Literature at the University of Minnesota and Assistant Professor at the Universidad de San Marcos in Lima, Peru. He has published several essays on Peruvian literature and is currently preparing his dissertation on colonial Latin American literature.

Bernardita Llanos. Assistant Professor of Latin American Literature at Denison University. She has recently finished her dissertation, "América y la defensa de España en el teatro popular del siglo XVIII español," and has published articles on colonial literature and on the subject of women and the Spanish Enlightenment. Her current research interests include a comparative approach to colonial and Spanish peninsular theater.

Walter D. Mignolo. Professor of Latin American Literature, Semiotics and Literary Theory at the University of Michigan. Founder and editor of *Dispositio: Revista Hispánica de Semiótica Literaria*. Author of several books and articles, among them *Textos, modelos y metáforas* (1984); *Teoría del texto e interpretación de textos* (1986); "Teorías literarias o de la literatura: ¿Qué son y para qué sirven?," in *Teorías de la literatura en la actualidad*, G. Reyes, ed. (forthcoming). He is presently completing a book entitled *Representing the New World: Literacy, Territoriality and Colonization*.

José Piedra. Associate Professor of Romance Studies and Director of the Hispanic American Studies Program at Cornell University. He has published in *New Literary History, Diacritics*, and other leading journals. The essay "Loving Columbus" is part of his book project *The Erotics of Conquest*.

Mary Louise Pratt. Professor in the Departments of Spanish and Portuguese and Comparative Literature at Stanford University, where she teaches courses on literary and discourse theory, Latin American literature, and the history of women and print culture in Latin America. She is the author of books and articles on linguistic approaches to literature, language and ideology, and colonial discourse. Most recently she coedited a special issue of *Nuevo Texto Crítico* on the subject of "América Latina: Mujer, escritura, praxis" (4.2, 1989), and coauthored the volumes *Women, Culture and Politics in Latin America* and *Amor Brujo: Images and Culture of Love in the Andes*. Her latest book is *Imperial Eyes: Studies in Travel Writing and Transculturation* (1991).

Eloise Quiñones Keber. Associate Professor of Art History at Baruch College of the City University of New York. She is the coauthor of *Art of Aztec Mexico: Treasures of Tenochtitlan* (1983), coeditor of *The Work of Bernardino de Sahagún: Pioneer Ethnographer of Aztec Mexico* (1988), and author of numerous articles on Aztec art before and after the Conquest. She has recently completed a book on the *Codex Telleriano-Remensis*, a sixteenth-century Aztec manuscript painted and annotated in colonial Mexico, and is now working on a study of Aztec and European images of the Spanish Conquest.

Roberto Reis. Associate Professor of Brazilian Literature and Culture at the University of Minnesota. He has published numerous essays on authors such as Machado de Assis, Graciliano Ramos, João Cabral de Melo Neto, Guimarães Rosa, and Clarice Lispector. Recently he has been working on authoritarianism in Brazilian cultural discourses. Among his books are *A permanência do círculo* (1987), a study on hierarchy in the Brazilian novel, and *The Pearl Necklace* (1992).

Nicholas Spadaccini. Professor of Hispanic Studies and Comparative Literature at the University of Minnesota. He has written especially on Cervantes, the picaresque novel, and Spanish Golden Age drama, edited several Spanish classics, and coedited books of literary theory and criticism, including *Literature among Discourses* (1986); *The Institutionalization of Literature in Spain* (1987); *Autobiography in Early Modern Spain* (1988); *1492-1992: Re/Discovering Colonial Writing* (1989); *Cervantes's Exemplary Novels and the Adventure of Writing* (1990); and *The Politics of Editing* (1992). *Through the Shattering Glass: Cervantes and the Self-made World* (coauthored) is forthcoming from the University of Minnesota Press.

Margarita Zamora. Associate Professor of Spanish and Latin American and Iberian Studies at the University of Wisconsin, Madison. She is author of *Language, Authority, and Indigenous History in the* Comentarios reales de los incas (1988) and *Reading Columbus* (1993).

Index

compiled by Donna Buhl LeGrand   \